FINANCIAL INSTITUTIONS MANAGEMENT

A MODERN PERSPECTIVE

THE IRWIN SERIES IN FINANCE

FINANCIAL MANAGEMENT

Block and Hirt
Foundations of Financial Management
Seventh Edition

Brooks
Fingame: The Financial Management Decision Game
Third Edition

Bruner
Case Studies in Finance: Managing for Corporate Value Creation
Second Edition

Fruhan, Kester, Mason, Piper, and Ruback
Case Problems in Finance
Tenth Edition

Harrington
Corporate Financial Analysis: Decisions in a Global Environment
Fourth Edition

Helfert
Techniques of Financial Analysis
Eighth Edition

Higgins
Analysis for Financial Management
Third Edition

Jones
Introduction to Financial Management
First Edition

Kallberg, Parkinson
Corporate Liquidity: Management and Measurement
First Edition

Ross, Westerfield, and Jaffe
Corporate Finance
Third Edition

Ross, Westerfield, and Jordan
Fundamentals of Corporate Finance
Second Edition

Schary
Cases in Financial Management
First Edition

Stonehill and Eiterman
Finance: An International Perspective
First Edition

White
Financial Calculator Applications
First Edition

INVESTMENTS

Bodie, Kane, and Marcus
Essentials of Investments
First Edition

Bodie, Kane, and Marcus
Investments
Second Edition

Bolster
The Wall Street Journal: Applications in Finance
1994 Edition

Cohen, ZInbarg, Zeikel
Investment Analysis and Portfolio Management
Fifth Edition

Hirt and Block
Fundamentals of Investment Management
Fourth Edition

Lorie, Dodd, and Kimpton
The Stock Market: Theories & Evidence
Second Edition

MarketBase, Inc.
MarketBase^{SM-E}
First Edition

Shimko
The Innovative Investor, Version 2.0
First Edition

FINANCIAL INSTITUTIONS AND MARKETS

Rose
Readings on Financial Institutions and Markets
Sixth Edition

Rose
Money and Capital Markets: The Financial System in an Increasingly Global Economy
Fifth Edition

Rose
Commercial Bank Management: Producing and Selling Financial Services
Second Edition

Rose and Kolari
Financial Institutions: Understanding & Managing Financial Services
Fourth Edition

Saunders
Financial Institutions Management: A Modern Perspective
First Edition

REAL ESTATE

Berston
California Real Estate Practice
Sixth Edition

Berston
California Real Estate Principles
Sixth Edition

Brueggeman and Fisher
Real Estate Finance and Investments
Ninth Edition

Smith and Corgel
Real Estate Perspectives: An Introduction to Real Estate
Second Edition

Shenkel
Real Estate Finance
First Edition

FINANCIAL PLANNING AND INSURANCE

Allen, Melone, Rosenbloom, and VanDerhei
Pension Planning: Pensions, Profit-Sharing, and Other Deferred Compensation Plans
Seventh Edition

Crawford and Beadles
Life Insurance Law
Seventh Edition

Crawford
Life Insurance Law
LOMA Edition

Hirsch and Donaldson
Casualty Claims Practice
Fifth Edition

Kapoor, Dlabay, and Hughes
Personal Finance
Third Edition

Kellison
Theory of Interest
Second Edition

Rokes
Human Relations in Handling Insurance Claims
Revised Edition

FINANCIAL INSTITUTIONS MANAGEMENT

A MODERN PERSPECTIVE

Anthony Saunders

John M. Schiff Professor of Finance
Salomon Center
Stern School of Business
New York University

Burr Ridge, Illinois
Boston, Massachusetts
Sydney, Australia

© RICHARD D. IRWIN, INC., 1994

All rights reserved. No part of this publication may be
reproduced, stored in a retrieval system, or transmitted,
in any form or by any means, electronic, mechanical,
photocopying, recording, or otherwise,
without the prior written permission of the publisher.

Sponsoring editor: *James M. Keefe*
Developmental editor: *Jennifer Eddy*
Marketing manager: *Ron Bloecher*
Project editor: *Paula M. Buschman*
Production manager: *Ann Cassady*
Designer: *Mercedes Santos*
Art coordinator: *Heather Burbridge*
Art studio: *Jay Benson Studios*
Compositor: *Weimer Graphics, Inc.*
Typeface: *10/12 Times Roman*
Printer: *Von Hoffman*

Library of Congress Cataloging-in-Publication Data

Saunders, Anthony.
    Financial institutions management: a modern perspective / by Anthony Saunders.
        p.   cm. — (The Irwin series in finance)
    Includes bibliograhical references and index.
    ISBN 0–256–11056–5
        1. Financial institutions—United States—Management.   2. Risk management —United States.
    3. Financial services industry—United States—Management.   I. Title.   II. Series.
HG181.S33   1994
332.1'068—dc20   93–5597

Printed in the United States of America

2 3 4 5 6 7 8 9 0 VH 0 9 8 7 6 5 4

This book is dedicated to
Pat, Nicholas, and Emily
and to my parents Meyer
and Evelyn.

Anthony Saunders

Anthony Saunders is the John M. Schiff Professor of Finance at the Stern School of Business at New York University. Having received his Ph.D. from the London School of Economics, Professor Saunders has taught both undergraduate and graduate level courses at NYU since 1978. Throughout his academic career his teaching and research has specialized in financial institutions and international banking. He is currently on the Executive Committee of the Salmon Brothers Center for the Study of Financial Institutions. He has also served as a visiting professor all over the world, including INSEAD, the Stockholm School of Economics, and the University of Melbourne.

Professor Saunders currently holds positions on the Board of Academic Consultants of the Federal Reserve Board of Governors as well as the Council of Research Advisors for the Federal National Mortgage Association. In addition, Dr. Saunders has acted as a visiting scholar and as the Comptroller of the Currency at the Federal Reserve Bank of Philadelphia. He also held a visiting position in the research department of the International Monetary Fund. He is the editor of the *Journal of Financial Markets, Instruments and Institutions* as well as the associate editor of eight other journals including *Financial Management* and the *Journal of Banking and Finance*. His research has been published in all of the major money and banking journals and in several books. In addition, he has authored or co-authored several professional books.

PREFACE

The financial services industry is undergoing great changes. Not only are the boundaries between traditional industry sectors, such as commercial banking and investment banking, breaking down but competition is becoming increasingly global in nature. There are many forces contributing to this breakdown in inter-industry and inter-country barriers, including financial innovation, technology, taxation, and regulation. It is in this context that this book is written.

Although the traditional nature of each sector's product activity is analyzed, a greater emphasis is placed on *new* areas of activities such as asset securitization, off-balance-sheet banking, international banking, and so on.

This text takes an innovative approach and focuses on managing return and risk in modern financial institutions (FIs). *Financial Institutions Management's* central theme is that the risks faced by FI managers and the methods and markets through which these risks are managed are becoming increasingly similar whether the institution is chartered as a commercial bank, a savings bank, an investment bank, or an insurance company.

Similar to any stockholder-owned corporation, the goal of FI managers should always be to maximize the value of the financial intermediary. However, pursuit of value maximization does not mean that risk management can be ignored.

Indeed, modern FIs are in the risk management business. As we discuss in this book, in a world of perfect and frictionless capital markets, FIs would not exist and individuals would manage their own financial assets and portfolios. But since real-world financial markets are not perfect, FIs provide the positive function of bearing and managing risk on behalf of their customers through the pooling of risks and the sale of their services as risk specialists. Thus, just as a shoe manufacturer has to manage an inventory of shoe leather, the FI has to manage an inventory of risk.

Intended Audience

Financial Institutions Management: A Modern Perspective is aimed at the upper level undergraduate and an MBA audience. Occasionally, in Chapters 6, 7, 8, and 21, there are more technical sections which are marked with an asterisk. These sections may be included or dropped from chapter reading, depending on the rigor of the course, without harming the continuity of the chapters.

Main Features

Throughout the text special features have been added to encourage student interaction with the text and aid in absorbing the material. Some of these features include:

- **Learning objectives** which open each chapter and alert the student to what they can expect to learn from the chapter discussion.
- **Bold key terms and marginal glossary** which emphasize the main terms and concepts throughout the chapter. They emphasize the most important terms and aid in studying.
- **Concept questions** which allow the student to test themselves on the main concepts within each major chapter section.
- **Professional Perspective boxes** featuring financial practitioners and how they apply some of the topics throughout the text.
- **Integrative problem material** that covers all the main topics within the chapter.

Ancillaries

To assist in course preparation the following ancillaries are offered:

- Instructor's Manual/Test Bank includes detailed chapter contents, complete solutions to end of chapter question and problem material and additional problems for test material.
- Computest, our computerized version of the test bank, allows the instructor to pick and choose the order and amount of questions to include for each test.

Organization

Since our focus is on return and risk and the sources of that return and risk, this book relates ways in which the managers of modern FIs can expand return with a managed level of risk to achieve the best, or most favorable, return-risk outcome for FI owners.

Chapters 1 and 2 provide an overview describing the key balance sheet and regulatory features of the major sectors of the U.S. financial services industry. We discuss depository institutions in Chapter 1 and other financial institutions in Chapter 2. Chapter 3 takes an analytical look at how financial intermediation benefits today's economy.

In Chapter 4 we start the risk measurement section with an overview of the risks facing a modern FI. In Chapters 5, 6, and 7, we investigate the net interest margin as a source of profitability and risk, with a focus on the effects of interest rate volatility and the mismatching of asset and liability durations on FI risk exposure.

In Chapter 8, we look at the measurement of credit risk and how this risk adversely impacts an FI's profits through losses and provisions against the loan and debt security portfolio. Modern FIs do more than generate returns and bear risk through traditional maturity mismatching and credit extensions. They also are increasingly engaging in off-balance-sheet activities to generate fee income (Chapter 9), making technological investments to reduce costs (Chapter 10), pursuing foreign exchange activities and overseas financial investments (Chapter 11), and engaging in sovereign lending and securities activities (Chapter 12). Each of these has implications for the size and variability of an FI's profit and/or its revenues. In addition, as a by-product of the provision of their interest rate and credit intermediation services, FIs face liquidity risk. We analyze the special nature of this risk in Chapter 13.

In Chapter 14, we begin the risk management section by looking at ways in which FIs can insulate themselves from risk. At the core of FI risk insulation is the size and adequacy of the owners' capital stake, which is the focus of Chapter 14. In Chapter 15, we go on to consider the role of deposit insurance and other guarantee schemes as mechanisms for deterring liquidity problems in FIs, especially in preventing runs, panics, and eventual insolvencies. Chapters 16 and 17 analyze how and why both product and geographic diversification can improve an FI's return-risk performance and the impact of regulation on the diversification opportunity set. Chapters 18 through 22 review various new markets and instruments that have been innovated or engineered to allow FIs to better manage three important types of risk: interest rate risk, credit risk, and foreign exchange risk. These markets and instruments and their strategic use by FIs include futures and forwards (Chapter 18); options, caps, floors, and collars (Chapter 19); swaps (Chapter 20); securitization (Chapter 21); and loan sales (Chapter 22). In Chapter 23, we describe the role and use of asset and liability management as a device to control liquidity risk exposure.

Acknowledgments

Finally, I would like to thank a number of colleagues without whose help this book would never have been written. In no particular order, they are Linda Allen, Mitch Berlin, Allen Berger, and Greg Udell. Linda Allen wrote the end of chapter problems, the Instructors Manual and the Test Bank. Also of great help were the book reviewers whose painstaking comments and advice guided the book through its second and third revisions.

George Benston
Emory University

William A. Christiansen
Florida State University

Marcia M. Cornett
Southern Methodist University

Robert A. Eisenbeis
University of North Carolina

David Ely
San Diego State University

Joseph E. Finnerty
University of Illinois—Champaign/Urbana

Gary Gorton
University of Pennsylvania—Wharton

John R. Hall, Jr.
University of Missouri—Columbia

Gerald A. Hanweck	George G. Kaufman
George Mason University	*Loyola University—Chicago*
David W. Johnson	George W. Kutner
University of Northern Colorado	*Marquette University*
Edward J. Kane	Dennis Lasser
Boston College	*State University of New York—Binghamton*

I very much appreciate the contributions of Jennifer Eddy, Joanne Dorff, and Mike Junior at Irwin, my research assistant Abon Mazumdar, and my secretary Robyn Vanterpool. Without Robyn's diligence and accurate reproduction of my scrawl into typed script, the project would never have been completed on time.

Anthony Saunders

LIST OF PROFESSIONAL PERSPECTIVE BOXES

BRIEF CONTENTS

CONTENTS

PART III

MANAGING RISK

INTRODUCTION

THE FINANCIAL SERVICE INDUSTRY

Depository Institutions

Learning Objectives

In this chapter you learn about two major groups of financial intermediaries (FIs): commercial banks and thrifts or so-called depository institutions. The major activities of each group are described (including their balance sheets) so you can gain an appreciation of the similarities and differences between these groups. For example, depository institutions compete in many of the same markets and face similar types of risk. This chapter also explains the regulators and the major laws governing the activities of each FI group. In Chapter 2, we analyze other FIs in a similar fashion.

Introduction

The theme of this book is that the risks faced by modern FIs are becoming increasingly similar, as are the techniques used to measure and manage these risks. In this chapter we begin by describing two major FI groups, commercial banks and thrifts, which are also called depository institutions because a significant proportion of their funds come from customer deposits. Our attention focuses on three major characteristics of each group: (1) size, structure, and composition of the industry group; (2) balance sheets and recent trends; and (3) regulation. A final section is an overview of the similarities of the risk exposures among these FIs.

Commercial Banks

Size, Structure, and Composition of the Industry

At the end of 1991, the United States had 11,519 commercial banks. Even though this may seem a large number, in fact the number of banks has been shrinking due to consolidations via mergers and departures from the industry due to failures. For example, in 1985 there were 14,416 banks and in 1989, 12,744.

Note the size distribution of the commercial banking industry in Table 1–1. As can be seen, there are many small banks. In fact, 10,897 banks or 95 percent accounted for approximately 23.8 percent of the assets of the industry in 1991. Often called community banks, these smaller banks—under $500 million in asset size—tend to specialize in retail or consumer banking, such as providing residential mortgages and consumer loans and in accessing the local deposit base. The majority of

TABLE 1–1 U.S. Commercial Banks, 1991

Year	$0–$25 million	$25–$50 million	$50–$100 million	$100–$500 million	$500 million–$1 billion	$1 billion+
Number of Banks	2,846	3,092	2,750	2,209	257	365
Percent of U.S. Banks	24.7%	26.8%	23.9%	19.2%	2.2%	3.2%
Total assets ($ billions)	$44.2	$108.3	$188.0	$444.4	$173.7	$2,331.9
Percent of U.S. total assets	1.3%	3.3%	5.7%	13.5%	5.3%	70.9%

SOURCE: Federal Reserve Bank of Atlanta, *Economic Review,* May–June 1992.

Federal Funds Market
An interbank market for short-term borrowing and lending of bank reserves.

Money Center Bank
A bank that has a heavy reliance on nondeposit or borrowed sources of funds.

banks in the largest two size classes ($500 million and above) are often either regional or super-regional banks. They engage in a more complete array of commercial banking activities encompassing consumer and residential lending as well as commercial and industrial lending (so-called C and I loans) both regionally and nationally. In addition, the big banks access markets for purchased funds—such as the interbank or **federal funds market**—to finance their lending and investment activities. However, some of the very biggest banks often have the separate title, **money center banks.** For example, Salomon Brothers equity research department identified 10 banking organizations as comprising the money center bank group: Bank of New York, Bankers Trust, Chase Manhattan, Chemical, Citicorp, J. P. Morgan, Republic NY Corporation, Bank of Boston, First Chicago, and Continental Bank Corporation.[1]

It is important to note that asset or lending size does not necessarily make a bank into a money center bank. Thus, BankAmerica Corporation with $128 billion in loans in 1992 (the second largest U.S. bank organization) is not a money center bank while Republic NY Corporation (with only $7 billion in loans) is a money center bank. What makes a bank a money center bank is partly location and partly its heavy reliance on nondeposit or borrowed sources of funds.[2] In fact, because of its extensive retail branch network, Bank of America—the subsidiary bank of BankAmerica Corporation—tends to be a net supplier of funds on the interbank market (federal funds market). By contrast, money center banks such as J. P. Morgan and Bankers Trust have no retail branches and rely almost entirely on wholesale and borrowed funds as sources of funds or liabilities.

The bigger banks tend to fund themselves in national markets and to lend to larger corporations. This means that the spreads or margins they can earn between their cost of funds and earnings on assets are often narrower than those of smaller community banks, which are often sheltered from competition in highly localized markets. For example, in 1991 the smallest banks were operating with an adjusted net interest margin (NIM)—the difference between the return on assets and cost of funds adjusted for defaults—of 4.29 percent compared to 2.74 percent for the largest banks. Because the NIM is an important component of a bank's overall profit margin, the

---

[1]These banking organizations are mostly holding companies that own and control the shares of a bank. Thus Citicorp is the bank organization (holding company) that owns and controls Citibank (the bank subsidiary).

[2]A money center bank is normally headquartered in New York, Chicago, or San Francisco. These are the traditional national and regional centers for correspondent banking services offered to smaller non-urban banks.

ROE
Return on equity is equal to an FI's net income divided by shareholders' equity.

ROA
Return on assets is equal to an FI's net income divided by its earning assets.

largest banks' **ROE** and **ROA** have generally been lower than that for the smallest banks (see Table 1–2).

Balance Sheet and Trends

Assets. Figure 1–1 shows the broad trends in the four principal earning asset areas of commercial banks: business loans (or commercial and industrial loans), securities, mortgages, and consumer loans. Although business loans were the major asset in bank balance sheets between 1965 and 1990, there has been a sudden drop in volume (as a proportion of the balance sheet) since 1990. This drop has been mirrored by an offsetting rise in securities holdings and mortgages. These trends reflect a number of secular and temporary influences. One important secular influence has been the growth of the commercial paper market that has become an alternative funding source to commercial bank loans for major corporations. Another has been the securitization of mortgages—the pooling and packaging of mortgage loans for sale in the form of bonds. A more temporary influence has been the so-called credit crunch and decline in the demand for business loans as a result of the economic downturn and recession of the 1989–92 period.

Look at the detailed balance sheet for all U.S. commercial banks as of October 28, 1992, in Table 1–3. Total loans amount to $2.26 trillion and fall into four broad classes: business or commercial and industrial ($.6 trillion); commercial and residential real estate ($.88 trillion); individual, such as consumer loans for auto purchases and credit card debt ($.356 trillion); and all other loans, such as lesser developed country (LDC) loans ($.256 trillion). Of the investment security portfolio of $.78 trillion, U.S. government securities, such as Treasury bonds, comprised $.62 trillion with other securities (in particular, municipal securities and investment grade corporate bonds) making up the rest. The balance sheet also distinguishes between those securities held by banks for trading purposes, normally for less than one year, and those

TABLE 1–2

Year	All Banks	$0–$25 million	$25–50 million	$50–$100 million	$100–$500 million	$500 million– $1 billion	$1 billion+
Percentage Return on Assets *(Insured commercial banks by consolidated assets)*							
1987	0.09%	0.26%	0.46%	0.66%	0.73%	0.51%	−0.15%
1988	0.83	0.36	0.61	0.77	0.80	0.58	0.89
1989	0.50	0.60	0.73	0.88	0.91	0.88	0.35
1990	0.50	0.60	0.71	0.81	0.79	0.77	0.39
1991	0.55	0.64	0.75	0.86	0.85	0.56	0.45
Percentage Return on Equity *(Insured commercial banks by consolidated assets)*							
1987	1.49%	2.75%	5.39%	8.02%	9.93%	7.51%	−2.80%
1988	13.51	3.79	6.96	9.15	10.53	8.67	16.40
1989	7.85	6.15	8.14	10.12	11.81	12.72	6.21
1990	7.81	6.02	7.81	9.29	10.14	10.37	6.86
1991	8.21	6.46	8.10	9.68	10.78	7.85	7.49

SOURCE: Federal Reserve Bank of Atlanta, *Economic Review,* May-June 1992.

FIGURE 1–1

Portfolio shift: American commercial banks' financial assets

Percent of total

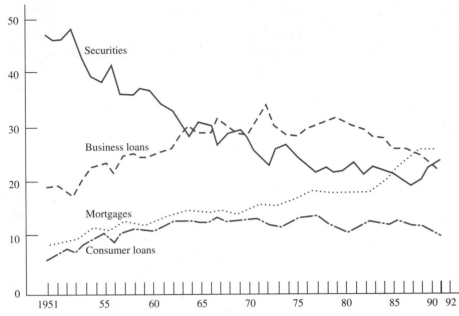

SOURCE: Federal Reserve Bank of San Francisco.

held for longer-term investment purposes. The large money center banks are often active in the secondary market trading of government securities, reflecting their important role as primary dealers in government securities at the time of Treasury security auctions.

The major inference we can draw from this asset structure is that credit or default exposure is a major risk faced by modern commercial bank managers.

Liabilities.   Commercial banks have two major sources of funds other than the equity provided by owners: deposits and borrowed or other liability funds. The major difference between banks and other firms, especially other financial service firms, is their high leverage. For example, banks had an average ratio of equity to assets of 6.68 percent in 1991; this implies 93.32 percent of assets were funded by debt, either deposits or borrowed funds.

Note in Table 1–3, the aggregate balance sheet of U.S. banks, that deposits amounted to $2.48 trillion and borrowings and other liabilities were $.49 and $.34 trillion respectively. Of the total stock of deposits, transaction accounts comprised 29 percent, or $.72 trillion. **Transactions accounts** are checkable deposits that either bear no interest (so-called demand deposits) or are interest bearing (most commonly called **NOW accounts** or negotiable order of withdrawal accounts). Since their introduction in 1980, interest-bearing checking accounts—especially NOW accounts—have dominated the transaction accounts of banks. However, since there are limitations imposed on the ability of corporations to hold such accounts and there are minimum balance requirements for NOW accounts, noninterest-bearing demand deposits are still held. The second major segment of deposits is retail or household savings and time deposits, normally individual account holdings of less than $100,000.

Transaction Accounts
The sum of noninterest-bearing demand deposits and interest-bearing checking accounts.

NOW account
An interest-bearing checking account.

**TABLE 1–3 Balance Sheet (All U.S. Commercial Banks)
As of October 28, 1992 (in millions)**

Assets			
Loans and securities...................................			$3,083,082
Investment securities.............................		$781,185	
U.S. government securities		$618,057	
Other		163,068	
Trading account assets			41,140
U.S. government securities		24,924	
Other securities		3,592	
Other trading account assets		12,624	
Total loans...			2,260,818
Interbank loans..		157,123	
Loans excluding interbank		2,103,695	
Commercial and industrial...................	$601,186		
Real estate...	888,839		
Revolving home equity	$73,706		
Other	815,133		
Individual...	356,923		
All Other	256,748		
Total cash assets.......................................			203,683
Balances with Federal Reserve Banks		24,519	
Cash in vault		31,658	
Demand balances at U.S. depository institutions..		29,985	
Cash items...		73,333	
Other cash assets.....................................		44,188	
Other assets...			287,228
Total Assets...			$3,573,993
Liabilities			
Total deposits			$2,478,756
Transaction accounts..............................		$718,206	
Demand, U.S. government....................	$2,522		
Demand, depository institutions	39,037		
Other demand and all checkable deposits	676,647		
Savings deposits excluding checkable		738,848	
Small time deposits................................		645,000	
Time deposits over $100,000		376,703	
Borrowings			491,820
Treasury tax and loan notes		16,221	
Other		475,599	
Other liabilities			339,918
Total liabilities			$3,310,494
Residual (assets less liabilities).................			263,499

SOURCE: *Federal Reserve Bulletin*, January 1993, p. A19.

Important components of bank retail savings accounts are passbook savings and money market deposit accounts introduced in 1982.[3] These two deposit categories combined comprise 56 percent of the total deposits. However, this disguises an important trend in the supply of these deposits to banks. Specifically, retail savings and

---

[3]The $100,000 ceiling is the cap for explicit coverage under bank deposit insurance. We discuss this in more detail in Chapter 15.

Money Market Mutual Fund
A specialized (mutual fund) FI that offers deposit-like interest-bearing claims to savers.

Negotiable CDs
Fixed-maturity interest-bearing deposits with face values over $100,000 that can be resold in the secondary market.

time deposits have been falling in recent years largely as a result of competition from **money market mutual funds.** These funds pay a competitive rate of interest based on wholesale money market rates by pooling and investing funds (see Chapter 2), while requiring relatively small denomination investments.

The third major source of funds is time deposits over $100,000; these amounted to $.38 trillion, or approximately 15 percent of the stock of deposits in October 1992. These are primarily **negotiable certificates of deposit** (deposit claims with promised interest rates and fixed maturities of at least 14 days) which can be resold to outside investors in an organized secondary market. As such, they are usually distinguished from retail time deposits by their negotiability and secondary market liquidity.

Nondeposit liabilities comprise borrowings and other liabilities which together total 25 percent of all bank liabilities, or $.83 trillion. These categories include a broad array of instruments such as purchases of federal funds (bank reserves) on the interbank market and repurchase agreements (temporary swaps of securities for federal funds) at the short end of the maturity spectrum to the issuance of notes and bonds at the longer end.[4]

Overall, the liability structure of bank balance sheets tends to reflect a shorter maturity structure than the asset portfolio with relatively more liquid instruments—such as deposits and interbank borrowings—used to fund less liquid assets. Thus, maturity mismatch or interest rate risk and liquidity risk are key exposure concerns for bank managers.

Off-Balance-Sheet Activities.   Looking at the balance sheet alone tends to disguise many fee-related activities conducted by banks off-the-balance sheet. These include issuing various types of guarantees (such as letters of credit) that often have a strong insurance underwriting element and making commitments to lend in the future for a fee. They also involve engaging in futures, forward, options, and swap transactions that are not reflected in the current balance sheet because it is a fixed picture of the bank's outstanding assets and liabilities today. As we discuss in Chapter 9, off-balance-sheet activities are increasing in importance compared to the on-balance-sheet activities of many of the nation's largest banks. This is due to increased competition from other FIs and financial instruments in traditional areas of activity—commercial lending and deposit taking—as well as to fee, maturity (or duration) gap management, and regulatory incentives to move off-balance sheet. As will be discussed, these activities expose banks to new and important credit and other risks.

Regulation

The Regulators.   Unlike other countries that have one or sometimes two regulators, U.S. banks may be subject to the supervision and regulations of up to four separate regulators. The key regulators are the Federal Deposit Insurance Corporation (FDIC), the Comptroller of the Currency (COC), the Federal Reserve System (FRS), and state bank regulators.

Next, we can look at the principal roles played by each. For a full description of their regulatory powers, look at the appendix to this chapter.

The FDIC.   Established in 1933, the Federal Deposit Insurance Corporation insures the deposits of member banks. In so doing, it levies insurance premiums on member

---

[4]These instruments are explained in greater detail in later chapters, especially Chapter 23.

banks, manages the deposit insurance fund, and carries out bank examinations. Further, when an insured bank is closed, the FDIC acts as the receiver and liquidator—although the closure decision itself is technically in the hands of the bank chartering or licensing agency such as the COC. Because of the problems in the thrift industry and the insolvency of the savings and loan (S&L) insurance fund (FSLIC) in 1989, the FDIC now manages both the commercial bank insurance fund and the savings and loan insurance fund. The Bank Insurance fund is called BIF and the S&L fund, SAIF (Savings Association Insurance Fund).

As of the third quarter of 1992, only three commercial banks with combined assets of $243 million were not insured by the FDIC. The remaining 11,492 banks, with assets of $3,481.5 billion, were members of the FDIC's BIF fund. (See Figure 1–2.)

Comptroller of the Currency (COC).   COC is the oldest bank regulatory agency; established in 1863, it is a subagency of the U.S. Treasury. Its primary function is to charter so-called national banks as well as to close them. In addition, COC examines national banks and has the power to approve or disapprove their merger applications. However, instead of seeking a national charter, banks can be chartered by 1 of 50 individual state bank regulatory agencies. The choice of being a nationally chartered or state-chartered bank lies at the foundation of the **dual banking system** in the United States. While most large banks such as Citibank choose national charters, this is not always the case. For example, Morgan Guaranty, the money center bank subsidiary of J. P. Morgan is chartered as a state bank under New York State law. In the third quarter of 1992, 3,622 banks were *nationally* chartered and 7,870 *state* chartered, with approximately 57 percent and 43 percent of total commercial bank assets respectively.

Federal Reserve System.   Apart from being concerned with the conduct of monetary policy, as this country's central bank the Federal Reserve also has regulatory power over some banks and, when relevant, their holding company parents. As shown in Figure 1–2, all nationally chartered banks are automatically members of the Federal Reserve system; 960 of the state-chartered banks have also chosen to become members. Since 1980, all banks have had to meet the same noninterest bearing reserve requirements whether they are members of the Federal Reserve System (FRS) or not. The primary advantages of FRS membership are direct access to the federal funds

Dual Banking System
The coexistence of both nationally and state-chartered banks in the United States.

FIGURE 1–2

Bank regulators

Insured commercial banks (FDIC-BIF)

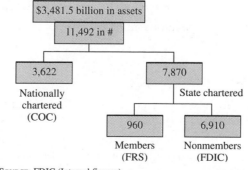

SOURCE: FDIC (Internal figures).

wire transfer network for nationwide interbank borrowing and lending of reserves and to the discount window for lender of last resort borrowing of funds. Finally, many banks are often owned and controlled by parent **holding companies;** for example, Citicorp is the parent holding company of Citibank (a national bank). Because the holding company's management can influence decisions taken by a bank subsidiary and thus influence its risk exposure, the Federal Reserve System regulates and examines bankholding companies as well.

Holding Company
A parent company that owns a controlling interest in a subsidiary bank or other FI.

Regulations.   Commercial banks are among the most regulated firms in the U.S. economy. Because of the inherent special nature of banking and banking contracts—we discuss these in Chapter 3—regulators have imposed numerous restrictions on their products and geographic activities. In Table 1–4, we list the major laws from the McFadden Act of 1927 to the FDIC Improvement Act of 1991 and describe the key features of each briefly.

Even though we will go into greater detail about these regulations in Chapters 14 through 17, we now note the major objectives of each of these laws. The 1927 McFadden Act sought to restrict interstate bank branching while the 1933 Glass-Steagall Act sought to separate commercial banking from investment banking by limiting the powers of commercial banks to engage in securities activities. Restrictions on the nonbank activities of commercial banks were strengthened by the Bank Holding Company Act of 1956 and its 1970 Amendments that limited the ability of a bank's parent holding company to engage in commercial, insurance, and other nonbank financial service activities. The 1978 International Banking Act extended federal regulation, such as the McFadden and Glass-Steagall Acts, to foreign branches and agencies in the United States for the first time, thereby seeking to level the competitive playing field between domestic and foreign banks. The 1980 DIDMCA and the 1982 DIA are mainly deregulation acts, in that they eliminated interest ceilings on deposits and allowed banks (and thrifts) new liability and asset powers.[5] As we discuss in the next section on thrifts, this deregulation is blamed, in part, for the thrift crisis that resulted in widespread failures and the insolvency of FSLIC in 1989.

Nonbank Bank
Undertakes many of the activities of a commercial bank without meeting the legal definition of a bank.

The Competitive Equality in Banking Act (CEBA) 1987 sought to impose controls over a growing number of **nonbank banks** that were established to get around interstate banking restrictions and restrictions on nonbank ownership of banks imposed under the 1927 McFadden and the 1956 Bank Holding Company Acts. In 1989, Congress responded to the problems of thrift banks and the collapse of FSLIC with the passage of FIRREA. In 1991, Congress enacted FDICIA to deal with a large number of bank failures and the threatened insolvency of the FDIC and the commercial bank insurance fund. These acts sought to pull back from some of the deregulatory elements of the 1980 DIDMCA and 1982 DIA. Thus, the most recent legislation has strengthened regulatory control and intervention.

Concept Questions

    1. Why are banks' commercial and industrial (business) loans declining in balance sheet importance?

---

[5]In particular, Regulation Q ceilings on bank deposit rates were phased out in stages between March 1980 and March 1986.

TABLE 1–4   Major Bank Laws (Major Features)

1927 The McFadden Act:

1. Made branching of nationally chartered banks subject to the same branching regulations as state-chartered banks.
2. Liberalized national banks' securities underwriting activities, which previously had to be conducted through state-chartered affiliates.

1933 The Banking Acts of 1933:

1. The Glass-Steagall Act generally prohibited commercial banks from underwriting securities with four exceptions:
   a. Municipal general obligation bonds.
   b. U.S. government bonds.
   c. Private placements.
   d. Real estate loans.
2. In addition, the acts established the FDIC to insure bank deposits.

1956 The Bank Holding Company Act:

1. Restricted the banking and nonbanking acquisition activities of multibank holding companies.
2. Empowered the Federal Reserve to regulate multibank holding companies by:
   a. Determining permissible activities.
   b. Exercising supervisory authority.
   c. Exercising chartering authority.
   d. Conducting bank examinations.

1970 Amendments to the Bank Holding Company Act of 1956:

1. Extended the BHC Act of 1956 to one-bank holding companies.
2. Restricted permissible BHC activities to those "closely related to banking."

1978 International Banking Act

1. Regulated foreign bank branches and agencies in the United States.
2. Subjected foreign banks to the McFadden and Glass-Steagall Acts.
3. Gave foreign banks access to fedwire, the discount window, and deposit insurance.

1980 Depository Institutions Deregulation and Monetary Control Act (DIDMCA)

1. Set a six-year phase out for Regulation Q interest rate ceilings on small time and savings deposits.
2. Authorized NOW accounts nationwide.
3. Introduced uniform reserve requirements for state and nationally chartered banks.
4. Increased the ceiling on deposit insurance coverage from $40,000 to $100,000.
5. Allowed federally chartered thrifts to make consumer and commercial loans (subject to size restrictions).

1982 Garn-St Germain Depository Institutions Act (DIA)

1. Introduced money market deposit accounts (MMDAs) and super NOW accounts as interest rate-bearing savings accounts with limited check writing features.
2. Allowed federally chartered thrifts more extensive lending powers and demand deposit taking powers.
3. Allowed sound commercial banks to acquire failed savings banks.
4. Reaffirmed limitations on bank powers to underwrite and distribute insurance.

1987 Competitive Equality in Banking Act (CEBA)

1. Redefined the definition of a *bank* to limit the growth of nonbank banks.
2. Sought to recapitalize the Federal Savings and Loan Insurance Corporation (FSLIC).

1989 Financial Institutions Reform Recovery and Enforcement Act (FIRREA)

1. Limited savings banks' investments in nonresidential real estate, required divestiture of junk bond holdings (by 1994), and imposed a restrictive asset test to qualify as a savings bank (the qualified thrift lender test or QTL).
2. Equalized the capital requirements of thrifts and banks.
3. Replaced FSLIC with FDIC-SAIF.

4. Replaced the Federal Home Loan Bank Board as the charterer of federal savings and loans with the Office of Thrift Supervision (OTS), an agency of the Treasury.
5. Created the Resolution Trust Corporation (RTC) to resolve failed and failing savings banks.

1991 Federal Deposit Insurance Corporation Improvement Act (FDICIA)

1. Introduced prompt corrective action (PCA), requiring mandatory interventions by regulators whenever a bank's capital falls.
2. Introduced risk-based deposit insurance premiums beginning in 1993.
3. Limited the use of "too big to fail" bailouts by federal regulators for large banks.
4. Extended federal regulation over foreign bank branches and agencies in the Foreign Bank Supervision and Enhancement Act (FBSEA).

2. What is the definition of a money center bank?
3. Is there any link between the 1927 McFadden Act and the large number of banks in the United States?
4. Do we really need *three* federal regulators for banks?
5. Why are banks' leverage ratios higher and their equity-asset ratios lower than those of commercial firms?
6. What is the most important bank asset in current balance sheets?

Thrifts

Thrift institutions comprise three different groups of FIs: savings and loan associations (S&Ls), savings banks (SBs) and credit unions (CUs). They are usually grouped together because they not only provide important mortgage and/or lending services to households but also are important recipients of household savings. Historically, S&Ls have concentrated mostly on residential mortgages, while credit unions focused on consumer loans. Savings banks have been operated as more diversified S&Ls having a large concentration of residential mortgage assets, but holding commercial loans, corporate bonds, and corporate stock as well. In the next sections, we review each of these groups in turn.

Savings and Loans (S&Ls)

Size, Structure, and Composition of the Industry. The S&L industry prospered throughout most of the 20th century; these specialized institutions made long-term residential mortgages backed by short-term savings deposits. This was made possible largely because of the Federal Reserve's policy of smoothing or targeting interest rates—especially in the 1960s and 1970s until October 1979—and the generally upward-sloping shape of the yield curve, or the term structure of interest rates. There were periods, such as the early 1960s, when the yield curve sloped downwards.[6] But, for most of the post-Second World War period, the upward-sloping yield curve meant that the interest rates on 30-year residential mortgage assets exceeded short rates on savings and time deposit liabilities. Moreover, significant shocks to interest rates were generally absent due to the Fed's policy of interest rate smoothing.

---

[6]Under so-called operation twist that sought to decrease long-term rates and increase short-term rates by altering the amount of short-term relative to long-term debt outstanding.

President Clinton's Agenda for Financial Institutions

Gillian Garcia

Despite its initial slowness in making appointments to financial regulatory agencies, the Clinton administration has several financial sector incentives. They derive from its principal focus—improving the economy. Soon after the election, Clinton's economic summit drew attention to the impediments the credit crunch presents to economic growth. Comptroller of the Currency Eugene Ludwig has spearheaded an interagency project to eliminate counterproductive overregulation to ease the crunch.

To date, the administration has not proposed legislation to reverse any components of the two major financial sector bills passed during the Bush administration nor has it supported rollback bills now before Congress. These major financial acts were the Financial Institutions Reform, Recovery, and Enforcement Act (FIRREA) of 1989, which provided money for the S&L cleanup, and the FDIC Improvement Act (FDICIA) of 1991, which imposed tighter discipline on the banking industry and reformed deposit insurance. The Treasury Department has prodded the House to join the Senate in authorizing additional funds for the Resolution Trust Corporation and the Savings Association Insurance Fund to complete the S&L cleanup.

Other components of the president's initiatives for the financial services industry address the social aspects of banking. For example, bankers who complain of overregulation typically cite the Community Reinvestment Act (CRA) as the most burdensome and ineffective regulation. So, the president plans to revamp the CRA program to emphasize that insured banks and thrifts must meet the credit needs of all the communities they serve, including the low-income communities in both rural and urban areas.

Also, the administration has announced its intention to end discrimination in mortgage lending. Section 1211 of FIRREA required insured lenders to report to their primary federal regulator the "cen-sus tract, income level, racial characteristics and gender" of mortgage applicants and the outcome of their applications. Subsequent Federal Reserve studies have used this data to provide strong evidence of discrimination against African Americans and Hispanic mortgage applicants. The Office of the Comptroller of the Currency (OCC) has instituted a program to identify national banks guilty of discriminaton. To ascertain whether everyone receives equal treatment, OCC conducts controlled experiments in which African American or Hispanic couples and white couples ("testers") apply for credit at the same institution.

Still unclear is whether the Clinton administration will adopt any of the industry's proposals to enhance the value of the bank charter by permitting interstate branching, repealing the Glass Steagall Act, unifying banking and commerce, and consolidating the regulatory system. The chairmen of the House and Senate banking committees favor waiting to see if FIRREA and FDICIA have succeeded in reforming the deposit insurance system and protecting taxpayers from additional losses before enacting legislation that will modernize the banking system. They also favor consolidating the regulatory system in one independent agency.

BIOGRAPHICAL SUMMARY

Gillian (Jill) Garcia is currently a member of the staff of the Senate Banking Committee and a distinguished Adjunct Professor in the Business School at Georgetown University. Initially, she was an Assistant Professor at the University of California at Berkeley. While on leave at the Office of the Comptroller of the Currency in Washington, she developed an interest in financial legislation. Subsequently she co-authored two books with Professor Thomas Cargill of the University of Nevada, one on the Depository Institutions Deregulation and Monetary Control Act of 1980 and the other on the Garn-St Germain Act of 1982; both were published by the Hoover Institution. She became a senior economist at the Federal Reserve Bank of Chicago and then returned to Washington to create a group of economists at the U.S. General Accounting Office to monitor the bank and thrift crises for Congress. While at GAO, she wrote *The Federal Reserve: Lender of Last Resort* with Elizabeth Plautz. From GAO, she moved to the Senate to participate in legislation to reform the banking and thrift industries. She has recently begun her book about the political economy of financial reform.

At the end of the 1970s slightly less than 4,000 S& Ls had assets of approximately $.6 trillion. Over the October 1979 to October 1982 period, however, the Federal Reserve radically changed its monetary policy strategy by targeting bank reserves rather than interest rates in an attempt to lower the underlying rate of inflation (see Chapter 5 for more details). The Fed's restrictive monetary policy action led to a sudden and dramatic surge in interest rates with rates on T-bills rising as high as 16 percent. This increase in short-term rates and the cost of funds had two effects: first, S&Ls faced negative interest spreads or net interest margins in funding much of their long-term residential mortgage portfolios over this period. Second, they had to pay more competitive interest rates on savings deposits to prevent **disintermediation** and the reinvestment of these funds in money market mutual fund accounts. Their ability to do this was constrained by the Federal Reserve's **Regulation Q ceilings** that limited the rates S&Ls could pay on traditional passbook savings accounts and retail time deposits.[7]

In part to ameliorate the effects of rising rates and disintermediation on the S&L industry, Congress passed the DIDMCA and DIA (see Table 1–4); these expanded the deposit-taking and asset-investment powers of S&Ls. On the liability side, S&Ls were allowed to offer NOW accounts and more market rate sensitive liabilities, such as money market deposit accounts, to limit disintermediation and to compete for funds. On the asset side, they were allowed to offer floating or adjustable rate mortgages and to a limited extent expand into consumer and commercial lending. In addition, many state chartered thrifts—especially in California, Texas, and Florida—received wider investment powers that included real estate development loans often made through special-purpose subsidiaries. Note the structural shifts in S&L balance sheets between 1977 and 1982 in Table 1–5 and the effects on thrift industry profits in Table 1–6.

For many S&Ls the new powers created safer and more diversified institutions. For a small but significant group whose earnings and shareholders' capital was being eroded in traditional lines of business, however, it meant the opportunity to take more risks in an attempt to return to profitability. This risk-taking or moral hazard behavior was accentuated by the policies of the S&L insurer, FSLIC. It chose not to close capital depleted, economically insolvent S&Ls (a policy of **regulator forbearance**) and to maintain deposit insurance premium assessments independent of the risk of the S&L institution (see Chapter 15).[8] As a result, there was an increasing number of failures in the 1982–89 period aligned with rapid asset growth of the industry. Thus, while S&Ls decreased in number from 4,000 in 1980 to 2,600 in 1989 or by 35 percent, the assets of S&Ls actually doubled from $.6 trillion to $1.2 trillion over the same period.

The mounting number of failures, especially in 1988 and 1989, depleted the resources of FSLIC to such an extent that by 1989 it was massively insolvent. The resulting legislation—the FIRREA of 1989—abolished FSLIC and created a new insurance fund (SAIF) under the management of the FDIC. In addition, the act created the Resolution Trust Corporation (RTC) to close the most insolvent S&Ls.[9] Further, FIRREA strengthened the capital requirements of S&Ls and constrained their nonmortgage-related asset-holding powers under a newly imposed qualified thrift lender or **QTL test.**

Disintermediation
Withdrawal of deposits from S&Ls and other depository institutions and their reinvestment elsewhere.

Regulation Q Ceiling
An interest ceiling imposed on small savings and time deposits at banks and thrifts up until 1986.

Regulator Forbearance
A policy of not closing economically insolvent FIs but allowing them to continue in operation.

QTL Test
Qualified thrift lender test that sets a floor on the mortgage- related assets held by thrifts (currently 65 percent).

---

[7]These Regulation Q ceilings were usually set at rates of 5¼ or 5½ percent.

[8]We discuss moral hazard behavior and the empirical evidence regarding such behavior in more detail in Chapter 15.

[9]As of 1993, the RTC had resolved or closed more than 700 savings banks.

TABLE 1–5   Balance Sheets of Savings and Loans: Percent of total assets and liabilities

Item	1977	1982
Liabilities		
Fixed ceiling liabilities	87.3%	22.0%
Passbook and NOW accounts	33.9	15.6
Fixed ceiling time deposits	53.4	6.4
Market ceiling small time deposits	0.0	52.8
Money market certificates	0.0	28.6
Small saver certificates	0.0	19.3
Other small time deposits	0.0	4.9
Discretionary liabilities	8.6	23.2
Large time deposits	2.1	8.1
FHLB advances	4.7	10.3
Other borrowings	1.8	4.6
Other liabilities	4.0	2.0
Assets		
Mortgage assets	86.0	81.1
Fixed rate	86.0	74.9
Adjustable rate	0.0	6.2
Nonmortgage loans	2.3	2.6
Cash and investments	9.2	11.2
Other assets	2.5	5.1

SOURCE: *Federal Reserve Bulletin,* December 1982.

TABLE 1–6   Net Income at Thrift Institutions

Amounts in billions of dollars; percentages at annual rates

Year	FSLIC-insured savings and loan associations		All operating mutual savings banks	
	Amount	As a percent of average assets	Amount	As a percent of average assets
1970	.9	.57	.2	.27
1971	1.3	.71	.4	.48
1972	1.7	.77	.6	.60
1973	1.9	.76	.6	.54
1974	1.5	.54	.4	.35
1975	1.4	.47	.4	.38
1976	2.3	.63	.6	.45
1977	3.2	.77	.8	.55
1978	3.9	.82	.9	.58
1979	3.6	.67	.7	.46
1980	.8	.14	−.2	−.12
1981	−4.6	−.73	−1.4	−.83
H1	−1.5	−.49	−.5	−.56
H2	−3.1	−.97	−.9	−1.10
1982–H1	−3.3	−1.01	−.8	−.92

NOTE: H = Half-year.
SOURCE: *Federal Reserve Bulletin,* December 1992.

As a result of the closing of weak S&Ls and the strengthening of capital requirements, the industry has shrunk significantly both in numbers and in asset size in the 1990s. Thus, S&Ls decreased from 2,600 in 1989 to 2,013 in June 1992 (by 22 percent) and assets have shrunk from $1.2 trillion to $.84 trillion (by 30 percent).

Balance Sheet and Recent Trends.   Even in its new shrunken state, concerns have been raised about the future viability of the S&L industry in traditional mortgage lending areas. This is partly due to intense competition for mortgages from other financial institutions, such as commercial banks and specialized mortgage bankers. It is also due to the securitization of mortgages into mortgage-backed security pools by government-sponsored enterprises, which we discuss further in Chapter 21.[10] In addition, long-term mortgage lending exposes an FI to significant credit, interest rate, and liquidity risks.

A recent study has found that surviving thrifts have improved their profit margin (6.93 percent in 1992 compared to 4.51 percent in 1987) and reduced their leverage while maintaining a relatively stable level of asset turnover.[11] Nevertheless, this improved performance has been aided by the relatively low interest rate levels in the early 1990s, which has helped S&Ls to expand their net interest margin. The unresolved question is whether S&Ls could survive another period of sharply rising interest rates as in the early 1980s, given their restrained powers of asset diversification and heavy reliance on mortgage assets required by the QTL test for these institutions.[12]

In Table 1–7, we show the balance sheet of S&Ls as of August 1992. On this balance sheet, mortgages and mortgage-backed securities (securitized pools of mortgages) comprise 74 percent of total assets. As noted earlier, the FDICIA uses the qualified thrift lender test to establish a minimum holding of 65 percent in mortgage-related assets for S&Ls. Reflecting the enhanced lending powers established under the 1980 DIDMCA and 1982 DIA, commercial loans and consumer loans amounted to 1.6 and 4.3 percent of assets, respectively. Finally, S&Ls are required to hold cash and investment securities for liquidity purposes and to meet regulator-imposed reserve requirements. In August 1992, cash and securities holdings amounted to 14.5 percent of total assets.

On the liability side of the balance sheet, small time and savings deposits are still the predominant source of funds, with balances less than $100,000 accounting for approximately 90 percent of the $.67 trillion in deposits; the total number of deposit accounts amount to 72.7 million. The second most important source of funds is from the Federal Home Loan Banks (FHLBs) of which there are 12; these, in turn, are owned by the S&Ls themselves. Because of their size and government sponsored status, FHLBs have access to wholesale money markets for notes and bonds and can relend the funds borrowed on these markets to S&Ls at a small markup over wholesale cost. Other borrowed funds include repurchase agreements and direct federal fund borrowings. Finally, net worth is the book value of the equity holders' capital contribution; it amounted to 6.5 percent in August 1992.

---

[10]The major enterprises are GNMA, FNMA, and FHLMC.

[11]Rossi, "The Viability of the Thrift Industry," OTS, Washington, D. C., December 1992.

[12]FIRREA required 70 percent of S&L assets to be mortgage related. FDICIA reduced this to 65 percent.

TABLE 1–7

S&L INSTITUTIONS INSURED BY SAIF
BALANCE SHEET
As of August 1992 (in millions)

Assets		
Mortgages		$512,047
Mortgage-backed securities		120,417
Contra-assets to mortgage assets[1]		11,143
Commercial loans		13,520
Consumer loans		37,115
Contra-assets to nonmortgage loans		905
Cash and investment securities		124,145
Other		61,066
Total assets		$856,169
Liabilities and Net Worth		
Savings capital (deposits)		$672,354
Borrowed money		110,110
FHLB	$62,225	
Other	47,885	
Other		20,526
Net worth		53,179
Total liabilities and net worth		$856,169

[1]Contra-assets are credit-balance accounts that must be subtracted from the corresponding gross asset categories to yield net asset levels. Contra-assets to mortgage assets, mortgage loans, contracts, and pass-through securities—include loans in process, unearned discounts and deferred loan fees, valuation allowances for mortgages "held for sale," and specific reserves and other valuation allowances. Contra-assets to nonmortgage loans include loans in process, unearned discounts and deferred loan fees, and specific reserves and valuation allowances.
SOURCE: *Federal Reserve Bulletin,* January 1993, p. A27.

Regulation.   The two main regulators of S&Ls are the Office of Thrift Supervision and the FDIC–SAIF Fund.

The Office of Thrift Supervision.   Established in 1989 under FIRREA, the office charters and examines all federal S&Ls. Further, where S&Ls are held by parent holding companies, it supervises the holding companies as well. State-chartered S&Ls, of which there were 635 in 1992, are regulated by state agencies rather than the Office of Thrift Supervision (OTS).

The FDIC–SAIF Fund.   Also established in 1989 under FIRREA and in the wake of FSLIC insolvency, the FDIC oversees and manages the Saving Association Insurance Fund (SAIF).

Concept Questions

1. How do adjustable rate mortgages help S&Ls?
2. Why should S&Ls with little or no equity capital seek to take more risk than well-capitalized S&Ls?
3. Why could it be argued that the QTL test makes S&Ls more rather than less risky?
4. Are S&Ls likely to be more or less exposed to interest rate risk than banks? Explain your answer.

Savings Bank

Size, Structure, and Composition of the Industry.   Traditionally, savings banks were established as mutual organizations in those states that permitted such organizations. These states are largely confined to the East Coast such as New York, New Jersey, and the New England states. In recent years, many of these institutions—similar to S&Ls—have switched from mutual to stock charters. In addition, less than 20 have switched to federal charters. In the third quarter of 1992, 332 state-chartered mutual savings banks had $.215 trillion in assets; their deposits are insured by the FDIC under the BIF. This distinguishes savings banks from S&Ls, whose deposits are insured under the FDIC–SAIF.

Balance Sheet and Recent Trends.   Notice the major similarities and differences between S&Ls and savings banks in Table 1–8, which shows their respective balance sheets for the third quarter of 1992. Savings banks have a heavy concentration of 71 percent in mortgage loans and mortgage-backed securities, but this is less than the S&Ls' 79 percent in these assets. Over the years, savings banks have been allowed to diversify more into corporate bonds and stocks; their holdings are 8 percent compared to just over 2 percent for S&Ls. On the liability side, the major difference is that savings banks have more passbook savings accounts and fewer time deposits than S&Ls; nevertheless, small retail deposits are the dominant source of funding for both.

Regulation.   Savings banks may be regulated at both the federal and state levels.

The FDIC-BIF.   Savings banks are insured under the FDIC's BIF and are thus subject to supervision and examination by the FDIC.

Other Regulators.   State-chartered savings banks (the vast majority) are regulated by state agencies. Those savings banks adopting federal charters are subject to the regulations of the OTS (the same as S&Ls).

Concept Question

1. List four characteristics that differentiate savings banks from S&Ls.

Credit Unions

Size, Structure, and Composition of the Industry and Recent Trends.   Credit unions (CUs) are the most numerous of the institutions that comprise the thrift segment of the FI industry. Moreover, they have been less affected by the crisis in the thrift industry than savings banks or savings and loans. This is because more than 65 percent of their assets are in small consumer loans, often for amounts less than $10,000. In addition, CUs tend to hold large amounts of government securities (more than 25 percent of their assets) and very small amounts of residential mortgages. Their lending activities are funded by savings deposits contributed by credit union members who share some common thread or bond of association usually geographical or occupational in nature. For an occupational example, the Federal Reserve Board of Governors has a credit union because all its members are central bankers.

TABLE 1–8

SAVINGS BANKS AND S&Ls
Assets and Liabilities
September 30, 1992

	BIF-Insured Savings Banks		SAIF-Insured S&Ls	
	$ Millions	*Percent*	*$ Millions*	*Percent*
Assets				
Cash and due..	$3,886	1.81	$11,130	1.34
U.S. Treasury and federal agency obligations	15,761	7.33	28,205	3.40
Mortgage loans	123,776	57.58	503,433	60.62
MBS (includes CMOs, POs, IOs)....................	29,382	13.67	156,349	18.83
Bonds, notes, debentures and other securities .	14,007	6.52	15,661	1.89
Corporate stock...	2,967	1.38	2,710	0.33
Commercial loans..	5,467	`2.54	12,459	1.50
Consumer loans	7,216	3.36	36,590	4.41
Other loans and financial leases.....................	1,105	0.51	618	0.07
Other assets..	11,416	5.31	63,267	7.62
Total assets...	214,981	100.00	830,422	100.00
Liabilities				
Savings deposits	78,009	36.29	176,045	21.20
Time deposits..	86,259	40.12	420,383	50.62
Transaction deposits	16,703	7.77	57,313	6.90
Borrowings and mortgage warehousing	11,057	5.14	80,629	9.71
Federal funds purchased and repos.................	4,395	2.04	20,026	2.41
Other liabilities	2,108	0.98	19,711	2.37
Total liabilities...	198,530	92.35	774,107	93.22
Net worth*	16,451	7.65	56,316	6.78
Total liabilities and net worth	214,981	100.00	830,422	100.00
Number of banks..	332		2022	

*Includes limited life preferred stock for BIF-insured state charter savings and co-op banks and redeemable preferred stock and minority interest for SAIF-insured institutions and BIF-insured FSE.
Totals may not add due to rounding.
SOURCE: Savings and Community Bankers of America, Washington, D. C. (Internal figures).

Also, many universities have credit unions. In the third quarter of 1992, more than 13,500 credit unions had assets of $265 billion. This compares to $155 billion in assets in 1987, or a growth rate of 71 percent. Individually, credit unions tend to be very small with a median size of $3 million in 1991 compared to $49 million for banks and $102 million for noncredit union thrifts.[13]

Regulation.   Like savings banks and S&Ls, credit unions can be federally or state chartered. Approximately two thirds of credit unions are federally chartered and subject to National Credit Union Administration (NCUA) regulation. In addition, through its insurance fund (NCUIF) NCUA provides deposit insurance guarantees of up to $100,000 for insured credit unions. Currently, the NCUIF covers 98 percent of all credit union deposits.

---

[13]See Marilyn Little, Federal Reserve Bank of Kansas City, *Financial Industry Trends 1992.*

Concept Questions

1. Why have credit unions prospered in recent years compared to S&Ls and savings banks?
2. What is the major asset held by credit unions?

Summary

This chapter has provided an overview of the major activities of commercial banks and thrifts. Both sets of institutions rely heavily on deposits to fund their activities, although borrowed funds are becoming increasingly important for the largest institutions. Historically, commercial banks have concentrated on commercial or business lending and on investing in securities, while thrifts have concentrated on mortgage lending. This difference is being eroded due to competitive forces, regulation, and changing financial and business technology. Indeed, at the end of 1992, the largest group of assets in commercial bank portfolios were mortgages. This reliance on long-term lending (such as mortgages) and short-term funding means that the interest rate, credit, liquidity, and other risks faced by banks and thrifts are becoming more similar than different. The measurement and management of such exposures are the major themes of Chapters 4 through 23 of this book.

Questions and Problems

1. What are the major sources of funds for commercial banks in the U.S.? What are the major uses of funds for commercial banks in the U.S.? For each of your answers, specify where the item appears on the balance sheet.

2. Contrast the activities of money center commercial banks with superregional and regional banks. Contrast the activities of small commercial banks.

3. Contrast the profitability of small commercial banks with that of large money center banks. What would account for this difference?

4. How did the Financial Institutions Reform, Recovery, and Enforcement Act (FIRREA) of 1989 and the Federal Deposit Insurance Corporation Improvement Act (FDICIA) of 1991 reverse some of the key features of earlier legislation?

5. How would you explain the recent decline in the size of the thrift industry?

6. What are the three major types of thrift FIs? What are their similarities? Differences?

7. What happened to the value of a the thrift charter in the period of time since October 1979? How has this shift contributed to the "thrift crisis"?

8. How did the two major pieces of banking legislation of the early 1980s propose to rescue the thrift industry?

9. What shortcomings in the Depository Institutions Deregulation and Monetary Control Act of 1980 (DIDMCA) and the Garn-St. Germain Depository Institutions Act of 1982 (DIA) led to their failure to rescue the thrift industry?

10. In Table 1–7 you can see that S&Ls held $120,417 million of mortgage-backed securities as of August 1992. If thrifts are in the business of originating mortgages, why are they holding mortgage-backed securities on their balance sheets?

11. Using the Du Pont decomposition of return on equity (ROE), what is the major source of thrift profitability?

APPENDIX
DEPOSITORY INSTITUTIONS AND THEIR REGULATORS

	Chartering and Licensing 1.	*Branching* 2. Intrastate
A. National banks	Comptroller	Comptroller
B. State member banks	State authority	Federal Reserve and state authority
C. State nonmember banks, insured	State authority	FDIC and state authority
D. Noninsured state banks	State authority	State authority
E. Insured savings associations, federal (1)	OTS	OTS
Insured savings associations, state (2)	State authority	OTS and state authority
F. Uninsured savings associations, state	State authority	State authority
G. Credit unions, federal	NCUAB	(5)
Credit unions, state	State authority	State authority
H. Bank holding companies	Federal Reserve and state authority	Federal Reserve and state authority
I. Savings association holding companies	OTS and state authority (3)	OTS & state authority
J. Foreign branches of U.S. banks, national and state members	Federal Reserve and state authority	N/A
Foreign branches of U.S. banks, insured state nonmembers	State authority	N/A
K. Edge Act corporations	Federal Reserve	Federal Reserve
Agreement corporations	State authority (4)	Federal Reserve
L. U.S. branches and agencies of foreign banks—federal	Comptroller	Comptroller and FDIC (6)
U.S. branches and agencies of foreign banks—state	State authority	State authority and FDIC (6)

The Matrix provides an overview of primary regulators of depository institutions as of April 1992. It is not intended to cover each area of regulatory responsibility in detail. Further, the Matrix and accompanying footnotes should not be considered either a substitute for or an interpretation of the regulations. Regulatory agencies should be consulted for answers to specific questions.

(1) Federal savings associations include any thrift institution such as federal savings banks, federally chartered under Section 5 of the Home Owners' Act.

(2) State savings associations include any state chartered savings bank, savings and loan association, building and loan association, homestead association, or cooperative bank.

(3) Savings association holding companies are required to register with the OTS.

(4) Agreement corporations are subject to the restrictions on powers established by the Federal Reserve for Edge Act corporations.

(5) Federal credit unions are not required to receive NCUA approval before opening a branch.

(6) The establishment of federal branches and agencies is subject to the within-state branching restrictions of the McFadden Act. The establishment of state branches or agencies is regulated by state banking law. A foreign bank may relocate any insured branch within the state without the prior written consent of the FDIC.

(7) While the McFadden Act prevents interstate branching by national and state member banks, banks can provide certain services on an interstate basis.

(8) While the McFadden Act's interstate branching restrictions are not applicable to insured state nonmember and noninsured state banks, state laws generally prohibit branching by out-of-state banks.

	Mergers, Acquisitions and Consolidations		Reserve Requirements
3. Interstate	**4. Intrastate**	**5. Interstate**	**6.**
(7)	Comptroller (11)	(19)	Federal Reserve (21)
(7)	Federal Reserve and state authority (12)	(19)	Federal Reserve (21)
(8)	FDIC and state authority (13)	FDIC and state authority	Federal Reserve (21)
(8)	State authority (14)	State authority (14)	Federal Reserve (21)
OTS (9)	OTS	OTS (9, 15)	Federal Reserve (21)
OTS and state authority	OTS and state authority (15)	OTS and state authority	Federal Reserve (21)
State authority	State authority	State authority	Federal Reserve (21)
(5)	NCUA	NCUA	Federal Reserve (21)
State authority	NCUA and state authority (16)	NCUA and state authority (16)	Federal Reserve (21)
Federal Reserve and state authority	Federal Reserve and state authority	Federal Reserve and state authority (20)	N/A
OTS and state authority	OTS and state authority	OTS and state authority	N/A
N/A	N/A	N/A	(22)
N/A	N/A	N/A	(22)
Federal Reserve	Federal Reserve (17)	Federal Reserve (17)	Federal Reserve (21)
Federal Reserve	Federal Reserve (17)	Federal Reserve (17)	Federal Reserve (21)
Comptroller and Federal Reserve (10)	Comptroller and Federal Reserve (18)	(18)	Federal Reserve (21)
State authority and Federal Reserve (10)	FDIC or Federal Reserve and state authority (18)	(18)	Federal Reserve (21)

(9) Federal savings associations are prohibited from out-of-state branching unless they qualify as domestic building and loan associations under the tax laws or meet certain other requirements.

(10) Foreign banks with state or federal branches or agencies (or commercial lending companies or bank subsidiaries) are not permitted to establish a federal or state branch or agency outside their home state unless: (a) it is permitted by law in the state in which it will operate and (b) in the case of a branch, an agreement with the Federal Reserve has been entered that will limit deposits at the nonhome state branch to those permitted to Edge Act corporations.

(11) The Comptroller must approve the merger or acquisition if the resulting bank is a national bank. However, if a noninsured bank merges into a national bank, the FDIC must approve the merger.

(12) The Federal Reserve must approve the merger or acquisition if the resulting bank is a state member bank. However, if a noninsured bank merges into a state member bank, the FDIC must approve the merger.

(13) The FDIC must approve the merger or acquisition if the resulting bank is an insured state nonmember bank or if a noninsured bank merges into an insured state nonmember bank.

(14) In addition to state authority, the FDIC must approve mergers or acquisitions between insured depository institutions and noninsured institutions.

(15) The OTS must approve the merger or acquisition if the resulting institution is an insured savings association. However, if a noninsured institution merges into an insured savings association, the FDIC must approve the merger.

	Access to the Discount Window 7.	Deposit Insurance 8.	Supervision and Examination 9.
A. National bank	Federal Reserve (23)	FDIC	Comptroller (27)
B. State member banks	Federal Reserve (23)	FDIC	Federal Reserve and state authority (27)
C. State nonmember banks, insured	Federal Reserve (23)	FDIC	FDIC and state authority
D. Noninsured state banks	Federal Reserve (23)	None or state insurance fund (24)	State authority
E. Insured savings associations, federal (1)	Federal Home Loan Bank and Federal Reserve (23)	FDIC	OTS (27, 28)
Insured savings associations, state (2)	Federal Home Loan Bank and Federal Reserve (23)	FDIC	OTS and state authority (27, 28)
F. Uninsured savings associations, state	Federal Home Loan Bank and Federal Reserve (23)	None or state insurance fund (24)	State authority (28)
G. Credit unions, federal	Central Liquidity Facility and Federal Reserve (23)	Credit Union Share (25)	NCUA
Credit unions, state	Central Liquidity Facility and Federal Reserve (23)	Credit Union Share or state insurance fund (25)	State authority
H. Bank holding companies	N/A	N/A	Federal Reserve
I. Savings association holding companies	N/A	N/A	OTS
J. Foreign branches of U.S. banks, national and state members	N/A	N/A	Comptroller or Federal Reserve (29)
Foreign branches of U.S. banks, insured state nonmembers	N/A	N/A	FDIC or state authority (29)
K. Edge Act corporations	N/A	N/A	Federal Reserve
Agreement corporations	N/A	N/A	Federal Reserve and state authority
L. U.S. branches and agencies of foreign banks—federal	Federal Reserve (23)	FDIC (26)	Comptroller and Federal Reserve (27, 30)
U.S. branches and agencies of foreign banks—state	Federal Reserve (23)	FDIC (26)	FDIC, state authority and Federal Reserve (27, 30)

(16) The NCUA must approve the merger or acquisition if the resulting credit union is federally insured.

(17) The Federal Reserve supervises acquisitions made by Edge Act corporations and agreement corporations. Agreement corporations may merge as permitted by state authority.

(18) The International Banking Act of 1978 makes foreign banks that have branches or agencies in the U.S. subject to the provisions of the Bank Holding Company Act of 1956 with respect to nonbank acquisitions. Acquisitions of banks are subject to the Bank Holding Company Act and the home state limitations imposed by the International Banking Act.

(19) The McFadden Act prevents interstate branching by national and state member banks.

(20) The Douglas Amerndment to the Bank Holding Company Act allows bank holding companies to acquire banks in other states if the state of the acquired bank specifically allows out-of-state holding companies to acquire in-state banks.

(21) Under the Depository Institutions Deregulation and Monetary Control Act of 1980, the Federal Reserve is required to set a uniform system of reserve requirements (Regulation D) for virtually all depository institutions. Noninsured state banks eligible for deposit insurance may be subject to reserve requirements. Regulation D provides that IBF deposits satisfying the requirements of that regulation are exempt from reserve requirements.

(22) Deposits at foreign branches of U.S. banks payable only outside the United States are generally not subject to reserve requirements.

(23) Nearly all depository institutions in the United States, including branches and agencies of foreign banks, have access to the discount window. These depository institutions are expected to make reasonable use of their usual sources of funds before requesting loans from Federal Reserve Banks. For example, savings associations and credit unions should first go to the Federal Home Loan Banks and the Central Liquidity Facility, respectively, for loans.

LEGEND:

FDIC	Federal Deposit Insurance Corporation	NCUA	National Credit Union Administration
FTC	Federal Trade Commission	Member	Member of the Federal Reserve System
Federal Reserve	Board of Governors of the Federal Reserve System/Federal Reserve Banks	N/A	Not applicable
		OCC	Office of the Comptroller of Currency
IBF	International Banking Facility	OTS	Office of Thrift Supervision

Prudential Limits, Safety, and Soundness	*Consumer Protection*	
10.	**11. Rulemaking**	**12. Enforcement**
Comptroller	Federal Reserve	Comptroller
Federal Reserve and state authority	Federal Reserve and state authority	Federal Reserve and state authority
FDIC and state authority	Federal Reserve and state authority	FDIC and state authority
State authority	Federal Reserve and state authority	State authority and FTC (31)
OTS and FDIC	Federal Reserve and OTS	OTS
OTS, FDIC and state authority	Federal Reserve, OTS, and state authority	OTS and state authority
State authority	Federal Reserve and state authority	State authority and FTC (31)
NCUA	Federal Reserve and state authority	NCUA
State authority	Federal Reserve and state authority	State authority and FTC (31)
Federal Reserve	Federal Reserve and state authority	FTC (31)
OTS	Federal Reserve and state authority	FTC (31)
Comptroller and Federal Reserve	N/A	N/A
FDIC and state authority	N/A	N/A
Federal Reserve	N/A	N/A
Federal Reserve	N/A	N/A
Comptroller	Federal Reserve and state authority	OCC or FTC
Federal Reserve or FDIC and state authority	Federal Reserve and state authority	OCC or FTC and state authority

(24) Deposits not insured by the FDIC may be insured by states or state-authorized insurance funds.

(25) Shares in all federal credit unions and many state credit unions are insured by the National Credit Union Share Insurance Fund, which is administered by the NCUA. Shares in some state credit unions may be insured by state or state-authorized insurance funds.

(26) Federal branches of foreign banks that accept retail deposits generally must obtain FDIC insurance. State branches of foreign banks that accept retail deposits generally must also obtain FDIC insurance if they are located in a state in which a state bank is required to have deposit insurance.

(27) The FDIC has some residual examination authority over all FDIC-insured depository institutions.

(28) Federally insured savings associations are supervised and examined by the OTS; nonfederally insured state savings associations by state authority.

(29) Foreign branches of national banks are supervised and examined by the OCC; foreign branches of state member banks by the Federal Reserve; foreign branches of insured state nonmember banks by the FDIC; and foreign branches of noninsured state nonmember banks by state authority.

(30) Federal branches and agencies are examined by the OCC; state branches insured by the FDIC are examined by the FDIC and state authority; and state noninsured branches and agencies are examined by state authority. The Federal Reserve has residual examining authority over all banking activities of foreign banks.

(31) Enforcement of federal consumer regulations is generally left to the FTC where the institution is not otherwise a federally insured depository institution.

SOURCE: Public Information Department, Federal Reserve Bank of New York, 33 Liberty Street, New York, NY 10045.

2

THE FINANCIAL
SERVICE INDUSTRY

Other Financial Institutions

Learning Objectives

In this chapter you will learn about the activities and regulation of financial institutions other than depository institutions. In particular, you will gain an understanding of the life insurance, property-casualty insurance, and investment banking industries as well as the finance company and mutual fund industries. Despite the apparently diverse nature of their activities, these FIs often face risk exposures similar to those faced by depository institutions.

Introduction

As in Chapter 1, we describe the main features of other FIs by concentrating on (1) the size, structure, and composition of the industries in which they operate; (2) balance sheets and recent trends; and (3) regulations.

Life Insurance Companies

Size, Structure, and Composition of the Industry

At the end of 1990, the United States had 2,153 life insurance companies compared to 1,758 in 1980. The aggregate assets of life insurance companies were $1.4 trillion at the end of 1990 compared to $.48 trillion in 1980.

Life insurance allows individuals and their beneficiaries to protect against losses in income either through premature death or retirement. By pooling risks, life insurance transfers income-related uncertainties from the insured individual to a group. While life insurance may be the core activity area, modern life insurance companies also sell annuity contracts, manage pension plans, and provide accident and health insurance. We discuss these different activity lines in the following sections.

Life Insurance. The four basic classes or lines of life insurance are distinguished by the manner in which they are sold or marketed to purchasers. These classes are (1) ordinary life, (2) group life, (3) industrial life, and (4) credit life. Of the life insurance policies in force in the United States in 1990, ordinary life accounted for 57.1 percent, group life for 40 percent, industrial life for 0.25 percent, and credit life for 2.65 percent of a total contract value in force of $9 trillion.

Ordinary Life.   Ordinary life insurance involves policies marketed on an individual basis, usually in units of $1,000, on which policy makers make periodic premium payments. Despite the enormous variety of contractual forms, there are essentially five basic contractual types. The first three are traditional forms of ordinary life insurance, and the last two are newer contracts that originated in the 1970s and 1980s due to increased competition for savings from other segments of the financial services industry. The three traditional contractual forms are term life, whole life, and endowment life. The two newer forms are variable life and universal life. The key features of each of these contractual forms are identified as follows:

• **Term Life.** A term life policy is the closest to pure life insurance with no savings element attached. Essentially, the individual receives a payout contingent on death during the coverage period. The term of coverage can vary from as little as 1 year to 40 years or more.

• **Whole Life.** A whole life policy protects the individual over an entire lifetime. In return for periodic or level premiums, the individual's beneficiaries receive the face value of the life insurance contract on death. Thus, there is certainty that if the policyholder continues premium payments the insurance company makes a payment—unlike term insurance. As a result, whole life has a savings element as well as a pure insurance element.

• **Endowment Life.** An endowment life policy combines both a pure (term) insurance element with a savings element. It guarantees a payout to the beneficiaries of the policy if death occurs during some endowment period (e.g., prior to reaching retirement age). An insured person who lives to the endowment date receives the face amount of the policy.

• **Variable Life Insurance.** Unlike traditional policies that promise to pay the insured the fixed or face amount of a policy should a contingency arise, variable life insurance invests fixed premium payments in mutual funds of stocks, bonds, and money market instruments. Usually, policyholders can choose mutual fund investments to reflect their risk preferences. Thus, variable life provides an alternative way to build savings compared to the more traditional policies such as whole life because the value of the policy increases or decreases with the asset returns of the mutual fund in which premiums are invested.

• **Universal Life and Variable Universal Life.** Universal life allows both the premium amounts and the maturity of the life contract to be changed by the insured, unlike traditional policies that maintain premiums at a given level over a fixed contract period. In addition, for some contracts firms invest premiums in money, equity, or bond mutual funds—as in variable life insurance—so that the savings or investment component of the contract reflects market returns. In this case, the policy is called variable universal life.

Group Life Insurance.   Group life insurance covers a large number of insured persons under a single policy. Usually issued to corporate employers, these policies may be either contributory or noncontributory for the employees themselves. Cost economies are the principal advantage of group life over ordinary life policies. Cost economies occur due to mass administration of plans, lower costs for evaluating individuals through medical screening and other rating systems, and reduced selling and commission costs.

Industrial Life.   Industrial life insurance currently represents a very small area of coverage. Industrial life usually involves weekly payments directly collected by representatives of the companies. To a large extent, the growth of group life insurance has led to the demise of industrial life as a major activity class.

Credit Life.   Credit life insurance is sold to protect lenders against a borrower's death prior to repayment of a debt contract such as a mortgage or car loan. Usually the face amount of the insurance policy reflects the outstanding principal and interest on the loan.

Other Life Insurer Activities.   Three other major activities of life insurance companies are the sale of annuities, private pension plans, and accident and health insurance.

Annuities.   Annuities represent the reverse of life insurance activities. While life insurance involves different contractual methods to *build up* a fund, annuities involve different methods of *liquidating* a fund, such as paying out a fund's proceeds. As with life insurance contracts, many different types of annuity contracts have been developed. Specifically, they can be sold to an individual or group and on either a fixed or variable basis by being linked to the return on some underlying investment portfolio. Individuals can purchase annuities with a single payment or payments spread over a number of years. Payments may be structured to start immediately or can be deferred. These payments may cease on death or continue to be paid to beneficiaries for a number of years after death. As of the end of 1990, nearly 6 million people in the United States held annuities with a combined value of $81 billion.

Private Pension Funds.   Insurance companies offer many alternative pension plans to private employers in an effort to attract this business away from other financial service companies such as commercial banks and securities firms. Some of their innovative pension plans are based on guaranteed investment contracts (GICs). This means the insurer guarantees not only the rate of interest credited to a pension plan over some given period—for example, five years—but also the annuity rates on beneficiaries' contracts. Other plans include immediate participation and separate account plans that follow more aggressive investment strategies than traditional life insurance. At the end of 1990, life insurance companies were managing $713 billion in pension fund assets, equal to 39 percent of all private pension plans.

Accident and Health Insurance.   While life insurance protects against mortality risk, accident and health insurance protect against morbidity or ill-health risk. Some $58.2 billion in net premiums were written by life and health companies in the accident-health area in 1990. The major activity line is group insurance, providing health insurance coverage to corporate employees. Other coverages include credit health plans, whereby individuals have their debt repayments insured against unexpected health contingencies and various types of renewable, nonrenewable, and guaranteed health and accident plans for individuals. In many respects, the loss exposures faced by insurers in accident and health lines are more similar to those faced under property-casualty insurance than under traditional life insurance (see section on Property-Casualty Insurance).

Balance Sheet and Recent Trends

Because of the long-term nature of their liabilities (due to the long-term nature of life insurance policyholders' claims) and the need to generate competitive returns on the

TABLE 2–1   Life Insurance Company Assets
Distribution of Assets of U.S. Life Insurance Companies

| Year | Government Securities | Corporate Securities | | Mortgages | Real Estate | Policy Loans | Misc. Assets | Total |
		Bonds	Stocks					
Amount (000,000 omitted)								
1917	$ 562	$ 1,975	$ 83	$ 2,021	$ 179	$ 810	$ 311	$ 5,941
1920	1,349	1,949	75	2,442	172	859	474	7,320
1925	1,311	3,022	81	4,808	266	1,446	604	11,538
1930	1,502	4,929	519	7,598	548	2,807	977	18,880
1935	4,727	5,314	583	5,357	1,990	3,540	1,705	23,216
1940	8,447	8,645	605	5,972	2,065	3,091	1,977	30,802
1945	22,545	10,060	999	6,636	857	1,962	1,738	44,797
1950	16,118	23,248	2,103	16,102	1,445	2,413	2,591	64,020
1955	11,829	35,912	3,633	29,445	2,581	3,290	3,742	90,432
1960	11,815	46,740	4,981	41,771	3,765	5,231	5,273	119,576
1965	11,908	58,244	9,126	60,013	4,681	7,678	7,234	158,884
1970	11,068	73,098	15,420	74,375	6,320	16,064	10,909	207,254
1975	15,177	105,837	28,061	89,167	9,621	24,467	16,974	289,304
1976	20,260	120,666	34,262	91,552	10,476	25,834	18,502	321,552
1977	23,555	137,889	33,763	96,848	11,606	27,556	21,051	351,722
1978	26,552	156,044	35,518	106,167	11,764	30,146	23,733	389,924
1979	29,719	168,990	39,757	118,421	13,007	34,825	27,563	432,282
1980	33,015	179,603	47,366	131,080	15,033	41,411	31,702	479,210
1981	39,502	193,806	47,670	137,747	18,278	48,706	40,094	525,803
1982	55,516	212,772	55,730	141,989	20,624	52,961	48,571	588,163
1983	76,615	232,123	64,868	150,999	22,234	54,063	54,046	654,948
1984	99,769	259,128	63,335	156,699	25,767	54,505	63,776	722,979
1985	124,598	296,848	77,496	171,797	28,822	54,369	71,971	825,901
1986	144,616	341,967	90,864	193,842	31,615	54,055	80,592	937,551
1987	151,436	405,674	96,515	213,450	34,172	53,626	89,586	1,044,459
1988	159,781	480,313	104,373	232,863	37,371	54,236*	97,933	1,166,870
1989	178,141	538,063	125,614	254,215	39,908	57,439	106,376	1,299,756
1990	210,846	582,597	128,484	270,109	43,367	62,603	110,202	1,408,208

Policy Loans
Loans made by an insurance company to its policyholders using their policies as collateral.

Policy Reserves
A liability item for insurers that reflects their expected payment commitments on existing policy contracts.

Surrender Value of a Policy
The cash value of a policy received from the insurer if a policyholder surrenders the policy prior to maturity. The cash surrender value is normally only a portion of the contract's face value.

savings elements of life insurance products, life insurance companies concentrate their asset investments at the longer end of the maturity spectrum. Look at Table 2–1, where we show the distribution of life insurance assets.

As you can see, in 1990 15 percent of assets were invested in government securities, 50.5 percent in corporate bonds and stocks, and 19.2 percent in mortgages, with other loans—including **policy loans**—comprising the balance. The major trends have been a long-term increase in the proportion of bonds and a decline in the proportion of mortgages in the balance sheet.

The aggregate balance sheet for the life insurance industry at the end of 1991 is in Table 2–2. Looking at the liability side of the balance sheet, we see that $.879 trillion, or 58 percent, of total liabilities and capital are net **policy reserves.** These reserves are based on actuarial assumptions regarding the insurers' expected future liability commitments to pay out on present contracts including death benefits, matured endowments (lump sum or otherwise), and the cash **surrender values of policies.** Even though the actuarial assumptions underlying policy reserves are normally very conservative, unexpected fluctuations in future required payouts can

TABLE 2–1   (concluded)

Year	Government Securities	Corporate Securities Bonds	Corporate Securities Stocks	Mortgages	Real Estate	Policy Loans	Misc. Assets	Total
Percent								
1917	9.6%	33.2%	1.4%	34.0%	3.0%	13.6%	5.2%	100.0%
1920	18.4	26.7	1.0	33.4	2.3	11.7	6.5	100.0
1925	11.3	26.2	.7	41.7	2.3	12.5	5.3	100.0
1930	8.0	26.0	2.8	40.2	2.9	14.9	5.2	100.0
1935	20.4	22.9	2.5	23.1	8.6	15.2	7.3	100.0
1940	27.5	28.1	2.0	19.4	6.7	10.0	6.3	100.0
1945	50.3	22.5	2.2	14.8	1.9	4.4	3.9	100.0
1950	25.2	36.3	3.3	25.1	2.2	3.8	4.1	100.0
1955	13.1	39.7	4.0	32.6	2.9	3.6	4.1	100.0
1960	9.9	39.1	4.2	34.9	3.1	4.4	4.4	100.0
1965	7.5	36.7	5.7	37.8	3.0	4.8	4.5	100.0
1970	5.3	35.3	7.4	35.9	3.0	7.8	5.3	100.0
1975	5.2	36.6	9.7	30.8	3.3	8.5	5.9	100.0
1976	6.3	37.5	10.7	28.5	3.3	8.0	5.7	100.0
1977	6.7	39.2	9.6	27.5	3.2	7.8	6.0	100.0
1978	6.8	40.0	9.1	27.2	3.0	7.8	6.1	100.0
1979	6.9	39.1	9.2	27.4	3.0	8.1	6.3	100.0
1980	6.9	37.5	9.9	27.4	3.1	8.6	6.6	100.0
1981	7.5	36.8	9.1	26.2	3.5	9.3	7.6	100.0
1982	9.4	36.2	9.5	24.1	3.5	9.0	8.3	100.0
1983	11.7	35.4	9.9	23.1	3.4	8.3	8.2	100.0
1984	13.8	35.8	8.8	21.7	3.6	7.5	8.8	100.0
1985	15.0	36.0	9.4	20.8	3.5	6.6	8.7	100.0
1986	15.4	36.5	9.7	20.6	3.4	5.8	8.6	100.0
1987	14.5	38.8	9.3	20.4	3.3	5.1	8.6	100.0
1988	13.7	41.2	8.9	20.0	3.2	4.6	8.4	100.0
1989	13.7	41.4	9.7	19.5	3.1	4.4	8.2	100.0
1990	15.0	41.4	9.1	19.2	3.1	4.4	7.8	100.0

*Excludes some $600 million of policy loans securitized during 1988.

NOTE: Beginning with 1962, these data include the assets of separate accounts.

SOURCES: *Spectator Year Book* and American Council of Life Insurance, *Life Insurance Fact Book,* 1991.

occur; that is, underwriting life insurance is risky. For example, mortality rates—and life insurance payouts—might unexpectedly increase above those defined by historically based mortality tables due to a catastrophic epidemic illness such as AIDS. To meet unexpected future losses, the life insurer holds a capital and surplus reserve fund with which to meet such losses. The capital and surplus reserves of life insurers in 1990 were $.106 trillion or 7 percent of total assets.[1] Another important life insurer liability, GICs are short- and medium-term debt instruments sold by insurance companies to fund their pension plan business ($.122 trillion).

In recent years, life insurance companies have been under pressure to generate higher returns for savers and to invest long term to better match their relatively long term liability exposures such as life insurance coverages. This has led a small but

---

[1]An additional line of defense against unexpected underwriting losses is the insurer's investment income from its asset portfolio (net asset returns were 8.89 percent in 1990), plus any new premium income flows.

TABLE 2–2

LIFE INSURANCE INDUSTRY
Balance Sheet
As of December 31, 1991
(in thousands)

Assets

Bonds	$ 768,097,199
Preferred stock	10,068,581
Common stock	57,007,510
Mortgage loans	256,045,495
Real estate	34,948,306
Policy loans	61,705,483
Cash and deposits	5,856,019
Short-term investments	40,510,782
Other invested assets	27,074,417
Life and annuity premium due	10,584,079
Accident and health premium due	4,907,330
Accrued investment income	20,029,935
Separate account assets	204,600,265
Other assets	18,789,965
Total assets	$1,520,225,365

Liabilities and Capital/Surplus

Net policy reserves		$ 878,913,737
Policy claims		18,090,047
Policy dividend accumulations		18,570,096
Dividend reserve		12,316,097
Policyholder premiums		4,757,188
Guaranteed interest contracts		122,287,371
Other contract deposit funds		78,337,280
Commissions, taxes, expenses		11,621,416
Securities valuation reserve		18,568,301
Other liabilities		48,486,275
Separate account business		202,380,799
Total capital and surplus		105,896,758
Capital	$ 3,367,770	
Treasury stock	(374,061)	
Paid-in and contributed surplus	33,081,994	
Contingency reserve	5,968,271	
Unassigned surplus	55,410,167	
Other surplus	6,465,085	
Other reserves	1,977,532	
Total liabilities and capital/surplus		$1,520,225,365

SOURCE: *A. M. Best's Aggregates and Averages,* Life-Health, 1992, p. 11.

Junk Bonds
A corporate bond rated less than investment grade by bond rating agencies.

significant number of life insurance companies to expand their holdings of low-quality **junk bonds** and to invest heavily in long term mortgage loans for commercial property development. The sharp decline in property values especially in Texas, the Northeast, and California and, to a lesser extent, the decline in junk bond values following the bankruptcy of Drexel Burnham Lambert (the primary sponsor of junk bonds) has raised concerns about the credit, interest rate, and liquidity risk exposures of some large life insurance companies. As a result, insurance company regulators have imposed constraints on life insurers holdings of low-quality junk bonds in their asset portfolios and more forcefully monitor life insurers real estate loan portfolios.

Regulation

The most important legislation affecting the regulation of life insurance companies is the McCarran-Ferguson Act of 1945 that confirms the primacy of state over federal regulation of insurance companies. Thus, unlike the depository institutions we discussed in Chapter 1, that can be chartered either at the federal or state levels, chartering of life insurers is done entirely at the state level. In addition to chartering, state insurance commissions supervise and examine insurance companies using a coordinated examination system developed by the National Association of Insurance Commissioners (NAIC). Other than supervision and examination, states also promote life insurance guaranty funds. In most cases, these are not permanent funds (like the FDIC) but rather involve required contributions from insurance companies to compensate the policyholders of an insurer after a failure has taken place.

Concept Questions

1. What is the difference between a life insurance contract and an annuity contract?
2. What is the major source of life insurance underwriting risk?
3. Why do life insurance companies invest in long-term assets?

Property-Casualty Insurance

Size, Structure, and Composition of the Industry

Currently some 3,800 companies sell property-casualty (PC) insurance with approximately 900 firms writing PC business in all or most of the United States. Collectively, the top 15 firms have just under a 50 percent share of the overall PC market, with the top 5 having a 25 percent share.[2] In terms of the worldwide volume of PC insurance, U.S. firms wrote some 38 percent of the premiums.[3] The total assets of the PC industry as of December 1991 were $.6 trillion, or approximately 40 percent of the life insurance industry's assets.

PC Insurance.   Property insurance involves insurance coverages related to the loss of real and personal property. Casualty—or, perhaps, more accurately liability—insurance concerns protection against legal liability exposures. However, distinctions between the two broad areas of property and liability insurance are increasingly becoming blurred. This is due to the tendency of PC insurers to offer multiple activity line coverages combining features of property and liability insurance into single policy packages; for example, homeowners multiple peril insurance. Later we describe the key features of the main PC lines briefly. Note, however, that some PC activity lines are marketed as different products to both individuals and commercial firms (e.g., auto insurance) while other lines are marketed to one specific group (e.g., boiler and machinery insurance targeted at commercial purchasers). To

---

[2]*Property/Casualty Insurance Fact Book,* Insurance Information Institute, Washington, D.C., 1990, p. 12.

[3]Ibid., p. 13.

understand the importance of each line in premium income earned in the 1980s, look at Table 2–3. Specifically, important lines include:

Fire Insurance and Allied Lines. Protects against the perils of fire, lightning, and removal of property damaged in a fire.

Homeowners Multiple Peril Insurance. Protects against multiple perils of damage to a personal dwelling and personal property as well as liability coverage against the financial consequences of legal liability due to injury done to others. Thus, it combines features of both property and liability insurance.

Commercial Multiple Peril Insurance. Protects commercial firms against perils similar to homeowners multiple peril insurance.

Marine Insurance. Is divided into *inland* and *ocean marine* and is largely concerned with protection against damage to or loss in the transportation of goods or real property by water.

Automobile Liability and Physical Damage Insurance. Provides protection against (1) losses resulting from legal liability due to the ownership or use of the vehicle (auto liability) and (2) theft or damage to vehicles (auto physical damage).

TABLE 2–3   Property and Casualty Insurance—Premiums and Losses, by the Line of Insurance: 1980 to 1988 (in $ millions)

Line of Insurance	Premiums Earned					Losses Incurred				
	1980	*1985*	*1986*	*1987*	*1988*	*1980*	*1985*	*1986*	*1987*	*1988*
Total	86,612	131,115	166,637	182,982	194,188	61,813	114,376	133,041	141,512	146,487
Auto liability	19,324	33,546	42,116	46,431	50,000	14,647	31,870	37,929	41,525	43,313
Auto, physical damage	12,765	23,515	28,182	29,849	31,913	8,904	17,286	19,019	18,962	20,383
Workers' compensation	14,067	17,168	19,870	23,674	25,863	10,097	15,448	18,893	21,758	23,845
Liability, other than auto	6,532	9,115	16,163	19,272	19,103	4,516	10,455	14,910	16,703	15,670
Commercial multiple peril	6,658	10,148	14,336	16,159	17,018	3,822	8,738	8,840	8,919	9,669
Homeowners multiple peril	9,175	13,413	15,164	15,721	16,526	6,634	10,637	10,702	10,132	10,857
Fire and allied lines	4,981	5,109	6,852	7,195	6,553	3,193	3,304	3,764	3,562	3,422
Reinsurance	3,089	4,788	6,828	6,530	7,026	2,461	4,318	5,649	5,531	5,345
Inland marine	2,180	3,315	3,758	3,986	4,069	1,439	2,058	1,791	1,859	2,009
Health	2,845	3,082	2,713	3,732	4,263	2,538	2,824	2,640	4,609	3,629
Surety and fidelity	1,170	1,771	2,038	2,238	2,390	614	1,414	1,224	1,377	950
Malpractice	1,009	1,913	2,512	2,876	3,000	1,022	3,020	2,963	2,909	2,634
Ocean marine	1,035	1,115	1,123	1,235	1,237	857	830	763	831	869
Farmowners	518	727	1,108	837	784	409	576	862	532	510
Aircraft	162	472	659	768	710	126	381	456	595	514
Boiler and machinery	372	497	597	648	637	145	204	245	237	324
Product liability	–	362	1,002	424	890	–	320	910	276	646
Financial guaranty	–	–	272	268	409	–	–	284	211	442
Earthquake	46	131	190	228	286	3	13	22	73	35
Burglary and theft	135	117	123	121	114	60	40	36	34	28
Glass	34	29	30	26	29	20	8	10	8	11
Other	515	782	1,001	764	1,368	306	632	1,131	869	1,382

– Represents zero.

Source: The National Underwriter Co., Cincinnati, Ohio, *Argus F. C. & S. Chart,* annual (copyright) and *Statistical Abstract of the United States, 1991* (Washington, D.C.: U.S. Government Printing Office, 1992), p. 21.

Liability Insurance (other than auto). Provides either individuals or commercial firms with protection against non-automobile-related legal liability. For commercial firms, this includes protection against liabilities relating to their business operations (other than personal injury to employees covered by workers compensation insurance) and product liability hazards.

Reinsurance. Insurers generally set retention limits on the amount of risk exposure they are willing to face on any PC policy or line. To facilitate their ability to write large contracts while limiting their risk exposure, primary insurers can cede some of the risk and premium income to another insurance company, the reinsurer.

Balance Sheet and Recent Trends

The Balance Sheet and Underwriting Risk.   The balance sheet of PC firms at the end of 1991 is shown in Table 2–4. Looking at their liabilities, we can see that major components are the reserves set aside to meet expected losses from *underwriting* the PC lines just described, while the loss adjustment expense item relates to expected administrative and related costs of adjusting (settling) these claims. The two items combined comprise 51 percent of total liabilities and capital.

To understand how and why this reserve is established, we need to understand the risks of underwriting PC insurance. In particular, PC underwriting risk results when the premiums generated on a given insurance line are insufficient to cover (1) the claims (losses) incurred insuring the peril and (2) the administrative expenses of providing that insurance (legal expenses, commissions, taxes, etc.) after taking into account the investment income generated between the time premiums are received and the time claims are paid. Thus, underwriting risk may result from (1) unexpected increases in loss rates, (2) unexpected increases in expenses, and/or (3) unexpected decreases in investment yields or returns. Next, look more carefully at each of these three areas of PC underwriting risk.

Loss Risk. The key feature of claims loss exposure is the actuarial *predictability* of losses relative to premiums earned. This predictability depends on a number of characteristics or features of the perils insured. Specifically:

• **Property versus Liability.** In general, the maximum level of losses are more predictable for property lines than liability lines. For example, the monetary value of the loss or damage to an auto is relatively easy to calculate while the upper limit to the losses an insurer might be exposed to in a product liability line, such as asbestos damage to workers' health under other liability insurance, might be difficult if not impossible to estimate.

• **Severity versus Frequency.** In general, loss rates are more predictable on low-severity high-frequency lines than on high-severity low-frequency lines. For example, losses in fire, auto, and homeowners peril lines tend to be events expected to occur with high frequency and to be independently distributed across any pool of insured. Furthermore, the dollar loss of each event in the insured pool tends to be relatively small. Applying the law of large numbers, the expected loss potential of such lines—the **frequency of loss** times the extent of the damage (**severity of loss**) may be estimable within quite small probability bounds. Other lines, such as earthquake and financial guarantee insurance, tend to insure very low probability (frequency) events. Here the probabilities are not always stationary, the individual risks in the insured pool are not independent, and the severity of the loss could be potentially enormous.

Frequency of Loss
The probability of a loss occurring.

Severity of Loss
The size of the loss.

TABLE 2–4

Balance Sheet (Property-Casualty Industry)
As of December 31, 1991

Assets

Unaffiliated investments		$488,058,272
Bonds	$368,012,182	
Preferred stocks	9,806,122	
Common stocks	58,141,615	
Mortgage loans	6,164,925	
Real estate investment	1,749,887	
Collateral loans	36,003	
Cash on hand and on deposit	5,334,093	
Short-term investments	25,601,306	
Other invested assets	5,310,521	
Accrued interest	7,901,618	
Investments in affiliates		28,772,422
Real estate, offices		5,635,206
Premium balances		49,101,160
Reinsurance funds		3,071,149
Reinsurance recoverable		10,216,821
Federal income taxes recoverable		1,663,086
Electronic data processing equipment		1,884,575
Receivables from affiliates		4,549,310
Association accounts		2,179,743
Receivable uninsured accident and health plans		6,652
Future investment income on loss reserves		244,516
Other assets		6,062,166
Total assets		$601,445,078

Liabilities and Capital/Surplus

Losses		$257,711,909
Loss adjustment expenses		49,428,906
Reinsurance payable on paid losses		1,382,411
Commissions, taxes, expenses		7,744,375
Federal income taxes		1,908,160
Borrowed money		1,293,455
Interest on borrowed money		32,661
Unearned premiums		84,572,401
Dividends to stockholders		279,141
Dividends to policyholders		1,481,519
Reinsurance funds		8,460,294
Loss portfolio transfer (assumed)		360,496
Loss portfolio transfer (ceded)		(845,448)
Amounts retained for others		2,034,761
Foreign exchange rate adjustments		376,529
Drafts outstanding		3,612,375
Payable to affiliates		3,823,508
Payable for securities		1,357,227
Amounts held for uninsured accident and health plans		66
Discount on loss reserve		(364,273)
Other liabilities		12,578,324
Conditional reserves		5,558,718
Policyholders' surplus		158,657,564
Capital paid-up	$ 6,927,089	
Guaranty funds	313,746	
Assigned funds	70,440,534	
Unassigned funds	80,976,194	
Total liabilities and capital/surplus		$601,445,078

SOURCE: *A. M. Best's Aggregates and Averages,* Property-Casualty, 1992.

Long-Tail Loss
A claim that is made some time after a policy was written.

This means that estimating expected loss rates (frequency times severity) is extremely difficult in these coverage areas.

• **Long-Tail versus Short-Tail**. Some liability lines suffer from a long-tail risk exposure phenomenon that makes estimation of expected losses difficult. This **long-tail loss** arises in policies where the peril occurs during a coverage period but a claim is not made or reported until many years later. Losses incurred but not reported have caused insurers significant problems in lines such as medical malpractice and other liability insurance where product damage suits (e.g., the Dalkon shield case and asbestos cases) have mushroomed many years after the event occurred and the coverage period expired.[4]

• **Product Inflation versus Social Inflation.** Loss rates on all PC property policies are adversely affected by unexpected increases in inflation. Such increases were triggered, for example, by the oil price shocks of 1973 and 1978. However, in addition to a systematic unexpected inflation risk in each line, there may be line-specific inflation risks as well. The inflation risk of property lines is likely to reflect the approximate underlying inflation risk of the economy. Liability lines may be subject to social inflation, as reflected in juries' willingness to award punitive and other liability damages at rates far above the underlying rate of inflation. Such social inflation has been particularly prevalent in commercial liability and medical malpractice insurance and has been directly attributed by some analysts to faults in the U.S. civil litigation system.

Loss Ratio
Measures the ratio of pure losses incurred to premiums earned.

The **loss ratio** measures the actual losses incurred on a line. It measures the ratio of losses incurred to premiums earned. Thus, a loss ratio of less than 100 means that premiums earned were sufficient to cover losses incurred on that line. For example, over the 1978–88 period the mean loss ratio on all PC lines was 69.35.[5]

Expense Risk. The two major sources of expense risk to PC insurers are loss adjustment expenses (LAE) and commissions and other expenses. Loss adjustment expenses relate to the costs surrounding the loss settlement process; for example, many PC insurers employ adjusters who determine the liability of the insurer and the size of the adjustment or settlement to be made. The other major area of expense occurs in the commission costs paid to insurance brokers and sales agents and other expenses related to the acquisition of business.

These two sources of expense account for significant portions of premiums. In 1988, for example, the ratio of loss adjustment expense to premiums earned was 11.9 percent, and the ratio of commissions and other acquisition expenses to premiums written was 17.3 percent. These compare to a simple loss ratio on all lines of 66.4 percent in that year. Clearly, sharp rises in LAE, commissions, and other operating costs can rapidly render an insurance line unprofitable.

Combined Ratio
Measures the overall underwriting profitability of a line and is equal to the loss ratio plus the ratios of loss adjustment expenses to premiums earned, and commission and other acquisition costs to premiums written minus any dividends paid to policyholders as a proportion of premiums earned.

A common measure of the overall underwriting profitability of a line, which includes both loss and expense experience, is the **combined ratio.** Technically, the combined ratio is equal to the loss ratio plus the ratios of LAE to premiums earned, commissions, and other acquisition costs and general expense costs to premiums written, adjusted for any dividends paid to policyholders as a proportion of premiums earned. If the combined ratio is less than 100, premiums alone are sufficient to cover both losses and expenses related to the line.

If premiums are insufficient and the combined ratio exceeds 100, the PC insurer must rely on investment income on premiums for overall profitability. For example,

---

[4]In some product liability cases, such as those involving asbestos, the nature of the risk being covered was not fully understood at the time many of the policies were written.

[5]*A. M. Best's Aggregates and Averages,* Property-Casualty, 1989, p. 2.

over the 1979–1988 period, the combined ratio was on average 108.36, indicating that premiums alone were insufficient to cover the costs of both losses and expenses related to writing PC insurance.

Investment Yield/Return Risk. As noted earlier, when the combined ratio is more than 100, overall profitability can only be ensured by a sufficient investment return on premiums earned. That is, PC firms invest premiums in assets between the time they are received and paid out to meet claims. For example, over the 1979–88 period, average net investment income to premiums earned (or the PC insurers investment yield) was 8.92 percent. As a result, the overall average profitability (or **operating ratio**) of PC insurers was 99.44. It was equal to the combined ratio (108.36) minus the investment yield (8.92), indicating that PC insurers were marginally profitable over this period.[6] However, slightly lower returns on investments—8 percent rather than 8.92 percent—would have meant that underwriting PC insurance would have been marginally unprofitable. Thus, the behavior of interest rates and default rates on PC insurers' investments are crucial to the PC insurers' overall profitability. That is, measuring and managing credit and interest rate risk are key concerns of PC managers.

Given the importance of investment returns to PC insurers' profitability, we can see from Table 2–4 that bonds—both treasury and corporate—dominated the asset portfolios of PC insurers. Bonds comprised more than 61 percent of total assets and 75 percent of financial assets (so-called affiliated investments) in 1991.

Finally, if pure losses, LAE, and other costs are higher and investment yields are lower than expected so that operating losses are incurred, PC insurers carry a significant amount of surplus reserves (policyholder surplus) to reduce the risk of insolvency. In 1991, the ratio of policyholder surplus to assets was 26.4 percent.

Recent Trends.   The period since 1987 has not been very profitable for the PC industry. In particular, the combined ratio (the measure of loss plus cost risk) increased from 104.6 in 1987 to 116 in 1992—see Figure 2–1—which is the highest ratio since 1985. The major reason for this rise has been a succession of catastrophes from Hurricane Hugo in 1989, the San Francisco earthquake in 1991, the Oakland fires of 1991, to the more than $10 billion in losses incurred in Florida as a result of Hurricane Andrew in 1991. In the terminology of PC insurers, the industry is in the trough of an **underwriting cycle**, or underwriting conditions are hard.

The traditional reaction to such losses or poor profit results has been the exit from the industry—through failure or otherwise—of less profitable firms and a rapid increase in premiums among the remaining firms.[7] Historically, this has resulted in a fall in the combined ratio, as premiums rise, and an improvement in the operating ratio and PC industry profitability. As the underwriting profitability cycle approaches its peak, however, new entrants to the industry emerge. These new entrants compete by cutting premiums and lowering underwriting quality standards, thus setting the stage for a downturn in the cycle again. On average, underwriting cycles measured from peak to peak can last anywhere from 6 to 10 years.[8]

---

[6]Since the operating ratio was less than 100.

[7]In 1992, 59 PC insurers failed compared to 52 in 1985. Although, failures represented .5 percent of premiums in 1992 compared to 1.5 percent in 1985. For example, *The Economist* (March 20, 1993, p. 86) reports that premiums rose 10 to 20 percent in Florida in 1992 and reinsurance costs by 50 percent in the first three months of 1993.

[8]There are numerous competing theories of the underwriting cycle and what triggers PC insurers' behavior. See *Yale Journal of Regulation* 5, no. 2, Summer 1988, pp. 367–516, for an excellent review of these theories.

Operating Ratio
A measure of the overall profitability of a PC insurer; it equals the combined ratio minus the investment yield.

Underwriting Cycle
The tendency of profits in the PC industry to follow a cyclical pattern.

FIGURE 2–1

The PC insurers combined ratio 1980–1992

Still Rising American insurers' combined ratio*

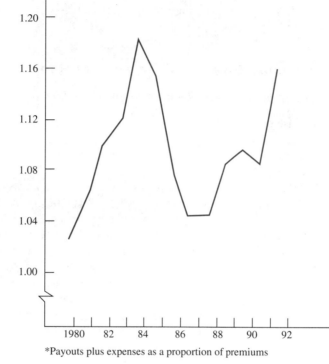

*Payouts plus expenses as a proportion of premiums

SOURCE: A.M. Best, *The Economist,* March 20, 1993, p. 86.

Regulation

As with life insurance companies, PC insurers are chartered by states and regulated by state commissions. In addition, state guaranty funds provide some protection to policyholders should an insurance company fail. The National Association of Insurance Commissioners (NAIC) also provides various services to state regulatory commissions. These include a standardized examination system called IRIS (Insurance Regulatory Information System) to identify insurers with loss, combined, and other ratios operating outside normal ranges.

An additional burden that PC insurers face in some activity lines—especially auto insurance and worker compensation insurance—is rate regulation. That is, given the public utility nature of some insurance lines, state commissioners set ceilings on premiums and premium increases, usually based on a specific cost of capital and line risk exposure formulas for the insurance supplier. This has led to some insurers leaving states such as New Jersey, Florida, and California which have the most restrictive regulations.

Concept Questions

1. Why do PC insurers hold more capital and reserves than life insurers?
2. Why are PC insurers' assets, on average, shorter in maturity than life insurers assets?

3. Suppose the pure loss ratio is 80 percent, the LAE and other expense ratio is 27 percent, and investment yields are 11 percent. Is the PC insurer profitable? What is its operating ratio?

4. Why does the combined ratio tend to behave cyclically?

Securities Firms and Investment Banks

Size, Structure, and Composition of the Industry

Because of the emphasis on securities trading and underwriting, the size of the industry is usually measured by the equity capital of the firms participating in the industry. This amounted to $43.4 billion at the end of 1992, supporting total assets of $.744 trillion.

Beginning in 1980 and up to the stock market crash of October 19, 1987, the number of firms in the industry expanded dramatically from 2,933 in 1980 to 6,722 in 1987. The aftermath of the crash saw a major shakeout with firms declining to 5,206 by the third quarter of 1992, or a decline of 23 percent since 1987.

The firms in the industry can be divided along a number of dimensions. First are the largest firms, the so-called national full-line firms who service both retail customers (especially in acting as broker-dealers) and corporate customers (such as new issue underwriting). The major national full-line firm is Merrill Lynch.[9] Second are the national full-line firms that specialize more in corporate finance and are highly active in trading securities such as Goldman Sachs, Salomon Brothers, and Morgan Stanley. Third, the rest of the industry comprises

1. Specialized investment bank subsidiaries of commercial bank holding companies (such as J. P. Morgan).

2. Specialized **discount brokers** that effect trades for customers without offering investment advice or tips (such as Charles Schwab).[10]

3. Regional securities firms that are often subdivided into large, medium, and small categories and concentrate on servicing customers in a particular region such as New York or California.

Next, we discuss the five key activity areas for securities firms.[11]

Investing. Investing involves not only managing pools of assets such as closed- and open-ended mutual funds but also managing pension funds in competition with life insurance companies. Securities firms can manage such funds either as agents for other investors or as principals for themselves. The objective in funds management is to choose asset allocations to beat some return-risk performance benchmark.[12]

Investment Banking. Investment banking refers to activities related to underwriting and distributing new issues of debt and equity. New issues can be either primary, the first-time issues of companies sometimes called **IPOs** for initial public

Discount Broker
A stockbroker that conducts trades for customers but does not offer investment advice.

IPO
An initial or first-time public offering of debt or equity by a corporation.

---

[9]The second largest until 1993 was Shearson Lehman. In 1993, the Shearson part of the firm was sold by American Express (the parent company) to Primerica Corporation. This left Lehman Brothers as a more specialized and smaller investment banking arm of American Express.

[10]Discount brokers usually charge lower commissions than full-service brokers such as Merrill Lynch.

[11]See Bloch (1990) and Schwartz (1991) for similar lists.

[12]Such as the "securities market line" given the funds "beta."

Private Placement
A securities issue placed with one or a few large institutional investors.

offerings, or secondary issues, which are the new issues of seasoned firms whose debt or equity is already trading. Securities underwritings can be undertaken through either public or private offerings. In a private offering, the investment banker acts as a **private placement** agent for a fee, placing the securities with one or a few large institutional investors such as life insurance companies.[13] In a public offering, the securities may be underwritten either on a best-efforts or a firm commitment basis and the securities offered to the public at large. With best-efforts underwriting, investment bankers act as *agents* on a fee basis related to their success in placing the issue. In firm commitment underwriting, the investment banker acts as a *principal,* purchasing the securities from the issuer at one price and seeking to place them with public investors at a slightly higher price. Finally, in addition to investment banking operations in the corporate securities markets, the investment banker may participate as an underwriter (primary dealer) in government, municipal, and mortgage-backed securities.

Market Making. Market making involves creating a secondary market in an asset. Thus, in addition to being primary dealers in government securities and underwriters of corporate bonds and equities, investment bankers make a secondary market in these instruments. Market making can involve either agency or principal transactions. *Agency* transactions are two-way transactions on behalf of *customers;* for example, acting as a *stockbroker* or dealer for a fee or commission such as the bid-ask spread. In *principal* transactions, the market maker seeks to profit on the price movements of securities and takes either long or short inventory positions for its own account. Or, an inventory position may be taken to stabilize the market in the securities.[14]

Trading. Trading is closely related to the market making activities just described, where a trader takes an active net position in an underlying instrument or asset. There are at least four types of trading activities:

1. *Position trading* involves purchases of large blocks of securities to facilitate smooth functioning of the secondary markets in such securities.

2. *Pure arbitrage* entails buying an asset in one market at one price and selling it immediately in another market at a higher price.

3. *Risk arbitrage* involves buying blocks of securities in anticipation of some information release—such as a merger or takeover announcement or a Federal Reserve interest rate announcement.[15]

4. *Program trading* is associated with seeking a risk arbitrage between a cash market price (e.g., the Standard & Poor's 500 Stock Market Average) and the *futures* market price of that instrument.[16]

As with many activities of securities firms, such trading can be conducted on behalf of a customer as an agent or on behalf of the firm as a principal.

---

[13]See, *Federal Reserve Bulletin,* February 1993, for an excellent description of the private placement market. Issuers of privately placed securities do not have to register with the SEC since they are made only to large sophisticated investors.

[14]In general, full-service investment banks can become market makers in stocks on NASDAQ, but have been prevented until recently from acting as market-making specialists on the NYSE.

[15]It is termed *risk arbitrage* because if the event does not actually occur, the trader stands to lose money; for example, if a merger does not take place or the Federal Reserve does not change interest rates.

[16]For example, buying the cash S&P index and selling futures contracts on the S&P index. Since stocks and futures contracts trade in different markets, their prices are not always equal.

FIGURE 2–2

Commission income as a percentage of total revenues

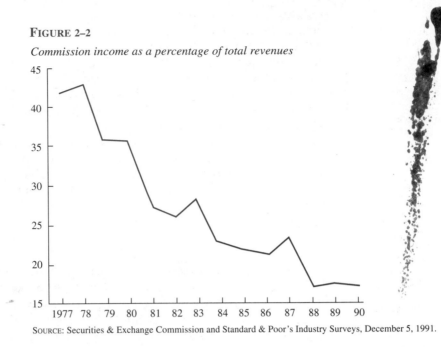

SOURCE: Securities & Exchange Commission and Standard & Poor's Industry Surveys, December 5, 1991.

Back-Office and Other Service Functions. These functions include custody and escrow services, clearance and settlement services, and research and advisory services; for example, giving advice on mergers and acquisitions (M&A). In performing these functions, the securities firm normally acts as an agent for a fee.

Balance Sheet and Recent Trends

A major effect of the 1987 stock market crash was a sharp decline in stock market trading volume and, thus, in brokerage commissions earned by securities firms over the 1987–90 period. However, the decline in brokerage commissions actually began in 1977 as part of a secular fall in the importance of commission income, as a percentage of revenues, for securities firms as a result of the abolition of fixed commissions on securities trades by the Securities and Exchange Commission (SEC) in May 1975 and the fierce competition for wholesale commissions and trades that followed (see Figure 2–2).[17]

Also affecting the profitability of the securities industry were the decline in new equity issues over the 1987–90 period and bond and equity underwriting in general. This was partly a result of the stock market crash, partly due to a decline in mergers and acquisitions, and partly due to investor concerns about junk bonds following the Michael Milken–Drexel Burnham Lambert scandal, which resulted in that firm's failure.

Since 1990, however, the securities industry has shown a resurgence in profitability.[18] The two principal reasons for this have been enhanced fixed income trading profits and increased growth in new issue underwritings. Since 1987, securities firms in the aggregate have nearly tripled their holdings of fixed income securities

---

[17]Although a sharply increased volume of equities trading in 1992 returned commissions to 1987 levels, this may be a temporary phenomenon.

[18]Total profits increased from −$162 million in 1990 to more than $7,500 million in 1992.

TABLE 2–5   U.S. Corporate Underwriting Activity
(in $ billions)

	Straight Corporate Debt	Convertible Debt	Asset-Backed Debt	Total Debt	High-Yield Bonds	Common Stock	Preferred Stock	Total Equity	All IPOs	True IPOs	Closed-End IPOs	Total Underwritings
1980	$36.7	$4.4	$0.5	$41.6	$1.4	$12.8	$3.2	$16.0	$1.4	$1.4	—	$57.6
1981	35.1	4.7	0.5	40.3	1.2	13.9	1.7	15.6	3.1	3.1	—	55.9
1982	39.5	3.2	1.1	43.8	2.5	14.0	5.4	19.4	1.3	1.3	—	63.2
1983	37.4	6.1	8.4	51.9	7.4	37.0	8.5	45.5	12.5	12.5	—	97.4
1984	53.2	4.1	12.1	69.4	14.0	9.2	4.0	13.2	3.9	3.8	$0.1	82.6
1985	76.4	7.5	20.8	104.7	14.2	24.7	8.6	33.3	8.5	8.4	0.1	138.0
1986	149.8	10.1	67.8	227.7	31.9	43.2	13.9	57.1	22.3	18.1	4.2	284.8
1987	117.8	9.9	91.7	219.4	28.1	41.5	11.4	52.9	24.0	14.3	9.7	272.3
1988	120.3	3.1	113.8	237.2	27.7	29.7	7.6	37.3	23.6	5.7	17.9	274.5
1989	134.1	5.5	135.3	274.9	25.3	22.9	7.7	30.6	13.7	6.1	7.6	305.5
1990	106.9	4.8	178.9	290.6	1.4	19.2	4.7	23.9	10.2	4.6	5.6	314.4
1991	200.6	7.5	299.0	507.1	10.0	56.0	20.0	76.0	25.1	16.5	8.6	583.1
1992												
Jan	36.4	0.8	43.0	80.2	1.6	6.6	0.9	7.5	3.0	2.1	0.9	87.7
Feb	18.5	0.6	29.4	48.4	1.3	7.5	4.9	12.4	3.8	2.3	1.4	60.8
Mar	20.7	1.4	39.9	62.0	4.6	7.8	1.3	9.2	4.3	3.5	0.8	71.2
Apr	19.8	0.3	28.7	48.8	3.5	6.7	1.6	8.2	3.2	2.7	0.5	57.0
May	27.8	0.4	44.1	72.3	3.9	6.7	3.0	9.7	2.5	2.2	0.3	82.0
June	31.0	0.7	39.2	70.9	4.4	7.5	3.1	10.5	3.8	2.1	1.7	81.4
July	35.5	0.2	44.0	79.7	4.9	5.3	2.6	7.9	4.0	2.6	1.4	87.6
Aug	23.1	0.2	32.8	56.1	2.8	4.5	1.7	6.3	3.0	1.2	1.8	62.4
Sept	27.2	0.3	45.1	72.7	3.1	4.3	1.9	6.2	2.4	0.7	1.7	78.8
YTD '91	142.6	6.1	222.8	371.6	3.5	36.8	9.7	46.5	15.0	9.4	5.6	418.1
YTD '92	240.0	5.0	346.1	591.1	30.1	56.8	21.0	77.8	29.9	19.3	10.6	668.9
% Change	68.3%	−18.4%	55.3%	59.1%	770.4%	54.1%	117.3%	67.3%	99.8%	105.2%	90.8%	60.0%

NOTE: High-yield bonds is a subset of straight corporate debt. IPOs is a subset of common stock; true and close-end fund IPOs are subsets of all IPOs.
SOURCE: Securities Data Company and Securities Industry Association, *Security Trends* 18, No. 7, October 19, 1992.

(corporate bonds, foreign, mortgage-backed, and Treasuries) in a successful strategic move to enhance trading profits. Indeed, in 1992 bond trading profits accounted for 20 percent of industry revenues and exceeded brokerage commission revenues. However, a heavy reliance on fixed income trading can also produce losses if interest rates move in a direction other than expected. For example, Salomon Brothers announced major trading losses on their bond trading activities in February 1993. Thus, interest rate risk is now a focal area of investment bank risk exposure.

The growth in underwriting activity over the 1990–92 period is evident from the fact that the total dollar value of underwriting activity grew from $314 billion in 1990 to $583 billion in 1991 and to $668.9 in the third quarter of 1992. As you can see in Table 2–5, new issue activity more than doubled in two years.

Note the current importance of securities trading and underwriting on the 1992 consolidated balance sheet of securities firms in Table 2–6. Looking at the asset portfolio, securities and spot commodities owned accounted for 30 percent of assets, while reverse repurchase agreements—securities borrowed for temporary purposes (especially trading) in exchange for cash—accounted for 35 percent of assets.

TABLE 2–6

SECURITIES FIRMS
Balance Sheet
As of December 31, 1992
(in $ millions)

Assets		
Cash..		$ 3,207.6
Segregated cash...		4,854.2
Receivables—Brokers, dealers, clearing organizations		181,175.9
Receivables: Failed to deliver	7,530.7	
Receivables: Securities borrowed	161,244.7	
Receivables: Omnibus accounts...	944.5	
Receivables: Clearing organizations	2,700.8	
Receivables: Other	8,755.2	
Receivables from customers..		43,313.9
Receivables from noncustomers...		3,229.2
Reverse repurchase agreements		262,554.9
Securities and spot commodities owned		223,379.4
Bankers acceptances, CDs, commercial paper..........................	5,690.9	
U.S. and Canadian government obligations..............................	149,101.7	
State and municipal government obligations	8,490.5	
Corporate obligations..	41,861.5	
Stocks and warrants...	11,144.3	
Options...	844.3	
Arbitrage	3,684.9	
Other securities	1,612.1	
Spot commodities..	488.0	
Exempted securities (FOCUS IIA Only)...................................	02.9	
Debt securities (FOCUS IIA Only)	258.3	
Securities owned not readily marketable...		1,979.1
Other investments not readily marketable...		110.1
Securities borrowed under subordinated agreements		50.3
Secured demand notes...		263.2
Exchange memberships..		286.0
Investments in subsidiaries, affiliates and partnerships		5,276.6
Property, furniture and equipment..		3,255.6
Other assets...		11,235.8
Total Assets...		$744,171.8
Liabilities		
Bank loans payable		$ 28,476.2
Repurchase agreements...		384,067.7

<small>SOURCE: Securities Industry Association (internal figures).</small>

With respect to liabilities, repurchase agreements were the major source of funds; these are securities temporarily lent in exchange for cash received. Repurchase agreements amounted to 51 percent of total liabilities and equity. The other major sources of funds were securities sold short for future delivery, broker-call bank loans, and shareholders' equity.

Regulation

The primary regulator of the securities industry is the Securities and Exchange Commission (the SEC) established in 1934. Two self-regulatory organizations are also involved in the day-to-day regulation of trading practices on the exchanges: they monitor trading abuses (such as insider trading) as well as securities firms' capital

---

TABLE 2–6   (concluded)

Payables—Brokers, dealers, clearing organizations......................		52,693.3
Payables: Failed to receive.................................	7,383.4	
Payables: Securities loaned................................	39,738.5	
Payables: Omnibus accounts..............................	668.4	
Payables: Clearing organizations	558.0	
Payables: Other	4,345.0	
Payables to customers		56,858.8
Payables: Securities accounts	49,954.0	
Payables: Commodities accounts	6,904.8	
Payables to noncustomers		3,722.2
Payables: Securities accounts.............................	2,866.0	
Payables: Commodities accounts	856.2	
Securities sold short..		121,694.1
Accounts payable and accrued liabilities		32,227.4
Drafts payable..	2,679.6	
Accounts payable	7,016.6	
Income taxes payable..	393.4	
Deferred income taxes......................................	260.6	
Accrued expenses, other liabilities.....................	15,698.4	
Other payables and accrued liabilities.................	5,837.5	
Accounts payable and accrued liabilities (FOCUS IIA)	341.3	
Notes and mortgages payable...		21,018.3
Subordinated liabilities		14,928.4
Cash borrowings...	14,568.7	
Securities borrowed..	0.0	
Secured demand notes.......................................	239.1	
Exchange memberships......................................	24.4	
Other (Not qualified for net capital)...................	96.2	
Total Liabilities		$715,686.4
Ownership Equity		
Equity: Sole proprietorship		0.0
Equity: Partnership...		4,558.5
Equity: Corporation..		23,926.9
Preferred stock	392.9	
Common stock	1,060.2	
Additional paid-in capital..................................	13,319.7	
Retained earnings...	9,263.7	
Less treasury stock	−109.6	
Total Ownership Equity		28,485.4
Total Liabilities and Ownership Equity..................................		$744,171.8

(solvency positions). They are the New York Stock Exchange (NYSE) and the National Association of Securities Dealers (NASD), the latter responsible for trading in the over-the-counter markets such as NASDAQ. The SEC also lays down rules governing securities firms' underwriting and trading activities. For example, SEC Rule 415 on *shelf-offerings* allows larger corporations to register their new issues with the SEC up to two years in advance.[19] SEC Rule 144A defines the boundaries between public offerings of securities and private placements of securities.

---

[19]They are called shelf-offerings because after registering the issue with the SEC, the firm can take the issue "off the shelf" and sell it to the market when conditions are the most favorable; for example, when interest rates are low in the case of debt issues.

TABLE 2–7

U.S. FINANCE COMPANIES
Balance Sheet
As of December 31, 1991
(in $ billions)

Assets		
Accounts receivable, gross..		$480.3
Consumer..	$121.9	
Business...	292.6	
Real estate..	65.8	
Less reserves for unearned income	(55.1)	
Less reserves for losses...	(12.9)	
Accounts receivable net...	412.3	
All other...		149.0
Total assets...		$561.2
Liabilities and Capital		
Bank loans..		42.3
Commercial paper...		159.5
Debt due to parent..		34.5
Debt not elsewhere classified..		191.3
All other liabilities		69.0
Capital, surplus, and undivided profits		64.8
Total liabilities and capital..		$561.2

NOTE: Figures do not add exactly due to rounding.
SOURCE: *Federal Reserve Bulletin,* January 1993, p. A35.

Finally, the Securities Investor Protection Corporation (SIPC) protects investors against losses of up to $500,000 on securities firm failures. This guarantee fund was created following the passage of the Securities Investor Protection Act in 1970 and is based on premium contributions from member firms.

Concept Questions

1. Securities firms are increasingly building up their long-term bond portfolios and funding these with short-term repurchase agreements. What is the risk of this strategy?
2. What is the difference between pure arbitrage and risk arbitrage in investment banking?
3. Is high stock price volatility necessarily bad for securities firms?
4. How are the risks of bond trading related to the volatility of interest rates?

Finance Companies

Size, Structure, and Composition of the Industry

Factoring
The process of purchasing accounts receivable from corporations (often at a discount) usually with no recourse to the seller should the receivables go bad.

Finance companies have been among the fastest growing FI groups in recent years. At the end of 1991, their assets stood at $.56 trillion. The two major types of finance companies are (1) those specializing in making installment and other loans, especially auto loans, to consumers and (2) diversified finance companies making consumer loans in addition to providing financing to corporations, especially through equipment leasing and **factoring**.

The industry is quite concentrated with the largest 20 firms accounting for more than 80 percent of its assets. In addition, many of the largest finance companies such as General Motors Acceptance Corporation (GMAC) tend to be wholly owned or captive subsidiaries of major manufacturing companies. Thus, a major role of a **captive finance company** is to provide financing for the purchase of products manufactured by the parent, such as GM cars. At the end of 1990, 7 of the top 20 companies were captives.

Captive Finance Company
A finance company wholly owned by a parent corporation.

Balance Sheet and Recent Trends

In recent years, the fastest growing areas of asset business have been in the nonconsumer finance areas, especially leasing and business loans. The growth in leasing was encouraged by tax incentives provided under the 1981 Economic Recovery Act. Over the 1980–90 period leasing grew, on average, at more than 17 percent per annum.

To finance this asset growth, finance companies have primarily relied on short-term commercial paper and longer-term notes and bonds. In particular, unlike banks and thrifts, finance companies cannot issue deposits. In the short-term commercial paper market, finance companies are now the largest issuers with many having direct sale programs in which commercial paper is sold directly to mutual funds and other institutional investors on a continuous day-by-day basis. Most commercial paper issues have maturities of 30 days or less, although it can be issued with maturities of up to 270 days.[20]

In Table 2–7 we show the balance sheet of finance companies as of the end of 1991. As you can see, business and consumer loans (called accounts receivable) are the major assets; commercial paper and other debt (long-term debt) are the major liabilities.

Regulation

Because finance companies do not accept deposits, they are not subject to the oversight of any specific federal or state regulators. That is, they are much less regulated than banks or thrifts. However, since they are heavy borrowers in the capital markets, they need to signal their solvency and safety to investors. This is usually done by holding much higher equity or capital-asset ratios, and therefore, lower leverage ratios than banks. For example, the 1991 aggregate balance sheet (Table 2–7) shows a capital-assets ratio of 11.5 percent for finance companies—almost twice the size of that held by banks in the same year. Also, some finance companies use default protection guarantees from their parent companies and/or guarantees, such as letters of credit or lines of credit, purchased for a fee from high-quality commercial or investment banks.

Concept Questions

1. Since finance companies seem to compete in the same lending markets as banks, why aren't they subject to the same regulations as banks?

---

[20]Commercial paper issued with a maturity longer than 270 days has to be registered with the SEC (i.e., it is treated the same as publicly placed bonds).

2. Do finance companies mismatch the maturities of their assets and liabilities as much as banks?

3. Is business lending a more important asset for banks or for finance companies?

Mutual Funds

Size, Structure, and Composition of the Industry

The first mutual fund was founded in Boston in 1924. The industry grew very slowly at first; by 1970 360 funds held about $50 billion in assets. Due to the advent of money market mutual funds in 1972, tax-exempt money market mutual funds in 1979, and an explosion of special purpose stock, bond and derivative funds there has been a dramatic growth in the number of funds and in the asset size of the industry. At the end of 1991, more than 3,400 different funds had total assets of $1.2 trillion. In terms of asset size, the mutual fund industry is slightly smaller than the life insurance industry and about 40 percent the size of the commercial banking industry. This makes mutual funds the third most important FI group in the United States measured by asset size.

The mutual fund industry itself is usually divided into two sectors: short-term funds and long-term funds. Short-term funds comprise taxable money market mutual funds and tax-exempt money market mutual funds. In Figure 2–3, we show the growth of bond, income, and equity funds relative to money market funds over the 1989–91 period. At the end of 1991, 59.9 percent of all mutual fund assets were in long-term funds (27.3 percent equity and 32.6 percent bonds and income); the remaining funds, or 40.1 percent, were in money market mutual funds. As you can see in Figure 2–3, the proportion invested in long-term versus short-term funds can vary quite considerably over time. For example, the decline in short-term funds and the growth in long-term funds in 1991 reflects the decline in short-term interest rates and the rise in equity returns during that year.

The aggregate figures for bond, income, and equity funds tend to obscure the fact that there are many different funds in these groups. Indeed, regulations require that mutual fund managers specify the investment objectives of their funds in a prospectus sent to potential investors. Currently, the Investment Company Institute (the trade organization for mutual funds) classifies 19 major categories of investment objectives for long-term funds. These objectives are in Table 2–8 along with the assets allocated to each major category in 1990 and 1991.

The rationale for mutual funds existence is to achieve superior diversification through fund and risk pooling compared to that achieved by the individual small investor on his or her own. As a simple example, wholesale CDs sell in minimum denominations of $100,000 each and often pay higher interest rates than passbook or small time deposits. By pooling funds in a money market mutual fund, small investors can gain access to wholesale money markets and instruments and, therefore, to potentially higher returns.

The return the investor gets from investing in mutual fund shares reflects three aspects of the underlying portfolio of mutual fund assets: First, income and dividends are earned on those assets: second, capital gains occur when assets are sold by the mutual fund at prices higher than the purchase price; and third, capital appreciation in

FIGURE 2–3

Mutual fund total net assets
(in $ billions)

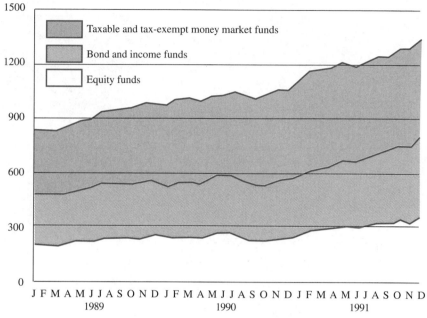

SOURCE: *Mutual Fund Fact Book,* Investment Company Institute, Washington, D.C., 1992, p. 6.

Marked-to-Market
Adjusting asset and balance sheet values to reflect current market prices.

NAV
The net asset value of a mutual fund is equal to the market value of the assets in the mutual fund portfolio divided by the number of shares outstanding.

Open-Ended Mutual Fund
The supply of shares in the fund are not fixed but can increase or decrease daily with purchases and redemptions of shares.

Closed-End Investment Companies
Specialized investment companies that invest in securities and assets of other firms but have a fixed supply of shares outstanding themselves.

REIT
A real estate investment trust. A closed-end investment company that specialized in investing in mortgages, property, or real estate company shares.

Load Fund
A mutual fund with an upfront sales or commission charge that has to be paid by the investor.

the underlying values of the assets held in the fund's portfolio. With respect to capital appreciation, mutual fund assets are normally **marked-to-market** daily. This means that the managers of the fund calculate the current value of each mutual fund share by computing the daily market value of the fund's total asset portfolio and then dividing this amount by the number of mutual fund shares outstanding. The resulting value is called the net-asset value (**NAV**) of the fund. This is the price the investor gets when selling shares back to the fund that day or buying any new shares in the fund. Most mutual funds are **open-ended** in that the number of shares outstanding fluctuates daily with the amount of share redemptions and new purchases. This contrasts to most regular corporations traded on stock exchanges and to **closed-end investment companies**, which have fixed quantities of shares outstanding at any given time. For example, real estate investment trusts (**REITs**) are closed-end investment companies that specialize in investment in real estate company shares and/or in buying mortgages.[21]

An investor who buys a mutual fund share may be subject to a sales charge— sometimes as large as 8.5 percent. In this case, the fund is called a **load fund**. Other funds, that directly market shares to investors, do not use sales agents working for commissions and have no upfront commission charges; these are called *no-load* funds. In general, these funds retain a small percentage of investable funds to meet distribution costs and other operating costs. Such annual fees are known as

---

[21]At the end of 1991, closed-end investment companies had assets of $53 billion. Many have become specialized country funds investing in shares in countries such as Argentina, Brazil, or Mexico. The shares of these closed-end funds are traded on NYSE or in the over-the-counter market.

TABLE 2–8   **Mutual Fund Assets**
              Classified by Investment Objective—Year-End
              (in $ billions)

Investment Objective	1990	1991	Percent Change
Aggressive growth	$ 35.4	$ 63.3	+78.8%
Growth	68.1	105.0	+54.2
Growth & income	86.9	129.5	+49.0
Precious metals	3.1	2.9	–6.8
International	14.3	19.1	+33.6
Global-equity	13.5	17.3	+28.1
Income-equity	22.3	29.3	+31.4
Option/income	2.2	1.4	–36.4
Flexible portfolio	6.7	10.0	+49.3
Balanced	12.8	20.2	+57.8
Income-mixed	18.9	25.6	+35.5
Income-bond	15.9	27.5	+73.0
U.S. government income	75.6	96.9	+28.2
GNMA	29.0	36.6	+26.2
Global bond	12.4	26.8	+116.1
Corporate bond	12.3	15.5	+26.0
High-yield bond	18.9	26.1	+38.1
Long-term municipal bond	70.7	88.3	+24.9
State municipal bond—long-term	49.5	65.8	+32.9
*Total long-term funds	$568.5	$807.1	+42.0%

SOURCE: *Mutual Fund Fact Book,* Investment Company Institute, Washington, D.C., 1992, p. 6.

12b–1 Fees
Fees relating to the
distribution costs of
mutual fund shares.

12b–1 fees after the SEC rule covering such charges. Annual fees can run as high as 1.25 percent.

Balance Sheet and Recent Trends

Look at the distribution of assets of money market mutual funds in 1991 in Table 2–9. As you can see, the average maturity of assets is a very short 50 days. Short maturity asset holdings are an objective of these funds to retain their deposit-like nature. In fact, most money market mutual fund shares have their values fixed at $1. Asset value fluctuations due to interest rate changes and any small default risk and capital gains or losses on assets are adjusted for by increasing or reducing the number of $1 shares owned by the investor. The major assets owned by money market funds are commercial paper such as that issued by finance companies (see Section IV), repurchase agreements, and short-term Treasury securities.

Note the asset composition of long-term mutual funds in Table 2–10. As might be expected, it reflects the popularity of different types of bond or equity funds at that time. Underscoring the attractiveness of equity funds in 1991 was the fact that stocks comprised 40 percent of total long-term mutual fund asset portfolios. U.S. Treasury securities and municipal bonds were the next most popular assets.

Regulation

The SEC is the primary regulator of mutual funds. Specifically, the Securities Act of 1933 requires a mutual fund to file a registration statement with the SEC and to set

TABLE 2–9   Money Market Fund Asset Composition
Year-End 1991
(in $ billions)

U.S. Treasury bills	$47.6
Other Treasury securities	32.1
Other U.S. securities	41.3
Repurchase agreements	68.2
Commercial bank CDs	6.1
Other domestic CDs	26.9
Eurodollar CDs	21.6
Commercial paper	187.6
Bankers acceptances	4.3
Cash reserves	−0.2
Other	14.2
Total Net Assets	$449.7
Average maturity (days)	50
Number of funds	553

SOURCE: *Mutual Fund Fact Book,* Investment Company Institute, Washington, D.C., 1992, p. 31.

TABLE 2–10   Portfolio Composition of Equity, Bond, and Income Funds
Year-End 1991
(in $ billions)

Common stock	$328.1
Preferred stock	6.6
Warranty and rights	1.0
Options	0.4
Municipal bonds (long-term)	147.7
Municipal bonds (short-term)	13.6
Other taxable debt	84.5
U.S. gov't. sec. (long-term)	170.1
U.S. gov't. sec. (short-term)	21.3
Liquid assets	25.5
Others	8.3
Total Net Assets	$807.1

SOURCE: *Mutual Fund Fact Book,* Investment Company Institute, Washington, D.C., 1992, p. 32.

rules and procedures regarding the fund's prospectus sent to investors. In addition, the Securities Exchange Act of 1934 makes the purchase and sale of mutual fund shares subject to various antifraud provisions. The 1934 Act also appointed the National Association of Securities Dealers (NASD) to supervise mutual fund share distributions.

In 1940, Congress passed the Investment Advisers Act and Investment Company Act. The Investment Advisers Act regulates the activities of mutual fund advisers. The Investment Company Act sets out rules to prevent conflicts of interest, fraud, and excessive fees or charges for fund shares.

In recent years, the passage of the Insider Trading and Securities Fraud Enforcement Act of 1988 has required mutual funds to develop mechanisms and procedures to avoid insider trading abuses. In addition, the ability of mutual funds to conduct their business may be affected by the Market Reform Act of 1990 passed in the wake of the 1987 stock market crash. This act allows the SEC to introduce circuit breakers to halt trading on exchanges and to restrict program trading when it deems necessary. Finally, most states have also passed securities laws regulating the sale of mutual fund shares.

Concept Questions

1. What type of mutual fund—defined by its objectives—might be appropriate for a 25-year-old investor who doesn't need to cash in his or her shares for at least 10 years? Explain your answer.
2. Suppose the Federal Reserve radically tightens monetary policy. How is this likely to affect the allocation of funds among money market mutual funds, bond funds, and equity funds?
3. Are money market mutual funds exposed to credit risk or default risk on their assets?

FIGURE 2–4

Share of all intermediary assets

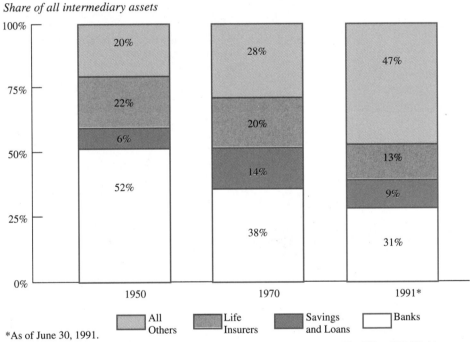

*As of June 30, 1991.

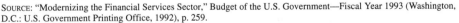

SOURCE: "Modernizing the Financial Services Sector," Budget of the U.S. Government—Fiscal Year 1993 (Washington, D.C.: U.S. Government Printing Office, 1992), p. 259.

Summary

This chapter has provided an overview of (1) the size, structure, and composition, (2) the balance sheet and recent trends, and (3) the regulation of the major groups of nondepository FIs in the United States. The current market shares of the overall intermediation pie and the trends in these shares are summarized in Figure 2–4. Clearly, the most striking trend has been the decline in the share of depository institutions since the Second World War compared to the other FIs as a group. We discuss possible reasons for this trend in Chapter 3.

The major theme of this book is the measurement and management of FI risks. In particular, although we might categorize or group FIs and label them life insurance companies, PC insurance companies, and so on, in fact they face risks that are more common than different. Specifically, all the FIs described in this chapter (1) hold some assets that are potentially subject to default or credit risk, (2) tend to mismatch the maturities of their balance sheets to a greater or lesser extent, and are thus exposed to interest rate risk. Moreover, all are exposed to some degree of saver withdrawal or liquidity risk depending on the type of claims sold to liability holders. And, most are exposed to some type of underwriting risk whether through the sale of insurance, the sale of securities, or issuing various types of credit guarantees on or off the balance sheet.

Finally, all are exposed to operating cost risks because the production of financial services requires the use of real resources and back-office support systems.

In the rest of this textbook, we investigate the ways in which managers of FIs are measuring and managing this inventory of risks to produce the best return-risk trade-off for shareholders in a increasingly competitive and contestable market environment.

Questions and Problems

1. What are the similarities and differences among the four basic lines of life insurance products?

2. How can you use life insurance and annuity products to create a steady stream of cash disbursements and payments so as to avoid either the payment or receipt of a single lump sum cash amount?

3. *a.* Calculate the annual cash flows on a $1 million 20 year fixed payment annuity earning a guaranteed 8 percent p.a. if payments are to begin at the end of the current year.

    b. Calculate the annual cash flows on a $1 million 20 year fixed payment annuity earning a guaranteed 8 percent p.a. if payments are to begin at the end of five years.

4. Distinguish between insurance company Guaranteed Investment Contracts (GICs) and bank Certificates of Deposit (CDs). What are their similarities? Differences?

5. Contrast the balance sheet of depository institutions with that of a typical life insurance company.

6. How do insurance companies earn profits? Use the method by which insurance companies generate profits to explain their involvement in the junk bond market.

7. *a.* If the simple loss ratio on a line of property insurance is 73 percent, the loss adjustment expense is 12.5 percent, and the ratio of commissions and other acquisitions expenses 18 percent, is this line profitable?

    b. How does your answer to part (a) change if investment yields are 9 percent?

8. Contrast the activities of securities firms with depository institutions.

9. What are the five major activity areas for security firms and how were they impacted by the stock market crash of 1987?

10. Why do you think that finance companies have been among the fastest growing FI groups in recent years?

3

WHY ARE FINANCIAL INTERMEDIARIES SPECIAL?

Learning Objectives

In this chapter you are going to learn why financial institutions are different from commercial firms. That is why, for example, the failure of a large bank may have more serious effects on the economy than the failure of a large steel or car producer. We explain how financial institutions—especially banks—provide a special set of services to households and firms. We also discuss why their very specialness results in increased regulation and regulatory oversight that other corporations do not require. This imposes a regulatory burden on FIs. Thus, regulation can and does affect the efficiency with which financial institutions produce financial services.

Introduction

Of all private corporations, financial intermediaries (FIs) are singled out for special regulatory attention.[1] To justify such regulation, advocates usually argue that FIs provide special functions or services and that major disturbances to, or interferences with, these functions can lead to adverse effects on the rest of the economy—what economists call **negative externalities**.[2] We first examine this specialness question in general; that is, what are the special functions FIs—both depository institutions and nondepository institutions—provide? How do these functions benefit the economy? Second, we investigate what makes some FIs more special than others. Third, we look at how unique and longlived the special functions of FIs really are.

Negative Externality
An action by an economic agent imposing costs on other economic agents.

Financial Intermediaries Specialness

To understand the important economic function played by FIs, imagine a simple world in which FIs do not exist. In such a world, households generating excess savings by consuming less than they earn would have the basic choice: they could hold cash as an asset or invest in the securities issued by corporations. In general, corporations issue securities to finance their investments in real assets and to cover the gap

---

[1] Some public utility suppliers such as gas, electric, telephone, and water companies are also singled out for regulation because of the special nature of their services and the costs imposed on society if they fail.

[2] A good example of a negative externality is the costs faced by small businesses in a one-bank town should the local bank fail. These businesses could find it difficult to get financing elsewhere and their customers may be similarly disadvantaged. As a result, the failure of the bank may have a negative or contagious effect on the economic prospects of the whole community resulting in lower sales, production, and employment.

FIGURE 3–1

Flow of funds in a world without FIs

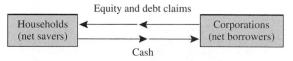

Equity and debt claims

| Households (net savers) | | Corporations (net borrowers) |

Cash

between their investment plans and their internally generated savings such as retained earnings.

As shown in Figure 3–1, in such a world savings would flow from households to corporations; in return, financial claims (equity and debt securities) would flow from corporations to household savers.

In an economy without FIs, the level of fund flows between the household savers and the corporate sector is likely to be quite low. There are several reasons for this. Once they have lent money to a firm by buying its financial claims, households need to monitor or check the actions of the firm. They must be sure that the firm's management neither absconds with nor wastes the funds on any projects with low or negative net present values. Such monitoring actions are extremely costly for any given household because they require considerable time and expense to collect sufficiently high-quality information relative to the size of the average household savers' investment. Given this, it is likely that each household would prefer to leave the monitoring to others; in the end, little or no monitoring would be done. The resulting lack of monitoring would reduce the attractiveness and increase the risk of investing in corporate debt and equity.

In the real world, bondholders partially alleviate these problems by requiring restrictive clauses or **covenants** in bond contracts. Such covenants restrict the risky nature of projects that a firm's management can undertake. Bond holders also hire a bond trustee to oversee compliance with these covenants. However, the enforcement and monitoring of covenants are still quite costly, especially if the debt is long term and renewed infrequently.

The relatively long-term nature of corporate equity and debt also creates a second disincentive for household investors to hold the direct financial claims issued by corporations. Specifically, given the choice between holding cash and long-term securities, the households may well choose to hold cash for **liquidity** reasons, especially if they plan to use savings to finance consumption expenditures in the near future.

Finally, even though real-world financial markets provide some liquidity services by allowing households to trade corporate debt and equity securities among themselves, investors also face a **price risk** on sale of securities and the secondary market trading of securities involves various transaction costs. That is, the price at which household investors can sell securities on secondary markets such as the New York Stock Exchange may well differ from the price they initially paid for the securities.

Because of (1) monitoring costs, (2) liquidity costs, and (3) price risk, the average household saver may view investment in corporate securities as an unattractive proposition and prefer either not to save or to save in the form of cash. This aversion of households toward directly holding securities issued by corporations is clearly evident from the U.S. flow of funds tables. The Federal Reserve produces flow of funds tables each quarter to show aggregate changes in the asset and liability positions for various important sectors in the economy. For example, between 1986 and 1989 direct net acquisition of equity by households was negative (an average of negative $110.25 billion a year) while their net acquisition of corporate bonds declined from

Covenant
Legal clauses in a bond contract that require the issuer of bonds to take or avoid certain actions.

Liquidity
The ease of converting an asset into cash.

Price Risk
The risk that the sale price of an asset will be lower than the purchase price of the asset.

FIGURE 3–2

Flow of funds in a world with FIs

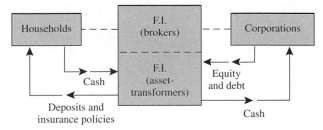

$39.3 billion in 1986 to $11.3 billion in 1989. Although these figures include the October 1987 crash when the risks of holding securities increased dramatically, they are symptomatic of a trend in which households are moving their asset portfolios away from corporate securities in general. If the direct purchase of securities were the only way households could invest in firms, such trends could have serious implications for the growth of the corporate sector of the economy as well as for its competitive performance.

However, the economy has developed an alternative and indirect way to channel household savings to the corporate sector. This is to channel savings via FIs. Due to the costs of monitoring, liquidity, and price risk, as well as for some other reasons explained later, savers often prefer to hold the financial claims issued by FIs rather than those issued by corporations.

Consider Figure 3–2 which is a closer representation than Figure 3–1 of the world in which we live and the way funds flow in our economy. Notice how financial intermediaries or institutions are standing or intermediating between, the household and corporate sectors.

These intermediaries fulfill two functions; any given FI might specialize in one or the other or might do both simultaneously. The first function is the brokerage function; when acting as a pure broker, an FI acts as an agent for the saver in providing information and transaction services. For example, full-service securities firms (e.g., Merrill Lynch) carry out investment research and make investment recommendations for their retail (or household) clients as well as conducting the purchase or sale of securities for commission fees. Discount brokers (e.g., Charles Schwab) carry out the purchase or sale of securities at better prices and with greater efficiency than household savers could achieve by trading on their own. Independent insurance brokers identify the best types of insurance policies that household savers can buy to fit their savings-retirement plans. In fulfilling a brokerage function, the FI plays an extremely important role by reducing transaction and information costs or imperfections between households and corporations. Thus, the FI encourages a higher rate of savings than would otherwise exist.

Asset Transformer
An FI issues financial claims that are more attractive to household savers than the claims directly issued by corporations.

Primary Securities
Securities issued by corporations and backed by the real assets of those corporations.

The second function is the asset transformation function. In acting as an **asset transformer**, the FI issues financial claims far more attractive to household savers than the claims directly issued by corporations. That is, for many households the financial claims issued by FIs dominate those issued directly by corporations due to lower monitoring costs, lower liquidity costs, and lower price risk. In acting as asset transformers, FIs purchase the financial claims issued by corporations—equities, bonds, and other debt claims called **primary securities**—and finance these purchases by selling financial claims to household investors and other sectors in the form of deposits, insurance policies, and so on. The financial claims of FIs may be considered

TABLE 3–1   Simplified Commercial Firm and FI Balance Sheets

Commercial Firm		Financial Intermediary	
Assets	*Liabilities*	*Assets*	*Liabilities*
Real assets (Plant, machinery)	Primary securities (Debt, equity)	Primary securities (Debt, equity)	Secondary securities (Deposits and insurance policies)

Secondary Securities
Securities issued by FIs and backed by primary securities.

secondary securities because these assets are backed by the primary securities issued by commercial corporations that in turn invest in real assets.

Simplified balance sheets of a commercial firm and an FI are shown in Table 3–1. Note that in the real-world FIs hold a small proportion of their assets in the form of real assets such as bank branch buildings. These simplified balance sheets reflect a reasonably accurate characterization of the operational differences between commercial firms and FIs.

How can FIs purchase the direct or primary securities issued by corporations and profitably transform them into secondary securities more attractive to household savers? This question strikes at the very heart of what makes FIs special and important to the economy. The answer lies in the ability of FIs to better resolve the three costs facing the saver who chooses to invest directly in corporate securities.

Information Costs

One problem faced by an average saver directly investing in a commercial firm's financial claims is the high cost of information collection. Household savers must monitor the actions of firms in a timely and complete fashion after purchasing securities. Failure to monitor exposes investors to **agency costs**. That is, the risk that the firm's owners or managers would take actions with the saver's money contrary to the promises contained in the covenants of its securities contracts. One solution to this problem is for a large number of small savers to place their funds with a single FI. This FI groups these funds together and invests in the direct or primary financial claims issued by firms. This agglomeration of funds resolves a number of problems. First, the large FI now has a much greater incentive to collect information and monitor actions of the firm because it has far more at stake than any small individual household. This alleviates the free-rider problem that exists when small household savers leave it to each other to collect information and monitor the actions of the firms. In a sense, small savers have appointed the FI as a **delegated monitor** to act on their behalf.[3] Not only does the FI have a greater incentive to collect information but the average cost of collecting information is also lower. For example, the cost to a small investor of buying a $100 broker's report may seem inordinately high, for a $10,000 investment. For an FI with $10 million under management, however, the cost seems trivial. Such economies of scale of information production and collection tend to enhance the advantages to savers of using FIs rather than directly investing themselves.

Agency Costs
Costs relating to the risk that the owners and managers of firms that receive savers' funds will take actions with those funds contrary to the best interests of the savers.

Delegated Monitor
An economic agent appointed to act on behalf of smaller agents in collecting information and/or investing funds on their behalf.

---

[3]For a theoretical modeling of the delegated monitor function, see D. W. Diamond "Financial Intermediaries and Delegated Monitoring," *Review of Economic Studies* 51, 1984, pp. 393–414; and J. H. Boyd and E. C. Prescott, "Financial Intermediary—Coalitions," *Journal of Economic Theory* 38, 1986, pp. 211–32.

Second, associated with the greater incentive to monitor and the costs involved in failing to monitor appropriately, FIs may develop new secondary securities that enable them to monitor more effectively. Thus, a richer menu of contracts may improve the monitoring abilities of FIs. Perhaps, the classic example of this is the bank loan. Bank loans are generally shorter-term debt contracts than bond contracts. This short-term nature allows the FI to exercise more monitoring power and control over the borrower. In particular, the information the FI generates regarding the firm is frequently updated as its loan renewal decisions are made. When bank loan contracts are sufficiently short term, the banker becomes almost like an insider to the firm regarding informational familiarity with its operations and financial conditions. Indeed, this more frequent monitoring often replaces the need for the relatively inflexible and hard-to-enforce covenants found in bond contracts.[4] Moreover, by acting as a partial corporate insider and sending favorable information signals regarding the firm and its performance through bank loan renewals, the holders of outside debt and equity (such as traditional corporate securities) also benefit by acting on this information, as can firms who are then able to issue their securities at a lower cost. Thus, by acting as a delegated monitor and producing better and more timely information, FIs reduce the degree of information imperfection and asymmetry between the ultimate sources and users of funds in the economy.

Liquidity and Price Risk

In addition to improving the flow and quality of information, FIs provide financial or secondary claims to household savers. Often, these have superior liquidity attributes compared to primary securities such as corporate equity and bonds. For example, banks and thrifts issue transaction account deposit contracts with a fixed principal value (and often a guaranteed interest rate) that can be withdrawn immediately on demand by household savers. Money market mutual funds issue shares to household savers that allow them to enjoy almost fixed principal (deposit-like) contracts while often earning higher interest rates than bank deposits. Even life insurance companies allow policyholders to borrow against their policies held with the company at very short notice. The real puzzle is still how FIs, such as depository institutions, can offer highly liquid and low price risk contracts to savers on the liability side of their balance sheets, while investing in relatively illiquid and higher price-risk securities issued by corporations on the asset side. Furthermore, how can FIs be confident enough to guarantee they can provide liquidity services to investors and savers when they themselves invest in risky asset portfolios? And, why should savers and investors believe FI's promises regarding the liquidity of their investments?

Diversify
The ability of an economic agent to reduce risk by holding a number of securities in a portfolio.

The answers to these questions lie in the ability of FIs to **diversify** away some but not all of their portfolio risks. The concept of diversification is familiar to all students of finance: basically, as long as the returns on different investments are not perfectly *positively* correlated, by exploiting the benefits of size FIs diversify away significant amounts of portfolio risk—especially the risk specific to the individual firm issuing any given security. Indeed, experiments in the United States and United Kingdom have shown that diversifying across just 15 securities can bring significant

---

[4]For a further description and discussion of the special or unique nature of bank loans, see E. Fama, "What's Different about Banks?" *Journal of Monetary Economics* 15, 1985, pp. 29–39; and C. James, "Some Evidence on the Uniqueness of Bank Loans," *Journal of Financial Economics* 19, 1987, pp. 217–35.

diversification benefits to FIs and portfolio managers.[5] Further, as the number of securities in an FI's asset portfolio increases, portfolio risk falls, albeit at a diminishing rate. What is really going on here is that FIs exploit the law of large numbers in their investments, whereas due to their small size, many household savers are constrained to holding relatively undiversified portfolios. This risk diversification allows an FI to predict more accurately its expected return on its asset portfolio. A domestically and globally diversified FI may be able to generate an almost risk-free return on its assets. As a result, it can credibly fulfill its promise to households to supply highly liquid claims with little price or capital value risk. A good example of this is the ability of a bank to offer highly liquid demand deposits—with a fixed principal value—as liabilities while at the same time investing in risky loans as assets. As long as an FI is sufficiently large to gain from diversification and monitoring, its financial claims are likely to be viewed as liquid and attractive to small savers when compared to direct investments in the capital market. The smaller and the less diversified an FI becomes, the less able it is to credibly promise household savers that its financial claims are highly liquid and of low capital risk. Specifically, the less diversified the FI, the higher the probability that it will default on its liability obligations and the more risky and illiquid are its claims.[6] In reality, the majority of financial institution failures are small FIs that are relatively undiversified product-wise and geographically. For example, there were widespread failures of smaller U.S. banks, thrifts, and insurance companies in the Southwest during the slump in oil and gas prices in the 1980s.[7]

Other Special Services

The preceding discussion has concentrated on three general or special services provided by FIs reducing household savers' monitoring costs, increasing their liquidity, and reducing their price-risk exposure. Next, we discuss two other special services provided by FIs: reduced transaction costs and maturity intermediation or asset transformation.

Reduced Transaction Cost.   Just as FIs provide potential economies of scale in information collection, they also provide potential economies of scale in transaction costs. For example, since May 1, 1975, fixed commissions for equity trades on the NYSE have been abolished. As a result, small retail buyers face higher commission charges or transaction costs than large wholesale buyers. By grouping their assets in FIs that purchase assets in bulk—such as in mutual funds and pension funds—household savers can reduce the transaction costs of their asset purchases. In addition, bid-ask (buy-sell) spreads are normally lower for assets bought and sold in large quantities.

Maturity Intermediation.   An additional dimension of FIs' ability to reduce risk by diversification is that they can better bear the risk of mismatching the maturities of

---

[5]For a review of such studies see Chapter 2, E. J. Elton and M. J. Gruber, *Modern Portfolio Theory and Investment Analysis,* 3rd ed. (New York: John Wiley & Sons, 1987).

[6]For a theoretical modeling of the link between credible deposit contracts and diversification, see J. H. Boyd and E. C. Prescott, "Financial Intermediary—Coalitions," *Journal of Economic Theory* 38, 1986, pp. 211–32.

[7]Nevertheless, in the 1980s 9 out of the 10 biggest banking organizations in Texas also had to be closed, merged, or reorganized, in large part because of their undiversified exposures to the heavily oil and gas-dependent Texas economy.

Part I   Introduction

their assets and liabilities than small household savers. Thus, FIs offer maturity intermediation services to the rest of the economy. Specifically by maturity mismatching, FIs can produce new types of contracts, such as long term mortgage loans to households, while still raising funds with short-term liability contracts. Further, while such mismatches can subject an FI to interest rate risk (see Chapters 5 to 7), a large FI is better able to manage this risk through its superior access to markets and instruments for hedging such as securitization (Chapter 21); futures (Chapter 18); swaps (Chapter 20); and caps, floors, and collars (Chapter 19).

Concept Questions

1. What are the three major risks to household savers from direct security purchases?
2. What are two major differences between brokers (such as security brokers) and depository institutions (such as commercial banks)?
3. What are primary securities and secondary securities?
4. What is the link between asset diversification and the liquidity of deposit contracts?

Other Aspects of Specialness

The theory of the flow of funds points to three principal reasons for believing FIs are special along with two other associated reasons. In reality, academics, policymakers, and regulators identify other areas of specialness relating to certain specific functions of FIs or groups of FIs. We discuss these next.

The Transmission of Monetary Policy

The highly liquid nature of bank and thrift deposits has resulted in their acceptance by the public as the most widely used medium of exchange in the economy. As you can see from the notes to Table 3–2, at the core of the three most commonly used definitions of the money supply—M1, M2, and M3—lie bank and/or thrift deposit contracts. Because the liabilities of depository institutions are a significant component of the money supply that impacts the rate of inflation, depository institutions and commercial banks play a key role in the *transmission of monetary policy* from the central bank to the rest of the economy. That is, banks are the conduit through which monetary policy actions impact the rest of the financial sector and the economy in general.

Credit Allocation

A further reason why FIs are often viewed as special is that they are the major, and sometimes only, source of finance for a particular sector of the economy preidentified as being in special need of finance. Policymakers in the United States and a number of other countries such as the United Kingdom have identified *residential real estate* as needing special subsidies. This has enhanced the specialness of FIs that most commonly service the needs of that sector. In the United States, S&Ls and savings banks have traditionally served the credit needs of the residential real estate sector. In a

TABLE 3–2   Money Stock, Liquid Assets, and Debt Measures
(Billions of Dollars, Averages of Daily Figures)

	Seasonally Adjusted			
Item	*1988 Dec.*	*1989 Dec.*	*1990 Dec.*	*1991 Dec.*
Measures				
1 M1	786.9	794.1	826.1	898.1
2 M2	3,071.1	3,227.3	3,339.0	3,439.8
3 M3	3,923.1	4,059.8	4,114.6	4,171.0
4 L	4,677.1	4,890.6	4,965.2	4,988.1
5 Debt	9,326.3	10,076.7	10,751.3	11,200.4

NOTES: Composition of the money stock measures and debt is as follows:

M1: (1) currency outside the Treasury, Federal Reserve Banks, and the vaults of depository institutions; (2) travelers checks of nonbank issuers; (3) demand deposits at all commercial banks other than those due to depository institutions, the U.S. government, and foreign banks and official institutions, less cash items in the process of collection and Federal Reserve float; and (4), other checkable deposits (OCDs), consisting of negotiable order of withdrawal (NOW) and automatic transfer service (ATS) accounts at depository institutions, credit union share draft accounts, and demand deposits at thrift institutions. Seasonally adjusted M1 is computed by summing currency, travelers checks, demand deposits, and OCDs, each seasonally adjusted separately.

M2: M1 plus (1) overnight (and continuing-contract) repurchase agreements (RPs) issued by all depository institutions and overnight Eurodollars issued to U.S. residents by foreign branches of U.S. banks worldwide, (2) savings (including MMDAs) and small time deposits (time deposits—including retail RPs—in amounts of less than $100,000, and (3) balances in both taxable and tax-exempt general purpose and broker-dealer money market funds. Excludes individual retirement accounts (IRAs) and Keogh balances at depository institutions and money market funds. Also excludes all balances held by U.S. commercial banks, money market funds (general purpose and broker-dealer), foreign governments and commercial banks, and the U.S. government. Seasonally adjusted M2 is computed by adjusting its non-M1 component as a whole and then adding this result to seasonally adjusted M1.

M3: M2 plus (1) large time deposits and term RP liabilities (in amounts of $100,000 or more) issued by all depository institutions, (2) term Eurodollars held by U.S. residents at foreign branches of U.S. banks worldwide and at all banking offices in the United Kingdom and Canada, and (3) balances in both taxable and tax-exempt, institution-only money market funds. Excludes amounts held by depository institutions, the U.S. government, money market funds, and foreign banks and official institutions. Also excluded is the estimated amount of overnight RPs and Eurodollars held by institution-only money market funds. Seasonally adjusted M3 is computed by adjusting its non-M2 component as a whole and then adding this result to seasonally adjusted M2.

L: M3 plus the nonbank public holdings of U.S. savings bonds, short-term Treasury securities, commercial paper, and bankers acceptances, net of money market fund holdings of these assets. Seasonally adjusted L is computed by summing U.S. savings bonds, short-term Treasury securities, commercial paper, and bankers acceptances, each seasonally adjusted separately, and then adding this result to M3.

Debt: Debt of domestic nonfinancial sectors consists of outstanding credit market debt of the U.S. government, state and local governments, and private nonfinancial sectors. Private debt consists of corporate bonds, mortgages, consumer credit (including bank loans), other bank loans, commercial paper, bankers acceptances, and other debt instruments. Data are derived from the Federal Reserve Board's flow of funds accounts. Debt Data are based on monthly averages. This sum is seasonally adjusted as a whole.

SOURCE: *Federal Reserve Bulletin*, January 1993, table A14.

similar fashion, farming is an especially important area of the economy in terms of the overall social welfare of the population. The U.S. government has even directly encouraged financial institutions to specialize in financing this area of activity through the creation of Federal Farm Credit Banks.

Intergenerational Wealth Transfers or Time Intermediation

The ability of savers to transfer wealth between youth and old age and across generations is also of great importance to the social well-being of a country. Because of this, life insurance and pension funds are often especially encouraged, via special taxation relief and other subsidy mechanisms to service and accommodate these needs.

Payment Services

Depository institutions such as banks and thrifts are special in that the efficiency with which they provide payment services directly benefits the economy. Two important payment services are check-clearing and wire-transfer services. For example, on any given day approximately 1.7 trillion of payments are effected through Fedwire and CHIPS, the two large wholesale payment wire networks in the United States. Any breakdowns in these systems would likely produce gridlock to the payment system with resulting harmful effects to the economy.

Denomination Intermediation

Both money market and debt/equity mutual funds are special because they provide services relating to denomination intermediation. Because they are sold in very large denominations, many assets are either out of reach of individual savers or would result in savers holding highly undiversified asset portfolios. For example, the minimum size of a negotiable CD is $100,000 and commercial paper (short-term corporate debt) is often sold in minimum packages of $250,000 or more. Individually, a saver may be unable to purchase such instruments. However, by buying shares in a money market mutual fund along with other small investors, household savers overcome the constraints to buying assets imposed by large minimum denomination sizes. Such indirect access to these markets may allow small savers to generate higher returns on their portfolios as well.

Concept Questions

1. Why does the need for denomination intermediation arise?
2. What are the two major sectors that society has identified as deserving special attention in credit allocation?
3. Why is monetary policy transmitted through the banking system?

Specialness and Regulation

The general areas of FI specialness include:

- Information services.
- Liquidity services.
- Price-risk reduction services.
- Transaction cost services.
- Maturity intermediation services.

Areas of institution-specific specialness are as follows:

- Money supply transmission (banks).
- Credit allocation (thrifts, farm banks).

- Intergenerational transfers (pensions funds, life insurance companies).
- Payment services (banks, thrifts).
- Denomination intermediation (mutual funds, pension funds).

Failure to provide these services, or a breakdown in their efficient provision, can be costly to both the ultimate sources (households) and users of savings (firms). The *negative externalities* affecting firms and households when something goes wrong in the FI sector of the economy makes a case for regulation. Thus, bank failures may destroy household savings and at the same time restrict a firm's access to credit. Insurance company failures may leave households totally exposed in old age to catastrophic illnesses and sudden drops in income on retirement. Further, individual FI failures may create doubts in savers' minds regarding the stability and solvency of FIs in general and cause panics and even runs on sound institutions. In addition, racial, sexual, age, or other discrimination—such as mortgage **redlining**—may unfairly exclude some potential financial service consumers from the marketplace. This type of market failure needs to be corrected by regulation. Although regulation may be socially beneficial, it also imposes private costs, or a regulatory burden, on individual FI owners and managers. Consequently, regulation is an attempt to enhance the social welfare benefits and mitigate the social costs of the provision of FI services. The private costs of regulation relative to its private benefits, for the producers of financial services, is called the **net regulatory burden**.[8]

Six types of regulation seek to enhance the net social welfare benefits of financial intermediaries' services. These are (1) safety and soundness regulation, (2) monetary policy regulation, (3) credit allocation regulation, (4) consumer protection regulation, (5) investor protection regulation, and (6) entry and chartering regulation. Regulation can be imposed at the federal or the state level and occasionally at the international level as in the case of bank capital requirements (see Chapter 14).

Redlining
The procedure by which a banker refuses to make loans to residents living inside given geographic boundaries.

Net Regulatory Burden
The difference between the private costs of regulations and the private benefits for the producers of financial services.

Safety and Soundness Regulation

To protect depositors and borrowers against the risk of FI failure due, for example, to a lack of diversification in asset portfolios, regulators have developed layers of protective mechanisms. In the first layer of protection are requirements encouraging FIs to diversify their assets. Thus, banks are required not to make loans exceeding more than 15 percent of their own equity capital funds to any one company or borrower. A bank that has 6 percent of its assets funded by its own capital (and therefore 94 percent by deposits) can lend no more than 0.9 percent of its assets to any one party.

The second layer of protection concerns the minimum level of capital or equity funds that the owners of an FI need to contribute to the funding of its operations. For example, bank and thrift regulators are concerned with the minimum ratio of capital to assets while property-casualty insurers are concerned with the minimum ratio of capital to premiums. The higher the proportion of capital contributed by owners, the greater the protection against insolvency risk to outside liability claimholders, such as depositors and insurance policyholders. This is because losses on the asset portfolio due, for example, to the lack of diversification are legally borne by the equity holder first, and only after equity is totally wiped out by outside liability holders.[9]

---

[8]Other regulated firms such as gas and electric utilities also face a complex set of regulations imposing a net regulatory burden on their operations.

[9]Thus, equity holders are junior claimants and debt holders senior claimants to an FI's assets.

Consequently, by varying the required degree of equity capital, FI regulators can directly affect the degree of risk exposure faced by nonequity claimholders in FIs. (See Chapter 14 for more discussion on the role of capital in FIs.)

The third layer of protection is the provision of guarantee funds such as the Bank Insurance Fund (BIF) for banks, the Savings Association Insurance Fund (SAIF) for savings and loans, the Security Investors Protection Corporation (SIPC) for securities firms, and the state guarantee funds established (with regulator encouragement) to meet insolvency losses to small claimholders in the life and property-casualty industries. By protecting FI claimholders, when an FI collapses and owners' equity or net worth is wiped out, these funds create a demand for regulation of the insured institutions to protect the funds' resources (see Chapter 15 for more discussion). For example, the FDIC monitors and regulates participants in both BIF and SAIF.

The fourth layer of regulation is monitoring and surveillance itself. Whether banks, securities firms, or insurance companies, regulators subject all FIs to varying degrees of monitoring and surveillance. This involves on-site examination as well as the FI's production of accounting statements and reports on a timely basis for off-site evaluation. Just as savers appoint FIs as delegated monitors to evaluate the behavior and actions of ultimate borrowers, society appoints regulators to monitor the behavior and performance of FIs.

Finally, note that regulation is not without costs for those regulated. For example, society's regulators may require FIs to have more equity capital than private owners believe is in their own best interests. Similarly, producing the information requested by regulators is costly for FIs because it involves the time of managers, lawyers, and accountants. Again, the socially optimal amount of information may differ from an FI's privately optimal amount.

As noted earlier, the differences between the private benefits to an FI from being regulated—such as insurance fund guarantees—and the private costs it faces from adhering to regulation—such as examinations—is called the *net regulatory burden.* The higher the net regulatory burden on FIs, the more inefficiently they produce any given set of financial services from a private (FI) owner's perspective.

Monetary Policy Regulation

Outside Money
That part of the money supply directly produced by the government or central bank, such as notes and coin.

Inside Money
That part of the money supply produced by the private banking system.

Another motivation for regulation concerns the special role banks play in the transmission of monetary policy from the Federal Reserve (the central bank) to the rest of the economy. The problem is that the central bank directly controls only the quantity of notes and coin in the economy—called **outside money**—whereas the bulk of the money supply is bank deposits—called **inside money**. In theory, a central bank can vary the quantity of cash or outside money and directly affect a bank's reserve position as well as the amount of loans and deposits it can create without formally regulating the bank's portfolio. In practice, regulators have chosen to impose formal controls.[10] In most countries, regulators commonly impose a minimum level of

---

[10]In classic central banking theory, the quantity of bank deposits (D) is determined as the product of the banking system's required (or desired) ratio of cash reserves to deposits (r) times the quantity of bank reserves (R) outstanding, where R is comprised of notes and coin plus bank deposits held on reserve at the central bank, $D = rR$. Thus by varying R, given a relatively stable reserve ratio (r), the central bank can directly affect D, the quantity of deposits or inside money which, as just noted, is a large component of the money supply. Even if not required to do so by regulation, banks would still tend to hold some cash reserves as a liquidity precaution against the sudden withdrawal of deposits or sudden arrival of new loan demand.

required cash reserves to be held against deposits. Since January 1991, in the United States this reserve has been 3 percent against the first $46.8 million of a bank's transaction accounts (demand deposits, NOW accounts, etc.) and 10 percent against transaction accounts exceeding $46.8 million.[11] No reserves are currently required to be held against time and savings deposits. Some argue that imposing such reserve requirements makes the control of the money supply and its transmission more predictable. Such reserves also add to an FI's *net regulatory burden* if they are more than the institution believes are necessary for its own liquidity purposes. In general, whether banks or insurance companies, all FIs would choose to hold some cash reserves—even noninterest bearing—to directly meet the liquidity and transaction needs of their customers. For well-managed FIs, however, this optimal level is normally low, especially if the central bank (or other regulatory body) does not pay interest on required reserves. As a result, FIs often view required reserves as similar to a tax and as a positive cost of undertaking intermediation.

Credit Allocation Regulation

Credit allocation regulation supports the FI's lending to socially important sectors such as housing and farming. These regulations may require an FI to hold a minimum amount of assets in one particular sector of the economy or, alternatively, to set maximum interest rates, prices, or fees to subsidize certain sectors. Examples of asset restrictions include the qualified thrift lender test (QTL) requiring thrifts to hold 65 percent of their assets in residential mortgage-related assets to retain a thrift charter, and insurance regulations, such as those in New York State that set maximums on the amount of foreign or international assets in which insurance companies can invest. Examples of interest rate restrictions are the usury laws set in many states on the maximum rates that can be charged on mortgages and/or consumer loans, and regulations (now abolished) such as the Federal Reserve's Regulation Q maximums on time and savings deposit interest rates.

Such price and quantity restrictions may have justification on social welfare grounds—especially if society has a preference for strong (and subsidized) housing and farming sectors. However, they can also be harmful to FIs that have to bear the private costs of meeting many of these regulations. To the extent that the net private costs of such restrictions are positive, they add to the costs and reduce the efficiency with which FIs undertake intermediation.

Consumer Protection Regulation

Congress passed the Community Reinvestment Act (CRA) and the Home Mortgage Disclosure Act (HMDA) to prevent discrimination in lending. For example, since 1975 the HMDA has assisted the public in determining whether banks and other mortgage-lending institutions were meeting the needs of their local communities. HMDA is especially concerned about discrimination on the basis of age, race, sex, or income. Since 1990, depository institutions have reported on a standardized form to their chief federal regulator the reasons why credit was granted or denied. To get some idea of the information production cost of regulatory compliance in this area, the Federal Financial Institutions Examination Council processed information on 6.4

---

[11]The dollar amount subject to the 3 percent reserve requirement is adjusted each year for deposit growth. In 1993, it had risen to $46.8 million.

million mortgage transactions from almost 9,300 institutions during March to August in 1991.[12] (The council is a federal supervisory body comprising the members of the Federal Reserve, the Federal Deposit Insurance Corporation, and the Office of the Comptroller of the Currency.) Many analysts believe that community and consumer protection laws are imposing a considerable net regulatory burden on FIs without offsetting social benefits that enhance equal access to mortgage and lending markets.

Investor Protection

A considerable number of laws protect investors who use investment banks directly to purchase securities and/or to indirectly access securities markets through investing in mutual or pension funds. Various laws protect investors against abuses such as insider trading, lack of disclosure, outright malfeasance, and breach of fiduciary responsibilities. Important legislation affecting investment banks and mutual funds are the Securities Acts of 1933 and 1934 and the Investment Company Act of 1940. As with consumer protection legislation, compliance with these acts can impose a net regulatory burden on FIs.

Entry Regulation

The entry and activities of FIs are also regulated. Increasing or decreasing the cost of entry into a financial sector affects the profitability of firms already competing in that industry. Thus, the industries heavily protected against new entrants by high direct costs (e.g., through capital contribution) and high indirect costs (e.g., by restricting individuals who can establish FIs) of entry produce bigger profits for existing firms than those in which entry is relatively easy. In addition, regulations define the scope of permitted activities under a given charter. The broader the set of financial service activities permitted under a given charter, the more valuable that charter is likely to be. Thus, barriers to entry and regulations pertaining to the scope of permitted activities affect the *charter value* of an FI and the size of its net regulatory burden.

Concept Questions

1. What six major types of regulation do FIs face?
2. Define the concept of net regulatory burden.
3. Why should more regulation be imposed on FIs than on other types of private corporation?

The Changing Dynamics of Specialness

At any moment in time, each FI supplies a set of financial services (brokerage-related, asset transformation-related, or both) and is subject to a given net regulatory burden. As the demands for the special features of financial services change due to changing preferences and technology, one or more areas of the financial services

---

[12]As reported in Federal Reserve Bank of Atlanta, *Financial Update* 4, no. 4 (1991), p. 1.

industry become less profitable. Similarly, changing regulations can increase or decrease the net regulatory burden faced in supplying financial services in any given area. These demand, cost, and regulatory pressures are reflected in changing market shares in different financial service areas as some contract and others expand. Clearly, an FI seeking to survive and prosper must be flexible enough to move to growing financial service areas and away from those that are contracting. If regulatory activity restrictions inhibit or reduce the flexibility with which FIs can alter their product mix, this would reduce their competitive ability and the efficiency with which financial services are delivered. That is, activity barriers within the financial services industry may reduce the ability to diversify and potentially add to the net regulatory burden faced by FIs.

Trends in the United States

In Table 3–3, we show the changing shares of total assets in the U.S. financial services industry from 1946 to 1990. A number of important trends are clearly evident: most apparent is the decline in the total share of depository institutions. Specifically, the share of commercial banks declined from 57.3 to 31.2 percent between 1946 and 1990 while the share of thrifts (mutual savings banks, savings and loans, credit unions) grew marginally from 12.6 to 14.7 percent over the period. Similar to banks, life insurance companies witnessed a secular decline in their share from 20.3 to 13.1 percent with other (property-casualty) insurance companies growing from 3 to 5 percent.

The most dramatic trends are the increased shares of pension funds and investment companies. Pension funds (private plus state and local) increased their asset share from 2.7 to 18.3 percent while investment companies (real estate investment trusts, mutual funds, and money market mutual funds) increased from 0.6 to 10.4 percent.

Pension funds and investment companies differ from banks and insurance companies in that they give savers cheaper access to the direct securities markets. They

TABLE 3–3   Financial Assets of Selected Financial Institutions (Percent of Total)

Institutions	1946	1950	1960	1970	1980	1990
Commercial banks	57.3%	51.2%	38.3%	38.6%	36.7%	31.2%
Savings and loan associations	4.4	5.8	11.9	12.9	15.4	10.2
Mutual savings banks	8.0	7.6	6.9	5.9	4.2	2.5
Credit unions	0.2	0.3	1.0	1.3	1.7	2.0
Life insurance companies	20.3	21.3	19.3	15.0	11.5	13.1
Private pension funds	1.5	2.4	6.4	8.3	11.6	10.9
State and local pension funds	1.2	1.7	3.3	4.5	4.9	7.4
Other insurance companies	3.0	4.0	4.4	3.7	4.3	5.0
Finance companies	2.1	3.2	4.6	4.8	5.0	5.3
Real estate investment trusts	0.0	0.0	0.0	0.3	0.1	0.1
Mutual funds	0.6	1.1	2.8	3.5	1.5	5.7
Money market mutual funds	0.0	0.0	0.0	0.0	1.9	4.6
Securities brokers and dealers	1.5	1.4	1.1	1.2	1.1	2.0
Total*	100.0	100.0	100.0	100.0	100.0	100.0
Total (in billions)	$234.	$294.	$600.	$1,342.	$4,040.	$10,751.

*NOTE: Columns may not add to exactly 100% because of rounding.

SOURCE: Board of Governors of the Federal Reserve System, *Flow of Funds Accounts*, various editions.

do so by exploiting the comparative advantages of size and diversification, with the transformation of financial claims, such as maturity transformation, a lesser concern. Thus, open-ended mutual funds buy stocks and bonds directly in financial markets and issue to savers shares whose value is linked in a direct pro rata fashion to the value of the mutual funds asset portfolio. Similarly, money market mutual funds invest in short-term financial assets such as commercial paper, CDs, and Treasury bills and issue shares linked directly to the value of their underlying portfolio. To the extent that these funds efficiently diversify, they also offer price risk protection and liquidity services as well.

The maturity and return characteristics of the financial claims issued by pension and mutual funds closely reflect the maturities of the direct equity and debt securities portfolios in which they invest. In contrast, banks, thrifts, and insurance companies have lower correlations between their asset portfolio maturities and the promised maturity of their liabilities. Thus, banks may partially fund a 10-year commercial loan with demand deposits; a thrift may fund 30-year conventional mortgages with three-month time deposits; and a life insurance company, the purchase of 30-year junk bonds with a 7-year fixed-interest guaranteed investment contract (GIC).

To the extent that the financial services market is efficient and these trends reflect the forces of demand and supply, they indicate a current trend: savers increasingly prefer investments that closely mimic diversified investments in the *direct* securities markets over the transformed financial claims offered by traditional FIs. This trend may also indicate that the net regulatory burden on traditional FIs—such as banks and insurance companies—is higher than that on pension funds and investment companies. As a result, traditional FIs are unable to produce their services as cost efficiently as previously.

International Trends

Interestingly, the movement of household savers away from traditional FIs toward holding assets in pension funds or other similar savings vehicles is an international phenomenon. Figure 3–3 shows the changing composition of household financial assets between 1980 and 1987 in the United States, Japan, West Germany, and Britain.

As you can see, in all four countries the shares of savings and demand deposits decreased and the shares of pension and insurance funds increased. The relative decline of traditional FI products is most dramatic in Japan, as that country started to liberalize its bond and equity markets beginning in the early 1980s. The Big Bang liberalization of the capital markets in Britain took place in October 1986. The United Kingdom revoked many of the controls on the structure and ownership of securities firms and the markets in which they participated. This action also appears to have accelerated the decline in relative shares of traditional deposit products in that country. Note also in Figure 3–3 the actions of household savers in Japan and West Germany. Apart from seeking more direct access to the securities markets through investment companies and pension funds, these savers bypassed the FI sector altogether by increasing their direct holdings of corporate debt and equity.

Future Trends

The growth of mutual and pension funds coupled with investors' recent focus on direct investments in primary securities may be the beginning of a secular trend away from intermediation as the most efficient mechanism for savers to channel funds to borrowers. While this trend may reflect changed investors' preferences toward risk and return,

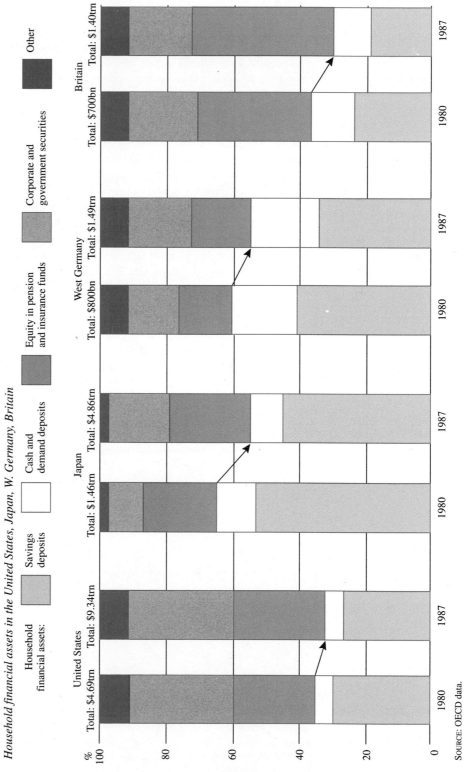

Source: OECD data.

67

it may also reflect a decline in the relative costs of direct securities investment versus investment via FIs. Certainly, the net regulatory burden faced by traditional FIs in the United States has been high. This has limited the ability of traditional FIs to diversify into areas such as mutual funds that are expanding at a fast rate; it leaves them to specialize in declining markets with decreasingly valuable charters. Since the early 1970s, there has been a generally downward long term trend in the ratio of the market value of equity to the book value of equity for large banks in the United States. This **market-to-book ratio** is depicted in Figure 3–4 for large banks over the period 1951–87.

Recent regulatory changes in the United States are partially alleviating the net regulatory burden by allowing FIs to move across traditional product boundaries and lines. As a result, bank profitability in the early 1990s has been better than in much of the 1980s. Nevertheless, the direct financial markets are evolving even faster; due to technological advances, the costs of direct access by savers is ever falling. A good example of this is the private placement market, where securities are directly sold by corporations to investors without underwriters and with a minimum of public disclosure about the issuing firm. Privately placed bonds and equity have traditionally been the most illiquid of securities, with only the very largest FIs or institutional investors being able or willing to buy and hold them in the absence of a secondary market. In April 1990, the Securities and Exchange Commission amended Regulation 144A. This allowed large investors to begin trading these privately placed securities among themselves even though, in general, privately placed securities do not satisfy the stringent disclosure and informational requirements imposed by the SEC on approved publicly registered issues. While the SEC defined the large investors able to trade privately placed securities as those with assets of $100 million or more—which excludes all but the very wealthiest household savers—it is reasonable to ask how long

Market-to-Book Ratio
The ratio of the market value of a firm's equity to the book value of that equity. This ratio reflects the market premium (if greater than one) or discount (if less than one) that investors are willing to pay to own the firm's equity. These premiums or discounts reflect the market or investors' views about the future profitability of a firm or industry.

FIGURE 3–4

Ratio of market value of equity to book value of equity, 1952–87

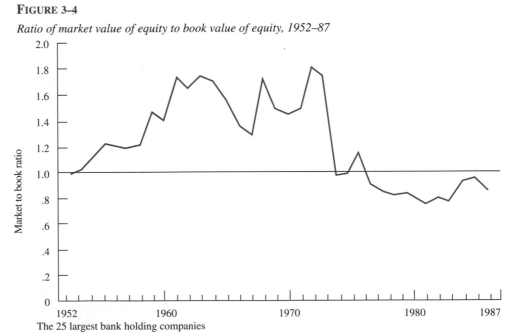

The 25 largest bank holding companies

SOURCE: J. H. Boyd and A. H. Rolnick, *A Case for Reforming Federal Deposit Insurance*, Federal Reserve Bank of Minneapolis, Annual Report, 1988.

this size restriction will stay in effect. As they get more sophisticated and the costs of information acquisition fall, savers will increasingly demand access to the private placement market. In such a world, savers would have a choice not only between the secondary securities from FIs and the primary securities publicly offered by corporations but also between publicly offered (registered) securities and privately offered (unregistered) securities.

To some extent, this choice set is already available to the smaller investor willing to consider investing in bonds issued by corporations and foreign governments offshore. Specifically, Eurodollar bonds are dollar-denominated bonds issued mainly in London and other European centers such as Luxembourg. Since they are issued outside U.S. territory, they do not have to be registered with the SEC. Only the highest-grade corporations issue these bonds because the problems of monitoring and covenant enforcement exclude more risky firms. Eurodollar bonds can even be resold in the United States 90 days after issue. In addition, they are available in small denominations of $1,000, pay coupon interest gross (i.e., do not deduct taxes at the source), and guarantee owners' anonymity because they are issued in bearer form. Secondary trading is quite deep and facilitated by two clearing systems: Euroclear is operated by Morgan Guaranty and CEDEL by a consortium of banks. As international barriers to investing fall and global financial service firms and markets become more available to small investors, the charter values, franchise, or specialness of traditional FIs is likely to become of less and less value.

Concept Questions

1. Is the share of bank and thrift assets growing as a proportion of total FI assets in the United States?
2. What are the fastest growing FIs in the United States?
3. Are trends in FI asset shares in Germany, the United Kingdom, and Japan similar or different to those in the United States?
4. Define privately placed securities and Eurobonds.

Summary

This chapter has described the various factors and forces impacting financial intermediaries and the specialness of the services they provide. These forces suggest that in the future, FIs that have historically relied on making profits by performing traditional special functions such as asset transformation and the provision of liquidity services will need to expand into selling financial services that interface with direct security market transactions such as asset management, clearance, settlement, and underwriting services. This is not to say that specialized or niche FIs cannot survive, but rather that only the most efficient FIs will prosper as the competitive value of a specialized FI charter declines.

Questions and Problems

1. What are the major functions of financial intermediaries?
2. How can financial intermediaries afford to issue financial claims that have superior liquidity to securities market claims?
3. From the perspective of society, apply cost benefit analysis to government regulation of the FI industry by enumerating the benefits FIs provide to society and weighing them against the costs to society. Relate the cost benefit analysis to emerging trends in financial intermediation.

4. From the perspective of the FI, apply cost benefit analysis to the FI industry. Relate this cost benefit analysis to emerging trends in financial intermediation.

5. If financial markets operated perfectly and costlessly, financial intermediaries would not exist. State whether you agree or disagree and why.

6. FIs are among the most heavily regulated firms in private industry. Explain why.

7. How would financial and economic transactions differ if there were no FIs?

8. Why are investors generally averse to holding securities directly?

9. What is meant by maturity intermediation?

10. Why do you think pension funds and investment companies have been growing rapidly in recent years at the expense of "traditional" banks and insurance companies?

II

MEASURING RISK

RISKS OF FINANCIAL INTERMEDIATION

Learning Objectives

In this chapter we introduce the fundamental risks faced by the modern FI. In later chapters, we analyze these risks more deeply, but for the moment we simply identify the key features and sources of these risks. By the end of this chapter you should have a basic understanding of the variety and complexity of the risks facing managers of modern FIs.

Introduction

The modern FI faces at least seven risks in conducting its brokerage and asset transformation services:

- Interest rate risk.
- Credit risk.
- Off-balance-sheet risk.
- Technology/operational risk.
- Foreign exchange rate risk.
- Country/sovereign risk.
- Liquidity risk.

We examine each of these risks in more detail in the sections that follow.

Interest Rate Risk

Chapter 3 discussed asset transformation as a key special function of FIs. Asset transformation involves buying primary securities and issuing secondary securities. The primary securities purchased by FIs often have different maturity and liquidity characteristics than the secondary securities they sell. In mismatching the maturities of assets and liabilities as part of their asset transformation function, FIs potentially expose themselves to interest rate risk.

Consider, for example, an FI that issues liabilities of one-year maturity to finance the purchase of assets with a two-year maturity. We show this in the following time lines:

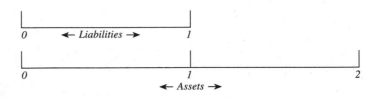

Suppose the cost of funds (liabilities) for an FI is 9 percent per annum and the interest return on an asset is 10 percent per annum. Over the first year, the FI can lock in a profit spread of 1 percent (10 percent – 9 percent) by borrowing short-term (for one year) and lending long-term (for two years). However, its profits for the second year are uncertain. If the level of interest rates does not change, the FI can *refinance* its liabilities at 9 percent and lock in a 1 percent profit for the second year as well. There is always a risk, however, that interest rates could change between years one and two. If interest rates were to rise and the FI could only borrow new one-year liabilities at 11 percent in the second year, its profit spread in the second year would actually be negative; that is, 10 percent – 11 percent = –1 percent. The positive spread earned in the first year by the FI from holding assets with a longer term than its liabilities would be offset by a negative spread in the second year. As a result, whenever an FI holds longer-term assets relative to liabilities, it potentially exposes itself to **refinancing risk.** This is the risk that the cost of rolling over or reborrowing funds could be more than the returns earned on asset investments. The classic example of this mismatch in recent years has been executed by the U.S. thrifts or savings banks.

An alternative balance sheet structure would have the FI borrowing for a longer term than the assets in which it invests. Using a similar example, suppose the FI borrowed funds at 9 percent per annum for two years and invested the funds in an asset that yields 10 percent for one year. This is shown as follows:

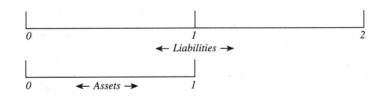

As before, the bank locks in a one-year profit spread of 1 percent, the difference between the 9 percent cost of funds and the 10 percent return on assets in the first year. At the end of the first year, the asset matures and the funds that have been borrowed for two-years have to be reinvested. Suppose interest rates fall between the first and second years so that in the second year the return on assets is 8 percent. The FI would face a loss or negative spread in the second year of 1 percent (that is, 8 percent asset return minus 9 percent cost of funds), this would offset the positive 1 percent spread in the first year. Thus, the FI was exposed to **reinvestment risk;** by holding shorter-term assets relative to liabilities, it faced uncertainty about the interest rate at which it could reinvest funds borrowed for a longer period. In recent years, good examples of this exposure have been banks operating in the Euromarkets that have borrowed fixed-rate deposits while investing in floating-rate loans; that is, loans whose interest rates were changed or adjusted frequently.

Refinancing Risk
The risk that the cost of rolling over or reborrowing funds will rise above the returns being earned on asset investments.

Reinvestment Risk
The risk that the returns on funds to be reinvested will fall below the cost of funds.

In addition to a potential refinancing or reinvestment risk that occurs when interest rates change, an FI faces *market value* risk as well. Remember that the market value of an asset or liability is conceptually equal to the discounted future cash flows from that asset. Therefore, rising interest rates increase the discount rate on those cash flows and reduce the market value of that asset or liability. Conversely, falling interest rates increase the market values of assets and liabilities. Moreover, mismatching maturities by holding longer-term assets than liabilities means that when interest rates rise, the market value of the FI's assets fall by a greater amount than its liabilities. This exposes it to the risk of economic loss and insolvency.

If holding assets and liabilities with mismatched maturities exposes them to reinvestment or refinancing and market value risks, FIs can be approximately hedged or protected against interest rate changes by matching the maturity of their assets and liabilities. This has resulted in the general philosophy that matching maturities is somehow the best policy for FIs averse to risk. Note that matching maturities works against an active asset-transformation function for FIs. That is, FIs cannot be asset transformers and direct balance sheet hedgers at the same time. While reducing exposure to interest rate risk, matching maturities may also reduce the profitability of being FIs because any returns from acting as specialized risk-bearing asset transformers are eliminated. Finally, matching maturities only hedges interest rate risk in a very approximate rather than complete fashion. The reasons for this are technical, relating to the difference between the average life (or duration) and maturity of an asset or liability and whether the FI partly funds its assets with equity capital as well as liabilities. In the preceding simple example, the FI financed its assets completely with borrowed funds. In the real world, FIs use a mix of debt liabilities and stockholders' equity to finance asset purchases. When assets and debt liabilities are not equal, hedging risk (i.e., insulating an FI's stockholders' equity values) may be achieved by not exactly matching the maturities (or average lives) of assets and liabilities. We discuss these issues more fully in Chapters 5 through 7 and the methods and instruments to hedge interest rate risk in Chapters 18 through 21.[1]

Concept Questions

1. Define refinancing risk.
2. Define maturity matching.
3. Why does a rise in the level of interest rates adversely affect both the market value of assets and liabilities?

---

[1]We assumed in our example that interest payments are paid only at the end of each year and could only be changed then. In reality, many loan and deposit rates adjust frequently or float as market rates change. For example, suppose a bank makes a one-year loan whose interest rate and interest rate payments are adjusted each quarter while fully funding the loan with a one-year CD that pays principal and interest at the end of the year. Even though the maturity of the loan and CD are equal to a year, the FI would not be fully hedged in a cash flow sense against interest rate risk since changes in interest rates over the year affect the cash flows (interest payments) on the loan but not on deposits.

In particular, if interest rates were to fall, the FI might lose on the loan in terms of net interest income (interest revenue minus interest expense). The reason for this loss is that the average life of the loan in a cash flow sense is less than that of the deposit because cash flows on the loan are received, on average, earlier than those paid on the deposit.

Credit Risk

Credit risk arises because promised cash flows on the primary securities held by FIs may or may not be paid in full. If the principal on all financial claims held by FIs was paid in full on maturity and interest payments were made on their promised dates, FIs would always receive back the original principal lent plus an interest return. That is, they would face no credit risk. Should a borrower default, both the principal loaned and the interest payments expected to be received are at risk. As a result, many financial claims issued by corporations and held by FIs promise a limited or fixed upside return. This takes the form of interest payments to the investor, with a high probability, and a large downside risk (loss of loan principal and promised interest) with a much smaller probability. Good examples of financial claims issued with these return risk trade-offs are fixed-income coupon bonds issued by corporations and bank loans. In both cases, an FI investing in these claims earns the coupon on the bond or the interest promised on the loan if no borrower default occurs. On default, the FI earns zero interest on the asset and may lose all or part of the principal lent depending on its ability to access some of the borrower's assets through bankruptcy and insolvency proceedings.

Look at the probability distribution of dollar returns from an FI investing in risky loans or bonds in Figure 4–1. As you see, the spike in the distribution indicates a high probability (but less than one) of repayment of principal and promised interest in full. Problems with cash flows at the corporate level can result in varying degrees of default risk. These range from partial or complete default on interest payments— the range between principal and principal plus interest in Figure 4–1—and partial or complete default on the principal lent, the range between principal and zero. Given this limited upside return and long-tailed downside risk, it is incumbent on FIs to estimate expected default risk on bonds and loans held as assets and to demand risk premiums on those securities equal to that risk exposure.

The return distribution for credit risk suggests that FIs need to both monitor and collect information about any firms whose assets are in their portfolios. Thus, managerial efficiency and credit risk management strategy affect the shape of the loan return distribution. Moreover, the credit risk distribution in Figure 4–1 is for an investment in a single asset exposed to default risk. One of the advantages FIs have over individual household investors is the ability to diversify some credit risk away by exploiting the law of large numbers in their asset investment portfolios (see Chapter 3). In the framework of Figure 4–1, diversification across assets exposed to credit risk moderates the long tailed downside risk of the return distribution. For a well-diversified FI, the shape of the return distribution on a portfolio of securities exposed to credit or default risk looks more like that in Figure 4–2.

FIs earn the maximum dollar return when all bonds and loans pay off interest and principal in full. In reality, some loans or bonds default on interest payments or principal payments or both. Thus, the mean return on the asset portfolio would be less than the maximum possible in a risk free, no default case. The effect of risk diversification is to truncate or limit the probabilities of the bad outcomes in the portfolio. As you can see in Figure 4–2, portfolio diversification tightens the range of outcomes on the negative side. The return distribution looks more like a symmetric or bell-shaped normal distribution. In effect, diversification reduces individual **firm specific credit risk,** such as the risk specific to holding the bonds or loans of General Motors or IBM, while leaving the FI still exposed to **systematic credit risk,** such as factors that increase the default risk of all firms in the economy. We describe methods

Firm Specific Credit Risk
The risk of default of the borrowing firm associated with the specific types of project risk taken by that firm.

Systematic Credit Risk
The risk of default associated with general economy wide or macroconditions affecting all borrowers.

FIGURE 4–1

The return distribution on risky debt (loans/bonds)

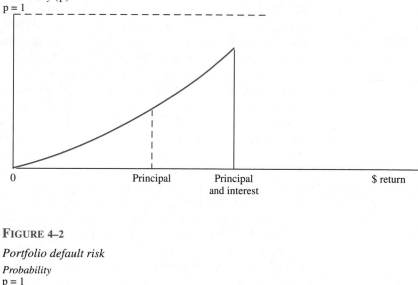

FIGURE 4–2

Portfolio default risk

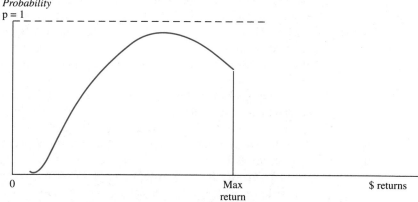

to measure the default risk of individual corporate claims such as bonds and loans as well as portfolios of such claims in Chapter 8.

Concept Questions

1. Define credit risk.
2. Can all credit risk be diversified away?

Off-Balance-Sheet Risk

One of the most striking trends in modern FIs has been the growth in their off-balance-sheet activities. An off-balance-sheet activity, by definition, does not appear on the current balance sheet because it does not concern holding a *current primary* claim (asset) or the issuance of a *current secondary* claim (liability). Instead, off-balance-sheet activities affect the *future* shape of an FI's balance sheet in that they involve the creation of contingent assets and liabilities. As such, accountants place them "below the bottom line" when they report an FI's balance sheet. A good example of an off-balance-sheet activity is the issuance of stand by **letter of credit** guarantees by insurance companies and banks to back the issuance of municipal bonds. Many state and local governments could not issue such securities without *letter of credit guarantees* promising principal and interest payments to investors by the bank or insurance company should the municipality default on its obligations. Thus, the letter of credit guarantees payment should a municipal government (e.g., New York State) face financial problems in paying either the promised interest payments and/or principal on the bonds it issues. If a municipal government's cash flow is sufficiently strong to pay off the principal and interest on the debt it issues, the letter of credit guarantee issued by an FI expires unused. Nothing appears on the FI's balance sheet today or in the future. However, the fee earned for issuing the letter of credit guarantee appears on the FI's profit and loss statement.

As a result, the ability to earn fee income while not loading up or expanding the balance sheet has become an important motivation in FIs pursuing off-balance-sheet business. Unfortunately, this activity is not risk free. Suppose the municipal government defaults on its bond interest and principal payments. Then the contingent liability or guarantee the FI issued becomes an actual or real balance sheet liability. That is, the FI has to use its own equity to compensate investors in municipal bonds. Indeed, significant losses in off-balance-sheet activities can cause an FI to fail, just as major losses due to balance sheet default and interest rates risks can cause a bank to fail.

Letters of credit are just one example of off-balance-sheet activities. Others include loan commitments by banks; mortgage servicing contracts by thrifts; and positions in forwards, futures, swaps, options, and other derivative securities by almost all FIs. While some of these activities are structured to reduce an FI's exposure to credit, interest rate, or foreign exchange risks, mismanagement or inappropriate use of these instruments can result in major losses to FIs. We detail the specific nature of the risks of off-balance-sheet activities more fully in Chapter 9.

Letter of Credit
A credit guarantee issued by an FI for a fee on which payment is contingent on some future event occurring, most notably default of the agent that purchases the letter of credit.

Concept Questions

1. Why are letter of credit guarantees an off-balance-sheet item?
2. What is the similarity between selling guarantees and selling insurance?

Technology and Operational Risk

Technological innovation has been a major concern of FIs in recent years. In the 1980s and 1990s banks, insurance companies, and investment companies have all sought to improve operational efficiency with major investments in internal and external communications, computers, and an expanded technological infrastructure. Good examples are the automated teller machine (ATM) networks developed by banks at the retail level and the automated clearing houses (ACH) and wire transfer payment networks such as the clearinghouse interbank payments system (CHIPS) developed at the wholesale level. Indeed, a global financial service firm such as

Economies of Scale
The degree to which an FI's average unit costs of producing financial services fall as its output of services increase.

Economies of Scope
The degree to which an FI can generate cost synergies by producing multiple financial service products.

Citicorp has operations in more than 80 countries connected in real time by a proprietary-owned satellite system. The objective of technological expansion is to lower operating costs, increase profits, and capture new markets for the FI. In current terminology, it is to allow the FI to better exploit potential economies of scale and economies of scope in selling its products. **Economies of scale** imply an FI's ability to lower its average costs of operations by expanding its output of financial services. **Economies of scope** imply an FI's ability to generate cost synergies by producing more than one output with the same inputs. For example, an FI could use the same information on the quality of customers stored in its computers to expand the sale of both loan products and insurance products. That is, the same information (e.g., age, job, size of family, income, etc.), can identify both potential loan and life insurance customers.

Technology risk occurs when technological investments do not produce the anticipated cost savings in economies of scale or scope. Diseconomies of scale, for example, arise because of excess capacity, redundant technology, and/or organizational bureaucratic inefficiencies (red tape) that get worse as an FI grows. Diseconomies of scope arise when an FI fails to generate perceived synergies or cost savings through major new technology investments. We describe the measurement and evidence of economies of scale and scope in FIs in Chapter 10. Technological risk can result in major losses in the competitive efficiency of an FI and ultimately result in its long-term failure. Similarly, gains from technological investments can produce performance superior to rivals' as well as allow an FI to develop new and innovative products enhancing its long-run survival chances.

Operational risk is partly related to technology risk and can arise whenever existing technology malfunctions or back-office support systems break down. For example, major banks use the federal funds market to both sell to, and buy funds from, other banks for periods as short as a day. Their payment messages travel along a wire transfer network called Fedwire. Suppose the Bank of New York wished to lend federal funds to a California bank. It would transmit an electronic message instructing the Federal Reserve Bank of New York to deduct reserves from its account and send a message by Fedwire to credit the California borrowing bank's account at its own Federal Reserve Bank. Thus, funds would be credited to Bank of America's account at the Federal Reserve Bank of San Francisco. Normally, this system functions highly efficiently; occasionally, risk exposures such as that actually faced by the Bank of New York in 1985 can arise. Specifically, the Bank of New York's computer system failed to register incoming payment (funds borrowed) messages on Fedwire but still processed outbound (funds lent) messages. As a result, at the end of the day the bank faced a huge net payment position on funds lent that it had to settle with other banks. The Bank of New York could only do this by arranging emergency loans from the Federal Reserve. Even though such computer glitches are rare, their occurrence can cause major dislocations in the FIs involved and potentially disrupt the financial system in general.

Back-office support systems combine labor and technology to provide clearance, settlement, and other services to back the underlying on- and off-balance-sheet transactions of FIs. Prior to 1975, most transactions among securities firms and their customers were paper based. As the market volume of trades rose, severe backlogs in settling and clearing transactions occurred because of the general inefficiency of decentralized paper-based systems. Such problems stimulated the development of centralized depositories as well as computerized trading and settlement in the securities industry.

Concept Questions

1. Define economies of scale.
2. Define economies of scope.
3. How constant are bank production functions over time?

Foreign Exchange Risk

Increasingly, FIs have recognized that both direct foreign investment and foreign portfolio investments can extend the operational and financial benefits available from purely domestic investments. Thus, U.S. pension funds now hold approximately 5 percent of their assets in foreign securities; this is projected to rise to 10 percent by the end of the 1990s, Japanese pension funds currently hold more than 30 percent of their assets in foreign securities plus an additional 10 percent in foreign currency deposits. To the extent that the returns on domestic and foreign investments are imperfectly correlated, there are potential gains for an FI that expands its asset holdings and liability funding beyond the domestic frontier.

The returns on domestic and foreign direct investing and portfolio investments are not perfectly correlated for two reasons: The first is that the underlying technologies of various economies differ as do the firms in those economies. For example, one economy may be agriculture based while another is industry based. Given different economic infrastructures, one economy could be expanding while another is contracting. The second reason is that exchange rate changes may not be perfectly correlated across countries. This means the dollar-deutsche mark exchange rate may be appreciating while the dollar-yen exchange rate may be falling.

One potential benefit from an FI becoming increasingly global in its outlook is the ability to expand abroad directly or to expand a financial asset portfolio to include foreign securities as well as domestic securities. Even so, undiversified foreign expansion—such as establishing operations in only one country or buying the securities of corporations in only one country—exposes an FI to foreign exchange risk in addition to interest rate risk and default risk.

To see how foreign exchange risk arises, suppose a U.S. FI makes a loan to a British company in pounds sterling (£). Should the British pound depreciate relative to the U.S. dollar, the principal and interest payments received by U.S. investors would be devalued in dollar terms. Indeed, were the British pound to fall far enough over the investment period, when cash flows were converted back into dollars, the overall return could be negative. That is, on the conversion of principal and interest payments from sterling into dollars, foreign exchange losses can offset the promised value of local currency interest payments at the original exchange rate at which the investment occurred.

In general, an FI can hold assets denominated in a foreign currency and/or issue foreign liabilities. Consider an FI that holds both British pound loans as assets and funds them with British pound certificates of deposit. Suppose that a U.S. FI funded more British loans in pounds than it raised in pound liabilities through issuing pound sterling CDs. The difference between the £100 million in pound loans and £80 million in pound CDs is funded by dollar CDs (i.e., £20 million pounds worth of dollar CDs). See Figure 4–3.

In this case, the U.S. FI is *net long* £20 million in British assets; that is, it holds more foreign assets than liabilities. The U.S. FI would suffer losses if the exchange

FIGURE 4–3
The foreign asset and liability position: A net long asset position in pounds

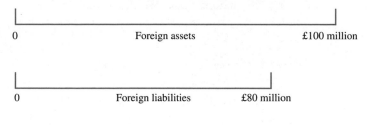

FIGURE 4–4
The foreign asset and liability position: A net short asset position in pounds

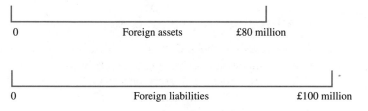

rate for pounds falls or depreciates against the dollar over this period. In dollar terms, the value of the British pound loan assets would fall or decrease in value by more than the British pound CD liabilities. That is, the FI is exposed to the risk that its net foreign assets may have to be liquidated at an exchange rate lower than the one that existed when the FI entered into the foreign asset-liability position.

Instead, the FI could have £20 million more foreign liabilities than assets; then it would be holding a *net short* position in foreign assets, as shown in Figure 4–4.

In this second case, the FI would be exposed to foreign exchange risk if the pound appreciated against the dollar over the investment period. This is because the cost of its British pound liabilities in dollar terms would rise faster than the return on its pound assets. Consequently, to be approximately hedged the FI must match its assets and liabilities in each foreign currency.

Note that the FI is only approximately hedged unless we also assume that it holds foreign assets and liabilities of exactly the same maturity.[2] Consider what happens if the FI matches the size of its foreign currency book (British pound assets = British pound liabilities = £100 million in that currency) but mismatches the maturities so that the pound sterling assets are of six-month maturity and the liabilities are of three-month maturity. The FI would then be exposed to foreign interest rate risk; the risk that British interest rates would rise when it has to roll over its £100 million British CD liabilities at the end of the third month. Consequently, an FI that matches both the size and maturities of its exposures in assets and liabilities of a given currency is hedged or immunized against foreign currency and foreign interest rate risk. To the extent that FIs mismatch their portfolios and maturity exposures in different currency assets and liabilities, both foreign currency risk and foreign interest rate

---

[2]Technically speaking, hedging requires matching the durations (average lives of assets and liabilities) rather than simple maturities.

risks are present. As already noted, if foreign exchange rate and interest rate changes are not perfectly correlated across countries, an FI can diversify away part, if not all, of its foreign currency risk. We discuss the measurement and evaluation of an FI's foreign currency risk exposure in depth in Chapter 11.

Concept Questions

1. A U.S. bank is net long in deutsche mark (DM) assets. If the DM appreciates against the dollar, will the bank gain or lose?
2. A U.S. bank is net short in DM assets. The DM appreciates against the dollar, will the bank gain or lose?

Country or Sovereign Risk

As we noted in the previous section, a globally oriented FI that mismatches the size and maturities of its foreign assets and liabilities would be exposed to foreign currency and foreign interest rate risks. Even beyond these risks and even when investing in dollars, investing in assets in a foreign country can expose an FI to a third foreign investment risk, country or sovereign risk. Country or sovereign risk is a more serious credit risk than that faced by an FI which purchases domestic assets such as the bonds and loans of domestic corporations. For example, when a domestic corporation is unable or unwilling to repay a loan, as a claimholder an FI usually has recourse to the bankruptcy courts and eventually may recoup at least a portion of its original investment as the assets of the defaulted firm are liquidated or restructured. By comparison, a foreign corporation may be unable to repay the principal or interest on its issued claims even if it would like to. Most commonly, the government of the country may prohibit payment or limit payments due to foreign currency shortages and political reasons. In recent years, the governments of Argentina, Peru, and Brazil have imposed restrictions with various degrees of stringency on the debt repayments of domestic corporations and government agencies in hard currencies such as dollars to overseas investors. In the event of such restrictions or outright prohibitions on payment, the FI claimholder has little if any recourse to the local bankruptcy courts or an international civil claims court. The major leverage available to an FI to ensure or increase repayment probabilities is its control over the future supply of loans or funds to the country concerned. However, such leverage may be very weak in the face of a collapsing country and currency; one recent example of this is Russia. Chapter 12 discusses how country risk is measured and considers possible financial market solutions to the country risk exposure problems of a globally oriented FI.

Concept Questions

1. Can a bank be subject to sovereign risk if it only lends to AAA or the highest quality foreign corporations?
2. What is the major way an FI can discipline those countries that threaten not to repay their loans?

Liquidity Risk

Liquidity risk arises whenever an FI's liability holders, such as depositors or insurance policyholders, demand immediate cash for their financial claims. When liability holders demand cash immediacy—that is, put their financial claim back to the FI—the FI must either borrow additional funds or sell off assets to meet the demand for the withdrawal of funds. The most liquid asset of all is cash, and FIs can use this asset to directly meet liability holders' demands to withdraw funds. Although, FIs minimize their cash assets because such holdings earn no interest, low holdings are generally not a problem. Day-to-day withdrawals by liability holders are usually predictable and FIs can normally expect to borrow additional funds to meet any shortfalls of cash on the money and financial markets.

However, there are times when an FI can face a liquidity crisis. Due to either a lack of confidence in the FI or some seasonal unexpected need for cash, liability holders may demand *larger* withdrawals than normal. When all or many FIs are facing similar abnormally large cash demands, the cost of additional funds rises and their supply becomes restricted or unavailable. As a consequence, FIs may have to sell some of their less liquid assets to meet the withdrawal demands of liability holders. This results in a more serious liquidity risk; some assets with thin markets generate lower prices when the sale is immediate than if the FI had longer to negotiate the sale. As a result, the liquidation of some assets at low or "fire-sale" prices could threaten the solvency of an FI. Good examples of such illiquid assets are bank loans to small firms. Such serious liquidity problems may eventually result in a run situation in which all liability claimholders seek to withdraw their funds simultaneously from the FI. This turns the FI's liquidity problem into a solvency problem and can cause it to fail.

We examine the nature of normal, abnormal, and run-type liquidity risks and their impact on banks, thrifts, insurance companies, and other FIs in more detail in Chapter 13.

Concept Questions

1. Give two reasons why an FI may face a sudden liquidity crisis.
2. What is meant by a "fire-sale" of assets?

The Interaction of Risks

This chapter has described in very elementary terms the major risks facing a modern FI. These risks are operational and financial, domestic and international, as well as on- and off-balance sheet. Even though the previous discussion has described them independently, in reality these risks are often interdependent. For example, when interest rates rise, corporations find it more difficult to maintain promised payments on their debt. Thus, over some range of interest rate movements, credit risk and interest rate risks are positively correlated. Similarly, foreign exchange rate changes and interest rate changes are also highly correlated. This means FI managers are faced with making trade-offs among these various risks.

Concept Question

1. What is the likely interaction between foreign exchange risk and country risk?

Other Risks

In this chapter we have concentrated on seven major risks continuously impacting FI managers' decision-making processes and risk management strategies. However, various other risks, often of a more discrete type, impact an FI's profitability and risk exposure as well. Discrete risks might include a sudden change in taxation—such as the Tax Reform Act of 1986—that subjected banks to a minimum corporate tax rate of 20 percent (the alternative minimum tax) and limited their ability to expense the cost of funds used to purchase tax-free municipal bonds. Such changes can affect the attractiveness of some types of assets over others as well as the liquidity of the balance sheet. For example, banks' demand for municipal bonds to hold as assets fell quite dramatically following the 1986 tax law change and the municipal bond market became quite illiquid for a time.[3]

Other discrete risks—often called event risks—involve sudden and unexpected changes in financial market conditions due to war, revolution, or sudden collapse such as the 1929 and 1987 stock market crashes. These have a major impact on an FI's risk exposure. Other event risks include theft, malfeasance, and breach of fiduciary trust; all of these can ultimately cause an FI to fail or be severely harmed.

Finally, more general macroeconomic risks such as increased inflation, inflation volatility, and unemployment can all feed back and directly and indirectly impact the FI's level of interest rate, credit, and liquidity risk exposure. For example, inflation was very volatile in the 1979–82 period in the United States. Interest rates reflected this volatility. During periods in which an FI faces high and volatile inflation and interest rates, its interest rate risk exposure from mismatching its balance sheet maturities tends to rise. Its credit risk exposure also rises because borrowing firms with fixed price product contracts often find it difficult to keep up their loan interest payments when inflation and interest rates rise abruptly.

---

[3]Other examples might include the forced disinvestment of S&L junk bond portfolios and the exclusion of accounting for goodwill from equity capital as part of the FIRREA 1989 reform package.

Summary

This chapter has provided an overview of the seven major risks faced by modern FIs. The chapters that follow analyze each of these major risks in greater detail, beginning with interest rate risk.

Questions and Problems

1. The sales literature of a mutual fund claims that the fund has no risk exposure because it invests exclusively in default risk-free federal government securities. Is this claim true? Why or why not?

2. Characterize the risk exposure(s) of the following FI transactions by choosing one or more of the following:

    i. Interest rate risk

   ii. Credit risk

  iii. Off-balance-sheet risk

  iv. Technology risk

    v. Foreign exchange rate risk
   vi. Country/sovereign risk
  vii. Liquidity risk

a. A bank finances a $20 million 5-year fixed-rate commercial loan by selling 1-year certificates of deposit.

b. An insurance company invests its policy premiums in a long-term municipal bond portfolio.

c. A German bank sells two-year fixed-rate notes to finance a two-year fixed-rate loan to a Polish entrepreneur.

d. A British bank acquires an Australian bank so as to facilitate clearing operations.

e. A mutual fund completely hedges its interest rate risk exposure using forward contingent contracts.

f. A bond dealer uses his own equity to buy Brazilian debt on the bond market for less developed countries (LDCs).

g. The bond dealer sold the Brazilian debt in question *f.*

h. A bank sells a package of its mortgage loans as mortgage backed securities.

i. A bank funds its asset portfolio consisting of commercial loans by issuing demand deposits.

3. Discuss how off-balance-sheet risk can encompass several of the other six sources of risk exposure.

4. Discuss how the availability of international computerized payments systems creates both risk and opportunity.

5. Assume a bank invested $50 million in a two-year asset paying 10 percent interest per annum and simultaneously issued a $50 million one-year liability paying 8 percent interest per annum. What would be the impact on the bank's net interest income if, at the end of the first year, all interest rates increased by one percentage point?

6. If international capital markets are well-integrated and operate efficiently, will banks be exposed to foreign exchange risk? What are the sources of foreign exchange risk for FIs?

7. Discuss the interrelationships among the different sources of bank risk exposure.

8. If it were feasible, would it be optimal for banks to be totally free of risk exposure?

9. Megabank, Ltd., issued a $100 million one-year maturity Euromark CD, denominated in German deutsche mark (DM). On the same date, $60 million was invested in a deutsche mark-denominated loan and $40 million in a U.S. Treasury bill. The exchange rate on this date was 1.7382 DM/$. Assume no repayment of principal; today's exchange rate is 1.3905 DM/$:

   a. What is the current value of the Euromark CD principal in dollars and deutsche marks?

   b. What is the current value of the German loan principal in dollars and deutsche marks?

   c. What is the current value of the U.S. Treasury bill in dollars and deutsche marks?

   d. What is Megabank's profit/loss from this transaction in dollars and deutsche marks?

10. Banks have greater exposure to liquidity risk than do mutual funds. Is this statement true?

5

INTEREST RATE RISK
The Maturity Model

Learning Objectives

Chapter 5 is the first of three chapters on interest rate risk measurement. Here you are introduced to the sources of interest rate risk and the impact this risk has on an FI's balance sheet. You will learn that at the heart of interest rate risk is the tendency of many modern FIs to mismatch the maturities of their assets and liabilities. Further, we show that this mismatching can give rise to significant interest rate exposure and insolvency risk. Finally, we discuss the problems caused by measuring interest rate risk exposure by looking only at the maturity mismatch.

Introduction

Chapter 4 established that while performing their asset-transformation functions, FIs often mismatch the maturities of their assets and liabilities. In so doing, they expose themselves to interest rate risk and the risk of **insolvency.** For example, in recent years a large number of thrifts have suffered economic insolvency (i.e., the **net worth** or equity of their owners has been eradicated) due to major movements or shifts in interest rates. Indeed, all FIs tend to mismatch their balance sheet maturities to some degree; however, the Federal Reserve's monetary policy is also a key determinant of interest rate risk.

Insolvency
When the market value net worth of the bank is reduced to zero or is negative.

Net Worth
The value of the FI to its owners; this is equal to the difference between the market value of assets and liabilities.

The Central Bank and Interest Rate Risk

Underlying the movement of interest rates is the strategy of the central bank or the Federal Reserve. If the Federal Reserve smooths or targets the level of interest rates, unexpected interest rate shocks and interest rate volatility tend to be small. Accordingly, the risk exposure to an FI from mismatching the maturities of its assets and liabilities also tends to be small. On the other hand, to the extent that the Federal Reserve targets the supply of bank reserves and is willing to let interest rates find their own levels, the volatility of interest rates can be very high. In Figure 5–1, a chart shows the yields of U.S. 91-day T-bills for the 1950–92 period. The first observation is that the degree of volatility appears to have increased over time. The second is that the relative degree of volatility, or interest rate uncertainty, is directly linked to the Federal Reserve's monetary policy strategy. Specifically, between October 1979 and October 1982, the Federal Reserve targeted bank reserves during the so-called nonborrowed reserves target regime.[1] The volatility of interest rates in this period was far greater than in the two regimes surrounding this period. Note how the Federal Reserve targeted interest rates during the 1970 to October 1979 period and smoothed interest rates after October 1982 under the so-called borrowed reserves targeting regime. Indeed, the 1979–82 period was the genesis for the interest rate risk problems facing those thrifts that specialized in making long-term conventional mortgage loans funded by short-term deposits such as CD's.[2]

The secular increase in the volatility of interest rates and the risk that the Federal Reserve may return to a more overtly reserve targeting regime similar to 1979–82 puts the measurement and management of interest rate risk at the head of the problems facing modern financial institution managers. In this chapter and chapters 6 and 7, we analyze the different ways an FI might measure the gap exposure it faces in running a mismatched maturity book of assets and liabilities in a world of interest rate volatility.

In particular, we concentrate on three ways, or models, of measuring the asset-liability gap exposure of an FI:

The maturity model (Chapter 5).

The duration model (Chapter 6).

The repricing (or funding gap) model (Chapter 7).

Also, Chapter 7 discusses the interest rate gap models used by *bank regulators.*

The Maturity Model

Book Value Accounting
The assets and liabilities of the FI are reported according to their historic values and thus are insensitive to changes in market rates.

In most countries, FIs report their balance sheets using **book value accounting.** This records the historic values of securities purchased, loans made, and liabilities sold. For example, for U.S. banks, investment assets (i.e., those expected to be held for more than a year) are recorded at book values while those assets expected to be used for trading (held for less than one year) are reported according to market values.[3] The recording of market values means that assets or liabilities are revalued to reflect current market conditions. Thus, if a fixed-coupon bond had been purchased at $100 per $100 of face value in a low-interest rate environment, a rise in current market rates reduces the present value of the cash flows from the bond to the investor. Such a rise also reduces the price—say to $97—at which it could be sold in the secondary market today. That is, marking-to-market, implied by the **market value accounting** method, reflects economic reality or the true values of assets and liabilities if the FI's portfolio were to be liquidated at today's securities prices rather than at the prices when the assets and liabilities were originally purchased or sold.

Market Value Accounting
The assets and liabilities of the FI are revalued according to the current level of interest rates.

---

[1]For more details, see A. Saunders and T. Urich, "The Effects of Shifts in Monetary Policy and Reserve Accounting Regimes on Bank Reserve Management Behavior in the Federal Funds Market," *Journal of Banking and Finance* 12, 1988, pp. 523–35.

[2]Certificates of deposit are usually issued with maturities of less than one year.

[3]More accurately, they are reported at the lower of cost or current market value (LOCOM). However, both the SEC and the Financial Accounting Standards Board (FASB) have strongly advocated that FIs switch to market value accounting in the near future.

FIGURE 5–1

Yields of 91-day U.S. T-bills

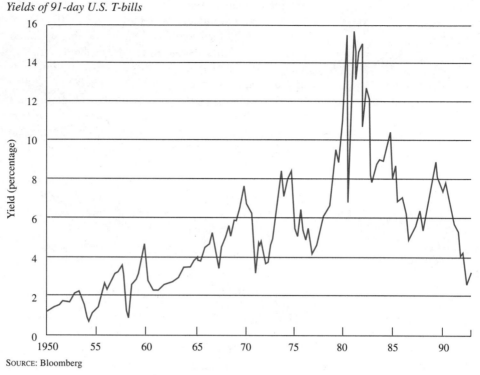

SOURCE: Bloomberg

The Maturity Model: An Example

Consider the value of a bond held by an FI that has one year to maturity, one single annual coupon of 10 percent (C) plus a face value of 100 (F) to be paid on maturity, and a current yield (R) to maturity (reflecting current interest rates) of 10 percent. The price of the one year bond, P_1^B, is

$$P_1^B = \frac{F+C}{(1+R)} = \frac{100+10}{1.1} = 100$$

Suppose that the Federal Reserve tightens monetary policy so that the required yield on the bond rises instantaneously to 11 percent. The market value of the bond falls to:

$$P_1^B = \frac{100+10}{1.11} = 99.10$$

Thus, the market value of the bond is now only $99.10 per $100 of face value, while its original book value was $100. The FI has suffered a capital loss (ΔP_1) of $0.90 per $100 of face value in holding this bond, or,

$$\Delta P_1 = 99.10 - 100 = -0.90\%$$

This example simply demonstrates the fact that:

$$\frac{\Delta P}{\Delta R} < 0$$

A rise in the required yield to maturity reduces the price of fixed-income securities held in FI portfolios. Note that if the bond under consideration were issued as a liability by the FI (e.g., a fixed-interest deposit such as a CD) rather than being held as an asset, the effect is the same; the market value of the FI's deposits would fall. However, the economic interpretation is different. Although rising interest rates that reduce the market value of assets is bad news, the reduction in the market value of liabilities is good news for the FI. The economic intuition is straightforward. Suppose the bank issued a one-year deposit with a promised interest rate of 10 percent and principal or face value of $100.[4] When the current level of interest rates is 10 percent, the market value of the liability is 100:

$$P_1^D = \frac{100 + 10}{(1.1)} = 100$$

Should interest rates on new one-year deposits rise instantaneously to 11 percent, the bank has gained by locking in a promised interest payment to depositors of only 10 percent. The market value of the bank's liability to its depositors would fall to $99.10; alternatively, this would be the price the bank would need to pay the depositor if it repurchased the deposit in the secondary market:

$$P_1^D = \frac{100 + 10}{1.11} = 99.10$$

That is, the bank gained from paying only 10 percent on its deposits rather than 11 percent if they were newly issued after the rise in interest rates.

As a result, in a market value accounting framework rising interest rates generally lower the market values of both assets and liabilities on an FI's balance sheet. Clearly, falling interest rates have the reverse effect, they increase the market values of both assets and liabilities.

In the preceding example, both the bond and deposit were of one-year maturity. We can easily show that if the bond or deposit had a two-year maturity with the same annual coupon rate, the same increase in market interest rates from 10 to 11 percent would have had a more *negative* effect on the market value of the bond's price. That is, before the rise in required yield:

$$P_2^B = \frac{10}{(1.1)} + \frac{10 + 100}{(1.1)^2} = 100$$

after the rise in market interest rates yields from 10 to 11 percent,

$$P_2^B = \frac{10}{(1.11)} + \frac{10 + 100}{(1.11)^2} = 98.29$$

and

$$\Delta P_2 = 98.29 - 100 = -1.71\%$$

This example demonstrates another general rule of portfolio management for FIs: the *longer* the maturity of a fixed income asset or liability, the greater is its fall in price and market value for any given increase in the level of market interest rates:

---

[4]In this example, we assume for simplicity that the promised interest rate on the deposit is 10 percent. In reality, for returns to intermediation to prevail the promised rate on deposits would be less than the promised rate (coupon) on assets.

Figure 5–2

The relationship between ΔR, maturity, and ΔP

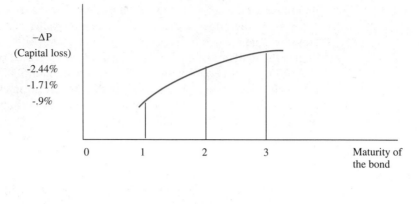

$$\frac{\Delta P_1}{\Delta R} < \frac{\Delta P_2}{\Delta R} < ..... < \frac{\Delta P_{30}}{\Delta R}$$

Note, however, that while a two-year bond's fall in price is greater than the one-year bond's, the difference between the two price falls $\Delta P_2 - \Delta P_1$, is $-1.71\% - (-0.9\%)$ $= -0.81\%$. The fall in a 3-year, 10 percent coupon bond's price when yield increases to 11 percent is $- 2.44$ percent. Thus, $\Delta P_3 - \Delta P_2 = -2.44\% - (-1.71\%) = -0.73\%$. This establishes an important result: While P_3 falls more than P_2 and P_2 falls more than P_1, the size of the capital loss increases at a diminishing rate as we move into the higher maturity ranges. This effect is graphed in Figure 5–2.

So far, we have shown that for an FI's fixed-income assets and liabilities:

1. A rise (fall) in interest rates generally leads to a fall (rise) in the market value of an asset or liability.
2. The longer the maturity of a fixed-income asset or liability, the greater the fall (rise) in market value for any given interest rate increase (decrease).
3. The fall in the value of longer-term securities increases at a diminishing rate for any given increase in interest rates.

The Maturity Model with a Portfolio of Assets and Liabilities

The preceding general rules can be extended beyond an FI holding an individual asset or liability to holding a portfolio of assets and liabilities. Let M_A be the weighted-average maturity of an FI's assets and M_L the weighted-average maturity of an FI's liabilities such that

$$M_i = W_{i1}M_{i1} + W_{i2}M_{i2+.....+}W_{in}M_{in}$$

where

M_i = The weighted-average maturity of an FI's assets (liabilities), $i = A \ or \ L$

W_{ij} = The importance of each asset (liability) in the asset (liability) portfolio as measured by the market value of that asset (liability) position relative to the market value of all the assets (liabilities)

M_{ij} = The maturity of the *j*th asset (or liability), $j = l .... n$

This equation shows that the maturity of a portfolio of assets or liabilities is a weighted-average of the maturities of assets or liabilities that comprise that portfolio. In a portfolio context, the same three principles prevail as for an individual security:

1. A rise in interest rates generally reduces the market values of an FI's asset and liability portfolios.
2. The longer the maturity of the asset or liability portfolio, the greater the fall in value for any given interest rate increase.
3. The fall in value of the asset or liability portfolio increases with its maturity at a diminishing rate.

Given the preceding, the net effect of rising or falling interest rates on an FI's balance sheet depends on the extent and direction in which the FI mismatches the maturities of its asset and liability portfolios. That is, whether its maturity gap, $M_A - M_L$, is greater than, equal to, or less than zero.

Consider the case where $M_A - M_L > 0$; that is, the maturity of assets is longer than the maturity of liabilities. This is the case for most commercial banks and thrifts. These FIs tend to hold large amounts of relatively longer-term fixed-income assets such as conventional mortgages, consumer loans, commercial loans, and bonds, while issuing shorter-term liabilities, such as certificates of deposit with fixed interest payments promised to the depositors.[5]

TABLE 5–1   The Market Value Balance Sheet of a Bank

Assets	Liabilities
Long-term assets (A)	Short-term liabilities (L)
	Net worth (E)

Look at the simplified portfolio of a representative bank in Table 5–1 and notice that all assets and liabilities are marked-to-market; that is, we are using a market value accounting framework. Note that in the real world, reported balance sheets differ from Table 5–1 because historic or book value accounting rules are used. In Table 5–1, the difference between the market value of the bank's assets (A) and the market value of its liabilities such as deposits (L) is called the net worth or true equity value (E) of the bank. This is the economic value of the bank owners' stake in the FI. In other words, the money the owners would get if they could liquidate the bank's assets and liabilities at today's prices in the financial markets by selling off loans, bonds, and repurchasing deposits at the best prices. This is also clear from the balance sheet identity:

$$E = A - L$$

---

[5]These assets generate periodic interest payments, such as coupons, that are fixed over the assets' life. In Chapter 6, we discuss interest payments fluctuating with market interest rates, such as on an adjustable rate mortgage.

TABLE 5–2   Initial Values of a Bank's Assets and Liabilities

Assets	Liabilities
A = 100 (long term)	90 = L (short term)
	10 = E
100	100

TABLE 5–3   A Bank's Market Value Balance Sheet after a Rise in Interest Rates of 1% with Longer-Term Assets

Assets	Liabilities
A = 97.56	L = 89.19
	E = 8.37
or ΔE = ΔA − ΔL	
−1.63 = (−2.44) − (−0.81)	

Suppose that initially the bank's balance sheet looks like Table 5–2. As has been demonstrated earlier, when interest rates rise the market values of both assets and liabilities fall. However, in this example with more long-term assets than liabilities, the market value of the asset portfolio (A) falls by more than the market value of the liability portfolio (L). The value of the bank's net worth is the difference between the market value of its assets and liabilities:

$$\Delta E \quad = \quad \Delta A \quad - \quad \Delta L$$

ΔE	=	ΔA	−	ΔL
(change in	=	(change in	−	(change in
bank net		market value		market value
worth)		of assets)		of liabilities)

To see the effect on bank net worth of having longer term assets than liabilities, suppose the bank in Table 5–2 had $100 million invested in three-year, 10 percent coupon bonds and raised $90 million with one-year deposits paying a promised interest rate of 10 percent. We showed earlier that if market interest rates rise by 1 percent from 10 to 11 percent, the value of three-year bonds falls by 2.44 percent while the value of one-year deposits falls by 0.9 percent. In Table 5–3, we depict this fall in asset and liability market values and the associated effects on bank net worth.

Because the bank's assets have a three-year maturity compared to its one-year maturity liabilities, the value of its assets have fallen by more than the its liabilities. The net worth of the bank declines from $10 million to $8.37 million, a loss of $1.63 million, or 16.3 percent! Thus, it is clear that with a *maturity gap* of two years,

$$M_A - M_L = 2 \text{ years}$$
$$(3) - (1)$$

a one percentage point rise in interest rates can cause the bank's owners or stockholders to take a big hit to their net worth. Indeed, if a 1 percent rise in interest rates leads

TABLE 5–4   **A Bank Becomes Insolvent after a 7 Percent Rate Increase**

Assets	Liabilities
A = 84.53	L = 84.62
	E = −0.09
or ΔE = ΔA − ΔL	
−10.09 = −15.47 − (−5.38)	

TABLE 5–5   **A Bank with an Extreme Maturity Mismatch**

Assets	Liabilities
A = 100	L = 90 (1-year deposits)
(30-year discount bonds)	E = 10

to a fall of 16.3 percent in the bank's net worth, it is not unreasonable to ask how large an interest rate change would need to occur to render the bank economically insolvent by reducing its owners' equity stake or net worth to zero. That is, what increase in interest rates would make ΔE fall by 10 so that all the owners' net worth is eliminated, such that after the interest rate rise:

$$E \leq 0.$$

For the answer to this question, look at Table 5–4. If interest rates were to rise a full 7 percent from 10 to 17 percent, the market value balance sheet would look similar to Table 5–4. As you can see, the bank's equity (E) falls by just over 10, rendering the FI economically insolvent.[6]

Deep-Discount Bonds
Often called zero-coupon bonds because they do not pay any coupon interest over the life of the bond. Instead they make a single payment of principal or face value on maturity.

Suppose the bank had adopted an even more extreme maturity gap by investing all its assets in 30-year **deep-discount bonds** while continuing to raise funds by issuing 1-year deposits with promised interest payments of 10 percent as shown in Table 5–5. Deep-discount bonds pay $100 face value on maturity and no coupon interest in the intervening period. The price (P_{30}) an investor is willing to pay today for the bond becomes the present value of the $100 face value to be received in 30 years' time. Assuming annual compounding and a current level of interest rates of 10 percent,

$$P_{30} = \frac{\$100}{(1.1)^{30}} = \$5.73$$

Thus, an FI manager would be willing to pay $5.73 per $100 of face value. If interest rates were to rise by 1 percent as we have shown, the market value of the

---

[6]Here we are talking about economic insolvency. The legal and regulatory definition may vary depending on what type of accounting rules are used. In particular, under the recently passed Federal Deposit Insurance Corporation Improvement Act or FDICIA (November 1991), a bank is required to be placed in conservatorship by regulators when the book value of its net worth falls below 2 percent. However, the true or market value of net worth may well be less than this figure at that time.

bank's one-year deposit liabilities would fall by 0.9 percent. However, the fall in the price of the 30-year discount bond asset would be to:

$$P_{30} = \frac{\$100}{(1.11)^{30}} = \$4.37$$

Or, as a percentage change $(\Delta P_{30}/P_{30})\% = -23.73\%$.

Look at Table 5–6 to see the effect on the market value balance sheet and the bank's net worth after a rise of 1 percent in interest rates. It is clear from Table 5–6 that a mere 1 percent increase in interest rates completely eliminates the bank's 10 in net worth and renders it completely and massively insolvent (net worth is -12.92 after the rise in rates). Given this example, you should not be surprised that savings and loans with 30-year fixed-rate mortgages as assets and one-year and less CDs as liabilities suffered badly during the 1979–82 period when interest rates rose so dramatically.

TABLE 5–6 **The Effect of a 1 Percent Rise in Interest Rates on the Net Worth of a Bank with an Extreme Asset and Liability Mismatch**

Assets	Liabilities
$A = 76.27$	$L = 89.19$
	$E = -12.92$
or ΔE =	ΔA – ΔL
$-22.92 = (-23.73) - (-0.81)$	

From the preceding examples, you might infer that the best way for an FI to **immunize** or protect itself from interest rate risk would be for its managers to match the maturities of its assets and liabilities. That is, to construct its balance sheet so that its **maturity gap,** the difference between the weighted-average maturity of its assets and liabilities, is zero:

$$M_A - M_L = 0$$

However, as we discuss next, maturity matching does not always protect an FI against interest rate risk.

Immunize
Immunization occurs when an FI's equity holders are fully protected or hedged against interest rate risk.

Maturity Gap
The difference between the weighted-average maturities of an FI's assets and liabilities.

Concept Questions

1. What would be the effect on the FI's net worth if it held one-year discount bonds (with a yield of 10 percent) as assets in the preceding example?
2. Explain your finding in question 1.

Maturity Matching Does Not Always Eliminate Interest Rate Risk Exposure

While a strategy of matching asset and liability maturities moves the bank in the direction of hedging itself against interest rate risk, it is easy to show that this strategy does not always eliminate all interest rate risk for an FI. Indeed, we show in Chapter

6 that immunization against interest rate risk requires the bank to take into account:

1. The **duration** or average life of asset or (liability) cash flows, rather than the maturity of assets and liabilities.
2. The degree of leverage in the bank's balance sheet; that is, the proportion of assets funded by liabilities (such as deposits) rather than equity.

Duration
The average life of an asset or liability, or more technically, the weighted-average time to maturity using the relative present values of the asset or liability cash flows as weights.

Hedging
Reducing interest rate risk and thus the exposure of the FI by taking appropriate managerial actions.

We show next, using a simple example, that an FI choosing to directly match the maturities of its assets and liabilities does not necessarily achieve a perfect **hedge,** or protection for its equity holders against interest rate risk. Consider the example of a bank that issues a one-year CD to a depositor. This CD has a face value of $100 and an interest rate promised to depositors of 15 percent. Thus, on maturity at the end of the year, the bank has to repay the borrower $100 plus $15 interest, or $115, as shown in Figure 5–3.

Suppose the bank lends $100 for one year to a corporate borrower at a 15 percent annual interest rate. However, contractually the bank requires half of the loan ($50) to be repaid after six months and the last half to be repaid at the end of the year. Note that although the maturity of the loan = maturity of the deposit = 1 year, the cash flow earned on the loan may be greater or less than the $115 required to pay off depositors, depending on what happens to interest rates over the one-year period. You can see this in Figure 5–4.

At the end of the first six months, the bank receives a $50 repayment in loan principal plus $7.5 in interest (100 × ¹/₂ year × 15 percent) for a total midyear cash flow of $57.5. At the end of the year, the bank receives $50 as the final repayment of loan principal plus $3.75 interest ($50 × ¹/₂ year × 15 percent) plus the reinvestment income earned from relending the $57.5 received six months earlier. If interest rates do not change over the period, the bank's extra return from its ability to

FIGURE 5–3

One-year CD cash flows

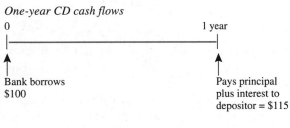

FIGURE 5–4

One-year loan cash flow

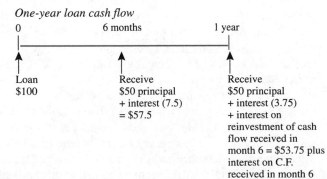

TABLE 5–7   **Cash Flow on a Loan with a 15 Percent Interest Rate**

Cash flow at $\frac{1}{2}$ year	
Principal	$ 50.00
Interest	7.50
Cash flow at 1 year	
Principal	$ 50.00
Interest	3.75
Reinvestment income	4.3125
	$115.5625

TABLE 5–8   **Cash Flow on the Loan when the Beginning Rate of 15 Percent falls to 12 Percent**

Cash flow at $\frac{1}{2}$ year	
Principal	$ 50.00
Interest	7.50
Cash flow at 1 year	
Principal	$ 50.00
Interest	3.75
Reinvestment income	3.45
	$114.70

reinvest part of the cash flow for the last six months would be ($57.5 × $\frac{1}{2}$ × 15 percent) = 4.3125. We summarize the total cash flow on the bank's one-year loan in Table 5–7.

As you can see by the end of the year the cash paid in on the loan exceeded the cash paid out on the deposit by $0.5625. The reason for this is the ability of the bank to reinvest part of the principal and interest over the second-half of the year at 15 percent. Suppose that instead of interest rates staying unchanged at 15 percent throughout the whole one year period, they had fallen to 12 percent over the last six months in the year. This fall in rates would affect neither the promised deposit rate of 15 percent nor the promised loan rate of 15 percent because they are set at time 0 when the deposit and loan were originated and do not change throughout the year. What is affected is the bank's reinvestment income on the $57.5 cash flow received on the loan at the end of six months. It can only be relent for the final six months of the year at the new lower interest rate of 12 percent (see Table 5–8).

The only change to the asset cash flows for the bank are from the reinvestment of the $57.5 received at the end of six months at the lower interest rate of 12 percent. This produces the smaller reinvestment income of $3.45 ($57.5 × $\frac{1}{2}$ × 12 percent) rather than $4.3125 when rates stayed at 15 percent throughout the year. Rather than making a profit of $0.5625 from intermediation, the bank loses $0.3. Note that this loss occurs due to interest rates changing, even when the FI had matched the maturity of its assets and liabilities, $M_A = M_L = 1$ year.

Despite the matching of maturities, the FI is still exposed to interest rate risk because the *timing* of the *cash flows* on the deposit and loan are not perfectly matched. In a sense, the cash flows on the loan are received, on average, earlier than on the deposit where all cash flows occur at the end of the year. In the next chapter we show that only by matching the average lives of assets and liabilities and taking into account the precise timing of arrival of cash flows can an FI immunize itself against interest rate risk. In a cash flow sense, the average life, or *duration* of an asset or liability usually, but not always, differs from its maturity. In particular, we demonstrate in the next chapter that for our simple one-year maturity deposit and one-year maturity loan case that maturity and duration differ. While the maturity of the deposit (M_D) equals the maturity of the loan (M_L), the duration of the loan (D_L) is less than the duration of the deposit (D_D). This duration mismatch exposes an FI to interest rate risk.

Concept Questions

1 Suppose the average maturity of an FI's assets are less than its liabilities and interest rates fall. Will its net worth rise or fall?

2. Would the FI in the above example be exposed to interest rate risk if its deposits paid interest semiannually rather than annually?

Summary

In this chapter, we have introduced one of the simplest methods of measuring the interest rate risk exposure of an FI, the maturity model. We showed that by mismatching the maturities of assets and liabilities an FI exposes its equity holders/owners to a risk of insolvency. Because the maturity model ignores the timing of the arrival of cash flows on assets and liabilities, it is an incomplete measure of the interest rate exposure of an FI. More complete and accurate measures are duration and the duration gap which are explained in the next chapter.

Questions and Problems

1. The Central Bank utilizes monetary policy to effect the level of economic activity. Assume that the economy is in a recession and the Central Bank has decided to use monetary policy to increase the level of economic activity. What are the two alternative approaches available to the Central Bank to accomplish this monetary policy goal? Compare the two approaches to monetary policy concentrating on their relative impacts on the volatility of interest rates. Are these two approaches to monetary policy mutually exclusive? Why or why not?

2. How did the increased rate volatility of the 1979-1982 period create interest rate problems for thrifts?

3. Why is it important to utilize market, as opposed to book, values in financial decision making for FIs?

4. What are some advantages of utilizing book values as opposed to market values?

5. List three possible explanations for a reduction in the market value of a purchased financial security below book values.

6. Evaluate the prices of the following pure discount (zero coupon) bonds:

   a. $1,000 face value received in 5 years yielding an annual rate of 8%.

   b. $10,000 face value received in 3 years yielding an annual rate of 6%.

   c. $100,000 face value received in 10 years yielding an annual rate of 13%.

   d. $1,000,000 face value received in 2 years yielding an annual rate of 7%.

e. $1,000,000 face value received in 6 months yielding an annual rate of 7%.

7. Calculate the value of each of the bonds in question 6 if all yields increased by 1%.

8. Calculate the percentage price changes for each of the bonds in question 6 if all yields increased by 1% (as in question 7).

9. What can you conclude about bond price volatility from your answer to question 8?

10. If the bonds in question 6 were coupon instruments selling at par, calculate the annual coupon payment for each bond.

11. Calculate the prices of each of the coupon bonds in question 10 if all yields increased by 1%.

12. Calculate the percentage price changes for each of the bonds in question 11 if all yields increased by 1%. (Recall that the coupon bonds were originally priced at par.)

13. Compare your answers to questions 8 and 12. What can you conclude about bond price volatility?

14. Consider a five year coupon bond with a face value of $1,000 paying an annual coupon of 15%.

   a. If the current market yield is 8%, what is the bond's price?

   b. If the current market yield increases by 1%, what is the bond's new price?

   c. Using your answers to parts *a* and *b*, what is the percentage change in the bond's price as a result of the 1% increase in interest rates?

15. Compare your answers to questions 8, 12, and 14. What can you conclude about bond price volatility?

16. Consider the following FI balance sheet.

M. Match, Inc. ($000)

Assets		Liabilities	
2 yr. T-note	$175	1 yr. CP	$135
15 yr. muni	$165	5 yr. note	$160

NOTES: All securities are selling at par (equal to book value). The 2-year Treasury notes yield 5%; the 15-year municipal bonds yield 9%; the 1-year commercial paper issue pays 4.5%; and the 5-year notes pay 8%. Assume that all instruments have annual coupon payments.

   a. What is the value of M. Match, Inc.'s equity?

   b. What is the weighted average maturity of the FI's assets?

   c. What is the weighted average maturity of the FI's liabilities?

   d. What is the FI's maturity gap?

   e. What does your answer to part *d* imply about the interest rate risk exposure of M. Match, Inc?

   f. Calculate the values of all four securities on M. Match, Inc.'s balance sheet if all interest rates increase by 2%.

   g. What is the impact on the equity of M. Match, Inc.? Calculate the percentage change in the value of equity.

   h. What would be the impact on M. Match, Inc.'s interest rate risk exposure if its liabilities paid interest semiannually as opposed to annually?

17. An insurance company issues a $100,000 1-year note paying 7% annually in order to finance the acquisition of a $100,000 1-year corporate loan paying 9% semiannually. (The loan contract requires the corporate borrower to pay half of the principal at the end of six months and the rest at the end of the year.)

   a. What is the insurance company's maturity gap? What does the maturity model state about interest rate risk exposure given the insurance company's maturity gap?

   b. Immediately after the insurance company makes these investments, all interest rates increase by 3%. What is the impact on the asset (corporate loan) cash flows? What is the impact on the liability (1 year note) cash flows? What is the impact on the insurance company's net interest income?

   c. Assume instead that all interest rates decline by 3% immediately after the insurance company makes the above investments. What is the impact on the asset (corporate loan) cash flows? What is the impact on the liability (1 year note) cash flows? What is the impact on the insurance company's net interest income?

   d. Are the maturity model's conclusions about interest rate risk exposure in part *a* correct? (Use your answer to part *b*.) Why or why not?

6

INTEREST RATE RISK
The Duration Model

Learning Objectives

In this second of three chapters on measuring interest rate risk, we explain the concept of *duration*. You will see that duration and the duration gap are more accurate measures of an FI's interest rate risk exposure than the simple maturity model. You will also learn how the duration model can be used to analyze the interest rate risks of various FIs. The final part of the chapter also discusses some of the problems of applying the duration model to real-world FIs.

Introduction

We begin by presenting the basic arithmetic needed to calculate the duration of an asset or liability. Then, we analyze the economic meaning of the number we calculate for duration. This number, which measures the average life of the asset or liability, also has an *economic* meaning as the interest sensitivity (or interest elasticity) of that asset or liability's value. Next, we show how duration can immunize or protect an FI against interest rate risk. Finally, we examine some problems in applying the duration measure to real-world FIs.

Calculating Duration

Duration is a more complete measure of an asset or liability's interest rate sensitivity than maturity because it takes into account the time of arrival of all cash flows as well as the asset or liability's maturity. Consider the example of the one-year loan at the end of Chapter 5. This loan had a 15 percent interest rate and required repayment of half the $100 in principal at the end of six months and the other half at the end of the year. The promised cash flows (*CF*) received by the bank from the borrower at the end of one-half year and at the end of the year appear in Figure 6–1.

FIGURE 6–1

Promised cash flows on the one-year loan

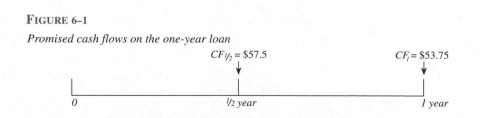

$CF_{1/2} = \$57.5$ $CF_1 = \$53.75$

| 0 | 1/2 year | 1 year |

FIGURE 6–2

PV of the cash-flows from the loan

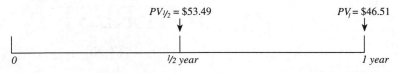

$CF\tfrac{1}{2}$ is the \$50 promised repayment of principal plus the \$7.5 promised interest payment. CF_1 is the promised cash flow at the end of year and is equal to the second \$50 promised principal repayment plus \$3.75 promised interest (\$50 $\times$ $\tfrac{1}{2}$ $\times$ 15%). To compare the relative sizes of these two cash flows, we should put them in the same dimensions. This is because \$1 of principal or interest received at the end of a year is worth less to the bank in terms of the time value of money than \$1 of principal or interest received at the end of six months. Since interest rates are 15 percent per annum, the present values of the two cash flows are:

$$CF_{\frac{1}{2}} = \$57.5 \qquad PV_{\frac{1}{2}} = \$57.5/(1.075) = \$53.49$$

$$CF_1 = \$53.75 \qquad PV_1 = \$53.75/(1.075)^2 = \$46.51$$

$$CF_{\frac{1}{2}} + CF_1 = \$111.25 \qquad PV_{\frac{1}{2}} + PV_1 = \$100.00$$

Note that since $CF\tfrac{1}{2}$, the cash flows received at the end of one-half year, are received earlier they are discounted at $(1 + \tfrac{1}{2}R)$; this is smaller than the discount rate on the cash flow received at the end of the year $(1 + \tfrac{1}{2}R)^2$.[1]

In Figure 6–2 we summarize the *PVs* of the cash flows from the loan.

Technically speaking, duration is the *weighted-average* time to maturity using the relative present values of the cash flows as weights. As Figure 6–2 shows, we receive some cash flows at one-half year and some at one year. In duration analysis, we weight the time at which cash flows are received by the relative importance in present value terms of the cash flows arriving at each point in time. In present value terms, the relative importance of the cash flows arriving at time $t = \tfrac{1}{2}$ year and time $t = 1$ year are as follows:

Time (t)	Weight (x)			
½ year	$X_{\frac{1}{2}} = \dfrac{PV_{\frac{1}{2}}}{PV_{\frac{1}{2}} + PV_1}$	$= \dfrac{53.49}{100.00}$	= .5349	= 53.49%
1 year	$X_1 = \dfrac{PV_1}{PV_{\frac{1}{2}} + PV_1}$	$= \dfrac{46.51}{100.00}$	= .4651	= 46.51%
			1.0	100%

In present value terms, 53.49 percent of cash flows on the loan are received at the end of six months ($t = \tfrac{1}{2}$) and 46.51 percent at the end of the year ($t = 1$). By definition, the sum of the (present value) cash flow weights must equal one:

---

[1] We use here the Treasury formula for calculating the present values of cash flows on a security that pays cash flows semiannually.

FIGURE 6–3

PV of the cash flows of the deposit

$$X_{\frac{1}{2}} + X_1 = 1$$
$$.5349 + .4651 = 1$$

We can now calculate the duration (D) or the average life of the loan using the present value of its cash flows as weights:

$$D_L = X_{\frac{1}{2}}\left(\frac{1}{2}\right) + X_1(1)$$
$$= .5349\left(\frac{1}{2}\right) + .4651(1) = .7326 \text{ years}$$

Thus, while the maturity of the loan is one year, its duration or average life in a cash flow sense is only .7326 years. The duration is less than maturity because in present value terms 53.49 percent of the cash flows are received at the end of one-half year. Note that duration is measured in years since we weight the time (t) at which cash flows are received by the relative present value importance of cash flows ($X_{\frac{1}{2}}, X_1$, etc.)

To learn why the bank was still exposed to interest rate risk while matching maturities under the maturity model in the example at the end of Chapter 5, we next calculate the duration of the one-year, 15 percent interest certificate of deposit. The bank promises to make all cash payments to depositors at the end of the year; that is, $CF_1 = \$115$, which is the promised principal and interest repayment to the depositor. Since weights are calculated in present value terms:[2]

$$CF_1 = \$115, PV_1 = \$115/1.15 = \$100$$

We show this in Figure 6–3. Because all cash flows are received at the end of the year, $X_1 = PV_1/PV_1 = 1$, the duration of the deposit is

$$D_D = X_1 \cdot (1)$$
$$D_D = 1 \cdot (1) = 1 \text{ year}$$

Thus, only when all cash flows are paid or received at the end of the period with no intervening cash flows does duration equal maturity. This example also illustrates that while the maturity gap between the deposit and the loan is zero, the duration gap is positive:

$$M_D - M_L = 1 - 1 = 0$$
$$D_D - D_L = 1 - .7326 = .2674 \text{ years}$$

As will become clearer, to measure and to hedge interest rate risk the bank needs to manage its duration gap, rather than its maturity gap.

---

[2]Since the CD is like an annual coupon bond, the annual discount rate is $1/1 + R = 1/1.15$.

A General Formula for Duration

You can calculate the duration for any fixed income security using this general formula:[3]

$$D = \frac{\displaystyle\sum_{t=1}^{N} CF_t \cdot DF_t \cdot t}{\displaystyle\sum_{t=1}^{N} CF_t \cdot DF_t} = \frac{\displaystyle\sum_{t=1}^{N} PV_t \cdot t}{\displaystyle\sum_{t=1}^{N} PV_t}$$

where

CF_t = Cash flow received on the security at end of period t

N = The last period in which the cash flow is received

DF_t = The discount factor = $1/(1 + R)^t$, where R is the yield or current level of interest rates in the market

$\displaystyle\sum_{t=1}^{N}$ = summation sign for addition of all terms from $t = 1$ to $t = N$

PV_t = The present value of the cash flow at the end of period t which equals $CF_t \times DF_t$

To help you fully understand this formula, we look at some examples next.

The Duration of a Six-Year Eurobond

Eurobonds pay coupons *annually*. Suppose the annual coupon is 8 percent, the face value of the bond is $1,000, and the current yield to maturity (R) is also 8 percent. We show the calculation of its duration in Table 6–1.

The Duration of a Two-Year U.S. Treasury Bond

U.S. Treasury bonds pay coupon interest semiannually. Suppose the annual coupon

TABLE 6–1   The Duration of a Six-Year Eurobond with 8 Percent Coupon and Yield

t	CF_t	DF_t	$CF_t \times DF_t$	$CF_t \times DF_t \times t$
1	80	0.9259	74.07	74.07
2	80	0.8573	68.59	137.18
3	80	0.7938	63.51	190.53
4	80	0.7350	58.80	235.20
5	80	0.6806	54.45	272.25
6	1,080	0.6302	680.58	4,083.48
			1,000.00	4,992.71

$$D = \frac{4,992.71}{1,000} = 4.993 \text{ years}$$

---

[3]In the following material, a number of useful examples and formulas were suggested by G. Hawawini of INSEAD. For more discussion of the duration model and a number of those examples, see G. Hawawini, "Controlling the Interest Rate Risk of Bonds: An Introduction to Duration Analysis and Immunization Strategies," *Finanzmarket and Portfolio Management* 1, 1986–87, pp. 8–18.

rate is 8 percent, the face value is $1,000, and the annual yield to maturity R is 12 percent. See Table 6–2 for the calculation of the duration of this bond.[4]

Next, we look at two other types of bonds that are useful in understanding duration.

The Duration of a Zero-Coupon Bond

In recent years, the U.S. Treasury has created zero-coupon bonds by stripping individual coupons and the principal from regular Treasury bonds and selling them to investors as separate securities. Elsewhere, such as in the Eurobond markets, corporations have issued discount or zero-coupon bonds directly. U.S. T-bills and commercial paper are usually issued on a discount basis and are further examples of discount bonds. These bonds sell at a discount from face value on issue and pay the face value (e.g., $1,000 on maturity). The current price an investor is willing to pay for such a bond is equal to its present value, or

$$P = \frac{1000}{(1+R)^N}$$

where R is the required annually compounded yield to maturity, N is the number of periods to maturity, and P, the price. Because there are no intervening cash flows such as coupons between issue and maturity, the following must be true:

$$D_B = M_B$$

that is, the duration of a discount instrument equals its maturity.

The Duration of a Consol Bond

Although consol bonds have yet to be issued in the United States, they are of theoretical interest in exploring the differences between maturity and duration. A consol bond is a bond that pays a fixed coupon each year. The novel feature of this bond is that it *never* matures, that is, it is a perpetuity.

TABLE 6–2   **The Duration of a Two-Year U.S. Treasury Bond with 8 Percent Coupon and 12 Percent Yield**

t	CF_t	DF_t	$CF_t \times DF_t$	$CF_t \times DF_t \times t$
½	40	.9434	37.74	18.87
1	40	.8900	35.60	35.60
1½	40	.8396	33.58	50.37
2	1040	.7921	823.78	1,647.56
			930.70	1,752.4

$$D = \frac{1752.4}{930.70} = 1.88 \text{ years}$$

---

[4]Here we use the Treasury formula for discounting bonds with semiannual coupons: $(1 + \tfrac{1}{2}R)^x$ where x is the number of semiannual coupon payments. Thus, at $t = \frac{1}{2}$, the discount rate is (1.06), at $t = 1$ the discount rate is $(1.06)^2$, and so on.

$$M_c = \infty$$

In fact, consol bonds that were issued by the British government in the 1890s to finance the Boer Wars in South Africa are still outstanding. However, while its maturity is theoretically infinity, the formula for the duration of a consol bond is[5]

$$D_c = 1 + \frac{1}{R}$$

where R is the required yield to maturity. Suppose the yield curve implies $R = 5$ percent, then the duration of the consol bond would be:

$$D_c = 1 + \frac{1}{.05} = 21$$

Thus, while maturity is infinite, duration is finite. Moreover, as interest rates rise, the duration of the consol bond falls. For example, consider the 1979–82 period when some yields rose to around 20 percent on long-term government bonds, then

$$D_c = 1 + \frac{1}{.2} = 6 \text{ years}$$

Concept Questions

1. Calculate the duration of a one-year, 8 percent coupon, 10 percent yield bond that pays coupons quarterly.
2. Why were Treasury strips (discount bonds) introduced in the early 1980s?

Features of Duration

From the preceding examples, we derive three important features of duration relating to the maturity, yield, and coupon interest of the security being analyzed.

Duration and Maturity

Duration *increases* with the maturity of a fixed-income asset or liability, but at a *decreasing* rate,

$$\frac{\partial D}{\partial M} > 0 \quad \frac{\partial D^2}{\partial^2 M} < 0$$

To see this, look at Figure 6–4, where we plot duration against maturity for a three year, six year, and consol bond using the *same yield of 8 percent* for all three and assuming an annual coupon of 8 percent on each bond.

---

[5]For reasons of space, we do not provide formal proof here. Interested readers might refer to Hawawini, "Controlling the Interest Rate Risk."

FIGURE 6–4

Duration versus maturity

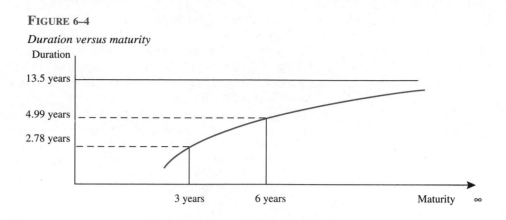

Duration and Yield

Duration decreases as yield increases:

$$\frac{\partial D}{\partial R} < 0$$

To prove this, consider the consol bond: When $R = 8$ percent, as we show in Figure 6–4, D = 13.5 years. If R increased to 9 percent, then $D = 12.11$ years. This makes sense intuitively because higher yields discount later cash flows more heavily and the relative importance, or weights, of those later cash flows decline when compared to earlier cash flows on an asset or liability.

Duration and Coupon Interest

The higher the coupon or promised interest payment on the security, the lower its duration.

$$\frac{\partial D}{\partial C} < 0$$

This is due to the fact that the larger the coupons or promised interest payments, the quicker cash flows are received by investors and the higher the present value weights of those cash flows in the duration calculation.

Concept Questions

1. Which has the longest duration, a 30-year, 8 percent zero-coupon or discount bond, or an 8 percent infinite maturity consol bond?
2. Do high coupon bonds have high or low durations?

The Economic Meaning of Duration

So far we have calculated duration for a number of different fixed-income assets and liabilities. Now we are ready to make the direct link between the number measured in years we call duration and the interest rate sensitivity of an asset or liability, or of an FI's entire portfolio.

Duration is a *direct* measure of the interest rate sensitivity or elasticity of an asset or liability. In other words, the larger the numerical value of D that is calculated for an asset or liability, the more sensitive the price of that asset or liability is to changes or shocks in interest rates.

Consider the following equation showing that the current price of a bond is equal to the present value of the coupons and principal payment on the bond, where

P = Price on the bond
C = Coupon (annual)
R = Yield to maturity
N = Number of periods to maturity
F = Face value of bond

$$P = \frac{C}{(1+R)} + \frac{C}{(1+R)^2} + ... + \frac{C+F}{(1+R)^N} \tag{1}$$

We want to find out how the price of the bond (P) changes when yields (R) rise. We know that bond prices fall, but we want to derive a direct measure of the size of this fall (i.e., its degree of price sensitivity).

Taking the derivative of the bond's price (P) with respect to the yield to maturity (R), we get:

$$\frac{dP}{dR} = \frac{-C}{(1+R)^2} + \frac{-2C}{(1+R)^3} + ... + \frac{-N(C+F)}{(1+R)^{N+1}} \tag{2}$$

By rearranging, we get:

$$\frac{dP}{dR} = -\frac{1}{1+R}\left[\frac{C}{(1+R)} + \frac{2C}{(1+R)^2} + ... + \frac{N[C+F]}{(1+R)^N}\right] \tag{3}$$

We have shown that duration (D) is the weighted-average time to maturity using the present value of cash flows as weights; that is, by definition:

$$D = \frac{1 \cdot \dfrac{C}{(1+R)} + 2 \cdot \dfrac{C}{(1+R)^2} + ... + N \cdot \dfrac{(C+F)}{(1+R)^N}}{\dfrac{C}{(1+R)} + \dfrac{C}{(1+R)^2} + ... \dfrac{(C+F)}{(1+R)^N}} \tag{4}$$

Since the denominator of the duration equation is simply the price (P) of the bond which is equal to the present value of the cash flows on the bond, then:

$$D = \frac{1 \cdot \dfrac{C}{(1+R)} + 2 \cdot \dfrac{C}{(1+R)^2} + ... + N \cdot \dfrac{C+F}{(1+R)^N}}{P} \tag{5}$$

multiplying both sides of this equation by P, we get

$$P \cdot D = 1 \cdot \frac{C}{(1+R)} + 2 \cdot \frac{C}{(1+R)^2} + ... + N\frac{C+F}{(1+R)^N} \tag{6}$$

The term on the right side of Equation 6 is the same term as that in square-brackets in Equation 3. Substituting Equation 6 into Equation 3, we get:

$$\frac{dP}{dR} = -\frac{1}{1+R}[P \cdot D] \tag{7}$$

By cross-multiplying,

$$\frac{dP}{dR} \cdot \frac{1+R}{P} = -D \tag{8}$$

or, alternatively

$$\frac{\dfrac{dP}{P}}{\dfrac{dR}{(1+R)}} = -D \tag{9}$$

The economic interpretation of Equations 8 and 9 is that the number D is the *interest-elasticity* or sensitivity of the security's price to small interest rate changes. That is, it describes the percentage price fall of a bond (dP/P) for any given (present value) increase in required interest rates or yields ($dR/1 + R$).

Equations 8 and 9 can be rearranged in another useful way for interpretation regarding interest sensitivity:

$$\frac{dP}{P} = -D\left(\frac{dR}{1+R}\right) \tag{10}$$

Equation 10 and Figure 6–5, its graphic representation, show that for small changes in interest rates, bond prices move *in an inversely proportional* fashion according to the size of D. Next, we use duration to measure the interest sensitivity of an asset or liability.

The Six-Year Eurobond

Consider the example of the six-year Eurobond with an 8 percent coupon and 8 percent yield. We determined in Table 6–1 that its duration was approximately $D = 4.99$ years. Suppose that yields were to rise by one basis point (one hundredth of one percent) from 8 to 8.01 percent, then:

$$\frac{dP}{P} = -(4.99)\left(\frac{.0001}{1.08}\right)$$
$$= -.000462$$
$$\text{or} \quad -0.0462\%$$

FIGURE 6–5

The relationship between price changes and yield changes on a bond

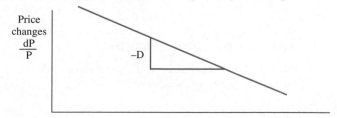

Yield changes (dR / 1+R)

The bond price had been $1,000, which was the present value of a six-year bond with 8 percent coupons and 8 percent yield. However, the duration model predicts the price of the bond would fall to $999.538 after the increase in yield by one basis point.[6]

The Consol Bond

Consider the consol bond with an 8 percent coupon, an 8 percent yield, and a calculated duration of 13.5 years. Thus,

$$\frac{dP}{P} = -(13.5)\left(\frac{.0001}{1.08}\right)$$

$$= -.00125$$

or a -0.125% price fall

As you can see, for any given change in yields, long-duration securities suffer a greater capital loss or receive a greater capital gain than short-duration securities.

SemiAnnual Coupon, Two-Year Maturity, Treasury Bond

For fixed-income assets or liabilities whose interest payments are received semiannually or more frequently than annually, the formula in Equation 10 has to be slightly modified. For semiannual payments:

$$\frac{dP}{P} = -D\left[\frac{dR}{1 + \frac{1}{2}R}\right]$$ (11)

The only difference between (11) and (10) is the introduction of a $\frac{1}{2}$ in the discount rate term $1 + \frac{1}{2}R$ to take into account the semiannual payments of interest.

Recall the two-year T bond with semiannual coupons whose duration we derived in Table 6–2 as 1.88 years when annual yields were 8 percent. A one-basis-point rise in interest rates would have the following predicted effect on its price:

$$\frac{dP}{P} = -1.88\left[\frac{.0001}{1.04}\right]$$

$$= -.00018$$

or a .018 percent price fall.

Concept Questions

1. What is the relationship between the duration of a bond and the interest elasticity of a bond?
2. How would the formula in Equation 11 have to be modified to take into account quarterly coupon payments and monthly coupon payments?

Duration and Immunization

So far, you have learned how to calculate duration and that the duration measure has economic meaning as it indicates the interest sensitivity or elasticity of an asset

---

[6]That is, the price would fall by .0462 percent, or by $0.462.

or liability's value. For FIs, the major relevance of duration is as a measure for managing interest rate risk exposure. Also important is duration's role in allowing the FI to immunize its balance sheet or some subset of that balance sheet against interest rate risk. In the following sections, we consider two examples of how FIs can use the duration measure for immunization purposes. The first is its use by insurance company and pension fund managers to help meet promised cash flow payments to policyholders or beneficiaries at a particular time in the future. The second is its use to immunize or insulate the whole balance sheet against interest rate risk.

Duration and Immunizing Future Payments

Frequently, pension fund and life insurance company managers face the problem of structuring their asset investments so they can pay out a given cash amount to policyholders in some future period. The classic example of this is an insurance policy that pays the holder some lump sum on reaching retirement age. The risk to the life insurance company manager is that interest rates on the funds generated from investing the retiree's premiums could fall. Thus, the target or promised amount could not be met from the accumulated returns on the premiums invested. In effect, the insurance company would be forced to draw down its reserves and net worth to meet its payout commitments. (See Chapter 2 for a discussion of this risk.)

Suppose that we are in 1994 and the insurer has to make a guaranteed payment to an investor in five years time, 1999. For simplicity, we assume that this target guaranteed payment is $1,469, a lump-sum policy payout on retirement. Of course, realistically this payment would be much larger, but the underlying principles of the example do not change by scaling up or down the payout amount.

To immunize or protect itself against interest rate risk, the insurer needs to determine which investments would produce a cash flow of exactly $1,469 in five years' time regardless of what happens to interest rates in the immediate future. The FI investing either in a five-year maturity and duration zero-coupon bond or a coupon bond with a five-year duration, would produce a $1,469 cash flow in five years, no matter what happens to interest rates in the immediate future. Next, we consider the two strategies: buying five-year deep discount bonds and buying five-year duration coupon bonds.

Buy Five-Year Maturity Discount Bonds. Given a $1,000 face value, an 8 percent yield, and assuming annual compounding the current price per five-year discount bond would be:

$$P = 680.58 = \frac{1000}{(1.08)^5}$$

That is, a price of $680.58 per bond. If the insurer bought 1.469 of these bonds at a total cost of $1,000 in 1994, these investments would produce exactly $1,469 on maturity in five years ($1,000 × $(1.08)^5$ = $1,469). The reason is that the duration of this bond portfolio exactly matches the target horizon for the insurer's future liability to its policyholders. Intuitively, since no intervening cash flows or coupons are paid by the issuer of the zero-coupon discount bonds, future changes in interest rates have no reinvestment income effect. Thus, the return would be unaffected by intervening interest rate changes.

Suppose no five-year discount bonds exist. Then the portfolio manager may seek to invest in appropriate duration coupon bonds to hedge interest rate risk. In this example, the appropriate investment would be in five-year duration coupon-bearing bonds.

Buy a Five-Year Duration Coupon Bond. We demonstrated earlier in Table 6–1 that a six-year maturity Eurobond paying 8 percent coupons with an 8 percent yield to maturity had a duration of 4.99 years, or approximately 5 years. By buying this six-year maturity/five-year duration bond in 1994 and holding it for five years until 1999, the term exactly matches the target horizon of the insurer. The cash flows generated at the end of five years would be $1,469 whether interest rates stay at 8 percent or instantaneously rise to 9 percent or fall to 7 percent. Thus, buying a coupon bond whose duration exactly matches the time horizon of the insurer also immunizes the insurer against interest rate changes.

Interest Rates Remain at 8 Percent. The cash flows received by the insurer on the bond if interest rates stay at 8 percent throughout the five years would be:

1. Coupons, 5 × $80	$ 400
2. Reinvestment income	69
3. Proceeds from sale of bond at end of the fifth year	1,000
	$1,469

This is how to calculate each of the three components of the insurer's income from the bond investment:

1. *Coupons.* The $400 from coupons is simply the annual coupon of $80 received in each of the five years.
2. *Reinvestment income.* Because the coupons are received annually, they can be reinvested at 8 percent as they are received generating an additional cash flow of $69.[7]
3. *Bond sale proceeds.* The proceeds from the sale are calculated by recognizing that the six-year bond has just one year left to maturity when it is sold by the insurance company at the end of the fifth year. That is,

----

[7] Receiving annual coupons of $80 is equivalent to receiving an annuity of $80. There are tables and formulas that help us calculate the value of $1 received each year over a given number of years and that can be reinvested at a given interest rate. The appropriate terminal value of receiving $1 a year for five years and reinvesting at 8 percent can be determined from the Future Value of an Annuity Factor (FVAF) Tables (see appendix at end of book) whose general formula is:

$$FVAF_{n,R} = \left[\frac{(1+R)^n - 1}{R} \right]$$

In our example:

$$FVAF_{5,8\%} = \left[\frac{(1+.08)^5 - 1}{.08} \right] = 5.867$$

Thus, the reinvestment income for $80 of coupons per year is
Reinvestment income = (80 × 5.867) − 400 = 469 − 400 = 69.
Note we take away $400 since we have already counted the simple coupon income (5 × $80).

What fair market price can the insurer expect to get when selling the bond at the end of the fifth year with one year left to maturity? A buyer would be willing to pay the present value of the $1,080—final coupon plus face value—to be received at the end of the one remaining year, or

$$P_5 = \frac{1080}{1.08} = \$1,000$$

Thus, the insurer would be able to sell the one remaining cash flow of $1,080 to be received in the bond's final year, for $1,000.

Next, we show that since this bond has a duration of five years exactly matching the insurer's target period, even if interest rates were to instantaneously fall to 7 percent or rise to 9 percent, the expected cash flows from the bond would still exactly sum to $1,469. That is, the coupons + reinvestment income + principal at the end of the fifth year would be immunized. In other words, the cash flows on the bond would be protected against interest rate changes. In the following sections are examples of rates falling from 8 to 7 percent and rising from 8 to 9 percent.

Interest Rates Fall to 7 Percent. In this example with falling interest rates, the cash flows over the five years would be:

1. Coupons, 5 × $80 $ 400
2. Reinvestment income   60
3. Bond sale proceeds   1,009
                             ─────────
                             $1,469

As you can see, the total proceeds over the five years are unchanged from when interest rates were 8 percent. To see why this occurs, consider what happens to the three parts of the cash flow when rates fall to 7 percent:

1. *Coupons.* Are unchanged since the insurer still gets five annual coupons of $80 = $400.
2. *Reinvestment income.* The coupons can now only be reinvested at the lower rate of 7 percent. Reinvestment income is only $60.[8]
3. *Bond sale proceeds.* When the six-year maturity bond is sold at the end of the fifth year with one cash flow of $1,080 remaining, investors would now be willing to pay more:

$$P_5 = \frac{1080}{1.07} = 1,009$$

That is, the bond can be sold for $9 more than when rates were 8 percent. The reason is that investors can only get 7 percent on newly issued bonds while this older bond was issued with a higher coupon of 8 percent.

By comparing reinvestment income with bond sale proceeds, you can see that the fall in rates has produced a *gain* on the bond sale proceeds of $9. This exactly offsets

---

[8] $FVAF_{5,7\%} = \left[\dfrac{(1+.07)^5 - 1}{.07} \right] = 5.751$

Reinvestment income = (5.751 × 80) − 400 = 60, which is $9 less than when rates were 8 percent.

the loss of reinvestment income of $9 due to reinvesting at a lower interest rate. Thus, total cash flows remain unchanged at $1,469.

Interest Rates Rise to 9 Percent. In this example with rising interest rates, the proceeds from the bond investment are

    1. Coupons, 5 × $80 $ 400
    2. Reinvestment income [(5.985 × 80) − 400]   78
    3. Bond sale proceeds (1080/1.09)   991
                                                      $1,469

Notice that the rise in interest rates from 8 to 9 percent leaves the final terminal cash flow unaffected at $1,469. The rise in rates has generated $9 extra reinvestment income ($78 − $69), but the price at which the bond can be sold at the end of the fifth year has declined from $1,000 to $991 equal to a capital loss of $9. Thus, the gain in reinvestment income is exactly offset by the capital loss on the sale of the bond.

    This example demonstrates that matching the duration of a coupon bond—or any fixed-interest rate instrument such as a loan or mortgage—to the FI's target or investment horizon *immunizes* it against instantaneous shocks to interest rates. The gains or losses on reinvestment income that result from an interest rate change are exactly offset by losses or gains from the bond proceeds on sale.

Concept Question

    1. Would the FI in the preceding example been immunized if rates had fallen to (*a*) 6 percent and (*b*) risen to 10 percent?

Immunizing the Whole Balance Sheet of an FI

So far, we have looked at the durations of individual instruments and how we can select individual fixed-income securities to protect FIs such as life insurance companies and pensions funds with certain precommitted liabilities such as future pension plan payouts. The duration model can also evaluate the overall interest rate exposure for an FI; that is, measure the *duration gap* on its balance sheet.

The Duration Gap for a Financial Institution. To estimate the overall duration gap, we determine first the duration of an FI's asset portfolio and the duration of its liability portfolio. These can be calculated as

$$D_A = X_{1A} D_1^A + X_{2A} D_2^A + \ldots + X_{nA} D_n^A$$

and,

$$D_L = X_{1L} D_1^L + X_{2L} D_2^L + \ldots + X_{nL} D_n^L$$

where

$$X_{1j} + X_{2j} \ldots + X_{nj} = 1 \text{ and } j = A, L$$

    The *X*'s in the equation are the proportions of each asset or liability held in the respective asset and liability portfolios. Thus, if new 30-year Treasury bonds were 1 percent of a life insurer's portfolio and D_1^A the duration of those bonds was equal to 9.25 years, then $X_{1A} D_1^A = .01(9.25) = 0.0925$. More simply, the duration of a portfolio of assets or liabilities is a market value weighted-average of the individual durations of the assets or liabilities on the FI's balance sheet.[9]

Consider an FI's simplified market value balance sheet:

Assets	Liabilities
$A = 100$	$L = 90$
	$E = 10$
100	100

From the balance sheet:

$$A = L + E$$

$$\text{and } \Delta A = \Delta L + \Delta E$$

$$\text{or, } \Delta E = \Delta A - \Delta L$$

That is, when interest rates change, the change in the FI's net worth is equal to the difference between the change in the market values of assets and liabilities on each side of the balance sheet. This should be familiar from our discussion of the maturity model in Chapter 5. The difference here is that we want to relate the sensitivity of an FI's net worth (ΔE) to its duration mismatch rather than its maturity mismatch. As we have already shown, duration is a more accurate measure of the interest rate sensitivity of an asset or liability than maturity.

Since $\Delta E = \Delta A - \Delta L$, we need to determine how ΔA and ΔL—the changes in the market values of assets and liabilities on the balance sheet—are related to duration.[10]

From the duration model:

$$\frac{\Delta A}{A} = -D_A \frac{\Delta R}{(1 + R)} \tag{12}$$

$$\frac{\Delta L}{L} = -D_L \frac{\Delta R}{(1 + R)} \tag{13}$$

Here we have simply substituted $\Delta A/A$ or $\Delta L/L$, the proportional change in the market values of assets or liabilities, to replace $\Delta P/P$, the change in any single bond's price and D_A or D_L, the duration of the FI's asset or liability portfolio, to replace D_i, the duration on any given bond, deposit, or loan. The term $\Delta R/(1 + R)$ reflects the shock to interest rates as before. These equations can be rewritten as:

$$\Delta A = -D_A \cdot A \cdot \frac{\Delta R}{(1 + R)} \tag{14}$$

---

[9]This derivation of an FI's duration gap closely follows G. Kaufman, "Measuring and Managing Interest Rate Risk: A Primer," Federal Reserve Bank of Chicago, *Economic Perspectives,* 1984, pp. 16–29.

[10]In what follows we use the Δ (change) notation instead of d (derivative notation) to recognize that interest rate changes tend to be discrete rather than infinitesimally small. For example, in real-world financial markets, the smallest observed rate change is usually one basis point or 1/100th of 1 percent.

and

$$\Delta L = -D_L \cdot L \cdot \frac{\Delta R}{(1+R)} \tag{15}$$

Since, $\Delta E = \Delta A - \Delta L$, we can substitute these two expressions into this equation:

$$\Delta E = \left(-D_A \cdot A \cdot \frac{\Delta R}{(1+R)}\right) - \left(-D_L \cdot L \cdot \frac{\Delta R}{(1+R)}\right) \tag{16}$$

Assuming that the level of rates and expected shock to interest rates are the same for both assets and liabilities,[11]

$$\Delta E = \left[-D_A A + D_L L\right]\frac{\Delta R}{(1+R)} \tag{17}$$

or

$$\Delta E = -\left[D_A A - D_L L\right]\frac{\Delta R}{(1+R)} \tag{18}$$

To rearrange the equation in a slightly more intuitive fashion, we multiply and divide both the terms $D_A A$ and $D_L L$ by A (assets):

$$\Delta E = -\left[D_A \frac{A}{A} - D_L \frac{L}{A}\right] \cdot A \cdot \frac{\Delta R}{(1+R)} \tag{19}$$

$$\Delta E = -\left[D_A - D_L k\right] \cdot A \cdot \frac{\Delta R}{(1+R)} \tag{20}$$

Where $k = L/A$ is a measure of the FI's leverage; that is, the amount of borrowed funds or liabilities rather than owners' equity used to fund its asset portfolio. The effect of interest rate changes on the market value of an FI's equity or net worth (ΔE) breaks down into three effects:

1. *The leverage adjusted duration gap* $= [D_A - D_L k]$. This gap is measured in years and reflects the degree of duration mismatch in an FI's balance sheet. Specifically, the larger this gap *in absolute terms,* the more exposed the FI is to interest rate shocks.
2. *The size of the FI.* The term A measures the size of the FI's assets. The larger the scale of the FI, the larger the dollar size of the potential net worth exposure from any given interest rate shock.
3. *The size of the interest rate shock* $= \Delta R/(1 + R)$. The larger the shock, the greater the FI's exposure.

Given this, we express the exposure of the net worth of the FI as $\Delta E = -$ [Adjusted duration gap] $\times$ Asset size $\times$ Interest rate shock.

While interest rate shocks are largely external to the bank and often result from changes in the Federal Reserve's monetary policy (as discussed in the first section of Chapter 5), the size of the duration gap and the size of the FI are under the control of management.

---

[11]This assumption is standard in "Macauley" duration analysis. While restrictive, this assumption can be relaxed. However, if this is done, the duration measure changes as is discussed later in this chapter.

Using an example, the next section explains how a manager can use information on an FI's duration gap to restructure its balance sheet to immunize its stockholders against interest rate risk.

Duration Gap Measurement and Exposure: An Example. Suppose, the FI manager calculates that:

$$D_A = 5 \text{ years}$$
$$D_L = 3 \text{ years}$$

Then the manager learns from an economic forecasting unit that rates are expected to rise from 10 to 11 percent in the immediate future; that is,

$$\Delta R = 1\% = .01$$
$$1 + R = 1.10$$

The FI's initial balance sheet is assumed to be:

Assets ($M)	Liabilities ($M)
A = 100	L = 90
	E = 10
100	100

The FI's manager would calculate the potential loss to equity holders' net worth (E) if the forecast of rising rates proves true, as follows:

$$\Delta E = -\left(D_A - kD_L\right) \cdot A \cdot \frac{\Delta R}{(1+R)}$$

$$= -\left(5 - (.9)(3)\right) \times \$100 \text{ m.} \times \frac{.01}{1.1} = -2.09 \text{ million}$$

The bank could lose $2.09 million in net worth if rates rose by 1 percent. Since the FI started with $10 million, the loss of $2.09 million is almost 21 percent of its initial net worth. The market value balance sheet after the rise in rates by 1 percent would look like this:

Assets ($M)	Liabilities ($M)
A = 95.45	L = 87.54
	E = 7.91
95.45	95.45

Even though the rise in interest rates would not push the FI into economic insolvency, it reduces the FI's net worth-to-assets ratio from 10 (10/100) to 8.29 percent (7.91/95.45). To counter this effect, the manager might reduce the FI's adjusted duration gap. In an extreme case, the gap might be reduced to zero,

$$\Delta E = - [\,0\,] \times A \times \Delta R/(1 + R) = 0$$

To do this, the FI should not directly set $D_A = D_L$ which ignores the fact that the bank's assets (A) do not equal its borrowed liabilities (L), and that k is not equal to 1. To see the importance of factoring in leverage, suppose the manager increased the duration of the FI's liabilities to five years, the same as D_A, then:

$$\Delta E = - [5 - (.9)(5)] \times 100 \text{ m.} \times (.01/1.1) = - \$0.45 \text{ million.}$$

The FI would still be exposed to a loss of \$0.45 million if rates rose by 1 percent. An appropriate strategy would involve changing D_L until:

$$D_A = D_L k = 5 \text{ years}$$
$$\Delta E = -[5 - (.9)5.55] \times 100 \text{ m.} \times (.01/1.1) = 0$$

The appropriate strategy would be for the FI manager to set $D_L = 5.55$ years, or slightly longer than $D_A = 5$ years to compensate for the fact that only 90 percent of assets are funded by borrowed liabilities with the other 10 percent by equity. Note that the FI manager has at least three other ways to reduce the adjusted duration gap to zero:

1. *Reduce D_A.* Reduce D_A from 5 years to 2.7 years (equal to $D_L k$ or 3(.9)) such that:

$$[D_A - kD_L] = [2.7 - (.9)(3)] = 0$$

2. *Reduce D_A and increase D_L.* Shorten the duration of assets and lengthen the duration of liabilities at the same time. One possibility would be to *reduce D_A* to 4 years and to *increase D_L* to 4.44 years such that:

$$[D_A - kD_L] = [4 - (.9)(4.44)] = 0$$

3. *Change k and D_L.* Increase k (leverage) from .9 to .95 and increase D_L from 3 years to 5.26 years, such that:

$$[D_A - kD_L] = [5 - (.95)(5.26)] = 0$$

Concept Question

1. Suppose $D_A = 3$ years, $D_L = 6$ years, $k = .8$, and $A = \$100$ million; what is the effect on owners' net worth if $\Delta R/(1 + R)$ rises by 1 percent?

Immunization and Regulatory Considerations

In the above section we assumed that the FI manager wants to structure the duration of assets and liabilities to immunize the equity or net worth stake (E) of the FI's equity owners from interest rate shocks. However, regulators periodically monitor the solvency or net worth position of FIs. As we discuss in greater detail in Chapter 14 on capital adequacy, regulators set minimum target ratios for a bank's net worth. The simplest is the ratio of bank capital (net worth) to its assets, or

$$\frac{E}{A} = \text{Capital (net worth) ratio}$$

While this target has normally been formulated in book value accounting terms for banks, it is evaluated in a market value context for investment banks. Also, the SEC has long advocated a capital ratio based on market value accounting for U.S. banks.

Suppose that the FI manager is close to the minimum regulatory required E/A ratio (e.g., 4 percent for banks), and wants to immunize against any fall in this ratio should interest rates rise.[12] That is, the immunization target is no longer $\Delta E = 0$ when rates change but $\Delta(E/A) = 0$.

Obviously, immunizing ΔE cannot be the same strategy as immunizing $\Delta(E/A)$ the net worth ratio. As a result, the FI manager has a problem. A portfolio constructed to immunize ΔE would have a different duration match from that required to immunize $\Delta(E/A)$. Or, more simply, the manager could satisfy either the FI's stockholders or the regulators *but not both* simultaneously.

More specifically, when the objective is to immunize ΔE, to set $\Delta E = 0$, the FI manager should structure the balance sheet so that

$$D_A = kD_L$$

By comparison, to immunize the net worth ratio, to set $\Delta(E/A) = 0$, the manager needs to set:

$$D_A = D_L$$

In this scenario, the leverage adjustment effect (k) drops out.[13] If $D_A = 5$, then immunizing the net worth ratio would require setting $D_L = 5$.

Applying the Duration Model to Real-World FI Balance Sheets*

Critics of the duration model have often claimed it is difficult to apply in real-world situations. However, as we show in the following sections, duration measures and immunization strategies are useful in most real-world situations. In fact, the model recently proposed by the Federal Reserve (and the Bank for International Settlements) to monitor bank interest rate risk taking, which we discuss in Chapter 7, is heavily based on the duration model. Next, we look at the various criticisms of the duration model and discuss ways in which a modern FI manager would deal with them in practice.

Duration Matching Can Be Costly*

Critics charge that although in principle an FI manager can change D_A and D_L to better immunize the FI against interest rate risk, restructuring the balance sheet of a large complex FI can be both time-consuming and costly. While this argument may have been true historically, the growth of purchased funds, asset securitization, and loan sales markets have considerably eased the speed and lowered the transaction

---

[12]In actuality, banks face three required minimum capital ratios. The 4 percent rule used in this example is for the leverage ratio (see Chapter 14 for more details).

[13]See Kaufman, "Measuring and Managing Interest Rate Risk: A Primer," for a proof.

costs of major balance sheet restructurings. (See Chapters 21, 22, and 23 for a discussion of these strategies.) Moreover, an FI manager could still manage risk exposure using the duration model by employing techniques other than direct portfolio rebalancing to immunize against interest rate risk. Managers can get many of the same results of direct duration matching by taking positions in the markets for derivative securities, such as futures and forwards (Chapter 18), options, caps, floors, and collars (Chapter 19), and swaps (Chapter 20).

Immunization Is a Dynamic Problem*

Immunization is an aspect of the duration model that is not well understood. Let's go back to the earlier immunization example where an insurer sought to buy bonds providing an accumulated cash flow of $1,469 in five years no matter what happened to interest rates. We showed that buying a six-year maturity, 8 percent coupon bond with a five-year duration would immunize the insurer against an instantaneous change in interest rates. The word *instantaneous* is very important here. This means a change in interest rates immediately after purchasing the bond. However, interest rates can change at any time over the holding period. Further, the duration of a bond changes as time passes; that is, as it approaches maturity or the target horizon date. Not only that, but duration changes at a different rate than real or calendar time.

To see this time effect, consider the initially hedged position where the insurer bought the five-year duration (six-year maturity), 8 percent coupon bond in 1994 to match its cash flow target of $1,469 in 1999. Suppose the FI manager puts the bond in the bottom drawer of a desk and doesn't think about it for a year, believing the insurance company's position is fully hedged. After one year has passed, the manager opens the drawer of the desk and finds the bond. Knowing the target date is now only four years away, the manager calculates the duration of the bond. Imagine the manager's shock upon finding that the same 8 percent coupon bond with an 8 percent yield and only five years left to maturity has a duration of 4.31 years. This means the insurance company is no longer hedged; the 4.31-year duration of this bond portfolio *exceeds* the investment horizon of four years. As a result, the manager has to restructure the bond portfolio to remain immunized. One way to do this would be to sell some of the five-year bonds (4.31-year duration) and buy some bonds of shorter duration so that the overall duration of the investment portfolio is 4 years.

For example, suppose the insurer sold 50 percent of the five-year bond with a 4.31-year duration and invested the proceeds in zero-coupon bonds with a remaining maturity and duration of 3.69 years. Because duration and maturity are the same for discount bonds, the duration of the asset portfolio would be:

$$D_A = [4.31 \times .5] + [3.69 \times .5] = 4 \text{ years}$$

This simple example demonstrates that immunization based on duration is a dynamic strategy. In theory, it requires the portfolio manager to continuously rebalance the portfolio to ensure the duration of the investment portfolio exactly matches the investment horizon (i.e., the duration of liabilities). Because continuous rebalancing may not be easy to do and involves costly transaction fees, most portfolio managers only seek to be approximately dynamically hedged against interest rate changes by rebalancing at discrete intervals such as quarterly.

FIGURE 6–6

Duration versus true relationship

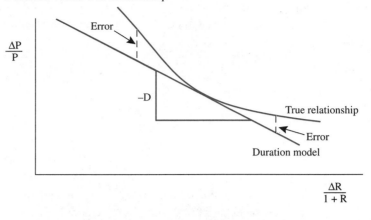

Large Interest Rate Changes and Convexity*

Duration accurately measures the price sensitivity of fixed-income securities for small changes in interest rates of the order of one basis point. But suppose that interest rate shocks are much larger, of the order of 2 percent or 200 basis points? Then, duration becomes a less accurate predictor of how much the prices of securities will change and, therefore, a less accurate measure of interest rate sensitivity. Looking at Figure 6–6, you can see the reason for this. Note first the change in a bond's price due to yield changes according to the duration model; and second, the true relationship, as calculated directly, using the exact present value calculation for bond valuation.

The duration model predicts that the relationship between rate shocks and bond price changes will be proportional to *D* (duration). However, by precisely calculating the true change in bond prices, we would find that for large interest rate increases, duration overpredicts the *fall* in bond prices while for large interest rate decreases it underpredicts the *increase* in bond prices. That is, the duration model predicts symmetric effects for rate increases and decreases on bond prices. As Figure 6–6 shows, in actuality for rate increases the *capital loss effect* tends to be smaller than the *capital gain* effect for rate decreases. This is the result of the bond price-yield relationship exhibiting a property called **convexity** rather than *linearity* as assumed by the basic duration model.

Note that convexity is a desirable feature for an FI manager to capture in a portfolio of assets. Buying a bond or a portfolio of assets exhibiting a lot of convexity or bentness in the price-yield curve relationship is similar to buying partial interest rate risk insurance. Specifically, high convexity means that for equally large changes of interest rates up and down (e.g., plus or minus 2%), the capital gain effect of a rate decrease more than offsets the capital loss effect of a rate increase. As we show later, all fixed-income assets or liabilities exhibit some convexity in their price-yield relationships.[14]

Convexity
The degree of curvature of the price-yield curve around some interest rate level.

---

[14]To be more precise, fixed-income securities without special option features such as callable bonds or mortgage-backed securities. A callable bond tends to exhibit negative convexity (or concavity) as do some mortgage-backed securities.

To see the importance of accounting for the effects of convexity, in assessing the impact of large rate changes on an FI portfolio, consider the six-year Eurobond with an 8 percent coupon and yield. According to Table 6–1, its duration is 4.99 years and its current price P_0 will be $1,000 at a yield of 8 percent,

$$P_0 = \frac{80}{(1.08)} + \frac{80}{(1.08)^2} + \frac{80}{(1.08)^3} + \frac{80}{(1.08)^4} + \frac{80}{(1.08)^5} + \frac{1,080}{(1.08)^6} = \$1,000$$

This is point A in the price-yield curve in Figure 6–7.

If rates rise from 8 to 10 percent, the duration model predicts that the bond price will fall by 9.2457 percent, that is:

$$\frac{\Delta P}{P} = -4.99\left(\frac{.02}{1.08}\right) = -9.2457\%$$

or, from a price of $1,000 to $907.543 (see point B in Figure 6–7). However, calculating the exact change in the bond's price after a rise in yield to 10 percent we find:

$$P_1 = \frac{80}{(1.1)} + \frac{80}{(1.1)^2} + \frac{80}{(1.1)^3} + \frac{80}{(1.1)^4} + \frac{80}{(1.1)^5} + \frac{1,080}{(1.1)^6} = \$912.895$$

This is point C in Figure 6–7. As you can see, the true or actual fall in price is less than the predicted fall by $5.352. This means there is just over a 0.5% error using the duration model. The reason for this is the natural convexity to the price yield curve as yields rise.

Reversing the experiment reveals the duration model would predict that the bond's price would rise by 9.2457 percent if yields fell from 8 to 6 percent, resulting in a predicted price of $1,092.457. (See point D in Figure 6–7.) By comparison, the true or actual change in price can be computed as $1,098.347 by estimating the present value of the bond's coupons and its face value with a 6 percent yield (see point E in Figure 6–7). The duration model has underpredicted the bond price increase by $5.89 or by over 0.5 percent of the true price increase.

FIGURE 6–7

The price-yield curve for the six-year Eurobond

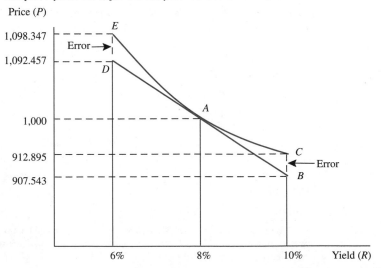

An important question for the FI manager is whether a 0.5 percent error is big enough to be concerned about. This depends on the size of the interest rate change and the size of the portfolio under management. Clearly 0.5 percent of a large number will still be a large number!

So far, we have established these three characteristics of convexity:

1. *Convexity is desirable.* The greater the convexity of a security or a portfolio of securities, the more insurance or interest rate protection an FI manager has against rate increases and the greater the potential gains following interest rate falls.

2. *Convexity and duration.* The larger the interest rate changes and the more convex a fixed-income security or portfolio, the greater the error the FI manager faces in using just duration (and duration matching) to immunize exposure to interest rate shocks.

3. *All fixed-income securities are convex.*[15] To see this, we can take the six-year, 8 percent coupon, 8 percent yield bond and look at two extreme price-yield scenarios. What is the price on the bond if yield falls to zero, and what is its price if yield rises to some very large number, such as infinity?

When $R = 0$:

$$P = \frac{80}{(1+0)} + ... + \frac{1,080}{(1+0)^6} = \$1,480$$

The price is just the simple undiscounted sum of the coupon values and the face value. Since yields can never go below zero, $1,480 is the maximum possible price for the bond.

When $R = \infty$:

$$P = \frac{80}{(1+\infty)} + ... + \frac{1,080}{(1+\infty)^n} \approx 0$$

As the yield goes to infinity, the bond price falls asymptotically toward zero, but by definition a bond's price can never be negative. Thus, zero must be the minimum bond price (see Figure 6–8).

Since convexity is a desirable feature for assets, the FI manager might ask: Can we measure convexity? And, can we incorporate this measurement in the duration model to adjust for or offset the error in prediction due to its presence? The answer to both questions is yes.

Theoretically speaking, duration is the slope of the price-yield curve; and convexity, or curvature, is the change in the slope of the price-yield curve. Consider the total effect of a change in interest rates on a bond's price as being broken into a number of separate effects. The precise mathematical derivation of these separate effects is based on a Taylor series expansion which you probably remember from your math classes. Essentially, the first-order effect (dP/dR) of an interest rate change on the bond's price is the price-yield curve slope effect which is measured by duration. The second-order effect (dP^2/d^2R) measures the change in the slope of the price-yield curve; this is the curvature or convexity effect. There are also third, fourth, and

---

[15]This applies to fixed income securities without special option features such as calls or puts.

FIGURE 6–8

The natural convexity of bonds

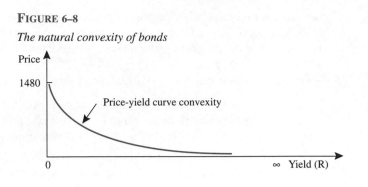

higher order effects from the Taylor series expansion, but for all practical purposes these can be ignored.

We have noted that overlooking the curvature of the price-yield curve may cause errors in predicting the interest sensitivity of our portfolio of assets and liabilities, especially when yields change by large amounts. We can adjust for this by explicitly recognizing the second-order effect of yield changes by measuring the change in the slope of the price-yield curve around a given point. Just as D (duration) measures the slope effect (dP/dR) we introduce a new parameter to measure the curvature effect (dP^2/d^2R) of the price-yield curve.

The resulting equation predicting the change in a security's price ($\Delta P/P$) is

$$\frac{\Delta P}{P} = -D\frac{\Delta R}{(1+R)} + \frac{1}{2}CX(\Delta R)^2 \qquad (21)$$

or

$$\frac{\Delta P}{P} = -MD\,\Delta R + \frac{1}{2}CX(\Delta R)^2 \qquad (22)$$

Modified Duration
Duration divided by 1 + R.

The first term in Equation 21 is the simple duration model that over- or underpredicts price changes for large changes in interest rates, and the second term is the second-order effect of interest rate changes; that is, the convexity or curvature adjustment. In Equation 21, the first term D can be divided by $1 + R$ to produce what practitioners call **modified duration** (*MD*). You can see this in Equation 22. This form is more intuitive because we multiply *MD* by the simple change in R (ΔR) rather than the discounted change in R ($\Delta R/1 + R$). In the convexity term, the number $\frac{1}{2}$ and $(\Delta R)^2$ result from the fact that the convexity effect is the second-order effect of interest rate changes while duration is the first-order effect. The parameter *CX* reflects the degree of curvature in the price-yield curve at the current yield level; that is, the degree to which the *capital gain effect* exceeds the *capital loss effect* for an equal change in yields up or down. At best, the FI manager can only approximate the curvature effect by using a parametric measure of *CX*. Even though calculus is based on infinitesimally small changes, in financial markets the smallest change in yields normally observed is one basis point or a 1/100th of 1 percent change. One possible way to measure *CX* is introduced next.

As just discussed, the convexity effect is the degree to which the capital gain effect more than offsets the capital loss effect for an equal increase and decrease in interest rates at the current interest rate level. In Figure 6–9, we depict yields changing

FIGURE 6–9

Convexity and the price yield curve

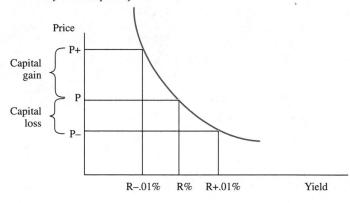

upward by one basis point ($R + .01\%$) and downward by one basis point ($R - .01\%$). Because convexity measures the curvature of the price-yield curve around the rate level R percent, it intuitively measures the degree to which the capital gain effect of a small yield decrease exceeds the capital losses effect of a small yield increase.[16] Definitionally, the CX parameter equals:

$$CX = \text{Scaling Factor} \left(\begin{array}{ccc} \text{The capital loss} & & \text{The capital} \\ \text{from a one-basis-} & & \text{gain from a} \\ \text{point rise in} & + & \text{one-basis-point} \\ \text{yield (negative} & & \text{fall in yield} \\ \text{effect).} & & \text{(positive effect).} \end{array} \right)$$

The sum of the two terms in the brackets reflects the degree to which the capital gain effect exceeds the capital loss effect for a small one-basis-point interest rate change down and up. The scaling factor normalizes this measure to account for a larger 1 percent change in rates. Remember, when interest rates change by a large amount, the convexity effect is important to measure. A commonly used scaling factor is 10^8 so that:[17]

$$CX = 10^8 \left[\frac{\Delta P-}{P} + \frac{\Delta P+}{P} \right]$$

Calculation of CX*

To calculate the convexity of the 8 percent coupon, 8 percent yield, six-year maturity Eurobond which had a price of $1,000:[18]

---

[16]We are trying to approximate, as best we can, the change in the slope of the price-yield curve at R percent. In theory, the changes are infinitesimally small (dR); but in reality, the smallest yield change normally observed is one basis point (ΔR).

[17]This is consistent with the effect of a 1 percent (100 basis points) change in rates.

[18]You can easily check that $999.53785 is the price of the six-year bond when rates are 8.01 percent and $1,000.46243 is the price of the bond when rates fall to 7.99 percent. Since we are dealing in small numbers and convexity is sensitive to the number of decimal places assumed, use at least five decimal places in calculating the capital gain or loss. In fact, the more decimal places used, the greater the accuracy of the CX measure.

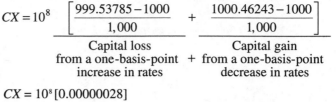

$$CX = 10^8 [0.00000028]$$
$$CX = 28$$

This value for CX can be inserted into the bond price prediction equation with the convexity adjustment:

$$\frac{\Delta P}{P} = -MD \, \Delta R + \frac{1}{2}(28) \, \Delta R^2$$

Assuming a 2 percent increase in R (from 8 to 10 percent),

$$\frac{\Delta P}{P} = -\left(\frac{4.99}{1.08}\right).02 + \frac{1}{2}(28)(.02)^2$$
$$= -.0924 + .0056 = -.0868 \quad \text{or} \quad -8.68\%$$

The simple duration model (the first term) predicts a 2 percent rise in interest rates will cause the bond's price to fall by 9.24 percent. However, for large changes in yields, the duration model overpredicts the price fall. The duration model with the second-order convexity adjustment predicts a price fall of 8.68 percent; it adds back 0.56 percent due to the convexity effect. This is much closer to the true fall in the six-year, 8 percent coupon bond's price if we calculated this using 10 percent to discount the coupon and face value cash flows on the bond. The true value of the bond price fall is 8.71 percent. That is, using the convexity adjustment reduces the error between predicted value and true value to just a few basis points.[19]

In Table 6–3, we calculate various properties of convexity, where

N = Time to maturity
R = Yield to maturity
C = Annual coupon
D = Duration
CX = Convexity

Part 1 of Table 6–3 shows that as the bond's maturity (N) increases so does its convexity (CX). As a result, long-term bonds have more convexity—which is a desirable property—than short-term bonds. This property is similar to that possessed by duration.[20]

Part 2 of Table 6–3 shows that coupon bonds of the same maturity (N) have less convexity than zero-coupon bonds. However, for coupon bonds and discount or zero-coupon bonds of the same duration, part 3 of the table shows the coupon bond has more convexity. We depict the convexity of both in Figure 6–10.

---

[19]In actuality, one might use the third moment of the Taylor series expansion to reduce this small error (8.71 percent versus 8.68 percent) even further. In practice, few people do this.

[20]Note that the CX measure differs according to the level of interest rates. For example, we are measuring CX in Table 6–3 when yields are 8 percent. If yields were 12 percent, the CX number changes. This is intuitively reasonable as the curvature of the price-yield curve differs at each point on the price-yield curve. Note that duration also changes with the level of interest rates.

FIGURE 6–10

Convexity of a coupon versus a discount bond with the same duration

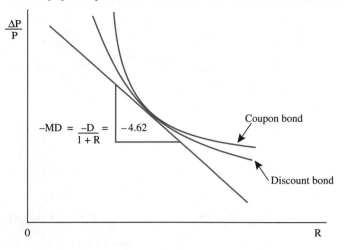

TABLE 6–3   Properties of Convexity

1. Convexity increases with bond maturity			2. Convexity varies with coupon		3. For same duration, zero-coupon bonds less convex than coupon bonds	
Example			Example		Example	
A	B	C	A	B	A	B
$N = 6$	$N = 18$	$N = \infty$	$N = 6$	$N = 6$	$N = 6$	$N = 5$
$R = 8\%$	$R = 8\%$	$R = 8\%$	$R = 8\%$	$R = 8\%$	$R = 8\%$	$R = 8\%$
$C = 8\%$	$C = 8\%$	$C = 8\%$	$C = 8\%$	$C = 0\%$	$C = 8\%$	$C = 0\%$
$D = 5$	$D = 10.12$	$D = 13.5$	$D = 5$	$D = 6$	$D = 5$	$D = 5$
$CX = 28$	$CX = 130$	$CX = 312$	$CX = 28$	$CX = 36$	$CX = 28$	$CX = 25.72$

Finally, before leaving convexity we might look at one important use of the concept by managers of insurance companies, pension funds, and mutual funds. Remembering that convexity is a desirable form of interest rate risk insurance, FI managers could structure an asset portfolio to maximize its desirable effects. As an example, consider a pension fund manager with a 15-year payout horizon. To immunize the risk of interest rate changes, the manager purchases bonds with a 15-year duration. Consider two alternative strategies to achieve this:

Strategy 1: Invest 100 percent of resources in a 15-year deep discount bond with an 8 percent yield.

Strategy 2: Invest 50 percent in the very short-term money market (federal funds) and 50 percent in 30-year deep-discount bonds with an 8 percent yield.

The duration (D) and convexities (CX) of these two asset portfolios are

Strategy 1: $D = 15$, $CX = 206$

FIGURE 6–11

Barbell strategy

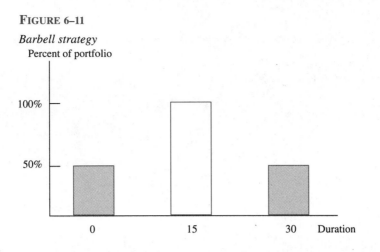

Strategy 2:[21] $D = \frac{1}{2}(0) + \frac{1}{2}(30) = 15$, $CX = \frac{1}{2}(0) + \frac{1}{2}(797) = 398.5$

Strategies 1 and 2 have the same durations, but strategy 2 has a greater convexity. Strategy 2 is often called a barbell portfolio as shown in Figure 6–11 by the shaded bars.[22] Strategy 1 is the unshaded bar. To the extent that the market does not price (or fully price) convexity, the barbell strategy dominates the direct duration matching strategy (number one).[23]

Concept Questions

1. Calculate the convexity of an 8 percent yield zero-coupon bond with a face value of $1,000 and a maturity of 14 years.
2. Calculate the convexity of an 8 percent yield, 8 percent coupon, three-year maturity Eurobond with a face value of $1,000.

The Problem of the Flat Term Structure*

We have been calculating simple or Macauley's duration, which was named after an economist who was among the first to develop the *duration* concept. A key assumption of the simple duration model is that the yield curve or the term structure of interest rates is flat and that when rates change, the yield curve shifts in a parallel fashion. We show this in Figure 6–12.

---

[21]The duration and convexity of one-day federal funds is approximately zero.

[22]This is called a barbell because the weights are equally loaded at the extreme ends of the duration range or bar as in weight-lifting.

[23]In a world in which convexity is priced, the long-term 30-year bond's price would rise to reflect the competition among buyers to include this more convex bond in their barbell asset portfolios. Thus buying bond insurance—in the form of the barbell portfolio—would involve an additional cost to the FI manager. In addition to be hedged, in both a duration and convexity sense, the manager should not choose the convexity of the asset portfolio without seeking to match it to the convexity of its liability portfolio. For further discussion of the convexity "trap" that results when an FI mismatches it's asset and liability convexities see, James H. Gilkeson and Stephen D. Smith, "The Convexity Trap: Pitfalls in Financing Mortgage Portfolios and Related Securities," The Federal Reserve Bank of Atlanta, *Economic Review,* November/December 1992, pp. 14–27.

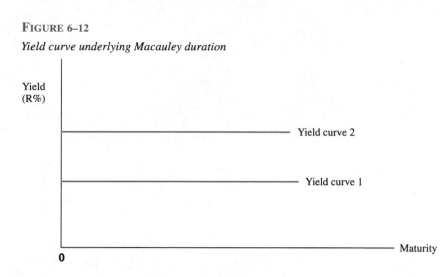

FIGURE 6–12

Yield curve underlying Macauley duration

In the real world, the yield curve can take many shapes and at best may only approximate a flat yield curve. If the yield curve is not flat, using simple duration could be a potential source of error in predicting asset and liability interest rate sensitivities. Many models can deal with this problem. These models differ according to the shapes and shocks to the yield curve which are assumed.

Suppose the yield curve is not flat but shifts in such a manner that the yields on different maturity or discount bonds change in a proportional fashion.[24] Consider calculating the duration of the six-year Eurobond when the yield curve is not flat at 8 percent. Instead, the yield curve looks like that in Figure 6–13.

Suppose that the yield on one-year discount bonds rises. Assume also that the discounted changes in longer maturity discount bond yields are just proportional to the change in the one-year discount bond yield:

$$\frac{\Delta R_1}{1+R_1} = \frac{\Delta R_2}{1+R_2} = \ldots\ldots\ldots = \frac{\Delta R_6}{1+R_6}$$

Given this quite restrictive assumption, we can prove that the appropriate duration measure of the bond—call it D^*—can be derived by discounting the coupons and principal value of the bond by the discount rates or yields on appropriate maturity zero-coupon bonds. Given the discount bond yield curve plotted in Figure 6–13, D^* is calculated in Table 6–4.[25]

Notice that D^* is 4.92 years while simple Macauley duration (with an assumed flat 8 percent yield curve) is 4.99 years. D^* and D differ because by taking into account the upward-sloping yield curve in Figure 6–13, the later cash flows are discounted at higher rates than the flat yield curve assumption underlying Macauley's measure D.

---

[24]We are interested in the yield curve on discount bonds because these yields reflect the time value of money for single payments at different maturity dates. Thus, we can use these yields as discount rates for cash flows on a security to calculate appropriate present values of its cash flows and its duration.

[25]For more details, see Hawawini, "Controlling the Interest Rate Risk;" and G. O. Bierwag, G. G. Kaufman, and A. Toevs, "Duration: Its Development and Use in Bond Portfolio Management," *Financial Analysts Journal* 39, 1983, pp. 15–35.

FIGURE 6–13

Nonflat yield curve

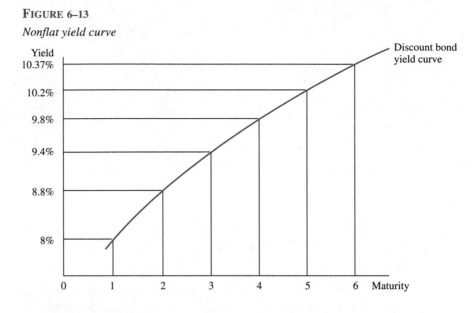

TABLE 6–4   Duration with an Upward Sloping Yield Curve

t	CF	DF	$CF \times DF$	$CF \times DF \times t$
1	80	$\dfrac{1}{(1.08)} = 0.9259$	74.07	74.07
2	80	$\dfrac{1}{(1.088)^2} = 0.8448$	67.58	135.16
3	80	$\dfrac{1}{(1.094)^3} = 0.7637$	61.10	183.3
4	80	$\dfrac{1}{(1.098)^4} = 0.6880$	55.04	220.16
5	80	$\dfrac{1}{(1.102)^5} = 0.6153$	49.22	246.1
6	1,080	$\dfrac{1}{(1.103)^6} = 0.5553$	599.75	3,598.50
			906.76	4,457.29

$$D = \frac{4,457.29}{906.76} = 4.91562$$

With respect to the FI manager's problem, choosing to use D^* instead of D does not change the basic problem except for a concern with the gap between the D^* on assets and leverage-weighted liabilities, that is:

$$D_A^* - k D_L^*$$

However, remember the D^* was calculated under very restrictive assumptions about the yield curve. If we change these assumptions in any way, the measure of D^* changes.[26]

---

[26]A number of authors have identified other nonstandard measures of duration for more complex yield curve shapes and shifts. See, for example, Bierwag, Kaufman, and Toevs, "Duration: Its Development."

TABLE 6–5	**Duration and Rescheduling**			
t	*CF*	*DF*	*CF × DF*	*CF × DF × t*
1	0	.9259	0	0
2	160	.8573	137.17	274.34
3	80	.7938	63.51	190.53
4	80	.7350	58.80	235.21
5	80	.6806	54.45	272.25
6	1,080	.6302	680.58	4,083.48
			994.51	5,055.81

Thus

$$D = \frac{5,055.81}{994.51} = 5.0837 \text{ years}$$

*The Problem of Default Risk**

The models and the duration calculations we have looked at assume that the issuer of bonds or the borrower of a loan pays the promised interest and principal with a probability of one. That is, we assume no default or delay in the payment of cash flows. In the real world, problems with principal and interest payments are common and lead to restructuring and workouts on debt contracts as bankers and bond trustees renegotiate with borrowers. That is, the borrower reschedules or recontracts interest and principal payments rather than defaulting outright. If we view default risk as synonymous with the rescheduling of cash flows to a later date, this is quite easy to deal with in duration models.

Consider the six-year, 8 percent coupon, 8 percent yield Eurobond. Suppose the issuer gets into difficulty and cannot pay the first coupon. Instead, the borrower and FI agree that the unpaid interest can be paid in year two. This alleviates part of the cash flow pressure on the borrower while lengthening the duration of the bond from the FI's perspective (see Table 6–5). The effect of rescheduling of the first interest payment is to increase duration from approximately 5 years to 5.08 years.

More generally, an FI manager unsure of the future cash flows because of future default risk might multiply the promised cash flow (CF_t) by the probability of repayment (p_t) in year t to generate expected cash flows in year t—$E(CF_t)$.[27]

$$E(CF_t) = p_t \times CF_t$$

Chapter 8 suggests a number of ways to generate these repayment probabilities. Once the cash flows have been adjusted for default risk, a duration measure can be directly calculated in the same manner as the Macauley formula (or D^*) except that $E(CF_t)$ replaces CF_t.

Floating Rate Loans and Bonds*

The duration models we have looked at assume that the interest rates on loans or the coupons on bonds are fixed at issue and remain unchanged until maturity. However,

---

[27]The probability of repayment is between 0 and 1.

FIGURE 6–14

Floating rate note

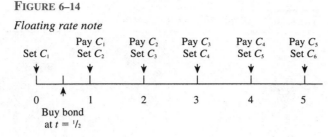

many bonds and loans carry floating interest rates. Examples include loan rates indexed to LIBOR (London Interbank Offered Rate) and adjustable-rate mortgages (ARMs) whose rates can be indexed to Treasury or other securities yields. Moreover, in the 1980s many banks and security firms either issued or underwrote perpetual floating-rate notes (FRNs). These are like consol bonds in that they never mature; unlike consols, their coupons fluctuate with market rates. The FI manager, who wants to analyze overall gap exposure, may ask: What are the durations of such floating-rate securities? The duration of a floating-rate instrument is generally the time interval between the purchase of the security and the time when the next coupon or interest payment is readjusted to reflect current interest rate conditions. We call this the time to repricing of the instrument.

For example, suppose the investor bought a perpetual floating-rate note. These floating rate notes (FRNs) never mature. At the beginning of each year, the FI sets the coupon rate paid at the end of that year. Suppose the investor buys the bond in the middle of the first year ($t = \frac{1}{2}$) rather than at the beginning (see Figure 6–14).

The present value of the bond from time of purchase is[28]

$$P = \frac{C_1}{(1+1/2R)} + \frac{C_2}{(1+1/2R)(1+R)} + \frac{C_3}{(1+1/2R)(1+R)^2} + \frac{C_4}{(1+1/2R)(1+R)^3}$$
$$+ \frac{C_5}{(1+1/2R)(1+R)^4} + \ldots\ldots + \frac{C_\infty}{(1+1/2R)(1+R)^\infty}$$

Note three important aspects of this present value equation: First, the investor has to wait only a half year to get the first coupon payment—hence the discount rate is $(1 + \frac{1}{2}R)$. Second, the investor only knows with certainty the size of the first coupon C_1 which was preset at the beginning of the first coupon period to reflect interest rates at that time. The FI set the first coupon rate six months before the investor bought the bond. Third, the other coupons on the bond, C_2, C_3, C_4, C_5, ...C_∞, are unknown at the time of purchase because they depend on the level of interest rates at the time they are reset—see Figure 6–14.

To derive the duration of the bond, one can rewrite the cash flows at one-half year onward as:

$$P = \frac{C_1}{(1+1/2R)} + \frac{1}{(1+1/2R)}\left[\frac{C_2}{(1+R)} + \frac{C_3}{(1+R)^2} + \frac{C_4}{(1+R)^3} + \frac{C_5}{(1+R)^4} + \ldots + \frac{C_\infty}{(1+R)^{\infty-1}}\right]$$

---

[28]This formula follows the Euro-bond convention that any cash flows received in less than one full coupon period's time are discounted using simple interest. Thus we use $1 + \frac{1}{2}R$ rather than $(1+R)^{1/2}$ for the first coupon's cash-flow in the example above. Also see, Ronald A Grobel, "Understanding the Duration of Floating Rate Notes," Salomon Brothers, New York, 1986.

where P is the present value of the bond (the bond price) at one-half year, the time of purchase.

The term in brackets is the present value or fair price (P_1) of the bond if it were sold at the end of year one, the beginning of the second coupon period. As long as the variable coupons match fluctuations in yields or interest rates, the present value of the cash flows in the square bracket is unaffected by interest rate changes. Thus:

$$P = \frac{C_1}{(1+1/2R)} + \frac{P_1}{(1+1/2R)}$$

Since C_1 is a fixed cash flow preset before the investor bought the bond and P_1 is a fixed cash flow in present value terms, buying this bond is similar to buying two single-payment deep-discount bonds each with a maturity of six months. Because the duration of a deep-discount bond is the same as its maturity, this FRN bond has:

$$D = \text{$^1/_2$ year}$$

As indicated earlier, a half year is exactly the time interval between when the bond was purchased and when it was first repriced.[29]

Demand Deposits and Passbook Savings*

Core Deposits
Deposits that remain in a depository institution for relatively long periods.

Many banks and thrifts hold large amounts of checking and passbook savings account liabilities. This is especially true for smaller banks. The problem in assessing the durations of such claims is that their maturities are open-ended and many demand deposit accounts do not turn over very frequently. Although demand deposits allow holders to demand cash immediately—suggesting a very short maturity—many tend to retain demand deposit balances for lengthy periods. In the parlance of banking, they behave as if they were a bank's **core deposits.** A problem arises because defining the duration of a security requires defining its maturity. Yet, demand deposits have open-ended maturities. One way for an FI manager to get around this problem is to analyze the runoff, or the turn-over characteristics, of the FI's demand and passbook savings account deposits. For example, suppose the manager learned that, on average, each dollar in demand deposit accounts turned over five times a year. This suggests an average turn-over or maturity per dollar of around 73 days.[30]

A second method is to consider demand deposits as bonds that can be instantaneously put back to the bank in return for cash. As instantaneously putable bonds, the duration of demand deposits is approximately zero.

---

[29]Another case might be where an FI manager bought a bond whose coupon floated but repaid fixed principal (many loans are priced like this). Calculating the duration on this bond or loan is straightforward: First, we have to think of it as two bonds: a floating rate bond that pays a variable coupon (C) every year and a deep-discount bond that pays a fixed amount (F) on maturity. The duration of the first bond is the time between purchase and the first-coupon reset date: $D = \text{$^1/_2$ year}$ as in the preceding example. While the duration of the deep-discount bond equals its maturity, $D =$ three years for a three-year bond. The duration of the bond as a whole is the weighted average of a half year and three years where the weights (w_i) reflect the present values of respectively the coupon cash flows and face value cash flow to the present value of the total cash flows (the sum of the two present values). Thus:

$$D = w_i (\text{$^1/_2$}) + (1 - w_i)(3).$$

[30]That is, 365 days/5 = 73 days.

A third approach is more directly in line with the idea of duration as a measure of interest rate sensitivity. It looks at the withdrawal sensitivity of demand deposits ($\Delta DD/DD$) to interest rate changes (ΔR). Because demand deposits and to a lesser extent passbook savings deposits pay either low explicit or **implicit interest**—where implicit interest takes forms such as subsidized checking fees—there tends to be enhanced withdrawals and switching into higher yielding instruments as rates rise. You can use a number of quantitative techniques to test this sensitivity including linear and nonlinear time series regression analysis.[31]

Implicit Interest
Payment of interest in kind such as through subsidized check clearing services.

Concept Questions

1. What is the effect of an upward sloping yield curve on the measurement of duration?
2. How do you measure the duration of a perpetual floating-rate note?
3. What are three ways you might figure out the duration of a demand deposit?

---

[31]Such analysis might employ ($\Delta DD/DD$) as the dependent variable and interest changes as the independent variable in a time series regression. For a very sophisticated model along these lines see "The OTS Market Value Model," OTS, Washington, D.C., 1992, pp. 5.T.-1 to 5.T.-4.

Summary

This chapter has analyzed the duration model approach to measuring interest rate risk. The duration model is superior to the simple maturity model in that it incorporates the timing of cash flows as well as maturity effects into a simple measure of interest rate risk. The duration measure could be used to immunize a particular liability as well as the whole FI balance sheet. We also identified a number of potential problems in applying the duration model in real-world scenarios. However, the duration model is fairly robust and can deal with a large number of real-world complexities.

In the next chapter we discuss how the Federal Reserve proposes to use duration analysis to examine the risk exposure of U.S. commercial banks. This follows an analysis of the current model used by U.S. bank regulators, the repricing or funding gap model. The key difference between the repricing model and the duration and maturity models is that the repricing model is firmly based on book value accounting principles while the maturity and duration models are based on market value accounting principles.

Questions and Problems

1. What is the price of a newly auctioned five-year Treasury note with a coupon of 7 percent and a yield of 7.05 percent? (Hint: All Treasury notes and bonds pay interest semiannually.)

2. *a.* What are all of the promised cash flows on a $1,000 1 year loan yielding 10 percent p.a. that pays interest and principle quarterly?
   b. What is the present value of the loan if interest rates are 10 percent p.a.?
   c. What is the present value of the loan if interest rates are 8 percent p.a.?

3. Calculate the duration of the loan in question 2 assuming yields of both 10 percent and 8 percent p.a.

4. Calculate the impact of a 75-basis-point increase in interest rates on the following securities' prices using duration, convexity, and the exact solution:
   a. Four-year, 6 percent annual coupon note selling at par.
   b. Four-year, 6 percent annual coupon note selling at $94.976 per $100 face value.
   c. Six-year, 3 percent annual coupon bond selling at par.
   d. Six-year, 12 percent annual coupon bond selling at par.

5. Calculate durations of the following securities:
   a. Two-year, 6 percent quarterly coupon selling at par.

b. Three-year, 12 percent annual coupon selling at $90 per $100 face value.

c. Four-year, 8 percent annual coupon selling at par.

6. Calculate the duration of a two-year Euro-note with $100,000 par value and an annual coupon rate of 10 percent if today's yield to maturity is 11.5 percent. What would the duration be if today's yield was 5.5 percent? (Hint: Interest is to be paid annually.)

7. a. Use duration to calculate the approximate price change if interest rates increase by 10 basis points for the notes in question 6.

b. Use the mechanics of bond valuation to calculate the exact price change if interest rates increase by 10 basis points for the notes in question 6.

c. Why are your answers for parts a and b different?

8. How would the incorporation of convexity change your answer to question 7a?

9. a. What is the duration of a consol bond with a required yield to maturity of 7 percent p.a.? 3 percent p.a.? 12 percent p.a.?

b. What can you conclude from your answers to part a?

10. a. Calculate the duration of a five-year Treasury bond with a 10 percent semiannual coupon selling at par.

b. What is the duration of the Treasury bond if the yield to maturity is 14 percent paid annually?

c. What is the duration of the bond if the yield to maturity is 16 percent paid annually?

d. What can you conclude about the relationship between duration and yield to maturity?

11. a. What is the duration of a two-year Treasury note with a 10 percent semiannual coupon selling at par?

b. What is the duration of an 11-year Treasury bond with a 10 percent semiannual coupon selling at par?

c. Use your answers to questions 11a and b and question 10 to draw conclusions about the relationship between duration and time to maturity.

12. a. Calculate the modified duration of the bonds in question 11.

b. If all interest rates increase by 10-basis-points, what is the impact on the price of the 2-year and 11-year Treasury bonds? (That is, $\Delta R/(1+R) = .001$.)

13. a. Calculate the semiannual payment on a $100,000, five-year maturity, 10 percent yield fully amortized loan. (A fully amortized security has no principal payment at maturity. Each coupon payment contains both an interest and principal payment.)

b. What is the duration of the loan in part a?

c. Compare the duration of the amortizing loan with the duration of the five-year Treasury bond in question 10.

14. a. Using the duration approximation, what is the impact of a 200-basis-point increase in annual interest rates on the price of the U.S. Treasury bond in Table 6–2?

Contrast your answer with the exact price using bond valuation.

b. Calculate the convexity of the bond in Table 6–2. What is your estimate of the bond's price after the 200-basis-point increase in yields after you adjust for convexity?

c. Recompute your answers to questions 14a and 14b assuming a 200-basis-point decrease in yields.

15. Calculate the duration gaps of FIs with the following asset and liability portfolios:

a. $250 million in assets with duration of 4.5 years; $500 million in assets with duration of 11 years; $350 million of liabilities with duration of .75 years; $300 million of liabilities with duration of 3 years.

b. $50 million in assets with duration of .5 years; $200 million in assets with duration of 3 years; $150 million of liabilities with duration of .75 years; $50 million of liabilities with duration of 1.5 years.

c. What is the interest rate risk exposure of the FIs in parts a and b?

16. a. Calculate the duration gap of the following position: *Asset:* $1 million invested in 30-year, 10 percent semiannual coupon Treasury bonds selling at par; and *Liability:* $900,000 financing obtained from a 2-year, 7.25 percent semiannual coupon note selling at par.

b. What is the impact on equity values if all interest rates fall 20 basis points? That is,

$$\frac{\Delta R}{1+\frac{R}{2}} = -.002.$$

17. Use the data provided for Gotbucks Bank, Inc., to answer questions a through e.

Gotbucks Bank, Inc. (in millions)

Assets		Liabilities	
Cash	30	Core deposits	20
Federal funds	20	Federal funds	50
Loans (floating)	105	Euro CDs	130
Loans (fixed)	65	Equity	20
	220		220

NOTES TO THE BALANCE SHEET: Currently, the federal funds rate is 8.5 percent. Variable rate loans are priced at 4 percent over LIBOR (currently at 11 percent). Fixed-rate loans are all five-year maturities with 12 percent interest, paid annually. Core deposits are all fixed-rate for two years, at 8 percent paid annually. Euros currently pay 9 percent per annum.

a. What is the duration of Gotbucks Bank's (GBI) fixed-rate loan portfolio if the loans are priced at par?

b. If the average time to repricing of GBI's floating-rate loans (including federal fund assets) is .36 years, what is the duration of the bank's assets? (Note that the duration of cash is zero.)

c. What is the duration of GBI's core deposits if they are priced at par?

d. If the time to repricing of GBI's Euro CD and federal fund liabilities is .401 years, what is the duration of the bank's liabilities?

e. What is GBI's duration gap? What is the bank's interest rate risk exposure? If *all* yields increase by 1 percent, what will be the impact on the market value of GBI's equity? (That is, $\Delta R/(1 + R) = .01$ for all assets and liabilities.)

18. An insurance company issued a $90 million one-year, note at 8 percent add on annual interest (paying one coupon at the end of the year) and used the proceeds to fund a $100 million face value two-year commercial loan at 10 percent annual interest. Immediately after these transactions were (simultaneously) undertaken, all interest rates went up 150 basis points!

    a. What happened to the market value of the insurance company's loan investment? (Get a precise answer.)

    b. What is the duration of the commercial loan investment when it is first issued?

    c. Use the duration approximation to answer question 18*a.*

    d. Use the convexity adjustment to correct your answer to question 18*c.*

    e. What happened to the market value of the insurance company's $90 million liability? (Get a precise answer.)

    f. What is the duration of the insurance company's liability when it is first issued?

    g. Use the duration approximation to answer question *e.*

    h. What is the net effect on the market value of the insurance company's equity? (Get a precise answer.)

    i. How could you have used the insurance company's duration gap to estimate the answer to question 18*h*?

19. Use this balance sheet information to answer the following questions:

Balance Sheet (dollars in thousands)

	Duration (Years)	Amount
T-bills	.5	$ 90
T notes	.9	55
T bonds	*x*	176
Loans	7	2,724
Deposits	1	$2,092
Federal funds	.01	238
Equity		715

NOTES: Treasury bonds are five-year maturities paying 6 percent semiannually and selling at par.

a. What is the duration of the Treasury bond portfolio? (Calculate the value of *x* in the balance sheet.)

b. What is the duration of all the assets?

c. What is the duration of all the liabilities?

d. What is the FI's duration gap? What is the FI's interest rate risk exposure?

e. If the entire yield curve shifted upward 50-basis-points ($\Delta R = .0050$), what is the impact on the FI's market value of equity?

$$\frac{\Delta R}{1 + R} = .0050$$

f. If the entire yield curve shifted downward 25-basis-points ($\Delta R = -.0025$), what is the impact on the FI's market value of equity?

$$\frac{\Delta R}{1 + R} = -.0025$$

7

INTEREST RATE RISK
The Repricing Model

Learning Objectives

In this chapter, you will learn about a third model or way of measuring an FI's gap or exposure to interest rate risk; the repricing model. You will learn the strengths and weaknesses of this model. Once you have an appreciation of these, you can better understand the Federal Reserve's recent proposal to use the duration model, which we discussed in Chapter 6, to monitor the interest rate risk exposures of U.S. commercial banks.

Introduction

In this chapter, we analyze the repricing model, sometimes called the funding gap model. Then, we compare and contrast it to the duration model. Until recently, U.S. bank regulators had generally based their evaluations of bank interest rate risk exposures on the repricing model. As we explain in this chapter, however, this model has some serious weaknesses compared to the duration and market-value based models. Currently, the Federal Reserve has developed a new measure of exposure grounded on the duration model. The FDIC Improvement Act passed at the end of 1991 required the use of a new measure of interest rate exposure by regulators that will be implemented in 1994.[1] We discuss the actual mechanics of this replacement for the repricing model at the end of this chapter.

The Repricing Model

Repricing Gap
The difference between those assets whose interest rates will be repriced or changed over some future period (rate-sensitive assets) and liabilities whose interest rates will be repriced or changed over some future period (rate-sensitive liabilities).

The repricing or funding gap model is essentially a book value accounting cash flow analysis of the **repricing gap** between the interest revenue earned on an FI's assets and the interest paid on its liabilities over some particular period. This contrasts with the market-value-based maturity and duration models discussed in Chapters 5 and 6.

In recent years, the Federal Reserve has required commercial banks to report quarterly on schedule RC–J of the call report, the repricing gaps for assets and liabilities with these maturities:

1. One day
2. > one day to three months
3. > three months to six months

---

[1]Originally, the FDICIA of 1991 required implementation of the new measure by June 19, 1993, at the latest. However, differences among the three bank regulators according to the finer details of the model have delayed implementation until 1994 (see *American Banker,* July 28, 1993, p. 2).

TABLE 7–1 **Repricing Gaps (in millions)**

	Assets	Liabilities	Gaps
1. one day	$ 20	$ 30	$−10
2. one day—three months	30	40	−10
3. three months—six months	70	85	−15
4. six months—12 months	90	70	+20
5. one year—5 years	40	30	+10
6. over five years	10	5	+5
	$260	$260	0

    4. > 6 months to 12 months

    5. > one year to five years

    6. > five years

Under this reporting scheme, a bank calculated the gaps in each maturity bucket (or bin) by looking at the rate sensitivity of each asset and each liability on its balance sheet. Rate sensitivity here means the time to repricing of the asset or liability. More simply, it means how long the FI manager has to wait to change the posted rates on any asset or liability.

In Table 7–1, we show how the assets and liabilities of a bank are categorized into each of the six previously defined buckets according to their time to repricing.

While the cumulative gap over the whole balance sheet must by definition be zero, the advantage of the repricing model lies in its information value and its simplicity in pointing to an FI's *net interest income exposure* (or earnings exposure) to interest rate changes at different maturity buckets.[2]

For example, the one-day gap indicates a negative $10 million difference between assets and liabilities being repriced in one day. Assets and liabilities that are repriced each day are likely to be interbank borrowings on the federal funds or repurchase agreement markets (see Chapter 1). Thus, this gap indicates a rise in the federal funds rate would lower the bank's *net interest income* because the bank has more rate-sensitive liabilities than assets in this bucket. In other words, it has purchased more short-term funds (such as federal funds) than it has lent. Specifically, let

ΔNII_i =   Change in net interest income in the ith bucket.

GAP_i =   The dollar size of the gap between the book value of assets and liabilities in maturity bucket i.

ΔR_i =   The change in the level of interest rates impacting asset and liabilities in the ith bucket; then,

ΔNII_i = $(GAP_i) \Delta R_i = (RSA_i − RSL_i) \Delta R_i$

In this first bucket, if the gap is negative $10 million and federal fund rates rise by 1 percent, the annualized change in the bank's future net interest income is

$$\Delta NII_i = (− \$10M) \times .01 = − \$100,000$$

As you can see, this approach is very simple and intuitive. Remember from Chapters 5 and 6, however, that capital or market value losses occur when rates rise. The capital loss effect that is measured by both the maturity and duration models is

---

[2]If we include equity capital as a long-term (over five years) liability.

TABLE 7–2 Simple Bank Balance Sheet (in millions)

Assets		Liabilities	
1. Short-term consumer loans (one-year maturity)	$ 50	1. Equity capital fixed	$ 20
2. Long-term consumer loans (2-year maturity)	25	2. Demand deposits	40
3. Three-month treasury bills	30	3. Passbook savings	30
4. Six-month Treasury notes	35	4. Three-month CDs	40
5. Three-year Treasury bonds	70	5. Three-month bankers acceptances	20
6. 10-year, fixed-rate mortgages	20	6. Six-month commercial paper	60
7. 30-year, floating-rate mortgages (rate adjusted every nine months)	40	7. One-year time deposits	20
		8. Two-year time deposits	40
	$270		$270

lost here. The reason is that in the book value accounting world of the repricing model, assets and liability values are reported at their *historic* values or costs. Thus, interest rate changes only affect interest income or interest costs; that is, net interest income.[3]

The FI manager can also estimate cumulative gaps (*CGAP*) over various repricing categories or buckets. A common cumulative gap of interest is the one-year repricing gap estimated from Table 7–1 as:

$$CGAP = (-10) + (-10) + (-15) + 20 = -15$$

If ΔR_i is the average rate change affecting assets and liabilities that can be repriced within a year, the cumulative effect on the bank's net interest income is

$$\Delta NII_i = (CGAP)\,\Delta R_i$$
$$= (-15)\,(.01) = -\$150,000$$

We can now look at how an FI manager would calculate the cumulative one-year gap from a balance sheet. Remember that the manager asks: Will or can this asset or liability have its interest rate changed within the next year? If the answer is yes, it is a rate-sensitive asset or liability; if the answer is no, it is not rate sensitive.

Consider the simplified balance sheet facing the FI manager in Table 7–2. Rather than the original maturities, the maturities are those remaining on different assets and liabilities at the time the repricing gap is estimated.

Rate Sensitive Assets

Looking down the asset side of the balance sheet, these four are one-year rate-sensitive assets (RSA):

1. *Short-term consumer loans $50M.* These are repriced at end of the year and just make the one-year cutoff.

---

[3]For example, a 30-year bond purchased 10 years ago when rates were 13 percent would be reported as having the same book (accounting) value as when rates are 7 percent. In a market value world, the gains and losses to asset and liability values would be reflected in the balance sheet as rates change.

2. *Three-month T-bills $30M.* These are repriced on maturity (rollover) every three months.

3. *Six-month T-notes $35M.* These are repriced on maturity (rollover) every six months.

4. *30-Year floating-rate mortgages $40M.* These are repriced (i.e., the mortgage rate is reset) every nine months. Thus, these long-term assets are rate-sensitive assets in the context of the repricing model with a one-year repricing horizon.

Summing these four items produces one-year rate-sensitive assets (RSA) of $155 million.

Rate Sensitive Liabilities

Looking down the liability side of the balance sheet, these four liability items clearly fit the one-year rate or repricing sensitivity test:

1. *Three-month CDs $40M.* These mature in three months and are repriced on rollover.

2. *Three-month bankers acceptances $20M.* The same as applies to CDs.

3. *Six-month commercial paper $60M.* These mature and are repriced every six months.

4. *One-year time deposits $20M.* Get repriced right at the end of the one-year gap horizon.

Summing these four items produces one-year rate-sensitive liabilities (RSL) of $140 million.

Note that demand deposits (or transaction accounts in general) were not included here. We can make strong arguments for and against their inclusion as rate-sensitive liabilities (RSL).

Against Inclusion: The explicit interest rate on demand deposits is zero by regulation. Further, while the rate on transaction accounts such as NOW accounts is positive, the rates paid by banks are very sticky. Moreover, many demand deposits act as **core deposits** for banks, meaning they are a long-term source of funds.

For Inclusion: Even if they pay no explicit interest rates, they do pay implicit interest in the form of the bank not charging fully for checking services through fees. Further, if interest rates rise, individuals draw down (or run off) their demand deposits forcing the bank to replace them with higher-yielding, interest-bearing, rate-sensitive funds. This is most likely to occur when the interest rates on alternative instruments are high. In such an environment, the opportunity cost of holding funds in demand deposit accounts is likely to be larger than in a low-interest-rate environment.

Very similar arguments for and against inclusion can be made for retail passbook savings accounts. Although Federal Reserve Regulation Q ceilings on the maximum rates for these accounts were abolished in March 1986, banks still adjust these rates only infrequently. However, savers tend to withdraw funds from these accounts when rates rise forcing banks into more expensive fund substitutions.[4]

Core Deposits
Those deposits that act as long-term sources of funds for an FI.

---

[4]The Federal Reserve's repricing report has traditionally viewed transaction accounts and passbook savings accounts as rate-*in*sensitive liabilities as we have done in this example.

The four repriced liabilities of $40 + $20 + $60 + $20 sum to $140 million and the four repriced assets of $50 + $30 + $35 + $40 sum to $155 million. Given this, the cumulative one-year repricing gap (*CGAP*) for the bank is:

CGAP = One-year, rate-sensitive assets − one-year rate-sensitive liabilities
CGAP = RSA − RSL
CGAP = $155 − $140 = $15 million

This can also be expressed as a percentage of assets:

$$\frac{CGAP}{A} = \frac{\$15M}{\$270M} = .056 = 5.6\%$$

Expressing the repricing gap in this way is useful since it tells us: (1) the direction of the interest rate exposure (positive or negative CGAP) and (2) the scale of that exposure as indicated by dividing the gap by the asset size of the institution.

In our example, the bank has 5.6 percent more rate-sensitive assets than liabilities in the one year and under bucket. If the rates rise by +1 percent, the *CGAP* would project the annual change in net interest income (Δ*NII*) of the bank as approximately:

$$
\begin{aligned}
\Delta NII &= CGAP \times \Delta R \\
&= (\$15 \text{ million}) \times .01 \\
&= \$150,000
\end{aligned}
$$

Look at the one-year percentage gaps of various large regional and money center banks over a period of interest rate volatility in Table 7–3.

Notice that some banks take quite large interest rate gambles relative to their asset size. For example, the average one-year repricing gap of Bank of America was −11.95 percent between the last quarter of 1983 and the third quarter of 1984. If interest rates had fallen over the period, its net interest income would have risen. However, if rates had risen, Bank of America would have been exposed to significant net interest income losses due to the cost of refinancing its large amount of rate-sensitive liabilities. As it turned out, Bank of America was lucky—or its interest rate forecasts were correct—in that rates actually fell over this period.

You can see from the preceding discussion that the rate sensitivity gap can be a useful tool for managers and regulators in identifying interest rate risk-taking or exposure. Nevertheless, the repricing gap model has a number of serious weaknesses.[5]

Concept Questions

1. Why do some banks have positive gaps while others have negative gaps in Table 7–3?
2. How can banks change the size and direction of their gaps so quickly?

Weaknesses of the Repricing Model

Market Value Effects

As we have discussed earlier, interest rate changes have a market value effect in

---

[5]See Brewer, "Bank Gap Management," for an excellent analysis of the repricing model and its strengths and weaknesses.

TABLE 7–3   **Rate Sensitivity Gap as a Percentage of Total Assets**

| | 1983 | 1984 | | |
	Fourth Quarter	First Quarter	Second Quarter	Third Quarter
Bank of America	−11.4%	−10.5%	−13.8%	−12.1%
Bank of New York	6.6	7.2	5.8	0.8
Bankers Trust Company	3.9	5.9	−1.1	1.7
Chase Manhattan Bank	9.0	−2.7	−3.5	−5.0
Chemical Bank	1.9	2.2	−2.8	−1.0
Citibank	−1.8	−3.1	−2.9	−3.6
First Interstate Bank, CA.	−1.8	−1.8	−0.3	−0.2
First National Bank of Boston	−0.9	−2.5	−1.1	−0.4
First National Bank of Chicago	−4.1	−9.0	−6.9	−8.6
Interfirst Bank, Dallas	−4.2	−5.3	−2.5	−5.0
Irving Trust Company	−4.0	2.5	4.7	2.0
Manufacturers Hanover Trust	5.9	5.4	4.6	2.7
Marine Midland Bank	−1.9	−7.5	−5.8	−4.2
Mellon Bank	−3.2	2.0	4.3	4.2
Morgan Guaranty Trust Co.	−2.4	−1.4	−0.7	−4.0
National Bank of Detroit	0.8	−0.2	0.7	1.0
North Carolina National Bank	−2.1	3.2	2.2	2.2
RepublicBank, Dallas	2.4	3.6	1.2	2.1
Security Pacific National Bank	−4.1	−4.7	−4.6	−6.8
Wells Fargo Bank	−1.9	−5.7	−5.9	−4.9
Average	−0.3	−1.1	−1.4	−1.9

*One-year rate-sensitivity gap.

Rate-sensitive assets include all assets repricing or maturing within one year and comprise loans and leases, debt security, and other interest-bearing assets.

Rate-sensitive liabilities are all those liabilities scheduled to reprice or mature within one year and include domestic time certificates of deposits of $100,000 or more, all other domestic time deposits, total deposits in foreign offices, money market deposit accounts, Super NOWs, and demand notes issued to the U.S. Treasury.

Source: Salomon Brothers, "Bank Analysts Rate Sensitivity Quarterly Handbook First Quarter 1984," July 27, 1984; "Bank Analysts Quarterly Handbook Third Quarter 1984," January 29, 1985; and E. Brewer, "Bank Gap Management and the Use of Financial Futures," Federal Reserve Bank of Chicago, *Economic Perspectives,* March–April 1985.

addition to an income effect on asset and liability values. The repricing model ignores the former—implicitly assuming a book value accounting approach. As such, the repricing gap is only a *partial* measure of the true interest rate exposure of an FI.

Over Aggregation

The problem of defining buckets over a range of maturities ignores information regarding the distribution of assets and liabilities within that bucket. For example, the dollar value of rate-sensitive assets and liabilities within any maturity bucket range may be equal; however, on average, liabilities may be repriced toward the end of the bucket's range while assets may be repriced toward the beginning.

Look at the simple example for the three-month-six-month bucket in Figure 7–1. Note that $50 million more rate-sensitive assets than liabilities are repriced between months three and four, while $50 million more liabilities than assets are repriced between months five and six. The bank in its call report would show a zero repricing gap for the three month–6 month bucket (+50 + (− 50) = 0). But, as you can easily

FIGURE 7–1

The over aggregation problem: The three- to six-month bucket

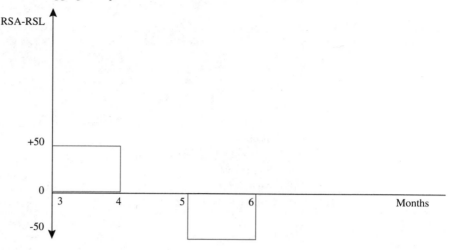

see, the bank's assets and liabilities are *mismatched* within the bucket. Clearly, the shorter the range over which bucket gaps are calculated, the smaller is this problem. If an FI manager calculated one-day bucket gaps out into the future, this would give a very good idea of the net interest income exposure to rate changes. Reportedly, many large banks have internal systems that indicate their repricing gaps on any given day in the future (e.g., 252 days' time, 1,329 days' time, etc.). This suggests that although regulators only require the reporting of repricing gaps over relatively wide maturity bucket ranges, FI managers could set in place internal information systems to report the daily future patterns of such gaps.[6]

The Problem of Runoffs

Runoffs
Periodic cash flow of interest and principal amortization payments on long-term assets such as conventional mortgages that can be reinvested at market rates.

In the simple repricing model in the first section, we assumed that all consumer loans matured in one year or that all conventional mortgages matured in 30 years' time. In reality, the bank continuously originates and retires consumer and mortgage loans as it creates and retires deposits. For example, today some 30-year original maturity mortgages may only have one year left before they mature; that is, they are in their 29th year. In addition, virtually all long-term mortgages pay at least some principal back to the bank each month. As a result, the bank receives a **runoff** cash flow from its conventional mortgage portfolio that can be reinvested at current market rates; that is, this runoff component is rate sensitive. The bank manager can easily

---

[6]Another way to deal with the over-aggregation problem is by adjusting the buckets for the time to interest rate repricing within the bucket. Let RSA and RSL be rate-sensitive assets and liabilities in a bucket, let R denote initial interest rates on an asset or liability, and K new interest rates after repricing. Let t be the proportion of the bucket period for which the asset's (liability's) old interest rate (R) is in effect, and thus, $1-t$ is the proportion of the bucket period in which the new interest rate (K) is in operation:

$$\Delta NII = RSA \left[(1+R_A)^{t_A} \cdot (1+K_A)^{1-t_A} \right] - RSL \left[(1+R_L)^{t_L} \cdot (1+K_L)^{1-t_L} \right]$$

See Brewer, "Bank Gap Management," for more details.

TABLE 7–4 **Runoffs of Different Assets and Liabilities**

	Assets				Liabilities		
Item	$ Amount Runoff in Less Than One Year	$ Amount Runoff in More Than One Year		Item	$ Amount Runoff in Less Than One Year	$ Amount Runoff in More Than One Year
1. Short-term consumer loans	$ 50	—		1. Equity	—	$20
2. Long-term consumer loans	5	$20		2. Demand deposits	$ 30	10
3. Three-month T-bills	30	—		3. Passbook savings	15	15
4. Six-month T-bills	35	—		4. Three-month CDs	40	—
5. Three-year notes	10	60		5. Three-month bankers acceptances	20	—
6. 10-year mortgages	2	18		6. Six-month commercial paper	60	—
7. 30-years floating-rate mortgages	40	—		7. One-year time deposits	20	—
				8. Two-year time deposits	20	20
	$172	$98			$205	$65

deal with this in the repricing model by identifying for each asset and liability item the proportion that will runoff, reprice, or mature within the next year. For example, consider Table 7–4.

Notice in this table that while the original maturity of an asset or liability may be long-term, these assets and liabilities still generate some cash flows that can be reinvested at market rates. Table 7–4 is a more sophisticated measure of the one year repricing gap that takes into account the cash flows received on each asset and liability item during that year. Adjusted for runoffs, the repricing gap is

$$\text{GAP} = \$172 - \$205 = -\$33$$

Note that the runoffs themselves are not independent of interest rate changes. Specifically, when interest rates rise, many people may delay repaying their mortgages (and the principal on those mortgages) causing the runoff amount of $2 in Table 7–4 to be overly optimistic. Similarly, when interest rates fall, people may prepay their fixed-rate mortgages to refinance at a lower interest rate. Then, runoffs could balloon to a number much greater than $2. This sensitivity of runoffs to interest rate changes is a further weakness of the repricing model.

Concept Questions

1. What is meant by a runoff?
2. What are three major problems with the repricing model?

The New Regulatory Approach to Interest Rate Risk Measurement*

Congress passed the Federal Deposit Insurance Corporation Improvement Act (FDICIA) at the end of 1991 in the wake of record numbers of bank and thrift failures. This act required federal regulators to revise capital adequacy standards for banks and to revise the way they measure the interest rate risk exposure of banks. We describe the capital adequacy standards and the role of capital as an insurance fund to protect against risks more fully in Chapter 14. Here, we concentrate on the methodology underlying the Federal Reserve's original proposal for a new method of measuring interest rate risk, and how this improves on the repricing model.

As discussed in the last section, bank regulators have historically relied on the book-value-based repricing model to measure bank interest sensitivity gaps and, thus, their interest rate risk exposure. In contrast, the Federal Reserve's new method is closely related to the duration model discussed in Chapter 6. The methodology may be best understood by going through the Federal Reserve's original example.[7]

Step 1.   Each bank sorts its assets and liabilities into a number of buckets or tranches as it does with the repricing model. Each tranche represents either the maturity date of that asset or liability or the date at which it will be repriced by having its contractual interest rate reset. The six maturity buckets in Table 7–5 are

> Up to three months
>
> Greater than three months up to and including one year
>
> Greater than one year up to and including three years
>
> Greater than three years up to and including seven years
>
> Greater than 7 years up to and including 15 years
>
> Over 15 years

Also included would be off-balance-sheet items such as forwards, futures, options, and swaps, which we discuss in a later chapter. For the moment, recognize that changing interest rates can affect the market values of off-balance-sheet positions as well as on-balance-sheet positions. As we show in Table 7–5, only *net* off-balance-sheet positions (long or bought minus short or sold) are reported in each maturity bucket. For the bank in the example, off-balance-sheet net positions are quite small but this is not always so, as we discuss in Chapter 9.

As you can also see in Table 7–5, for a number of items such as time deposits, the simple total dollar amounts are reported in each bucket. For securities and loans, leases and acceptances, however, the Fed has three categories of assets:

> Amortizing assets (e.g., conventional mortgages)
>
> Nonamortizing assets (e.g., coupon-bearing bonds)
>
> Deep-discount assets (e.g., zero-coupon bonds)

---

[7]For more details see the Federal Reserve Press Release on July 30, 1992. The new regulations were meant to be in place by June 19, 1993. However, because of disputes among the Federal Reserve, the OCC, and the FDIC the new scheme is unlikely to be in effect before the end of 1994. In its proposed rule-making announcement of March 26, 1993, the Federal Reserve adjusted its duration model to allow for convexity. Thus, the final scheme is likely to measure market-value risk exposures allowing for both the duration and convexity of assets and liabilities.

TABLE 7–5 Interest Rate Risk Reporting Schedule (in thousands)

Reporting Institution: *Example Bank*   Reporting Date: *12/31/9X*

		Remaining Time before Maturity or Interest Rate Adjustment					
	Total	*Up to Three Months*	*> 3 Months <= 1 Year*	*> 1 Year <= 3 Years*	*> 3 Years <= 7 Years*	*> 7 Years <= 15 Years*	*Over 15 Years*
I. Interest-Bearing Assets							
1. Cash and balance	$13,200	$13,200					
2. Securities (including trading)							
a. Amortizing	42,169		$1,950	$4,050	$4,332	$12,907	$18,930
b. Nonamortizing	32,099	1,234	4,478	7,533	8,654	5,250	4,950
c. Deep-discount coupons							
d. High-risk mortgage securities	3,000						
3. Federal funds sold and securities purchased for resale	500	500					
4. Loans, leases, and acceptances							
a. Amortizing	37,053	1,536	10,444	10,812	6,442	5,569	2,250
b. Nonamortizing	52,766	10,202	13,510	12,791	6,359	6,854	3,050
5. Total interest bearing assets	180,787	26,672	30,382	35,186	25,787	30,580	29,180
II. All Other Assets	2,463						
III. Total Assets	$183,250						
IV. Interest-Bearing Liabilities							
1. Interest-bearing deposits							
a. NOW accounts	$27,405		$19,183	$8,222			
b. MMDA accounts	26,270		18,389	7,881			
c. Savings	14,398			10,079	$4,319		
d. Time deposits	71,023	$23,083	42,853	5,087			
2. Federal funds purchased and securities sold for repurchase							

	Total	Up to Three Months	> 3 Months < = 1 Year	> 1 Year < = 3 Years	> 3 Years < = 7 Years	> 7 Years < = 15 Years	Over 15 Years
3. Other borrowed funds	127				127		
4. Total interest-bearing liabilities	139,223	$23,083	$80,425	$31,269	$4,446		
V. Noninterest-Bearing Liabilities							
1. Demand deposits	26,611	$4,050	$14,578	$7,983			
2. Other liabilities	860						
VI. Total Liabilities	$166,694						
VII. Equity Capital	$16,556						
VIII. Net Off-Balance-Sheet Positions							
1. Amortizing		$100		($100)			
2. Nonamortizing			$50	$50			

Memoranda	Carrying Value	Market Value	Mkt Value + 100 BPs	Mkt Value – 100 BPs
High-risk securities evaluated:	$2,000	$2,000	$2,160	$1,800
High-risk securities not evaluated:	$1,000			

SOURCE: Federal Reserve Press Release, July 30, 1992, Table 1.

Remember from Chapter 6 that the durations, and thus interest rate sensitivities of securities and loans, can differ significantly. Specifically, a 30-year amortizing mortgage loan usually pays off some principal and interest each payment period, normally monthly. *Amortizing* means some principal is paid off on a regular basis over the life of the loan, rather than in one bullet or balloon payment on maturity. Because its cash flows are spread evenly throughout its life, an amortizing 30-year asset has a relatively short duration of four to six years. This short duration is enhanced if market rates fall and the mortgagee pays off the loan early to refinance the mortgage at a lower rate. By comparison, a conventional 30-year bond, which has 10 percent semiannual coupons and pays a fixed face value on maturity in 30 years, has a duration of a little over 9.5 years when yields are 10 percent. Finally, a 30-year zero-coupon bond has a duration equal to its maturity of 30 years. Clearly, the distribution of a bank's assets among amortizing, nonamortizing, and deep-discount bonds has a major effect on the overall duration of its assets (D_A).[8]

For liabilities, the major distinction is between sources of funds that have market-sensitive interest rates (such as time deposits) and core deposits such as demand deposits, other transaction accounts (NOW accounts), and savings accounts with low or sticky interest rates and open-ended maturities. The Fed's proposed method allows banks to allocate their core deposits in maturity buckets according to their withdrawal or turnover experience subject to the following constraints:

1. Under the assumption that transaction accounts are used by banks to fund their noninterest-bearing reserve balances and currency and coin, an equal amount of demand deposits would be slotted into the shortest time bucket. If demand deposit balances are insufficient, other core deposits would be used.

2. Residual demand deposits, MMDA, and NOW account balances can be distributed across any of the first three time buckets provided that no more than 30 percent of the total of these balances are slotted in the one to three year time bucket.

3. Savings account balances can be distributed across any of the first four time buckets provided that no more than 30 percent of the total of these balances are slotted in the three to seven year time bucket.[9]

Step 2.   The next step is to derive duration-based risk weights to multiply against the dollar values in each maturity bucket. This tells us how much each asset or liability bucket's market value would fall should interest rates rise. The system implies four sets of duration-based risk weights for each bucket, one each for the three types of assets—amortizing, nonamortizing, and deep-discount—and a single risk weight for all types of liabilities. Note the appropriate weights in the middle of Table 7–6 under the heading IRR weights.

To understand the economic meaning of the weights, look at the weights in the greater than three-year less than or equal to seven-year bucket (the fourth column).

---

[8]High-risk mortgage securities are also segregated. In the example, they are equal to $3,000. To assess their interest rate risk they are treated either as deep-discount bonds or are market evaluated, by analyzing the effects of a 100-basis-point change in interest rates on their value (see memoranda item in Table 7–5).

[9]See the Federal Reserve Press Release of July 30, 1992. The March 1993 proposal changed the maximum allotment for demand deposits, MMDA and NOW accounts in the one–three year bucket to 40%. The maximum allotment for savings accounts was changed to 40% for the longest time bucket.

TABLE 7–6 Interest Rate Risk Weighting Calculations (in thousands)

Balance Sheet Summary (from reporting schedule)		Remaining Time before Maturity or Interest Rate Adjustment					
	Total	Up to Three Months	>3 Months <=1 Year	>1 Year <=3 Years	>3 Years <=7 Years	>7 Years <=15 Years	Over 15 Years
1. Total Assets	$183,250						
2. Other assets and high-risk securities evaluated	$4,463						
3. Total interest-bearing assets	$178,787	$26,672	$30,382	$35,186	$25,787	$30,580	$30,180
4. Amortizing assets	$79,222	$1,536	$12,394	$14,862	$10,774	$18,476	$21,180
5. Nonamortizing assets	$98,565	$25,136	$17,988	$20,324	$15,013	$12,104	$8,000
6. Deep-discount assets	$0	$0	$0	$0	$0	$0	$0
7. High-risk securities not evaluated	$1,000						$1,000
8. Total Liabilities	$166,694						
9. Other liabilities and DDAs	$27,471	$4,050	$14,578	$7,983	$4,446		
10. Interest-bearing liabilities	$139,223	$23,083	$80,425	$31,269		$0	$0
11. Net Worth (Gap)	$16,556	($461)	($64,621)	($4,066)	$21,341	$30,580	$30,180
12. Off-Balance-Sheet Positions							
13. Amortizing OBS items		$100	$0	($100)		$0	$0
14. Nonamortizing OBS items		$0	$50	$50		$0	$0

IRR Weights

	Up to Three Months	>3 Months <=1 Year	>1 Year <=3 Years	>3 Years <=7 Years	>7 Years <=15 Years	Over 15 Years
15. Amortizing assets	0.08%	0.25%	0.90%	2.15%	3.20%	4.30%
16. Nonamortizing assets	0.12%	0.55%	1.75%	3.85%	6.60%	8.90%
17. Deep-discount assets	0.12%	0.60%	1.90%	4.75%	10.50%	21.40%
18. Liabilities	0.12%	0.55%	1.80%	4.10%	7.50%	11.00%

Weighted Positions

	Total	Up to Three Months	>3 Months <=1 Year	>1 Year <=3 Years	>3 Years <=7 Years	>7 Years <=15 Years	Over 15 Years
19. Weighted amortizing assets	$1,899.58	$1.23	$30.99	$133.76	$231.64	$591.23	$910.74
20. Weighted nonamortizing assets	$2,573.63	$30.16	$98.93	$355.67	$578.00	$798.86	$712.00
21. Weighted deep-discount assets:	$0.00	$0.00	$0.00	$0.00	$0.00	$0.00	$0.00
22. Weighted high-risk sec. not evaluated	$214.00						$214.00
23. Total risk-weighted assets	$4,687.22	$31.39	$129.92	$489.43	$809.64	$1,390.10	$1,836.74
24. Total risk-weighted liabilities	$1,443.90	$32.56	$522.52	$706.54	$182.29	$0.00	$0.00
25. Risk-weighted off-balance-sheet position	$0.33	$0.08	$0.28	($0.02)	$0.00	$0.00	$0.00
26. High-risk security evaluated (+ 100 BPs)	($160.00)						
27. Net risk-weighted position	$3,083.65	($1.09)	($392.32)	($217.13)	$627.36	$1,390.10	$1,836.74

IRR Measure

Net risk weighted position as a percent of assets = 1.68% = Level of IRR

Source: Federal Reserve Press Release, July 30, 1992, Table 2.

We see from the Table 7–6 that the weights in this bucket are

(line 15) Amortizing assets 2.15%

(line 16) Nonamortizing assets 3.85

(line 17) Deep-discount assets 4.75

(line 18) Liabilities 4.10

Note that the midpoint of this time band is five years, so that the average asset or liability in this bucket should have a remaining maturity of five years.

The duration of a five-year deep-discount bond is

$$D = 5 \text{ years.}$$

However, the weights in Table 7–6 are *modified* durations. A modified duration is simply D divided by 1 plus yield to maturity.[10] Since in the United States interest on bonds is paid twice a year, we derive modified duration as

$$MD = \frac{D}{(1 + R/2)}$$

Now, assuming yields on discount bonds to be 10 percent as they are in the Fed's example:

$$MD = \frac{5}{(1 + (.10/2))} = 4.76$$

If we round to the nearest .05 years, then $MD = 4.75$. We know from the duration model that:

$$\frac{\Delta P}{P} = -MD \cdot \Delta R$$

Suppose interest rates were to rise by 1 percent, which is not an unreasonable number given recent interest rate volatility experience:

$$\frac{\Delta P}{P} = -4.75\% = -(4.75) \times 1\%$$

That is, the value of deep-discount assets in the three- to seven-year maturity bucket would fall by 4.75 percent. Looking at line 6 in Table 7–6, note the bank in the example has no discount bonds in this category. Thus, the bank would have no exposure to an interest rate shock in that bucket ($0 \times (-4.75\%) = $0 on line 21, column 4). However, line 5 indicates the bank does have $15,013 of nonamortizing assets (loans and bonds) in the three- to seven-year range. The duration of five-year bonds with a (semiannual coupon) and yield of 10 percent is approximately 4.05 years. Its modified duration is

---

[10]The reason for using modified duration (*MD*) is that by writing the duration equation as:

$$\Delta P/P = \frac{-D}{(1 + R)} \cdot \Delta R = -MD \cdot \Delta R$$

rather than

$$\Delta P/P = -D \cdot \frac{\Delta R}{(1 + R)}$$

the banker can think in terms of the effects of rate changes (ΔR) rather than discounted rate changes ($\Delta R/1 + R$).

$$MD = \frac{4.05}{(1+(.10/2))} = 3.86 \text{ years or } 3.85 \text{ rounding to the nearest .05 years.}$$

Thus a 1 percent rise in interest rates leads to:

$$\frac{\Delta P}{P} = -3.85\% = -(3.85) \times 1\%$$

Since the bank has $15,013 of these assets (line 5) and the *MD* of these assets is 3.85 (line 16), the market value of these assets would fall by $15,013 $\times$ (-3.85%) = $-$578 if rates rise by 1 percent. The loss of $578 in market value is shown in line 20 column 4.

For amortizing assets, such as conventional mortgages, calculating the durations is more difficult because of potential prepayments of mortgages. For the three- to seven-year range, a mortgage-backed security measures the modified duration of an asset that pays monthly interest and principal repayments with a remaining life of five years. As you can see on line 15 in Table 7–6, the modified duration of such assets in the three- to seven-year bucket is 2.15 years and the fall in value of the amortizing loan portfolio for a 1 percent increase in rates would be $10,774 $\times$ (-2.15%) or $231.64. This is shown on line 19 in Table 7–6.

Finally, for liabilities there is one modified duration interest rate risk weight in each maturity bucket. For the three- to seven-year bucket, this weight is 4.1 percent, as shown in line 18 of Table 7–6. This assumes a five-year deposit paying an effective 7.25 percent coupon rate semiannually; 7.25 percent was also the average cost of U.S. banks' interest-bearing liabilities in 1991. As a result, a rise of 1 percent in interest rates reduces the market value of liabilities by 4.1 percent times $4,446, or by $182.29. Remember, a reduction in the market value of liabilities is a good thing.

Combining the asset market value effect (ΔA) and the liability market value effect (ΔL), the loss or negative effect on the bank's net worth (ΔE) of a 1 percent rise in rates in the three- to seven-year bucket would be:

$$
\begin{array}{ccccc}
\Delta A & - & \Delta L & = & \Delta E \\
[\$0 + \$578 + 231.64] & - & [\$182.29] & = & \$627.36
\end{array}
$$

As shown on line 27, the market value of the bank's net worth would fall by $627.36 in this bucket if rates were to rise by 1 percent.[11]

Looking at Table 7–6, notice that a rise in rates of 1 percent has different effects in each bucket. In the shorter-term buckets, where there are more liabilities than assets, the bank actually gains when rates rise; for example, by $392.32 in the 3 month–1 year bucket, as shown on line 27. By contrast, the bank normally loses net worth in the longer-term buckets; $1,836.74 in the over-15-year bucket on line 27.

The total of the aggregate negative effect on the bank's net worth of a 1 percent rise in rates appears on line 27 in column 1; it simply sums each of the net worth losses and gains in each of the six buckets. (Note that a gain is in brackets.) Overall, a 1 percent rise in rates reduces the net worth (ΔE) of the bank by $3,083.65, or as a percent of assets by 1.68 percent, and as a percent of original net worth by 18.625 percent.

---

[11]The number of $627.36 has been rounded up from $627.35.

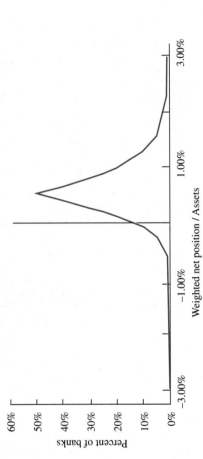

FIGURE 7–2

Estimated levels of IRR as of 12/31/91 (11,916 banks)

Core deposit assumptions = Cash offset with DDA's; MMDA's, Nows & DDA's up to 1–3 yrs.; Savings up to 3–7 yrs.
No more than 30% of core deposit balances in the maximum allowable time band

Percentiles	1%	5%	10%	20%	25%	30%	40%	50%	60%	70%	75%	80%	90%	95%	99%
IRR levels	-0.59%	-0.24%	-0.07%	0.13%	0.20%	0.27%	0.40%	0.52%	0.65%	0.80%	0.89%	0.99%	1.30%	1.58%	2.29%

Mean = 0.58%   Standard deviation = 0.58%

SOURCE: Federal Reserve Press Release, July 30, 1992, Chart 1.

In its proposals, the Fed views a net worth loss-to-asset ratio exceeding 1 percent as potentially dangerous and would require the bank to hold more capital as protection against losses.[12] Look at the distribution of interest rate risk exposures across all U.S. banks at the end of 1991 in Figure 7–2. As you can see, approximately 20 percent had interest rate risk exposures exceeding 1 percent of their assets.

Concept Questions

1. Why do amortizing assets have lower durations than nonamortizing assets?
2. What is the difference between modified duration and duration?
3. Why should regulators monitor an FI's interest rate risk exposure?

---

[12]The rule proposes additional capital for this bank equal to $(1.68\% - 1\%) \times \text{assets} = .68\% \times \$183,250 = \$1,246.1$.

Summary

In this chapter we evaluated a third model for measuring an FI's interest rate gap, the repricing model. Because of the book value approach underlying this model, it concentrates only on the net interest income effects of rate changes and ignores the market value effects. As such, it gives a partial and potentially misleading picture of an FI's interest rate risk exposure. Consequently, Congress has required the Fed to adopt a measure of bank interest rate risk exposure more firmly based on the duration model and market valuation of assets and liabilities. As we showed in Chapter 6, the duration model gives a more complete picture of the interest sensitivity of an FI's assets and liabilities since it takes into account both the interest income effects and capital value effects of rate changes. By comparison, the repricing model only looks at interest income effects.

Questions and Problems

1. *a.* The repricing model requires specification of the length of the repricing period. Why must a time period be specified? How does the choice of the repricing period impact the delineation between rate-sensitive and fixed-rate assets and liabilities?
   b. What determines the optimal length of the repricing period? What are the shortcomings of very short repricing periods?
   c. What are the shortcomings of very long repricing periods?

2. Calculate the repricing gap and impact on net interest income of a 1 percent increase in interest rates for the following positions:
   a. Rate sensitive assets = $100 million. Rate sensitive liabilities = $50 million.
   b. Rate sensitive assets = $50 million. Rate sensitive liabilities = $150 million.
   c. Rate sensitive assets = $75 million. Rate sensitive liabilities = $70 million.

   d. Compare the interest rate risk exposure of the institutions in parts *a, b,* and *c.*

3. Which of the following assets or liabilities fit the one-year rate or repricing sensitivity test?
   a. Ninety-one day U.S. Treasury bills.
   b. One-year U.S. Treasury notes.
   c. Twenty-year U.S. Treasury bonds.
   d. Twenty-year floating rate corporate bonds with annual repricing.
   e. Thirty-year floating rate mortgages with annual repricing.
   f. Thirty-year floating rate mortgages with biannual repricing.
   g. Overnight federal funds.
   h. Nine-month fixed rate CDs.
   i. One-year fixed rate CDs.
   j. Five-year floating rate CDs with annual repricing.
   k. Common stock

4. Use the following data to answer questions *a* through *c.*

Givebucks Bank, Inc. (in millions)

Assets		Liabilities	
Rate sensitive	$50	Rate sensitive	$70
Fixed rate	50	Fixed rate	20
		Equity	10

Notes: All rate-sensitive assets currently earn 10 percent interest per annum. All fixed-rate assets earn 7 percent per annum. Rate-sensitive liabilities currently pay 6 percent per annum, while fixed-rate liabilities offer 6 percent annual interest.

a. What is Givebucks Bank's current net interest income?

b. What will the net interest income be if interest rates increase by 2 percent?

c. What is Givebucks' repricing or funding gap? Use it to check your answer to part *b*.

5. Use the following information about a hypothetical government security dealer named J. P. Mersal Citover to answer questions *a* through *e*. (Market yields are in parentheses.)

J. P. Mersal Citover (dollars in millions)

Assets		Liabilities	
Cash	$10	Overnight repos (7.00%)	$170
T-bills: 30 day (7.05%)	75	Subordinated Debt:	
T-bills: 91 day (7.25%)	75	7 year fixed at (8.55%)	150
T notes: 2 year (7.50%)	50	Equity	15
T bonds: 10 year (8.96%)	100		
Municipal notes:	25		
5 year quarterly floating rate (8.20%)			

a. What is the repricing or funding gap if the planning period is 30 days? 91 days? 2 years? (Recall that cash is a noninterest earning asset.)

b. What is the impact over the next 30 days on net interest income if all interest rates rise by 50 basis points?

c. If the duration of assets is 3.41 years and the duration of liabilities is 3.5 years, what is J. P. Mersal Citover's duration gap?

d. What conclusions regarding J. P. Mersal Citover's interest rate risk exposure can you draw from the duration gap in your answer to question 3*c*? From the repricing or funding gap (30-days planning period) in your answer to question 3*a*?

e. Approximately how will the market value of the Treasury bill portfolio change if all interest rates increase by 50 basis points?

6. Assume a planning period of 120 days when answering questions *a* through *e*.

Assets		Rate
30-year, fixed-rate mortgages: $11 million		10%
90-day, fixed-rate loans: $35 million		9%
Property: $4 million		

Liabilities and Equity	Rate
Demand deposits: $12 million	0%
Federal funds: $30 million	7%
Equity: $8 million	

a. Calculate the above bank's repricing or funding gap.

b. What is the bank's net interest income?

c. Suppose that all interest rates decrease by 50 basis points over the planning period, what will be the impact on net interest income?

d. Suppose that all interest rates increase by 1 percent over the planning period, what will be the impact on net interest income?

e. What is the bank's interest rate risk exposure and how can the bank protect itself from unanticipated reductions in net interest income?

7. Consider the following balance sheet for Universal Insurance Company before answering questions *a* through *e*.

Universal Insurance Company (in thousands)

Assets		Liabilities	
3-month Treasury bills	$ 75	6-month GICs	$1,200
9-month Treasury bills	55	2-year notes	500
2-year Treasury notes	205	20-year bonds	13
15-year Treasury bonds	555	Equity	200
10-year municipals	93		
15-year corporate debt	930		

a. What is the repricing gap over the 0- to three-month maturity bucket?

b. What is the repricing gap over the three-month to one-year maturity bucket?

c. What is the repricing gap over the one-year to three-year maturity bucket?

d. What is the cumulative repricing gap? When is the cumulative repricing gap zero?

e. Calculate the impact on net interest income if interest rates increase 20 basis points for the four repricing gaps in questions 2*a* through *d*.

The Federal Reserve Interest Rate Risk model risk weights on nonamortizing and deep-discount assets are derived using modified durations of average maturity par value Treasury bonds with 10 percent coupons. (The average maturity is equal to the midpoint of the maturity bucket. All interest is assumed to be paid semiannually. Recall that modified duration is simply duration divided by one plus the semiannual rate of return.)

8. *Challenge Question*

Spot rates are:
One-year CD: 7.80
Two-year CD: 7.95
One-year municipal note: 7.95
Two-year municipal note: 8.15
Overnight federal funds: 8.075

a. Using the preceding term structure, describe the leveraged transaction with the highest interest spread. (Recall that a typical transaction for an FI consists of the simultaneous purchase of an interest-earning asset financed with the issuance of a financial liability.)

b. What is the interest rate risk exposure of the transaction in part *a*?

c. If all interest rates increase 50 basis points at the end of one year, what are the cash flows at the end of each of the first and second years? (Hint: Use implied forward rates to form expectations about future spot rates for one-year CDs.)

d. List two transactions that have no interest rate risk exposure. What are the cash flows over the life of the investment?

9. Calculate the IRR weighted positions using the Fed's interest rate risk weighting calculations for the following balance sheet positions:

   a. $100 million two-month amortizing assets.

   b. $45 million two-year non-amortizing assets.

   c. $500,000 five-year deep discount assets.

   d. $125,000 10-year liabilities.

   e. $5 million nine-month deep discount assets.

10. Derive the risk weights for the two categories of assets in the up-to-three-month maturity bucket.

11. Derive the risk weights for the two categories of assets in the one- to three-year maturity bucket.

12. Derive the risk weights for the two categories of assets in the 7–15 year maturity bucket.

13. Challenge Question: Derive the risk weights for the two categories of assets in the 3 month–1 year maturity bucket.

14. *Challenge Question*

   a. Risk weights for amortizing assets with maturity under seven years are derived using the duration of a standard monthly amortizing instrument with a remaining maturity equal to the midpoint of the time band in the maturity bucket and a coupon and yield equal to the effective yield on the industry's earning assets. Assume that yield to be 10 percent paid annually. Calculate the risk weight on amortizing assets for the one- to three-year maturity bucket.

   b. Compare your calculations with the actual risk weight for these assets. What can you conclude about the effective yield on the industry's earning assets?

Liability risk weights from the Federal Reserve Interest Rate Risk model are derived from modified durations of average maturity par value Treasury bonds with 7.25 percent coupons. (The average maturity is equal to the midpoint of the maturity bucket. All interest is assumed to be paid semiannually.)

15. Derive the risk weight for liabilities in the three-month maturity bucket.

16. Derive the risk weight for liabilities in the one- to three-year maturity bucket.

17. Derive the risk weight for liabilities in the three- to seven-year maturity bucket.

18. Derive the risk weight for liabilities in the 7–15 year maturity bucket.

19. Use the following Interest Rate Risk Reporting Schedule to determine the bank's:

   a. Risk-weighted assets (amortizing).

   b. Risk-weighted assets (nonamortizing).

   c. Risk-weighted assets (discount).

   d. Risk-weighted liabilities.

   e. Risk-weighted off-balance-sheet items. (Assume that the risk weight for all off-balance-sheet items is .5 percent.)*

   f. Net risk-weighted position. (Assume that the risk weight for all high-risk items is 1 percent.)

   g. Risk-weighted position as a percent of assets.

   h. Risk-weighted position as a percent of capital.

   i. Is the bank in compliance with the new interest rate risk guidelines? Why or why not? What action, if any, must the bank undertake to comply with the regulations?

Interest Rate Risk Reporting Schedule
(dollars in thousands)

	Up to 3 mos	3 mos–1 yr	1–3 yr
Assets			
Amortizing	0	295	7,474
Nonamortizing	0	0	247
Discount	123,190	10,154	2,345
Liabilities	2,748,000	1,479,020	1,235,667
Off Balance Sheet Items	−585,033	−4,928	843

	3–7 yr	7–15 yr	> 15 yrs
Assets			
Amortizing	2,345	324,965	5,143,266
Nonamortizing	282,803	2,957	0
Discount	0	0	0
Liabilities	358,911	0	0
Off Balance Sheet Items	0	0	0

High Risk Items   Total = 1,900

[*These do not reflect the numbers in the Federal Reserve proposal, but are used here for simplicity.]

8

CREDIT RISK

Learning Objectives

In this chapter you will learn about credit risk. In particular, you will understand which factors lead to defaults on loans and other debt securities as well as on other contractual agreements. Since default risk can seriously threaten the solvency of an FI, it is crucial that managers measure default risk exposure before entering into contracts with borrowers and other counterparties. In this chapter we analyze a number of different approaches to measuring credit risk and explain their strengths and weaknesses.

Introduction

In this chapter, we look at different approaches to assessing and measuring credit or default risk. Such measurement is crucial if an FI is to (1) price a loan or value a bond correctly and (2) set appropriate limits on the amount of credit it extends to any one borrower or the loss exposure it accepts from any particular counterparty. Before we do this, we look at the types of loans—as well as the characteristics of loans—made by U.S. FIs.

Credit Quality Problems

Junk Bond
A bond rated as speculative or less than investment grade by bond-rating agencies such as Moody's.

In recent years, the poor credit quality of many FIs' lending and investment decisions has raised a great deal of attention. In the 1980s there were tremendous problems with bank loans to less developed countries (LDCs) as well as thrift and bank residential and farm mortgage loans. In the early 1990s, attention has switched to the problems of commercial real estate loans, to which banks, thrifts, and insurance companies are all exposed, and **junk bonds.** For example, in 1991 both Executive Life Insurance Company and Capital Life Insurance Company were placed under regulatory supervision by state regulators due to large losses on their junk bond portfolios. Banks have also reported increased loan charge offs and rising nonperforming loans. For example, note in Table 8–1 that banks' nonperforming loans increased from 2.97 percent of total loans in 1989 to 3.76 percent in 1991.[1]

---

[1]Nonperforming loans are defined as loans past due 90 days or more and loans that are not accruing interest due to problems of the borrower.

TABLE 8–1 Nonperforming Loans as a Percentage of Total Loans (insured commercial banks by consolidated assets)

Year	All Banks	$0–$25 million	$25–$50 million	$50–$100 million	$100–$500 million	$500 million–$1 billion	$1 billion +
1987	3.63%	3.63%	3.10%	2.72%	2.27%	2.48%	4.08%
1988	3.11	2.98	2.66	2.31	2.01	2.52	3.44
1989	2.97	2.59	2.31	2.10	1.96	2.09	3.32
1990	3.38	2.25	2.14	2.01	2.05	2.32	3.85
1991	3.76	2.12	2.08	2.03	2.19	2.73	4.34

SOURCE: Federal Reserve Bank of Atlanta, *Economic Review,* July-August 1992, p. 41.

Credit quality problems, in the worst case, can result in FI insolvency. Or, they can result in such a significant drain on capital and net worth that an FI's growth prospects and its ability to compete with other domestic and international FIs are adversely affected.

However, credit risk doesn't only apply to traditional areas of lending and bond investing. As banks and other FIs have expanded into credit guarantees and other off-balance-sheet activities (see Chapter 9), new types of credit risk exposure have arisen causing concern among managers and regulators. Thus, credit risk analysis is now important for a whole variety of contractual agreements between FIs and counterparties.[2]

Types of Loan

Although most FIs make loans, the types of loan made and the characteristics of these loans differ considerably. In this section, we concentrate on analyzing the major types of loans made by U.S. commercial banks. Remember from Chapters 1 and 2, however, that other FIs, such as thrifts and insurance companies, are also heavily engaged in lending, especially in the real estate area. We also discuss important aspects of their loan portfolios.

In Table 8–2, we show a recent breakdown of the aggregate loan portfolio of U.S. commercial banks into four broad classes: commercial and industrial (C&I), real estate, individual, and all other. We briefly look at each of these loan classes in turn.

Commercial and Industrial Loans

The broad figures in Table 8–2 disguise a great deal of heterogeneity in the commercial and industrial loan portfolio. Indeed, commercial loans can be made for periods as short as a few weeks to as long as eight years or more. They can be made in quite small amounts such as $100,000 to small businesses or in packages as large as $10 million or more to major corporations. In addition, they can be secured or unsecured. A **secured loan** is one backed by specific assets of the borrower; if the borrower defaults, the lender has a first lien or claim on those assets. In the terminology of finance, secured debt is senior to an **unsecured loan** or junior debt that has only a

Secured Loan
A loan that is backed by a first claim on certain assets (collateral) of the borrower if default occurs.

Unsecured Loan
A loan that only has a general claim to the assets of the borrower if default occurs.

---

[2]This is one of the reasons for bank regulators' new approach to setting capital requirements against credit-risk (see Chapter 14).

TABLE 8–2   Types of U.S. Bank Loans, September 2, 1992 (dollars in billions)

	Amount	Percent
Total Loans*	$2,094	100.0%
C&I	599	28.6
Real estate	882	42.1
Individual	358	17.1
Other	255	12.2

*Excluding interbank loans
SOURCE: *Federal Reserve Bulletin,* January 1993, Table A.19.

general claim on the assets of the borrower should default occur. As we explain later in this chapter, there is normally a trade-off between the security or collateral backing of a loan and the loan interest rate or risk premium charged by the lender on a loan.[3]

In addition, loans can be made at either fixed rates of interest or floating rates. A fixed-rate loan has the rate of interest set at the beginning of the contract period. This rate remains in force over the loan contract period no matter what happens to market rates. Suppose, for example, IBM borrowed $10 million at 10 percent for one year, but the bank's cost of funds rose over the course of the year. Because this is a fixed-rate loan, the bank bears all the interest rate risk. This is why many loans have floating-rate contractual terms. The loan rate can be periodically adjusted according to a formula so that the interest rate risk is transferred in large part from the bank to the borrower. As might be expected, longer-term loans are more likely to be made under floating-rate contracts than relatively short-term loans.

Finally, loans can be made either spot or under commitment. A **spot loan** is made by the bank and the borrower uses or takes down the whole loan amount immediately. With a **loan commitment,** by contrast, the lender makes an amount of credit available such as $10 million; the borrower has the option to take down any amount up to the $10 million at any time over the commitment period. In a fixed-rate loan commitment, the interest rate to be paid on any takedown is established at the time the loan commitment contract originates. In a floating-rate commitment, the borrower pays the loan rate in force at the time at which the loan is actually taken down. For example, suppose that the $10 million IBM loan was made under a one-year loan commitment. At the time the loan commitment was originated (say January 1994) IBM borrows nothing. Instead, it waits until six months have passed (say June 1994) before it takes down the whole $10 million. IBM would pay the loan rate in force as of June 1994. We discuss the special features of loan commitments more fully in Chapter 9.

To get some idea of the basic characteristics of C&I loans, the Federal Reserve surveys more than 400 banks each quarter. In Table 8–3, we show the major characteristics in a recent lending survey. As you can see, there were more short-term (under one year) C&I loans than long-term loans. Also, short-term loans are more likely to be fixed rate than long-term loans and are less likely to be backed or secured by collateral.

Spot Loan
The loan amount is withdrawn by the borrower immediately.

Loan Commitment
A credit facility with a maximum size and a maximum period of time over which the borrower can withdraw funds.

[3]A recent empirical study has confirmed such a trade-off; see A. Berger and G. Udell, "Lines of Credit, Collateral and Relationship Lending in Small Firm Finance," Working Paper, Stern Business School, New York University, March 1993.

TABLE 8–3 **Characteristics of Commercial Loan Portfolios,**
            May 4–8, 1992

	Long-Term Loans	*Short-Term Loans (under one year)*
Amount outstanding	$5.67 billion	$39.21 billion
Average size of loan	$231,000	$297,000
Weighted-average maturity	45 months	61 days
Percent of which fixed rate	22.3%	53.2%
Percent of loans secured by collateral	70.6%	45%

SOURCE: *Federal Reserve Bulletin,* September 1992.

Finally, as we noted in Chapter 1, commercial loans are declining in importance in bank loan portfolios. The major reason for this has been the rise in nonbank loan substitutes, especially commercial paper. Commercial paper is a short-term debt instrument issued by corporations either directly or via an underwriter to purchasers in the financial markets, such as money market mutual funds. By using commercial paper, a corporation can sidestep banks and the loan market while raising funds at rates often below those banks charge. Moreover, since only the largest corporations can tap the commercial paper market, banks are left facing a pool of increasingly smaller and more risky borrowers in the C&I loan market. This makes credit risk evaluation more important today than ever before. As of September 1992, the total commercial paper outstanding was $549 billion compared to C&I loans of $599 billion.

Real Estate Loans

Real estate loans include primarily mortgage loans but also some revolving home equity loans (approximately 8 percent of the real estate loan portfolio).[4] We show the distribution of mortgage debt for U.S. banks for the second quarter of 1992 in Table 8–4.

As you can see, for banks and thrifts residential mortgages are still the largest component of the real estate loan portfolio; until recently, however, commercial real estate mortgages have been the fastest growing component of real estate loans.[5] Moreover, commercial real estate loans make up more than 80 percent of life insurance companies' real estate portfolios. These loans have caused banks, thrifts, and insurance companies significant default and credit risk problems in recent years.

As with C&I loans, the characteristics of residential mortgage loans differ widely. These include the size of loan, the ratio of the loan to the property's price—the loan price or loan value ratio, and the maturity of the mortgage. Also important characteristics are the fees and charges on the loan, such as commissions, discounts, and points paid by the borrower or the seller to obtain the loan.[6] In addition, the contractual mortgage rate differs according to whether the mortgage has a fixed rate or a

---

[4]Under home equity loans, borrowers use their homes as collateral backing for loans.

[5]Thrifts' proportion of one- to four-family loans as a percent of their real estate mortgage portfolio was 77 percent in the second quarter of 1992.

[6]Points are a certain percentage of the face value of the loan paid up-front, as a fee, by the borrower to the lender.

TABLE 8–4 The Distribution of U.S. Commercial
Bank Real Estate Mortgage Debt
(Second Quarter 1992)

	Percent
One- to four-family residences	56.2%
Multifamily residences	4.3
Commercial	37.3
Farm	2.2
	100%

SOURCE: Federal Reserve Bulletin, January 1993, Table A.37.

TABLE 8–5 Contractual Terms on Conventional
New Home Mortgages, October 1992
(dollars in thousands)

Purchase price	$148.4
Amount of loan	$113.6
Loan price ratio (percent)	78.7%
Maturity (years)	24.8
Fees and charges (percent of loan amount)	1.62%
Contract rate (percent)	7.72%

Adjustable Rate Mortgage (ARMs) A mortgage whose interest rate adjusts with movements in an underlying market index interest rate.

floating rate, also called an adjustable rate. **Adjustable rate mortgages (ARMs)** have their contractual rates periodically adjusted to some underlying index such as the one-year T bond rate. The proportion of fixed-rate to ARM mortgages in FI portfolios varies with the interest rate cycle. In low-interest-rate periods, borrowers prefer fixed rate to ARM mortgages. As a result, the proportion of ARMs to fixed-rate mortgages can vary considerably over the rate cycle. In Figure 8–1, note the behavior of ARMs over one recent interest rate cycle.

Table 8–5 includes a summary of the major contractual terms on conventional fixed-rate mortgages as of October 1992.

Residential mortgages are very long-term loans with an average maturity of approximately 25 years. To the extent that house prices can fall below the amount of the loan outstanding—that is, the loan to value ratio rises—the residential mortgage portfolio can also be susceptible to default risk. For example, during the collapse in real estate prices in Houston, Texas, in the late 1980s, many house prices actually fell below prices in the early 1980s. This led to a dramatic surge in the proportion of mortgages defaulted on and eventually foreclosed by banks and thrifts.

Individual (Consumer) Loans

Another major type of loan is the individual or consumer loan such as personal and auto-loans. Commercial banks, finance companies, retailers, savings banks, and gas companies also provide consumer loan financing through credit cards such as Visa, MasterCard and proprietary credit cards issued by Sears, Mobil, and AT&T. As of September 1992, banks had an approximately 44.75 percent share of the total U.S. consumer loan market.

Conventional commitment rates

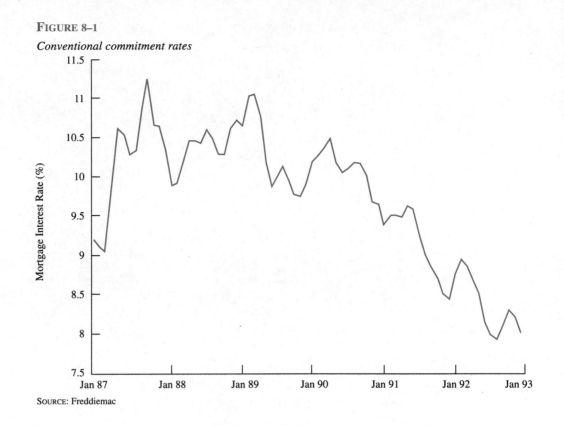

SOURCE: Freddiemac

TABLE 8–6   **Types of Consumer Loan at Commercial Banks, September 1992**

	Percent
Automobile	33.4%
Revolving	39.3
Other	27.3
	100%

SOURCE: *Federal Reserve Bulletin,* January 1993, Table A.38.

TABLE 8–7   **Interest Rate Terms on Consumer Loans, August 1992**

	Percent
48-month car loan	9.15%
24-month personal	13.94
120-month mobile home	12.57
Credit card	17.66

FIGURE 8–1 (CONCLUDED)

ARMs' share of total loans closed

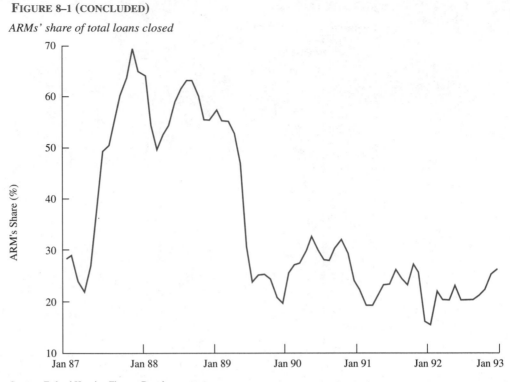

SOURCE: Federal Housing Finance Board.

In Table 8–6 are the three major classes of consumer loans at U.S. banks. The largest class of loans is revolving consumer loans, which include credit card debt. With a **revolving loan,** the borrower has a credit line on which to draw as well as to repay up to some maximum over the life of the credit contract. In recent years, banks have normally faced default rates of between 2 and 5 percent on their credit card outstandings. Such relatively high default rates again point to the importance of risk evaluation prior to the credit decision. The other major class of consumer loans is for new or used automobile purchases. Finally, other consumer loans include fixed-term consumer loans such as 24-month personal loans as well as loans to purchase mobile homes.

In Table 8–7, we show indicative rates on car, personal, mobile home, and credit card loans as of August 1992. These rates differ widely depending on features such as collateral backing, maturity, default rate experience, and noninterest rate fees. In addition, competitive conditions in each market as well as regulations such as state-imposed **usury ceilings** all affect the rate structure for consumer loans.

Revolving Loan
A credit line on which a borrower can both draw and repay many times over the life of the loan contract.

Usury Ceilings
State-imposed ceilings on the maximum rate FIs can charge on consumer and mortgage debt.

Other Loans

The other loans category can include a wide variety of borrowers and types. These include other banks, nonbank financial institutions (such as call loans to investment banks), state and local governments, foreign banks, and sovereign governments.[7] We discuss sovereign loans in Chapter 12.

---

[7]A call loan is a loan contract enabling the lender (e.g., the bank) to request repayment of a loan at any time in the contract period. A noncallable loan leaves the timing of the repayment in the hands of the borrower subject to the limit of the maturity of the loan. For example, most broker loans to investment banks are callable within the day and have to be repaid immediately at the bank lender's request.

Concept Questions

1. Will more ARMs be originated in a high- or low-interest environment? Explain your answer.
2. In Table 8–7, why are credit card loan rates much higher than car loan rates?

The Return on a Loan

The Contractually Promised Return on a Loan

The previous description of loans makes it clear that a number of factors impact the promised return an FI achieves on any given loan. These factors include:

1. The interest rate on the loan.
2. Any fees relating to the loan.
3. The credit risk premium on the loan.
4. The collateral backing of the loan.
5. Other nonprice terms (especially compensating balances and reserve requirements).

Compensating Balances
A proportion of a loan that a borrower is required to hold on deposit at the lending institution.

Compensating balances are a proportion of a loan that a borrower cannot actively use for expenditures. Instead, these balances have to be kept on deposit at the FI. For example, a borrower facing a 10 percent compensating balance requirement on a $100 loan would have to place $10 on deposit (traditionally on demand deposit) with the bank and could use only $90 of the $100 borrowed. This requirement raises the effective cost of loans for the borrower since the deposit rate earned on compensating balances is less than the borrowing rate. Thus, compensating balance requirements act as an additional source of return on lending for an FI.[8] Consequently, while credit risk may be the most important factor ultimately affecting the return on a loan, these other factors should not be ignored by FI managers in evaluating loan profitability and risk. Indeed, FIs can compensate for high credit risk in a number of ways other than charging a higher explicit interest rate or risk premium on a loan or restricting the amount of credit available. In particular, higher fees, high compensating balances, and increased collateral backing all offer implicit and indirect methods of compensating an FI for lending risk.

Next, we look at an example of how the promised return on a C&I loan might vary by choosing specific noninterest rate terms. Suppose a bank makes a spot one-year, $1 million loan. The loan rate is set at:

$$\text{Base lending rate} = 12\% = L$$
$$\text{plus}$$
$$\text{Risk premium} = \underline{2\% = m}$$
$$14\% = L + m$$

LIBOR
The London Interbank Offered Rate, which is the rate for interbank dollar loans in the offshore or Eurodollar market of a given maturity.

Prime Lending Rate
The base lending rate periodically set and reset by banks.

The base lending rate (L) could reflect the bank's marginal cost of funds, such as the commercial paper rate, the federal funds rate, or the London Interbank Offered Rate **LIBOR.** Alternatively, it could reflect the **prime lending rate.** Traditionally, the prime rate was the rate charged to the bank's lowest risk customers. Now, it is more of a base rate from which positive or negative risk premiums can be added. In other

---

[8]They also create a more stable supply of deposits and, thus, mitigate liquidity problems.

words, the best and largest borrowers now commonly required to pay below prime rate so as to be competitive with the commercial paper market.[9]

Suppose the bank also:

1. Charges a $1/_8$% loan origination fee (f) to the borrower.
2. Imposes a 10 percent compensating balance requirement (b) to be held as noninterest-bearing demand deposits.
3. Pays reserve requirements (R) of 10 percent imposed by the Federal Reserve on the bank's demand deposits including any compensating balances.

Then, the contractually promised gross return on the loan, k, per dollar lent would equal:[10]

$$1+k=1+\frac{f+(L+m)}{1-[b(1-R)]}$$

This formula might need some explanation. The numerator is the promised gross cash inflow to the FI per dollar reflecting fees plus interest. In the denominator, for every \$1 in loans the FI lends, it retains b as noninterest-bearing compensating balances. Thus $1 - b$ is the cash outflow from the bank ignoring reserve requirements. However, since b (compensating balances) are held by the borrower at the bank as demand deposits, the Federal Reserve requires the bank to hold noninterest-bearing reserves at the rate R against these compensating balances. Thus, the net benefit from compensating balances has to take into account noninterest-bearing reserve requirements. The net outflow by the bank per \$1 of loans is $1 - [b(1 - R)]$ or 1 minus the reserve adjusted compensating balance requirement.

Plugging in the numbers from our example into this formula we have:[11]

$$1+k=1+\frac{.00125+(.12+.02)}{1-[(.10)(.9)]}$$

$$1+k=1+\frac{.14125}{.91}$$

$$1+k=1.1552 \text{ or } k=15.52\%$$

This is, of course, greater than the simple promised interest return on the loan, $L + m = 14\%$.

In the special case where fees (f) are zero and the compensating balance (b) is zero,

$$f = 0$$
$$b = 0$$

the contractually promised return formula reduces to

$$1 + k = 1 + (L + m)$$

---

[9] For more information on the prime rate, see P. Nabar, S. Park, and A. Saunders, "Prime Rate Changes: Is There an Advantage in Being First?" *Journal of Business* 66, 1993, pp. 69–92.

[10] This formula ignores present value aspects that could easily be incorporated. For example, fees are earned in up-front undiscounted dollars while interest payments and risk-premiums are normally paid on loan maturity and, thus, should be discounted by the bank's cost of funds.

[11] If we take into account the present value effects on the fees and the interest payments and if we assume that the bank's discount rate (d) was $12^1/_2$ percent, then the $L + m$ term needs to be discounted by $1 + d = 1.125$ while fees (as up-front payments) are undiscounted. In this case, k is 13.81 percent.

That is, the credit risk premium is the fundamental factor driving the promised return on a loan once the base rate on the loan is set.

Note that as credit markets have become more competitive, both origination fees (*f*) and compensating balances (*b*) are becoming less important. For example, where compensating balances are still charged, the bank may now require them to be held as time deposits, and they earn interest. As a result, borrowers' opportunity losses from compensating balances have been reduced to the difference between the loan rate and the compensating balance time-deposit rate. Further, in most nondomestic dollar loans made offshore, compensating balance requirements are very rare.[12]

The Expected Return on the Loan

The promised return on the loan $(1 + k)$ that the borrower and lender contractually agreed upon includes both interest rate and noninterest rate features such as fees. Therefore, it may well differ from the expected and, indeed, actual return on a loan. Default risk is the risk of the borrower being unable or unwilling to fulfill the terms promised under the loan contract. It is usually present to some degree or other in all loans. Thus, at the time the loan is made, the *expected* return $(E(r))$ per dollar loaned is related to the promised return by:

$$E(r) = p\,(1 + k)$$

where *p* is the probability of repayment of the loan. To the extent *p* is less than 1, default risk is present. This means the FI manager must (1) set the risk premium (*m*) sufficiently high to compensate for this risk and (2) recognize that setting high risk premiums as well as high fees and base rates may actually reduce the probability of repayment (*p*). That is, *k* and *p* are not independent. Indeed, over some range, they may be negatively related. As a result FIs usually have to control for credit risk along two dimensions: the price or promised return dimension $(1 + k)$ and the quantity or credit availability dimension. In general, the quantity dimension controls credit risk differences on retail loans more than the price dimension when compared to wholesale loans. We discuss the reasons for this in the next section. This is then followed by a section that evaluates different ways in which FI managers can assess the appropriate size of *m,* the risk premium on a loan. This is the key to pricing wholesale loan and debt risk exposures correctly.

Concept Questions

1. Calculate the promised return (*k*) on a loan if the base rate is 13 percent, the risk premium is 2 percent, the compensating balance requirement is 5 percent, fees are $1/_2$ percent, and reserve requirements are 10 percent.

---

[12]For a number of interesting examples using similar formulas, see John R. Brick, *Commercial Banking: Text and Readings* (Haslett, Mich.: Systems Publication Inc., 1984), Chap. 4. If compensating balances held as deposits paid interest at 8 percent $(r_d = 8\%)$ then the numerator (cash flow) of the bank in the example would be reduced by $b \times r_d$, where $r_d = .08$ and $b = .1$. In this case, the $k = 14.64\%$. This assumes that the reserve requirement on compensating balances held as time- deposits (*R*) is 10 percent. However, while currently reserve requirements on demand deposits are 10 percent, the reserve requirement on time-deposits is 0 percent (zero). Recalculating, but assuming R = 0 and interest of 8 percent on compensating balances, we find $k = 14.81$ percent.

2. What is the expected return on this loan if the probability of default is 5 percent?

Retail versus Wholesale Credit Decisions

Retail

Because of their small dollar size in the context of an FI's overall investment portfolio and the higher costs of collecting information on household borrowers, most loan decisions made at the retail level tend to be reject or accept decisions. All borrowers who are accepted are often charged the same rate of interest and by implication the same risk premium. For example, a wealthy individual borrowing from a bank to finance the purchase of a Rolls-Royce is likely to be charged the same auto loan rate as a less wealthy individual borrowing to finance the purchase of a Honda. In the terminology of finance, retail customers are more likely to be sorted or rationed by loan quantity restrictions rather than by price or interest rate differences. Residential mortgage loans provide another good example. While two borrowers may be accepted for mortgage loans, an FI discriminates between them according to the loan price ratio—the amount it is willing to lend relative to the market value of the house being acquired—rather than by setting a different mortgage rate.[13]

Wholesale

Credit Ration
Restrictions on the quantity of loans made available to an individual borrower.

Generally, at the retail level an FI controls its credit risks by **credit rationing,** rather than by using a range of interest rates or prices. At the wholesale level, FIs use both interest rates and credit quantity to control credit risk. Thus, when banks quote a prime lending rate (L) to certain business borrowers, lower-risk customers are charged a lending rate below the prime-lending rate. More risky borrowers are charged an additional markup on prime, or a default risk premium (m), to compensate the FI for the additional risk involved.

Even though over some range of credit demand, FIs may be willing to loan funds to lower-quality wholesale borrowers as long as they are compensated by high enough interest rates, too high lending rates can backfire on the FI as discussed earlier. For example, a borrower charged 15 percent for a loan—a prime rate of 10 percent plus a risk premium of 5 percent—may be able to repay only by using the funds to invest in highly risky investments with some small chance of a big payoff. However, by definition, many high-risk projects fail to pay off and the borrower may default. In an extreme case, the FI receives neither the promised interest nor the original principal lent. This suggests that very high contractual interest rate charges on loans may actually reduce an FI's expected return on loans, because high interest rates induce the borrower to invest in risky projects.[14] Alternatively, only borrowers with risky projects might be interested in borrowing at high interest rates, with low-

---

[13]However, as the cost of information falls, and comprehensive databases on individual household's creditworthiness are developed, the size of a loan for which a single interest rate becomes optimal will shrink.

[14]In the context of the previous section, a high k on the loan reflecting a high base rate (L) and risk premium (m) can lead to a lower probability of repayment (p) and thus a lower $E(r)$ on the loan, where $E(r) = p(1 + k)$.

FIGURE 8–2

The relationship between the promised loan rate and expected return on the loan

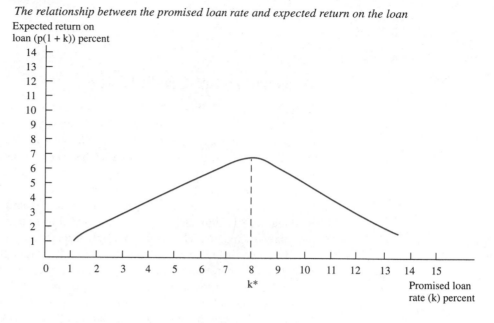

risk borrowers dropping out of the potential borrowing pool at high-rate levels. This lowers the average quality of the pool of potential borrowers. We show these effects in Figure 8–2.[15]

At very low contractual interest rates (k), borrowers do not need to take high risks in their use of funds and those with relatively safe investment projects use bank financing. As interest rates increase, borrowers with fairly safe low-return projects no longer think it is profitable to borrow from FIs. Alternatively, they may switch to higher-risk investment projects to have a chance of being able to payoff the loan. In terms of Figure 8–2, when interest rates rise above k^*, the additional expected return earned by the FI through higher interest rates (k) is increasingly offset by an increase in the expected default risk on the loan ($1 - p$). In other words, an FI charging wholesale borrowers loan rates in the 9 to 15 percent region can earn a *lower* expected return than an FI charging 8 percent.

This relationship between interest rates and the expected returns on loans suggests that beyond some interest-rate level it may be best for the FI to *credit-ration* its wholesale loans; that is, to not make loans or make fewer loans. Rather than seeking to ration by price by charging higher and higher risk premiums to borrowers, the FI can establish an upper ceiling on the amounts it is willing to loan to maximize its expected returns on lending. In the context of Figure 8–2, borrowers may be charged interest rates up to 8 percent with the most risky borrowers also facing more restrictive limits or ceilings on the amounts they can borrow at any given interest rate.

Concept Questions

1. Can a bank's return on its loan portfolio increase if it cuts its loan rates?

---

[15]See also J. Stiglitz and A. Weiss, "Credit Rationing in Markets with Imperfect Information," *American Economic Review* 71, 1981, pp. 393–410.

2. What might happen to the expected return on a wholesale loan if a bank eliminates its fees and compensating balances in a low-interest rate environment?

Measurement of Credit Risk

To calibrate the default risk exposure of its credit and investment decisions as well as to assess its credit risk exposure in off-balance-sheet contractual arrangements, such as loan commitments an FI manager needs to measure the probability of borrower default. The ability to do this largely depends on the amount of information the FI has about the borrower. At the retail level, much of the information needs to be collected internally or purchased from external credit agencies such as American Management Systems. At the wholesale level, these information sources are bolstered by publicly available information such as certified accounting statements, stock and bond prices, and analysts' reports. Thus, for a publicly traded company more information is produced and available to an FI than for a small, single-proprietor corner store. The availability of more information, and the lower average cost of collecting such information, allows FIs to use more sophisticated and usually more quantitative methods in assessing default probabilities for large borrowers compared to small borrowers. However, advances in technology and information collection are making quantitative assessments of even smaller borrowers increasingly feasible and less costly.[16]

Covenants
Restrictions written into bond and loan contracts either limiting or encouraging the borrower's actions that affect the probability of repayment.

In principle, FIs can use very similar methods and models to assess the probabilities of default on both bonds and loans. Even though loans tend to involve fewer lenders to any single borrower as opposed to multiple bondholders, in essence both loans and bonds are contracts that promise fixed (or indexed) payments at regular intervals in the future. Loans and bonds stand ahead of the borrowing firm's equity holders in terms of the priority of their claims should things go wrong. Also, bonds like loans include **covenants** restricting or encouraging various actions to enhance the probability of repayment. A common restrictive covenant included in many bond and loan contracts limits the amount of dividends a firm can pay to its equity holders. Clearly, for any given cash flow, a high dividend payout to stockholders means that less is available for repayments to bondholders and lenders. Moreover, bond yields, like wholesale loan rates, usually reflect risk premiums that vary with the perceived quality of the borrower and the collateral or security backing of the debt. Given this, FIs can use many of the following models that analyze default risk probabilities either in making lending decisions or when considering investing in corporate bonds offered either publicly or privately.[17]

Default Risk Models

Economists, bankers, and analysts have employed many different models to assess the default risk on loans and bonds. These vary from the relatively qualitative to the

---

[16]These advances include database services and software for automating credit assessment provided by companies such as Dun & Bradstreet.

[17]For more discussion of the similarities between bank loans and privately placed debt, see M. Berlin and L. Mester, "Debt Covenants and Renegotiation," *Journal of Financial Intermediation* 2, 1992, pp. 95–133.

highly quantitative. Further, these models are not mutually exclusive, in that an FI manager may use more than one to reach a credit pricing or loan quantity rationing decision. We analyze a number of these models in the next sections starting with the most simple.

Qualitative Models

In the absence of publicly available information on the quality of borrowers, the FI manager has to assemble information from private sources—such as credit and deposit files—and/or purchase such information from external sources—such as credit rating agencies. This information helps a manager to make an informed judgment on the probability of default of the borrower and also to price the loan or debt correctly.

In general, the amount of information assembled varies with the size of the potential debt exposure and the costs of collection. However, a number of key factors enter into the credit decision. These include (1) *borrower-specific* factors that are idiosyncratic to the individual borrower and (2) *market-specific* factors impacting on all borrowers at the time of the credit decision.

Borrower Specific Factors

Reputation.   The borrower's reputation involves the borrowing-lending history of the credit applicant. If over time the borrower has established a reputation for prompt and timely repayment, this enhances the applicant's attractiveness to the FI. A long-term customer relationship between a borrower and lender forms an **implicit contract** regarding borrowing and repayment that extends beyond the formal explicit legal contract on which borrower-lender relationships are based. The importance of reputation, which can only be established over time through repayment and observed behavior, works to the disadvantage of small, newer borrowers. This is one of the reasons why initial public offerings of debt securities by small firms often require higher yields than offerings of older, more seasoned firms.[18]

Leverage.   A borrower's **leverage** or capital structure—the ratio of debt to equity—affects the probability of its default. This is because large amounts of debt, such as bonds and loans, increase the borrower's interest charges and pose a significant claim on its cash flows. As shown in Figure 8–3, relatively low debt equity ratios may not significantly impact the probability of debt repayment. Yet, beyond some point the risk of bankruptcy increases as does the probability of some loss of interest or principal for the lender. Thus, highly leveraged firms, such as firms recently engaged in leveraged buyouts (LBOs) financed in part by FIs' provision of junk bonds or below-investment-grade debt, may find it necessary to pay higher risk premiums on their borrowings if they are not rationed in the first place.[19]

Implicit Contract
Long-term customer relationship between a borrower and lender based on reputation.

Leverage
The ratio of a borrower's debt to equity.

---

[18]For the link between bank finance and the cost of initial public offerings of securities, see C. James and P. Weir, "Borrowing Relationships, Intermediation, and the Costs of Issuing Public Securities," *Journal of Financial Economics* 28, 1992, pp. 149–71.

[19]However, S. J. Grossman and O. D. Hart argue that high debt (leverage) may be a signal of managerial efficiency and may, in fact, lower bankruptcy risk. Similar arguments have been made about the efficiency incentives for managers in junk-bond-financed LBOs. That is, firms with a lot of debt have to be "lean and mean" to meet their repayment commitments. See "Corporate Financial Structure and Managerial Incentives," in *The Economics of Information and Uncertainty,* ed. J. McCall (Chicago: Chicago University Press, 1982).

FIGURE 8–3

The relationship between the cost of debt, the probability of default, and leverage

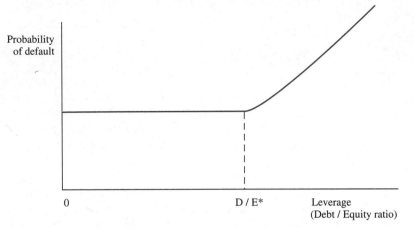

Volatility of Earnings.   As with leverage, a highly volatile earnings stream increases the probability that the borrower cannot meet fixed interest and principal charges for any given capital structure. Consequently, newer firms, or firms in high-tech industries with a high earnings variance over time are less attractive than those with long and more stable earnings histories.

Collateral.   As discussed earlier, a key feature in any lending and loan-pricing decision is the degree of collateral or assets backing the security of the loan. Many loans and bonds are backed by specific assets should a borrower default on repayment obligations. Mortgage bonds give the bondholder first claim to some specific piece of property of the borrower, normally machinery or buildings; debentures give a bondholder a more general and more risky claim to the borrower's assets. Subordinated debentures are even riskier because their claims to the assets of a defaulting borrower are junior to both those of mortgage bondholders and debenture bondholders. Similarly, loans can either be secured (collateralized) or unsecured (uncollateralized).[20]

Market Specific Factors

The Business Cycle.   The position of the economy in the business cycle phase is enormously important to an FI in assessing the probability of borrower default. For example, during recessions firms in the consumer durable goods sector, that produce autos, refrigerators, or houses do relatively badly compared to those in the nondurable goods sector producing tobacco and foods. People cut back on luxuries during a recession but are less likely to cut back on necessities such as food. Thus, corporate borrowers in the consumer durable goods sector of the economy are especially prone to default risk. Interestingly, the earnings of the biggest junk bond issue to date, that of RJR-Nabisco, are largely dependent on the relatively recession-

---

[20]However, collateralized loans are still subject to some default risk unless these loans are significantly overcollateralized; that is, assets are pledged with market values exceeding the face value of the debt instrument.

proof nondurable goods sectors, food and tobacco. Because of cyclical concerns, FIs are more likely to increase the relative degree of credit rationing in recessionary phases. This has especially adverse consequences for smaller borrowers with limited or no access to alternative credit markets such as the commercial paper market.

The Level of Interest Rates.   High interest rates indicate restrictive monetary policy actions by the Federal Reserve. FIs not only find funds to finance their lending decisions scarcer and more expensive but also must recognize that high interest rates are correlated with higher credit risk in general. As discussed earlier, high-interest-rate levels may encourage borrowers to take excessive risks and/or encourage only the most risky customers to borrow.

So far, we have delineated just a few of the qualitative borrower and economy-specific factors an FI manager may take into account in deciding on the probability of default on any loan or bond.[21] Rather than letting such factors enter into the decision process in a purely subjective fashion, the FI manager may weight these factors in a more objective or quantitative manner. We discuss alternative quantitative models to measure credit risk next.

Concept Question

1. Make a list of 10 key borrower characteristics you would assess before making a mortgage loan.

Credit Scoring Models

Credit scoring models use data on observed borrower characteristics either to calculate the probability of default or to sort borrowers into different default risk classes. By selecting and combining different economic and financial borrower characteristics, an FI manager may be able to:

1. Numerically establish which factors are important in explaining default risk.
2. Evaluate the relative degree or importance of these factors.
3. Improve the pricing of default risk.
4. Be better able to screen out bad loan applicants.
5. Be in a better position to calculate any reserves needed to meet expected future loan losses.

To employ credit scoring models in this manner, the manager must identify objective economic and financial measures of risk for any particular class of borrower. For consumer debt, the objective characteristics in a credit scoring model might include income, assets, age, occupation, and location. For example, First Data Resources uses 48 different borrower characteristics to evaluate the probability of credit card defaults. For corporate debt, financial ratios such as the debt equity ratio are usually key factors. After data are identified, a statistical technique quantifies or scores the default risk probability or default risk classification.

---

[21]More generally, J. F. Sinkey identifies five Cs of credit that should be included in any subjective (qualitative) credit analysis: character (willingness to pay), capacity (cash flow), capital (wealth), collateral (security), and conditions (economic conditions). See *Commercial Bank Financial Management—In the Financial Services Industry,* 4th ed. (New York: Macmillian Publishing, 1992).

Credit scoring models include these four broad types: (1) linear probability models, (2) logit models, (3) probit models and (4) linear discriminant analysis. Next, take a brief look at each of these models, their major strengths, and weaknesses.

Linear Probability Model.   The linear probability model uses past data, such as accounting ratios, as inputs into a model to explain repayment experience on old loans. The relative importance of the factors used in explaining past repayment performance then forecast repayment probabilities on new loans; that is, for assessing p the probability of repayment discussed in the second and third sections.

Briefly, we divide old loans (i) into two observational groups, those that defaulted ($Z_i = 1$) and those that did not default ($Z_i = 0$). Then, we relate these observations by linear regression to a set of j causal variables (X_{ij}) that reflect quantitative information about the ith borrower, such as leverage or earnings. We estimate the model by linear regression of this form:[22]

$$Z_i = \sum_{j=i}^{n} \beta_j X_{ij} + \text{error}$$

where β_j is the estimated importance of the jth variable (leverage) in explaining past repayment experience.

If we then take these estimated β_js and multiply them with the observed X_{ij} for a prospective borrower, we can derive an expected value of Z_i for the prospective borrower. That value can be interpreted as the probability of default for the borrower: $E(Z_i) = (1 - p_i) = $ expected probability of default, where p_i is the probability of repayment on the loan.

While this technique is straightforward as long as current information on the X_{ij} is available for the borrower, its major weakness is that the estimated probabilities of default can often lie outside the interval zero to one. The logit and probit models discussed next overcome this weakness by restricting the estimated range of default probabilities to lie between zero and one.

Concept Question

1. Suppose the estimated linear probability model looked as follows: $Z = 0.3 X_1 + 0.1 X_2 + $ error,

   where $X_i = $ debt equity ratio and $X_2 = $ total assets/working capital ratio. Suppose for a prospective borrower $X_1 = 1.5$ and $X_2 = 3.0$. What is the projected probability of default for the borrower?

The Logit Model.*   The logit model constrains the cumulative probability of default on a loan to lie between zero and one and assumes the probability of default to be logistically distributed according to the functional form:

$$F(Z_i) = \frac{1}{1 + e^{-Z_i}}$$

---

[22]See C. G. Turvey, "Credit Scoring for Agricultural Loans: A Review with Applications," *Agricultural Finance Review* 51, 1991, pp. 43–54.

where *e* stands for exponential, $F(Z_i)$ is the cumulative probability of default on the loan, and Z_i is estimated by regression in a similar fashion to the linear probability model. Basically, we can estimate a projected value for Z_i for a prospective borrower from a regression model in the same fashion as the linear probability model. Then we can plug it into the right side of the logistic function. This directly produces a value for $F(Z_i)$ which can be interpreted as the cumulative probability of default. Its major weakness is the assumption that the cumulative probability of default takes on a particular functional form that reflects a logistic function.[23] We show this in Figure 8–4.

The Probit Model.*   The probit model also constrains the projected probability of default to lie between zero and one, but differs from the logit model in assuming that the probability of default has a (cumulative) normal distribution rather than the logistic function shown in Figure 8–4. However, when multiplied by a fixed factor, logit estimates may produce approximately correct probit values.[24]

Linear Discriminant Models.   While linear probability, logit models, and probit models all estimate or project a value for the expected probability of default, should a loan be made, discriminant models divide borrowers into high or low default risk classes contingent on their observed characteristics (X_j).

For example, consider the discriminant analysis model developed by E. I. Altman for publicly traded manufacturing firms in the United States. The indicator variable Z is an overall measure of the default risk classification of the borrower. That, in turn, depends on the values of various financial ratios of the borrower (X_j) and the weighted importance of these ratios based on the past observed experience of defaulting versus nondefaulting borrowers derived from a discriminant analysis model.[25]

That is, Altman's discriminant function takes the form:

$$Z = 1.2\,X_1 + 1.4\,X_2 + 3.3\,X_3 + 0.6\,X_4 + 1.0\,X_5$$

where

$$X_1 = \text{Working capital/total assets ratio}$$
$$X_2 = \text{Retained earnings/total assets ratio}$$
$$X_3 = \text{Earnings before interest and taxes/total assets ratio}$$
$$X_4 = \text{Market value of equity/book value of long-term debt ratio}$$
$$X_5 = \text{Sales/total assets ratio}$$

The higher the value of Z, the lower the default risk classification of the borrower.[26] Thus, low or negative values of Z may be evidence of the borrower being a member of a relatively high default risk class.

---

[23]See Turvey, "Credit Scoring," for more details.

[24]G. S. Madalla suggests multiplying the logit $F(Z_i)$ by .551; see *Limited-Dependent and Qualitative Variables in Econometrics* (Cambridge: Cambridge University Press, 1983). T. Amemiya suggests .625; see "Qualitative Response Models: A Survey," *Journal of Economic Literature* 19, 1981, pp. 483–536. See also Turvey, "Credit Scoring," for more discussion on the transformation of logit estimates into probit estimates.

[25]See E. I. Altman, "Managing the Commercial Lending Process," in *Handbook of Banking Strategy,* eds. R. C. Aspinwall and R. A. Eisenbeis (New York: John Wiley, 1985), pp. 473–510.

[26]Working capital is current assets minus current liabilities.

FIGURE 8–4

Logit model

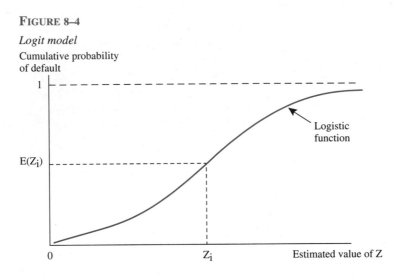

Suppose that the financial ratios of a potential borrowing firm took the following values:

$$X_1 = .2$$
$$X_2 = 0$$
$$X_3 = -.20$$
$$X_4 = .10$$
$$X_5 = 2.0$$

The ratio X_2 is zero and X_3 is negative, indicating that the firm has had negative earnings or losses in recent periods. Also, X_4 indicates the borrower is highly leveraged. However, the working capital ratio (X_1) and the sales asset ratio (X_5) indicate the firm is reasonably liquid and is maintaining its sales volume. The Z score provides an overall score or indicator of the borrower's credit risk since it combines and weights these five factors according to their past importance in explaining borrower default. For the borrower in question:

$$Z = 1.2(.2) + 1.4(0) + 3.3(-.20) + 0.6(.10) + 1.0(2.0)$$
$$Z = 0.24 + 0 - .66 + 0.06 + 2.0$$
$$Z = 1.64$$

According to Altman's credit scoring model, any firm with a Z score of less than 1.81 should be placed in the high default risk region.[27] Thus, the FI should not make a loan to this borrower until it improves its earnings.

There are, however, a number of problems in using the discriminant analysis model to make credit risk evaluations.[28] The first problem is that this model usually discriminates only between two extreme cases of borrower behavior, no default and default. As discussed in Chapter 4, in the real world there are various gradations of default from nonpayment or delay of interest payments (nonperforming assets) to outright default on all promised interest and principal payments. This suggests that a

---

[27]Discriminant analysis models produce such a switching point, $Z = 1.81$. See Turvey, "Credit Scoring," for more details.

[28]Most of these criticisms also apply to the linear probability, logit and probit models.

more accurate or finely calibrated sorting among borrowers may require defining more classes in the discriminant analysis model.

The second problem is that there is no obvious economic reason to expect the weights in the discriminant function—or more generally, the weights in any credit scoring model—to be constant over any but very short periods. The same concern also applies to the variables (X_j). Specifically, due to changing real and financial market conditions, other borrower-specific financial ratios may come to be increasingly relevant in explaining default risk probabilities. Moreover, the linear discriminant model assumes that the X_j variables are independent of one another.[29]

The third problem is that these models ignore important hard-to-quantify factors that may play a crucial role in the default or no default decision. For example, the reputational characteristics of the borrower and the implicit contractual nature of long-term borrower-lender relationships could be important borrower-specific characteristics as could macrofactors such as the phase of the business cycle. These variables are often ignored in credit scoring models. Moreover, credit scoring models rarely use publicly available information, such as the prices in asset markets in which the outstanding debt and equity of the borrower are already traded.[30] The credit risk models that follow use *financial theory* and *financial market* data to make inferences about default probabilities on debt instruments. Consequently, these models are most relevant in evaluating lending to, or purchasing debt issues from, larger borrowers of the corporate sector.

Concept Question

1. Suppose that $X_3 = .5$ in the preceding discriminant model example; show how this would change the default risk classification of the borrower.

Term Structure Derivation of Credit Risk

One market-based method of assessing credit risk exposure and default probabilities is to analyze the risk premiums inherent in the current structure of yields on corporate debt or loans to similar risk-rated borrowers. Rating agencies categorize corporate bond issuers into seven major classes according to perceived credit quality. The first four quality ratings, AAA, AA, A, and BBB, indicate investment-quality borrowers. For example, the Office of the Comptroller of the Currency, which regulates national banks, restricts the ability of banks to purchase securities rated outside these classes. By comparison, in recent years thrift and insurance company regulators have permitted these FIs to purchase noninvestment-grade securities with ratings such as BB, B, and CCC. These three classes are known as high-yield or junk bonds. Different quality ratings are reflected in the degree to which corporate bond yields exceed those implied by the Treasury (credit risk free) yield curve.

---

[29]Recent work in nonlinear discriminant analysis has sought to relax this assumption. Moreover, work with neural networks, which are complex computer algorithms seeking links or correlations between the X_j variables to improve on Z classifications, show some promise. See P. K. Coats and L. F. Fant, "Recognizing Financial Distress Patterns: Using a Neural Network Tool," Working Paper, Department of Finance, Florida State University, September 1992.

[30]For example, S. C. Gilson, K. John and L. Lang show that three years of low or negative stock returns can usefully predict bankruptcy probabilities. In fact, this market-based approach is supplementary to the market-based information models discussed in later Sections. See "An Empirical Study of Private Reorganization of Firms in Default," *Journal of Financial Economics,* 1990, pp. 315–53.

FIGURE 8–5

Yield spreads between corporate debt and T bonds, 1980–89

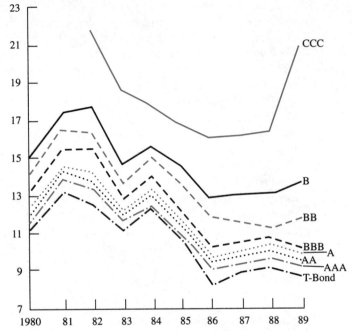

SOURCE: *Standard & Poor's Bond Guides,* 1973–1990 and E. I. Altman, "How 1989 Changed the Hierarchy of Fixed Income Security Performance," in *Recent Developments in Finance,* ed. A. Saunders (Homewood, Ill.: Business One Irwin, 1990), pp. 19–30.

Treasury Strips and Zero-Coupon Corporate Bonds
Bonds that are created or issued bearing no coupons and only a face value to be paid on maturity. As such they are issued at a large discount from face value. (Also called deep-discount bonds.)

Look at these spreads for coupon-bearing bonds in Figure 8–5 for the 1980s. Similar yield curves might also be constructed for **Treasury strips and zero-coupon corporate bonds** if sufficient issues are available. Because Treasury strips and zero-coupon corporates are single payment discount bonds, it may be possible to extract required credit risk premiums and implied probabilities of default from actual market data on interest rates. That is, the spreads between risk free deep-discount bonds issued by the Treasury and deep-discount bonds issued by corporate borrowers of differing quality may reflect perceived credit risk exposures of corporate borrowers for single payments at different times in the future.

Next, we look at the simplest case of extracting an implied probability of default for an FI considering buying one-year bonds from, or making one-year loans to, a risky borrower. Then, we consider multiyear loans and bonds. In each case, we show that we can extract a market view of the credit risk—the probability of default—of an individual borrower.

Probability of Default on a One-Period Debt Instrument.   Assume that the FI requires an expected return on a one year corporate debt security at least equal to the risk free return on Treasury bonds of one year's maturity. Let p be the probability that the corporate debt, both principal and interest, will be repaid in full; therefore, $1 - p$ is the probability of default. If the borrower defaults, the FI is assumed to get nothing. By denoting the promised return on the one-year corporate security as $1 + k$ and on the credit risk free Treasury security as $1 + i$, the FI manager would just be indifferent between corporate and Treasury securities when,[31]

$$p(1 + k) = 1 + i$$

or, the expected return on corporate securities is equal to the risk free rate. Suppose that:

$$i = 10\%$$

and

$$k = 15.8\%$$

This implies that the probability of repayment on the security as perceived by the market, is

$$p = \frac{1+i}{1+k} = \frac{1.100}{1.158} = .95$$

If the probability of repayment is .95, this implies a probability of default $(1 - p)$ equal to .05. Thus, in this simple one-period framework a probability of default of 5 percent on the corporate bond (loan) requires the FI to set a risk premium of 5.8 percent,[32]

$$\Phi = k - i = 5.8\%$$

Clearly, as the probability of repayment (p) falls and the probability of default $(1 - p)$ increases, the required spread Φ, between k and i increases.

This analysis can easily be extended to the more realistic case where the FI does not expect to lose all interest and all principal, if the corporate borrower defaults.[33] Realistically, the FI lender can expect to receive some partial repayment even if the borrower goes into bankruptcy. For example, Altman has estimated that when firms default on their junk bonds, the investor receives, on average, around 40 cents on the dollar.[34] As discussed in the second section, many loans and bonds are secured or collateralized by first liens on various pieces of property or real assets should a borrower default. Let γ be the proportion of the loan's principal and interest that is collectable on default, where in general γ is positive. For example, in the junk bond case, γ is approximately .4.

The FI manager would set the expected return on the loan to equal the risk free rate in the following manner:

$$\gamma(1 + k) \cdot (1 - p) + p(1 + k) = 1 + i$$

The new term here is $\gamma(1 + k) \cdot (1 - p)$; this is the payoff the FI expects to get if the borrower defaults.

---

[31]This assumes that the FI manager is not risk averse; that is, applies risk neutral valuation methods.

[32]In the real world, a bank could partially capture this required spread in higher fees and compensating balances rather than only in the risk premium. In this simple example, we are assuming away compensating balances and fees. However, they could easily be built into the model.

[33]See J. B. Yawitz, "Risk Premia on Municipal Bonds," *Journal of Financial and Quantitative Analysis* 13, 1977, pp. 475–85 and J. B. Yawitz, "An Analytical Model of Interest Rate Differentials and Different Default Recoveries," *Journal of Financial and Quantitative Analysis* 13, 1977, pp. 481–90.

[34]E. I. Altman, "Measuring Corporate Bond Mortality and Performance," *Journal of Finance* 44, 1989, pp. 909–22.

As might be expected, if the loan has collateral backing such that $\gamma > 0$, the required risk premium on the loan would be less for any given default risk probability $(1 - p)$. Collateral requirements are a method of controlling default risk; they act as a direct substitute for risk premiums in setting required loan rates. To see this, solve for the risk premium Φ between k (the required yield on risky corporate debt) and i the risk free rate of interest:

$$k - i = \Phi = \frac{(1+i)}{(\gamma + p - p\gamma)} - (1+i)$$

If $i = 10$ percent and $p = .95$ as before, but the FI can expect to collect 90 percent of the promised proceeds if default occurs ($\gamma = .9$), then the required risk premium $\Phi = 0.6$ percent.

Interestingly, in this simple framework γ and p are perfect substitutes for each other. That is, a bond or loan with collateral backing of $\gamma = .7$ and $p = .8$ would have the same required risk premium as one with $\gamma = .8$ and $p = .7$. An increase in collateral γ is a direct substitute for an increase in default risk (i.e., a decline in p). You can see these trade-offs in Figure 8–6, where point A is $\gamma = .7$ and $p = .8$ and point B is $\gamma = .8$ and $p = .7$.

Probability of Default on a Multiperiod Debt Instrument.*   We can extend this analysis to derive the credit risk or default probabilities occurring in the market for longer-term loans or bonds. For the simple one-period loan or bond, the probability of default $(1 - p)$ was

$$1 - p = 1 - \left[\frac{1+i}{1+k}\right]$$

or

FIGURE 8–6

The trade-off between risk premiums and collateral

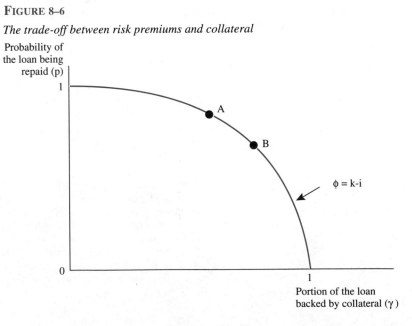

$$1 - p = 1 - \left[\frac{1.10}{1.158} \right]$$

$$1 - p = .05$$

Suppose that the FI manager wanted to find out the probability of default on a two-year bond.[35] To do this, the manager must estimate the probability that the bond would default in the second year conditional on the probability that it does not default in the first year. The probability that a bond would default in any one year is clearly conditional on the fact the default hasn't occurred earlier. The probability that a bond would default in any one year is the **marginal default probability** for that year. For the one-year loan, $1 - p_1 = .05$ is the marginal and total or cumulative probability (Cp) of default in year one. However, for the two-year loan, the marginal probability of default in the second year ($1 - p_2$) can differ from the marginal probability of default in the first year ($1 - p_1$). Later we discuss ways in which p_2 can be estimated by the FI manager, but for the moment suppose that $1 - p_2 = .07$. Then,

$$1 - p_1 = .05 = \text{probability of default in year 1.}$$

$$1 - p_2 = .07 = \text{probability of default in year 2.}$$

The probability of the borrower surviving—not defaulting at any time between now (time 0) and the end of period 2—is $p_1 \times p_2 = (.95)(.93) = .8835$. The **cumulative default probability** at some time between now and the end of year 2 is

$$Cp = 1 - [(p_1)(p_2)]$$

$$Cp = 1 - [(.95)(.93)] = .1165$$

There is a 11.65 percent probability of default over this period.

We have seen that we can estimate p_1 by taking the ratio of the yield on one-year discount T bonds to the yield on one-year discount corporate bonds in a particular risk class. Given the presence of both one- and two-year discount bonds for Treasury issues and corporate issues of a particular risk class, we can derive p_2 from the term structure of interest rates.[36] Consider Figure 8–7.

As you can see, yield curves are rising for both Treasury issues and corporate issues. We want to extract from these yield curves the *market's expectation* of the multiperiod default rates for corporate borrowers classified in the grade B rating class.[37]

Look first at the Treasury yield curve. The condition of **no arbitrage** by investors requires that the return on buying and holding the two-year treasury discount

Marginal Default Probability
The probability that a borrower will default in any given year.

Cumulative Default Probability
The probability that a borrower will default over a specified multiyear period.

No Arbitrage
The inability to make a profit without taking risk.

---

[35]For more details of this approach, see R. Litterman and T. Iben, "Corporate Bond Valuation and the Term Structure of Credit Spreads," *Journal of Portfolio Management,* 1989, pp. 52–64.

[36]Important assumptions underlying this model are that (1) the expectations theory of interest rates hold (there are no liquidity premium or preferred habitat effects on yield curves); (2) transaction costs are small; (3) calls, sinking fund, and other option features are absent; and (4) discount yield curves exist or can be extracted from coupon-bearing yield curves. See Chapter 20 for a detailed explanation of such a derivation.

[37]To use this model, one has to place borrowers in a rating class. One way to do this for unrated firms would be to use the Z score model to calculate a Z ratio for this firm. E. I. Altman has shown that there is a high correlation between Z scores and Standard & Poor's and Moody's bond ratings. Once a firm is placed in a bond rating group (e.g., B) by the Z score model, the term structure model can be used to infer the expected (implied) probabilities of default for the borrower at different times in the future. See "Valuation, Loss Reserves, and Pricing of Commercial Loans," Working Paper, Salomon Brothers Center, New York University, 1992.

FIGURE 8–7

Corporate and treasury discount bond yield curves

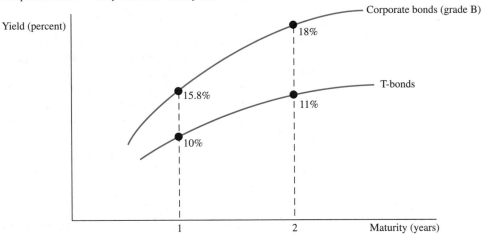

bond to maturity should just equal the expected return from investing in the current one-year discount T bond and reinvesting the principal and interest in a new one-year discount T bond at the end of the first year at the expected one-year **forward rate.** That is

Forward Rate
A one-period rate of interest expected on a bond issued at some date in the future.

$$(1 + i_2)^2 = (1 + i_1)(1 + f_1) \tag{1}$$

The term on the left side is the return from holding the two-year discount bond to maturity. The term on the right side results from investing in two successive one-year bonds, where i_1 is the current one-year bond rate, and f_1 is the expected one-year bond rate or forward rate next year. Since we can observe directly from the T bond yield curve the current required yields on one- and two-year Treasuries, $i_1 = 10$ percent, $i_2 = 11\%$, we can directly infer the market's expectation of the one-year T bond rate next period or the one-year forward rate, f_1:

$$1 + f_1 = \frac{\left(1 + i_2\right)^2}{\left(1 + i_1\right)} = \frac{(1.11)^2}{(1.1)} = 1.12 \tag{2}$$

$$\text{or} \quad f_1 = 12\%$$

The expected rise in one-year rates from 10 percent (i_1) this year to 12 percent (f_1) next year reflects investors' perceptions regarding inflation and other factors that directly affect the time value of money.

We can use the same type of analysis with the corporate bond yield curve to infer the one-year forward rate on corporate bonds (grade B in this example). The current yield curve indicates that appropriate one-year discount bonds are yielding k_1 equal to 15.8 percent and two-year bonds are yielding $k_2 = 18$ percent. The one-year rate expected on corporate securities (c_1) one year into the future reflects the market's default risk expectations for this class of borrower as well as the more general time value factors also affecting f_1:

$$1 + c_1 = \frac{\left(1 + k_2\right)^2}{1 + k_1} = \frac{(1.18)^2}{1.158} = 1.202 \tag{3}$$

$$\text{or} \quad c_1 = 20.2\%$$

TABLE 8–8   Treasury-Corporate Rates and Rate Spreads

	Current One-Year Rate	*Expected One-Year Rate*
Treasury	10.0%	12.0%
Corporate (B)	15.8	20.2
Spread	5.8	8.2

We summarize these calculations in Table 8–8. As you can see, the expected spread between one-year corporate bonds and treasuries in one year's time is higher than the spread for current one-year bonds. The expected rates on one-year bonds can generate an estimate of the expected probability of repayment on one-year corporate bonds in one year's time, or what we have called p_2:

$$p_2 = \left[\frac{1+f_1}{1+c_1}\right] = \frac{[1.12]}{[1.202]} = .9318 \tag{4}$$

Thus, expected probability of default in year 2 is

$$1 - p_2 = 1 - .9318 = .0682$$
$$\text{or } 6.82\%$$

In a similar fashion, the one-year rates expected in two years' time can be derived from the Treasury and corporate term structures. The probability of repayment on one-year loans originated in two years' time is

$$p_3 = \left[\frac{1+f_2}{1+c_2}\right]$$

where f_2 is the expected yield on new one-year discount bonds issued by the Treasury two years from today and c_2 is the expected yield on new one-year corporate discount bonds issued two years from today. Thus, we can derive a whole term structure of expected future one-year default probabilities for grade B corporate debt issues as shown in Figure 8–8.

The default risk probabilities in the example and Figure 8–8 are only pertinent to debt issues by borrowers in the grade B risk class. As noted earlier, bond and loan rating agencies recognize at least seven different quality classes of corporate securities. A curve similar to that in Figure 8–8 can be derived for each class of debt: AAA, AA, A, BBB, BB, B, and CCC. In Figure 8–8, the curves for AAA through BB would lie below—have lower default probabilities—than the curve for B grade debt. The default risk curve for grade CCC debt would lie above the B grade debt curve. We have drawn the default risk curve as upward sloping implying that the market expects default rates to be rising. Possibly, investors perceive a future recession in which grade B borrowers would find it increasingly difficult to repay their debt. This need not be the case. If the market perceives better times ahead, such as a major business expansion, the default risk curve in Figure 8–8 would be downward sloping.

The probabilities we have estimated are marginal probabilities conditional on default not occurring in a prior period. We also discussed the concept of the *cumulative probability* of default that would tell the FI the probability of a loan or bond

FIGURE 8–8

Term structure of default probabilities for grade B borrowers

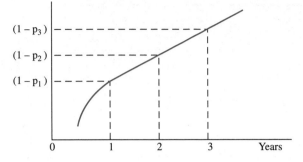

investment defaulting over a particular time period. In the example developed earlier, the cumulative probability that corporate grade B bonds would default over the next two years is

$$Cp = 1 - [(p_1)(p_2)]$$
$$Cp = 1 - [(.95)(.9318)] = 11.479\%$$

As with the credit scoring approach, using this model creates some potential problems. Its principal advantages are that it is clearly forward looking and based on market expectations. Moreover, if there are liquid markets for Treasury and corporate discount bonds—such as Treasury strips and corporate zeros—then we can easily estimate expected future default rates. However, while the market for Treasury strips is now quite deep, the market for corporate discount bonds is quite small. Although a discount yield curve for corporate bonds could be extracted mathematically from the corporate bond coupon yield curve, these bonds are not very actively traded. Given this, the FI manager might have to consider an alternative way to use bond or loan data to extract default rate probabilities for all but the very largest corporate borrowers. We consider a further possible alternative next.

Mortality Rate Derivation of Credit Risk

Mortality Rate
Historic default rate experience of a bond or loan.

Marginal Mortality Rate
The probability of a bond or loan dying (defaulting) in any given year of issue.

Rather than extracting *expected* default rates from the current term structure of interest rates, the FI manager may analyze the *historic* or past default risk experience, the **mortality rates,** of bonds and loans of a similar quality. Consider calculating p_1 and p_2 using the mortality rate model.[38] Here, p_1 is the probability of a grade B bond or loan surviving the first year of its issue, thus $1 - p_1$ is the **marginal mortality rate** or the probability of the bond or loan dying or defaulting in the first year of issue. While p_2 is the probability of the loan surviving in the second year given that default has not occurred during the first year, $1 - p_2$ is the marginal mortality rate for the second year. Thus, for each grade of corporate borrower quality, a marginal mortality rate (MMR) curve can show the historical default rate experience of bonds in any specific quality class in each year after issue on the bond or loan.

---

[38]For further reading, see Altman, "Measuring Corporate Bond Mortality;" "How 1989 Changed," and "Valuation Loss Reserves, and Pricing."

FIGURE 8–9

Hypothetical marginal mortality rate curve for grade B corporate bonds

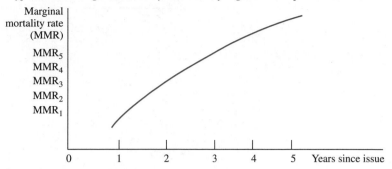

SOURCE: E. I. Altman, *Default Risk, Mortality Rates, and the Performance of Corporate Bonds* (Charlottesville, Va.; The Research Foundation of the ICFA), 1989.

Note in Figure 8–9 that as grade B bonds age, their probability of dying in each successive year increases. Of course, in reality, any shape to the mortality curve is possible. It is possible that MMRs can be flat, decline over time, or show a more complex functional form. These marginal mortality rates can be estimated from actual data on bond and loan defaults. Specifically, for grade B quality bonds:

$$MMR_1 = \frac{\text{Total value of grade B bonds defaulting in year 1 of issue.}}{\text{Total value of grade B bonds outstanding in year 1 of issue.}}$$

$$MMR_2 = \frac{\text{Total value of grade B bonds defaulting in year 2 of issue.}}{\begin{array}{c}\text{Total value of grade B bonds outstanding in year 2 of issue}\\ \text{adjusted for defaults, calls, sinking fund redemptions, and}\\ \text{maturities in the prior year.}\end{array}}$$

For example, using this concept Altman has estimated that the average MMRs for grade B bonds in their first and second years of issue, as measured over the 1971–88 period, were

$$MMR_1 = 1.40\%$$
$$MMR_2 = 0.65\%$$

Consequently, while on average 1.4 percent of grade B bonds were defaulted on in their first year of issue, this rate actually fell to 0.65 percent in the second year of issue. We show the marginal and **cumulative mortality rates** of each quality class in Table 8–9 for the period 1971–88.

Cumulative Mortality Rate
The probability of a bond or loan dying (defaulting) over a given multiyear period.

The mortality rate approach has a number of conceptual and applicability problems. Probably the most important of which is that like the credit scoring model it produces historic or backward looking measures. Also, the estimates of default rates and, therefore, implied future default probabilities tend to be highly sensitive to the period over which the FI manager calculates the MMRs. In addition, the estimates tend to be sensitive to the number of issues and the relative size of issues in each investment grade.

Finally, note that while the preceding example has concentrated on calculating the mortality rates for bonds, an FI manager can directly apply this analysis to loans. All that is needed is historic information on the default rates on loans by different risk classes or types of borrower. Most FIs maintain records of this nature.

TABLE 8–9 Adjusted Mortality Rates by Original Standard & Poor's Bond Rating (Defaults and Issues, 1971–88)

						Years after Issuance (percentage)					
Original Rating		*1*	*2*	*3*	*4*	*5*	*6*	*7*	*8*	*9*	*10*
AAA	Yearly	0.00	0.00	0.00	0.00	0.00	0.15%	0.05%	0.00	0.00	0.00
	Cumulative	0.00	0.00	0.00	0.00	0.00	0.15	0.21	0.21%	0.21%	0.21%
AA	Yearly	0.00	0.00	1.39%	0.33%	0.20%	0.00	0.27	0.00	0.11	0.13
	Cumulative	0.00	0.00	1.39	1.72	1.92	1.92	2.18	2.18	2.29	2.42
A	Yearly	0.00	0.39%	0.32	0.00	0.00	0.11	0.11	0.07	0.13	0.00
	Cumulative	0.00	0.39	0.71	0.71	0.71	0.82	0.93	1.00	1.13	1.13
BBB	Yearly	0.03%	0.20	0.12	0.26	0.39	0.00	0.14	0.00	0.21	0.80
	Cumulative	0.03	0.23	0.35	0.61	1.00	1.00	1.14	1.14	1.34	2.13
BB	Yearly	0.00	0.50	0.57	0.26	0.53	2.79	3.03	0.00	0.00	3.48
	Cumulative	0.00	0.50	1.07	1.34	1.86	4.59	7.48	7.48	7.48	10.70
B	Yearly	1.40	0.65	2.73	3.70	3.59	3.86	6.30	3.31	6.84	3.70
	Cumulative	1.40	2.04	4.72	8.24	11.54	14.95	20.31	22.95	28.22	30.88
CCC	Yearly	1.97	1.88	4.37	16.35	2.06	0.00	0.00	0.00	0.00	0.00
	Cumulative	1.97	3.81	8.01	23.05	24.64	24.64	24.64	24.64	24.64	24.64

Note: Adjusted for changes in population (cohort groups) due to defaults, calls, and sinking fund redemption.
Source: E. I. Altman, *Default Risk, Mortality Rates, and the Performance of Corporate Bonds* (Charlottesville, Va.: The Research Foundation of the ICFA), 1989.

Concept Questions

1. In Table 8–9, the CMR over five years for CCC rated bonds is 24.64 percent. Check this calculation using the individual year MMRs.
2. Why would any FI manager buy bonds that have a CMR of 24.64 percent? Explain your answer.

Option Models of Default Risk*

Theoretical Framework. In recent years, following the pioneering work of Merton, Black and Scholes, and others, we now recognize that when a firm raises funds either by issuing bonds or increasing its bank loans, it holds a very valuable default or repayment option.[39] That is, if a borrower's investment projects fail so it cannot repay the bondholder or the bank, it has the option of defaulting on its debt repayment and turning any remaining assets over to the debtholder. Because of limited liability for equity holders, the borrower's loss is limited, on the downside, by the amount of equity invested in the firm.[40] On the other hand, if things go well, the borrower can keep most of the upside returns on asset investments after the promised principal and interest on the debt have been paid.

The Borrower's Payoff from Loans. Look at the payoff function for the borrower in Figure 8–10, where *S* is the size of the initial equity investment in the firm, *B* is the

---

[39]R. C. Merton, "On the Pricing of Corporate Debt: The Risk Structure of Interest Rates," *Journal of Finance* 29, 1974, pp. 449–70; F. Black and M. Scholes, "The Pricing of Options and Corporate Liabilities," *Journal of Political Economy* 81, 1973, pp. 637–59.

[40]Given limits to losses in personal bankruptcy, a similar analysis can be applied to retail and consumer loans.

FIGURE 8–10

The payoff function to corporate borrowers (stockholders)

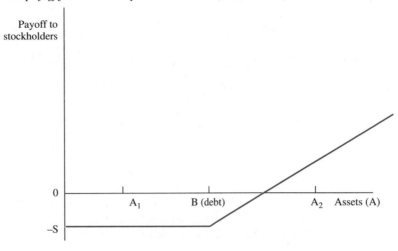

value of outstanding bonds or loans (assumed for simplicity to be issued on a discount basis) and A is the market value of the assets of the firm.

If the investments in Figure 8–10 turn out badly, the stockholder-owners of the firm would default on the firm's debt, turn its assets (such as A_1) over to the debt holders, and lose only their initial stake in the firm (S). By contrast, if the firm does well and the assets of the firm are valued highly (A_2), the firm's stockholders would pay off the firm's debt (OB) and keep the difference ($A_2 - B$). Clearly, the higher A_2 is relative to B, the better off are the firm's stockholders. Given that borrowers face only a limited downside risk of loss of their equity investment but a very large potential upside return if things turn out well, equity is analogous to buying a call option on the assets of the firm.

The Debtholder's Payoff from Loans.   Consider the same loan or bond issue from the perspective of the bank or bondholder. The maximum amount the bank or bondholder can get back is B, the promised payment. However, the borrower who possesses the default or repayment option would only rationally repay the loan if $A > B$, that is, if the market value of assets exceed the value of promised debt repayments. A borrower whose asset value falls below B would default and turn over any remaining assets to the debt holders. Thus, the payoff function to the debt holder tends to be the mirror image of that of the borrower, as shown in Figure 8–11.

After investment has taken place, if the value of the firm's assets resemble points to the right of B, the face value of the debt—such as A_2—the debt holder or bank would be paid off in full and receive B. On the other hand, if asset values fall in the region to the left of B—such as A_1—the debt holder would receive back only those assets remaining as collateral, thereby losing $B - A_1$. Thus, the value of the loan from the perspective of the lender is always the minimum of B or A, or min $[B, A]$. That is, the payoff function to the debt holder is similar to writing a put option on the value of the borrower's assets with B, the face-value of debt, as the *exercise price*. If $A > B$, the loan is repaid and the debt holder earns a small fixed return (similar to the premium on a put option) which is the interest rate implicit in the discount bond. If $A < B$, the borrower defaults and the debt holder stands to lose both interest and

FIGURE 8–11

Payoff function to the debt holder (the bank) from a loan

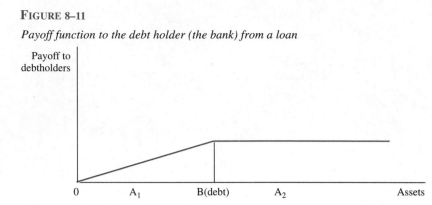

principal. In the limit, default for a firm with no assets left results in debt holders losing all their principal and interest. In actuality, if there are also costs of bankruptcy, the debt holder can potentially lose even more than this.

Applying the Option Valuation Model to the Calculation of Default Risk Premiums.   Merton has shown that in the context of the preceding options framework it is quite straightforward to express the market value of a risky loan made by a lender to a borrower as:[41]

$$F(\tau) = Be^{-i\tau} [(1/d) N (h_1) + N(h_2)] \tag{6}$$

where

τ = The length of time remaining to loan maturity. That is, $\tau = T - t$ where T is the maturity date and time t is today.

d = The borrowers leverage ratio measured as $Be^{-i\tau}/A$ where the market value of debt is valued at the rate i, the risk free rate of interest.

$N(h)$ = A value computed from the standardized normal distribution statistical tables. This value reflects the probability that a deviation exceeding the calculated value of h will occur.

$h_1 = -[1/_2 \sigma^2\tau - ln (d)]/\sigma \sqrt{\tau}$

$h_2 = -[1/_2 \sigma^2\tau + ln (d)]/\sigma \sqrt{\tau}$

σ^2 = Measures the asset risk of the borrower. Technically, the variance of the rate of change in the value of the underlying assets of the borrower.

More important, written in terms of a yield spread, this equation reflects an equilibrium default risk premium that the borrower should be charged. That is:

$$k(\tau) - i = (-1/\tau) ln [N(h_2) + (1/d) N (h_1)] \tag{7}$$

where

$k(\tau)$ = Required yield on risky debt

ln = Natural logarithm

---

[41]See Merton, "On the Pricing of Corporate Debt."

i = Risk-free rate on debt of equivalent maturity (here one period)

Thus, Merton has shown that the lender should adjust the required risk premium as d and σ^2 change, that is, as leverage and asset risk change. Specifically, he shows:

$$\frac{\partial\left[k(\tau) - i\right]}{\partial d} > 0$$

$$\frac{\partial\left[k(\tau) - i\right]}{\partial \sigma} > 0$$

The lender or bondholder should require a higher default risk premium as d and σ increases for any given borrower. Alternatively, borrowers with relatively high d and high σ should be placed in higher credit risk classes.

An Option Model Application

B = $100,000[42]

τ = 1 year

i = 5 percent

d = 90% or .9

σ = 12%

Substituting these values into the equations for h_1 and h_2 and solving for the areas under the standardized normal distribution, we find:

$$N(h_1) = .174120$$
$$N(h_2) = .793323$$

where

$$h_1 = \frac{-\left[\frac{1}{2}(.12)^2 - \ln(.9)\right]}{.12} = -.938$$

and

$$h_2 = \frac{-\left[\frac{1}{2}(.12)^2 + \ln(.9)\right]}{.12} = +.818$$

The current market value of the loan is

$$L(t) = Be^{-i\tau}\left[N(h_2) + (1/d)N(h_1)\right]$$

$$= \frac{\$100,000}{1.05127}\left[.793323 + (1.1111)(.17412)\right]$$

$$= \frac{\$100,000}{1.05127}\left[.986788\right]$$

$$= \$93,866.18$$

and the required risk spread or premium is

---

[42]This numerical example is based on D. F. Babbel, "Insuring Banks against Systematic Credit Risk," *Journal of Futures Markets* 9, 1989, pp. 487–506.

$$k(\tau) - i = \left(\frac{-1}{\tau}\right) \ln\left[N(h_2) + (1/d)N(h_1) \right]$$

$$= (-1) \ln[.986788]$$

$$= 1.33\%$$

Thus, the risky loan rate $k(\tau)$ should be set at 6.33 percent when the risk free rate (i) is 5 percent.

Theoretically, this model is an elegant tool for extracting premiums and default probabilities; it also has important conceptual implications regarding which variables to focus on in credit risk evaluation (e.g., leverage (d) and risk (σ^2)). Even so, this model has a number of real-world implementation problems. Probably the most significant is the assumption of continuously traded claims on the assets of the borrower. Since many loans are never or, at best, infrequently traded, this assumption is difficult to accept in many real-world applications (see Chapter 22 on the market for loan sales). Moreover, the value of σ^2—the volatility of the underlying assets of the borrower—plays a crucial role in setting the equilibrium risk premium. The value of option-based premiums is extremely sensitive to errors made in measuring σ^2.[43] Moreover, volatility itself is variable over time.[44]

Concept Questions

1. Which is the only credit risk model discussed in this section that is really forward looking?
2. How should the posting of collateral by a borrower affect the risk premium on a loan?
3. What are three major problems with the Z score model of credit risk evaluation?
4. How should the risk premium on a loan be affected if there is a reduction in a borrower's leverage and the underlying volatility of its earnings?

Loan Portfolio Diversification

The models discussed previously are different ways an FI manager could measure the default risk on individual debt instruments such as loans or bonds. In this section, we concentrate on the ability of an FI manager to internally measure and control aggregate credit risk exposure of the FI in a portfolio context.

Portfolio Diversification and Modern Portfolio Theory

To the extent that an FI manager holds widely traded loans and bonds as assets, portfolio diversification models could measure and control the FI's overall credit risk exposure in aggregate. Suppose that the manager can calculate periodic returns on each

---

[43]See, for example, D. Pyle, "Pricing Deposit Insurance: The Effects of Mismeasurement," Working Paper, University of California at Berkeley, 1983.

[44]See L. Canina and S. Figlewski on the problems of estimating stochastic volatility: "The Informational Content of Implied Volatility," *Review of Financial Studies* (forthcoming).

loan or bond in the FI's portfolio; assets such as equity are normally widely traded and their returns can easily be calculated from stock market data.[45] Such data may come from observing bond prices directly, the prices of similar bonds or loans traded in secondary debt markets, or internally imputing fair market values. Once price data have been constructed, the manager can calculate periodic expected or mean returns ($\overline{R}_i$) on the i individual debt instruments.[46]

After calculating the individual security return series, the FI manager can compute the expected return on a portfolio of assets as:

$$R_p = \sum_{i=1}^{N} X_i \, \overline{R}_i \tag{8}$$

In addition, we can calculate the variance of returns or risk of the portfolio from:

$$\sigma_p^2 = \sum_{i=1}^{n} X_i^2 \, \sigma_i^2 \; + \; \sum_{i=1}^{n} \sum_{\substack{j=1 \\ i \ne j}}^{n} X_i \, X_j \, \sigma_{ij} \tag{9}$$

where

R_p = The expected or mean return on the asset portfolio
Σ = Summation sign
$\overline{R}_i$ = The mean return on the ith asset in the portfolio
X_i = The proportion of the asset portfolio invested in the ith asset
σ_i^2 = The variance of returns on the ith asset
σ_{ij} = The covariance of returns between the ith and jth assets

The fundamental lesson of modern portfolio theory is that by taking advantage of its size, an FI can diversify away considerable amounts of credit risk as long as the returns on different assets are imperfectly correlated.[47]

Indeed, regulators view loan concentrations or lack of loan diversification such as oil and gas loans in Texas, as a major cause of FI failure. In particular, the Federal Deposit Insurance Corporation Improvement Act, passed in 1991, required federal bank regulators to put in place a monitoring and measurement system for bank loan concentrations.

Consider the σ_p^2 in equation 9. If many loans have negative covariances of returns (σ_{ij} are negative)—that is, when one borrower's loans do badly, another's do well—the sum of the individual credit risks of loans viewed independently would overestimate the risk of the whole portfolio. This is what we meant in Chapter 3, when we stated that by pooling funds, FIs can take advantage of the law of large numbers in their investment decisions.

---

[45]Due to regulatory reasons, banks generally do not hold equities in their balance sheets, although equities are an important part of the portfolios of life insurance companies, pension funds, and mutual funds.

[46]In a recent study applying portfolio theory to the commercial loan portfolio, T. L. Gollinger and J. B. Morgan calculate returns using data published by the Loan Pricing Corporation. Pricing data include market average-loan pricing by size, industry, and loan purpose. They also calculate return on assets (ROA) for loan types. Interestingly, in measuring risk (or the variance) of loan returns, the authors employed average industry Z scores rather than the variance of the ROA. See "Calculation of an Efficient Frontier for a Commercial Loan Portfolio," *Journal of Portfolio Management,* Winter 1993, pp. 39–46.

[47]One objection to using modern portfolio theory for loans is that the returns on individual loans are not normally or symmetrically distributed. In particular, most loans have limited upside returns and long-tail downside risks (see the discussion in Chapter 4).

FIGURE 8–12

FI portfolio diversification

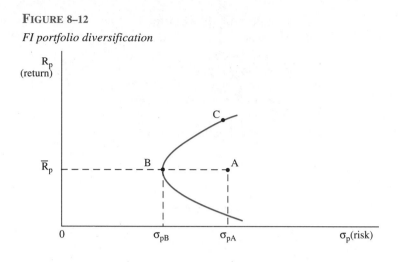

Look at the advantages of diversification in Figure 8–12. Note that *A* is an undiversified portfolio with heavy investment concentration in just a few loans or bonds. By fully exploiting diversification potential with bonds or loans whose returns are negatively correlated, or that have a low positive correlation with those in the existing portfolio, the FI manager can lower the credit risk on the portfolio from σ_{pA} to σ_{pB} while earning the same expected return. That is, portfolio *B* is the efficient (lowest risk) portfolio associated with portfolio return level R_p. By varying the required portfolio return level R_p up and down, the manager can identify a whole frontier of efficient portfolio mixes of loans, bonds, and equity. Each portfolio mix is efficient in the sense that it offers the lowest risk level to the FI manager at each possible level of portfolio returns. However, as you can see in Figure 8–12, of all possible efficient portfolios that can be generated, portfolio *B* produces the lowest possible risk level for the FI manager. That is, it maximizes the gains from diversifying across all available loans and bonds so that the manager cannot reduce the risk of the portfolio below σ_{pB}. For this reason, σ_{pB} is usually labelled the **minimum risk portfolio.**

Minimum Risk Portfolio
Combination of assets that reduces the variance of portfolio returns to the lowest feasible level.

Even though *B* is clearly the minimum *risk* portfolio, it does not generate the highest returns. Consequently, portfolio *B* may only be chosen by the most risk averse FI managers; that is, those whose sole objective is to minimize portfolio risk regardless of the portfolio's return. Most portfolio managers have some desired return-risk trade off in mind; they are willing to accept more risk if they are compensated with higher expected returns.[48] One such possibility would be portfolio *C* in Figure 8–12. This is an efficient portfolio, in that the FI manager has mixed loans, bonds, and other assets to produce a portfolio risk level that is a minimum for that

---

[48]The point that is chosen depends on the risk aversion of managers and the degree of separation of ownership from control. If the FI is managed by agents who perform the task of maximizing the value of the firm, they act as risk neutral agents. They would know that stockholders, who are well-diversified, could through homemade diversification hold the shares of many firms to eliminate borrower specific risk. Thus, managers would seek to maximize expected return subject to any regulatory constraints on risk-taking behavior (i.e., they would likely pick a point in the region *C* in Figure 8–12). However, if managers are risk averse because of their human capital invested in the FI and make lending decisions based on their own risk preferences rather than those of the stockholders, they are likely to choose a relatively low-risk portfolio, something closer to the minimum risk portfolio. For more on agency issues and bank risk taking, see A. Saunders, E. Strock, and N. G. Travlos, "Ownership Structure, Deregulation, and Bank Risk Taking," *Journal of Finance* 45, 1990, pp. 643–54.

higher expected return level; this portfolio dominates all other portfolios that can produce the same expected return level.

Portfolio theory is a highly attractive tool, especially for mutual fund managers who invest in widely traded assets. Still, over and above the intuitive concept that diversification is generally good, a question arises as to its applicability for small banks and thrifts. These FIs often hold significant amounts of regionally specific nontraded or infrequently traded loans and bonds. At best, these FIs may be able to use only very simplified forms of portfolio diversification models. We look at a modified form of portfolio theory next.

Partial Applications of Portfolio Theory*

Direct application of modern portfolio theory is often difficult for depository institutions lacking information on market prices of assets. Sufficient loan volume data may be available to allow managers to construct modified portfolio models to analyze the overall concentration or credit risk exposure of the FI.[49] Such loan volume data includes:

1. *Commercial Bank Call Reports.* These reports to the Federal Reserve classify loans as real estate, agriculture, commercial and industrial, depository institutions, individuals, state and political subdivisions, and international. Produced for individual banks, these data can be aggregated to get estimates of the national allocation of loans among categories or types.

2. *Shared National Credit.* A national database on commercial and industrial loans that breaks loan volume into two-digit Standard Industrial Classification (SIC) codes. For example, loans made to SIC code 49 are loans to public utilities. Because this database provides a national picture of the allocation of loans across sectors, it is analogous to the market portfolio or basket of commercial and industrial loans.

These data, therefore, provide *market benchmarks* with which an individual bank can compare its own internal allocations of loans across major leading sectors such as real estate, and C&I. For example, the Shared National Credit (SNC) database provides a market benchmark of the allocation of loans across various industries or borrowers.

By comparing its own allocation, or the proportions (X_{ij}), it allocates to loans in any specific area with the national allocations across borrowers (X_i), where i designates different loan groups, the jth FI can measure the extent to which it deviates from the market portfolio benchmark. This indicates the degree to which it has developed *loan concentrations* or relatively undiversified portfolios in various areas.

For example, consider Table 8–10. In this table, we evaluate the first level of the loan asset allocation problem, which is the amount to be lent to each major loan sector or type. Here we show hypothetical numbers for four types of loans: real estate, commercial and industrial, individual, and others. Column 1, shows the loan allocation proportions at the national level for all banks; this is the market portfolio allocation. Column 2 lists the allocations assumed to be chosen by bank A; and Column 3, the allocations chosen by bank B.

---

[49]This partial application of portfolio theory was first suggested by J. B. Morgan, "Managing a Loan Portfolio Like an Equity Fund," *Bankers Magazine,* January–February 1989, pp. 228–35.

Note that bank A has concentrated loans more heavily in C&I lending than the national average, while bank B has concentrated loans more heavily in lending to individuals. To calculate the extent to which each bank deviates from the national benchmark, we use the standard deviation of banks A and B's loan allocations from the national benchmark. Of course, the national benchmark may be inappropriate as the relevant market portfolio for a very small regional bank or thrift. In this case, the FI could construct a regional benchmark from the Call Report data of banks in a given regional area such as the American southwest or alternatively a peer group benchmark of banks of a similar asset size and location.

We calculate the relative measure of loan allocation deviation as:[50]

$$\sigma_j = \sqrt{\frac{\sum_{i=1}^{4}\left(X_{ij} - X_i\right)^2}{N}} \tag{11}$$

where

σ_j = The standard deviation of bank j's asset allocation proportions from the national benchmark

X_{ij} = The asset allocation proportions of the jth bank

X_i = The national asset allocations

N = The number of observations or loan categories, $N = 4$

The relevant calculation for the example in Table 8–10 is in Table 8–11.

As you can see, bank B deviates significantly from the national benchmark due to its heavy concentration in individual loans. This is not necessarily bad; a bank may specialize in this area of lending due to its comparative advantage in information collection and monitoring of personal loans (perhaps due to its size or location). The standard deviation simply provides a manager with a measure of the degree to which an FI's loan portfolio composition deviates from the national average or benchmark. Nevertheless, to the extent that the national composition of a loan portfolio represents a more diversified market portfolio because it aggregates across all banks, the asset proportions derived nationally (the X_i) are likely to be closer to the *most efficient portfolio composition* than are the X_is of the individual bank. This partial use of modern portfolio theory provides an FI manager with a feel for the relative degree of loan

TABLE 8–10   Allocation of the Loan Portfolio to Different Sectors (in percentages)

	(1) National	(2) Bank A	(3) Bank B
Real estate	10%	15%	10%
C&I	60	75	25
Individuals	15	5	55
Others	15	5	10
	100%	100%	100%

[50]For small samples such as this, it is really more appropriate to divide through equation (11) by $N - 1$ rather than N.

TABLE 8–11   Measures of Loan Allocation Deviation from the National Benchmark Portfolio

	Bank A	Bank B
$(X_{1j} - X_1)^2$	$(.05)^2 = .0025$	$(0)^2 = 0$
$(X_{2j} - X_2)^2$	$(.15)^2 = .0225$	$(-.35)^2 = .1225$
$(X_{3j} - X_3)^2$	$(-.10)^2 = .01$	$(.4)^2 = .16$
$(X_{4j} - X_4)^2$	$(-.10)^2 = .01$	$(-.05)^2 = .0025$
$\sum_{i=1}^{n}\left(X_{ij} - X_i\right)^2$	$\sum_{i=1}^{4} = .045$	$\sum_{i=1}^{4} = .285$
	$\sigma_A = 10.61\%$	$\sigma_B = 26.69\%$

concentration carried in the asset portfolio. Finally, although the preceding analysis has been described in terms of the loan portfolio of banks, any FI can use it for any asset group or, indeed, the whole asset portfolio whether the asset is traded or not. The key data needed is that of a peer group of regional or national financial institutions faced with similar investment decision choices.

Concept Questions

1. Suppose the returns on different loans were independent; would there be any gains from loan portfolio diversification?
2. How would I find the minimum risk portfolio in a modern portfolio theory framework?
3. Should FI managers select the minimum risk portfolio? If not why not?

Summary

This chapter has analyzed various approaches and models for assessing the credit risk on debt instruments such as loans and bonds that comprise significant proportions of an FI's portfolio of assets. These models can vary from the qualitative to the highly technical and quantitative. Which model or models an FI manager chooses depends in part on the data and information available to quantify risk as well as its costs.

Credit risk in a portfolio context may differ significantly from credit risk at the individual bond or loan level. That is, FIs can use their comparative advantage in size to exploit law-of-large-numbers gains from diversification.

Finally, these models might also measure credit risk exposure for contractual arrangements entered into off-the-balance sheet (see next chapter).

Questions and Problems

1. Bank regulators must assess bank safety and soundness by evaluating the bank's portfolio risk. How is the bank's credit assessment process similar to bank regulator's assessment of bank credit risk exposure? How is it different?

2. Differentiate between a spot loan and a loan made under commitment. Which loan is more likely to be a fixed, as opposed to a floating, rate? Why?

3. In recent years, commercial borrowers have found substitutes for bank loans to meet both their short-term and long-term financing needs. What are these credit substitutes? Why has bank lending been replaced by these credit alternatives for some borrowers? Why do some corporate borrowers continue to utilize bank loans to meet their financing needs? What is the impact on the banks of this commercial trend toward the use of securitized credit instruments?

4. Why is risk evaluation prior to credit approval important?

5. What determines bank loan rates?

6. Calculate the FI's annual rate of return on a loan if:

   a. Fees are .25 percent, the base loan rate is 10 percent annually, the borrower's risk premium is 2 percent, compensating balances are 5 percent, and reserve requirements are 10 percent.

   b. Fees are 10 basis points, the base loan rate is 5 percent annually, the borrower's risk premium is 4 percent, compensating balances are 0 percent, and reserve requirements are 10 percent.

   c. There are neither fees nor compensating balances. The base loan rate is 12 percent annually with a 50-basis-point risk premium. Reserve requirements are 10 percent.

7. Assume that the bank's marginal cost of funds (LIBOR) is 7 percent. (Answer each question cumulatively, using information from all of the previous parts of question 6.)

   a. What is the base lending rate?

   b. What is the loan rate if the risk premium is 4 percent?

   c. What is the loan rate if a 25 basis-point origination fee is charged?

   d. What is the loan rate if a 15 percent compensating balance is required?

   e. What is the loan rate if 10 percent reserve requirements are imposed?

8. Calculate the expected return on the loans in question 7 assuming a default probability of 3 percent.

9. If the default probability increases by 10 basis points for each percentage increase in the promised loan rate above the base lending rate, what is the expected loan rate on the loans in question 7? Why would the default rate increase as the promised loan rate increases? What is the impact on the lender's expected return?

10. a. Suppose the estimated linear probability model is: $Z = 1.1X_1 + .6X_2 + .5X_3 + error$, where $X_1 = .75$ is the borrower's debt/equity ratio; $X_2 = .25$ is the volatility of borrower earnings; and $X_3 = .15$ is the borrower's profit ratio. What is the projected probability of repayment for the borrower?

    b. What is the projected probability of repayment for the borrower in part *a* if the debt/equity ratio is 3.5?

11. Use the following financial statements to answer questions *a* through *c*:

ABC, Inc. Balance Sheet (in thousands)

Assets		Liabilities	
Cash	$20	Accounts payable	$30
Accounts receivable	90	Accrued taxes	30
Inventories	90	Notes payable	90
Fixed assets	500	Long-term debt	150
		Equity	400

ABC, Inc. Income Statement (in thousands)

Sales revenues	$500
Cost of goods sold	360
Interest	40
Taxes (at 56 percent)	56
Net income	44

   a. Evaluate Altman's discriminant function for ABC if the firm has a 50 percent dividend payout ratio and the market value of equity is equal to its book value. Recall that:

   - Net working capital = current assets minus current liabilities
   - Current assets = cash + accounts receivable + inventories
   - Current liabilities = accounts payable + accruals + notes payable + current portion of long-term debt
   - Gross profits = earnings before interest and taxes (EBIT) = revenues − cost of goods sold − depreciation
   - Taxes = [EBIT − interest](tax rate)
   - Net income = EBIT − interest − taxes
   - Retained earnings = net income (1 − dividend payout ratio)

   b. Should you approve ABC Inc.'s application to your bank for $500,000 for a capital expansion loan?

   c. If ABC's sales were $300,000 and the market value of equity fell to half its book value (assume cost of goods sold and interest unchanged), how would that change ABC's income statement? (Be sure to recompute ABC's tax liability.) Would your credit decision change?

   d. Critique Altman's discriminant model using your results in questions 11*b* and *c*.

12. Use Altman's discriminant function to determine whether to grant credit to Growth Resources, Inc., where:

Balance Sheet (in thousands)

Assets		Liabilities	
Cash	$125	Accounts payable	$50
Accounts receivable	275	Debt	950
Plant and equipment	900	Equity	600
Land	300		

Income Statement (in thousands)

Sales	$2,500
Cost of goods sold	1,000
Interest expense	95
Depreciation	90
Taxes	460

NOTES: Growth Resources pays no dividends. Equity is currently selling at twice its book value.

a. What are Growth Resources' retained earnings? What is the market value of equity?

b. Calculate Growth Resources' Z score. Should their loan application be approved?

13. If the rate on one-year U.S. Treasury securities is 6.5 percent, calculate the repayment probabilities and risk premiums for the following discount securities:

a. One-year AA-rated corporate note yielding 8.9 percent.

b. One-year Baa-rated corporate bond yielding 12.5 percent.

c. One-year junk bond yielding 18 percent.

14. Calculate the risk premium for the bonds in question 13 if the lender has a collateral backing of 25 percent (i.e., $\gamma = .25$). Compare your answer to your answers to question 13.

15. Calculate the term structure of default probabilities over three years using the following spot rates from the Treasury and corporate bond (pure discount) yield curves. Be sure to calculate both the annual marginal and the cumulative default probabilities. (All yields are annualized yields to maturity.)

	Spot 1 year	*Spot 2 year*	*Spot 3 year*
Treasury	5.0%	5.55%	7.0%
BBB/Baa Grade Corporate Debt	7.0%	8.1%	9.3%

16. a. Find the implied forward rate if a 175-day maturity Treasury security has a bond equivalent yield of 8.11 percent and a 93-day maturity Treasury security has a bond equivalent yield of 8.07 percent. (Use daily compounding on a 365-day/year basis.)

b. If 175-day maturity, A-rated corporate yields exceed same maturity Treasury yields by 55 basis points and 93-day, A- rated corporate yields exceed same maturity Treasury yields by 35 basis points, what is the implied probability of default on A-rated debt over the next 93 days? Over 175 days? (Use spot rates only.)

c. What is the implied forward rate on the A-rated corporate debt in question 16b? What is the implied default probability on 82-day maturity, A-rated debt to be issued in 93 days?

17. Compare the (a) qualitative methods of credit risk measurement to (b) Altman's discriminant analysis to (c) the term structure derivation to (d) the mortality rate derivation to (e) the option model of default risk. Be sure to discuss each model's data requirements as well as its effectiveness in forecasting future default rates.

18. An all-equity firm valued at $3 million is considering issuing two-year maturity pure discount debt in the

amount of $1 million. (Assume that the value of assets increases by the face value of the debt issue.) If the current risk free rate is 5 percent and the company's asset risk (variance) is .09, what is the market value of the firm's debt? (Hint: Use the options framework to compute the market value of the risky loan.) What is the risk-adjusted interest rate on the debt issue?

19. Complete the following adjusted mortality rates covering defaults and issues for the last five years.

Years after Issuance (in percents)

	1	*2*	*3*	*4*	*5*
AAA yearly	0		.05%		.11%
cumulative		0		.12%	
BBB yearly	.01%	.07%	.10		.20
cumulative				.33	

a. What happened to the rate of default for AAA-rated bonds over the years after issuance? For BBB-rated bonds?

b. What is the survival probability of AAA-rated bond five years after issuance? BBB-rated bonds?

c. What is the difference in cumulative default rates between AAA-rated and BBB-rated bonds three years after issuance?

20. Use the mortality model to determine both the annual and cumulative default rates for the following bond ratings (note that the default amounts are in millions and outstanding amounts are in billions):

Years after Issuance

Original Rating	*1*	*2*	*3*	*4*	*5*	*6*	*7*
AAA defaults	0	0	0	0	$1	$3	$4
Outstanding	$90	$88	$85	$80	77	72	66
AA defaults	0	0	0	5	7	8	9
Outstanding	85	82	81	78	75	71	66
A Defaults	0	0	2	4	8.5	10	11
Outstanding	100	98	92	89	85	79	75
BBB Defaults	40	31	47	26	39	35	33
Outstanding	55	52	51	50	48	45	41
BB Defaults	25	26	11	27	22	9	18
Outstanding	25	24	21	19	15	12	11
B Defaults	15	5	20	4	8	5	5
Outstanding	10	9	7	6	5	3	2
CCC Defaults	20	15	5	25	2	4	9
Outstanding	12	11	9	6	5	4	2

21. Consider the following loan portfolio; 50 percent real estate loans; 25 percent *C* and *I* loans; 25 percent loans to individuals. How does this loan portfolio deviate from the national average? (Use Table 8–10.)

OFF-BALANCE-SHEET ACTIVITIES

Learning Objectives

In this chapter you learn about FIs' off-balance-sheet activities and discover the nature of these activities. Recently their rate of growth has been extremely fast compared to more traditional on-balance-sheet activities. Many off-balance-sheet activities involve risks that add to the FI's overall risk exposure. However, some off-balance-sheet activities can hedge or reduce the interest rate, credit, and foreign exchange risks of FIs. That is, off-balance-sheet activities have both risk increasing and risk reducing attributes. In addition, off-balance-sheet activities are now an important source of fee income for many FIs.

Introduction

One of the most important choices facing an FI manager is the relative scale of an FI's on- and off-balance-sheet activities. On-balance-sheet activities are those most of us are aware of because they appear on the published asset and liability balance sheets of financial institutions. For example, a bank's deposits and holdings of bonds and loans are on-balance-sheet activities. By comparison, off-balance-sheet activities are less transparent and often invisible to all but the very informed investor or regulator. In accounting terms, off-balance-sheet items usually appear below the bottom-line, frequently just as footnotes to accounts. In economic terms, however, off-balance-sheet items are *contingent* assets and liabilities that affect the future, rather than the current, shape of an FI's balance sheet. As such, they directly impact the future profitability and solvency performance of the FI. Consequently, efficient management of these off-balance-sheet items is central to controlling overall risk exposure in a modern FI.

Off-Balance-Sheet Activities and FI Solvency

From a valuation perspective, off-balance-sheet assets and liabilities have the potential to produce positive or negative *future* cash flows. As a result, the true value of an FI's capital or net worth is not simply the difference between the market value of assets and liabilities on its balance sheet today but also reflects the difference between the current market value of off-balance-sheet or contingent assets and liabilities as well.

In this section we show how off-balance-sheet activities can affect the risk exposure and performance of an FI. The following section describes different types of off-balance-sheet activity and the risks associated with each.

An item or activity is an **off-balance-sheet (OBS) asset** if, when a contingent event occurs, the off-balance-sheet item moves onto the asset side of the balance sheet. Conversely, an item or activity is an **OBS liability** if when the contingent event occurs, the off-balance-sheet item moves onto the liability side of the balance sheet. As we discuss in more detail later, FIs sell various performance guarantees—especially guarantees that its customers will not default on their financial and other obligations. Examples of such guarantees include letters of credit and standby letters of credit. Should a customer default occur, the bank's contingent liability (its guarantee) becomes an actual liability and it moves onto the liability side of the balance sheet.

Since off-balance-sheet items are contingent assets and liabilities and they move on to the balance sheet with a probability less than one, their valuation is difficult and often highly complex. Because many off-balance-sheet items involve option features—the most common methodology has been to apply contingent claims/option pricing theory models of finance. For example, the Federal Reserve measures the interest rate risk of OBS options positions taken by banks in its interest rate risk measurement model (see Chapter 7). The Fed calculates the **delta of an option**—the sensitivity of an option's value to a unit change in the price of the underlying security—and then multiplies that with the notional value of the option's position. (The delta of an option is between 0 and 1). Thus, suppose an FI has bought call options on bonds with a face or **notional value** of $100 million and the delta is calculated at .25.[1] Then, the contingent asset value of this option position would be $25 million:

$$d = \text{delta of an option} \times \frac{\text{change in the option's price}}{\text{change in price of underlying security}} = \frac{dO}{dS} = .25$$

F = notional or face value amount of options = $100 million

The delta equivalent or contingent asset value = delta × face value of option = .25 × $100 million = $25 million. Of course, to figure the value of delta for the option, one needs an option pricing model such as Black-Scholes or a binomial model. In general, the delta of the option varies with the level of the price of the underlying security as it moves in and out of the money;[2] that is, $0 < d < 1$.[3] Note that if the FI sold options, these would be valued as a contingent liability.

Loan commitments and letters of credit are also off-balance-sheet activities that have option features.[4] Specifically, when the holder of a loan commitment or credit

---

Off-Balance-Sheet (OBS) Asset
When an event occurs, this item moves on to the asset side of the balance sheet.

Off-Balance-Sheet Liability
When an event occurs, this item moves on to the liability side of the balance sheet.

Delta of an Option
The change in the value of an option for a small unit change in the price of the underlying security.

Notional Value of an OBS Item
The face value of an OBS item.

---

[1]A one cent change in the price of the bonds underlying the call option leads to a 0.25 cent (or quarter cent) change in the price of the option.

[2]For example, an in-the-money call option is where the price of the underlying security exceeds the option's exercise price. An out-of-the money call option is where the price of the underlying security is less than the option's exercise price.

[3]In the context of the Black-Scholes model, the value of the delta on a call option is $d = N(d_1)$ where $N(.)$ is the cumulative normal distribution function and $d_1 = [ln(S/X) + (r + \sigma^2/2)T]/\sigma\sqrt{T}$.

[4]See, S. I. Greenbaum, H. Hong, and A. Thakor, "Bank Loan Commitments and Interest Rate Volatility," *Journal of Banking and Finance* 5, 1981, pp. 497–510; and T. Ho and A. Saunders, "Fixed Rate Loan Commitments, Takedown Risk, and the Dynamics of Hedging with Futures," *Journal of Financial and Quantitative Analysis* 18, 1983, pp. 499–516.

line decides to draw on that credit line, this person is exercising an *option to borrow.* Or, when the buyer of a guarantee defaults, this buyer is exercising a *default* option.

Given this, we can calculate in an approximate sense the current or market value of each OBS contingent asset and liability and their effect on an FI's solvency.

Consider Tables 9–1 and 9–2. In Table 9–1, the value of the FI's net worth (E) is calculated in the traditional way as the difference between the market values of its on-balance-sheet assets (A) and liabilities (L). As we discussed in Chapter 5,

$$E = A - L$$
$$10 = 100 - 90$$

Under this calculation, the market value of the stockholders' equity stake in the FI is 10 and the ratio of the FI's capital to assets (or capital assets ratio) is 10 percent. Regulators and FIs often use the latter ratio as a simple measure of solvency (see Chapter 14 for more details).

A truer picture of the FI's economic solvency should take into account both its visible on-balance-sheet and invisible OBS activities. Specifically, the FI manager needs to value contingent or future assets and liability claims as well as current assets and liabilities. In our example, the current market value of the FI's contingent assets (CA) is 50 while the current market value of its contingent liabilities (CL) is 55. Since contingent liabilities exceed contingent assets by 5, this difference is an additional obligation, or claim, on the net worth of the FI. That is, stockholders' true net worth (E) is really:

$$E = (A - L) + (CA - CL)$$
$$= (100 - 90) + (50 - 55)$$
$$= 5$$

rather than 10 when we ignored off-balance-sheet activities. Thus, economically speaking, contingent assets and liabilities are contractual claims that directly impact

TABLE 9–1   **Traditional Valuation of an FI's Net Worth**

Assets		Liabilities	
Market value of assets (A)	100	Market value of liabilities (L)	90
		Net worth (E)	10
	100		100

TABLE 9–2   **Valuation of an FI's Net Worth with On- and Off-Balance-Sheet Activities Valued**

Assets		Liabilities	
Market value of assets (A)	100	Market value of liabilities (L)	90
		Net worth (E)	5
Market value of contingent assets (CA)	50	Market value of contingent liabilities (CL)	55
	150		150

the value of the FI. Indeed, from both the stockholders' and regulators' perspectives, large increases in the value of off-balance-sheet liabilities can render the FI economically insolvent just as effectively as losses due to mismatched interest rate gaps and default or credit losses from on-balance-sheet activities.

Concept Questions

1. Define a contingent asset and a contingent liability.
2. Suppose that an FI had a market value of assets of 95 and market value of liabilities of 88. In addition, it had contingent assets valued at 10 and contingent liabilities valued at 7. What is the FI's true net worth position?

Returns and Risks of Off-Balance-Sheet Activities

In the early 1980s, rising losses on loans to less developed and Eastern European countries, rising interest rate volatility, and squeezed interest margins for on-balance-sheet lending due to nonbank competition induced many larger commercial banks to seek profitable OBS activities. By moving activities off the balance sheet, banks hoped to earn increased fee income to offset declining margins or spreads on their traditional intermediation business. At the same time, they could avoid regulatory costs or taxes since reserve requirements, deposit insurance premiums, and capital adequacy requirements were not levied on off-balance-sheet activities. Thus, banks had both earnings and regulatory tax-avoidance incentives to move activities off their balance sheets.[5]

The dramatic growth in OBS activities resulted in the Federal Reserve introducing a tracking scheme in 1983. As part of their quarterly call reports, banks began filling out schedule L on which they listed the notional size and variety of their off-balance-sheet activities. We show these off-balance-sheet activities and their distribution and growth for 1984 to 1989 in Table 9–3.

In Table 9–3, notice the relative growth of off-balance-sheet activities. By the end of 1989, the notional or face value of off-balance-sheet bank activities were $5,692 billion compared to $3,233.9 billion on-balance-sheet activities. While the notional value of OBS items overestimates their current market or contingent claims values, the growth of these activities is still nothing short of phenomenal.[6] Indeed, this phenomenal growth has pushed regulators into imposing capital requirements on such activities; that is, explicitly recognizing the solvency risk exposure to FIs from the pursuit of such activities . These capital requirements came into effect on January 1, 1993; we describe them in detail in Chapter 14.

From Table 9–3, you can see that the major off-balance-sheet activities for U.S. banks at the end of 1989 were

- Loan commitments.
- Standby letters of credit and letters of credit.

---

[5]For a modeling of the incentives to go off-balance-sheet due to capital requirements, see G. G. Pennacchi, "Loan Sales and the Cost of Bank Capital," *Journal of Finance* 43, 1988, pp. 375–96. Also, Chapters 21 and 22 go into further details on incentives relating to loan sales.

[6]This is because the contingent claims value is usually less than the face value of most contingent assets and liabilities.

- Futures, forward contracts, swaps, and options.
- When issued securities.
- Loans sold.

In the next section, we analyze these off-balance-sheet activities in more detail with particular attention being paid to the types of risk exposure an FI faces when engaging in such activities. As we discussed earlier, precise market valuation of these contingent assets and liabilities can be extremely difficult because of their complex contingent claim features and option aspects. At a very minimum, FI managers should understand not only the general features of the risk exposure associated with each major OBS asset and liability but also how each can impact the return and profitability of an FI.

Loan Commitments

These days most commercial and industrial loans are made by firms taking down prenegotiated lines of credit or loan commitments rather than borrowing spot loans (see Chapter 8's discussion on C&I loans). For example, recent estimates are that some 70 percent of all C&I loans have originated in this manner.[7]

A bank's loan commitment agreement is a contractual commitment to loan to a firm a certain maximum amount (say $10 million) at given interest rate terms (say 12 percent). The length of time over which the borrower has the option to take down this loan is also defined in the loan commitment agreement. In return for making this loan commitment, the bank may charge an upfront fee of, say, $1/8$ percent of the commitment size, or $12,500 in this example. In addition, the bank has to stand ready to supply the full $10 million at any time over the commitment period, say, one year. Meanwhile, the borrower has a valuable option to take down any amount between $0 and $10 million. The bank may also charge the borrower a **back-end fee** on any unused balances in the commitment line at the end of the period.[8] In this example, if the borrower only takes down $8 million in funds over the year and the fee on *unused* commitments is $1/4$ percent, the bank would generate additional revenue income of $1/4$ percent times $2 million or $5,000.

See Figure 9–1 for a summary of the structure of this loan commitment. Note that only when the borrower actually draws on the commitment do the loans made under the commitment appear on the balance sheet. Thus, when the $8 million loan is

Back-End Fee
The fee imposed on the unused component of a loan commitment.

FIGURE 9-1

The structure of a loan commitment

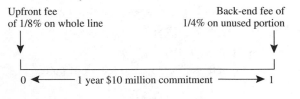

[7]M. Berlin, "Loan Commitments: Insurance Contracts in a Risky World," Federal Reserve Bank of Philadelphia, *Business Review,* May–June 1986, pp. 3–12.

[8]This is an excess capacity charge; see A. V. Thakor and G. Udell, "An Economic Rationale for the Pricing Structure of Bank Loan Commitments," *Journal of Banking and Finance* 11, 1987, pp. 271–90.

taken down exactly halfway through the one-year commitment period, only the balance sheet *six months later* would show a new $8 million loan being created. When the $10 million commitment is made at time 0, nothing shows on the balance sheet. Nevertheless, the bank must stand ready to make the full $10 million in loans on any day within the one-year commitment period; that is, at time 0 a new contingent claim on the resources of the bank was created.

This raises the question: What contingent risks are created by the loan commitment provision? At least four types of risk are associated with the extension of loan commitments: interest rate risk, take down risk, credit risk, and aggregate funding risk.

Interest Rate Risk.   Interest rate risk is a contingent risk emanating from the fact that the bank precommits to make loans available to a borrower over the commitment period at either: (1) some fixed interest rate as a fixed-rate loan commitment or (2) some variable rate as a variable-rate loan commitment. Suppose the bank precommits to lend $10 million at 12 percent over the year and its cost of funds rises. The cost of funds may well rise to such a level as to make the spread between the 12 percent commitment rate and the cost of funds negative or very small. Moreover, 12 percent may be much less than the rate the customer would have to pay if forced to borrow on the spot loan market under current interest rate conditions. When rates do rise over the commitment period, the FI stands to lose on its portfolio of fixed-rate loan commitments as borrowers exercise to the full their very valuable options to borrow at below-market rates.[9]

One way the FI can control this risk is by making commitment rates float with spot loan rates. For example, by making loan commitments indexed to the prime rate. If the prime rate rises over the commitment period, so does the cost of commitment loans to the borrower; that is, the borrower pays the market rate in effect at the time of drawing on the commitment. Nevertheless, this fixed formula rate solution does not totally eradicate interest rate risk on loan commitments. For example, suppose the prime rate rises by 1 percent but the cost of funds rises by 1.25 percent, the spread between the indexed commitment loan and the cost of funds narrows by .25 percent. This spread risk is often called **basis risk.**[10]

Basis Risk
The variable spread between a lending rate and a borrowing rate, or between any two interest rates or prices.

Take Down Risk.   Another contingent risk is take down risk. Specifically, in making the loan commitment, the FI must always stand ready to provide the maximum of the commitment line—$10 million in our example. The borrower has the flexible option to borrow anything between $0 and the $10 million ceiling on any business day in the commitment period. This exposes the FI to a degree of future liquidity risk or uncertainty. The FI can never be absolutely sure when during the commitment period, the borrower will arrive and demand the full $10 million or some proportion thereof in cash.[11] To some extent at least, the back-end fee on unused amounts is designed to create incentives for the borrower to take down lines

---

[9]In an options sense, the loans are in the money.

[10]Basis risk arises because loan rates and deposit rates are not perfectly correlated in their movements over time.

[11]Indeed, the borrower could come to the bank and borrow different amounts over the period (e.g., $1 million in month 1, $2 million in month 2, etc.). The only constraint is the $10 million ceiling. See Ho and Saunders (1983) for a modelling approach to take down risk. We discuss this liquidity risk aspect of loan commitments more in Chapter 13.

TABLE 9-3 Aggregate Volume of Off-Balance-Sheet Commitments and Contingencies by U.S. Commercial Banks, Annual data as of December (dollars in billions)

	Item No.	1984	1985	1986	1987	1988	1989	Distribution 1989
Commitments to lend	RCFD3423	$495.6	$542.4	$570.4	$611.6	$654.9	$685.7	12.0%
Future and forward contracts (exclude FX)								
Commitments to buy	RCFD3424	40	57.2	99.7	122.7	174.3	236.0	4.1
Commitments to sell	RCFD3425	28.3	40.5	79.6	137.6	234.4	284.9	5.0
When issued securities								
Commitments to buy	RCFD3434	4.3	4.4	9.8	2	6.8	11.6	0.2
Commitments to sell	RCFD3435	3.5	3.3	6.2	2.1	6.6	6.8	0.1
Standby contracts and other option contracts								
Obligations to buy under option contracts	RCFD3426	2.8	10.7	27.8	48.9	67.3	118.4	2.1
Obligations to sell under option contracts	RCFD3427	1.7	5	11.8	16.4	29.4	70.3	1.2
Commitments to buy FX (incl. $US), spot and forward	RCFD3415	584	735.2	890.8	1,504.1	1,683.2	2,249.4	39.5
Standby L/C and foreign office guarantees								
To U.S. addressees	RCFD3376	109.8	134.8	132.1	134.5	135.6	144.4	2.5
To non-U.S. addressees	RCFD3377	34	38.2	35.8	33.7	33.2	33.3	0.6
(Amount of these items sold to others via participations)	RCFD3378	15	18.2	18.5	19.6	19.2	20.1	0.4
Commercial L/C	RCFD3411	30	28.4	28.4	30.5	30.2	30.3	0.5
Participations in acceptances sold to others	RCFD3428	8.4	8.4	5.4	4.2	3.9	2.8	0.0
Participations in acceptances bought from others	RCFD3429	1.5	0.9	0.8	1.5	0.5	0.3	0.0
Securities borrowed	RCFD3432	2.7	3.5	5.4	5.9	6.7	6.8	0.1
Securities lent	RCFD3433	2.2	3.1	4	4.5	3.9	4.2	0.1
Other significant commitments and contingencies	RCFD3430	24.5	57.7	70.5	84.3	128.1	169.0	3.0
Memoranda:								
Loans originated and sold during period ending this quarter	RCFD3431	50.1	75.6	107.7	192.1	280.4	250.8	4.4
Loans purchased during period ending this quarter	RCFD3488	n/a	n/a	n/a	15.7	18.7	19.0	0.3
Notional value of all outstanding interest rate swaps	RCFD3450	n/a	186.1	366.6	714.9	928.6	1,348.1	23.7

Mortgages sold, with recourse								
FNMA and FHLMC residential mortgage loan pools								
O/S principal bal. of mortgages sold or swapped	RCFD3650	n/a	n/a	n/a	n/a	n/a	8.3	0.1
Amount of recourse exposure on these mortgages	RCFD3651	n/a	n/a	n/a	n/a	n/a	7.2	0.1
Private residential mortgage loans								
O/S principal bal. of mortgages sold	RCFD3652	n/a	n/a	n/a	n/a	n/a	2.1	0.0
Amount of recourse exposure on these mortgages	RCFD3653	n/a	n/a	n/a	n/a	n/a	0.2	0.0
Farmer Mac agricultural mortgage loan pools								
O/S principal bal. of mortgages sold	RCFD3654	n/a	n/a	n/a	n/a	n/a	0.0	0.0
Amount of recourse exposure on these mortgages	RCFD3655	n/a	n/a	n/a	n/a	n/a	0.0	0.0
Total, excluding memoranda items	RCFD2170	$1,438.4	$1,953.6	$2,471.3	$3,686.8	$4,445.9	$5,692.2	100.0%
Total assets (on-balance-sheet items)		$2,492.5	$2,707.6	$2,907.5	$2,955.2	$3,064.2	$3,233.9	

FX = foreign exchange

L/C = letter of credit

O/S principal bal. = outstanding principal balance

SOURCE: Call Reports (OCC, Ogilvie, October 1990). Source: Comptroller of the Currency

in full to avoid paying this fee. However, in actuality many lines are only partially drawn upon.[12]

Credit Risk.   FIs also face a degree of contingent credit risk in setting the interest or formula rate on a loan commitment. Specifically, the FI often adds a risk premium based on its current assessment of the creditworthiness of the borrower. For example, the borrower may be judged as a AA credit risk paying 1 percent over prime rate. However, suppose that over the one-year commitment period the borrowing firm gets into difficulty; its earnings decline so that its creditworthiness is downgraded to BBB. The problem for the FI is that the credit risk premium on the commitment had been preset to the AA level for the one-year commitment period. To avoid being exposed to dramatic declines in borrower creditworthiness over the commitment period, most FIs include an adverse material change in conditions clause under which the FI can cancel or reprice a loan commitment. However, exercising such a clause is really a last resort tactic for an FI because it may put the borrower out of business and result in costly legal claims for breach of contract.[13]

Aggregate Funding Risk.   Many large borrowing firms, such as GM, Ford, or IBM, take out multiple commitment or credit lines with many banks as insurance against future credit crunches. In a credit crunch, the supply of credit to borrowers is restricted possibly due to restrictive monetary policy actions of the Federal Reserve. Another cause is an increased aversion toward lending by FIs; that is, a shift to the left in the loan supply function at all interest rates. In such credit crunches, borrowers with long-standing loan commitments are unlikely to be as credit constrained as those

---

[12]See A. Melnick and S. Plaut, "Loan Commitment Contracts, Terms of Lending, and Credit Allocations," *Journal of Finance* 41, 1986, pp. 425–36.

It is quite easy to show how the unique features of loan commitments affect the promised return, $(1 + k)$, on a loan. In Chapter 8, we developed a model for determining $(1 + k)$ on a spot loan. This can be extended by allowing for partial take down and the upfront and back-end fees commonly found in loan commitments.

Let: L = interest on the loan = 12%
    m = risk premium = 2%
    f_1 = upfront fee on the whole commitment = $^1/_8$%
    f_2 = back-end fee on the unused commitment = $^1/_4$%
    b = compensating balance = 10%
    R = reserve-requirements = 10%
    t = expected (average) take down rate $(0 < t < 1)$ on the loan commitment = 75%

Then the general formula for the promised return $(1 + k)$ of the loan commitment is:

$$1+k = 1 + \frac{f_1 + f_2(1-t) + (L+m)t}{t - [bt(1-R)]}$$

$$1+k = 1 + \frac{.00125 + .0025(.25) + (.12 + .02).75}{.75 - [(.10)(.75)(.9)]}$$

$$1+k = 1 + \frac{.106875}{.682500} = 1.1566 \text{ or } k = 15.66\%$$

This formula closely follows that in Brick (1984) chap. 4. Note that for simplicity we have used undiscounted cash flows. Taking into account the time value of money means that we would need to discount both f_2 and $L + m$ since they are paid at the end of the period. If the discount factor (cost of funds) is $d = $ 10 percent, then $k = 14.25$ percent.

[13]Potential damage claims could be enormous if the borrower goes out of business and attributes this to the cancellation of loans under the commitment contract. There are also important reputational costs to take into account in canceling a commitment to lend.

without loan commitments. However, this also implies that aggregate demands by borrowers to take down loan commitments are likely to be greatest when the FI's borrowing and funding conditions are most costly and difficult. In difficult credit conditions, this aggregate commitment take down effect can raise the cost of funds above normal levels as many FIs scramble for funds to meet their commitments to customers. This is similar to the *externality* effect common in many markets when all participants simultaneously act together and affect the costs of each individual participant adversely.

The four contingent risk effects just identified—interest rate risk, take down risk, credit risk, and aggregate funding risk—all appear to imply that loan commitment activities increase the insolvency exposure of FIs that engage in such activities. However, an opposing view holds that loan commitment contracts may make an FI less risky than if it had not engaged in them. This view maintains that to be able to charge fees and sell loan commitments, or equivalent credit rationing insurance, the bank must convince borrowers that it will still be around to provide the credit needed in the *future*.[14] To convince borrowers in a credible fashion that an FI will be around to meet its future commitments, managers may have to adopt *lower* risk portfolios *today* than otherwise. By adopting lower risk portfolios, they increase the probability of meeting all long-term on- and off-balance-sheet obligations. Interestingly, a recent empirical study has confirmed that banks making more loan commitments have lower on-balance-sheet portfolio risk characteristics than those with relatively low levels of commitments.[15]

Commercial Letters of Credit and Standby Letters of Credit

Letters of Credit
Contingent guarantees sold by an FI to underwrite the trade or commercial performance of the buyer of the guarantee.

Standby Letters of Credit
Guarantees issued to cover contingencies that are potentially more severe and less predictable than contingencies covered under trade-related or commercial letters of credit.

In selling commercial **letters of credit** (LCs) and **standby letters of credit** (SLCs) for fees, FIs add to their contingent future liabilities. Both LCs and SLCs are essentially *guarantees* sold by an FI to underwrite the *performance* of the buyer of the guarantee (such as a corporation). In economic terms, the FI that sells LCs and SLCs is selling insurance against the frequency or severity of some particular future occurrence. Further, similar to the different lines of insurance sold by property-casualty insurers, LC and SLC contracts have differences in the severity and frequency of their risk exposures. We look next at the risk exposure to an FI from engaging in LC and SLC off-balance-sheet activities.

Commercial Letters of Credit.   Commercial letters of credit are widely used in both domestic and international trade. For example, to ease the shipment of grain between a farmer in Iowa and a purchaser in New Orleans, or to ease the shipment of goods between a U.S. importer and a foreign exporter. The FI's role is to provide a formal guarantee that payment for goods shipped or sold will be forthcoming in the future regardless of whether the buyer of the goods defaults on payment or not. We show a very simple LC example in Figure 9–2 for an international transaction between a U.S. importer and a German exporter.

Suppose the U.S. importer sent an order for $10 million worth of machinery to a German exporter as shown by arrow 1 in Figure 9–2. However, the German exporter may be reluctant to send the goods without some assurance or guarantee of being

---

[14]A. W. A. Boot and A. V. Thakor, "Off-Balance-Sheet Liabilities, Deposit Insurance, and Capital Regulation," *Journal of Banking and Finance* 15, 1991, pp. 825–46.

[15]R. B. Avery, and A. N. Berger, "Loan Commitments and Bank Risk Exposure," *Journal of Banking and Finance* 15, 1991, pp. 173–92.

FIGURE 9-2

A simple letter of credit transaction

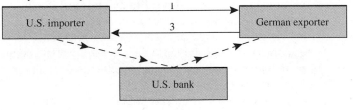

paid once the goods are shipped. The U.S. importer may promise to pay for the goods in 90 days but the German exporter may feel insecure either because it knows little about the creditworthiness of the U.S. importer, or because the U.S. importer has a low credit rating (say A or BBB). To persuade the German exporter to ship the goods, the U.S. importer may have to turn to a large U.S. bank with whom it has developed a long-term customer relationship. The U.S. bank can better appraise the creditworthiness of the U.S. importer due to its role as a lender and monitor. It can issue a contingent payment guarantee—that is, a letter of credit to the German exporter on the importer's behalf—in return for a letter of credit fee paid by the U.S. importer. In our example, the bank would send a LC to the German exporter guaranteeing payment for the goods in 90 days regardless of whether the importer defaults on its obligation to the German exporter. See arrow 2 in Figure 9–2. Implicitly, the bank is replacing the credit risk of the U.S. importer with its own credit risk guarantee. For this substitution to work effectively, in guaranteeing payment, the bank has to have a higher credit standing or better credit quality reputation than the U.S. importer. Once the bank issues the LC and sends it to the German exporter, the exporter ships the goods to the U.S. importer, as shown by arrow 3. In 90 days' time, the U.S. importer pays the German exporter for the goods sent with a very high probability and the bank keeps the fee as profit. The fee is, perhaps, 10 basis points of the face value of the letter of credit, or $10,000 in this example.

There is a small probability that the U.S. importer would be unable to pay the $10 million in 90 days and would default. Then, the bank would be obliged to make good on its guarantee. The cost of such a default could mean a payment of $10 million by the bank, although it would have a creditor's claim against the assets of the importer to offset this loss. Clearly, the LC fee should exceed the expected default risk on the LC, which is equal to the probability of default times the expected net payout on the LC, after adjusting for its ability to reclaim assets from the defaulting importer and any monitoring costs.

Standby Letters of Credit.   Standby letters of credit perform an insurance function similar to commercial and trade letters of credit. However, the structure and type of risk covered is different. FIs may issue standby letters of credit to cover contingencies that are potentially more *severe,* less *predictable* or frequent, and not necessarily trade related.[16] These include performance bond guarantees, whereby an FI may guarantee that a real estate development will be completed in some interval of time.

---

[16]G. O. Koppenhaver uses a similar definition to distinguish between LCs and SLCs. See "Standby Letters of Credit," Federal Reserve Bank of Chicago, *Economic Perspectives,* 1987, pp. 28–38.

Alternatively, it may offer default guarantees to back an issue of commercial paper (CP) or municipal revenue bonds to allow issuers to achieve a higher credit rating and a lower funding cost than otherwise.

Without credit enhancements, for example, many firms would be unable to borrow in the CP market or would have to borrow at a higher funding cost. P1 borrowers, who offer the highest quality commercial paper, normally pay 40 basis points less than P2 borrowers, the next quality grade. By paying a fee to a bank of perhaps 25 basis points, an FI guarantees to pay commercial paper purchasers' principal and interest on maturity should the issuing firm itself be unable to pay. The SLC backing of commercial paper issues normally results in the paper being placed in the lowest default risk class (P1) and the issuer saving up to 15 basis points on issuing costs. That is, 40 basis points (the P2 − P1 spread) minus the 25-basis-point SLC fee equals 15 basis points.

Note that in selling the SLCs, banks are directly competing with another of their off-balance-sheet products, loan commitments. Rather than buying a SLC from a bank to back a CP issue, the issuing firm might pay a fee to a bank to supply a loan commitment. This loan commitment would match the size and maturity of the commercial paper issue; for example, a $100 million ceiling and 45 days maturity. If on maturity, the commercial paper issuer had insufficient funds to repay the commercial paper holders, the issuer has the right to take down the $100 million loan commitment and to use these funds to meet CP repayments. Often, the upfront fees on such loan commitments are less than those on SLCs; therefore, many CP-issuing firms prefer to use commitments.

Finally, remember that U.S. banks are not the only issuers of SLCs. Not surprisingly, performance bonds and financial guarantees are an important business line of property-casualty insurers (often called surety and fidelity insurance—see box). Moreover, foreign banks are taking an increasing share of the U.S. market. The reason is that to credibly sell guarantees such as SLCs, the seller must have a better credit rating than the customer. In recent years, only one U.S. bank—Morgan Guaranty—has consistently had an AAA rating. Higher credit ratings not only make the guarantor more attractive from the buyer's perspective but also make the guarantor more competitive in that its cost of funds is lower than less creditworthy FIs.

Futures, Forwards, Swaps, and Option Contracts

Contingent credit risk is likely to be present when FIs expand their positions in forward, futures, swaps, and option contracts. This risk relates to the fact that the counterparty to one of these contracts may default on payment obligations, leaving the FI unhedged or naked and having to replace the contract at today's interest rates, prices, or exchange rates. Further, such defaults are most likely to occur when the counterparty is losing heavily on the contract and the FI is in the money on the contract. This type of default risk is much more serious for forward contracts than futures contracts. The reason is that forward contracts are nonstandard contracts entered into bilaterally by negotiating parties such as two banks and all cash flows are required to be paid at one time (on contract maturity). Thus, they are essentially over the counter (OTC) arrangements with no external guarantees should one or other party default on the contract. For example, a forward foreign exchange contract that promises to deliver £10 million in three months' time at the exchange rate $1.70 to £1 might be defaulted on by the contract seller if it costs $1.90 to purchase a £1 for delivery when the forward contract matures. By contrast, futures contracts are stan-

PROFESSIONAL PERSPECTIVES

Trade Credit Insurance

Paulette J. Truman
American International Underwriters

Accounts receivable is a critical component of a company's balance sheet and typically represents a significant portion of the firm's current assets. While most companies routinely insure against property loss, liability exposure, and other unpredictable events, accounts receivable often remains uninsured and therefore vulnerable to unexpected credit losses.

Fear that the leveraged buyouts of the 1980s will turn into the bankruptcies of the 1990s has driven many suppliers, especially in the retail apparel and steel industries, to purchase trade credit insurance. Because of high leverage and weak cash flow, these two industries have been especially vulnerable to insolvencies. Apparel manufacturers that shipped to Macy's department stores and subsequently incurred large credit losses due to Macy's bankruptcy probably wish that they had purchased trade credit insurance.

Trade credit insurance (also known as commercial credit insurance), offered by American International Underwriters (AIU) and a number of other diversified insurance companies, protects a supplier's trade receivables; that is, its right to receive payment from its customer (or buyer) for goods or services previously delivered to the buyer. The primary risk insured is the buyer's insolvency. Since the probability of insolvency loss cannot be actuarily determined as can the risks covered by the more typical lines of insurance such as property, casualty, and liability, trade credit risk can be properly evaluated only by analyzing the buyer's financial condition and studying industry trends and indicators.

In addition to protecting the insured's accounts receivable, trade credit insurance indirectly affords the buyer liquidity to carry on day-to-day operations. A distressed company, for example, relies heavily on its suppliers for trade credit, especially in cases where the company's banks are reluctant to extend adequate credit. Suppliers, in turn, may rely on trade credit insurance to transfer their customers' credit risk to the insurer.

The purpose of trade credit insurance, like many

continued

dardized contracts guaranteed by organized exchanges such as the New York Futures Exchange (NYFE). Futures contracts, like forward contracts, make commitments about the delivery of foreign exchange (or some other asset) at some future date. If a counterparty were to default on a future contract, however, the exchange assumes the position and the payment obligations of the defaulting party. Thus, unless the exchange itself is threatened by a systematic financial market collapse, futures are essentially default risk free.[17] In addition, default risk is reduced by the daily marking to market of contracts. This prevents the accumulation of losses and gains that occur with forward contracts. These differences are discussed in more detail in Chapter 18.

---

[17]More specifically, there are at least four reasons why the default risk of a futures contract is less than that of a forward contract: (i) daily marking to market of futures, (ii) margin requirements on futures that act as a security bond, (iii) price limits that spread out over time extreme price fluctuations and (iv) default guarantees by the futures exchange itself.

other types of insurance, is to protect the insured against unexpected, catastrophic losses, and not to encourage the insured to take risks that it would otherwise avoid. If a trade credit insurance policy were to completely shift the credit risk to the insurer, it would result in the insured having no economic incentive to exercise any restraint in shipping to financially unsound buyers. This situation can be avoided by requiring the insured to retain a significant portion of the risk through deductibles and coinsurance provisions. In addition, specific provisions are built into a policy to encourage the insured to act responsibly when extending credit to its buyers.

For example, at AIU we were recently faced with a situation where an insured wanted to continue to ship its product to its longtime steel customer (or buyer) after it became clear that the customer was in default under its bank loan agreements and was in an extremely precarious financial condition. The AIU policy required the insured to comply with its own credit and collection procedures before making any on-going shipments to a buyer. Because any further extension of trade credit to the steel company would have violated the insured's credit procedures, the insured itself would ultimately have borne the risk of extending additional credit because an insurance claim would likely have been denied by AIU under these circumstances. Thus, the trade credit policy served its purpose of protecting the insured from the risk of unexpected loss and indirectly providing the buyer with a source of credit as long as it remained a reasonable credit risk, but the policy discouraged the insured from shipping to the buyer after the buyer had clearly become distressed.

BIOGRAPHICAL SUMMARY

Paulette J. Truman is Credit Manager of American International Underwriters' (AIU) Trade and Political Risk Division. AIU is a marketing unit consisting of agencies and insurance companies wholly owned by American International Group, Inc. (AIG). With more than $12 billion in capital, AIG is the leading U.S.-based international insurance organization and the nation's largest underwriter of commercial and industrial coverages. Its member companies write property, casualty, marine, life, and financial services insurance in more than 100 countries and jurisdictions, and are engaged in a range of financial services businesses.

Ms. Truman joined AIU two years ago to focus her credit expertise on buyer risk analysis. She previously worked as a lending officer in the Europe/Middle East/Africa Department of Bankers Trust Company, specializing in trade finance. She prepared extensive credit risk evaluations of financial products extended to foreign agencies, banks, and corporations. Most recently, Ms. Truman was an investment banker at PaineWebber Incorporated working on cash flow and present value analysis of alternative debt structures for municipal bond underwritings.

Ms. Truman graduated from Stanford University with a B.A. in economics, and received an M.B.A. in finance from New York University. She also graduated from Bankers Trust Company's eight-month executive credit training program, which included intensive courses in accounting, credit analysis, and corporate finance.

The same is true for option contracts purchased or sold by an FI. If these are standardized options traded on exchanges, such as bond options, they are virtually default risk free.[18] If they are specialized options purchased over the counter such as interest rate caps (see Chapter 19), then some element of default risk exists.[19] Similarly, swaps are OTC instruments normally susceptible to counterparty risk (see Chapter 20).[20] In general, default risk on OTC contracts increases with the time to maturity of the contract, and the fluctuation of underlying prices, interest rates, or exchange rates.[21]

---

[18]Note that the options can still be subject to interest rate risk; see our earlier discussion on the delta on a bond option.

[19]Under an interest rate cap, in return for a fee the seller promises to compensate the buyer should interest rates rise above a certain level. If rates rise a lot more than expected, the cap seller may have an incentive to default to truncate the losses. Thus, selling a cap is similar to a bank selling interest rate risk insurance (see Chapter 19 for more details).

[20]In a swap, two parties contract to exchange interest rate payments or foreign exchange payments. If interest rates (or foreign exchange rates) move a lot, one party can be faced with considerable future loss exposure, creating incentives to default.

[21]Reputational considerations and the need for future access to markets for hedging deter the incentive to default (see Chapter 20 as well).

FIGURE 9-3

T-bill auction time line

Tuesday	Monday
size of	allotment of bills
auction announced	among bidders

Forward Purchases and Sales of When Issued Securities

When Issued (WI) Trading
Trading in securities prior to their actual issue.

Very often, banks and other FIs—especially investment banks—enter into commitments to buy and sell securities before issue. This is called **when issued (WI) trading.** These off-balance-sheet commitments can expose an FI to future or contingent interest rate risk.

Good examples of when issued commitments are those taken on in new T-bills in the week prior to the announcement of the T-bill auction results. Every Tuesday, on behalf of the Treasury, the Federal Reserve announces the auction size of new three- and six-month bills to be allotted the following Monday. See Figure 9–3.

Between the time the total auction size is announced on Tuesday and the bill allotments are announced on the following Monday, major T-bill dealers sell WI contracts. Normally, large investment banks and commercial banks are major T-bill dealers. They sell the yet-to-be-issued T-bills for forward delivery to customers in the secondary market at a small margin above the price they expect to pay at the primary auction. This can be profitable if the primary dealer gets all the bills needed at the auction at the appropriate price or interest rate to fulfill these forward WI contracts. A primary dealer that makes a mistake regarding the tenor of the auction faces the risk that the commitments entered into to deliver T-bills in the WI market can only be met at a loss. For example, an overcommitted dealer may have to buy bills from other dealers at a loss right after the auction results are announced to meet the WI T-bill commitments made to its customers.

This problem occurred when Salomon Brothers cornered or squeezed the market for new two-year Treasury bonds in 1990 by fixing the bids in the primary market. As a result, the Treasury instituted a wholesale reform program to change the way bills and bonds are auctioned.[22] Under the proposed reform program, Treasury securities are to be electronically auctioned using a single price, rather than the discriminating auction procedure traditionally used. Moreover, the number of dealers allowed to bid at these auctions will increase dramatically. Finally, should a squeeze be apparent, the Treasury will be able to increase the supply of bills or bonds by reopening the auction.

Loans Sold

We discuss the types of loans FIs sell, their incentives to sell, and the way in which they can be sold in more detail in Chapter 22. Increasingly, banks and other FIs originate loans on their balance sheets, but rather than holding them to maturity, quickly sell them to outside investors. These outside investors include other banks, insurance companies, mutual funds, or even corporations. In acting as loan originators and loan

---

[22]Under the auction rules, no bidder could bid for or attain more than 35 percent of an issue. However, by bidding using customers' names (without their knowledge) in addition to bidding under their own name, Salomon Brothers vastly exceeded the 35 percent limit.

sellers, FIs are operating more in the fashion of loan brokers than traditional asset transformers (see Chapter 3).

Recourse
The ability to put an asset or loan back to the seller should the credit quality of that asset deteriorate.

When an outside party buys a loan with absolutely no **recourse** to the seller of the loan, should the loan eventually go bad, loan sales have no off-balance-sheet contingent liability implications for FIs. Specifically, *no recourse* means that if the loan sold by the FI does go bad, the buyer of the loan has to bear the full risk of loss. In particular, the buyer cannot put the bad loan back to the seller or originating bank. Suppose the loan is sold with recourse. Then, loan sales present a long-term contingent credit risk to the seller. Essentially, the buyer of the loan holds a long-term option to put the loan back to the seller, which can be exercised should the credit quality of the purchased loan deteriorate. In reality, the recourse or nonrecourse nature of loan sales is often ambiguous. For example, some have argued that banks generally are willing to repurchase bad no recourse loans to preserve their reputations with their customers.[23] Obviously, reputational concerns may extend the size of a selling bank's contingent liabilities for off-balance-sheet activities.

Concept Questions

1. What are the four risks related to loan commitments?
2. What is the major difference between a commercial letter of credit and a standby letter of credit?
3. What is meant by counterparty risk in a forward contract?
4. Which is more risky for the bank, loan sales with recourse or loan sales without recourse?

Schedule L and Nonschedule L Off-Balance-Sheet Risks

So far, we have looked at five different off-balance-sheet activities that banks have to report to the Federal Reserve each quarter as part of their Schedule L section of the Call Report. Remember that many other FIs engage in these activities as well. Thus, thrifts, insurance companies, and investment banks all engage in futures, forwards, swaps, and options transactions of varying forms. Life insurers are heavily engaged in making loan commitments in commercial mortgages, property-casualty companies underwrite large amounts of financial guarantees, while investment banks engage in when issued securities trading. Moreover, the five activities just discussed are not the only off-balance-sheet activities that can create contingent liabilities or risks for an FI. Next, we introduce two others briefly and discuss them at greater length in later chapters.

Settlement Risk

FIs send the bulk of their wholesale dollar payments along wire transfer systems such as Fedwire and the Clearing House InterBank Payment System (CHIPS). Fedwire is a domestic wire transfer network owned by the Federal Reserve, while CHIPS is an

---

[23]G. Gorton and G. Pennacchi, "Are Loan Sales Really Off Balance Sheet?" in *Off-Balance-Sheet Activities,* ed. J. Ronen, A. Saunders, and A. C. Sondhi (New York: Quorum Books, 1989), pp. 19–40. We discuss loan sales in more detail in Chapter 22.

FIGURE 9–4

One and multibank holding company structures

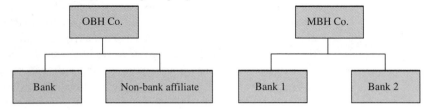

international and private network owned by 140 or so participating or member banks. Currently, over $1.7 trillion a day is transferred across these two networks.

Unlike the domestic Fedwire system, funds or payment messages sent on the CHIPS network *within* the day are provisional messages that become final and are settled only at the *end* of the day. Say that bank X sends a fund transfer payment message to bank Z at 11 A.M. EST. The actual cash settlement and physical transfer of funds between X and Z takes place at the end of the day, normally through transferring cash held in reserve accounts at the Federal Reserve banks. Because the transfer of funds is not finalized until the end of the day, bank Z, the message-receiving bank faces an *intraday* or within day settlement risk. Specifically, bank Z may assume the funds message received at 11 A.M. from bank X is for good funds and then on-lend them to Bank Y at 11:15 A.M. However, if bank X does not deliver the promised funds at the end of the day, bank Z may be pushed into a serious net funds deficit position when it is unable to meet its payment commitment to bank Y. Conceivably, its net debtor position may be large enough to exceed its capital and reserves, rendering it technically insolvent. Such a disruption might occur only if a major fraud were discovered in bank X's books during the day and it was closed the same day by bank regulators. That would make payment to bank Z impossible to complete at the end of the day. Alternatively, bank X might be transmitting funds it does not have in the hope of keeping its "name in the market" to be able to raise funds later in the day. However, other banks may revise their credit limits for this bank during the day, making it unable to deliver all the funds it promised to bank Z.

The essential feature of settlement risk is that bank Z is exposed to a within day or intraday credit risk that does not appear on its balance sheet. The balance sheet, at best, summarizes only the end of day closing position or book of a bank. Thus, intraday settlement risk is an additional form of off-balance-sheet risk facing FIs participating on private wholesale wire transfer system networks. (See Chapter 10 for a more detailed analysis of this risk and recent policy changes designed to reduce this risk.)

Affiliate Risk

Many FIs operate as holding companies. A holding company is a corporation that owns the shares (normally more than 25 percent) of other corporations. For example, Citicorp is a one bank holding company (OBHC) that owns all the shares of Citibank. Certain permitted nonbank activities such as data processing are engaged in through separately capitalized affiliates or companies also owned by Citicorp. Similarly, a number of other holding companies are multibank holding companies (MBHC) that own shares in a number of different banks. First InterState is a MBHC that holds shares in banks in more than 10 states. Look at these two organizational structures in Figure 9–4.

Legally, in the context of OBHCs, the bank and the nonbank affiliate are separate companies as are bank 1 and bank 2 in the context of MBHCs. Thus, in Figure 9–4, if the nonbank affiliate and bank 2 failed, they should have no effect on the financial resources of the bank in the OBHC or on bank 1 in the MBHC. This is the essence of the principle of corporate separateness underlying a legal corporation's limited liability in the United States. In reality, the failure of an affiliated firm or bank can impact another bank in a holding company structure in a number of ways. We discuss two ways next. First, *creditors* of the failed affiliate may lay a claim to the surviving bank's resources on the grounds that operationally in name or in activity, it is not really a separate company from the failed affiliate. This "estoppel argument" made under the law is based on idea that the customers of the failed institution are relatively unsophisticated in their financial affairs. That is, they could not distinguish between the failing corporation and its surviving affiliate due to name similarity or some similar such reason.[24] Second, *regulators* have tried to enforce a source of strength doctrine in recent years for large multibank holding company failures. Under this doctrine, directly challenging the principle of corporate separateness, the resources of sound banks may support those of failing banks. The Federal Reserve has tried to implement this principal, such as in MCorp's failure in Texas, but has generally been prevented from doing this by the courts.

If either of these breaches of corporate separateness are legally supported, the risks of a nonbank affiliate or an affiliated bank's activities impose a further contingent off-balance-sheet liability on a healthy bank. This is not only true for banks but also potentially true for many other FIs such as insurance companies and investment banks that adopt holding company organizational structures in which corporate separateness is in doubt.[25]

Concept Questions

1. What is the source of settlement risk on the CHIPS payments system?
2. What are two major sources of affiliate risk?

Off-Balance-Sheet Activities Are Not Always Risk Increasing

This chapter has emphasized that OBS activities may add to the riskiness of an FI's activities. Indeed, most contingent assets and liabilities have various characteristics that may accentuate the default and/or interest rate risk exposures of FIs. Even so, FIs use some OBS instruments—especially, forwards, futures, options, and swaps— to reduce or manage their interest rate risk, foreign exchange risk, and credit risk

---

[24]For example, suppose the failing nonbank affiliate was called Town Data Processing and the affiliated bank was called Town Bank.

[25]A good example is the failure of Drexel Burnham Lambert in February 1991. For a good discussion of affiliate risk in this case, see W. S. Haraf, "The Collapse of Drexel Burnham Lambert: Lessons for Bank Regulators," *Regulation,* Winter 1991, pp. 22–25.

exposures in a manner superior to that which would exist in their absence.[26] When used to hedge on-balance-sheet interest rate, foreign exchange, and credit risks, these instruments can actually work to reduce the overall insolvency risk of FIs. Although we do not fully describe the role of these instruments as hedging vehicles in reducing an FI's insolvency exposure until Chapters 18 through 20, you can now recognize the inherent danger in the overregulation of off-balance-sheet activities and instruments. For example, despite the risk that a counterparty might default on a forward foreign exchange contract, this risk is very small. It is probably much lower than the insolvency risk faced by an FI that did not use forward contracts to hedge foreign exchange assets against undesirable fluctuations in exchange rates. (See Chapter 11 for some examples of this.) As the regulatory costs of hedging rise, such as through the imposition of special capital requirements on such instruments (see Chapter 14), FIs may have a tendency to underhedge resulting in an increase, rather than a decrease, in FI insolvency risk.

Finally, fees from off-balance-sheet activities provide a key source of noninterest income for many FIs, especially the largest and most creditworthy. You can see the importance of such noninterest incomes for large banks in Table 10–1 in the next chapter. Thus, increased OBS earnings can potentially compensate for increased OBS risk exposure and actually reduce the probability of insolvency for some FIs.

---

[26]As we discuss in Chapter 18, there are strong tax disincentives to using derivatives for purposes other than direct hedging.

Summary

This chapter shows that the net worth or economic value of an FI as a going concern to its owners is linked not only to the value of its traditional on-balance-sheet activities but also to the contingent asset and liability values of its off-balance-sheet activities. Specifically, changes in the value of assets and liabilities both on and off the balance-sheet may render an FI economically insolvent. We also analyzed the risks of each major off-balance-sheet activity. The net result is that in assessing an FI's risk exposure both visible on-balance-sheet and invisible OBS activities need to be evaluated, measured, and managed. Finally, we pointed out that OBS activities are not simply risk increasing. On the one hand, they increase the fees and other income of an FI; on the other hand, they hedge the on-balance-sheet interest rate, foreign exchange, and credit risk exposures of an FI. This attractive feature of OBS activities is especially true of instruments such as futures, forwards, options, and swaps.

Questions and Problems

1. Classify the following items as either on-balance-sheet assets, on-balance-sheet liabilities, off-balance-sheet assets, off-balance-sheet liabilities, or capital accounts:
    a. Loan commitments.
    b. Loan loss reserves.
    c. Letters of credit.
    d. Bankers acceptance.
    e. Rediscounted bankers acceptance.
    f. Loan sales without recourse.
    g. Loan sales with recourse.
    h. Forward contracts to purchase.
    i. Forward contracts to sell.
    j. Swaps.
    k. Loan participations.
    l. Securities borrowed.
    m. Securities lent.
    n. Loss adjustment expense account (PC Insurers).
    o. Net policy reserves.
    p. Potential asbestos-related claims.
2. Enumerate the sources of FI risk exposure for all of the items in question 1.
3. List the sources of FI risk emanating from loan

commitments. Contrast the size of off-balance-sheet insolvency risk with the insolvency risk of traditional lending. If loan commitments expose the FI to greater risk than does traditional lending, how can you explain the observation that currently the majority of all commercial and industrial loans are originated from loan commitments?

4. Compare the off-balance-sheet activity of U.S. commercial banks with their on-balance-sheet activity. (Use Tables 1–3 and 9–3 to answer this question.)

   a. How does the size of bank loan commitments compare with total loans?

   b. How does the size of the banks' commitments on futures and forward contracts compare with trading account assets?

   c. How does the size of the banks' when-issued securities commitments compare with trading account assets?

   d. How does the size of the banks' letter of credit obligations compare with nondeposit liabilities?

5. An Italian shoe manufacturer exports a $1 million shipment of shoes to a U.S. retailer. Prior to shipment, the U.S. shoe retailer must send the Italian shoe manufacturer a letter of credit drawn on its bank. The shoes will be received and paid for in 30 days. The bank charges a fee of 5 basis points (of face value) for the letter of credit. The current 30-day discount yield is 5 percent per annum (calculated on a 365-day year basis). The price of a discount instrument is

$$P = FV \left(1 - \frac{dt}{365}\right)$$

where P = price, FV = face value, d = discount yield, and t = the number of days until maturity.

   a. What is the upfront fee received by the bank for the letter of credit?

   b. If the Italian shoe manufacturer chooses to cash in the letter of credit for an immediate cash inflow, perhaps to pay suppliers and workers, how much does it receive in U.S. dollars?

   c. If interest rates fall to 4.9 percent over the next 5 days (25 days until the shipment is received), how can the bank use the accepted letter of credit (BA) to lock in a positive spread?

   d. Record the bank's off- and on-balance-sheet entries at each stage of the transaction. What is the bank's total cash flow from this transaction? (Assume that the U.S. retailer does not default.)

6. Calculate the promised return on a loan commitment if:
   L = interest on the loan = 10 percent.
   m = risk premium = 5 percent.

f_1 = upfront fee on the entire commitment = 25 basis points.

f_2 = back-end fee on the unused commitment = 30 basis points.

b = compensating balances = 20 percent.

R = reserve requirements = 10 percent.

t = expected (average) takedown rate = 90 percent.

7. What is the total loan commitment fee for:

   a. A $100 million unused commitment with a 50-basis-point upfront fee and a 25-basis-point back-end fee?

   b. A 100 percent take down $50 million commitment with a 10- basis-point upfront fee and a 25-basis-point back-end fee?

   c. A 75 percent take down $10 million commitment with a 15-basis-point upfront fee and a 35-basis-point back-end fee?

   d. A 50 percent take down $75 million commitment with a 30-basis-point upfront fee and a 40-basis-point back-end fee?

8. How do off-balance-sheet commitments insure the FI's customers against risk exposure? What sources of risk are insured? Use examples of specific off-balance-sheet items.

9. In general, what determines the fees for off-balance-sheet items?

10. Using the total face value of off-balance-sheet commitments would overestimate their impact on FI profitability. Discuss the arguments supporting and refuting this statement.

11. The risk exposure associated with off-balance-sheet activities is considered independently of the risk exposure of the FI's on-balance-sheet items.

    a. Is this an appropriate risk measurement methodology?

    b. How are the on- and off-balance-sheet activities interrelated?

12. What factors determine the delta of the option to exercise off-balance-sheet contingencies?

13. What is the impact on off-balance-sheet activity of the recent increase in the global integration of financial intermediation?

14. Why do you think that financial products such as letters of credit evolved in the course of international trade?

15. How is affiliate risk affected by the growing diversity of FIs as the range of products and services offered by modern FIs are expanded?

16. How have electronic payments systems addressed the issue of settlement risk?

10

OPERATING COST AND TECHNOLOGY RISK

Learning Objectives

In this chapter you learn about the operating cost and technological risks affecting FIs. We demonstrate that FIs are not purely financial organizations; like regular corporations they have a real production or operating side as well. If the operating side of an FI is inefficiently managed, this becomes a potential source of failure risk and a drag on FI performance. We also discuss the relationships among size, technology, new product innovations, and FI costs.

Introduction

In Chapters 4 through 9, we have concentrated on the financial risks that arise as FIs perform their asset transformation and/or brokerage functions, either on or off the balance sheet. However, financial risk is only one part of the risk profile of a modern FI. Like regular corporations, FIs have a real or production side to their operations that results in additional costs and revenues. In this chapter, we focus on factors that impact the operational costs and risks of FIs and on the importance of managers optimally managing and controlling labor, capital, and other input sources and costs.

Technological Innovation and Profitability

Central to FIs' real or operating decisions are the costs of the inputs or the factors used in producing bank services both on and off the balance sheet. The two most important factors are labor (tellers, credit officers, etc.) and capital (buildings, machinery, furniture, etc.). Crucial to the efficient management and combination of these inputs resulting in financial outputs at the lowest possible cost is *technology*. Broadly defined, technology includes computers, visual and audio communication systems, and other information technology (IT). In Figure 10–1, we depict recent spending by U.S. banks on information technology. As you can see, it was running at close to $14 billion a year in 1990 and 1991 with the the top 35 banks as the biggest investors in such technology.

An efficient technological base for an FI can result in:

1. Lower costs by combining labor and capital in a more efficient mix.
2. Increased revenues by allowing a broader array of financial services to be produced or innovated and sold to customers.

FIGURE 10–1

The cost of keeping up
Spending on IT systems by American commercial
banks, $bn

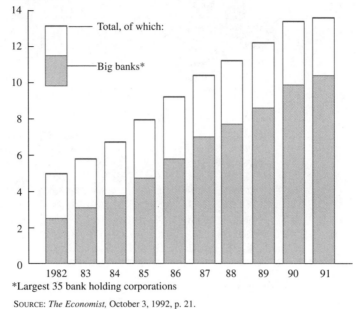

*Largest 35 bank holding corporations

SOURCE: *The Economist,* October 3, 1992, p. 21.

The importance of an FI's operating costs and the efficient use of technology impacting these costs is clearly demonstrated by this simplified profit function:

Income before taxes = Gross profit = (Interest income − Interest expense) +
(Other income − Noninterest expense) − Provision for loan losses

In Table 10–1 we break down the profit data for U.S. banks over the 1981–90 period into the different components impacting profits. Looking at 1990, you can see that interest income of $312,382 million and interest expense of $200,161 million produced net interest income of $112,221 million. However, U.S. banks also had total other income of $53,320 million (including service charges of $11,348 million) and noninterest expenses of $112,748 million, including other operating expenses of $61,919 million. Thus, bank's net other income was − $59,428 million. After taking into account provisions for loan losses of $30,296 million, and other (unreported) adjustments, income before taxes or gross profits of U.S. banks was $23,013 million.[1] Underscoring the importance of operating costs is the fact that noninterest expenses amount to 56.3 percent of interest expense and was 4.9 times gross profits in 1990.

Technology is important because well-chosen technological investments have the potential for increasing both the FI's net interest margin, or the difference between interest income and interest expense, and other net income. Therefore, it can directly improve profitability, as these examples show:

1. *Interest income* can increase if the FI sells a broader array of financial
   services due to technological developments. These may include cross-selling

---

[1] Due to adjustments not reported, gross profits are reported as $23,013 million rather than $22,497 million as calculated directly from Table 10–1.

TABLE 10–1   Earnings and Other Data for All Insured Banks
(In millions of dollars)

Financial Data	1981	1982	1983	R1984	R1985	R1986	R1987	R1988	1989	1990
Interest income	228,675	235,121	216,050	248,034	245,152	233,961	240,548	264,999	308,691	312,382
Interest expense	169,268	168,533	143,210	167,670	155,549	140,762	142,649	160,455	199,342	200,161
Net interest income	59,407	66,568	72,840	80,364	89,603	93,199	97,899	104,544	109,349	112,221
Provision for loan losses	5,059	8,291	10,614	13,704	17,504	21,538	36,534	15,990	28,806	30,296
Miscellaneous income	13,538	15,517	17,776	19,703	23,257	27,282	32,012	34,258	38,192	41,972
Service charges	3,905	4,573	5,399	6,518	7,333	7,908	8,659	9,323	10,151	11,348
Total other income	17,443	20,090	23,175	26,221	30,590	35,190	40,671	44,940	48,343	53,320
Personal expenses	27,927	31,218	33,636	36,463	39,467	42,262	44,463	45,595	48,129	50,827
Other operating expenses	25,528	29,913	32,761	36,448	41,664	46,259	50,684	53,011	56,612	61,919
Noninterest expenses	53,455	61,131	66,397	72,911	81,131	88,521	95,147	101,313	104,741	112,748
Income before taxes	20,149	19,172	18,995	19,824	23,063	22,115	8,286	34,838	24,918	23,013
Taxes	4,611	3,639	4,076	4,660	5,499	5,184	5,267	9,995	9,504	7,507
Net operating earnings	14,677	14,872	14,919	15,163	17,565	16,931	3,019	24,843	15,415	15,507
Net securities gains or losses	(861)	(661)	(30)	(146)	1,506	3,785	1,397	285	774	513
Average total assets (billion $)	1,933	2,101	2,245	2,401	2,559	2,753	2,883	2,959	3,112	3,264
Return on assets	0.76	0.71	0.67	0.64	0.70	0.62	0.11	0.82	0.51	0.50

R—Revised.
SOURCE: Federal Reserve Board and *Standard and Poor's Industry Surveys,* September 1992.

of financial products by computer matching customers and telemarketing of financial service products such as life insurance and bank products.

2. *Interest expense* can be reduced if access to markets for liabilities is directly dependent on the FI's technological capability. For example, Fedwire and CHIPS link the domestic and international interbank lending markets; they are based on interlocking computer network systems. Moreover, the ability of an FI to originate and sell commercial paper is increasingly computer driven. Thus, failure to invest in the appropriate technology may lock an FI out of a lower-cost funding market.[2]

3. *Other income* increases when fees for FI services, especially those from off-balance-sheet activities, are linked to the quality of the FI's technology. For example, letters of credit are now commonly electronically originated by customers; swaps, caps, options, and other complex derivatives are usually screen traded and valued using high-powered computers and algorithms. FIs could not offer innovative derivative products to customers without investments in suitable IT.

4. *Noninterest expenses* can be reduced if the collection and storage of customer information as well as the processing and settlement of numerous financial products are computer based rather than paper based. This is particularly true of security-related back-office activities.

---

[2]Not only corporations sell commercial paper. In recent years, approximately 75 percent of all commercial paper has been sold by financial firms such as bank holding companies, investment banks, and finance companies. Thus, commercial paper is now an important source of funds for many FIs.

Concept Question

1. Looking at Table 10–1, determine if noninterest expenses have been increasing or decreasing as a percent of total bank costs over the 1981–90 period.

The Impact of Technology on Wholesale and Retail Banking

Our previous discussion has established that modern technology has the potential to directly affect all profit producing areas of a modern FI. Next, we describe some specific technology-based products found in modern retail and wholesale banking. Note that this is far from a complete list.

Wholesale Banking Services

Probably the most important area where technology has impacted wholesale or corporate customer services is in banks' ability to provide cash management or working capital services. Cash management service needs have largely resulted from (1) corporate recognition that excess cash balances result in a significant opportunity cost due to lost or forgone interest and (2) the corporate need to know its cash or working capital position on a real time basis. Among the services modern banks provide to improve the efficiency with which corporate clients manage their financial positions are:

1. *Controlled disbursement accounts*—these checking accounts are debited early each day so corporations get an early insight into their net cash positions.
2. *Account reconciliation*—a checking feature that provides a record of which of the firm's checks have been paid by the bank.
3. *Wholesale lockbox*—a centralized collection service for corporate payments to reduce the delay in check clearing, or the **float**.[3]
4. *Funds concentration*—redirects funds from accounts in a large number of different banks or branches to a few centralized accounts at one bank.
5. *Electronic funds transfer*—includes overnight payments via CHIPS or Fedwire, automated payment of payrolls or dividends via automated clearinghouses (ACHs), and automated transmission of payments messages by SWIFT, an international electronic message service owned and operated by U.S. and European banks that instructs banks to make particular payments.
6. *Check deposit services*—such as encoding, endorsing, microfilming, and handling checks of customers.
7. *Electronic initiation of letters of credit*—allows customers in a network to access bank computers to initiate letters of credit.
8. *Treasury management software*—allows efficient management of multiple currency portfolios for trading and investment purposes.[4]

Float
The time between the deposit of a check and when funds become available for depositor use.

---

[3]The float is the time between when a check is received and when the funds are credited to the account; in other words, the time it takes a check to clear at a bank.

[4]One could add computerized pension fund management and advisory services to this list.

9. *Electronic data interchange*—A specialized application of electronic mail, allowing businesses to automatically transfer and transact invoices, purchase orders, and shipping notices using banks as clearinghouses.

Retail Banking Services

Retail customers have also demanded efficiency and flexibility in their financing of transactions. Using only checks or holding cash is often more expensive and time-consuming than making use of retail-oriented electronic payments technology. Some of the most important retail payment product innovations are:

1. *Automated teller machines (ATMs)*—these allow customers 24-hour access to their checking accounts. This can include payment of bills as well as withdrawals of cash. In addition, if the bank's ATMs are part of a bank network, such as CIRRUS, retail depositors can gain direct nationwide access to their deposit accounts by using the ATMs of other banks in the network to draw on their accounts.

2. *Point of sale debit cards*—for customers who choose not to use cash, checks, or credit cards for purchases, using debit card/point of sale terminals (POS) allows them to buy merchandise while the merchant avoids the check float and any delay in credit card receivables since the bank offering the debit card/POS service immediately and directly transfers funds from the customer's bank account to the merchant's bank accounts at time of card use. Unlike check or credit card purchases, the use of a debit card results in an immediate deduction of funds from the customers' checking accounts and transfer to the merchant's account.[5]

3. *Home banking*—usually connects customers to their deposit and brokerage accounts as well as provides a bill-paying service, all via personal computers.

4. *Preauthorized debits/credits*—includes direct payment into bank accounts of payroll checks as well as direct debits of mortgage payments and utility bills.

5. *Telephone bill paying*—allows direct transfer of funds from the customer's bank account to outside parties either by voice command or by touch-tone telephone.

In Exhibits 10–1, 10–2, and 10–3, we summarize the details of major private telecommunication investments (networks) by banks and other FIs that allow many of these products to be offered both domestically and internationally.

Concept Question

1. What is the link between interstate banking restrictions and the retail demand for electronic payment services?

---

[5]In the case of bank-supplied credit cards, the merchant normally gets compensated very quickly but not instantaneously by the credit card issuer (usually one or two days). The bank then holds an account receivable against the card user. However, even a short delay can represent an opportunity cost for the merchant.

EXHIBIT 10–1   The Largest U. S. Banks and Their Private Networks

Citibank, NA, of New York, is the largest U.S. bank and one of the few that offers a full range of retail and wholesale financial services around the world. During the 1980s, Citicorp developed 100 separate private networks, covering 92 countries. Each Citicorp business unit independently bought, developed, or contracted for networks. Beginning in January 1992, these are being combined into one global information network, or GIN. The goals are seamless technology integration, with common architecture and protocols, services across national borders, and reduced costs. The GIN will include voice, video, and data capabilities, will connect local-area networks (LANs) and wide-area networks (WANs), and will support value-added services such as electronic data interchange (EDI). The consolidation is expected to save $100 million per year within three years, by bulk purchases and leases and by eliminating some of the 1,500 network professionals. GIN was made feasible, Citicorp officials say, because of the evolution of ISDN (integrated services digital networks) and advances in frame-relay technology. In time, Citicorp may turn part of GIN over to a systems integrator or may have an outside entity manage or operate its systems ("outsourcing"). This is not, however, an explicit goal.

The Bank of America, the third-largest bank in the United States, has a packet-switched network to support its World Banking Division. The network is used to transmit data on loans and letters of credit, to supply financial information to officers and customers, to support on-line accounting, to send and receive international payments, and to receive customer instructions for business transactions.

Chase Manhattan, among the largest 10 banks in the United States, uses a private packet-switched network provided by Tymnet, which is owned by British Telecom.

Manufacturers Hanover Trust had a T1 (high-speed) backbone network providing transport among its U.S. locations, and a global X.25 packet-switching network based on Telenet (now Sprint hardware and software) connecting 52 cities in 27 foreign countries.

Bankers Trust offers no retail services but is a "merchant bank," i.e., a combination of investment bank and commercial (wholesale) bank. The bank's private network, created in 1982, is primarily a data network but carries some voice traffic on heavily used segments, such as between London and New York. There are also some 24-hour trading circuits for direct trading between countries where the business day overlaps (these differ from regular voice circuits because traders have open microphones on their desks activated by a distant trader using a 4-digit code). Satellite links are used for backup; Bankers Trust prefers terrestrial links to satellite links to avoid the several seconds delay which is disorienting for traders and may affect their ability to trade in volatile moments.

SOURCE: Office of Technology Assessment, *U.S. Banks and International Telecommunications Background Paper,* OTA–BP–TCT–100 (Washington, D.C.: U.S. Government Printing Office, September 1992), p. 8.

The Effects of Technology on Revenues and Costs

In the last section we described an extensive, yet incomplete list of current products or services being built around a strong technological base. Technological advances allow a bank or FI to offer such products to its customers and potentially to earn higher profits. The investment of resources in many of these products is risky, however, because product innovations may fail to attract sufficient business relative to the initial cash outlay and the future costs related to these investments once in place. In the terminology of finance, a number of technologically based product innovations may turn out to be *negative* net present value projects due to uncertainties over revenues and costs, and over how quickly rivals mimic or copy any innovation. Another factor is agency conflicts in which managers undertake growth-oriented investments to increase the size of an FI; such investments may be inconsistent with stockholders' value-maximizing objectives.[6] As a result, losses on

---

[6]A good example of the cost of failed technological innovation was the recent abandonment in the United Kingdom by British investment banks of a centralized computerized stock trading and settlement system called TAURUS. This had taken nearly 10 years to develop and even in 1993 was some two

---

EXHIBIT 10–2   Private Networks in Other Financial Industries

Not only banks but other kinds of financial institutions developed international private networks during the 1980s:

- One of the largest securities houses, Shearson Lehman, has private T1 networks between New York and London and between New York and Tokyo. These are primarily for data but some of the leased circuits are dedicated to voice. Data circuits go through three international hubs (New York, London, Tokyo) that have multiplexer concentrators to route messages to about 30 other locations. In London, there is a connection to SWIFT for funds transfer.

- American Express operates a network of 37 nodes linking 10,000 automated teller machines in 16 countries and 1.6 million point-of- sale terminals in 25 countries. Transaction authorization at these terminals is on-line and immediate.[1]

- A global money brokering firm uses only point-to-point lines—that is, dedicated open lines between the firm and its customers.[2] For domestic communications across state lines, it leases circuits on fiber-optic cables, provided by services vendors who house the firms' multiplexers on the vendors' premises. These communications are voice, referred to by the firm as "shouting down the pipe." For international service, the firm leases low bit-rate voice circuits; for example, it has 49 point-to-point lines to London. Other kinds of service are deemed not necessary and too expensive. A high bit-rate circuit might cost $2,500, compared with $700 for the voice circuits. The firm used satellites in the past, but the several seconds delay was disruptive for voice trading and it now uses cable.

- Reuters Ltd., a worldwide vendor of general news and financial data services delivers information services, predominantly financial market data, to customers around the world over leased lines and satellites. It has its own earth stations on Long Island, having been granted a license by the Federal Communications Commission. (In the United Kingdom, its home country, Reuters had to buy a company that already had a license in order to operate an earth station. In most of the rest of Europe, only post telephone and telegraph agencies can operate earth stations.)

[1] National Telecommunication and Information Administration. *Telecom 2000,* NTIA Special Publication 88-21, October 1988, p. 447.

[2] A brokering firm is an intermediary, bringing buyers and sellers together; in this case, the money brokering firm handles trades of foreign currency, overnight federal funds, Eurodollars, etc. Its customers are dealers located in banks or other large financial institutions. An official of the firm provided OTA with information in extended discussions but asked that the firm not be identified.

SOURCE: Office of Technology Assessment, *U.S. Banks and International Telecommunications Background Paper,* OTA–BP–TCT–100 (Washington, D.C.: U.S. Government Printing Office, September 1992), p. 9.

---

technological innovations and new technology could weaken an FI because scarce capital resources were invested in value-decreasing products.[7]

This raises the question: Is there direct or indirect evidence that technology investments updating the operational structure of FIs have either increased revenues or decreased costs? As you will note, most of the direct or indirect evidence has concerned the effects of size on financial firms' operating costs; indeed it is the largest FIs that appear to be investing most in IT and other technological innovations

---

years or more away from being operational. Its abandonment costs across U.K. FIs is estimated at up to £500 million.

[7] Standard capital budgeting techniques can be applied to technological innovations and new banking products.

Let, I_0 = the initial capital outlay for developing an innovation or product at time 0.

   R_i = the expected net revenues or cash flows from product sales in future years $i, i = 1 \ldots N$

   d = the bank's discount rate reflecting its risk-adjusted cost of capital

Thus, a negative net present value (NPV) project would result if

$$I_o > \frac{R_1}{(1+d)} + \ldots + \frac{R_N}{(1+d)^N}$$

EXHIBIT 10–3   Citicorp Moves into Electronic Services

Citibank is unusual among U.S. banks in emphasizing retail services overseas—i.e., services to individuals and households. Citibank has a retail presence in 11 countries in Europe, with 700 branches and 11,300 people; it serves 3 percent of all European households.

In the 1960s electronic communications allowed nonbanks to create financial instruments, such as money-market mutual funds invested in short-term government securities, that paid higher interest rates than banks could offer under existing regulations. Money flowed out of banks into these new kinds of investments. Corporations began to sell commercial paper directly to investors or to borrow from industry-owned finance companies. Banks were less often the intermediary between borrowers and lenders ("disintermediation").

Citicorp decided to shift its assets away from prime wholesale lending to computer based services. Citicorp created a time-sharing computer subsidiary, "Citishare," which developed the first comprehensive automated teller machine network in New York and later extended it across the country. It issued 20 million credit cards and purchased two other credit card companies. In the late 1970s Citicorp worked toward becoming a global, diversified company offering retail banking, commercial banking, investment, insurance, and information services. It entered joint ventures with NYNEX, RCA, and McGraw-Hill to offer electronic services to the home and to develop 24-hour trading systems. In 1985 Citicorp passed Bank of America to become the largest U.S. bank in terms of domestic deposits. The next year it bought a controlling interest in Quotron, an information services vendor specializing in financial market data.

SOURCES: David Lascelles, "Networking Without Frontiers," *Financial Times,* special section on international banking, May 9, 1990, p. 6; *Citibank World* 1, no. 2 (April 1992); and Office of Technology Assessment, *U.S. Banks and International Telecommunications Background Paper,* OTA–BP–TCT–100 (Washington, D.C.: U.S. Government Printing Office, September 1992), p. 12.

(see Figure 10–1). We begin by looking at the evidence on the product revenue side and then on the operating cost side. However, before looking at these revenue and cost aspects, we should stress that the success of a technologically related innovation cannot be evaluated independently from regulation and regulatory changes. To a large extent, the success of the retail and wholesale cash management products just described depend on continuing restrictions on interstate banking (see Chapter 15). For example, restrictions on U.S. banks' ability to branch across state lines creates problems for large corporations with national and international franchises; these firms need to consolidate and centralize their deposit funds for working capital purposes. Thus, innovations such as wholesale lockboxes and funds concentration are products that ease this problem. It is more than coincidence that cash management services have not reached the same degree of customer attraction in Europe as in the United States. One reason for this is that nationwide branching and banking is far more prevalent in European countries and interregional banking restrictions are notably absent.

As we discuss in greater length in Chapter 15, the United States is gradually moving toward a nationwide banking system. While the regulatory debate alters the playing fields for United States FIs, the revenue and cost functions for any particular

---

Clearly, the profitability of any product innovation is negatively related to the size of the initial set-up and development costs (I_0) and the bank's cost of capital (d) and positively related to the size of the stream of expected net cash flows (R_i) from selling the services.

For example, home banking might reasonably be viewed—with hindsight—as a negative NPV product for banks such as Bank of America and Chemical. Considerable resources (I_0) were sunk into its development in the 1980s at a time when these banks' cost of capital (d) was high. The realized net revenue streams (R_i) from home banking have been extremely disappointing to date.

product or innovation also shift. Thus, the success of technologically related innovations is directly affected by exogenous regulatory changes.[8] Of course, an astute FI manager should include expectations about regulatory changes in the cost and revenue (capital budgeting) calculus in the first place.

Technology and Revenues

One potential benefit of technology is that it allows an FI to cross-market both new and existing products to customers. Such joint selling doesn't require the FI to produce all the services sold within the same branch or financial services outlet. For example, a commercial bank may link up with an insurance company to jointly market each other's loan and insurance products. This arrangement has proved popular in Germany, where the second and third largest banks (Dresdner and Commerzbank) have developed sophisticated cross-marketing arrangements with large insurance companies. In the United States, Citicorp is using computerized information on its customers to cross-sell bank sponsored mutual funds, brokerage accounts, and insurance products. Unfortunately, concrete data are unavailable about the revenue synergy benefits from such ventures.

Technology also increases the rate of innovation of new products. In recent years, there have been many notable failures as well as successes. For example, despite large investments by banks, new product innovations such as POS/debit cards have found it hard to find a sufficiently large market. On the other hand, telephone bill paying, preauthorized debits and credits, including direct payroll systems, are proving to be high growth areas in modern banking.

Finally, we cannot ignore the issue of *service quality.* For example, while ATMs may potentially lower bank operating costs when compared to employing full-service tellers, the inability of machines to flexibly address customers' concerns and questions may drive retail customers away. That is, revenue losses may counteract any cost-savings effects. The continued growth and superior profit performance of small banks may well be due in part to customers' belief that overall service quality is higher with tellers who provide a human touch rather than the ATMs more common at bigger banks. We depict the recent growth of ATMs, home banking, and telephone related transactions at U.S. branches over the 1980–90 period in Figure 10–2.

Technology and Costs

Traditionally, FIs have considered the major benefits of technological advances to be on the cost side rather than the revenue side. After a theoretical look at how technology favorably or unfavorably affects an FI's costs, we look at the direct and indirect evidence of technology-based cost savings for FIs. In general, technology may favorably affect an FI's cost structure by allowing it to exploit either economies of scale or economies of scope.

Economies of Scale.   As financial firms grow bigger, generally the potential scale and array of the technology in which they can invest expands. As noted above and shown in Figure 10–1, the largest FIs have the biggest expenditures on technology-related innovations. If enhanced or improved technology lowers an FI's average costs of financial service production, then bigger FIs may have an **economy of scale**

Economies of Scale
As the output of an FI increases, its average costs of production fall.

---

    [8]Clearly, other regulatory restrictions—especially on the set of financial service activities FIs can undertake—can also affect the payoffs from technologically driven innovations.

FIGURE 10–2

Moving money
Billions of retail transactions in American banks

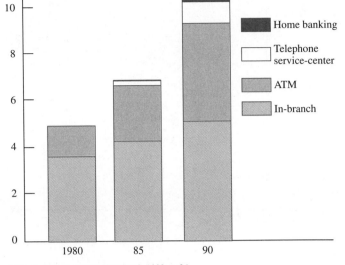

SOURCE: *The Economist,* October 3, 1992, p. 24.

advantage over smaller financial firms. Economies of scale imply that the unit or average cost of producing FI services in aggregate or some specific service such as deposits or loans falls as the size of the FI expands. See the graph in Figure 10–3.

In Figure 10–3, we show three different sized FIs. The average cost of producing an FI's output of financial services is measured as:

$$AC_i = \frac{TC_i}{S_i}$$

where

AC_i = Average costs of the *i*th bank
TC_i = Total costs of the *i*th bank
S_i = Size of the bank measured by assets, deposits, or loans[9]

As you can see in Figure 10–3, the largest FI (size *C*) has a lower average cost of producing financial services than smaller firms such as *B* and *A*. This means that at any given price for financial service firm products, firm C can make a bigger profit than either B or A. Alternatively, firm *C* can undercut B and A in price and potentially gain a larger market share. The long-run implication of economies of scale on the FI sector is that the larger and most cost efficient FIs will drive out smaller FIs leading to increased large firm dominance and concentration in financial services production. Such an implication is reinforced if time-related technological improvements increasingly benefit larger FIs over smaller FIs. For example, satellite technology and supercomputers, in which enormous technological advances are being made, may be available to only the largest FIs. The effects of improving technology over time, which is biased toward larger projects, is to shift the *AC* curve downward over time but with a bigger downward shift for large-sized FIs; see Figure 10–4.

---

[9]It is arguable that the size of the modern FI should be measured by including off-balance-sheet assets (contingent value) as well.

FIGURE 10–3

Economies of scale in FIs

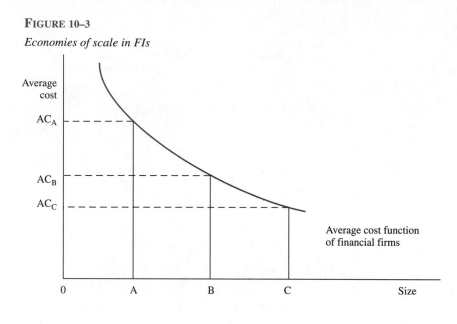

FIGURE 10–4

The effects of technological improvements

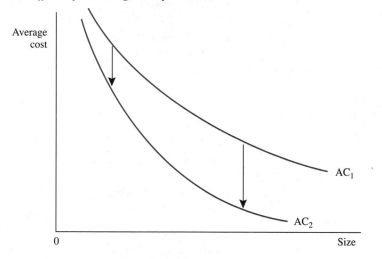

AC_1 is the hypothetical AC curve prior to technological innovations. AC_2 reflects the cost-lowering effects of technology on FIs of all sizes but with the greatest benefit accruing to those of the largest size.

As noted earlier, technological investments are risky; if they do not cover their costs of development through future revenues, they reduce the value of the FI and its net worth. On the cost side, large-scale investments may result in excess capacity problems and integration problems as well as cost overruns and cost-control problems. Then, small FIs with simple and easily managed computer systems and/or those leasing time on large FIs' computers without bearing the fixed costs of installation and maintenance may have an average cost advantage. In this case, large-sized FIs' technological investments result in higher average costs of financial service pro-

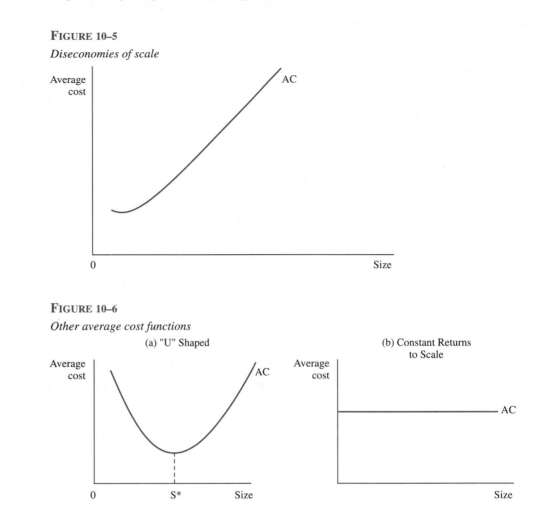

FIGURE 10–5

Diseconomies of scale

FIGURE 10–6

Other average cost functions

(a) "U" Shaped

(b) Constant Returns to Scale

Diseconomies of Scale
As the output of an FI increases, its average costs of production increase.

duction causing the industry to operate under conditions of **diseconomies of scale.** See this in Figure 10–5. Diseconomies of scale imply that smaller FIs are more cost efficient than bigger FIs and that in a freely competitive environment for financial services small FIs prosper.

At least two other possible shapes for the AC function exist; we show them in Figure 10–6. In panel *a* of Figure 10–6, the financial services industry reflects economies of scale at first and then diseconomies of scale as firms grow larger. This suggests a best or most efficient size for an FI at point *S** and that too much technology investment could be as bad as too little. In panel *b* of Figure 10–6, we have constant returns to scale. Any potential cost-reducing effects of technology are spread evenly over FIs of all sizes. That is, technology investment are neutral rather than favoring one size of FI over another.

Economies of Scope.   While technological investments may have good or bad effects on FIs in general, and these effects may well differ across FIs of different size, technology tends to be applied more in some product areas than others. That is, FIs are multiproduct firms producing services of different technological intensity. Moreover, technological improvements or investments in one financial service area (such as lending) may have incidental and synergistic benefits in lowering the costs of producing financial services in other areas (such as securities underwriting or brokerage). Specifically, computerization allows the storage and joint use of important information on customers and their needs. The simple *economy of scale* concept ignores these interrelationships among products and the "jointness" in the costs of producing financial products. In particular, the ability of FIs to generate synergistic cost savings across products is called *economies of scope* as opposed to economies of scale.

Technology may allow an FI to jointly use its input resources, capital and labor, to produce a set of financial services at a lower cost than if financial service products were produced independently of one another. Technically, let X_1 and X_2 be two financial products; each has one firm producing it as a specialized producer. That is, firm A produces only X_1 and no X_2, and firm B produces only X_2 and no X_1. The average cost functions (AC) of these firms are

$$AC_A[X_1, 0] \text{ and } AC_B[0, X_2]$$

Economies of Scope
The ability of FIs to generate synergistic cost savings through joint use of inputs in producing multiple products.

Economies of scope exist if these firms merge and jointly produce X_1 and X_2, and this joint production results in:

$$AC_{A+B}[X_1, X_2] < AC_A[X_1, 0] + AC_B[0, X_2]$$

That is, the cost of joint production via cost synergies is less than the separate and independent production of these services.

As an example, let TC_B be the total cost of a specialized bank producing lending services to a corporate client. Suppose the total operating costs of producing these services is $50,000 for a loan volume (L_B) of $10 million. Such costs include information collection and monitoring as well as account maintenance and processing. Thus, the average cost (AC_B) of loan production for the bank is

$$AC_B = \frac{TC_B}{L_B} = \frac{\$50,000}{\$10,000,000} = .005 = \frac{1}{2}\%$$

At the same time, a specialized investment bank is selling commercial paper for the same corporate customer. The total cost (TC_S) of the securities firm running the commercial paper operation is $10,000 for a $1 million issue ($P_S$). These costs include the cost of underwriting the issue as well as the costs of placing the issue with outside buyers. Thus:

$$AC_s = \frac{TC_s}{P_s} = \frac{\$10,000}{\$1,000,000} = .01 = 1\%$$

Consequently, the total average cost of separately producing the loan services through banks and the commercial paper issuance through the securities firm is

$$TAC = \frac{\$60,000}{\$11,000,000} = 0.54\%$$

Suppose, instead, a single financial services firm produced both $10 million of lending services and $1 million commercial paper issuance services for the same customer. For corporate customers, loans and commercial paper are source of funds substitutes. For a financial services firm to originate a loan and to originate commercial paper requires very similar expertise both in funding that issue as well as in credit risk assessment and monitoring. To the extent that most loans are quickly sold after origination, loan origination is very similar to the sale of commercial paper to outside buyers by the original underwriter. Common technologies in the loan and commercial paper production functions suggest that a single financial services firm simultaneously (or jointly) producing both loan and commercial paper services for the same client, should be able to do this at a lower average cost than the separate production of these services with specialized FIs.

Formally, if AC_{FS} is the total average cost of a nonspecialized financial services firm, then economies of scope would imply that:

$$AC_{FS} < TAC = 0.54\%$$

That is, the average costs of jointly producing many financial services may be less than the average costs of producing these products separately.

Diseconomies of Scope
The costs of joint production of FI services are higher than if they were produced independently.

Nevertheless, **diseconomies of scope** may occur instead. This is where FIs find costs actually higher from joint production of services than if they were produced independently. For example, suppose that an FI purchases some very specialized information-based technology to ease the loan production and processing function. Any excess capacity this system has could be employed by the FI in other service areas. However, this process could be a relatively inefficient technology for other service areas and add to the overall costs of production when compared to using a specialized technology for each service or product area.

Concept Questions

1. Does the existence of economies of scale for FIs mean that in the long run small FIs cannot survive?
2. If there are diseconomies of scope, do specialized FIs have a relative cost advantage or disadvantage over product-diversified FIs?
3. Make a list of the potential economies of scope or cost synergies if a commercial bank merged with an investment bank.

Testing for Economies of Scale and Economies of Scope

To test for economies of scale and economies of scope, FIs must clearly specify both the inputs into their production process and the cost of these inputs. Basically the two approaches to analyzing the cost functions of FIs are the production and the intermediation approaches.

The Production Approach

The production approach views FI's outputs of services as having two underlying inputs: labor and capital. If w = the wage costs of labor, r = the rental costs of capital, and y = the output of services, the total cost function (C) for the FI is

$$C = f(y, w, r)$$

The Intermediation Approach

The intermediation approach views the output of financial services as being produced by labor and capital as well as the funds the intermediary uses to produce intermediated services. Thus, deposit costs would be an input in banking and the thrift industry, while premiums or reserves would be inputs in insurance:

$$C = f(y, w, r, k)$$

where k reflects the cost of funds for the FI.

Empirical Findings on Economies of Scale and Scope

A large number of studies have examined economies of scale and scope in different financial service industry sectors.[9] We summarize these findings in Table 10–5.

    With respect to banks, most of the early studies failed to find economies of scale beyond the smallest bank size. More recently, better data sets and improved methodologies have suggested that economies of scale may exist for banks in the $100 million to $5 billion range. Many large-regional and super-regional banks fall in this size range. With respect to economies of scope, either among deposits, loans, and other traditional banking product areas or between on-balance-sheet products and off-balance-sheet products such as loan sales, the evidence is at best very weak that cost complementarities exist. Similarly, the smaller number of studies for nonbank financial service firms such as thrifts, insurance companies, and securities firms almost always report neither economies of scale nor economies of scope.

    Finally, a number of very recent studies have looked at the *dispersion* of costs in any given size class, rather than looking at the shape of the average cost functions. These efficiency studies find quite dramatic cost differences among banks, thrifts, and insurance companies in any given size class (e.g., $100 million asset size class, $200 million asset size class, etc.). Moreover, these studies find that sometimes as little as 5 percent of the cost differences among FIs in any size class can be attributed to economies of scale or scope.[10] This suggests that cost inefficiencies related to managerial ability and other hard-to-quantify factors may better explain cost differences and operating cost efficiencies among financial firms than technology related investments per se.

Implications for Technology Expenditures

There is an absence of any strong direct evidence that bigger multiproduct financial service firms enjoy cost advantages over smaller more specialized financial firms. Also, economies of scope and scale do not explain many of the cost differences

---

[9]Good reviews are found in J. A. Clark, "Economies of Scale and Scope at Depository Financial Institutions: A Review of the Literature," Federal Reserve Bank of Kansas City, *Economic Review,* September–October 1988, pp. 16–33, and L. Mester, "Efficient Production of Financial Services: Scale and Scope Economies," Federal Reserve Bank of Philadelphia, *Economic Review,* January–February 1987, pp. 15–25. Three major production function forms have been tested: the Cobb-Douglas, the trans-log, and the Box-Cox flexible functional form. For more details on the specific characteristics of these functions and estimation issues, see the references in Table 10–2.

[10]See A. Berger and D. Humphrey, "The Dominance of Inefficiencies over Scale and Product Mix in Banking," *Journal of Monetary Economics* 28, 1991, and the *Journal of Banking and Finance*, Special Issue on Efficiency (1993). The task for future research is to more precisely identify the source of these relative cost inefficiencies.

Efficiency in Banking

Allen N. Berger
Board of Governors of the Federal Reserve System

Bank efficiency is an important topic because it is both a powerful motivation for, and an important consequence of, changes in the banking industry. Bank merger applicants often cite efficiency gains as their primary motivation for consolidation. Further industry consolidation arises when inefficient banks, which cannot control their costs and revenues, go bankrupt and exit the industry.

A bank is fully efficient if it produces the output level and mix that maximizes profits and does so at the minimum possible cost. However, most banks are not fully efficient. There are a number of sources of inefficiency in banking. Many studies have investigated cost scale inefficiency—whether the costs per unit of output are unnecessarily high for particular bank sizes. The results generally suggest that the average cost curve in banking has a relatively flat U shape. Firms of medium size, $100 million to $5 billion in assets, have the lowest unit costs, while smaller and larger banks are somewhat less scale efficient. However, these inefficiencies usually do not amount to more than about 5 percent of costs, indicating that cost scale economies are relatively unimportant.

Another area of research has been cost scope efficiencies. Here, the goal is to determine whether it is cheaper to produce two or more outputs jointly in one consolidated firm or to produce them separately in multiple specializing firms. The results suggest that cost scope inefficiencies are quite small. Thus, neither scale nor scope of output appear to be very important sources of cost inefficiency.

The most important origin of cost problems in banking is X^m-inefficiency or differences in managerial ability to control costs for any given scale or scope of production. On average, banks' costs are about 20 percent above the efficient frontier.

That is, the average bank has costs about 20 percent higher than those of a "best-practice" firm producing the same output. Most of this is operational inefficiency, such as branch offices that use excessive labor, as opposed to financial inefficiency, where excessive interest rates are paid for funds.

Recently, researchers have used bank profits to measure inefficiency. Profits include revenue or output inefficiencies as well as cost or input inefficiencies. As just noted, full efficiency requires that the bank produce the profit-maximizing level and mix of output as well as minimizing costs for that output. A surprising result is that revenue inefficiencies may be as large as or larger than cost inefficiencies. Also surprising is that larger firms may be more efficient than smaller firms when revenue inefficiency is included. Thus, since bank size and product mix appear to matter greatly for revenue efficiency, but not for cost efficiency, banks seeking to improve efficiency should adjust output size and mix only if they improve revenues, and then concentrate on controlling costs for that output.

The opinions expressed do not necessarily reflect those of the Board of Governors, the Reserve Banks, or their staffs.

BIOGRAPHICAL SUMMARY

Allen N. Berger is a senior economist with the Board of Governors of the Federal Reserve System, where he conducts research on banking. Mr. Berger has published in a number of economics and finance journals, including the *Journal of Political Economy, American Economic Review, Journal of Monetary Economics, Review of Economics and Statistics,* and *Journal of Banking and Finance.* He currently serves as an associate editor of the *Journal of Banking and Finance* and the *Journal of Money, Credit and Banking,* and recently co-edited a special issue of the *Journal of Banking and Finance* on "The Efficiency of Financial Institutions." He received his Ph.D. in economics from the University of California, Berkeley, in 1983.

Economies of Scale and Scope

Loretta J. Mester
Federal Reserve Bank of Philadelphia

The banking industry has been undergoing a significant restructuring over the last several years. Since the mid-80s, the number of commercial banks has fallen by more than 2,000 as a result of failures and especially mergers, and average bank asset size has increased. Recently, several large banking organizations have merged—for example, Chemical and Manufacturers Hanover. A chief concern of the Federal Reserve and other bank regulators who must approve mergers is that restructuring could lead to a financial services industry that is too concentrated—one in which a handful of very large institutions could exert monopoly power. We also recognize restructuring might lead to an industry much more efficient in delivering financial services; that would help promote the safety and soundness of the industry.

To help analyze this issue, economists at the Fed and elsewhere have studied the banking industry's cost structure and, in particular, *scale and scope economies.* The degree of scale economies measures the percentage change in a firm's cost of production given a percent increase in the level of all its products. Scale economies exist when increasing the scale of operations reduces the average cost of production. Thus, a financial institution can become more efficient by increasing its operating scale until such economies are exhausted. Because a financial institution produces multiple outputs, in addition to identifying the optimal scale of operations, it must determine the optimal combination of products to minimize production cost. Is it more efficient to have financial supermarkets or financial boutiques?

The degree of scope economies measures the percentage change in production costs if a bank's products were produced by specialized firms as opposed to a single firm. If this measure is positive, scope economies exist and it is more efficient to have the bank produce the multiple products than to have several specialized banks producing the products. If the measure is negative, there are scope diseconomies and it is more efficient to have specialized banks.

Empirical studies of the banking industry suggest significant scale economies for banks with assets up to $100 million or so. There is mixed evidence concerning scale economies at large banks; if they exist, they don't seem to be large enough to be the sole motivator of the recent large bank mergers, or to put smaller banks at a competitive disadvantage. The empirical evidence shows there does not seem to be much in the way of scope economies or diseconomies, suggesting that banks that offer a variety of financial services and banks that offer just a few should be equally cost efficient. Thus, the empirical work seems to say that the consolidation trend could lead to a more efficient industry, as small banks merge and attain a more efficient size. But we shouldn't expect large cost savings from mergers of the largest banks. There appears to be room in the industry for both large and small, and also supermarket and boutique banks.

The views expressed here are those of the author and do not necessarily represent the views of the Federal Reserve Bank of Philadelphia or of the Federal Reserve System.

BIOGRAPHICAL SUMMARY
Loretta J. Mester is a research officer and economist in the Research Department of the Federal Reserve Bank of Philadelphia, which she joined in 1985. Dr. Mester provides economic forecasts, policy analysis, and regulatory analysis for the bank's senior management involved in monetary policy-making and bank regulatory policy-making. In addition, she conducts research on the organization of financial institutions, agency theory, and regulatory issues in banking. She supervises the bank's Working Paper series and economic research seminar program. Dr. Mester is also an Adjunct Assistant Professor of Finance at the Wharton School of the University of Pennsylvania, where she teaches banking.

Dr. Mester received her M.A. and Ph.D. in economics from Princeton University, where she held a National Science Foundation Fellowship. She earlier received her B.A. in mathematics and economics from Barnard College of Columbia University.

Dr. Mester has been published in professional journals, including the *Journal of Finance, RAND Journal of Economics, Journal of Money Credit, and Banking, Journal of Financial Intermediation, Journal of Banking and Finance,* and *Economics Letters,* and in the Philadelphia Fed's *Business Review.* She is a member of the American Economic Association and its Committee on the Status of Women in the Economics Profession, the American Finance Association, and the Econometric Society.

TABLE 10–2   **Economies of Scale and Scope in Financial Service Firms—The Evidence**

	Economies of Scale beyond Small Levels of Output (size)	Economies of Scope among Outputs
Domestic Banks		
Benston et al. 1983	No	No
Berger et al. 1987	No	No
Gilligan and Smirlock 1984	No	Yes
Gilligan, Smirlock, and Marshall 1984	No	Yes
Kolari and Zardkoohi 1987	No	No
Lawrence 1989	No	Yes
Lawrence and Shay 1986	No	No
Mester 1990	Yes	No
Noulas et al. 1990	Yes	?
Shaffer 1988	Yes	?
Hunter et al. 1990	Yes	No
Foreign Banks		
Yoshika and Nakajima 1987 (Japan)	Yes	?
Kim 1987 (Israel)	Yes	Yes
Saunders and Walter 1991 (Worldwide)	Yes	No
Thrifts		
Mester 1987	No	No
LeCompte and Smith 1990	No	No
Life Insurance		
Fields and Murphy 1989	Yes	No
Fields 1988	No	?
Securities Firms		
Goldberg et al. 1991	No	No

among FIs of the same size. These empirical findings raise questions as to the benefits of technology investments and technological innovation. While a majority of the studies in Table 10–2 are concerned with testing for economies of scope and scale rather than the benefits of technology, these results are consistent with the relatively low payoff from technological innovation. To the extent that benefits arise to large FIs, they may well be on the revenue generation/new product innovation side rather than on the cost side. Indeed, a recent study looking at output and input efficiencies for banks derived from the profit function found that large banks tend to be significantly more efficient in revenue generation than smaller banks and that such efficiencies may well offset scope and scale cost inefficiencies related to size.[11]

Moreover, the real benefits of technological innovation may also be long term and dynamic, related to the evolution of the U.S. payments system away from cash and checks and toward electronic means of payment. Such benefits are difficult to pick up in traditional economy of scale and scope studies which are largely static and ignore the more dynamic aspects of efficiency gains. This dynamic techno-

---

[11]A. Berger, D. Hancock, and D. B. Humphrey, "Bank Efficiency Derived from the Profit Function," *Journal of Banking and Finance* (forthcoming).

TABLE 10–3   Volume and Value Composition of U.S. Payments

Payment Instrument	Volume Composition (percentage)	Value Composition (percentage)	Average Dollar Value per Transaction
Nonelectronic	99.50%	21.50%	$ 247
Cash	70.41	1.54	25
Checks	25.14	19.80	910
Credit cards	3.13	.11	42
Money orders	.47	.03	67
Traveler's checks	.50	.02	35
Electronic	.35	78.50	258,993
ACH	.25	.39	1,800
ATM	.05	.00	70
POS	.01	.00	30
Wire transfers	.04	78.11	2,500,000

SOURCE: David B. Humphrey, "Payments System Risk, Market Failure, and Public Policy," in *The Payments Revolution: The Emerging Public Policy Issues,* ed. Elinor Solomon (Boston: Kluwer-Nijhoff Publishing, 1987), p. 84.

TABLE 10–4   Ratio of Fedwire and CHIPS Dollar Payments to Bank Reserves

	Average Daily Fedwire and CHIPS payments ($) / Bank Reserves
1970	2
1980	17
1983	38
1985	42
1992 (3rd quarter)	55

SOURCE: David B. Humphrey, "Future Directions in Payment Risk Reduction," *Journal of Cash Management,* 1988 and Office of Technology Assessment Calculations for 1992 (3rd quarter).

logical evolution not only has affected the fundamental role of FIs in the financial system but has also generated some new and subtle types of risks for FIs and their regulators. In the next section, we take a closer look at the effects of technology on the payments system.

Technology and the Evolution of the Payments System

To better understand the changing nature of the U.S. payments system, look at Table 10–3. As you can see, while nonelectronic methods—cash, checks, credit cards, money orders, and traveler's checks—accounted for 99.5 percent of transactions, this represented only 21.5 percent of the dollar *value* of transactions. By comparison, electronic methods of payment—automated clearinghouses, automated teller machines, point of sale terminals, and wire transfer systems—accounted for only .35

percent in volume, but 78.5 percent in value. Wire transfer systems alone accounted for 78.11 percent of all dollar transactions measured in value.

The two wire systems that dominate the payments system are Fedwire and the Clearing House Interbank Payment System (CHIPS). Fedwire is a wire transfer network linking more than 10,000 domestic banks with the Federal Reserve System. Banks use this network to make deposit and loan payments, to transfer book entry securities among themselves, and to act as payment agents on behalf of large corporate customers including other financial service firms. CHIPS is operated as a private network. At the core of the system are approximately 140 large U.S. and foreign banks acting as correspondent banks for a larger number of domestic and international banks in clearing mostly international payments (foreign exchange, Eurodollar loans, certificates of deposit).

Together, these two wire transfer networks have been growing at around 25 percent per annum. Indeed, since 1986 the combined value of payments sent over these two networks has often exceeded $1.7 trillion a day.[12] Another way to see the tremendous growth in these wire transfer payment networks is to compare their dollar payment values to bank reserves, as we do in Table 10–4. Thus, the value of wire transfers has increased more than 26-fold, relative to bank reserves, over the 1970–92 period.

Risks that Arise in a Wire Transfer Payment System

At least six important risks have arisen along with the growth of wire transfer systems. Some we touched on while discussing off-balance-sheet activities in Chapter 9; here we go into more detail.

Daylight Overdraft Risk

Some analysts and regulators view settlement or daylight overdraft risk as the greatest potential source of instability in the financial markets today. To better understand daylight overdrafts, look at Figure 10–7. It shows a typical daily pattern of net wire payment transfers—payments messages sent (debits) minus payment messages received (credits)—for a large money center bank using Fedwire.

Daylight Overdraft
When a bank's reserve account at the Fed becomes negative within the banking day.

Under the Federal Reserve Act, banks must maintain cash reserves on deposit at the Fed. For Fedwire settlement occurs at the end of the banking day at 6:30 P.M. EST. At that time, the Federal Reserve adjusts each member bank's reserve account to reflect that bank's net debit (credit) position with other banks.[13] Under current regulations, the end-of-day reserve position of a member bank cannot be negative. However, what is true at the end of the day is not true during the day; that is, the Fed allows banks to run real-time **daylight overdrafts** (or negative intraday balances) on their reserve accounts. These negative reserve balances arise under the current payments system because large banks and their customers often send payment messages repaying overnight loans and making interest payments at the beginning of the banking day and borrow funds (i.e., receive payment messages) toward the end of the banking day. For periods during the day, banks frequently

---

[12]See Office of Technology Assessment, *U.S. Banks and International Telecommunications.*
[13]Technically, CHIPS transactions settle on Fedwire between 4:30 and 6:30 P.M.

FIGURE 10–7

Daylight overdrafts on Fedwire

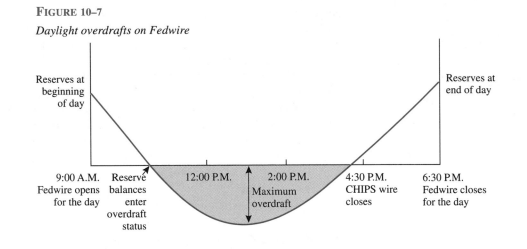

run daylight overdrafts on their reserve accounts at the Fed by having their payment outflow messages exceed their payment inflow messages (see Figure 10–7).

In effect, the Fed is implicitly lending banks within-day reserves. There are two other important institutional aspects to this process: First, until recently the Federal Reserve did not charge banks an explicit interest rate or fee for these daylight overdrafts. As a result, neither banks nor their large corporate customers had any incentive to economize on these transactions. Daylight Fedwire overdrafts were effectively free and therefore oversupplied.[14] Second, under Regulation J, the Federal Reserve guarantees payment finality for every wire transfer message. Therefore, if the representative bank in Figure 10–7 were to fail at 12:00 P.M., the Federal Reserve would be liable for all of the Fedwire transactions made by that bank until 12:00 P.M. This eliminates any risk that a payment message receiving bank or its customers would be left short of funds at the end of the day. Essentially, the Federal Reserve bears the Fedwire credit risk of bank failures by granting overdrafts without charging a market interest rate.

A good example of how technological failure or malfunctions can expose the Federal Reserve and the financial system to massive settlement risk exposure occurred in November 1985 at the Bank of New York. The Bank of New York (BONY) is a major dealer in government securities and uses Fedwire to pay for securities. Since the vast majority of U.S. Treasury securities are **book entry securities** (i.e., computerized accounts rather than paper claims), these would usually be transferred by securities Fedwire at the same time payments were made on cash Fedwire.[15] The problem occurred on November 20–21, 1985. On November 20, BONY had a very large number of securities transactions too extensive for its clearing and settlement software to handle in an efficient fashion. Indeed, because of a software breakdown it was still processing November 20 transactions the next day. As a result, BONY could not make any new securities deliveries the next day and therefore receive federal funds as payments. Its daylight overdraft on its reserve account started to build up throughout the day. Even though the Fed extended the hours of Fedwire, the

Book Entry Securities
Securities held in computerized account form rather than in paper form.

---

[14]Beginning in 1993, a small per annum interest charge was levied on a bank's maximum daily overdraft amounts. The maximum size of this charge is 0.25 percent and is to be phased in over a three-year period. This is clearly well below a bank's opportunity cost of funds.

[15]Technically, there are two Fedwires—one for securities and one for cash and reserve transfers.

software problem was still not solved late into the evening of the 21st. When settlement finally occurred early in the morning of the 22nd, the Federal Reserve had to extend a one-day loan to BONY equal to nearly two thirds of BONY's total domestic and worldwide assets and over 24 times the size of its primary equity capital. Clearly, failure to extend the loan would have resulted in a large number of settlement failures by BONY and other banks. The fact that the loan size was so enormous, relative to BONY's capital, is symptomatic of the type of risk exposure that can potentially arise on the wire transfer networks and the sensitivity of banks to operational and technological breakdowns.[16] In particular, it brings into focus the question of whether BONY could have survived without a Federal Reserve bail-out.

On CHIPS, net payment flows often take on a daily pattern similar to that in Figure 10–7 except that, as a privately owned pure net settlement system, the beginning-of-day position must be zero for all banks. As on Fedwire, big banks often run a daylight overdraft but this is generally larger and more pronounced early in the morning than on Fedwire. Again, large banks then seek to borrow funds in the afternoon to cover net debit positions created earlier in the day. While CHIPS does not charge banks explicit fees for running daylight overdrafts, a bank failing to settle at the end of the day is treated very differently than on Fedwire. On Fedwire all payments are in good funds, that is, the Federal Reserve guarantees the finality of any wire transfer at the time it is made. By contrast, on CHIPS, since it is a private network, all within-day transfers are provisional and only become final on settlement among CHIPS members at the end of the day. In this case, if a bank (bank Z) with a daylight overdraft were to fail, CHIPS might have to resolve this by unwinding all of the failing bank's transactions over that day with the other (N–1) remaining banks. Bank Z's individual failure could result in a systemic crisis in the banking and financial system among the remaining (N–1) banks in the system.

In particular, suppose bank Y would have been in a net creditor position at the end of the banking day had the failing bank settled. Bank Y may find that after bank Z's failure and any CHIPS unwinding of message transactions, it, too, cannot settle its transactions with the other remaining banks. As a result, all its transactions with those banks have to be unwound.[17] Such a process would have to continue until all banks could settle their transactions with each other. While no settlement failure has recently occurred on CHIPS,[18] any such failure could be potentially disastrous with financial ramifications far exceeding the October 1987 stock market crash.[19]

To lower this settlement risk problem and to introduce an element of payment finality, the members of CHIPS have contributed $4 billion to a special escrow fund. This fund became operational in 1991. CHIPS members can use this fund to replace the message commitments of any failed bank, therefore preventing the potentially disastrous unwinding effects just described. However, $4 billion is probably an

---

[16]This description of the BONY crisis is based on R. J. Herring, "Innovations to Enhance Liquidity: The Implications for Systemic Risk" (University of Pennsylvania, Wharton School, October 1992, Mimeographed).

[17]This would leave only N–2 banks.

[18]There was a failure in the early 1970s by the Herstatt Bank of Germany.

[19]Simulations by D. B. Humphrey of CHIPS unwinding following an assumed bank failure show that up to 50 banks might be unable to meet their payment obligations on CHIPS following any one bank's failure to settle implying a massive systematic collapse of the payment system. See "Payments Finality and Risk Settlement Failure," in *Technology and the Regulation of Financial Markets: Securities, Futures, and Banking,* ed. A. Saunders and L. J. White (Lexington, Mass.: Lexington Books, 1986), pp. 97–120.

insufficient amount to cover a major bank failure such as that of a U.S. money center bank. At the end of the day, it would probably be left to the Federal Reserve and other central banks to mount a rescue scheme to prevent an international failure contagion from spreading throughout the domestic and international financial system. Of course, this implies yet another subsidy from U.S. regulators and taxpayers to the private domestic and international banking system.

Because of these concerns, the FDICIA passed in 1991, required the Federal Reserve to implement Regulation F under which banks, thrifts, and foreign banks must develop internal procedures or benchmarks to limit their settlement and other credit exposures to depository institutions with which they do business (so-called correspondent banks). Accordingly, since December 1992 banks must normally limit their exposure to an individual correspondent to no more than 25 percent of the correspondent bank's capital. However, for adequately capitalized banks this can be raised to 50 percent, while no set benchmark is required for well-capitalized banks. Thus, the most solvent banks now find it easier to transact on the wire transfer networks and run daylight overdrafts than less well-capitalized banks.[20] In addition, as long as the benchmarks are adhered to, regulators' exposure to settlement risk is reduced.

International Technology Transfer Risk

In 1970, 7 of the top 10 banks in the world were from the United States. In 1993, not one U.S. bank made the top 20 when measured by assets. Yet, over this period the United States has been at the forefront in making technology investments and financial service innovations in the payments system. One possible reason for the relative decline of U.S. banks is that domestic payment system innovations face the risk of being nontransferable to other countries' financial systems due to different cultures, financial practices, and stages of technological development.

For example, the United States has been a major pioneer of ATMs (with more than 90,000 currently in place). Yet, such networks have grown relatively slowly in Germany because of prohibitive charges imposed for the use and leasing of domestic telephone lines.

This suggests that U.S. financial service firms have often been unable to transfer profitably domestic technological innovations to international markets to gain competitive advantage, at least in the short term.[21] By contrast, foreign financial service firms entering the U.S. market gain direct access to, and knowledge of, U.S. technology-based products at a very low cost. For example, since the passage of the International Banking Act in 1978, foreign banks have had direct access to U.S. Fedwire.

Crime and Fraud Risk

The increasing replacement of checks and cash as methods of payment or exchange by wire transfer has raised new problems regarding theft, data snooping, and white-collar crime. Because huge sums are transferred across the wire networks each day, and relatively few bank employees have specialized knowledge of personal

---

[20]See Federal Reserve Board of Governors Press Release, July 14, 1992, for more details.

[21]Longer-term benefits may yet be realized due to telecommunications deregulation globally and through better customer recruitment and marketing of products in foreign environments.

identification numbers (PINs) and other entry codes, the incentive for white-collar crime appears to have increased. For example, a manager at the Sri Lankan branch of BCCI reportedly stole a computer chip from a telex machine in the bank's Oman branch and used it to transfer $10 million from three banks in the United States and Japan to his own account in Switzerland.[22] In the future, greater bank and regulatory resources will have to be spent on surveillance and employee monitoring, as well as on developing fail-safe and unbreakable entry codes to wire transfer accounts, especially as a number of countries (such as in Europe) have passed data privacy laws.

Regulatory Risk

Usury Ceiling
Caps or ceilings on consumer and mortgage interest rates imposed by state governments.

The improvement in FIs' telecommunications networks also enhances the power of FIs vis-à-vis regulators, effectively aiding regulatory avoidance. Thus, as implied earlier, regulation not only can affect the profitability of technological innovations but it can also either spur or hinder the rate and types of innovation. For example, each state imposes usury ceilings on banks. **Usury ceilings** place caps and controls on the fees and interest rates that bankers can charge on credit cards, consumer loans, and residential mortgages. Because credit-card operations are heavily communications based and do not need to be located directly in the bank's market, the two states that now dominate the credit-card market are South Dakota and Delaware. These two states are among the most liberal regarding credit card fee and interest rate usury regulations.[23] A further example of regulatory avoidance has been the growth of banking in the relatively unregulated Cayman Islands. The 500 or more banks located there do most of their banking business via public and private telecommunications networks.[24] The growth of telecommunications networks and improvements in technology have changed, perhaps irreversibly, the balance of power between large multinational FIs and governments—both local and national—in favor of the former. This shift in power also creates incentives for countries to lower their regulations to attract entrants; that is, it increases the incentives for competitive deregulation. This trend may be potentially destabilizing to the market in financial services with the weakest regulators attracting the most entrants.[25]

Tax Avoidance

The development of international wire networks as well as international financial service firm networks have enabled FIs to shift funds and profits through internal pricing mechanisms, thereby minimizing their overall United States tax burden and maximizing their foreign tax credits. For example, prior to 1986 many large U.S. banks paid almost no corporate income taxes, despite large reported profits, by

---

[22]Office of Technology Assessment, *U.S. Banks and International Telecommunications,* Chap. 5, pp. 27–35.

[23]For example, Citibank, the U.S. bank with largest credit-card franchise has located its credit-card operations in South Dakota. See also I. Walter and A. Saunders for a discussion of trends in financial service firms leaving New York; "Global Competitiveness of New York City as a Financial Center," Occasional Papers in Business and Finance, Stern Business School, New York University, 1992.

[24]A major reason for the growth in Cayman Islands banking was the desire of large U.S. banks to avoid or reduce the cost of the Federal Reserve's noninterest-bearing reserve requirements. Many attribute its current popularity to drug or crime-related secret money transactions. See I. Walter, *Secret Money: The World of International Financial Secrecy* (London: George Allen and Unwin, 1985).

[25]A closely associated risk for regulators is that increased use of international wire transfer systems weaken the power of central banks to control the domestic money supply.

rapidly moving profits and funds across different tax regimes. This raised considerable public policy concerns and was a major reason underlying the 1986 tax reforms in the United States. These reforms imposed a minimum corporate income tax rate of 20 percent on U.S. banks and limited their ability to use foreign tax credits to offset their domestic income tax burdens.

Competition Risk

As financial services become more technologically based, they are increasingly competing with nontraditional financial service suppliers such as AT&T. For example, in addition to offering its own enhanced credit card in competition with bank-supplied credit cards, AT&T owns a finance company.[26] Also, once established, financial services technology can easily be purchased by nonfinancial firms. Thus, in 1992 General Motors also established a credit-card operation linked to the purchase of its vehicles at a discount. Currently, banks issue less than half of all new credit cards; much of the new business is going to nontraditional firms such as AT&T and General Motors. As a result, technology exposes existing FIs to the increased risk of erosion of their franchises as costs of entry fall and the competitive landscape changes.

Concept Questions

1. Give two reasons why daylight overdrafts create more of a risk problem for banks on CHIPS than on Fedwire.
2. Suggest two policy reforms through which the Federal Reserve could eliminate daylight overdraft risks on Fedwire.
3. What would be the social costs of the policies selected to answer question 2?
4. What are the six risks for FIs associated with the growth of wire transfer networks and payment systems?

---

[26]AT&T's universal card began operation in March 1990. It is both a credit card and a calling card. Its finance company subsidiary—AT&T Capital Corp—does leasing, project financing and small business lending.

Summary

This chapter has analyzed the operating cost side of FIs' activities including the growth of technology-based innovations in the financial services industry and the new types of risks that arise with such innovations. While technology-based investments can potentially result in new product innovations and lower costs, the evidence of such positive benefits is far from concrete. Specifically, a number of innovations have failed to find a market and the evidence on economies of scale and scope offer no strong support for innovation-based cost savings. Moreover, new and difficult risks appear to have been accentuated by modern technology. These include (1) settlement or daylight overdraft risk, (2) international technology transfer risk, (3) crime or fraud risk, (4) regulatory avoidance risk, (5) taxation avoidance risk, and (6) competition risk.

Questions and Problems

1. How has the globalization of financial intermediation impacted the cost and efficiency of operations?

2. How do the following FI services increase an FI's profitability? Choose from one or more of the four alternatives:

Increase interest income.
Decrease interest expense.
Increase operating income.
Decrease operating expense.

   a. Controlled disbursement accounts
   b. Wholesale lockbox
   c. Electronic funds transfer
   d. Check deposit services
   e. Treasury management software
   f. Automated teller machines (*ATMs*)
   g. Home banking

3. The United States has more than 12,000 commercial banks of widely disparate size and scope. What could you say about the cost structure of U.S. banks from this observation, assuming that the observed structure is not determined by regulatory intervention?

4. All companies attempt to improve the efficiency of their operations.

   a. How is this task more challenging for FIs than for nonfinancial firms?
   b. How is it easier for FIs than for nonfinancial firms?

5. Evaluate the net present value of the following cost savings proposals to determine whether the FI should undertake the project. The FI's total operating costs are currently $150 million annually. Out of this total, personnel costs are $100 million. The FI's cost of capital is 10 percent.

   a. Invest in a Local Area Network to access securities price information on a real-time basis: Expected cost savings = 10 percent of total annual costs. Projected project life span = five years. Initial cost = $50 million.
   b. Invest in a Wide Area Network to access global securities price information on a real-time basis: Expected cost savings = 15 percent of total annual

costs. Projected project life span = five years. Additional revenue projections = $5 million annually. Initial cost = $100 million.

   c. Provide all employees with a network of desktop workstations: Expected cost savings = 25 percent of personnel costs. Projected project life span = seven years. Initial cost = $80 million.

6. a. Would your investment decision on the project in question 5*a* change if the FI's cost of capital increased to 18 percent?
    b. Would your investment decision on the project in question 5*b* change if the initial cost increased by $5 million? (Cost of capital = 10 percent.)
    c. Would your investment decision on the project in question 5*c* change if the expected cost savings were only 10 percent of personnel costs? (Cost of capital = 10 percent.)

7. What do your answers to questions 5 and 6 suggest about cost-saving investment opportunities?

8. a. How does the recent trend toward greater diversity of FI activities impact the FI's cost of operations?
    b. As more FIs move from a mutual to a corporate form of ownership, how are operational costs likely to be affected?
    c. How does the increased incidence of takeovers and mergers affecting FIs impact operational efficiency?
    d. How does enhanced competitiveness in financial intermediation impact operational efficiency?

9. The advent of the information age creates an opportunity for as yet unexploited, but significant FI cost savings. Discuss.

10. The growth of an international bank, Bank of Credit and Commerce International (BCCI), exemplified the regulatory risk, fraud risk, and tax avoidance risk exacerbated by the proliferation of global technology. Discuss.

11

FOREIGN
EXCHANGE RISK

Learning Objectives

In this chapter you learn about FIs' exposure to foreign exchange risk. Foreign exchange risk arises for two main reasons. First, because FIs trade and deal in foreign currencies on behalf of their customers and for their own accounts. Second, because FIs invest in foreign currency assets and raise funds in foreign currency liabilities. Integral to this exposure is the tendency of FIs to hold net long (or short) positions in foreign currencies and foreign assets. You will learn that the more volatile are exchange rates, the more risky such exposures become.

Introduction

The globalization of the U.S. financial services industry has meant that FI managers are increasingly exposed to foreign exchange (FX) risk. Such risks can arise either directly through trading in foreign currencies, making foreign currency loans (a loan in sterling to a corporation), buying foreign-issued securities (U.K. sterling gilt-edged bonds or German mark government bonds), or by issuing foreign currency-denominated debt (sterling certificates of deposit) as a source of funds. In this chapter we evaluate the risks faced by FIs when assets and liabilities are denominated in foreign (as well as in domestic) currencies and when they take major positions as traders in the spot and forward foreign currency markets.

Sources of Foreign Exchange Risk Exposure

In recent years, the nation's largest commercial banks have been major players in foreign currency trading and dealing, with large money center banks such as Citicorp and J.P. Morgan also taking significant positions in foreign currency assets and liabilities. Table 11–1 shows the outstanding (dollar value) of U.S. banks' foreign assets and liabilities for the period 1988–92. The December 1991 figure for foreign assets is equal to 6.33 percent of the assets of the nation's 10 largest banks. In Table 11–2, we give a more detailed breakdown of the foreign currency positions of all U.S. banks in September of 1990 in five major currencies.

Spot Market for FX
The market in which foreign currency is traded for immediate delivery.

Forward Market for FX
The market in which foreign currency is traded for future delivery.

Looking at Table 11–2, columns 1 and 2 refer to U.S. banks' financial portfolio activities, the holding of assets and the issuing of liabilities denominated in foreign currencies. Columns 3 and 4 refer to foreign currency trading activities, the **spot and forward foreign exchange** contracts bought and sold in each major currency. As you can see, foreign currency trading dominates direct portfolio investments.

TABLE 11–1 Liabilities to, and Claims on, Foreigners Reported by Banks in the United States
Payable in Foreign Currencies (millions of dollars, end of period)

				1991		1992	
Item	1988	1989	1990	Sept.	Dec.	Mar.	June
1 Banks' liabilities	$74,980	$67,835	$70,477	$63,291	$75,129	$67,874	$70,764
2 Banks' claims	68,983	65,127	66,796	63,724	73,318	60,844	58,968
3 Deposits	25,100	20,491	29,672	29,812	26,192	23,269	23,462
4 Other claims	43,884	44,636	37,124	33,912	47,126	37,575	35,506
5 Claims of banks' domestic customers*	364	3,507	6,309	2,348	3,274	2,862	4,428

NOTE: Data on claims exclude foreign currencies held by U.S. monetary authorities.

*Assets owned by customers of the reporting bank located in the United States that represent claims on foreigners held by reporting banks for the accounts of the domestic customers.

SOURCE: *Federal Reserve Bulletin*, January 1993, Table 3.16, p. A5.

Even though the aggregate trading positions appear very large—127,118 billion yen being bought by U.S. banks—their overall or net exposure position can be relatively small.

FIs' overall FX exposure in any given currency can be measured by their net book or position exposure, which is measured in column 5 of Table 11–2 as:

$$\text{Net exposure}_i = (\text{FX assets}_i - \text{FX liabilities}_i) + (\text{FX bought}_i - \text{FX sold}_i).$$

$$\text{Net exposure}_i = Net \text{ Foreign Assets}_i + Net \text{ FX Bought}_i$$

Where: i = the ith currency

Clearly, an FI could match its foreign currency assets to its liabilities in a given currency and match buys and sells in its trading book in that foreign currency to avoid FX risk. Or, it could offset an imbalance in its foreign asset/liability portfolio by an opposing imbalance in its trading book so that its **net exposure** position in that currency would be zero.

Notice in Table 11–2 that U.S. banks had *positive* net FX exposure in Canadian dollars, Japanese yen, and the British pound, but *negative* net exposures in deutsche marks and Swiss francs. A *positive* net exposure position implies a U.S. FI is overall **net long in a currency** and faces the risk that the foreign currency will fall in value against the U.S. dollar, the domestic currency. A *negative* net exposure position implies that a U.S. FI is *net short* in a foreign currency and faces the *risk* that the foreign currency could rise in value against the dollar. Thus, failure to maintain a fully balanced position in any given currency exposes a U.S. FI to fluctuations in the FX rate of that currency against the dollar.

Even though we have given the FX exposures for U.S. banks only, most large nonbank FIs also have some FX exposure either through asset/liability holdings or currency trading. The absolute sizes of these exposures are smaller than for major U.S. money center banks. The reasons for this are threefold: smaller asset sizes, prudent man concerns,[1] and regulation.[2] For example, U.S. pension funds currently

Net Exposure
The degree to which a bank is net long (positive) or net short (negative) in a given currency.

Net Long in a Currency
Holding more assets than liabilities in a given currency.

_____

[1] Prudent man concerns are especially important for pension funds.

[2] For example, New York State restricts foreign asset holdings of New York-based life insurance companies to less than 10 percent of their assets.

TABLE 11–2   **Weekly U.S. Bank Positions in Foreign Currencies and Foreign Assets and Liabilities, September 26, 1990**
(In currency of denomination)

	(1)	*(2)*	*(3)*	*(4)*	*(5)*
	Assets	*Liabilities*	*FX Bought**	*FX Sold**	*Net Position*
Canadian dollars (millions)	24,819	25,100	102,224	101,568	375
German marks (millions)	124,442	126,870	1,094,497	1,104,173	−12,104
Japanese yen (billions)	15,050	12,864	127,118	128,747	557
Swiss francs (millions)	45,667	45,958	316,195	316,124	−220
British pounds (millions)	40,336	38,702	348,191	348,315	1,510

*Includes forward contracts.
SOURCE: *Treasury Bulletin*, March 1991, pp. 99–104.

invest approximately 9 percent of their asset portfolios in foreign securities and U.S. life insurance companies generally hold less than 10 percent of their assets in foreign securities. Interestingly, U.S. FIs' holdings of overseas assets are less than FIs in Japan and Britain (see Table 11–3).

Concept Questions

1. How is the net foreign currency exposure of an FI measured?
2. If a bank is long in deutsche marks (DM), does it gain or lose if the dollar appreciates in value against the DM?
3. A bank has £10 million in assets and £7 million in liabilities. It also bought £52 million in foreign currency trading. What is its net exposure in pounds?

Foreign Exchange Rate Volatility

As we discussed, we can measure the potential size of an FI's FX exposure by analyzing the asset, liability, and currency trading mismatches on its balance sheet. However, even if an FI mismatches its aggregate position in any currency, the dollar amount it stands to lose or gain also depends on the direction and underlying volatility of exchange rate movements. That is:

$$\text{Dollar loss/gain in currency } i = [\text{Net exposure in foreign currency } i]$$
$$\times \text{ Shock to the \$/Foreign currency } i \text{ exchange rate}$$

For example, in Table 11–2 U.S. banks had a net long position in British pounds of £1,510 million on September 26, 1990. Over that week the spot value of the pound

TABLE 11–3   **Foreign Investment of Private Sector Pension Assets**
(dollars in millions)

Country	1980		1985		1992* (projected)	
United States	$3,300	1%	$27,000	3%	$150,000	9%
United Kingdom	9,700	9	40,100	18	135,000	25
Japan	400	1	7,600	8	88,000	20
Netherlands	1,500	4	5,400	9	30,000	12
Canada	2,000	7	4,100	8	20,000	10
Switzerland	1,300	4	1,700	4	12,000	8
Australia	0	0	800	8	10,000	20
Hong Kong	1,200	60	2,400	60	9,000	65
Germany	500	2	1,000	3	9,000	6
Ireland	300	20	700	20	2,000	20
Belgium	275	25	800	30	1,800	35
France	75	1	200	2	600	3
New Zealand	0	0	0	0	400	8
Rest of World	100	2	600	3	1,200	10
Total	$20,650		$92,400		$469,000	

*Expressed in 1987 dollars. Assumes no change in foreign investment restrictions.
Source: InterSec Research Corp., March 1988.

depreciated against the dollar from $1.8938/£1 ($S_{t-1}$) to $1.8665/£1 ($S_t$). Expressed as a weekly percentage change:

$$\frac{S_t - S_{t-1}}{S_{t-1}} = \frac{1.8665 - 1.8938}{1.8938} = -.0144 \text{ or } -1.44\%$$

Spot Exchange Rate
The exchange rate between two currencies for immediate delivery at any given time.

where S_t is the dollar/pound **spot exchange rate** at the end of the week and S_{t-1} is the dollar/pound spot exchange rate at the beginning of the week. Since U.S. banks were net long in pounds, the dollar value of their positions fell by approximately:

Dollar loss/gain in currency i = [Net exposure in foreign currency i] ×
Shock to $/£ exchange rate = [£1510] × [1.8665 − $1.8938] = −$41.223 million.

Clearly, for any given net exposure position in a foreign currency the greater the volatility of foreign exchange rates, the greater the potential for losses or gains on any foreign currency position.

Figures 11–1 to 11–3 show monthly standard deviations in the dollar/yen, dollar/mark, and dollar/pound exchange rates over the 1957–91 period. Apart from major devaluations, such as the pound against the dollar in 1967, the volatility of exchange rates was small prior to 1971, as central banks intervened to smooth out currency fluctuations and to peg or fix exchange rates within fairly narrow bands around some agreed target rate. Beginning in 1971, central banks believed that they could no longer defend pegged exchange rates, especially when true exchange rate values deviated significantly from pegged exchange rate values. Under the Smithsonian Agreements in 1971 and 1973, major realignments of exchange rates took place; this was the beginning of the present system of relatively flexible or floating exchange rates. We show the effect of this structural change in exchange rate systems in

FIGURE 11–1

Japanese yen/U.S. dollar standard deviation (monthly)

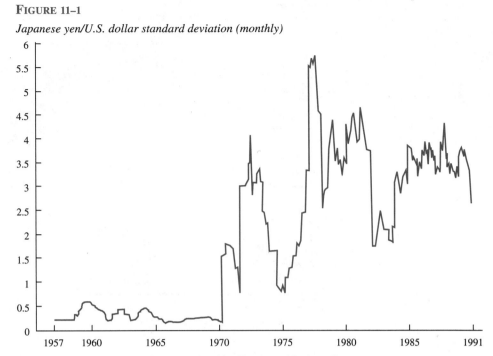

SOURCE: I. Giddy, A. Saunders, and I. Walter, "Securities Clearance and Settlement"
(Stern School of Business, New York University, 1993, Mimeographed), p. 26.

Figures 11–1 to 11–3; note the dramatic increase in FX volatility (the standard deviation of the exchange rate) after 1971. This suggests that mismatching a foreign currency position is far more risky under relatively flexible exchange rates than under a pegged or managed float system. Nevertheless, exchange rate volatility in the 1980s and in the early 1990s has been less than in the 1970s. There are several reasons for this. First was the creation of the European Monetary System among the major currencies of the European Community. The EC's eventual target is fixed exchange rates prior to the creation of a single currency or unit in the late 1990s. Second are attempts by the major industrialized countries—the group of seven—to set limits or bounds on the degree to which they are willing to allow currencies to fluctuate without combined and concerted intervention by central banks.[3] However, the collapse of the British pound in September 1992 and its realignment in the European Monetary System demonstrates the difficulties of achieving relatively fixed exchange rates when economic forces and foreign exchange traders determine that a currency is either over- or undervalued.[4]

We next take a closer look at the underlying determinants and risks of the two components of an FI's net exposure in a foreign currency: its foreign currency trading book and its foreign financial asset and liability book.

---

[3]Following the Louvre Agreement of 1987.

[4]For example, in September–October 1992 the British pound declined by approximately 20 percent against the dollar. Traders such as George Soros reputedly made $1 billion or more from speculating that the pound would devalue in this period. In addition, the French franc was allowed to depreciate against the DM in July 1993 and wider bands of fluctuation adopted for all major EMS currencies.

FIGURE 11–2

German mark/U.S. dollar standard deviation (monthly)

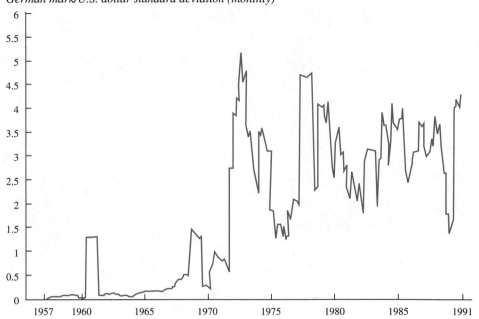

SOURCE: I. Giddy, A. Saunders, and I. Walter, "Securities Clearance and Settlement"
(Stern School of Business, New York University, 1993, Mimeographed), p. 25.

Foreign Currency Trading

The FX markets of the world have become the largest of all financial markets with
a turnover often exceeding $1 trillion a day. Moreover, the market is essentially a
24-hour market moving between Tokyo, London, and New York over the day.
Therefore, FX trading risk exposure continues into the night even when other
bank operations are closed.[5] This clearly adds to the risk from holding mismatched
FX positions. An FI's position in the FX markets generally reflects four trading
activities.

FX Trading Activities

1. The purchase and sale of foreign currencies to allow customers to partake in
   and complete international commercial trade transactions.
2. The purchase and sale of foreign currencies to allow customers (or the FI
   itself) to take positions in foreign real and financial investments.
3. The purchase and sale of foreign currencies for hedging purposes to offset
   customer (or FI) exposure in any given currency.
4. The purchase and sale of foreign currencies for speculative purposes through
   forecasting or anticipating future movements in FX rates.

---

[5]The Bank for International Settlements has estimated that the *average* daily volume of FX traded
worldwide was $800 billion a day in 1992.

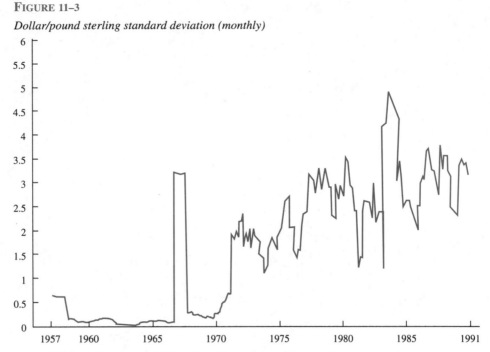

FIGURE 11–3

Dollar/pound sterling standard deviation (monthly)

SOURCE: I. Giddy, A. Saunders, and I. Walter, "Securities Clearance and Settlement"
(Stern School of Business, New York University, 1993, Mimeographed), p. 24.

Open Position
An unhedged position in a
particular currency.

In the first two activities, the FI normally acts for a fee as an *agent* of its customers and does not assume the FX risk itself. In the third activity, the FI acts defensively as a hedger to reduce FX exposure. Thus, risk exposure essentially relates to **open positions** taken as a principal for speculative purposes, the fourth activity. This is usually done by an FI taking an unhedged position in a foreign currency in its FX trading with other FIs. Specifically, many large commercial and investment banks make a market by quoting *two-way* bid and ask quotes in a foreign currency. The Federal Reserve estimates that 200 FIs are active market makers in foreign currencies in the U.S. FX market, with about 30 making a market in the five major currencies. FIs can make speculative trades directly with other FIs or arrange them through specialist FX brokers. The Federal Reserve Bank of New York estimated that approximately 44 percent of speculative or position trades were done through specialized brokers who receive a fee for arranging trades between FIs. Speculative trades can be instituted through a variety of FX instruments. Spot currency trades are the most common, with FIs seeking to make a profit on the difference between buy and sell prices or on movements in the bid/ask prices over time. However, FIs can also take speculative positions in foreign exchange forward contracts, futures, and options.

The Profitability of Foreign Currency Trading

Remember from the previous section that most profits or losses on foreign trading come from open position taking or speculation in currencies. Fees from market making—the bid-ask spread—or from acting as agents for retail or wholesale customers generally provide only a secondary or supplementary revenue source.

TABLE 11–4 Reported Foreign Exchange Income by Country

Country/Firm	1985 FX Income	1985 As Percent of Adjusted Income	1986 FX Income	1986 As Percent of Adjusted Income	1987 FX Income	1987 As Percent of Adjusted Income	1988 FX Income	1988 As Percent of Adjusted Income	1989 FX Income	1989 As Percent of Adjusted Income
United States—Millions of U.S. dollars										
Bankers Trust New York Corp.			$49.2	2.55%	$491.6	19.15%	$156.1	6.02%	$327.4	11.61%
Security Pacific Corp.			31.9	1.02	73.8	1.81	74.0	1.63	95.0	1.94
Manufacturers Hanover Corp.			36.0	1.04	63.0	1.88	103.0	2.64	95.0	3.00
J.P. Morgan & Co., Inc.			229.6	8.09	251.2	8.54	186.8	5.61	190.7	6.62
Chemical Banking Corp.			103.0	3.90	153.0	4.70	143.0	3.83	154.0	4.50
Chase Manhattan Corp.			199.3	4.21	213.8	4.38	239.9	4.36	193.8	3.91
Citicorp			412.0	3.94	453.0	3.61	616.0	4.72	471.0	3.42
First Chicago Corp.			94.0	4.94	119.0	6.16	149.0	6.66	76.0	3.11
BankAmerica Corp.			134.0	2.11	143.0	2.64	108.0	1.92	125.0	2.03
United States Sample Average Values			143.22	3.53	217.93	5.88	197.31	4.16	192.0	4.46
United States Sample Total FX Income			1,289.0		1,961.4		1,775.8		1,727.9	
Japan—Billions of Japanese yen										
Bank of Tokyo	47.8	16.49%	57.5	18.16%	77.2	24.31%	66.1	18.59%	NA	NA
Sumitomo Bank	NA	NA	NA	NA	61.4	10.90	63.3	9.23	129.4	20.04%
Dai-Ichi Kangyo Bank	NA	NA	NA	NA	29.0	5.37	56.2	9.64	38.4	7.44
Fuji Bank	NA	NA	24.3	4.89	26.6	4.83	27.7	4.69	54.4	9.53
Sanwa Bank	NA	NA	NA	NA	30.6	6.26	21.8	4.05	65.7	11.56
Mitsubishi Bank	NA	NA	22.2	5.04	24.5	5.02	17.1	3.06	30.4	6.01
Mitsubishi Trust & Banking	2.7	1.58	11.1	4.19	13.1	4.21	16.4	5.43	27.7	10.57
Industrial Bank of Japan	7.9	4.45	6.5	2.71	12.1	4.50	14.1	4.68	25.3	12.52
Mitsui Trust & Banking	1.9	1.38	-0.5	-0.23	2.1	0.82	7.7	3.13	13.6	5.95
Long-Term Credit Bank	4.6	3.57	2.1	1.13	3.3	1.49	6.4	2.64	1.0	0.73
Sumitomo Trust & Banking	5.8	3.21	9.2	3.62	17.8	5.64	5.9	2.03	6.5	2.47
Japan Sample Average Values	11.8	5.11	16.6	4.94	27.1	6.67	27.5	6.11	39.2	8.68
U.S. Dollar Equivalent*	$53.4		$103.8		$195.9		$214.4		$274.4	
Japan Sample Total FX Income	70.7		132.4		297.7		302.7		392.4	

*U.S. dollar equivalent calculated at average exchange rate over the year covered in the income statement.

SOURCE: Exchange rates from the *Federal Reserve Bulletin* and income figures provided by the Federal Reserve Bank of New York, "International Competitiveness of U.S. Financial Firms: Products, Markets, and Conventional Performance Measures," May 1991, p. 88B.

TABLE 11–5   **Standard Deviations and Correlations of Weekly Changes in the Natural Logarithms of Foreign Exchange Rates**
(January 5, 1984–December 28, 1989)

	German mark	French franc	Italian lira	Swiss franc	U.K. pound	Japanese yen	Canadian dollar
Standard Deviation:	1.70%	1.64%	1.55%	1.79%	1.76%	1.55%	.60%
Correlation with:							
German mark	1.00	.98	.96	.95	.79	.76	.20
French franc	.98	1.00	.96	.94	.80	.76	.21
Italian lira	.96	.96	1.00	.93	.77	.75	.21
Swiss franc	.95	.94	.93	1.00	.79	.80	.20
U.K. pound	.79	.80	.77	.79	1.00	.64	.27
Japanese yen	.76	.76	.75	.80	.64	1.00	.18
Canadian dollar	.20	.21	.21	.20	.27	.18	1.00

SOURCE: Bankers Trust

Note the importance of FX trading for some large U.S. and Japanese banks in Table 11–4. For large U.S. banks such as Bankers Trust, FX trading has become an extremely important source of income as it has concentrated on becoming a merchant, or trading, bank rather than a traditional commercial bank. However, FX trading income is a highly volatile source. Specifically for Bankers Trust, FX income as a percent of its total adjusted income varied from a low of 2.55 percent in 1986 to a high of 19.15 percent in 1987, with a standard deviation of 6.28 percent.[6]

Interestingly, Table 11–4 shows that a number of Japanese banks appear to be even more reliant than U.S. banks on FX trading as a source of income, especially Sumitomo Bank and the Industrial Bank of Japan.

Managing Foreign Trading Risk in a Portfolio Framework

Looking at individual currency mismatches may exaggerate the risk exposure of an FI taking an aggressive or open position in many currencies at the same time. In general, the exposure risk of a portfolio of currencies will be less than the sum of the risks of each currency position when viewed independently. To the extent that foreign exchange rate changes are negatively correlated across currencies, gains from trading or position taking in one FX area are offset by losses elsewhere. Thus, while the dollar is depreciating against one currency, it may be appreciating against others. That is, let σ_p^2 be the risk of a portfolio of foreign currencies held by a U.S. bank:

$$\sigma_p^2 = \sum_{i=1}^{n} X_i^2 \sigma_i^2 + \sum_{i=1}^{n} \sum_{\substack{j=1 \\ j \neq 1}}^{n} X_i X_j \rho_{ij} \sigma_i \sigma_j$$

where

X_i = The *net* position taken in the ith foreign currency (positive or negative)

---

[6]In 1993, over 80 percent of Bankers Trust's profits came from FX and securities trading. The five largest New York banks plus Bank of America made over $900 million from trading in that quarter representing 40 percent of their combined total profits. See *The New York Times*, "Europe Tumult Is U.S. Bank's Gain," August 4, 1993, pp. D1–D5.

TABLE 11–6 **Net Foreign Currency Trading**
(September 26, 1990)

Net FX Trading Position*	
Canadian dollars (millions)	+ 656
German mark (millions)	−9,676
Japanese yen (billions)	−1,629
Swiss francs (millions)	+ 71
British pounds (millions)	−124

*In local currencies.
SOURCE: *Treasury Bulletin*, March 1991, pp. 99–104.

σ_i = The volatility (standard deviation) of the ith exchange rate with the dollar

ρ_{ij} = The correlation coefficient between the ith and jth foreign currencies exchange rate with the dollar

Look at Table 11–5, the weekly correlations among foreign currency/dollar exchange rates over the period 1984–89. Clearly, with the exception of the Canadian dollar, major dollar/foreign currency exchange rates have been quite strongly positively correlated in recent years. This suggests that FIs may best achieve the gains from currency portfolio diversification by taking opposing net long and short positions in different currencies; for example, long in British pounds ($X_£$) and short in Japanese yen (X_J). This strategy is preferable to relying on opposing movements in the exchange rates themselves or negative correlations (ρ_{ij}) among foreign currency exchange rates. As we indicate in Table 11–2, the currency trading books of U.S. banks often reflect opposing net positions in different currencies. See Table 11–6.

Concept Questions

1. What are the four major FX trading activities?
2. In which trades do FIs normally act as agents and in which trades as principals?
3. If foreign exchange rates are highly correlated, how can FX diversification reduce an FI's risk?

Foreign Asset and Liability Positions

The second dimension of an FI's foreign exchange exposure results from any mismatches between its foreign financial asset and foreign financial liability portfolios. Foreign financial assets might include Swiss franc-denominated bonds, British pound gilt-edged securities, or even peso-denominated Mexican bonds. Foreign financial liabilities might include issuing British pound CDs or a yen-denominated bond in the Euromarkets to raise yen finance. The globalization of financial markets has created an enormous range of possibilities for raising finance in currencies other than the home currency. This is important for FIs that wish not only to diversify the source and use of funds but also to exploit imperfections in foreign banking markets that create opportunities for higher returns on assets or lower funding costs.

The Return and Risk of Foreign Investments

To understand the extra dimensions of return and risk from adding foreign currency assets and liabilities to an FI's portfolio, consider the following simple example:

Assets	Liabilities
$100 million U.S. loans (one year) in dollars	$200 million U.S. CDs (one year) in dollars
$100 million equivalent U.K. loans (one year) (loans made in sterling)	

Here a U.S. FI is raising all its liabilities in dollars but investing 50 percent in U.S. dollar assets and 50 percent in U.K. pound sterling assets.[7] In this example, the FI has matched the duration of its assets and liabilities ($D_A = D_L = 1$ year) but mismatched the currency composition of its asset and liability portfolios. Suppose the promised one-year U.S. CD rate is 8 percent to be paid in dollars at the end of the year. Suppose that one-year, credit risk free loans in the United States are yielding only 6 percent. The FI would face a negative spread of 2 percent from investing domestically.[8] Suppose, however, that credit risk free one-year loans are yielding 15 percent in the United Kingdom.

To invest in the United Kingdom, the FI decides to take 50 percent of its $200 million in funds and make one-year maturity U.K. sterling loans while keeping 50 percent of its funds to make U.S. dollar loans. To invest $100 million overseas in one-year loans in the United Kingdom, the U.S. FI has to undertake the following transactions:

1. At the beginning of the year, sell $100 million for pounds on the spot currency markets. If the exchange rate is $1.60 to £1, this translates into $100 million/1.6 = £62.5 million.

2. Take the £62.5 million and make one-year U.K. loans at a 15 percent interest rate.

3. At the end of the year, sterling revenue from these loans will be £62.5(1.15) = £71.875 million.[9]

4. Repatriate these funds back to the United States at the end of the year. That is, the U.S. bank sells the £71.875 million in the foreign exchange market at the spot exchange rate that exists at that time, the end of the year spot rate.

---

[7]For simplicity, we ignore the leverage or net worth aspects of the FI's portfolio.

[8]This is clearly an extreme example. In reality, it would likely exist only if there were major supply and demand imbalances in the deposit and loan markets and/or the bank in question was viewed as excessively risky by depositors. It should be noted that the basic principles demonstrated by this example would be unchanged if we were to assume a domestic loan rate exceeding 8 percent.

[9]No default risk is assumed.

Suppose that the spot foreign exchange rate has not changed over the year; it remains fixed at $1.60/£1, then the dollar proceeds from the U.K. investment would be:

£71.875 million × $1.60/£1 = $115 million or as a return:

$$\frac{\$115\ \text{million} - \$100\ \text{million}}{\$100\ \text{million}} = 15\%$$

Given this, the weighted return on the bank's portfolio of investments would be:

(.5)(.06) + (.5)(.15) = .105 or 10.5%

This exceeds the cost of the bank's CDs by 2.5 percent (10.5 % − 8%). However, suppose that at the end of the year the British pound had fallen in value relative to the dollar, or the U.S. dollar had appreciated in value relative to the pound. The returns on the U.K. loans could be far less than 15 percent even in the absence of interest rate or credit risk. For example, suppose the exchange rate had fallen from $1.60/£1 at the beginning of the year to $1.50/£1 at the end of the year when the bank needed to repatriate the principal and interest on the loan. At an exchange rate of $1.50/£1 the pound loan revenues at the end of the year translate into:

£71.875 million × $1.50/£1 = $107.8125 million

or as a return on the original dollar investment of:

$$\frac{\$107.8125 - \$100}{\$100} = .078125 = 7.8125\%$$

The weighted return on the bank's asset portfolio would be:

(.5)(.06) + (.5)(.078125) = .06906 = 6.906%

Here the bank would actually make a loss or have a negative interest margin on its balance-sheet investments since its cost of funds is 8 percent.

The reason for the loss is that the depreciation of the pound from $1.60 to $1.50 has offset the attractive high yield on British pound sterling loans relative to domestic U.S. dollar loans. If the pound had instead appreciated against the dollar over the year, say to $1.70/£1, then the U.S. bank would have generated a dollar return from its U.K. loans of:

£71.875 × $1.70 = $122.188 million

or a percentage return of 22.188 percent.

Then, the U.S. bank would receive a double benefit from investing in the United Kingdom, a high yield on the domestic British loans plus an appreciation in sterling over the one-year investment period.

Risk and Hedging

Since a manager cannot know in advance what the pound/dollar spot exchange rate will be at the end of the year, a portfolio imbalance or investment strategy where the bank is *net long* $100 million in pounds (or £62.5 million) is risky. As we discussed, the British loans would generate a return of 22.188 percent if the pound appreciated from $1.60 to $1.70 but produces a return of only 7.8125 percent if the pound depreciates in value against the dollar to $1.50.

There are, in principle, two major ways in which an FI manager can better control the scale of its FX exposure: on-balance-sheet hedging and off-balance-sheet hedging.

Hedging On Balance Sheet.   Suppose that instead of funding the $100 million investment in 15 percent British loans with U.S. CDs, the FI manager funds the British loans with $100 million equivalent one-year pound sterling CDs at a rate of 11 percent. Now the balance sheet of the bank would look like this:

Assets	Liabilities
$100 million U.S. loans (6%)	$100 million U.S. CDs (8%)
$100 million U.K. loans (15%) (loans made in sterling)	$100 million U.K. CDs (11%) (deposits raised in sterling)

This is a situation when the bank has both a matched maturity and currency foreign asset-liability book. We might now consider the bank's profitability or spreads between the return on assets and cost of funds under two scenarios: First, when the pound depreciates in value against the dollar over the year from $1.60/£1 to $1.50/£, and second, when the pound appreciates in value over the year from $1.60/£1 to $1.70/£.

The Depreciating Pound.   When the pound falls in value to $1.50/£, the return on the British loan portfolio is 7.8125 percent. Consider now what happens to the cost of $100 million in pound liabilities in dollar terms.

1. At the beginning of the year, the bank borrows $100 million equivalent in sterling CDs for one year at a promised interest rate of 11 percent. At an exchange rate of $1.60/£, this is a sterling equivalent amount of borrowing of $100/1.6 = £62.5.

2. At the end of the year, the bank has to pay back the sterling CD holders their principal and interest, £62.5 (1.11) = £69.375.

3. If the pound had depreciated to $1.50/£ over the year, the repayment in dollar terms would be £69.375 × $1.50/£1 = $104.06, or a dollar cost of funds of 4.06 percent.

Thus at the end of the year:

Average return on assets

$$(0.5)(0.6) + (0.5)(.078125) = .06906 = 6.906\%$$

U.S. asset return + U.K. asset return = Overall return

Average cost of funds

$$(0.5)(.08) + (0.5)(.0406) = .0603 = 6.03\%$$

U.S. cost of funds + U.K. cost of funds = Overall cost

Net return = Average return on assets − Average cost of funds

$$= 6.906\% - 6.03\% = 0.876\%$$

The Appreciating Pound.   When the pound appreciates over the year from \$1.60/£1 to \$1.70/£, the return on British loans was equal to 22.188 percent. Now consider the dollar cost of British one-year CDs at the end of the year when the U.S. FI has to pay the principal and interest to the CD holder:

$$£69.375 \times \$1.70/£1 = \$117.9375$$

or a dollar cost of funds of 17.9375 percent. Thus, at the end of the year:

Average return on assets

$$(0.5)(.06) + (0.5)(.22188) = .14094 \text{ or } 14.094\%$$

Average cost of funds

$$(0.5)(.08) + (0.5)(.179375) = .12969 \text{ or } 12.969\%$$

Net return = 14.094 − 12.969 = 1.125%

Thus, by directly matching its foreign asset and liability book, an FI can lock in a positive return or profit spread whichever direction exchange rates change over the investment period. Moreover, even if domestic U.S. banking is unprofitable due to an assumed negative 2 percent spread between the return on assets and the cost of funds, the bank could be profitable overall. It could lock in a positive spread—if it exists— between deposit rates and loan rates in overseas markets. In our example, there was a 4 percent positive spread between British one-year loan rates and deposit rates.

Note that for such imbalances in domestic spreads and foreign spreads to continue over long periods of time there would have to be significant barriers to entry facing financial service firms in overseas markets. Specifically, if real and financial capital is free to move, banks would increasingly withdraw from the U.S. market and reorient their operations toward the United Kingdom. Reduced competition would widen loan deposit interest spreads in the United States, while increased competition would contract U.K. spreads, until the profit opportunities from overseas activities disappeared. We discuss banks' abilities, and limits on their abilities, to engage in cross-border financial and real investments further in Chapter 17.[10]

Hedging with Forwards.   Instead of matching its \$100 million foreign asset position with \$100 million of foreign liabilities, the FI may have chosen to remain unhedged on the balance sheet. Instead, it could hedge by taking a position in the

---

[10]In the background of the previous example was the implicit assumption that the FI was also matching the durations of its foreign assets and liabilities. In our example, it was issuing one-year duration sterling CDs to fund one-year duration sterling loans. Suppose instead that it still had a matched book in size (\$100 million) but funded the one-year 15 percent British loans with three-month 11 percent sterling CDs:

$$D_{£A} - D_{£L} = 1 - .25 = .75 \text{ years}$$

Thus, sterling assets have a longer duration than sterling liabilities.

If British interest rates were to change over the year, the market value of sterling assets would change by more than the market value of sterling liabilities. This effect should be familiar from Chapter 6. More importantly, the bank would no longer be locking in a fixed return by matching the size of its foreign currency book since it would have to take into account its potential exposure to capital gains and losses on its sterling assets and liabilities due to shocks to British interest rates. In essence, an FI is only hedged against both foreign exchange rate and foreign interest rate risk if it matches both the size and durations of its foreign assets and liabilities in a specific currency. For a detailed discussion of this risk, see T. Grammatikos, A. Saunders, and I. Swary, "Returns and Risks of U.S. Bank Foreign Currency Activities," *Journal of Finance* 41, 1986, pp. 670–81.

forward market for foreign currencies, especially the one-year forward market for selling sterling for dollars. We discuss the nature and use of forward contracts by FI managers more extensively in Chapter 18; however, here we introduce them to show how they can insulate the FX risk of the bank in our example. Any forward position taken would not appear on the balance sheet; it would appear as a contingent off-balance-sheet claim, which we described as an item below the bottom line in Chapter 9. The role of the forward FX contract is to offset the uncertainty regarding the future spot rate on sterling at the end of the one-year investment horizon. Instead of waiting until the end of the year to transfer sterling back into dollars at an unknown spot rate, the FI can enter into a contract to sell forward its *expected principal and interest earnings on the loan, at today's* known **forward exchange rate** for dollars/pounds, with delivery of sterling funds to the buyer of the forward contract taking place at the end of the year. Essentially, by selling the expected proceeds on the sterling loan forward, at a known exchange rate today, the FI removes the future spot exchange rate uncertainty and thus the uncertainty relating to investment returns on the British loan. Consider the following transactional steps when the FI hedges its FX risk by selling its one-year sterling loan proceeds forward:

Forward Exchange Rate
The exchange rate agreed today for future (forward) delivery of a currency.

1. The U.S. bank sells $100 million for pounds at the *spot* exchange rate *today* and receives $100 million/$1.6/£ = £62.5 million.
2. The bank then immediately loans the £62.5 million to a British customer at 15 percent for one year.
3. The bank also sells the expected principal and interest pound proceeds from the loan forward for dollars at today's forward rate for one-year delivery. Let the current forward one-year exchange rate between dollars and pounds stand at $1.55/£ or at a 5 cent discount to the spot pound; as a percentage discount: ($1.6 − $1.55)/$1.6 = 3.125%).

This means that the forward buyer of sterling promises to pay:

£62.5 million (1.15) × $1.55/£ = £71.875 × $1.55/£ = $111.406 million

to the FI seller in one year when the bank delivers the £71.875 million proceeds of the loan to him (or her).

4. In one year the British borrower repays the loan to the bank plus interest in sterling (£71.875 million).
5. The bank delivers the £71.875 million to the buyer of the one-year forward contract and receives the promised $111.406 million.

Consider the economics of this transaction, barring a default on the loan by the sterling borrower or a reneging on the forward contract by the forward buyer of pounds. The bank knows from the very beginning of the investment period that it has locked in a guaranteed return on the British loan of:

$$\frac{\$111.406 - \$100}{\$100} = .11406 = 11.406\%$$

Specifically this return is fully hedged against any dollar/pound exchange rate changes over the one-year holding period of the loan investment. Given this return on British loans, *the overall expected return* on the bank's asset portfolio would be:

$$(.5)(.06) + (.5)(.11406) = .08703 \text{ or } 8.703\%$$

Since the cost of funds for the bank's $200 million U.S. CDs is 8 percent, it has been able to lock in a risk free return spread over the year regardless of spot exchange rate fluctuations between the initial overseas (loan) investment and repatriation of the foreign loan proceeds one year later.

In this example, it is profitable for the FI to increasingly get out of domestic U.S. loans and into hedged foreign U.K. loans since the hedged dollar return on foreign loans of 11.406 percent is so much higher than domestic loans' 6 percent. As the FI seeks to invest more in British loans, it would need to buy more spot sterling. This drives up the spot price of sterling in dollar terms to more than $1.60/£1. In addition, the bank would sell more sterling forward (the proceeds of these sterling loans) for dollars, driving down the forward rate to below $1.55/£1. The outcome would be a widening of the forward-spot rate spread on sterling, making forward hedged sterling investments less attractive than before. This process would go on until the 8 percent cost of bank funds just equals the forward hedged return on British loans. That is, no further profits could be made by borrowing in U.S. dollars and making forward contract-hedged investments in U.K. loans. This eventual equality between the cost of domestic funds and the hedged return on foreign assets looks like this:

$$1 + r_{ust}^{D} = \frac{1}{S_t} \cdot \left[1 + r_{ukt}^{L}\right] \cdot F_t$$

where

$1 + r_{ust}^{D}$ = is 1 plus the interest cost of U.S. CDs for the bank at time t.

S_t = is the $/£ spot exchange rate at time t.

$1 + r_{ukt}^{L}$ = is 1 plus the interest return on U.K. loans at time t.

F_t = the $/£ forward exchange at time t.

Suppose that $r_{ust}^{D} = 8$ percent and $r_{ukt}^{L} = 15$ percent as in our preceding example. As the bank moves into more British loans, suppose that the spot exchange rate for buying pounds rises from $1.60/£ to $1.63/£. In equilibrium, the forward exchange rate would have to fall to $1.5308/£ to eliminate completely the attractiveness of British investments to the U.S. FI manager. That is:

$$(1.08) = \left(\frac{1}{1.63}\right)[1.15](1.5308)$$

This is a *no-arbitrage* relationship in the sense that the hedged dollar return on foreign investments just equals the bank's dollar cost of domestic CDs.[11] We can re-express this relationship as:

$$\frac{r_{ust}^{D} - r_{ukt}^{L}}{1 + r_{ukt}^{L}} \simeq \frac{F_t - S_t}{S_t}$$

$$\frac{.08 - .15}{1.15} \simeq \frac{1.5308 - 1.63}{1.63}$$

$$-.0609 \simeq -.0609$$

---

[11]The return on U.K. loans still dominates that of U.S. loans, which is 6 percent in this example.

That is, the discounted spread between domestic and foreign interest rates would be reflected, in equilibrium, in a similar percentage spread between forward and spot exchange rates. In this form, the relationship is called the **interest rate parity theorem** (IRPT). The implication of this relationship is that in a competitive market for deposits, loans, and foreign exchange, the potential profit opportunities from overseas investment for the FI manager are likely to be small and fleeting. That is, long-term violations of this relationship are likely to occur only if there are major imperfections in international deposit, loan, and other financial markets including barriers to cross-border financial flows.

Interest Rate Parity Theorem
The discounted spread between domestic and foreign interest rates equals the percentage spread between forward and spot exchange rates.

Multicurrency Foreign Asset-Liability Positions

So far, we have used a one currency example of a matched or mismatched foreign asset-liability portfolio. Many FIs including banks, mutual funds, and pension funds hold multicurrency asset-liability positions. As for multicurrency trading portfolios, diversification across many asset and liability markets can potentially reduce the risk of portfolio returns and the cost of funds.

To the extent that domestic and foreign interest rates or stock returns for equities do not move strongly together over time, potential gains from asset-liability portfolio diversification can offset the risk of mismatching individual currency asset-liability positions. This may be especially important given the evidence of the high degree of correlation across foreign currency exchange rates over time (see Table 11–5).

Theoretically speaking, the one-period nominal interest rate (r_i) on fixed income securities in any particular country has two major components: First, the **real interest rate** reflects underlying real sector demands and supplies for funds in that currency. Second, the *expected inflation rate* reflects an extra amount of interest lenders demand from borrowers. This is to compensate lenders for the erosion in the principal (or real) value of the funds they lend due to inflation in goods prices expected over the period of the loan. Formally:[12]

Real Interest Rate
The difference between a nominal interest rate and the expected rate of inflation.

$$r_i = rr_i + i^e_i$$

where

$$r_i = \text{The nominal interest rate in country } i$$

$$rr_i = \text{The real interest rate in country } i$$

$$i^e_i = \text{The expected one-period inflation rate in country } i$$

If real savings and investment demand and supply pressures as well as inflationary expectations were closely linked or integrated across countries, we would expect to find that nominal interest rates are highly correlated across financial markets. For example, if due to the rebuilding of Eastern Europe and the strong demand for investment funds, German real interest rates rise, there may be a capital outflow from other countries toward Germany. This may lead to rising real and nominal interest rates in other countries as policymakers and borrowers try to mitigate the size of their capital outflows. On the other hand, if the world capital market is not very well integrated, quite significant nominal and real interest deviations may exist before

---

[12]This equation is often called the Fisher equation after the economist who first publicized this hypothesized relationship among nominal rates, real rates, and expected inflation. As shown, we ignore the small cross product term between the real rate and expected inflation rate.

TABLE 11–7   Correlations of Long-Term Government Bond Annual Returns in Local Currencies, 1961-1990

	Australia	Canada	France	Germany	Italy	Japan	Netherlands	Switzerland	United Kingdom	United States
Australia	1.00									
Canada	0.49	1.00								
France	0.52	0.61	1.00							
Germany	0.35	0.50	0.54	1.00						
Italy	0.41	0.39	0.73	0.30	1.00					
Japan	0.22	0.20	0.48	0.64	0.26	1.00				
Netherlands	0.45	0.74	0.62	0.80	0.35	0.55	1.00			
Switzerland	0.33	0.43	0.55	0.74	0.37	0.59	0.67	1.00		
United Kingdom	0.47	0.49	0.45	0.59	0.34	0.50	0.61	0.55	1.00	
United States	0.51	0.89	0.61	0.45	0.41	0.14	0.68	0.41	0.37	1.00

NOTE: Netherlands data begin in 1965, Japan in 1967, and Switzerland in 1965.

For each pair of countries, correlations are estimated over the longest period for which data are available for both countries.

SOURCE: R. G. Ibbotson and L. B. Siegel, "The World Bond Market: Market Values, Yields, and Returns," *Journal of Fixed Income*, June 1991, pp. 90–99.

equilibrating international flows of funds materialize. Foreign asset or liability returns are likely to be relatively weakly correlated and significant diversification opportunities exist.

In Table 11–7, we list the correlations among the annual returns on long-term bonds in 10 major bond markets for 1961–90. Looking at the last row for the United States, you can see that the correlations across bond markets vary from a high of .89, between the United States and Canada to a low of only .14 between the United States and Japan. The overall impression is that world bond markets are partially, but not fully, integrated and that an FI following a highly diversified international investment strategy can potentially reduce its exposure from single currency asset-liability mismatches.[13]

Concept Questions

1. The cost of one-year U.S. dollar CDs is 8 percent, one-year U.S. dollar bank loans yield 10 percent and U.K. sterling loans, 15 percent. The dollar/pound spot exchange is $1.50/£1 and the one-year forward exchange rate is $1.48/£1. Are one-year U.S. dollar loans more or less attractive than U.K. sterling loans?

2. Suppose the one year expected inflation rate in the United States is 8 percent and nominal one year interest rates are 10 percent. What is the real rate of interest?

---

[13]From the Fisher relationship, low correlations may be due to either weak correlations of real interest rates over time and/or inflation expectations.

Summary

This chapter has analyzed the sources of FX risk faced by modern FI managers. Such risks arise through mismatching foreign currency trading and/or foreign asset-liability positions in individual currencies. While such mismatches can

be profitable, if FX forecasts prove to be correct, unexpected outcomes and volatility can impose significant losses on an FI. They threaten its profitability and, ultimately, its solvency in a similar fashion to interest rate, credit, off-balance-sheet, and technology risks. We discussed possible ways to mitigate such risks including: direct hedging through matched foreign asset-liability books, hedging through forwards contracts, and hedging through foreign asset and liability portfolio diversification.

Questions and Problems

1. What is the net exposure of the following currency positions? (All amounts are in terms of currency of denomination.)

Currency	Assets	Liabilities	FX Bought	FX Sold
Dollar (m)	124,000	345,000	669,500	720,250
Yen (b)	707,900	592,444	935,000	651,000
Deutsche mark (m)	259,000	684,200	742,150	500,000

2. What is the foreign exchange rate shock for the following currencies?

   a. The British pound sterling rises against the U.S. dollar from $1.576 per dollar to $1.597 per dollar.

   b. The Japanese yen falls against the U.S. dollar from $.009 per yen to $.008 per yen.

   c. The deutsche mark rises against the U.S. dollar $.625 per deutsche mark to $.65 per deutsche mark.

3. What is the FX loss/gain for the positions in question 1 as a result of the exchange rate shocks in question 2?

4. Calculate the U.S. dollar and foreign currency exposures for the net positions held by U.S. banks in Table 11–2, using the following exchange rates:

   Currency (U.S. Dollar per Foreign Currency)

	S_{t-1}	S_t
Canadian dollar	$.7935	$.7928
German mark	.6270	.6258
Japanese yen	.0081	.0079
Swiss franc	.6925	.6908
British pound	1.5265	1.5295

5. A U.S.-based insurance company finances a £100 million three-year, 8 percent fixed-rate loan with three-year floating-rate U.S. dollar-denominated notes. The notes are repriced annually and are currently paying 6 percent per annum. Spot exchange rates are $1.6 per British pound.

   a. What are the sources of risk exposure associated with this transaction? What is the insurance company's net FX exposure?

   b. What are the annual cash flows associated with this transaction? (Assume no change in rates.)

   c. What is the breakeven future exchange rate at which the spread is reduced to zero? (Assume no change in interest rates.)

   d. If the British pound depreciates to $1.1/ £, then what

are the annual cash flows associated with the transaction? (Assume no change in interest rates.)

   e. If the British pound appreciates to $1.7/£, what are the annual cash flows associated with the transaction? (Assume no change in interest rates.)

   f. If there is no change in spot exchange rates but internationally all interest rates increase 100 basis points, what are the annual cash flows associated with the transaction?

   g. Discuss and contrast two ways the insurance company can hedge its FX risk exposure.

6. List some reasons why returns on domestic and foreign investments may not be perfectly correlated. How does this observation impact the integration of international financial markets?

7. The following are foreign currency positions for a U.S. FI expressed in local currencies.

Currency	Assets	Liabilities	FX Bought	FX Sold
Deutsche mark	96,440	75,000	44,900	205,500
Japanese yen	25,000	9,500	625,000	703,000
French franc	8,000	7,500	6,000	2,000

   a. What is the FI's net exposure in the deutsche mark?

   b. What is the FI's net exposure in the Japanese yen?

   c. What is the FI's net exposure in the French franc?

   d. How would you characterize the FI's risk exposure to fluctuations in the deutsche mark to dollar exchange rate?

   e. How would you characterize the FI's risk exposure to fluctuations in the yen to dollar exchange rate?

   f. How would you characterize the FI's risk exposure to fluctuations in the French franc to dollar exchange rate?

8. The following are net currency positions stated in U.S. dollars.

Currency	Net Position	Standard Deviation	Correlation
Canadian dollar	+US$125,000	1.30%	1.00
Deutsche mark	−US$25,000	1.70	.75
Japanese yen	+US$55,000	1.55	.77
British pound	+US$120,000	1.76	.81

Note: Net currency positions are foreign exchange bought minus foreign exchange sold restated in U.S. dollar terms.

   All correlation coefficients are for weekly changes in foreign exchange/US dollar rates between the foreign currency and the Canadian dollar. The standard deviation of the U.S. dollar is 1.51 percent. (For simplicity, assume that all the correlation coefficients except those just specified are zero.)

   a. How would you characterize the FI's risk exposure to fluctuations in the deutsche mark to dollar exchange rate?

   b. How would you characterize the FI's risk exposure to fluctuations in the yen to dollar exchange rate?

   c. How would you characterize the FI's risk exposure to fluctuations in the Canadian dollar to U.S. dollar exchange rate?

   d. How would you characterize the FI's risk exposure to fluctuations in the British pound to dollar exchange rate?

   e. What is the FI's total FX investment?

   f. What is the portfolio weight of the British pound in this FI's portfolio of foreign currency?

   g. What is the portfolio weight of the Canadian dollar in this FI's portfolio of foreign currency?

   h. What is the portfolio weight of the deutsche mark in this FI's portfolio of foreign currency?

   i. What is the portfolio weight of the Japanese yen in this FI's portfolio of foreign currency?

   j. If the correlation coefficients between each currency and the U.S. dollar were zero, what would be the risk (standard deviation) of this FI's portfolio of foreign currencies?

   k. Using the preceding correlation coefficients, what is the risk (standard deviation) of this FI's portfolio of foreign currencies?

   l. How can the FI decrease the risk of its FX portfolio?

9. If an FI wants to hedge its FX risk exposure, what are the advantages of hedging off the balance sheet as opposed to on the balance sheet? What are the disadvantages?

10. Why do FIs hedge their currency risk exposure? When is it undesirable to hedge? (Hint: Focus on the costs of putting on any hedge position.) What degree of currency hedging is optimal for the FI?

11. Suppose that the United States and the United Kingdom are in equilibrium with the spot exchange rate $S_t =$ US$1.60/£, the forward rate $F_t =$ US$1.55/£. Both countries have a real rate of interest equal to 3 percent. All rates are for one-year maturity. Assume that both interest rate parity and the Fisherian relationship hold.

   a. What is the nominal one-year interest rate in the United Kingdom?

   b. What is the nominal one-year interest rate in the United States?

   c. What is the one-year expected inflation rate in the United States?

   d. If forward rates fall to US$1.52/£ (with no change in spot rates), what can you infer?

   e. If there is no change in U.S. interest rates and no change in real rates of interest in both the United

States and the United Kingdom, what can you conclude about inflation expectations in the United Kingdom?

12. One-year risk free rates in the United States are 10 percent and one-year risk free rates in Germany are 8 percent. The spot exchange rate is DM2 per US$1. You have 1 million deutsche marks to invest.

   a. What are the risk free debt proceeds, at the end of one year, if you invest in Germany? State your answer in both dollars and deutsche marks.

   b. What are the risk free debt proceeds at the end of one year if you invest in the United States? State your answer in both dollars and deutsche marks.

   c. If you can lock in a forward exchange rate for delivery at the end of the year of DM1.9636 per US$1, would you invest in Germany or the United States?

   d. If you can lock in a forward exchange rate for delivery at the end of the year of DM1.5 per US$1, would you invest in Germany or the United States?

13. Assuming the no arbitrage condition holds, fill in the blanks in the following table. (All interest rates are assumed to be annual.)

Per Unit of Foreign Currency

FX Rate	Spot FX Rate	Forward Rate	U.S. Interest Rate	Foreign Interest Rate
£	US$2	US$1.994	*a*	10%
Yen	US$.008	*b*	8%	7.5%
DM	US$.57	US$.59	9.2%	*c*
FFr	*d*	US$.25	11%	11.4%

14. Consider the following balance sheet: (Assume that all instruments have maturities of one year with annual coupon payments.)

Assets	Liabilities
$1 million 1 year US 6% T-note	$5 million US 5% CDs
$4 million 1 year UK Loan.	(in dollars)
10% p.a. (in British pound sterling)	

   a. What is the interest rate risk exposure of this balance sheet position?

   b. Describe the currency risk exposure of this balance sheet postition.

   c. Spot exchange rates are 2 British pound sterling per dollar. What is the UK loan principal stated in pound sterling?

   d. If exchange rates are unchanged, what are the UK loan revenues at the end of the year? (State your answer in U.S. dollars and pound sterling.)

   e. What is the weighted return on the FI's asset portfolio? What is the net interest margin on this position? (Assume no change in FX rates.)

f. If the pound sterling falls to 1.90 British pound sterling per dollar, how do your answers to parts *d* and *e* change? (Calculate the loan revenues and net interest margin.)

g. If the pound sterling rises to 2.05 British pound sterling per dollar, how do your answers to parts *d*

and *e* change? (Calculate the loan revenues and net interest margin.)

h. How can the FI use the forward market to reduce exposure to FX rate changes?

i. If the FI hedged its currency risk exposure at a forward rate of 1.99 British pound sterling per dollar, calculate the end of year cash flows.

12

SOVEREIGN RISK

Learning Objectives

Country Risk Analysis
The analysis of the credit-worthiness of a sovereign nation.

In this chapter you learn about sovereign or country risk exposure and the special problems it creates for FIs. The absence of courts to enforce bankruptcy proceedings against a country means that **country risk analysis** is an important activity over and above the credit evaluations of individual borrowers we discussed in Chapter 8. We present and analyze several approaches to measuring country risk. In addition, we describe various ways FIs can and do limit their exposures to problem sovereign credits.

Introduction

In the 1970s, American and other countries' commercial banks rapidly expanded their loans to Eastern bloc, Latin American, and other less developed countries (LDCs). This was largely in response to their demand for funds beyond those provided by the World Bank and the International Monetary Fund (IMF), to aid their development, and the need to recycle petrodollar funds from huge dollar holders such as Saudi Arabia. In many cases, loans appear to have been made with little judgment regarding the credit quality of the sovereign country in which the borrower resided or whether that body was a government sponsored organization (such as Pemex) or a private corporation.

Debt Moratoria
Delay in repaying interest and/or principal on debt.

Loan Loss Reserves
Special reserves created on the balance sheet against which to write off bad loans.

The debt repayment problems of Poland and other Eastern bloc countries at the beginning of the 1980s and the **debt moratoria** announced by the Mexican and Brazilian governments in the fall of 1982 have had a major and long-lasting impact on commercial banks' balance sheets and profits. Indeed, at the time of the 1982 moratoria, the 10 largest U.S. money center banks alone had overall sovereign risk exposure of $56 billion, 80 percent of which was to Latin America. As a result, large banks such as Citicorp are still making provisions to their **loan loss reserves** as the value of these loans are written down in their portfolios. For example, in 1987 more than 20 U.S. banks announced major additions to their loan loss reserves in anticipation of future LDC loan charge offs, with Citicorp alone setting aside $3 billion.[1] This experience has confirmed the importance of assessing the country or sovereign risk of a borrowing country in making lending or other investment decisions such as buying foreign bonds. This is especially true as countries such as Chile and Mexico are endeavoring to reenter the international capital market again as their creditworthiness

---

[1] See T. Grammatikos and A. Saunders, "Additions to Bank Loan Loss Reserves: Good News or Bad News?" *Journal of Monetary Economics* 25, 1990, pp. 289–304.

improves. In Table 12–1, we show the year-end 1990 exposures of major money center banks.

In this chapter, we first define sovereign or country risk. We then look at measures of country risk to use as screening devices before making loans or other investment decisions. Finally, we look at the ways banks have reacted to their sovereign risk problems, especially by entering into **multiyear restructuring agreements (MYRA),** debt-equity swaps, loan sales, and **Brady bond** conversions as mechanisms to alleviate their sovereign risk problems. We describe and define these mechanisms in detail later in this chapter.

MYRA
A multiyear restructuring agreement which is the official terminology for a sovereign loan rescheduling.

Brady Bond
A bond that is swapped for an outstanding loan to a LDC.

Rescheduling
Changing the contractual terms of the loan such as its maturity and interest payments.

Credit Risk versus Sovereign Risk

To understand the difference between the sovereign risk and the credit risk on a loan or a bond, consider what happens to a domestic firm that refuses or is unable to repay its loans. The lender would probably seek to work out the loan with the borrower by **rescheduling** its promised interest and principal payments on the loan into the future. Ultimately, continued inability or unwillingness to pay would likely result in bankruptcy proceedings and eventual liquidation of the firm's assets. Consider next a dollar loan made by a U.S. bank to a private Mexican corporation. Suppose this first-class corporation has always maintained its debt repayments in the past. However, the Mexican economy and Mexican government's dollar reserve position is in bad shape. As a result, the Mexican government refuses to allow any further debt repayments to be made in dollars to outside creditors. This puts the Mexican borrower automatically into default even though, when viewed on its own, the company is a good credit risk. The Mexican government's decision is a *sovereign risk event* in large part independent of the credit standing of the individual loan to the borrower. Further, unlike the United States, where the lender might seek a legal remedy in the local bankruptcy courts, there is no international bankruptcy court to which the lender can take the Mexican government. That is, the lenders'

TABLE 12–1 LDC Exposure at Money Center Banks, as of December 31, 1990
(dollars in billions)

Bank	Medium and Long-Term LDC Loans	LDC Reserves	Reserves to LDC Loans Percentage	LDC Loans as Percentage of Loans	Adjusted* Reserves as Percentage of Adjusted LDC Loans
Citicorp	$7.6	$2.4	31%	4.9%	43%
Manufacturers Hanover	4.2	1.4	34	10.3	50
Chase Manhattan	4.0	1.6	40	5.4	59
BankAmerica	3.0	1.5	49	3.5	62
Bankers Trust	1.8E	1.3	72	8.4	NA
Chemical Banking	1.4	0.9	69	3.1	78
J.P. Morgan	1.3	1.3	100	4.7	100
First Chicago	0.3	NA	NA	1.1	74

*Net charge-offs added back to both loans and reserves. NA—Not available. E—Estimated.
SOURCE: *Standard and Poor's Industry Surveys*, September 1992, and November 1992, p. B29.

legal remedies to offset a sovereign country's default or moratoria decisions are very limited. For example, lenders can and have sought legal remedies in U.S. courts, but such decisions pertain only to the Mexican government or Mexican corporate assets held in the United States itself.

This situation suggests that making a lending decision to a party residing in a foreign country is a *two-step* decision. First, lenders must assess the underlying *credit quality* of the borrower, as would be done for a normal domestic loan, including setting an appropriate credit risk premium or credit ceiling (see Chapter 8). Second, lenders must assess the *sovereign risk quality* of the country in which the borrower resides. Should the credit risk or quality of the borrower be assessed as good but the sovereign risk assessed as bad, the loan should not be made. That is, in international lending or foreign bond investment decisions, considerations of sovereign risk should dominate considerations of private credit risk.

Concept Question

1. Why don't all countries default on their loans, given the absence of an international bankruptcy court?

Debt Repudiation versus Debt Rescheduling

There is a good deal of misunderstanding regarding the nature of a sovereign risk event. In general, a sovereign country's (negative) decisions on its debt obligations or the obligations of its public and private organizations may take two forms:

Repudiation
Outright cancellation of all current and future debt obligations by a borrower.

Repudiation **Repudiation** is an outright cancellation of all its current and future debt obligations. Since the Second World War, only China (1949), Cuba (1961), and North Korea (1964) have followed this course.[2] Repudiations on debt obligations were far more common before the Second World War as we discuss further later.

Rescheduling Rescheduling has been the most common form of sovereign risk event. Specifically, a country declares a moratorium or delay on its current and future debt obligations and then seeks to ease credit terms through a rescheduling of the contractual terms such as debt maturity or interest rates. Such delays may relate to the principal and/or the interest on the debt.

One of the interesting questions of international banking is why we have generally witnessed international debtor problems being met by reschedulings in the post-Second World War period, whereas a large proportion of debt problems were met with repudiations before the Second World War. A fundamental reason given for this difference in behavior is that most postwar international debt has been *bank loans* while before the war it was mostly in the form of foreign *bonds*.[3]

The increased importance of international loan rather than bond finance makes rescheduling more likely for reasons related to the inherent nature of international loan versus bond contracts. First, there are generally fewer banks in any international

[2]Some argue that Zimbabwe should be added to this list after it was created out of Rhodesia.
[3]See B. Eichengreen and R. Portes, "The Anatomy of Financial Crises," in *Threats to International Financial Stability*, ed. R. Portes and A. K. Swoboda (Cambridge: Cambridge University Press, 1987), pp. 10–51.

lending syndicate compared to thousands of geographically dispersed bondholders. The small number of lending parties makes renegotiation or rescheduling easier and less costly than when a borrower or a bond trustee has to get thousands of bondholders to agree to changes in the contractual terms on a bond.

Second, many international loan syndicates comprise the same groups of banks, which adds to bank cohesiveness in loan renegotiations and increases the probability of consensus being reached. For example, Citicorp has been chosen the lead bank negotiator by other banks in five recent loan reschedulings.[4]

Third, many international loan contracts contain cross-default provisions that if a country were to default on just one of its loans, all the other loans it has outstanding would automatically be put into default as well. Cross-default clauses prevent a country from selecting a group of weak lenders for special default treatment, and makes the outcome of any individual loan default decision potentially very costly for the borrower.

A further set of reasons why rescheduling is likely to occur on loans relates to the behavior of governments and regulators in lending countries. One of the overwhelming public policy goals in recent years has been to prevent large bank failures in countries such as the United States, Japan, Germany, and the United Kingdom. Thus, government-organized rescue packages for LDCs arranged either directly or indirectly via World Bank/IMF guarantees or the Brady Plan are ways of subsidizing large banks and/or reducing the incentives for LDCs to default on their loans. To the extent that banks are viewed as special (see Chapter 3), domestic governments may seek political and economic avenues to reduce the probability of foreign sovereign borrowers defaulting or repudiating on their debt contracts. Governments and regulators appear to view the social costs of default on international bonds as less worrisome than on loans. The reason is that bond defaults are likely to be more geographically and numerically dispersed in their effects and bondholders do not play a key role in the provision of liquidity services to the domestic economy.

Concept Question

1. Give four reasons why we see sovereign loans being rescheduled rather than repudiated.

Country Risk Evaluation

In evaluating sovereign risk, an FI can use alternative methods varying from the highly quantitative to the very qualitative. Moreover, as for domestic credit analysis, an FI may rely on outside evaluation services or develop its own internal evaluation models. Of course, to make a final assessment many models and sources may be used together because different measures of country risk are not mutually exclusive.

We begin by looking at the country risk assessment services available to outside investors and FIs: the *Euromoney Index* and the *Institutional Investor Index*. We then look at ways in which an FI manager might make internal risk assessments regarding sovereign risk.

---

[4]See Grammatikos and Saunders, "Additions to Bank Loan Loss Reserves."

Outside Evaluation Models

The *Euromoney Index*.   When originally published in 1979, the *Euromoney Index* was based on the spread in the Euromarket of the required interest rate on that country's debt over **LIBOR,** adjusted for the volume and maturity of the issue. More recently this has been replaced by an index based on a number of economic factors. See Table 12–2 for a list of the 29 countries with the highest risk ratings in 1993 along with a more detailed description of the sovereign risk index weighting system.

The *Institutional Investor Index*.   Normally published twice a year, this index is based on surveys of the loan officers of major multinational banks. These officers give subjective judgmental scores regarding the credit quality of given countries. Originally, the score was based on 10, but since 1980 it has been based on 100, where a score of 0 indicates certainty of default and 100, no possibility of default. The *Institutional Investor* then weighs the scores received from the officers surveyed by the exposure of each bank to the country in question. For the *Institutional Investor*'s country credit ratings as of March 1992, see Table 12–3.

Concept Question

1. Are the credit ratings of countries in the *Institutional Investor* rating scheme forward or backward looking?

Internal Evaluation Models

Statistical Models.   By far, the most common approach has been to develop sovereign country risk scoring models based on key economic ratios for each country similar to the domestic credit risk scoring models discussed in Chapter 8.

An FI analyst begins by selecting a set of macro and micro economic variables and ratios that might be important in explaining the probability of a country rescheduling. Then the analyst uses past data on rescheduling and nonrescheduling countries to see which variables best discriminate between those countries that rescheduled their debt and those that did not. This analysis helps the analyst identify a set of key variables that best explain rescheduling and a group of weights indicating the relative importance of these variables. In domestic credit risk analysis, we can employ discriminant analysis to calculate a Z score rating of the probability of corporate bankruptcy. Similarly in sovereign risk analysis, we can develop a Z score to measure the probability of a country rescheduling (see Chapter 8 for discussion of the Z score model).[5]

The first stage of this country risk analysis (CRA) is to pick a set of variables that may be important in explaining rescheduling probabilities. In many cases, analysts select more than 40 variables. Here we identify the variables most commonly included in sovereign risk probability models.[6]

LIBOR
The London Interbank Offered Rate. The rate charged on prime interbank loans on the Eurodollar market.

---

[5]Alternatively, analysts could employ linear probability, logit, or probit models.

[6]See, for example, K. Saini and P. Bates, "Statistical Techniques for Determining Debt-Servicing Capacity for Developing Countries: Analytical Review of the Literature and Further Empirical Results," Federal Reserve Bank of New York Research Paper No. 7818, September 1978.

TABLE 12–2 *Euromoney Country Risk Rankings for 1993*

March 93	Sept. 92	Country	Total Score	Economic Performance	Political Risk	Debt Indicators	Access to Bank Lending	Access to Short-Term Finance	Access to Capital Markets	Discount on Forfeiting	Credit Ratings	Debt in Default or Rescheduled
		Weighting		10	20	10	10	10	10	10	10	10
141	147	Zambia	20.29	1.93	4.04	7.03	0.10	0.50	2.00	0.00	0.00	4.69
142	146	Kyrgystan	19.91	2.61	5.53	0.00	0.00	1.00	2.00	0.00	0.00	8.77
143	159	Sierra Leone	19.71	1.37	4.47	8.45	0.00	0.50	0.00	0.00	0.00	4.93
144	149	Mongolia	19.20	2.17	7.02	0.00	0.00	0.00	0.00	0.00	0.00	10.00
145	122	Ukraine	19.17	2.30	5.11	0.00	0.00	1.00	2.00	0.00	0.00	8.77
146	136	Zaire	18.86	1.06	2.34	8.28	0.00	0.50	1.00	0.00	0.00	5.68
147	132	Belarus	18.75	2.30	4.68	0.00	0.00	1.00	2.00	0.00	0.00	8.77
148	134	Kazakhstan	18.55	2.73	4.04	0.00	0.00	1.00	2.00	0.00	0.00	8.77
149	129	Russia	18.13	2.17	4.68	0.00	0.00	0.50	2.00	0.00	0.00	8.77
150	142	Albania	17.77	1.49	1.28	0.00	0.00	3.00	2.00	0.00	0.00	10.00
151	167	Korea, North	16.73	1.18	2.55	0.00	0.00	3.00	0.00	0.00	0.00	10.00
152	144	Uzbekistan	16.37	2.05	2.55	0.00	0.00	1.00	2.00	0.00	0.00	8.77
153	160	Guyana	15.71	2.42	5.11	0.22	0.00	0.50	2.00	0.00	0.00	5.46
154	151	Congo	15.70	1.93	2.98	7.69	0.00	0.50	0.00	0.00	0.00	2.61
155	148	Georgia	15.57	1.40	3.40	0.00	0.00	2.00	0.00	0.00	0.00	8.77
156	143	Turkmenistan	15.28	1.74	2.77	0.00	0.00	1.00	1.00	0.00	0.00	8.77
157	168	Iraq	14.41	1.06	0.85	0.00	0.00	2.50	0.00	0.00	0.00	10.00
158	162	Liberia	14.17	0.68	1.49	8.36	0.00	0.50	1.00	0.00	0.00	2.14
159	156	Moldova	14.05	1.37	1.91	0.00	0.00	1.00	1.00	0.00	0.00	8.77
160	152	Tajikistan	13.80	1.12	1.91	0.00	0.00	1.00	1.00	0.00	0.00	8.77
161	153	Azerbaijan	13.66	1.61	1.28	0.00	0.00	1.00	1.00	0.00	0.00	8.77
162	154	Armenia	13.58	1.30	1.28	0.00	0.00	1.00	0.00	0.00	0.00	10.00
163	166	Somalia	12.94	0.00	2.13	6.85	0.00	0.50	0.00	0.00	0.00	3.45
163	164	Mozambique	12.83	0.99	2.34	5.31	0.00	0.50	0.00	0.00	0.00	3.68
165	169	Cambodia	12.15	0.87	1.28	0.00	0.00	0.00	0.00	0.00	0.00	10.00
166	158	Afghanistan	12.08	0.81	1.28	0.00	0.00	0.00	0.00	0.00	0.00	10.00
167	163	Sudan	9.66	0.43	1.06	7.66	0.00	0.50	0.00	0.00	0.00	0.00
168	161	Nicaragua	7.37	1.18	3.62	0.00	0.00	0.50	1.00	0.00	0.00	1.07
169	165	Cuba	6.75	0.56	3.19	0.00	0.00	3.00	0.00	0.00	0.00	0.00

TABLE 12–2 *(concluded)*

THE *EUROMONEY* COUNTRY RISK METHOD

The *Euromoney* country risk ranking will in the future be published every six months. The assessment uses ten categories which encompass three broad categories (analytical indicators, credit indicators, and market indicators). The different scores and figures for each category (as detailed below) are calculated into the weighted scores as follows: the highest figure in each category receives the full mark for the weighting. The lowest receives zero. The score for other figures is calculated proportionately according to the formula: Final score = (Weighting/(maximum figure−minimum figure)) × (figure − minimum figure). **The ranking table shows only the final scores after the calculation for weightings.**

The categories are:

Economic data (10% weighting). Taken from the *Euromoney* global economic projections 1993–94. The score is calculated from the sum of the overall economic performance evaluations for 1993 and 1994.

Political risk (20% weighting). *Euromoney* polled risk analysts, risk insurance brokers and bank credit officers. They were asked to give each country a score from 0 to 10. A score of 10 indicates nil risk of nonpayment, a score of 0 indicates that there is no chance of payments being made. Countries were scored in comparison both with each other and with previous years. Country risk was defined as the risk on nonpayment or nonservicing of payment for goods or services, loans, trade-related finance and dividends and the nonrepatriation of capital. This category does not take into account the creditworthiness of individual counterparties in each country.

Debt indicators (10% weighting). Scores are calculated from the following ratios taken from the World Bank World Debt Tables 1992–93: Debt service-to-export ratio (TDS/XGS); current account balance-to-GNP ratio (CAB/GNP); external debt-to-GNP ratio (EDT/GNP). Figures are the latest available, mostly for 1991. Scoring is calculated on the basis of (EDT/GNP) + (TDS/XGS × 2) − (CAB/GNP × 10), with the lower the score the better.

Because of the lack of consistent economic data for OECD and rich oil-producing countries, they all automatically score full points. Developing countries which do

not report debt data to the World Bank score zero. Successor states of countries which have split take the former country's figures.

Access to bank finance (10%). Calculated from disbursements of long-term private nonguaranteed debt in 1991 as a percentage of GNP. OECD countries automatically score 10. Source: World Bank World Debt tables 1992–93.

Access to short-term finance (10%). Score is calculated from: which OECD consensus group the country belongs to; whether the country is covered by US Exim or NCM. OECD consensus group: score 10 for Group I, 5 for Group II, 0 for Group III. Coverage from US Exim Bank and NCM: score from 10 to 0 depending on level of coverage available. A slightly different scoring method may mean that some countries for which coverage has not changed since September 1992 may have a different score.

Access to international bond and syndicated loan markets (10%). Analysis by *Euromoney* of syndicated loan and international bond issues since January 1989 and a judgment of how easy it would be for that country to tap the market now. 10 = no problem whatsoever; 8 = no problem on 95% of occasions; 6 = usually no problem; 4 = possible dependent on conditions; 2 = just possible in some circumstances; 0 = impossible.

Access to and discount on forfeiting (10%). Scored from a combination of the maximum tenor available (up to seven years) and the forfeiting spread over riskless countries such as the United States. Scores = maximum tenor minus spread. Countries for which forfeiting is not available score zero. Data supplied by Morgan Grenfell Trade Finance Limited.

Credit ratings (10%). Average of sovereign ratings from Moody's and Standard & Poor's. Countries without credit ratings or with less than BB–score 0. Countries with only a short-term rating score the equivalent of BBB.

Debt in default (10%). A score from 0 to 10 based on the amount of debt in default or which had to be rescheduled over the last three years. 0 = no nonpayments; 10 = all in default. Scores based on World Bank World Debt tables 1992–93.

SOURCE: *Euromoney*, March 1993, pp. 92–100.

TABLE 12–3 *Institutional Investor's 1992 Country Credit Ratings*

Rank (Sept 1991)	Rank (March 1992)	Country	Credit Rating	Six-Month Change	One-Year Change	Rank (Sept 1991)	Rank (March 1992)	Country	Credit Rating	Six-Month Change	One-Year Change
1	1	Switzerland	92.5	0.1	−0.6	37	36	Greece	47.6	0.5	−0.1
2	2	Japan	91.4	−0.9	−1.1	34	37	Czechoslovakia	47.1	−1.2	−3.1
3	3	Germany	90.4	0.5	−0.2	40	38	Kuwait	46.7	4.9	7.8
5	4	Netherlands	88.0	0.4	0.2	38	39	Cyprus	46.5	0.8	1.9
6	5	France	87.2	−0.1	−0.1	41	40	Chile	44.1	2.9	4.8
4	6	United States	87.0	−0.9	−0.3	39	41	Turkey	43.7	1.0	0.9
8	7	Austria	84.7	0.4	0.4	42	42	Hungary	41.7	0.7	0.6
7	8	United Kingdom	83.7	−1.1	−0.9	43	43	Mexico	41.0	2.4	3.1
9	9	Luxembourg	83.3	0.6	—	47	44	Venezuela	39.9	2.7	3.8
10	10	Canada	81.8	−0.9	−1.9	48	45	South Africa	39.3	2.3	2.9
11	11	Belgium	79.8	0.2	−0.1	46	46	Tunisia	38.7	1.2	−0.5
15	12	Singapore	78.6	0.8	1.0	50	47	Colombia	38.4	1.8	3.1
12	13	Italy	78.5	−0.6	−1.0	44	48	India	37.6	−0.8	−6.7
13	14	Norway	77.1	−1.3	−1.1	45	49	Barbados	37.4	−0.8	−0.8
14	15	Sweden	77.0	−1.4	−2.3	51	50	Israel	37.1	1.9	2.2
16	16	Taiwan	76.9	−0.2	−0.2	—	51	Botswana	35.4	—	—
18	17	Spain	76.2	0.6	0.2	53	52	Mauritius	33.3	−0.2	−1.0
19	18	Denmark	73.5	1.3	0.7	52	53	Algeria	33.1	−1.1	−4.8
17	19	Finland	72.9	−2.6	−4.2	54	54*	Papua New Guinea	32.1	−0.8	−2.0
21	20	Ireland	69.1	1.5	1.1	58	55*	Iran	32.1	3.7	5.6
20	21	South Korea	68.4	0.3	−0.3	55	56	Uruguay	32.0	0.7	2.2
22	22	Australia	66.7	0.1	−1.8	60	57*	Morocco	29.7	1.4	1.3
23	23	Hong Kong	65.8	2.2	1.3	49	58*	U.S.S.R.	29.7	−7.4	−14.6
24	24	Portugal	64.9	1.6	1.4	61	59	Libya	28.9	0.8	2.0
25	25	Thailand	62.8	0.3	−0.4	56	60	Trinidad & Tobago	28.5	−1.3	−1.1
27	26	Malaysia	62.6	0.7	1.1	57	61	Zimbabwe	28.3	−0.4	0.1
26	27	New Zealand	61.8	−0.2	−1.8	62	62	Pakistan	28.0	1.0	−0.7
28	28	Saudi Arabia	56.8	1.9	0.7	65	63*	Paraguay	27.0	0.4	0.7
29		United Arab Emirates	56.8	2.6	2.6	66	64*	Brazil	27.0	0.5	−0.4
31	30	China	54.4	1.3	2.9	63	65	Gabon	26.4	−0.4	0.0
30	31	Iceland	54.2	1.0	−0.2	59	66	Kenya	25.9	−2.4	−3.8
33	32	Qatar	51.3	1.5	1.2	68	67*	Philippines	25.7	1.2	0.9
32	33	Indonesia	50.6	0.2	0.2	—	68*	Estonia	25.7	—	—
35	34	Bahrain	49.4	1.3	0.0	64	69*	Romania	25.6	−1.0	−2.3
36	35	Oman	49.1	1.3	−0.4	68	70*	Poland	25.6	1.2	4.0

268

TABLE 12-3 (*concluded*)

70	71	Egypt	24.9	1.6	2.4
—	72	Latvia	23.9	—	—
—	73	Lithuania	23.7	—	—
78	74	Argentina	23.6	3.3	4.2
72	75	Costa Rica	23.4	1.0	1.9
75	75	Sri Lanka	23.4	1.5	1.4
73	77	Nepal	22.6	0.2	-0.5
71	78	Cameroon	21.9	-1.2	-2.4
81	79*	Nigeria	21.2	1.8	1.8
76	80*	Jordan	21.2	0.5	0.2
74	81	Bulgaria	21.1	-1.1	-6.7
80	82	Syria	20.3	0.8	1.0
79	83*	Ecuador	19.8	0.2	0.8
77	84*	Jamaica	19.8	-0.8	0.8
82	85	Swaziland	19.7	1.3	1.6
67	85	Yugoslavia	19.5	-5.0	-8.4
86	87	Panama	18.5	1.4	0.6
83	88	Senegal	17.8	0.0	-0.3
84	89	Guatemala	17.5	0.0	1.3
87	90*	Dominican Republic	17.2	0.2	0.3
89	91*	Bangladesh	17.2	0.7	-1.3
91	92*	Bolivia	17.2	2.1	3.2
—	93	Vietnam	16.8	—	—
88	94	Malawi	16.7	0.2	0.7
85	95	Côte d'Ivoire	16.6	-0.6	-1.6
90	96	Seychelles	15.7	-0.3	-0.1
—	97	Albania	15.5	—	—
96	98	Peru	14.3	2.1	2.0
94	99	Honduras	14.1	-0.3	0.5
93	100	Angola	14.0	-0.5	0.1
92	101	Myanmar	13.8	-1.2	—
95	102	Congo	13.7	-0.4	-0.3
97	103	Tanzania	12.5	0.5	1.7
99	104	El Salvador	11.8	0.8	1.1
100	105	Lebanon	11.4	1.2	2.9
102	106	Zambia	9.8	0.0	-0.1
98	107	Iraq	9.6	-2.1	-2.1
101	108	Zaire	9.2	-1.0	-0.4
103	109	Cuba	8.3	-0.6	-1.4
106	110	Grenada	8.0	0.0	-1.3
109	111	Mozambique	7.4	0.3	-0.3
105	112*	Haiti	7.2	-1.1	-0.8
108	113*	Nicaragua	7.2	0.1	0.2
104	114*	Liberia	7.0	-1.5	-1.5
107	115*	Ethiopia	7.0	-0.3	-1.1
110	116	Sierra Leone	6.7	-0.3	-0.6
112	117	North Korea	5.7	0.3	0.0
111	118	Sudan	5.6	-0.6	-1.0
113	119	Uganda	5.5	0.2	-0.2
		Global average rating including new countries	37.5	—	—
		Global average rating excluding new countries	38.2	0.3	0.2

*Order determined by actual results before rounding.

SOURCE: *Institutional Investor*, March 1992, p. 102.

The Debt Service Ratio (DSR).

$$\text{DSR} = \frac{\text{Interest plus amortization on debt}}{\text{Exports}}$$

An LDC's exports are its primary way of generating dollars and other hard currencies. The larger the debt repayments in hard currencies are in relation to export revenues, the greater the probability that the country will have to reschedule its debt. Thus, there should be a *positive* relationship between the size of the **debt service ratio** and the probability of rescheduling.

The Import Ratio (IR).

$$\text{IR} = \frac{\text{Total imports}}{\text{Total foreign exchange reserves}}$$

Many LDCs have to import manufactured goods since they cannot produce them without an adequately advanced infrastructure. In times of famine, even food becomes a vital import. To pay for imports, the LDC has to run down its stock of hard currencies, that is, its foreign exchange reserves. The greater its need for imports—especially vital imports—the quicker a country can be expected to deplete its foreign exchange reserves. Since the first use of reserves is to buy vital imports, the greater the ratio of imports to foreign exchange reserves, the higher the probability that the LDC will have to reschedule its debt repayments. This is because the repayment of foreign debtholders is generally viewed by countries as being less important than supplying vital goods to the domestic population. Thus, the **import ratio** and the probability of rescheduling should be *positively* related.

Investment Ratio (INVR).

$$\text{INVR} = \frac{\text{Real investment}}{\text{GNP}}$$

The **investment ratio** measures the degree to which a country is allocating resources to real investment in factories, machines, and so on rather than to consumption. On one hand, the higher this ratio is the more productive the economy should be in the future and the lower the probability that the country would need to reschedule its debt; this implies a *negative* relationship between INVR and the probability of rescheduling. An opposing view is that a higher investment ratio allows a LDC to build up its investment infrastructure. The higher ratio puts it in a stronger bargaining position with external creditors since the LDC would be less reliant on funds in the future and less scared about future threats of credit rationing by FIs should it request a rescheduling. This view argues for a *positive* relationship between the investment ratio and the probability of rescheduling, especially if the LDC invests heavily in import competing industries.[7]

Variance of Export Revenue (VAREX).

$$VAREX = \sigma^2_{ER}$$

---

[7]See S. Acharya and I. Diwan, "Debt Conversion Schemes of Debtor Countries as a Signal of Creditworthiness: Theory and Evidence" (Working Paper, Stern School of Business, New York University, June 1987).

Debt Service Ratio
The ratio of a country's interest and amortization obligations to the value of its exports.

Import Ratio
The ratio of a country's imports to its total foreign currency reserves.

Investment Ratio
The ratio of a country's real investment to its GNP.

An LDC's export revenues may be highly variable due to two risk factors. Quantity risk means the production of the raw commodities the LDC sells abroad such as coffee or sugar are subject to periodic gluts and shortages. Price risk means the international dollar prices at which the LDC can sell its exportable commodities are subject to high volatility as world demand and supply for a commodity such as copper varies. The more volatile an LDC's export earnings, the less certain creditors can be that at any time in the future it will be able to meet its repayment commitments. That is, there should be a positive relationship between σ^2_{ER} and the probability of rescheduling.

Domestic Money Supply Growth (MG).

$$MG = \frac{\Delta M}{M}$$

The faster the domestic growth rate of an LDC's money supply ($\Delta M/M$), the higher the domestic inflation rate and the weaker that country's currency becomes in domestic and international markets.[8] When a country's currency loses credibility as a medium of exchange, real output is often adversely impacted and increasingly it has to rely on hard currencies for both domestic and international payments. These inflation, output, and payment effects suggest a *positive* relationship between domestic money supply growth and the probability of rescheduling.

We can summarize the expected relationships among these five key economic variables and the probability of rescheduling (p) for any country as:

$$p = f = \left(DSR, \quad IR, \quad INVR, \quad VAREX, \quad MG.........\right)$$
$$\quad\quad\quad + \quad\quad + \quad\quad +or- \quad\quad + \quad\quad\quad +$$

After selecting the key variables, the FI manager normally places countries into two groups or populations:

$$P_1 = \text{Bad (Reschedulers)}$$

$$P_2 = \text{Good (Nonreschedulers)}$$

Then, the manager uses a statistical methodology, such as discriminant analysis, to identify which of these variables best discriminates between the population of rescheduling borrowers and that of nonrescheduling borrowers. Once the key variables and their relative importance or weights have been identified, the discriminant function can classify as good or bad current sovereign loans or sovereign loan applicants using currently observed values for the DSR, IR, and so on. Again, the methodology is very similar to the credit scoring models discussed in Chapter 8.

Problems with Statistical CRA Models. Even though this methodology has probably been one of the most common forms of CRA used by FIs, it is fraught with problems. Next, we discuss six of the major problems of using traditional CRA models and techniques. We do not imply in any way that these techniques should not be used, but rather that an FI manager should be aware of the potential pitfalls in using such models.

---

[8]The purchasing power parity theorem (PPP) argues that high relative inflation rates lead to a country's currency depreciating in value against other currencies.

Measurements of Key Variables.   Very often, the FI manager's information on a country's DSR or IR is out of date because of delays in collection of data and errors in measurement. For example, the Bank for International Settlements (BIS) collects aggregate loan volume data for countries; frequently this information is six months old or more before it is published. This example illustrates the problem: Citicorp may know today the current amount of its outstanding loans to Mexico but it is unlikely to know with any great degree of accuracy Mexico's total outstanding external loans and debt with every other lender in the world.

Moreover, these measurement problems are compounded by forecast errors when managers use these statistical models to predict the probabilities of rescheduling with future or projected values of key variables such as DSR or IR.

Population Groups.   Usually analysts seek to find variables that distinguish between only two possible outcomes: reschedulers and nonreschedulers. In actuality, a finer distinction may be necessary. For example, a distinction between those countries announcing a moratorium on only interest payments and those announcing a moratorium on both interest and principal payments. Thus, Peru, which has generally limited its total debt repayments to a small proportion of its export revenues, is a worse risk than a country that delayed the interest payments on its debt for a few months due to short-term foreign exchange shortages.

Political Risk Factors.   Traditionally, CRA statistical credit-scoring models incorporate only economic variables. While there may be a strong correlation between an economic variable such as money supply growth and rescheduling, the model may not capture very well purely political risk events such as *strikes, elections,* and *revolutions.* For example, the election of a strongly nationalist politician may reduce the probability of repayment and increase the probability of rescheduling. Quantitative measures of political risk, such as the number of labor strikes in any year, may have to be included to get better predictive power.

Portfolio Aspects.   Traditional CRA considers each country separately. However, many large banks with LDC or sovereign risk exposures hold a portfolio of LDC loans. In a portfolio context, the risk of holding a well-diversified portfolio of LDC sovereign loans may be smaller than having a portfolio heavily concentrated in nonoil-producing LDC loans. In particular the lender may distinguish between those key risk indicator variables having a *systematic* effect on the probability of repayment across a large number of sovereign countries and those variables having an *unsystematic* effect by impacting only one or a few countries.

One way to address this problem is to employ a portfolio framework for sovereign risk analysis. Such an analysis would identify those indicator variables that have a *systematic* impact across all borrowers' probability of repayment and those that tend to be country specific (or *unsystematic*).[9] The indicator variables that the FI manager should really be concerned with are the *systematic* variables since they cannot be diversified away in a multisovereign loan portfolio. By comparison, unsystematic or country specific risks can be diversified away. Consider this model:

---

[9] See L. S. Goodman, "Diversifiable Risks in LDC Lending: A 20/20 Hindsight View," *Studies in Banking and Finance* 3, 1986, pp. 249–62.

$$X_i = a_i + b_i \overline{X} + e_i$$

where

X_i = A key variable or country risk indicator for country i (e.g., the DSR for country i)

$\overline{X}$ = A weighted index of this key risk indicator across all countries to which the lender makes loans (e.g., the DSR for each country weighted by the shares of loans for each country in the bank's portfolio)

e_i = Other factors impacting X_i for any given country

Expressing this equation in variance terms:

$$\text{Var}(X_i) \quad = \quad b_i^2 \text{Var}(\overline{X}) \quad + \quad \text{Var}(e_i)$$

Total Risk   Systematic Risk   Unsystematic Risk

From this equation you can see that the total risk or variability of any given risk indicator for a country, such as the DSR for Nigeria, can be divided into a nondiversifiable *systematic* risk element that measures the extent to which that country's DSR moves in line with the DSRs of all other debtor countries, and an unsystematic risk element that impacts the DSR for Nigeria independently. The greater the size of the *unsystematic* element relative to the systematic risk element, the less important this variable is to the lender since it can be diversified away by holding a broad array of LDC loans.

L. S. Goodman found that for the 1970–83 period the DSR had a high systematic element across countries as did export revenue variance (VAREX); see Table 12–4.[10] This implies that when one LDC country was experiencing a growing debt burden relative to its exports, so were all others. Similarly, when commodity prices or world demand collapsed for one debtor country's commodity exports, the same occurred for other debtor countries as well. A possible reason for the high systematic risk of the DSR is the sensitivity of this ratio to rising nominal and real interest rates in the developed (or lending) countries. As we discussed in Chapter 11, international interest rates tend to be positively correlated over time. A possible reason for the high systematic risk of the export variance is the tendency of prices and world demands for commodities to reflect simultaneously economic conditions such as recessions and expansions in developed countries.

By comparison, money supply growth ($\Delta M/M$) and the import ratio appear to have low systematic elements.[11] This is not surprising since control over the money supply and use of domestic reserves are relatively discretionary variables for LDC governments. Thus, while Argentina may choose a money supply growth rate of 500 percent per annum, the Chilean government may choose a target rate of 10 percent per annum. Similarly, the Argentinian and Chilean economies may have very different demands for imports and the scale of vital imports may differ quite widely across LDCs. Using this type of analysis allows an FI manager to focus on relatively few variables, such as the DSRs and export variances, that affect the risk of the LDC sovereign loan portfolio.

Incentive Aspects. CRA statistical models often identify variables based on rather loose or often nonexistent analysis of the borrower or lender's incentives to

---

[10]Goodman, "Diversible Risks in LDC Lending…" (1986).
[11]Goodman, "Diversible Risks in LDC Lending…" (1986).

TABLE 12–4   Share of Systematic and Nonsystematic Variance of Exports
(in percentages)

	1971–1979		1971–1984		1979–1984*	
	Systematic	Nonsystematic	Systematic	Nonsystematic	Systematic	Nonsystematic
Argentina	28.9%	71.1%	27.1%	72.9%	8.2%	91.8%
Brazil	27.8	72.2	37.6	62.4	27.1	72.9
Chile	62.1	37.9	58.2	41.8	43.4	56.6
Ecuador	45.1	54.9	43.7	56.3	13.9	86.1
Mexico	45.0	55.0	49.0	51.0	—†	—†
Panama	17.2	82.8	16.6	83.4	17.2	82.8
Peru	47.3	52.7	44.4	55.6	61.0	39.0
Philippines	56.2	43.8	61.9	38.1	46.6	53.4
Yugoslavia	41.2	58.8	47.7	52.3	47.3	52.7
Venezuela	58.9	41.1	57.7	42.3	31.4	68.6
Uruguay	3.5	96.5	11.4	88.6	10.8	89.2
Morocco	50.8	49.2	53.9	46.1	29.8	70.2

*Using a dummy variable interaction term from 1979 on.
†Not meaningful.

Systematic and Nonsystematic Variance of the Debt Service/Export Ratio
(in percentages)

	1970–1979		1970–1983		1979–1983*	
	Systematic	Nonsystematic	Systematic	Nonsystematic	Systematic	Nonsystematic
Argentina	2.2	97.8	4.1	95.9	4.1	95.9
Brazil	94.0	6.0	58.1	41.9	55.8	44.2
Chile	64.0	36.0	56.1	43.9	57.2	42.8
Ecuador	41.6	58.4	27.0	73.0	24.7	75.3
Mexico	98.8	1.2	69.0	31.0	70.8	29.2
Panama	70.0	30.0	57.1	42.9	56.1	43.9
Peru	18.9	81.1	13.7	86.3	13.3	86.7
Philippines	78.3	21.7	36.2	63.8	34.9	65.1
Yugoslavia	34.5	65.5	31.9	68.1	32.0	68.0
Venezuela	43.9	56.1	18.1	81.9	16.5	83.5
Uruguay	0.1	99.9	0.3	99.7	0.1	99.9
Morocco	86.2	13.8	33.6	66.4	31.5	68.5

*Using a dummy variable interaction term from 1979 on.
SOURCE: L. S. Goodman, "Diversifiable Risks in LDC Lending . . ." (1986), p. 257.

reschedule. Rarely are the following questions asked: What are the *incentives or net benefits* to an LDC country seeking a rescheduling? What are the incentives or net benefits to an FI that grants a rescheduling? That is, what determines the demand for rescheduling by LDCs and the supply of rescheduling by FIs. Presumably, only when the benefits outweigh the costs for both parties does rescheduling occur. Consider these benefits and costs of rescheduling for the borrower on the one hand and the FI on the other:

The Borrower

Benefits
- By rescheduling its debt, the borrower lowers the present value of its future payments in hard currencies to outside lenders. This allows it to increase its consumption of foreign imports and/or to increase the rate of its domestic investment.

Costs
- By rescheduling now, the borrower may close itself out of the market for loans in the future. As a result, if it anticipates a number of high-growth investment opportunities in the future, it may be difficult or impossible to finance them.
- Rescheduling may result in significant interference with the borrower's international trade, since it would be difficult to gain access to instruments such as letters of credit, without which trade may be more costly.[12]

The Lender

Benefits
- After a loan has already been made, a rescheduling is much better than a borrower default. With a rescheduling, the bank lender may anticipate some present value loss of principal and interest on the loan; with an outright default, the bank stands to lose all its principal and future interest repayments.
- The bank can renegotiate fees and various other collateral and option features into a rescheduled loan.
- There may be tax benefits to a bank taking a recognized write down or loss in value on a rescheduled LDC loan portfolio.

Costs
- By rescheduling, loans become similar to long-term bonds or even equity, and the bank often becomes locked into a particular loan portfolio structure.
- Those banks with large amounts of rescheduled loans are subject to greater regulatory attention. For example, in the United States such banks may be placed on the regulators' problem list of banks.[13]

All of these relevant economic incentive considerations go into the demand for and the supply of rescheduling; however, it is far from clear how the simple statistical models just described incorporate this complex array of incentives. At a very minimum, statistical models should clearly reflect the underlying theory of rescheduling.[14]

Stability.   A final problem with simple statistical CRA models is one of stability. The fact that certain key variables may have explained rescheduling in the past does not mean that they would perform or predict well in the future. Over time, new variables and incentives affect rescheduling decisions, and the relative weights on the key variables change. This suggests that the FI manager must continuously update the CRA model to incorporate all currently available information and to ensure the best predictive power possible.

Concept Questions

1. Which sovereign risk indicators are the most important for a large FI, those with a high or those with a low systematic element across countries?

---

[12]See Chapter 9 on letters of credit.

[13]The problem list singles out banks for special regulatory attention. Normally, examiners rate a problem list bank a 4 or 5 on a rating scale of 1 to 5, where 1 is good and 5 is bad.

[14]See J. Bulow and K. Rogoff, "A Constant Recontracting Model of Sovereign Debt," *Journal of Political Economy* 97, 1989, pp. 155–78.

2. Make a list of five economic and three political variables you think should be included in any CRA of Russia.

Using Market Data to Measure Risk: The Secondary Market for LDC Debt

Since the mid-1980s, a secondary market for trading LDC debt has developed among large commercial and investment banks in New York and London. Indeed, trading in LDC loans often takes place in the high yield (or junk bond) departments of the participating banks.

These markets provide quoted prices for LDC loans and other debt instruments that an FI manager can use for CRA. Before we look at how this might be done, we describe the structure and development of the markets for LDC loans and related debt instruments including the determinants of market demand and supply.

The Structure of the Market.   The estimated worldwide stock of commercial banks' sovereign loans was approximately $350 billion in 1992, with trading volume rising from $135 billion in 1990 to $250 billion in 1992. This secondary market has considerably enhanced the liquidity of LDC loans on bank and other FI balance sheets.[15] These are the market players who sell and buy LDC loans:

Sellers

- Large banks willing to accept write-downs of loans on their balance sheets.
- Small banks wishing to disengage themselves from the LDC loan market.
- Banks willing to swap one country's LDC debt for another's to rearrange their portfolios of country risk exposures.

Buyers

- Wealthy investors, FIs, and corporations seeking to engage in debt-equity swaps or speculative investments.
- Banks seeking to rearrange their LDC balance sheets by reorienting their LDC debt concentrations.

Consider the quote sheets from Salomon Brothers in Tables 12–5 and 12–6; one is for May 2, 1988, and the other for November 12, 1992.

As you can see in Table 12–5—a relatively early stage of LDC loan market development—FIs such as investment banks and major commercial banks act as market makers quoting two-way bid-ask prices for LDC debt.[16] Thus, an FI or an investor could have bought $100 of Peruvian loans from Salomon for $9.00 in May 1988, or a

---

[15]LDC loans exchange hands when one creditor assigns the rights to all future interest payments and principal payments to a buyer. In most early market transactions, the buyer had to get the permission of the sovereign debtor country before the loan could be assigned to a new party. The reason for this was that the country may have concerns as to whether the buyer was as committed to any new money deals as part of restructuring agreements as the original lender. Most recent restructuring agreements, however, have removed the right of assignment from the borrower (the sovereign country). This has increased liquidity in the LDC loan market.

[16]Major market makers include the Dutch ING bank, as well as Lehman, Salomon Bros., Citibank, J.P. Morgan, Bankers Trust, and Merrill Lynch.

TABLE 12–5   Indicative Prices for Less Developed Country Bank Loans

Country	Indicative Cash Prices		Swap Index		Trading Commentary
	Bid	*Offer*	*Sell*	*Buy*	
Algeria	$91.00	$93.00	5.22	6.71	Longer-dated paper resurfacing as cash substitute in swaps.
Argentina	29.00	30.00	0.66	0.67	Less volume this period; consolidation exercise slows note trades.
Bolivia	10.00	13.00	0.52	0.54	Minimal current activity.
Brazil	53.00	54.00	1.00	1.02	Rally topping out as supply catches up with auction interest.
Chile	60.50	61.50	1.19	1.22	Market firm and rising as deal calendar fills.
Colombia	67.00	68.00	1.42	1.47	Resurgence of interest as high-quality exit.
Costa Rica	13.00	16.00	0.54	0.56	Market building reserves of patience to deal with this name again.
Dominican Rep.	17.00	20.00	0.57	0.59	Trading picks up at lower levels.
Ecuador	31.00	33.00	0.66	0.70	Occasional swaps surfacing.
Honduras	25.00	28.00	0.63	0.65	Viewed as expensive on a relative value basis.
Ivory Coast	30.00	33.00	0.67	0.70	Newly sighted by fee swappers.
Jamaica	33.00	36.00	0.70	0.73	Slow, but serious, inquiry continues.
Mexico	52.50	53.50	0.99	1.01	Prices continue upward drift on lower, lumpy flow.
Morocco	50.00	51.00	0.94	0.96	Fee swappers oblige sellers by jumping into the wider breach versus Latins.
Nicaragua	3.00	4.00	0.48	0.49	Avoided by the surviving court tasters.
Nigeria	28.50	30.50	0.66	0.68	Retail stonewalls dealer interest.
Panama	20.00	23.00	0.59	0.61	Recent bidding stirs the mud.
Peru	7.00	9.00	0.51	0.52	Debt-for-debt work-outs and debt-for-goods deals continue.
Philippines	52.00	53.00	0.98	1.00	Prices drift higher with good interest in non-CB names.
Poland	43.25	44.50	0.83	0.85	Somewhat slower trading this period.
Romania	82.00	84.00	2.61	2.94	Bidding improves on expectations of '88 principal payments.
Senegal	40.00	45.00	0.78	0.85	Trade talk more serious.
Sudan	2.00	10.00	0.48	0.52	Still on the mat.
Turkey	97.50	99.00	18.80	47.00	CTLD's remain well-bid.
Uruguay	59.50	61.50	1.16	1.22	Remains a patience-trying market.
Venezuela	55.00	55.75	1.04	1.06	Trading stronger as uptick in Chile brings swaps back into range.
Yugoslavia	45.50	47.00	0.86	0.89	More frequent trading.
Zaire	19.00	23.00	0.58	0.61	New interest develops.

SOURCE: Salomon Brothers Inc., May 2, 1988.

91 percent discount from face value. However, if selling the same loans to Salomon, the investor would have received only $7.00 per $100, or a 93 percent discount. The bid-ask spreads for certain countries were very large in this period; for example, Sudan's $2.00 bid and $10.00 ask was indicative of a serious lack of market demand for the sovereign loans of many countries.

The later quote sheet in Table 12–6 suggests a large number of changes in the structure of the market. Now there are three market segments: sovereign bonds, performing loans, and nonperforming loans.

Sovereign Bonds.   These reflect programs under which the U.S. and other banks have exchanged their dollar loans for dollar bonds issued by the relevant countries. These bonds have a much longer maturity than that promised on the original loans and a lower promised original coupon (yield) than the interest rate on the original loan. These loan for bond restructuring programs, also called debt for debt swaps, have developed through the auspices of the U.S. Treasury's 1989 Brady Plan

TABLE 12–6   Benchmark Bonds, November 12, 1992

Bonds	Coupon	Bid Price	1-Wk. Chg.	Offer Price	Bid Yield Current	Bid Yield Cash Flow	Bid Yield Stripped	Avg. Life (yrs.)	Final Maturity
Argentina Bonex '89	6L%	78.450	−1.150	78.650	5.18%	15.30%	15.30%	3.61	12/28/99
Argentina Par Bonds (W/I)*	4.00	37.875	−4.375	38.125	10.56	14.41	20.58	30.00	—
Argentina PDI (W/I)	6L + ¹³/₁₆	49.875	−3.875	50.125	8.90	19.76	19.76	9.00	—
Brazil IDU	6L + ¹³/₁₆	56.750	−0.250	57.750	14.76	21.30	21.30	6.08	01/01/01
Brazil Investment	6.00	43.000	−5.000	45.000	13.95	17.63	17.63	13.57	09/15/13
Brazil New Money	6L + ¹³/₁₆	73.000	−4.000	75.000	5.82	17.66	17.66	3.65	10/14/99
Costa Rica Series A	6.25	60.000	−2.000	62.000	10.42	12.81	13.69	12.75	05/21/10
Mexico Collat. of 3/08	6L + 1 ⁵/₈	86.250	−2.000	86.750	5.80	10.95	13.86	15.36	03/31/08
Mexico Par	6.25	62.375	−1.000	62.625	10.02	10.44	12.71	27.11	12/31/19
Mexico Discount	6L + ¹³/₁₆	79.500	−2.000	79.750	6.37	10.93	13.06	27.11	12/31/19
Nigeria Par	5.50, 6.25	36.875	−0.750	37.125	14.92	16.66	27.25	27.99	11/15/20
Philippine New Money	6L + ¹³/₁₆	63.000	−2.500	64.000	7.64	15.66	15.66	8.63	01/05/05
Philippine PIRB (W/I)†	4.25‡	53.000	−2.750	54.000	8.02	11.94	15.90	25.00	—
Venezuela Conversion	6L + ⁷/₈	56.750	−1.875	57.000	8.81	17.11	17.11	10.08	12/18/07
Venezuela Discount	6L + ¹³/₁₆	68.000	−1.000	69.500	6.43	12.59	15.74	27.37	03/31/20
Venezuela Par	6.75	58.000	−1.875	58.250	11.64	12.01	15.44	27.37	03/31/20
Venezuela NM Series A	6L + 1	56.000	−2.500	58.000	9.15	17.93	17.93	9.08	12/18/05
Venezuela FLIRB	5, 6, 7, 6L + ⁷/₈	56.000	−2.500	57.000	10.71	17.76	18.13	9.36	03/31/07

*The full coupon schedule is as follows: 4.00, 4.25, 5.00, 5.25, 5.50, 5.75, and 6.00.
†Principal Collateralized Interest Reduction when-issued bonds.
‡The full coupon schedule is as follows: 4.25, 5.25, 5.75, 6.25, 6.25, and 6.50.
L London Interbank Offered Rate.

Benchmark Loans, November 12, 1992

Performing Loans	Coupon	Bid Price	1-Wk. Chg.	Offer Price	Bid Yield Current	Bid Yield Cash Flow	Avg. Life (yrs.)	Final Maturity
Chile Rst. CB	6L + ⁷/₈%	91.000	0.000	93.000	5.63%	9.86%	8.78	12/01/05
Morocco Rst.	3L + ¹³/₁₆	43.875	−0.875	44.125	9.97	21.63	11.11	01/01/09

Nonperforming Loans	Bid Price	1-Wk. Chg.	Offer Price	Months in Arrears	Months Since Last Payment	Interest Convention
Argentina GRA	43.000	−3.500	45.000	42	1	Assigned
Bulgaria LC	9.000	7.000	11.000	20	22	—
Brazil MYDFA	27.625	−3.000	27.875	16	2	Retained
Ecuador MYRA	25.000	−2.500	26.000	43	8	Assigned
Ivory Coast	5.000	−0.500	7.000	59	60	Assigned
Panama	28.000	−3.500	30.000	51	51	Assigned
Peru Rst.	15.000	−0.250	16.000	89	50	Assigned
Poland DDRA	23.500	−1.125	23.750	38	16	Assigned
Vneshekonombank (Medium-Term)	18.000	0.000	21.000	9	10	—
Yugoslavia NBY	17.000	0.000	22.000	3	4	Retained

SOURCE: Salomon Brothers, Emerging Markets, Fixed Income Research, November 13, 1992.

TABLE 12–7 Brady Plans Completed (U.S. dollars in billions)

Countries	Bank Debt Covered under Brady Option	Debt Buyback Portion	Debt Converted to Bonds
Costa Rica	$1.46	$1.00	$0.460
Mexico	33.00	0	29.370
Philippines (1990)	2.10	1.30	0.715
Uruguay	1.98	1.00	0.980
Venezuela	19.30	1.40	17.900
Nigeria	5.80	3.78	2.020

Brady Plans in Final Stages (U.S. dollars in billions)

Countries	Bank Debt Covered under Brady Option	Debt Buyback Portion	Debt Converted to Bonds	Past Due Interest Arrears Converted to Bonds
Argentina	$31.0	$0	$23.00	$8.0
Brazil	52.5	0	44.00‡	8.5†
Philippines	4.8	1.25	3.55	0

*As of January 1992.

†Agreement completed in 1991.

‡Includes the parallel financing agreement and 1991–92 interest arrears.

Source: Salomon Brothers Inc. estimates.

and other international organizations such as the IMF. Once loans have been swapped for bonds by banks and other FIs, they can be sold on the secondary market. For example, 30-year Venezuelan discount bonds with a remaining life of 27.37 years had bid and ask prices of $68.00 and $69.50 per $100 of face value respectively.

As shown in the top panel of Table 12–7, approximately $50.5 billion of LDC loans have been converted into bonds under the Brady Plan. However as the bottom panel shows, plans are in process for Argentina, Brazil, and the Philippines to convert their loans into bonds as well. This would add another $88 billion to these bonds. To learn about the different Brady bonds, see Table 12–8.

These bond for loan swap programs, especially under the Brady Plan, aimed to restore LDCs' creditworthiness, and thus the value of bank holdings of such debt, by creating longer-term, lower fixed-interest but more liquid securities in place of shorter-term, floating-rate loans. The creation of these bonds has been helped by three factors: First, the assumption by LDC central banks of the various loans made to individual borrowers in that country.[17] Thus, for example, U.S. FIs' loans to Mexico, Brazil, and Argentina have been increasingly consolidated at the local central bank. As a result, a foreign FI such as Citibank becomes the owner or creditor of an account denominated in dollars at the LDC central bank.

Second, the frequent restructurings of the stock of LDC loans, along with their consolidation at the local central bank, has made loan terms increasingly homogeneous. For example, the August 1987 restructuring of Argentinian debt to a maturity

---

[17]Usually a local company or state organization swaps its dollar loans owed to a U.S. bank for a peso loan at the central bank. That is, the debt to the U.S. bank is transferred to the central bank of that country.

TABLE 12–8   Special Characteristics of Brady Bonds

Par Bonds: So named because they are exchanged dollar for dollar for existing debt, par bonds also are known as interest reduction bonds. Because the face amount of debt remains the same, debt relief is provided by a below market rate coupon. These bonds typically have principal and interest guarantees, a fixed coupon or coupon schedule, and bullet maturities of 25–30 years.

Discount Bonds: These bonds are named for the manner in which they are exchanged for loans. The debt holder receives a face amount of these bonds, which is reduced by the discount negotiated in the ' Brady agreement. Because of the discount, these bonds are also known as *principal reduction bonds*. Like the par bonds, discount bonds typically have principal and interest guaranteed and bullet maturities of 25–30 years. Since the principal was reduced, these bonds pay a "market" rate, usually LIBOR + 13/16.

Front-Loaded Interest Reduction Bonds (FLIRBs): These bonds usually have fixed coupons that step up from low levels for the first few years, after which they pay a floating rate. FLIRBs carry no principal collateral and their interest collateral is released after the step-up period. These bonds have amortization schedules that give them a shorter average life (about 10 years) than par or discount bonds to compensate investors for the lack of principal collateral.

New Money Bonds and Debt Conversion Bonds (DCBs): These bonds are generally issued together through the new money option of an exchange menu, which is designed to give debt holders an incentive to invest additional capital or "new money." For every dollar of new money bond that is purchased with cash, the investor may exchange existing debt for DCBs in a ratio negotiated in the Brady agreement (usually $4–6 dollars of DCBs for every dollar of new money). This provides an incentive to invest new money because the DCBs are usually made more attractive than the bonds available in other options. New money bonds and DCBs typically pay LIBOR + 7/8 and amortization schedules that give them a 10–15 year average life. The name "new money bond" also has been used for bonds issued both outside a Brady plan (Brazil) and as a prelude to a Brady plan (Philippines).

Principal Collateralization. In a number of Brady Plans, the U.S. Treasury has issued 30–year, zero–coupon bonds to collateralize the principal of the bonds. The market value of the principal guarantee, which tends to increase as the bond ages, depends on the yield of 30–year U.S. Treasury strips. The collateral has been paid for by a combination of International Monetary Fund (IMF) and World Bank loans, and the country's own reserves.

Rolling Interest Guarantees. In addition, in most Brady Plans, two or three semiannual interest payments are guaranteed by securities of at least double–A credit quality. All collateral is held by the New York Federal Reserve Bank in an escrow account to protect the investor against a temporary suspension of interest payments or default. If an interest payment is missed, the bond holder will receive the missed payment from the escrow account. Interest collateral is often referred to as "rolling interest guarantees"—if the interest collateral is not utilized, it will roll forward over the life of the bonds. The bonds are excluded by their terms from further new money requests.

Value Recovery Rights. Investors in the Mexican and Venezuelan bonds also may benefit from additional interest income from 1996 to maturity through value–recovery warrants, if both oil export volume and world oil prices increase. Attached to each bond is a series of value recovery rights entitling the holder to extra interest payments if the price of oil during a range of payment periods exceeds a certain price per barrel, adjusted for inflation. The holder may separate the right from the bond four years before the right's first payment.

SOURCE: Salomon Brothers, July 1992.

of 19 years and an interest rate of LIBOR + 13/16 percent involved the whole stock of Argentinian loans outstanding as of January 1986 or $30.5 billion.

Third, there has been an increasing demand by banks to make their LDC loan portfolios more liquid. In particular, by converting loans into Brady bonds, LDC assets become more liquid.[18] The reasons for this include the fact that these bonds are

---

[18]The Brady bond is usually created on an interest rate rollover date. On that date, the floating rate loans are usually converted into fixed-rate coupon bonds on the books of an agent bank. The agent bank is the bank that kept the records of loan ownership and distributed interest payments made by the LDC to individual bank creditors. Once converted, the bonds can start trading

often collateralized. Thus, the "Mexico Collat. of 03/08" bonds in Table 12–6 have their principal repayments collateralized by a U.S. Treasury bond maturing in March 2008 that is held in escrow. This means that foreign bondholders, such as U.S. FIs, are only exposed to Mexican default on interest payments on these bonds.[19]

Benchmark Performing Loans. In Table 12–6, benchmark performing loans are original or restructured outstanding sovereign loans on which the sovereign country is currently maintaining promised payments to lenders or debt holders. The discounts from $100 reflect expectations that these countries may face repayment problems in the future. Note the recent improvement in the creditworthiness of countries such as Chile by comparing the bid discount on its loans of 9 percent in 1992 (Table 12–6) with that of 39.5 percent in 1988 (Table 12–5).

Benchmark Nonperforming Loans. Benchmark nonperforming loans reflect the secondary market prices for the sovereign loans of countries where there are no interest or principal payments currently being made (see the months since last payment column in Table 12–6). Thus, the $5.00 bid price for Ivory Coast loans reflects the fact that, as of November 1992, no debt payments had been made for 60 months.

LDC Market Prices and Country Risk Analysis. By combining LDC asset prices with key variables, FI managers can potentially predict future repayment problems. For example, in the markets for which LDC debt is quite heavily traded such as Mexico and Brazil (both of whom have more than $80 billion in debts outstanding), these prices reflect the market consensus regarding the current and expected future cash flows on these loans and, implicitly, the probability of rescheduling or repudiation of these loans. Because market prices on LDC loans have been available monthly since 1985, the FI manager might construct a statistical CRA model to analyze which key economic and political variables or factors have driven changes in secondary market prices. Basically, this would involve regressing periodic changes in the prices of LDC debt in the secondary market on a set of key variables such as those described earlier in this section. In Table 12–9, consider the results of a recent study by E. Boehmer and W. L. Megginson of the factors driving the secondary market prices of 10 LDC countries over a 32-month period, July 1985– July 1988.

As you can see, the most significant variables affecting LDC loan sale prices over this period were a country's debt service ratios (TD/GNP and TD/EX), its import ratio (NIRES), its accumulated debt arrears (ARR), and the amount by which banks had already made loan loss provisions against these LDC loans (USP). Also important were variables that reflect debt moratoria for Peru and Brazil (PDUM and BDUM) and that indicate whether a debt-equity swap program was in place. Interestingly, debt-equity swap programs appear to depress prices. (We discuss these programs in the next section in more detail.)

Once managers have estimated a statistical model, they can use these parameters $\beta_1, \beta_2, \ldots \beta_5$ along with forecasts for a given LDC's debt service and other key variables to derive predicted changes in LDC asset prices (discounts). That is, this approach might allow the FI manager to come up with another set of forecasts regarding changes in sovereign risk exposure to a number of sovereign debtors.

---

[19]In fact, this instrument has hybrid sovereign risk: part U.S. and part Mexican. Due to its collateral backing, its price is high (86.25) compared to other Mexican bonds.

TABLE 12–9   Variables Affecting Secondary Market Prices

The following regression equation is estimated:

$$P_{it} = \beta_1 * \text{Intercept} + \beta_2 * \text{TDGNP}_{it} + \beta_3 * \text{TDEX}_{it} + \beta_4 * \text{NETDS}_{it} + \beta_5 * \text{NIRES}_{it} + \beta_6 * \text{INT}_t +$$
$$\beta_7 * \text{ARR}_{it} + \beta_8 * \text{USP}_t + \beta_9 * \text{BDUM}_{it} + \beta_{10} * \text{PDUM}_i + \beta_{11} * \text{CONVDUM}_{it} + U_{it}$$

where

TDGNP =	Ratio of total long-term debt to GNP
TDEX =	Ratio of total long-term debt to exports
NETDS =	Ratio of net exports to debt service
NIRES =	Ratio of net imports to hard currency reserves
INT =	Monthly London Interbank Offered Rate (a short-term interest rate)
ARR =	Level of incurred payment arrears
USP =	Cumulative developing country specific loan provisioning by U.S. banks
BDUM =	Unity for Brazil from January to December of 1987 and zero otherwise to capture the effects of the debt moratorium
PDUM =	Unity for Peru over the whole sampling period and zero otherwise to account for the unilateral limitation of debt service payments
CONVDUM =	Unity for all months in which a country maintained a legislation for debt-to-equity conversions

Parameter	Estimate	t-Statistic
Intercept	88.51760	13.47
TDGNP	-18.11610	-4.75
TDEX	-0.10437	-3.57
NETDS	-0.30754	-0.50
NIRES	5.79548	1.28
INT	0.22825	0.30
ARR	-0.00574	-2.68
USP	-0.00100	-13.69
BDUM	-10.92820	-6.61
PDUM	-36.07240	-8.31
CONVDUM	-5.43157	-6.75

Degrees of freedom: 309
Adjusted R^2: 0.96

SOURCE: E. Boehmer and W. L. Megginson, "Determinants of Secondary Market Prices for Developing Country Syndicated Loans," *Journal of Finance* 45, 1990, pp. 1517–40.

This approach is subject to many of the same criticisms made for the traditional statistical model of country risk prediction. Specifically, the parameters of the model may be unstable; and managers can measure variables, such as the DSR and the import ratio, only with error. In addition, the link between these key variables and the change in secondary market price is something of a black box in terms of links to the underlying theoretical incentives of borrowers and lenders to engage in future reschedulings or repudiations of their debt obligations.

Concept Questions

1. Briefly describe how a fall in a country's debt service ratio (DSR) and import ratio (IR) can be expected to affect the price of its LDC debt in the secondary market.

2. What are the three major sectors in the current secondary market for LDC debt?

3. What is a Brady bond?

Mechanisms for Dealing with Sovereign Risk Exposure

Earlier, we identified methods and models FI managers could use to measure sovereign risk exposure before making credit decisions. In this section, we take a closer look at the benefits and costs of using four alternative mechanisms to deal with problem sovereign credits once they have arisen. The four mechanisms are

1. Debt for equity swaps.
2. Restructuring of loans (MYRAs).
3. Sale of LDC loans on the secondary market.
4. Debt for debt swaps (Brady bonds).

While restructuring keeps the loans in the portfolio, the other three mechanisms change the fundamental nature of the FI's claim itself, or else remove it from the balance sheet.

Next, we take a detailed look at the mechanics of loan restructurings and debt equity swaps. As we have already described LDC loan sales and debt for debt swaps, we only summarize their benefits and costs here. Discussing each of these mechanisms, especially their benefits and costs, is important since an FI can choose among the four in dealing with a problem sovereign loan or credit.

Debt-Equity Swaps

The market for LDC loan sales has a close link to debt-equity swap programs arranged by certain LDCs, such as Chile and Mexico, with outside investors that wish to make equity investments in debtor countries.[20] Indeed, while banks are the major sellers of LDC loans, important buyers are parties who wish to engage in long-term equity or real investments in those debtor countries. For example, the 1985 Mexican debt-equity swap program allowed Mexican dollar loans to be swapped for Mexican equity in certain priority investment areas. These were the motor industry, tourism, and the chemical industry. A good example of an FI exploiting the opportunities of the Mexican debt-equity swap program was American Express bank which built seven hotels in Mexico as a result of debt-equity swaps.[21] As of 1992, the estimated annual amount of debt-equity swaps was around $10 billion.

To demonstrate the costs and benefits of a debt-equity swap for the FI and other parties participating in the transaction, we present a hypothetical example. Suppose in November 1992 Citibank had $100 million loans outstanding to Chile. Citibank could have sold those loans on the secondary market for a bid price of $91 million, or $91 per $100 (see Table 12–6). The advantage to Citibank from selling loans is removing these loans from its books and freeing up funds for other investments. However, Citibank has to accept a loss of $9 million on the loan. Given that the rest of the bank is profitable, this loss can be offset against other profits of the bank. Further, if the corporate tax rate is 34 percent, then Citibank's after-tax loss would be $9 (1 − .34) million = $5.94 million.

If this loan were sold to Salomon Brothers for $91 million, as market makers they would turn around and reoffer it to an outside buyer at a slightly higher price—

---

[20]For more details, see R. Grosse, "The Debt/Equity Swap in Latin America—In Whose Interest?" *Journal of International Financial Management and Accounting* 4, Spring 1992, pp. 13–39.

[21]Countries with debt equity swap programs include Argentina, Brazil, Chile, Costa Rica, Ecuador, Jamaica, Mexico, Uruguay, and Venezuela.

say of $93 million (or $93 per $100 of face value). Suppose IBM wants to build a computer factory in Chile and buys the $100 million face value loan from Salomon for $93 million for the purpose of financing the investments in Chile. Thus, Salomon earns a profit of $93 million − $91 million = $2 million, while IBM knows that Chile has a debt for equity swap program. This means that at a given exchange rate the Chilean government would allow IBM to convert the $100 million dollar loan it has purchased into local currency or pesos. However, the Chilean government would be willing to do this only if there is something in it for them. Thus, they may be willing to convert the dollars into pesos only at a 5 percent discount from the true free market dollar/peso exchange rate. Suppose the free market exchange rate were 380 Chilean pesos to a $1, then the Chilean government would only convert the dollars at 361 pesos to a $1. Thus, IBM would have to bear a 5 percent discount on the face value of the purchased loan.[22] That is, when converting the $100 million loan at the Chilean Central Bank, IBM would receive the $95 million equivalent in pesos. Remember that IBM had originally bought the loan for only $93 million on the secondary market. Thus, its net saving from this debt-equity conversion program is $2 million.[23] However, note that the $95 million is in pesos that have to be invested in Chilean equity, such as real estate or factories. In general, debt-equity swap investors face long periods before they can repatriate dividends (12 years in the Mexican case) and often large withholding taxes (55 percent in the Mexican case). Moreover, they face the risk of future expropriation or nationalization of those assets. Thus, the $2 million spread reflects IBM's expectations about such expropriation risks.

Finally, what does the Chilean government get out of this debt-equity swap program? On the one hand, it has retired relatively expensive hard-currency debt with local currency pesos at a discount. Implicitly, the Chilean government has retired a $100 million face value debt at a cost of $95 million in pesos; the difference reflects the debt-equity swap official exchange rate (361 pesos/$1) and the true exchange rate (380 pesos/$1). The cost to Chile is printing $95 million more pesos. This may lead to a higher domestic inflation rate, as well as facing increased foreign ownership and control of Chilean real assets as a result of IBM's equity purchases.

We depict the division of the original $100 million face value loan among the four parties as a result of the loan sale and debt-equity swap in Figure 12–1. As you can see, Citibank gets 91 percent of face value; Salomon Brothers, 2 percent; IBM, 2 percent; and Chile, 5 percent. That is, the 9 percent discount from face value accepted by Citibank is shared among three parties: the investment bank, the corporation involved in the debt-equity swap, and the sponsoring country's government.

One puzzle from the preceding example is why Citibank doesn't sidestep both the investment bank and IBM, and engage in a local currency debt for equity swap itself. That is, why doesn't Citibank directly swap its $100 million loan to Chile into the $95 million equivalent of local equity? The problem is that in the United States, Federal Reserve Regulation K places restrictions on the ability of U.S. banks to buy real equity or engage in commerce in overseas countries.[24] If a U.S. bank can buy and hold Chilean real assets, this might lower its potential losses from restructuring its

---

[22]In practice, debt-equity swaps convert into pesos at an official rate. This official rate is often less attractive than the rate quoted in official or unofficial parallel markets for private transactions.

[23]That is, in general, the swap is cheaper than direct local borrowing, if this is an available alternative.

[24]Limited amounts of equity purchases are allowed to specialized U.S. bank subsidiaries called Edge Act Corporations. Such corporations have been established since 1919 under the Edge Act to allow banks to finance international transactions. In 1987, the Federal Reserve approved bank acquisitions of 100 percent stakes in nonfinancial companies in 33 extremely poor LDCs as part of debt-equity swaps.

LDC loan portfolio. Nevertheless, note that while a loan sale directly removes a problem loan from the balance sheet, a debt for equity swap replaces that problem loan with a risky long-term peso-denominated equity position on its balance sheet. Thus, it is far from certain that the liquidity of the balance sheet has been improved through such a transaction.

Multiyear Restructuring Agreements (MYRA)

If a country is unable to keep its payments on a loan current, and an FI chooses to maintain the loan on its balance sheet rather than selling it or swapping it for equity or debt, the loan and its contractual terms would be rescheduled under a multiyear restructuring agreement (MYRA). A good example of a MYRA was the agreement reached between Argentina and its major creditors to restructure $30.5 billion of its loans in August 1987.

As with the loan sale, the debt-equity swap, and the debt for debt swap, the crucial question for an FI is how much it is willing to concede or give up to the borrower in the sovereign loan rescheduling process. The benefits and costs of this policy depend on a number of ingredients that are usually built into any MYRA including:

1. *The fee* charged by the bank to the borrower for the costs of restructuring the loan. This fee may be as high as 1 percent of the face value of the loan if a large lending syndicate is involved in the negotiations.
2. *The interest rate* charged on the new loan. This is generally lower than that on the original loan to ease the repayment cash flow problem of the borrower. (In the 1987 Argentinian case the restructured loan rate was set equal to LIBOR + 13 /16 percent.)
3. *A grace period* may be involved before interest and/or principal payments begin on the new loan. This is to give the borrower time to accumulate hard currency reserves to meet its debt interest and principal obligations in the future. In the Argentinian case, the grace period was set at seven years.
4. *The maturity* of the loan is lengthened normally to stretch out the interest and principal payments over a longer period. In the Argentinian case, the restructured loan's maturity was set at 19 years.
5. *Option features* are often built into the MYRA to allow the lender (and sometimes the borrower) to choose the currency for repayment of interest and/or principal.[25]

The following simple example demonstrates how these factors determine the degree of **concessionality** (the net cost) of a MYRA to an FI. In general, the net cost or degree of concessionality can be defined as:

Concessionality
The amount a bank gives up in present value terms as a result of a MYRA.

$$\text{Concessionality} = [\text{Present value of} - [\text{Present value of}$$
$$\text{original loan}] \quad \text{restructured loan}]$$

$$= PV_O - PV_R$$

Unfortunately, most of these countries do not operate debt-equity programs or have very little equity that is attractive. However, the American Express bank example of building seven hotels in Mexico illustrates a bank engaging in a direct debt-equity swap.

[25]For example, the lender may choose to be repaid in dollars or in yen. Such option features add value to the cash flow stream for either the borrower or lender depending on who can exercise the currency option.

FIGURE 12–1

Debt-equity swaps and loan sales

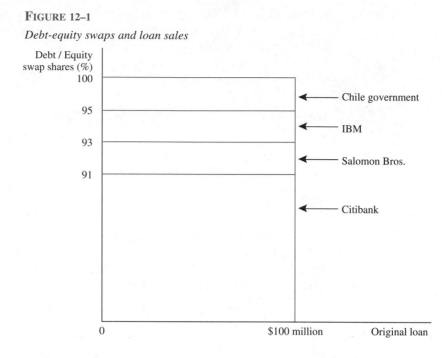

The lower the present value of the restructured loan relative to the original loan, the greater are the *concessions* the bank has made to the borrower; that is, the greater the cost of loan restructuring.

Suppose the original loan was $100 million for two years. And, under the terms of the original loan, the borrower was required to pay back $50 million principal at the end of the first year and $50 million at the end of the second year. That is, the loan was amortized equally over the two-year period. The interest rate charged on the loan was 10 percent and the bank's cost of funds was 8 percent. The present value of the original loan (PV_o) is

$$PV_o = \frac{(A_1 + I_1)}{(1+d)} + \frac{(A_2 + I_2)}{(1+d)^2}$$

where

A_i = principal paid back in year i = 1,2

I_i = interest paid in year i = 1,2

d = bank cost of funds (discount rate)

Thus,

$$PV_o = \frac{(50+10)}{(1.08)} + \frac{(50+5)}{(1.08)^2} = \$102.71 \text{ million}$$

That is, the present value of the loan is $102.71 million with a return of $102.71/$100 or 2.71 percent.

Suppose that a borrowing country is unable to meet its promised principal amortization and interest payments of $60 and $55 million in years one and two. To prevent default, the bank negotiates a MYRA that has the following terms:

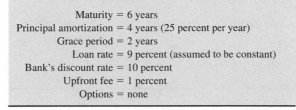

Maturity = 6 years
Principal amortization = 4 years (25 percent per year)
Grace period = 2 years
Loan rate = 9 percent (assumed to be constant)
Bank's discount rate = 10 percent
Upfront fee = 1 percent
Options = none

We look at each of these features of the MYRA in turn.

- *Maturity.* The maturity has been increased from two to six years, to allow the principal to be paid off over a longer time.
- *Amortization.* The principal is to be paid off over the last four years of the six-year period at 25 percent per year, or $25 million per year.
- *Grace period.* For the first two years of the restructured loan agreement, no principal payments are required of the borrower. (See Figure 12–2 for a summary of these three features.)
- *Loan interest rate.* The loan interest rate is lowered from 10 to 9 percent for the six-year period. Because no grace period is granted for interest payments, all appropriate interest payments have to be made on time.[26]
- *Bank cost of funds.* The bank's cost of funds or discount rate has increased to 10 percent to reflect depositors' and investors' concerns regarding the bank's solvency in light of its risky sovereign lending policies.
- *Upfront fee.* The bank charges an upfront fee, assumed to be equal to 1 percent of the face value of the loan, as compensation for the legal-contractual costs involved in the MYRA.
- *Option features.* For simplicity, no special currency conversion options for principal or interest are included in the MYRA.[27]

The present value of the restructured loan (PV_R) is[28]

$$PV_R = F + \frac{I_1}{(1+d)} + \frac{I_2}{(1+d)^2}$$

$$+ \frac{(A_3 + I_3)}{(1+d)^3} + \frac{(A_4 + I_4)}{(1+d)^4}$$

$$+ \frac{(A_5 + I_5)}{(1+d)^5} + \frac{(A_6 + I_6)}{(1+d)^6}$$

Substituting in the values from the previous example:

$$PV_R = 1 + \frac{9}{(1.10)} + \frac{9}{(1.10)^2} + \frac{(25+9)}{(1.10)^3} + \frac{(25+6.75)}{(1.10)^4}$$

---

[26]This assumption could easily be relaxed.

[27]We discuss the incorporation of such option features and their effects on the net cost of the MYRA later.

[28]This assumes that the FI rationally expects the borrower to maintain the restructured payments schedule.

FIGURE 12–2

Principal repayments (amortization schedule) on the old loan and the MYRA

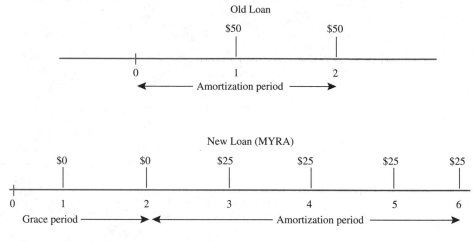

$$+\frac{(25+4.5)}{(1.10)^5}+\frac{(25+2.25)}{(1.10)^6}=\$97.55 \text{ million}$$

The present value of the loan has fallen to \$97.55 million. Therefore, bank concessionality $= PV_O - PV_R$

$$= \$102.71 - \$97.55$$
$$= \$5.16 \text{ million}$$

In present value terms, the bank has given up \$5.16 million in the MYRA. This value is very sensitive to the revised contractual terms and, in particular to d, the bank's discount rate. Suppose that bank investors viewed the bank as being too big to fail, believing that regulators would always bail out the bank should it get into trouble. Such a belief would mean that even with the onset of sovereign loan problems, the required returns on bank debt and equity (i.e., the bank's cost of funds) might remain unchanged at $d = 8$ percent.

Replacing the discount rate $d = 10$ percent with $d = 8$ percent in the preceding MYRA, we recalculate the PV_R as \$104.63 million. In present value terms, the bank actually gains from the restructuring by \$104.63 − \$102.71 = \$1.92 million.[29]

Also, as we noted earlier, many MYRAs contain option features that usually allow the lending bank to choose the currency in which it wishes to receive interest or principal. Occasionally, the borrower receives this option, but in most actual MYRAs this is rare. For example, in the 1985 Mexican MYRA, non-U.S. banks received the option of switching one half of their loans from dollars to their local currencies (yen, sterling, etc.). An FI that has this option reduces the degree of concessionality it makes under the MYRA. To illustrate the value of currency and interest rate options to the FI we use another simple example; see Figure 12–3.

Suppose a lender makes a one-year loan to a LDC borrower. At the end of the year, the lender has the option of being paid either \$10 million or £6.5 million;

---

[29]That the required return on a bank's equity and debt might not rise has some support from the findings of J. Madura and E. Zarruk that the announcement of the Brady Plan (debt for debt swaps) had a positive effect on bank equity values. See "Impact of the Debt Reduction Plan on the Value of LDC Debt," *International Review of Economics and Finance* 1, 1992, pp. 177–87.

that is, the lender can be paid either in dollars or in pounds. Also, suppose that the pound's expected spot exchange rate in dollars at the end of the year is equally likely to be either $1.50 or $1.60. If choosing to be repaid in dollars, the bank would receive $10 million regardless of the exchange rate. If the exchange rate at the end of the year is $1.60/£, the lender choosing to be repaid in British pounds receives £6.5 million. This could be converted into $10.4 million in the foreign exchange market (£6.5 × 1.6). Since this is more than $10 million, the bank would elect to be paid in pounds and receive the equivalent of $10.4 million. If the exchange rate at the end of the year is $1.50/£, then by choosing pounds the lender would end up with the equivalent of only $9.75 million, which is less than the $10 million to be repaid in dollars. The bank would be better off choosing to be repaid in dollars. Consequently, one exchange rate outcome would yield $10.4 million and the other, $10 million. Because either exchange rate outcome is assumed to be equally likely, the lender should expect to receive a cash flow of $10.2 million (1/2 × $10.4 plus 1/2 × $10).

In Figure 12–3, $p = .5$ reflects the equal probabilities that the exchange rate could be $1.60 or $1.50 in one year's time. In the upper arm of the probability tree, if the exchange rates rises to $1.60/£1, the bank would choose payment in pounds rather than dollars, £6.5 × 1.6 = $10.4 million is bigger than the $10 million payment in dollars. If the exchange rate is $1.50/£1—the lower arm of the probability tree—the lender would choose dollars, £6.5 × 1.5 = $9.75 million is less than the $10 million payment in dollars.

Thus, the value of the option is the discounted value of the expected cash flow in one year's time minus the cash flow without the option. That is, since the option pays off in one year's time, we need to discount it to derive its present value at the time of the MYRA. If the discount rate is 10 percent, then:

$$\text{Option value} = \frac{\left[\frac{1}{2}(10.4) + \frac{1}{2}(10)\right] - 10}{(1.1)}$$

$$= \frac{0.2}{1.1}$$

$$= \$0.1818 \text{ million}$$

Consequently, the inclusion of this type of currency option clause in a MYRA reduces the value of the lender's concessionality by $181,818. Further, the more volatile are exchange rates, the greater the value of such a currency option to the lender and the more costly it is to the borrower.[30]

Loan Sales

We described the third mechanism for dealing with problem sovereign loans, LDC loan sales, in some detail earlier in this chapter. Here we summarize the main benefits and costs for the FI. The first major benefit is that sale removes these loans from the balance sheet, and as such, frees up resources for other investments. Second, being able to sell these loans at a discount or loss signifies that the bank is sufficiently strong in the rest of its balance sheet to bear the cost. In fact, a number of studies have found that announcements of banks taking reserve additions against LDC

---

[30]In the context of concessionality, the value of this option should be added to PV_R to get the value of the restructured loan as a whole.

FIGURE 12–3

The value of a currency option to the FI (lender)

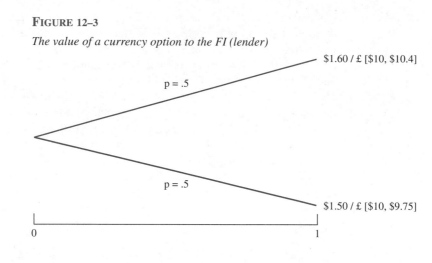

loans—prior to their charge off and sale—has a positive effect on bank stock prices.[31] Third, part of the loan sale loss is shared with the government because such losses provide a tax write-off for the lender.

The major cost is one of the loss itself—the tax-adjusted difference between the face value of the loan and its market value at the time of the sale. Further, many banks engaged in LDC loan sales in 1987 and 1988 after taking big loan-loss reserve additions in May–June 1987. Since 1988, and in particular in the 1991–93 period, the secondary market prices of many LDC countries—especially in Latin America—have risen in value by 20 to 30 percent. This suggests an additional cost related to loan sales, the optimal market timing of such sales, where FIs minimize the spread between the loan sale price and face value at the time of sale.

Debt for Debt Swaps (Brady Bonds)

The primary benefit of debt for debt swaps is that they transform an LDC loan into a highly marketable and liquid instrument—a bond. For example, FIs trade and clear Brady bonds (the most common debt for debt swap) in a similar fashion to most Eurobonds with relatively low transactions cost, small bid-ask spreads, and an efficient clearing and settlement system (via Euroclear and Cedel). In addition, because of full or partial collateral backing, these bonds are normally senior in status to any remaining LDC loans of that country. The major cost is that when the bond is swapped for the loan, it usually has a longer stated maturity and a fixed coupon set below the promised floating rate on the loan. Also, the swap of loan face value for debt face value is often less than dollar for dollar.

Choice between the Four Mechanisms

As described earlier in this section, FIs use four major mechanisms to deal with a problem sovereign LDC credit: a debt-equity swap, a MYRA, a loan sale, and a debt-debt (or loan-bond) swap. Each of these has a complex set of benefits and costs for an FI manager. Recent trends indicate how current FI managers evaluate the relevant benefits and costs. Specifically, debt for debt swaps and loan sales currently dominate

---

[31]See, for example, Grammatikos and Saunders, "Additions to Bank Loan Loss Reserves."

MYRAs and debt-equity swaps as sovereign loan risk exposure control mechanisms. Indeed, the combined annual volume for Brady bond and loan sales transactions exceeds $500 billion per annum. This can be compared to $10 billion in debt-equity swaps and an infrequent use of MYRAs among major creditor FIs in the 1990s.

Concept Questions

1. Make a list of the two major benefits and two major costs for an FI involved in debt-equity swaps, MYRAs, loan sales, and debt for debt swaps (Brady bonds).
2. Make up a list similar to that in question 1 from the perspective of the borrowing country.

Summary

This chapter has reviewed the problems FIs face from sovereign or country risk exposures. Sovereign risk is the risk of a foreign government limiting or preventing domestic borrowers in their jurisdiction from repaying the principal and interest on debt owed to external lenders. In recent years, this risk has caused enormous problems for U.S. banks lending to LDCs and Latin American and Eastern bloc countries. We reviewed various models for country risk analysis (CRA), including those produced by external monitoring agencies such as *Euromoney* and the *Institutional Investor* and those that could be constructed by an FI manager for internal evaluation purposes. Such statistical CRA models have problems and pitfalls. Finally, we analyzed the advantages and disadvantages of using four alternative mechanisms for dealing with problem sovereign credits from the perspective of the lender; namely, debt-equity swaps, MYRAs, loan sales, and debt-debt swaps.

Questions and Problems

1. The CRA Z score model uses key variables to assess the country's rescheduling probability. The values of these key variables are measured as of one particular point in time. What are the shortcomings introduced by this static methodology? How do predictive models attempt to incorporate these lags?

2. Relate the finding of high systematic risk across countries to the development of a secondary market for LDC debt.

3 *a.* What is the yield to maturity on a Chilean deep-discount sovereign bond with 25 years until maturity selling at $55 per $100 of face value?

   b. What is the price of an Australian deep-discount sovereign bond with 15 years until maturity yielding 4.2 percent annually?

4 *a.* What is the value of a five-year loan to Poland with a 10 percent annual coupon payment if there is only a 20 percent probability that the loan coupon payments will be made? (Current yields are 10 percent annually.) Assume principal payments are fully insured.

   b. Your FI holds $1 million of the loans in question 4*a* and you decide to sell them to a securities dealer. If the bid-ask spread in the secondary market is 5 percent (as a percentage of the ask price), what is the bid price of the loans? (Hint: Assume that the ask price is equal to the loan's present value.)

   c. What is the loss your FI books upon the sale of the loan? If your corporate tax rate is 25 percent, what is the after-tax loss? What is the cash value of the bid-ask spread?

   d. If your FI is a U.S. bank, why might you be willing to sell the loans at a discount of 5 percent?

   e. Calculate the securities dealer's profit if the loans are sold to a commercial firm at a discount (from ask price) of 2.5 percent.

   f. Currently, the exchange rate is 15,000 zlotys per U.S. dollar. The commercial firm intends to invest US$1 million in a joint venture with a Polish textile producer. The Polish government has offered the firm a debt-equity exchange rate of 14,000 zlotys per U.S. dollar. What is the profit to the commercial firm from the purchase of the debt?

g. What is the return to the Polish government of participating in the debt-equity swap? What are the costs?

h. Distribute the loan's face value among all the counterparties. (The total must sum to US$1 million.)

5. Prior to 1982, FIs acted as if they believed that there could never be a default on sovereign country debt. How did FI behavior encourage such beliefs?

6. When we talk of sovereign or country risk, we often speak of the risk of lending to developing countries (LDCs) as opposed to developed countries. Is this just chauvinism or are LDCs more susceptible to sovereign risk?

7. What is the cost of debt repudiation to the country? What is the cost of debt rescheduling to the country?

8. Critique the *Euromoney Index* evaluation model.

9. Critique the value of using the *Institutional Investor Index* to assess country risk exposure.

10. Analyze the following model. You estimate a linear probability model of sovereign country risk and obtain the following results:

$$P = 2.3DSR + .03IR - 1.1INVR + 1.9VAREX + 2.2MG$$

where

P is the probability of rescheduling

DSR is $\dfrac{Debt\ Payments}{Exports}$

IR is $\dfrac{Imports}{Foreign\ Exchange\ Reserves}$

$INVR$ is $\dfrac{Real\ Investment}{GNP}$

$VAREX$ is σ^2_{ER}

MG is $\dfrac{\Delta M}{M}$

11. First Global Bank holds loans to the following countries:

Country	DSR	b_i	Debt Amount
Ireland	0.55	.01	$95
Zaire	1.43	.99	15
Ivory Coast	1.05	.78	44
Hungary	1.11	.67	53

where debt amounts are in millions of dollars,

DSR_i is $\dfrac{Debt\ Payments}{Exports}$ for country i,

b_i is the coefficient on the following equation:

$$DSR_i = a_i + b_i DSR + e_i$$

DSR is the weighted average of the DSR variable for each of the four countries, e_i is the error term encompassing all other factors impacting DSR_i.

a. Calculate DSR.

b. How would you rank the countries with respect to default risk?

c. How does your answer to question 11*b* change if First Global is only concerned with portfolio risk?

d. How could First Global Bank reduce the sovereign country risk of its portfolio?

12. Compare the models in questions 10 and 11.

LIQUIDITY RISK

Learning Objectives

In this chapter you learn about liquidity risk. While liquidity risk arises for most FIs, it is generally more serious for banks and thrifts than for other institutions. A key reason for this is a deposit contract's unique characteristics. This is why depositors of banks perceived to be in trouble have very strong incentives to engage in bank runs. By contrast, incentives to engage in runs on FIs, such as mutual funds, are much weaker. An important reason for this is the difference in key contractual features between bank deposit and mutual fund contracts.

Introduction

In Chapters 4 through 12, you have seen how the major problems of interest rate risk, credit risk, off-balance-sheet risk, technology risk, foreign exchange risk, and sovereign risk can threaten the solvency of an FI. In this chapter we look at the problems created by liquidity risk.

Unlike the preceding risks that threaten the very solvency of an FI, liquidity risk is a normal aspect of the everyday management of an FI. Only in extreme cases do liquidity risk problems develop into solvency risk problems. Moreover, some FIs are more exposed to liquidity risk than others. At one extreme, banks and thrifts are highly exposed and in the middle are life insurance companies that are moderately exposed. At the other end are mutual and pension funds and property-casualty insurance companies with relatively low exposure. We examine the reasons for these differences in this chapter.

Causes of Liquidity Risk

Liquidity risk arises for two reasons—a liability side reason and an asset side reason. The liability side reason arises whenever an FI's liability holders, such as depositors or insurance policyholders, seek to cash in their financial claims immediately. When liability holders demand cash by withdrawing deposits, there is a need for the FI to borrow additional funds or to sell off assets to meet the withdrawal. The most liquid asset of all is cash; FIs use this asset to directly pay off claimholders who seek to withdraw funds. However, FIs tend to minimize their holdings of cash reserves as assets because they pay no interest. To generate interest revenues, most FIs invest in less liquid and/or longer maturity assets. While most assets can be turned into cash eventually, for some assets this can only be done at a high cost when the asset must be liquidated immediately. The price the asset holder has to accept for immediate sale may be far less than if there was a longer horizon over which to negotiate a sale. As a result, some assets may only be liquidated at low **fire-sale prices,** thus threatening the solvency of the FI. Alternatively, rather than liquidating assets, an FI may seek to purchase or borrow additional funds.

Fire-Sale Price
The price received for
an asset that has to be
liquidated (sold)
immediately.

The second source of liquidity risk arises on the asset side as a result of lending commitments. As we described in Chapter 9, a loan commitment allows a borrower to take down funds from an FI (over a commitment period) on demand. When a loan commitment is taken down, the FI has to fund it on the balance sheet immediately; this creates a demand for liquidity.[1] As with liability withdrawals, an FI can meet such a liquidity need either by running down its cash assets, selling off other liquid assets, or borrowing additional funds.

To analyze the differing degree of importance of liquidity risk across FIs, we next analyze liquidity risk problems faced by banks and thrifts, insurance companies, and mutual and pension funds.

Concept Question

1. Why is cash more liquid than loans for an FI?

Liquidity Risk at Banks and Thrifts

Liability Side Liquidity Risk

As we discussed in Chapter 5, typically a depository institution's balance sheet has a large amount of short-term liabilities, such as demand deposits and other transaction accounts, funding relatively long-term assets. Demand deposit accounts and other transaction accounts are contracts that give the holder the right to put their claims back to the bank on any given day and demand immediate repayment of the face value of their deposit claims in cash.[2] Thus, an individual demand deposit account holder with $10,000 in an account can turn up and demand cash immediately as readily as a corporation with $100 million in its demand deposit account. In theory at least, a bank that has 20 percent of its liabilities in demand deposits and other transaction accounts must stand ready to pay out that amount by liquidating its assets on any banking day. In Table 13–1 is an aggregate balance sheet of the assets and liabilities of U.S. commercial banks. As you can see in this table, total deposits are approximately 70 percent of total assets with 20 percent demand deposits and transaction accounts. By comparison, cash assets are only 6 percent of total assets. Also note that borrowed funds are 14.3 percent of total assets.

In reality, a depository institution knows that in normal times only a small proportion of depositors withdraw funds from their accounts, or put their account claims back to the bank, on any given day. Normally, most demand deposits act as

---

[1]In Chapter 9, we called this special type of liquidity risk take down risk.

[2]Accounts with this type of put option include demand deposits, NOW accounts (checking accounts with minimum balance requirements), and money market accounts (checking accounts with minimum balance and number of checks written restrictions). We describe these accounts in more detail in Chapter 23. Many savings account contracts give a bank some powers to delay withdrawals by requiring a certain number of days prior notification of withdrawal or by imposing penalty fees such as loss of interest.

TABLE 13–1   Assets and Liabilities of U.S. Banks, September 2, 1992
(in millions)

Assets		Liabilities	
Total securities	$ 816,064	Total deposits	$2,501,595
Total loans	2,265,015	Borrowings	513,471
Total cash assets	218,253	Other liabilities	577,965
Other assets	293,698		
	$3,593,030		$3,593,030

Source: *Federal Reserve Bulletin,* January 1993, Table 1.25.

Core Deposits
Those deposits that provide a bank with a long-term funding source.

Deposit Drains
The amount by which cash withdrawals exceed additions, a net cash outflow.

core deposits on a day-by-day basis, providing a relative long-term source of funds for an FI. Moreover, deposit withdrawals may in part be offset by the receipt of new deposits (and income generated on bank assets and off-balance sheet activities). Specifically, over time, a depository institution manager can predict the probability distribution of net **deposit drains** on any given normal banking day. Consider the two possible distributions in Figure 13–1.

As shown in panel *a* of Figure 13–1 the distribution is assumed to be strongly peaked at the 5 percent net deposit withdrawal level. That is, this FI expects approximately 5 percent of its net deposit funds to be withdrawn on any given day with the highest probability. In panel *a,* a net deposit drain means that a bank would be receiving insufficient additional deposits (and other cash inflows) to offset deposit withdrawals. For the banking industry to be growing, most banks would have a mean or average deposit drain where new deposit funds more than offset deposit withdrawals. Thus, the peak of the net deposit drain probability distribution would be at a point to the left of zero. See the −2 percent in panel *b,* where the bank would be receiving net cash inflows.

The bank in panel *a* has a mean or expected net positive drain on deposits, so its new deposit funds and other cash flows are expected to be insufficient to offset deposit withdrawals. The liability side of its balance sheet would be contracting. See Table 13–2 for a simple example of an actual 5 percent net drain of deposit accounts.

The two major ways in which the bank can meet this $5 million drain on deposits are liability management and/or reserve asset management.

Traditionally, bankers have relied on reserve asset management as the primary mechanism of adjustment. Today, many banks—especially the largest banks with access to the money market and other nondeposit markets for funds—rely on liability management to deal with the risk of cash shortfalls.

Liability Management.   If a manager uses liability management, the bank turns to markets for purchased funds, such as the federal funds market and/or the repurchase agreement markets, which are interbank markets for short-term loans. Alternatively, the bank could issue additional fixed maturity wholesale certificates of deposit or even sell some notes and bonds.[3] As long as the total amount of these

---

[3]The discount window is also a source of funds, but in emergency situations only. See the section on bank runs, the discount window, and deposit insurance and Chapter 15 for more discussion of the role of the discount window.

FIGURE 13–1

Distribution of net deposit drains

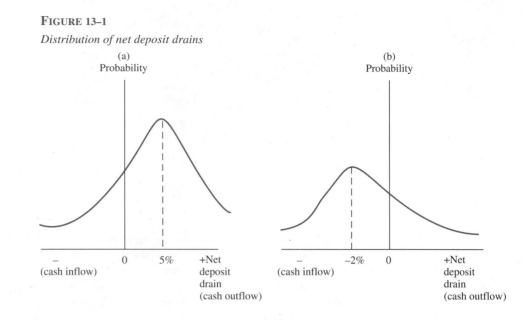

funds equaled $5 million, the bank in Table 13–2 could fully fund its net deposit drain. However, this can be expensive for the bank since it is paying *market rates* for funds in the wholesale money market to offset net drains on low-interest-bearing deposits.[4] Thus, the higher the cost of purchased funds relative to the rates earned on assets, the less attractive liability management becomes. In Table 13–3 is the bank's balance sheet if it responds to deposit drains by using liability management techniques and markets.

Note that liability management has allowed the bank to maintain its overall balance sheet size of $100 million, without disturbing the size and composition of the asset side of its balance sheet. That is, all the adjustments to the deposit drain take place on the liability side of the balance sheet. In other words, effective liability management can insulate the asset side of the balance sheet from normal drains in deposit accounts. This is one of the reasons for the enormous growth in bank liability management techniques and associated purchased fund markets such as fed funds, repurchase agreements, and CDs in recent years. We describe and discuss these instruments and liability management techniques in more detail in Chapter 23.

Reserve Asset Adjustment.   Instead of meeting the net deposit drain by borrowing in the wholesale money markets, the bank could liquidate some assets. Traditionally, banks have held cash reserves at the Federal Reserve and in their vaults for this very purpose. The Federal Reserve sets minimum reserve requirements for the cash reserves banks must hold. (Currently, the Fed requires 3 percent on the first $46.8 million and 10 percent on the rest of a bank's demand deposit and transaction account holdings.)[5] Even so, banks still tend to prudently hold excess reserve assets to meet

---

[4]While checking accounts pay no explicit interest, other transaction accounts such as NOW and money market accounts do. However, the rates paid are normally sticky and lie below purchased fund rates.

[5]As of April 2, 1992. The $46.8 million figure is adjusted annually along with the growth in bank deposits.

TABLE 13–2   The Effect of Net Deposit Drains on the Balance Sheet
(in millions)

Before the Drain				After the Drain			
Assets		Liabilities		Assets		Liabilities	
Assets	100	Deposits	70	Assets	100	Deposits	65
		Borrowed funds	10			Borrowed funds	10
		Other liabilities	20			Other liabilities	20
	100		100		100		95

TABLE 13–3   Adjusting to a Deposit Drain through Liability Management

Assets		Liabilities	
Assets	100	Deposits	65
		Borrowed funds	15
		Other liabilities	20
	100		100

liquidity drains. As an example, the United Kingdom has no official central bank-designated cash reserve requirements; even so, banks still hold 1 percent or more of their assets in cash reserves.

Suppose in our example that on the asset side of the balance sheet the bank normally held 9 percent of its assets in cash. We depict the situation before the net drain in liabilities in Table 13–4. As depositors withdraw $5 million in deposits, the bank can meet this directly by running down the cash held in its vaults or by withdrawing cash reserves called correspondent balances on deposit at other banks or at the Federal Reserve.[6] If the reduction in $5 million in deposit liabilities is met by a $5 million reduction in cash assets held by the bank, its balance sheet would look as in Table 13–5.

When the bank uses its cash reserve assets as the adjustment mechanism, both sides of its balance sheet contract; in this example, the bank's size shrinks from $100 to $95 million. The cost to the bank from using reserve asset adjustment—apart from shrinkage in bank size,[7] is that it has to hold excess noninterest-bearing assets on its balance sheet.[8] Thus, the cost is the forgone return (or opportunity cost) from being unable to invest these funds in loans and other higher income earning assets.

---

[6]Of the cash assets held by U.S. banks on September 2, 1992 totaling $218,253 million—see Table 13–1—balances held with Federal Reserve banks amounted to 12.9 percent; balances held at other depository institutions, 14.1 percent; and cash in the vault, 14.0 percent; other cash assets and items comprise the remainder.

[7]There is no empirical evidence showing a significant correlation between a bank's asset size and profits.

[8]Banks could hold highly liquid interest-bearing assets such as T-bills, but these are still less liquid than cash and immediate liquidation may result in capital value losses.

TABLE 13–4 **Composition of the Bank's Balance Sheet**

Assets		Liabilities	
Cash	9	Deposits	70
Other assets	91	Borrowed funds	10
		Other liabilities	20
	100		100

TABLE 13–5 **Reserve Asset Adjustment to Deposit Drain**

Assets		Liabilities	
Cash	4	Deposits	65
Other assets	91	Borrowed funds	10
		Other liabilities	20
	95		95

Finally, note that while reserve asset adjustment and liability management are alternative strategies for meeting deposit drains, a bank can also combine the two methods by using some liability management and some reserve adjustment to meet any given deposit drain.

Asset-Side Liquidity Risk

Just as deposit drains can cause a bank liquidity problems, so can the exercise, by borrowers, of their loan commitments and other credit lines. In Table 13–6, $5 million of a loan commitment is exercised on a particular day. As a result, $5 million in additional loans have to be funded on the balance sheet. Consider panel *a* in Table 13–6, the balance sheet before the commitment exercise, and panel *b,* the balance sheet afterward. In particular, the exercise of the loan commitment means that the banks need to provide $5 million in cash immediately to the borrower (other assets rise from $91 to $96 million). This can be done either by liability management (borrowing an additional $5 million in the money market and on-lending these funds to the borrower) or by reserve adjustment (running down the bank's own cash assets from $9 million to $4 million). We present these two policies in Table 13–7.

Measuring a Bank's Liquidity Exposure

Sources and Uses of Liquidity.   As discussed, a bank's liquidity risk can arise either from a drain on deposits or new loan demands and the subsequent need to meet these through liquidating assets or borrowing funds. Therefore, an FI manager must be able to measure the liquidity position on a daily basis if possible. A useful tool is a net liquidity statement that lists the sources and uses of liquidity and thus, provides a

TABLE 13–6   The Effects of Loan Commitment Exercise

(a) Before				(b) After			
Cash	9	Deposits	70	Cash	9	Deposits	70
Other assets	91	Borrowed funds	10	Other assets	96	Borrowed funds	10
		Other liabilities	20			Other liabilities	20
	100		100		105		100

TABLE 13–7   Adjusting the Balance Sheet to a Loan Commitment Exercise

(a) Liability Management				(b) Cash Reserve Asset Adjustment			
Cash	9	Deposits	70	Cash	4	Deposits	70
Other assets	96	Borrowed funds	15	Other assets	96	Borrowed funds	10
		Other liabilities	20			Other liabilities	20
	105		105		100		100

measure of an FI's net liquidity position. Look at such a statement for a hypothetical U.S. money center bank in Table 13–8.

The bank has three primary sources of liquidity: First, its cash-type assets such as T-bills can be sold immediately with little price risk and low transaction costs. Second, the maximum amount of funds it can borrow on the money/purchased funds market (this *internal* guideline is based on the manager's assessment of the credit limits the market is likely to impose on the bank). And third, any excess cash reserves over and above that held to meet regulatory imposed reserve requirements. As you can see, the bank's total sources of liquidity are $14,500 million. Compare this to the bank's *uses* of liquidity. In particular, the amount of borrowed or money market funds it has already utilized (e.g., fed funds, RPs borrowed) and the amount it has already borrowed from the Federal Reserve through discount window loans. These add up to $7,000 million. As a result, the bank has a positive net liquidity position of $7,500 million.

Peer Group Ratio Comparisons.   Another way to measure an FI's liquidity exposure is to compare certain key ratios and balance sheet features of the bank, such as its loans-deposits, borrowed funds-total assets, and commitment to lend-assets ratios, with banks of a similar size and geographic location. A high ratio of loans-deposits and borrowed funds-total assets means that the bank is placing a heavy reliance on the short-term money market, rather than core deposits, to fund loans. This could mean future liquidity problems if the bank is at or near its perceived borrowing limits in the purchased funds market. Similarly, a high ratio of loan commitments to assets indicates a need for a high degree of liquidity to fund any take downs of these loans. That is, high commitment banks often face more liquidity risk exposure than low commitment banks.

Financing Gap and the Financing Requirement.   A third way to measure liquidity risk exposure is to measure the bank's financing gap. As we discussed earlier,

TABLE 13–8   Net Liquidity Position

Sources of Liquidity	(in millions)
1. Total cash-type assets	$ 2,000
2. Maximum borrowed funds limit	12,000
3. Excess cash reserves	500
Total	$14,500
Uses of Liquidity	
1. Funds borrowed	$6,000
2. Federal Reserve borrowing	1,000
Total net liquidity	$7,500

even though demand depositors can withdraw their funds immediately, in normal circumstances they don't. On average, most demand deposits stay at banks for quite long periods—often two years or more.[9] Thus, a banker often thinks of the average deposit base including demand deposits as a core source of funds that over time can fund a bank's average amount of loans.

Financing Gap
The difference between a bank's average loans and average (core) deposits.

We define a **financing gap** (FGap) as:

$$\text{Financing gap} = \text{Average loans} - \text{Average deposits}$$

If this financing gap is positive, the bank has to fund it by running down its cash and liquid assets and/or borrowing funds on the money market. Thus:

$$\text{Financing gap} = -\text{Liquid assets} + \text{Borrowed funds}$$

We can reexpress this relationship as:

$$\text{Financing gap} + \text{Liquid assets} = \text{Financing requirement}$$

Financing Requirement
The financing gap plus a bank's liquid assets.

As expressed in this fashion, the liquidity and managerial implications of the **financing requirement,** are that some level of core deposits and loans as well as some amount of liquid assets determine the bank's borrowing or purchased fund needs. In particular, the larger a bank's financing gap and liquid asset holdings, the larger the amount of funds it needs to borrow on the money markets and the greater its exposure to liquidity problems from such a reliance.

We present an example of the relationship between the financing gap, liquid assets, and the borrowed funds financing requirement in Table 13–9. See also the following equation:

$$\text{Financing gap} + \text{Liquid assets} = \text{Financing requirement}$$
$$(5) \qquad\qquad (5) \qquad\qquad\qquad (10)$$

A rising financing gap can warn of future liquidity problems for a bank since it may indicate increased deposit withdrawals (core deposits falling below 20 in Table 13–9) and rising loans due to increased exercise of loan commitments (loans rising

---

[9]See Federal Reserve Board of Governors, "Risk-Based Capital and Interest Rate Risk," Press release, July 30, 1992.

TABLE 13–9   The Financing Requirement of a Bank
(in millions)

Assets		Liabilities	
Loans	$25	Core deposits	$20
		Financing gap	(5)
Liquid assets	5	Financing requirement (Borrowed funds)	10
	Total $30		Total $30

above 25). If the bank does not reduce its liquid assets, that is, they stay at 5, the manager would have to resort to more money market borrowings. As these borrowings rise, sophisticated lenders in the money market may be concerned about the creditworthiness of the bank. They may react by imposing higher risk premiums for borrowed funds or establishing stricter credit limits by not rolling over funds lent to the bank. If the banker's financing requirements exceed such limits, the bank is effectively insolvent. A good example of an excessive financing requirement resulting in bank insolvency was the failure of Continental Illinois in 1984.[10]

Liquidity Risk, Unexpected Deposit Drains, and Bank Runs

Under normal conditions, net deposit withdrawals or the exercise of loan commitments pose few liquidity problems for banks because borrowed fund availability or excess cash reserves are adequate to meet anticipated needs. For example, even in December and the summer vacation season when net deposit withdrawals are high, banks anticipate these *seasonal* effects through holding larger than normal excess cash reserves or borrowing more than normal on the wholesale money markets.

Major liquidity problems can arise, however, if deposit drains are abnormally *large* and unexpected. Such deposit withdrawal shocks may occur for a number of reasons, including:

1. Concerns about a bank's solvency relative to other banks.
2. Failure of a related bank leading to heightened depositor concerns about the solvency of other banks (the contagion effect).

---

[10]Continental Illinois, headquartered in Chicago, had a very small core deposit base due to restrictions on bank branching within the state. As a result, it had to rely extensively on borrowed funds such as fed funds, RPs and Eurodollar deposits (wholesale CDs from the offshore Euromarkets). As these borrowings grew, there were increased concerns about the bank's ability to meet its payment commitments—especially in view of a worsening loan portfolio. This resulted in an eventual refusal of a number of large money market lenders (such as Japanese banks) to renew or rollover their borrowed funds held by Continental Illinois on maturity. With the rapid withdrawal of such borrowed funds, Continental Illinois was unable to survive and was eventually taken over by the FDIC. For good detailed descriptions of the Continental Illinois failure, see I. Swary, "Stock Market Reaction to Regulatory Action in the Continental Illinois Crisis," *Journal of Business* 59, 1986, pp. 451–73; and L. Wall and D. R. Peterson, "The Effect of Continental Illinois' Failure on the Performance of Other Banks," *Journal of Monetary Economics*, 1990, pp. 77–99.

TABLE 13–10   **Bank Run Incentives**

	Assets		Liabilities
Assets	$90	Deposits	$100
			(100 × $1 each)

Bank Run
A sudden and unexpected increase in deposit withdrawals from a bank.

3. Sudden changes in investor preferences regarding holding nonbank financial assets (such as T-bills) relative to deposits.

Any sudden surge in net deposit withdrawals risks triggering a **bank run** that would eventually force a bank into insolvency.[11]

Deposit Drains and Bank Runs Liquidity Risk.   At the core of bank run liquidity risk is the fundamental and unique nature of the *demand deposit contract.* Specifically, demand deposit contracts are first come, first served, contracts in the sense that a depositor's place in line matters when withdrawing funds. In particular, a depositor either gets paid in full or gets nothing. To see this, suppose that a bank has 100 depositors who each deposited $1. Suppose that each has a reason to believe— correctly or incorrectly—that the bank has assets valued at only $90 on its balance sheet (see Table 13–10).

As a result, each depositor has an incentive to go to the bank quickly to with-draw his or her $1 deposit because the bank pays off depositors sequentially by liqui-dating its assets. If it has $90 in assets, it can pay off, in full, only the first 90 depositors in the line. The 10 depositors at the end of the line would get *nothing at all.* Thus, demand deposits are in essence either full pay or no pay contracts. We show the sequential nature of deposit withdrawals, and the importance of being first in line for our troubled bank in Figure 13–2.

Because demand deposit contracts pay off in full only a certain proportion of depositors when a bank's assets are valued at less than its deposits—and because depositors realize this—any line outside a bank should be joined immediately even if the depositor doesn't need cash today for normal consumption purposes.[12] Thus, even the bank's core depositors who don't really need to withdraw deposits for consump-tion needs, upon observing a sudden increase in the lines at their bank rationally seek to withdraw their funds immediately.

As a bank run develops, the demand for net deposit withdrawals grows. The bank might initially meet this by running down its cash reserves, selling off liquid or readily marketable assets such as T-bills and T bonds, and seeking to borrow in the money markets. As a bank run increases in intensity, more depositors join the with-drawal line, and a liquidity crisis develops. Specifically, the bank would find it diffi-cult, if not impossible, to borrow on the money markets at any price. Also, it would

---

[11]For more analysis regarding the details of bank runs, see D. W. Diamond and P. H. Dybvig, "Bank Runs, Deposit Insurance, and Liquidity," *Journal of Political Economy* 91, 1983, pp. 401–19; and G. Kaufman, "Bank Contagion: Theory and Evidence" (Loyola University, Center for Financial and Policy Studies, Working Paper 93–1, 1993).

[12]Here we are assuming no deposit insurance or discount window. The presence of deposit insurance and the discount window alters the incentives to engage in a bank run as we describe later in this chapter and in Chapter 15.

FIGURE 13–2

Place-in-line matters for bank depositors

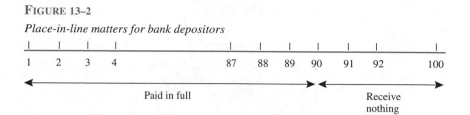

have sold off all its liquid assets, cash and bonds as well as any loans that are saleable (see Chapter 22). All the bank is likely to have left is relatively illiquid loans on the asset side of the balance sheet to meet depositor claims for cash. However, these loans can only be sold or liquidated at very large discounts from face value. For example, the Resolution Trust Corporation that is disposing of assets formerly held by failed thrifts has found it difficult to dispose of some commercial real estate loans at almost any price!

A bank needing to liquidate long-term assets at fire sale prices to meet continuing deposit drains faces the strong possibility that the proceeds from such asset sales would be insufficient to meet depositors' cash demands. The bank's liquidity problem would turn into a solvency problem; that is, the bank would have to close its doors.

The incentives for depositors to run first and ask questions later creates a fundamental instability in the banking system, such that an otherwise sound bank can be pushed into insolvency and failure by unexpectedly large depositor drains and liquidity demands. This is especially so in periods of contagious runs or **bank panics,** when depositors lose faith in the banking system as a whole and engage in a run on all banks by not materially discriminating among them according to their asset qualities.[13]

Bank Panic
A systemic or contagious run on the deposits of the banking industry as a whole.

Bank Runs, the Discount Window, and Deposit Insurance

Regulators have recognized the inherent instability of the banking system due to the all or nothing payoff features of the deposit contract. As a result, regulatory mechanisms are in place to ease the liquidity problems of banks and to deter bank runs and panics. The two major liquidity risk insulation devices are deposit insurance and the discount window. We discuss these in detail in Chapter 15. As we describe there, deposit insurance has effectively deterred bank panics since 1933, although the provision of deposit insurance has not been without other costs.

Concept Questions

1. List two benefits and two costs of using (i) liability management and (ii) reserve or cash assets to meet a deposit drain.

---

[13]See Kaufman, "Bank Contagion," for an excellent review of the nature and causes of bank runs and panics. There is strong evidence of contagious bank runs or panics in 1930–32 in the United States (see A. Saunders and B. Wilson, "Informed and Uninformed Depositor Runs and Panics: Evidence from the 1929–33 Period" (Working Paper, Salomon Center, New York University, March 1993). Such a panic also causes a flight to safe assets such as T-bills.

2. What are the three major sources of bank liquidity? What are the two major uses?

3. Which factors determine the financing requirement of an FI?

4. If a bank is in trouble, who are more likely to run first and why, retail depositors or wholesale depositors?

Liquidity Risk and Life Insurance Companies

Banks and thrifts are not the only FIs exposed to liquidity risk or run problems. Similar to banks, life insurance companies hold some cash reserves to meet policy cancellations and other working capital needs. In the normal course of business, premium income and returns on the asset portfolio would be sufficient to meet the cash outflows required when policyholders cash in or surrender their policies early. As with banks, the distribution or pattern of premium income minus policyholder liquidations is normally predictable. When premium income is insufficient, a life insurer can sell off some of its relatively liquid assets, such as government bonds. Here, bonds act as a buffer or reserve asset fund for the insurer. As with banks, concerns about the solvency of the insurer or insurance companies in general can result in a run where new premium income dries up and existing policyholders seek to cancel their policies by cashing them in for their **surrender values.**[14] To meet exceptional demands for cash, a life insurer could be forced to liquidate the less liquid assets in its portfolio, such as commercial mortgage loans and other securities, at potentially fire sale prices.[15] As with banks, forced asset liquidations can push an insurer into insolvency. A good example of an insurance company run occurred in 1991 on First Capital, a large California-based insurer. Losses on its junk bond portfolio raised regulator and policyholder concerns about the quality of its balance sheet. New policyholder premiums dried up and existing policyholders engaged in a run by seeking to cash in their policies for whatever surrender values they could get. To deter the run, the California State insurance regulator placed limits on the ability of existing policyholders to surrender their policies.[16]

Surrender Value
The amount received by an insurance policyholder when cashing in a policy early.

Liquidity Risk and Property-Casualty Insurers

As discussed in Chapter 2, property-casualty insurers sell policies insuring against certain contingencies impacting either real property or individuals. Unlike life insur-

---

[14]A surrender value is usually some proportion or percent less than 100 percent of the face value of the insurance contract.

Some insurance companies have also faced run problems resulting from their sale of guaranteed investment contracts (GICs). A GIC, similar to a long-term, fixed-rate bank deposit, is made by an investor with an insurance company. As market interest rates rose, many investors withdrew their funds and reinvested elsewhere in higher return investments. This created both liquidity and refinancing problems for life insurers that supplied such contracts and eventually led to restrictions on withdrawals.

[15]Note that life insurers also provide a considerable amount of loan commitments especially in the commercial property area. As a result, they face asset side loan commitment liquidity risk in a similar fashion to banks.

[16]State guarantee schemes also deter policyholder runs. In general, the level of coverage and the value of the guarantees are less than deposit insurance. We discuss these guarantee schemes in Chapter 15.

FIGURE 13–3

The supply of shares of an open-ended mutual fund

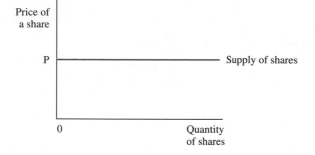

ers, the contingencies (and policy coverages) are relatively short-term, often one to three years. As a result, P-C insurers' assets tend to be shorter-term and more liquid than those of life insurers. Also, contracts and premium-setting intervals are usually relatively short term as well, so problems caused by policy surrenders are less severe. Their greatest liquidity exposure arises if policyholders cancel or fail to renew policies because of insolvency risk, pricing, or competitive reasons. This may result in their premium cash inflow, when added to their investment returns, being insufficient to meet policy claims. Or, large unexpected claims may materialize and exceed the flow of premium income and income returns from assets. Recent disasters such as Hurricane Andrew in 1991 and the blizzard of the century in 1993 have caused severe liquidity crises and failures among smaller P-C insurers.[17]

Mutual Funds

Mutual funds sell shares as liabilities to investors and invest the proceeds in assets such as bonds and equities. Mutual funds are open-ended and closed-ended. **Closed-end funds** issue a fixed number of shares as liabilities; unless the issuing fund chooses to repurchase them, the quantity of outstanding shares does not change. As discussed in Chapter 2, by far the majority of U.S. mutual funds are **open-end funds**; that is, they can issue an unlimited supply of shares to investors. Open-end funds must also stand ready to buy back previously issued shares from investors at the current market price for the fund's shares.

We show the supply function of open-ended mutual fund shares in Figure 13–3. Thus, at a given market price—$0P$ in Figure 13–3—the supply of open-ended fund shares is perfectly elastic. The price at which an open-ended mutual fund stands ready to sell new shares, or redeem existing shares, is the **net asset value** (NAV) of the fund. NAV is the current or market value of the fund's assets divided by the number of shares in the fund. A mutual fund's willingness to provide instant liquidity to shareholders while investing funds in equities, bonds, and other long-term instruments could expose it to liquidity problems similar to banks, thrifts, and life

Closed-end Fund
An investment fund that sells a fixed number of shares in the fund to outside investors.

Open-ended Fund
An investment fund that sells an elastic or nonfixed number of shares in the fund to outside investors.

Net Asset Value
The price at which mutual funds shares are sold (or can be redeemed). It equals the total market value of the assets of the fund divided by the number of shares in the fund outstanding.

---

[17]Also, claims may arise in long-tail lines where a contingency takes place during the policy period, but a claim is not lodged until many years later. One example is the claims regarding damage caused by asbestos contact.

TABLE 13–11   Run Incentives of Bank Depositors versus Mutual Fund Investors

Bank			Mutual Fund		
Assets		*Liabilities*	*Assets*		*Liabilities*
Assets	$90	$100 Deposits (100 depositors with $1 deposits)	Assets	$90	$100 Shares (100 shareholders with $1 shares)

insurance companies when withdrawals (or cashing in of mutual fund shares) rise to abnormally and unexpectedly high levels. However, the fundamental difference in the way mutual fund contracts are valued, compared to bank deposit and insurance policy contracts, mitigates the incentives for mutual fund shareholders to engage in runs. Specifically, if a mutual fund were to be liquidated, its assets would be distributed to mutual fund shareholders on a pro rata basis, rather than the first come, first served basis employed under deposit and insurance policy contracts.

To illustrate this difference, we can directly compare the incentives for mutual fund investors to engage in a run with those of bank depositors. In Table 13–11, we show a simple balance sheet of an open-ended mutual fund and a bank. When they perceive a bank's assets are valued below its liabilities, depositors have an incentive to engage in a run on the bank to be first in line to withdraw. In the example in Table 13–11, only the first 90 bank depositors would receive a dollar back for each dollar deposited. The last 10 would receive nothing at all.

Now consider the mutual fund with 100 shareholders who invested a total of $100 but whose assets are worth $90. If these shareholders tried to cash in their shares, *none* would receive $1 back. Instead, a mutual fund values its balance sheet liabilities on a market value basis; the price of any share liquidated by an investor is:

$$P = \frac{\text{Value of assets}}{\text{Shares outstanding}} = \text{NAV (net asset value)}$$

Thus, unlike deposit contracts that have fixed face values of $1, the value of a mutual fund's shares reflects the changing value of the fund's assets divided by the number of shares outstanding. In Table 13–11, the value of each shareholder's claim would be:

$$P = \frac{\$90}{100} = \$.9$$

That is, each mutual fund shareholder participates in the fund's loss of asset value on a *pro rata* or proportional basis. Technically, whether first or last in line, each shareholder who cashes in shares on any given day would receive the net asset value of the mutual fund. In this case, it is 90 cents, representing a loss of 10 cents per share. All mutual fund shareholders realize this and know that asset losses are shared among investors on a pro rata basis; there is no overall advantage to being first in line to withdraw, unlike for bank deposits.

This is not to say that mutual funds bear no liquidity risk, but rather that the incentives for mutual fund shareholders to engage in runs that produce the extreme form of liquidity problems faced by banks, thrifts, and life insurance companies are generally absent.[18] This has led some academics to argue for a restructuring of deposit contracts in a form more similar to mutual fund or equity contracts. This might also obviate the need for deposit insurance to deter bank runs.[19]

Concept Question

1. What problems would banks have if they offered deposit contracts of a mutual fund type rather than the traditional all or nothing demand deposit contract?

---

[18]For example, a sudden surge of mutual fund shareholder redemptions might require a mutual fund manager to sell off some of its less marketable bonds and equities at fire sale prices.

[19]See C. S. Jacklin, "Demand Deposits, Trading Restrictions, and Risk Sharing," in *Contractual Arrangements for Intertemporal Trade,* ed. E. Presscott and N. Wallace (Duluth: University of Minnesota, 1987). A common argument against this is that since deposits are money, and money is the unit of account in the economy, equity-type contracts could pose a problem if the value of a deposit were to fluctuate day to day. However, note that money market mutual funds offer depositlike contracts as well. As their NAV varies, they solve the fluctuating share value problem by setting the value of each share at $1 but allow the number of shares an individual holds to fluctuate so that the value of the individual's overall holdings moves in line with asset values, while the price of each money market mutual fund share remains at $1. A similar policy could be adopted for deposits at banks.

Summary

Liquidity risk, as a result of liability withdrawals, or loan commitment exercise is a common problem faced by FI managers. Well-developed policies for holding liquid assets or having access to markets for purchased funds are normally adequate to meet liability withdrawals. However, very large withdrawals can cause asset liquidity problems that can be compounded by incentives for liability claimholders to engage in runs at the first sign of a liquidity problem. These incentives for depositors and life insurance policyholders to engage in runs can push normally sound FIs into insolvency. Since such insolvencies have costs to society as well as to private shareholders, regulators have developed mechanisms such as deposit insurance and the discount window to alleviate liquidity problems. We discuss these mechanisms in detail in Chapter 15.

Questions and Problems

1. What factors exacerbate the liquidity risk exposure of:
   a. A bank?
   b. An insurance company?
   c. A mutual fund?

2. What factors mitigate the liquidity risk exposure of:
   a. A bank?
   b. An insurance company?
   c. A mutual fund?

3. How has the expansion of the FI's off-balance-sheet activities affected liquidity risk?

4. What are the pros and cons of the peer group ratio method of measuring liquidity risk?

5. How is the bank's distribution pattern of net deposit drains affected by:
   a. The holiday season?
   b. Summer vacations?
   c. A severe economic recession?
   d. Double-digit inflation?

6. *a.* How is interest rate risk related to liquidity risk for an FI?
   b. How does the general level of prices in the economy affect FI liquidity?

7. How are the financing requirements of an FI impacted if the market it serves has an economy that is rapidly

growing? How is liquidity risk affected? Contrast your answers with an FI in a contracting economic environment.

8. What is the impact on the bank's balance sheet if there is a $15 million net deposit drain? Show the bank's balance sheet if:

   a. The bank purchases liabilities.

   b. The reserve asset adjustment method is used to meet the liquidity shortfall.

Balance Sheet (in millions)

Assets		Liabilities	
Cash	$10	Deposits	$68
Loans	50	Equity	7
Securities	15		

9. Calculate the net liquidity position for the following FIs:

   a. Cash: $1 million; Maximum Borrowed Funds Limit: $3 million; Excess Cash Reserves: $.5 million; Funds Borrowed: $1.5 million; Federal Reserve Borrowing: 0.

   b. Cash: $.55 million; Maximum Borrowed Funds Limit: $1 million; Excess Cash Reserves: $.25 million; Funds Borrowed: $1.5 million; Federal Reserve Borrowing: $100,000.

   c. Compare the liquidity risks of the two FIs in parts a and b.

10. A bank has the following balance sheet in billions:

Assets		Liabilities	
Cash	$ 1	Demand deposits	$40
Loans	44	Net worth	5

   Loans have one year until maturity and are priced at par, paying 7 percent annual rates. Demand deposits are noninterest bearing.

   a. The bank experiences a run on its demand deposits. Deposit withdrawals are financed through asset sales.

If the bank attempts to conduct a fire sale of its loan portfolio by selling it in one day, the loans will be priced at a 35 percent annual rate. If the bank takes two days to package the loan sale, the loan sales rate falls to 10 percent annually. It will take three days for the bank to get the true market value of its loan portfolio. What is the value of the bank's loan portfolio on day 1? Day 2? Day 3? (Use annual interest rates.)

   b. How much do depositors receive if all attempt complete withdrawals of their balances on day 1? Day 2? Day 3? What would be the impact on the bank's net worth at each point in time? (Assume that regulators do not step in to close the bank.)

   c. How would your answer differ if this balance sheet was for a mutual fund? (Assume that all mutual fund investments are completely financed by fund shareholders; that is, there is no net worth.)

   d. Contrast the experience of bank depositors with the experience of mutual fund shareholders in the event of financial distress.

11. Consider the following bank balance sheet:

(in millions)

Assets		Liabilities	
Liquid assets	$ 20	Deposits	$1,800
Loans	2,550	Borrowed funds	xx
Property	330	Equity	150

   a. If stable core deposits are 90 percent of total deposits, what is the bank's financing gap?

   b. What is the amount of borrowed funds that the bank must have to meet its financing requirements?

   c. If stable core deposits are only 40 percent of total deposits, how do your answers to a and b change? How is the liquidity risk exposure of the bank affected?

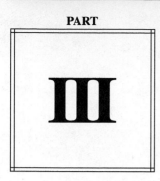

PART

III

MANAGING RISK

14

CAPITAL ADEQUACY

Learning Objectives

In this chapter you learn about the very important functions capital or equity plays in modern FIs. Not only does capital provide a source of funds in addition to deposits and other debt liabilities but it also protects the FI, its liability holders, and regulators against the risk of insolvency. That is, capital insulates an FI against exposure emanating from credit risk, interest rate risk, and so on. Further, you will learn how regulators measure the adequacy of an FI's capital and the types of action they take if an FI appears undercapitalized.

Introduction

Chapters 4 to 13 have examined the major areas of risk exposure facing a modern FI manager. These risks can emanate from both on- and off-balance-sheet (OBS) activities and be either domestic or international in source. To ensure survival, an FI manager needs to protect the institution against the risk of insolvency; that is, to shield it from risks sufficiently large to cause the institution to fail. The primary means of protection against the risk of insolvency and failure is an FI's capital. This leads to the first function of capital, namely:

1. To absorb unanticipated losses with enough margin to inspire confidence and enable the FI to continue as a going concern.

In addition, capital protects nonequity liability holders—especially those uninsured by an external guarantor such as the FDIC—against losses. This leads to the second function of capital:

2. To protect uninsured depositors in the event of insolvency and liquidation.

When FIs fail, regulators such as the FDIC have to intervene to protect insured claimants (see Chapter 15). The capital of an FI offers protection to insurance funds and ultimately the taxpayers who bear the cost of insurance fund insolvency. This leads to the third function of capital:

3. To protect FI insurance funds and the taxpayers.

Finally, just as for any firm, equity or capital is an important source of finance or funds for an FI. In particular, subject to regulatory constraints FIs have a choice between debt and equity to finance new projects and business expansion. Thus, the traditional factors that affect a business firm's choice of a capital structure—for instance, the tax deductibility of the interest on debt or the private costs of failure or insolvency—also interpose on the FI's capital decision.[1] This leads to a fourth function of capital:

4. To acquire the plant and other real investments necessary to provide financial services.[2]

In the following sections we mostly focus on the first three functions concerning the role of capital in reducing insolvency risk. We look briefly at the fourth function, equity capital and its cost as a funding source.

Concept Question

1. Why do banks hold capital? Which reasons are unique to banks?

The Cost of Equity Capital

Just as an FI competes for funds in the market for fixed income securities by offering claims such as deposits in competition with Treasury bills, Treasury bonds, and commercial paper, it must also compete in the market for equity capital. As we discussed in the preceding chapters, a bank's profitability reflects the net cash flows from its on- and off-balance-sheet activities. In turn, the value of a bank's stocks or equities sold in the capital market reflects the current and expected future dividends to be paid by the FI from these earnings, as for all firms. Thus,

$$P_0 = \frac{D_1}{(1+k)} + \frac{D_2}{(1+k)^2} + \ldots + \frac{D_\infty}{(1+k)^\infty}$$

where:

P_0 = Current price of the stock

D_i = Dividends expected in year $i = 1 \ldots n$

k = Discount rate or required return on the stock

We can also reexpress this as a price earnings (P/E) ratio. To see this, suppose that dividends are growing at a constant annual rate (g), so that:

$$D_1 = (1+g) \, D_0$$

$$D_2 = (1+g)^2 \, D_0$$

Then, Equation 1 reduces to:[3]

$$P_0 = \frac{D_0(1+g)}{k-g}$$

---

[1]See S. Ross and R. Westerfield, *Corporate Finance* (St. Louis, Mo.: Times Mirror-Mosby College Publishing, 1988).

[2]A fifth function might be added. This would focus on the role of capital regulation restraining the rate of asset growth.

[3]See F. K. Reilly, *Investment Analysis and Portfolio Management,* 3rd ed. (Chicago: Dryden Press, 1989), pp. 505–6.

FIGURE 14–1

Salomon Brothers bank composite relative price/earnings comparison,
1973-3Q 92E

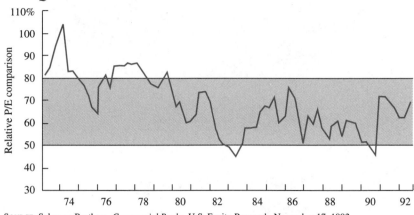

SOURCE: Salomon Brothers, *Commercial Banks,* U.S. Equity Research, November 17, 1992.

This is the well-known dividend growth model of stock price determination. Dividing both sides of Equation 2 by current earnings per share (E), we have

$$\frac{P_0}{E_0} = \frac{D_0/E_0\,(1+g)}{k-g}$$

The P/E Ratio
The price of a share per dollar of earnings.

Thus, the **P/E ratio**, or the price of a share per dollar of earnings, would be greater; the higher the dividend pay out ratio (D/E), the faster the growth in dividends (g) and the lower the required return on the firm's equity (k).[4] For any firm (including FIs), the higher the P/E ratio, the more investors are willing to pay for a dollar of earnings and the more attractive and cheaper equity is to issuers.

In Figure 14–1, we plot the P/E ratios of the 50 largest U.S. banks followed by Salomon Brothers (including the major money center, superregional, and regional banks) compared to the P/E ratio of the Standard & Poor's 500 Index over the 1973–92 period. As you can see, large bank P/E ratios have varied from between 50 and 80 percent of the P/E ratios for Standard & Poor's 500 firms. This means that equity capital has often been more expensive to raise for the nation's largest banks than for the average large nonbank firm. This may in turn reflect the perceived net regulatory burden that adversely impacts the attractiveness of bank stocks to investors (see Chapter 3). It has meant that FIs have had to bear the relatively high costs of additional equity issues when regulators have imposed minimum capital requirements that exceed capital holdings FIs privately view as optimal. Next, we discuss the rationale for regulators imposing such capital requirements and the economic role of equity capital in reducing insolvency risk.

Concept Questions

1. What factors might make an FI's price-earnings (P/E) ratio increase?
2. Why did bank's relative P/E ratios increase between 1990 and 1992?

---

[4]This is subject to $k > g$.

**TABLE 14–1 An FI's Market Value
Balance Sheet**

Assets		Liabilities	
Long-term securities	$ 80	Liabilities (short-term, floating-rate deposits)	$ 90
Long-term loans	20	Net worth	10
	$100		$100

Capital and Insolvency Risk

Capital

To see how capital protects an FI against insolvency risk, we have to define *capital* more precisely. The problem is that there are many definitions of capital; what an economist defines as capital may differ from an accountant's definition, which, in turn, can differ from the definition used by regulators. Specifically, the economic definition of a bank's capital or owners' equity stake in an FI is the difference between the market values of its assets and its liabilities. This is also called the **net worth** of an FI (see Chapter 5). While this is the economic meaning of capital, regulators have found it necessary to adopt different definitions of capital that depart by some greater or lesser degree from economic net worth. The concept of an FI's economic net worth is really a *market value accounting* concept. With the exception of the investment banking industry, regulatory defined capital and required leverage ratios are based in whole or in part on historical or **book value** accounting concepts.

    We begin by taking a look at the role of economic capital or net worth as an insulation device against two major types of risk: credit risk and interest rate risk. We then compare this market value concept with the book value concept of capital. Because it can actually distort the true solvency position of an FI, the book value of capital concept can be misleading to managers, owners, liability holders, and regulators alike. We also examine some possible reasons why FI regulators continue to rely on book value concepts in the light of such economic value transparency problems. Finally, we take a detailed look at the actual minimum capital requirements imposed by regulators in commercial banking, thrift or savings banking, P-C and life insurance, and investment banking.

The Market Value of Capital

To see how economic net worth or equity insulates an FI against risk, consider the following example. In Table 14–1, we have a simple balance sheet, where all the assets and liabilities of an FI are valued in **market value** terms at current prices on a **mark-to-market** basis (see Chapter 5). On a mark-to-market or market value basis, the economic value of the FI's equity is 10 which is the difference between the market value of its assets and liabilities. On a market value basis, the FI is economically solvent and would impose no failure costs on depositors or regulators if it were to be

Net Worth
A measure of an FI's capital that is equal to the difference between the market value of its assets and the market value of its liabilities.

Book Value
Basing asset and liabilities values on their historical costs.

Market Value or Marking-to-Market
Allowing balance sheet values to reflect current rather than historical prices.

TABLE 14–2 **The Market Value Balance Sheet after a Decline in the Value of Loans**

Assets		Liabilities	
Long-term securities	$ 80	Liabilities	$ 90
Long-term loans	12	Net worth	2
	$ 92		$ 92

liquidated today. Let's consider the impact of two classic types of FI risk, credit risk and interest rate risk, on this FI's net worth.

Market Value of Capital and Credit Risk.   In Table 14–1, an FI has 20 in long-term loans. Suppose that due to a recession, a number of these borrowers get into cash flow problems and are unable to keep up their promised loan repayment schedules. A decline in the current and expected future cash flows on loans lowers the market value of the loan portfolio held by the FI below 20. Suppose that loans are really worth only 12; that means the market value of the loan portfolio has fallen from 20 to 12. Look at the revised market value balance sheet in Table 14–2.

The loss of eight in the market value of loans appears on the liability side of the balance sheet as a loss of eight to an FI's net worth. That is, the loss of asset value is charged against the equity owners' capital or net worth. As you can see, the liability holders (depositors) are fully protected in that the total market value of their claims is still 90. This is because debt holders are senior claimants and equity holders are junior claimants. That is, equity holders bear losses on the asset portfolio first. In fact, in our example liability holders are only hurt when losses on the loan portfolio exceed 10, the net worth of the FI. Let's consider a larger credit risk shock, such that the market value of the loan portfolio plummets from 20 to 8, a loss of 12 (see Table 14–3).

This larger loss has rendered the FI insolvent; the market value of its assets (88) is now less than the value of its liabilities (90). The owners' net worth stake has been completely wiped out —reduced from 10 to −2, making the net worth negative. As a result, liability holders are hurt, but only a bit. Specifically, the first 10 of the 12 loss in value of the loan portfolio is borne by the equity holders. Only after the equity holders are wiped out, do the liability holders begin to lose. In this example, the economic value of their claims on the FI has fallen from 90 to 88, or a loss of 2 (a percentage loss of 2.22 percent). After insolvency and the remaining 88·in assets are liquidated, the depositors would only get 88/90 on the dollar, or 97.77 cents per $1 of deposits. Note here that we are ignoring deposit insurance.[5]

If the FI's net worth had been larger, say, 15 rather than 10 in the previous example, the liability holders would have been fully protected against loss.[6] This example

---

[5]In the presence of deposit insurance, the insurer, such as the FDIC, would bear some of the depositors' losses; for details see Chapter 15.

[6]In this case, the 12 loss reduces net worth to +3.

**TABLE 14–3   A Major Decline in the Value of
the Loan Portfolio**

Assets		Liabilities	
Long-term securities	$ 80	Liabilities	$ 90
Long-term loans	8	Net worth	−2
	$ 88		$ 88

clearly demonstrates the concept of net worth or capital as an insurance fund protecting liability holders, such as depositors, against insolvency risk. The larger the FI's net worth, relative to the size of its assets, the more insolvency protection or insurance there is for liability holders and liability guarantors such as the FDIC. This is why regulators focus on capital requirements such as the ratio of net worth to assets in assessing the insolvency risk exposure of an FI.

Concept Question

1. Why is an FI economically insolvent when its net worth is negative?

Market Value of Capital and Interest Rate Risk. Consider the same market value balance sheet in Table 14–1 after a rise in interest rates. As we discuss in Chapter 5, rising interest rates reduce the market value of the bank's long-term fixed income securities and loans while floating-rate instruments, if instantaneously repriced, find their market values largely unaffected. Suppose that the rise in interest rates reduces the market value of the FI's long-term securities investments from 80 to 75 and the market value of its long-term loans from 20 to 17. Because all deposit liabilities are assumed to be short-term floating-rate deposits, their market values are unchanged at 90.

After the shock to interest rates, the market value balance sheet might look as in Table 14–4. The loss of 8 in the market value of the FI's assets is once again reflected on the liability side of the balance sheet by a fall in the net worth of equity from 10 to 2. Thus, as for increased credit risk, losses in asset values due to adverse interest rate changes are borne first by the equity holders. Only if the fall in the market value of assets exceeded 10 would the liability holders, as senior claimants to the FI's assets, be adversely affected.

These examples show that market valuation of the balance sheet produces an economically accurate picture of the net worth and, thus, the solvency position of an FI. Credit risk and interest rate risk shocks that result in losses in the market value of assets are directly borne by the equity holders in the sense that such losses are charges against the value of their ownership claims in the FI. As long as the owners' capital or equity stake is adequate, or sufficiently large, liability holders (and implicitly regulators that back the claims of liability holders) are protected against insolvency risk. That is, if an FI were to be closed by regulators before its economic net worth became zero, neither liability holders nor those regulators guaranteeing the

TABLE 14–4 **The Market Value Balance Sheet after a Rise in Interest Rates**

Assets		Liabilities	
Long-term securities	$ 75	Liabilities	$ 90
Long-term loans	17	Net worth	2
	$ 92		$ 92

claims of liability holders would stand to lose. Thus, many academics and analysts have advocated the use of market value accounting and market value of capital closure rules for all FIs, especially in the light of the book value of capital rules associated with the savings and loan disaster.[7]

The Book Value of Capital

We contrast market value or economic net worth with book value of capital or net worth. As we discuss in later sections, book value capital and capital rules based on book values are most commonly used by FI regulators. In Table 14–5, we use the same initial balance sheet as in Table 14–1, but assume that assets and liabilities are now valued at their historical book values.

In Table 14–5, the 80 in long-term securities and 20 in long-term loans reflect the historic or original book values of those assets. That is, they reflect the values when the loans were made and bonds were purchased; this may have been many years ago. Similarly on the liability side, the 90 in liabilities reflects their historical cost, and net worth or equity is now the book value of the stockholders' claims rather than the market value of those claims. For example, the book value of capital—the difference between the book value of assets and liabilities—usually comprises the following four components in banking:

1. *Par value of shares:* the face value of the common stock shares issued by the FI (the par value is usually $1 per share) times the number of shares outstanding.

2. *Surplus value of shares:* the difference between the price the public paid for common stock or shares when originally offered (e.g., $5 share) and their par values (e.g., $1) times the number of shares outstanding.

3. *Retained earnings:* the accumulated value of past profits not yet paid out in dividends to shareholders. Since these earnings could be paid out in dividends, they are part of the equity owners' stake in the FI.

4. *Loan loss reserve:* a special reserve set aside out of retained earnings to meet expected and actual losses on the portfolio.

---

[7]See, for example, G. J. Benston and G. C. Kaufman, "Risk and Solvency Regulation of Depository Institutions: Past Policies and Current Options," Monograph Series in Finance and Economics, 1988–1 (New York University, Salomon Brothers, 1988); and L. J. White, *The S and L Debacle* (New York: Oxford University Press, 1991).

TABLE 14–5 Book Value of an FI's Assets and Liabilities

Assets		Liabilities	
Long-term securities	$ 80	Short-term liabilities	$ 90
Long-term loans	20	Equity	10
	$100		$100

Consequently, book value of capital = Par value + Surplus + Retained earnings + Loan loss reserves. As the example in Table 14–5 is constructed, the book value of capital equals 10. However, invariably the *book value of equity does not equal the market value of equity* (the difference between the market value of assets and liabilities).

You can see this by examining the effects of the same credit and interest rate shocks on the FI's capital position but assuming book value accounting methods.

The Book Value of Capital and Credit Risk.   Suppose that some of the 20 in loans are in difficulty regarding repayment schedules. We assumed in Table 14–2 that the revaluation of cash flows leads to an immediate downward adjustment of the loan portfolio's market value from 20 to 12, a market value loss of 8. By contrast, under historic book value accounting methods, such as Generally Accepted Accounting Principles or GAAP, FIs have greater discretion in reflecting or timing problem loan loss recognition on their balance sheets and thus in the impact of such losses on capital. Indeed, FIs may well resist writing down the values of bad assets as long as possible to try to present a more favorable picture to depositors and regulators. Such resistance might be expected if managers believe their jobs could be threatened when they recognize such losses. Only pressure from regulators such as bank, thrift, or insurance examiners may force loss recognition and write downs in the values of problem assets. For example, in recent years on-site examinations of property-insurance companies have taken place as infrequently as once every three years; regulators analyzed off-site balance sheet information only after delays as long as 18 months. While bank Call Report data and on-site examinations are more frequent, there is still a tendency to delay writing down the book values of loans. A good example is the writing off of Mexican and Brazilian loans.[8] This only began in earnest in 1987 even though these loans were in trouble as early as 1982. Moreover, in banking even loans declared substandard by examiners remain on the balance sheet at book value. A problem loan may require a writedown of only 50 percent, while only an outright loss requires a full 100 percent charge off against the bank's equity position.

Suppose that in our example of historical book value accounting the FI is forced to recognize a loss of three rather than eight on its loan portfolio. The 3 is a charge against the 10 of stockholders' book equity value. Technically, the three loss on

---

[8]The FDIC Improvement Act of 1991 requires annual bank examinations at a minimum. Banks produce Call Reports (balance sheet data) quarterly.

TABLE 14–6 The Effect of a Loan Loss Chargeoff against the Book Value of Equity

Assets		Liabilities	
Long-term securities	$80	Liabilities	$90
Long-term loans	17	Equity (Loss of 3 on loan loss reserve)	7
	$97		$97

assets would be charged off against the loan loss reserve component of equity.[9] The new book value balance sheet is in Table 14–6.

Concept Questions

1. What are the four major components of a bank's book equity?
2. Is book value accounting for loan losses backward or forward looking?

Book Value of Capital and Interest Rate Risk.   Although book value accounting systems do recognize credit risk problems, albeit only partially and usually with a long and discretionary time lag, their failure to recognize the impact of interest rate risk is more extreme.

In our market value accounting example in Table 14–5, a rise in interest rates lowered the market values of long-term securities and loans by 8 and led to a fall in the market value of net worth from 10 to 2. In a book value accounting world, when all assets and liabilities reflect their original cost of purchase, the rise in interest rates has no effect on the value of assets, liabilities, or the book value of equity. That is, the balance sheet remains unchanged; Table 14–5 reflects the position both before and after the interest rate rise. Consider thrifts that even though interest rates rose dramatically in the early 1980s were still reporting long-term fixed-rate mortgages at historical book values and, therefore, a positive book capital position. Yet, on a market value net worth basis, their mortgages were worth far less than the book values shown on their balance sheets. Indeed, more than half of the firms in the industry were economically insolvent—many massively so.[10]

The Discrepancy between the Market and Book Values of Equity

The degree to which the book value of an FI's capital deviates from its true economic market value depends on a number of factors, especially:

1. *Interest rate volatility:* the higher interest rate volatility, the greater the discrepancy.

---

[9]Banks normally get a tax shelter against the cost of the write-off, thus reducing its cost. If losses exceed the bank's loan loss reserves, it is likely to use its retained earnings as its next line of defense.

[10]See White, *The S and L Debacle.*

2. *Examination and enforcement:* the more frequent on-site and off-site examinations and the stiffer the examiner/regulator standards regarding charging off problem loans, the smaller the discrepancy.

In actual practice, for large publicly traded FIs we can get a good idea of the discrepancy between book values (BV) and market values (MV) of equity even when the FI itself doesn't mark its balance sheet to market.

Specifically, in an efficient capital market, investors can value the shares of an FI by doing an as-if market value calculation of the assets and liabilities of the FI. This valuation is based on its current and future net earnings or dividend flows (see the section on the cost of equity capital). The stock price of the FI reflects this valuation and, thus, the market value of its shares outstanding. The market value of equity per share is therefore:

$$MV = \frac{\text{Market value of shares outstanding}}{\text{Number of shares}}$$

By contrast, the historical or book value of the FI's equity per share (BV) is equal to:

$$BV = \frac{\text{Par value of equity } + \text{ Surplus value } + \text{ Retained earnings } + \text{ Loan loss reserves}}{\text{Number of shares}}$$

Market to Book Ratio
Shows the discrepancy between the stock market value of an FI's equity and the book value of its equity.

The ratio MV/BV is often called the **market to book ratio** and shows the degree of discrepancy between the market value of an FI's equity capital as perceived by investors in the stock market and the book value of capital on its balance sheet.

The lower this ratio, the more the book value of capital *overstates* the true equity or economic net worth position of an FI as perceived by investors in the capital market. To see the size of some of these differences, look at Figure 14–2, which shows a plot of the median MV/BV ratio for the banks included in the Salomon Brothers composite over the period 1980–92. Also, look at Table 14–7, which shows the market to book equity ratios for 35 banks followed by Salomon Brothers over the period 1990–92. As you can see, the median MV/BV ratio of the eight major money center banks fluctuated between 51.9 and 122 percent of book value even over a period as short as 1990–92.

Given such discrepancies, why do regulators and FIs continue to oppose the implementation of market value accounting? The foremost accounting standards body, the *Financial Accounting Standards Board,* has recommended such a move as has the Securities and Exchange Commission.

Concept Question

1. What does a market to book ratio that is less than one imply about an FI's performance?

Arguments against Market Value Accounting

The first argument against market value (MV) accounting is that it is difficult to implement. This may be especially true for small commercial banks and thrifts with large amounts of nontraded assets such as small loans in their balance sheets. When

FIGURE 14-2

Median price to book value for the Salomon Brothers bank composite, 1980–2Q 92

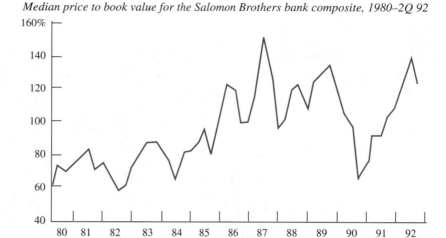

SOURCE: Salomon Brothers Inc.

it is impossible to get accurate market prices or values for assets, marking-to-market may only be done with error. A counterargument to this is that the error with market valuation of nontraded assets is still likely to be less than using original book or historical valuation. Further, with the growth of loan sales and asset securitization (see Chapters 21 and 22) indicative market prices are available on an increasing variety of loans.[11]

The second argument against market value accounting is that it introduces an unnecessary degree of variability into an FI's earnings announcements as paper capital gains and losses on assets are passed through the income statement. Critics argue that reporting unrealized capital gains and losses is distortionary if the FI actually plans to hold these assets to maturity. Insurers and bankers argue that in many cases they do hold loans and other assets to maturity and, therefore, never actually realize capital gains or losses. The counterargument is that FIs are increasingly trading, selling, and securitizing assets rather than holding them to maturity. Further, the failure to reflect capital gains and losses from interest rate changes means that the FI's equity position fails to reflect its true interest rate risk exposure.

The third argument against market value accounting is that FIs are less willing to take on longer-term asset exposures, such as commercial mortgage loans and C&I loans, if these assets have to be continuously marked-to-market to reflect changing credit quality and interest rates. For example, as shown in Chapter 5, long-term assets are more interest rate sensitive than short-term assets. The concern is that market value accounting may interfere with the FIs' special functions as lenders and monitors and may even result in (or accentuate) a major credit crunch. Of the three arguments against market value accounting, this one is probably the most persuasive to regulators concerned about small business finance and economic growth.[12]

---

[11]In 1993, Congress also proposed a number of initiatives to securitize small business loans using a public agency similar to the Government National Mortgage Association (GNMA), the public agency that facilitates residential mortgage securitization.

[12]This was a particularly sensitive issue in the early 1990s when a credit crunch was already perceived to exist and the proportion of C&I loans in bank portfolios was falling (also see Chapter 1).

TABLE 14–7   Historical Perspective of Market Price to Stated Book Value Ratios for 35 Banks

| | 1990 | | | | 1991 | | | | 1992 | | | | Bk. Val. Per Shr. |
	Mar	Jun	Sep	Dec	Mar	Jun	Sep	Dec	Mar	Jun	Sep	12 Nov	30 Sep 92
Bankers Trust NY	134.4%	144.9%	104.7%	141.3%	135.5%	141.1%	174.3%	182.5%	153.7%	156.5%	163.2%	169.6%	$39.07
Chase Manhattan	79.3	68.8	40.8	35.5	52.1	53.9	59.8	56.3	77.3	87.8	70.7	80.9	31.82
Chemical Banking	68.1	74.6	47.3	32.6	52.3	63.5	73.3	68.5	107.3	119.6	103.0	115.3	31.67
Citicorp	90.4	88.0	55.0	51.9	61.5	61.7	66.9	48.9	77.94	98.1	72.0	85.3	21.7
J. P. Morgan & Co.	154.9	148.2	132.7	175.5	178.1	193.1	208.3	233.3	189.5	175.7	186.1	190.2	33.45
Republic NY Corp.	128.3	129.9	99.7	124.0	137.3	144.7	157.7	158.4	135.0	127.5	133.1	137.7	32.4
Bank of Boston Corp.	54.4	47.3	35.2	32.5	47.6	39.7	53.6	61.6	93.6	124.4	96.9	111.5	20.52
First Chicago	86.2	81.5	47.5	45.5	60.8	57.6	72.3	70.6	82.4	100.8	96.7	100.5	32.85
Money Center Median	**86.2%**	**81.5%**	**53.2%**	**51.9%**	**61.5%**	**61.7%**	**72.6%**	**69.6%**	**100.4%**	**122.0%**	**100.0%**	**113.4%**	
Fleet Financial Group	118.7	104.1	68.1	62.3	90.9	121.6	127.3	137.1	135.9	133.1	130.4	150.0	$19.08
CoreStates Financial	147.3	149.5	97.3	125.0	140.4	145.4	162.0	170.4	155.9	168.5	167.8	168.6	30.02
Mellon Bank Corp.	91.7	85.7	63.9	83.3	89.3	100.1	109.0	111.5	120.6	122.8	122.1	137.1	35.64
PNC Financial Corp.	139.4	103.2	76.6	81.0	121.6	128.1	141.4	154.4	159.0	169.5	155.8	166.5	32.5
Banc One Corp.	177.7	169.0	129.9	153.2	192.5	201.0	226.1	226.5	239.0	228.8	218.0	236.9	20.47
National City Corp.	135.8	138.2	99.0	116.7	126.9	125.2	134.3	130.8	140.5	163.7	156.0	164.3	28.45
NBD Bancorp	128.1	131.3	106.5	129.4	151.9	130.1	155.5	165.0	154.0	150.2	154.8	149.5	18.98
First Bank System	106.0	111.0	87.2	97.6	128.9	132.2	144.2	163.5	175.4	167.8	149.8	158.4	16.10
Norwest Corp.	140.0	153.8	101.9	138.0	159.1	169.5	200.0	211.5	198.3	201.2	200.5	215.9	19.45
NationsBank	144.6	130.3	74.1	79.6	116.8	114.4	111.3	150.3	160.6	164.4	147.6	163.8	30.06
Wachovia Corp.	154.2	154.1	131.4	151.3	181.2	180.4	192.9	196.6	191.5	185.8	181.1	179.9	31.61
Barnett Banks	111.4	118.1	64.8	70.1	85.8	100.3	113.1	123.9	116.1	133.1	133.3	151.4	28.32
SunTrust Banks	125.9	116.6	95.2	125.1	145.4	158.1	189.3	200.2	177.0	195.7	138.6	140.8	28.77
BankAmerica Corp.	115.7	117.4	77.3	97.4	128.0	124.8	137.8	116.6	136.3	129.5	123.6	122.9	34.99
First Interstate	91.8	106.8	57.1	59.1	84.0	83.6	92.1	92.1	110.0	122.0	113.2	118.3	34.44
Wells Fargo & Co.	139.5	147.4	82.4	100.8	124.7	117.8	125.4	107.4	126.1	132.5	121.3	132.0	56.25
U.S. Bancorp	126.5	103.1	89.9	102.1	137.8	97.4	149.8	155.6	147.5	160.6	149.8	161.5	15.02
Regional Median	**127.3%**	**117.4%**	**82.4%**	**101.5%**	**127.5%**	**125.0%**	**139.6%**	**152.4%**	**154.0%**	**162.2%**	**148.7%**	**158.4%**	
35-Bank Median	**106.8%**	**99.5%**	**67.8%**	**76.7%**	**94.5%**	**93.4%**	**106.1%**	**111.0%**	**127.2%**	**142.1%**	**124.4%**	**135.9%**	

Source: Salomon Brothers Inc.

Actual Capital Rules

We have just discussed the advantages and disadvantages of book- and market-based measures of an FI's capital. As noted, most FI regulators have chosen some form of book value accounting standard to measure an FI's capital adequacy. The major exception is the SEC. Along with the NYSE and major stock exchanges, the SEC imposes on securities firms, retail brokers, and specialists a capital or net worth rule that is to all intents and purposes a market value accounting rule.

Next, we examine the capital adequacy rules imposed in key FI sectors: (1) commercial banking and thrifts, (2) P-C insurance, (3) securities firms, and (4) life insurance. Because many of these rules currently differ considerably across financial firms, the consolidation of the U.S. financial industry into financial conglomerates—or universal banks—on German or British lines would be more difficult than if market value accounting rules were adopted across all sectors of the financial services industry. There is, however, a clear movement toward similar risk-based capital rules in banking, the thrift industry, and insurance.

Capital Adequacy in the Commercial Banking and Thrift Industry

The FDIC Improvement Act of 1991 has required that banks and thrifts adopt essentially the same capital requirements. While there are some minor differences, the two industries have converged toward a level playing field as far as capital requirements are concerned. Given this, we concentrate on describing the recent evolution of capital requirements in commercial banking.

Since 1987, U.S. commercial banks have faced two different capital requirements: a capital-assets (leverage) ratio and a risk-based capital ratio that is in turn subdivided into a Tier I capital risk-based ratio and a total capital (Tier I plus Tier II capital) risk-based ratio. We describe these in more detail next.

The Capital Assets Ratio (or Leverage Ratio)

Leverage Ratio
Ratio of an FI's core capital to assets.

The capital assets or **leverage ratio** measures the ratio of a bank's book value of primary or core capital to its assets. The lower this ratio, the more leveraged it is. Primary or core capital is a bank's common equity (book value) plus qualifying cumulative perpetual preferred stock plus minority interest in equity accounts of consolidated subsidiaries.

With the passage of the FDIC Improvement Act in 1991, a bank's capital adequacy is assessed according to where its leverage ratio (*L*):

$$L = \frac{\text{Core capital}}{\text{Assets}}$$

places in one of five target zones. Note these in column 3 of Table 14–8.

If its leverage ratio is greater than 5 percent, it is well capitalized. If it is 4 percent or more, it is adequately capitalized; under 4 percent, it is undercapitalized; under 3 percent, significantly undercapitalized; and 2 percent or under, critically undercapitalized.

TABLE 14–8   Specifications of Capital Categories for Prompt Corrective Action (in percent)

	(1) *Total Risk-* *Based Ratio*		*(2)* *Tier 1 Risk-* *Based Ratio*		*(3)* *Tier 1 Leverage* *Ratio*		*Capital Directive/Other*
Well capitalized	10 or above	&	6 or above	&	5 or above	&	Not subject to a capital directive to meet a specific level for any capital measure
Adequately capitalized	8 or above	&	4 or above	&	4 or above*	&	Does not meet the definition of well capitalized
Undercapitalized	Under 8	or	Under 4	or	Under 4†		
Significantly undercapitalized	Under 6	or	Under 3	or	Under 3		
Critically undercapitalized							Ratio of tangible equity to total assets 2 or under‡

*3 percent or above for composite one-rated banks and savings associations that are not experiencing or anticipating significant growth.

†Under 3 percent for composite one-rated banks and savings associations that are not experiencing or anticipating significant growth.

‡Staff is proposing to define tangible equity as core capital elements plus cumulative perpetual preferred stock, net of all intangibles except limited amounts of purchased mortgage servicing rights.

SOURCE: Federal Reserve Board of Governors, September 10, 1993.

Associated with each zone is a mandatory set of actions as well as a set of discretionary actions that regulators have to take. The idea here is to put teeth into minimum capital requirements and to limit the ability of regulators to show forbearance to the worst capitalized banks. Analysts blame such forbearance and regulator discretion for the size of the losses being borne by taxpayers due to the widespread collapse of thrifts and the Federal Savings and Loan Insurance Corporation (FSLIC) in the 1980s and the current insolvency of the FDIC (see Chapter 15).

Prompt Corrective Action
Mandatory actions that have to be taken by regulators as a bank's capital ratio falls.

Since December 18, 1992, regulators must take specific actions—**prompt corrective action** (PCA)—whenever a bank falls outside of the zone 1 or well-capitalized category. Most important, a receiver must be appointed when its book value of capital to assets (leverage) ratio falls to 2 percent or under.[13] That is, receivership is mandatory even before the book value ratio falls to 0 percent.

Unfortunately, the leverage ratio has three problems as a measure of capital adequacy:

1. *Market value.* Even if a bank is closed when its leverage ratio falls below 2 percent, a 2 percent book capital-asset ratio could be consistent with a massive *negative* market value net worth. That is, there is no assurance that depositors and regulators (including taxpayers) are adequately protected against losses. Many thrifts that were closed with low book capital values in the 1980s had negative net worths on a market value basis exceeding 30 percent.

---

[13]Admittedly, there are a number of loopholes and delaying tactics managers and stockholders might exploit, especially through the courts.

2. *Asset risk.* By taking the denominator of the leverage ratio as total assets, it fails to take into account, even partially, the different credit and interest rate risks of the assets that comprise total assets.

3. *Off-balance-sheet activities.* Despite the massive growth in bank off-balance-sheet activities, no capital is required to be held to meet the potential insolvency risks involved with such contingent assets and liabilities.

Risk-Based Capital Ratios

Basel Agreement
The requirement to impose risk-based capital ratios on banks in major industrialized countries.

In light of the weaknesses of the simple capital-assets ratio just described, U.S. bank regulators formally agreed with other member countries of the Bank for International Settlements (BIS), to implement two new risk-based capital ratios for all commercial banks under their jurisdiction. The BIS phased in and fully implemented these risk-based capital ratios on January 1, 1993, under what has become known as the **Basel Agreement**.

Regulators currently enforce the Basel Agreement alongside the traditional leverage ratio. To be adequately capitalized, a bank has to hold a minimum total capital (Tier I core capital plus Tier II supplementary capital) to risk adjusted assets ratio of 8 percent, that is:

Total Risk-Based Capital Ratio
The ratio of the total capital to the risk-adjusted assets of an FI.

$$\textbf{Total risk-based capital ratio} = \frac{\text{Total capital (Tier I plus Tier II)}}{\text{Risk-adjusted assets}} \geq 8\%$$

In addition, the Tier I core capital component of total capital has its own minimum guideline:

Tier I Core Capital Ratio
The ratio of core capital to the risk-adjusted assets of an FI.

$$\textbf{Tier I (core) capital ratio} = \frac{\text{Core capital (Tier I)}}{\text{Risk-adjusted assets}} \geq 4\%$$

That is, of the 8 percent total risk-based capital ratio, a minimum of 4 percent has to be held in core or primary capital.[14]

Apart from their use to define adequately capitalized banks, risk-based capital ratios also define—along with the traditional leverage ratio—well capitalized, undercapitalized, significantly undercapitalized, and critically undercapitalized banks as part of the prompt corrective action program under the FDIC Improvement Act. As with the simple leverage ratio, for both the total risk-based capital ratio and the Tier I risk-based capital ratios, these five zones assess capital adequacy and the actions regulators are mandated to take. See Tables 14–8 and 14–9.

Unlike the simple capital-asset (leverage) ratio, however, the calculation of these risk-based capital adequacy measures is quite complex. Their major innovation is to distinguish among the different credit risks on the balance sheet as well as the credit risk inherent in instruments off the balance sheet through the use of a risk-adjusted assets denominator in these capital adequacy ratios. In a very rough fashion, these capital ratios mark-to-market the on- and off-balance-sheet positions of the bank to reflect its credit risk.[15] We discuss the limitations of these new risk-based ratios after we have taken a closer look at their calculation.

---

[14]The difference between the 8 percent and the 4 percent can be made up with noncore or other capital sources; see the description in Table 14–10.

[15]As we discuss later, interest rate risk will be integrated into the risk-based capital requirements in 1994 (see also Chapter 7).

TABLE 14–9 Summary of Prompt Corrective Action Provisions of the Federal Deposit Insurance Corporation Improvement Act of 1991

Zone	Mandatory Provisions	Discretionary Provisions
1. Well capitalized		
2. Adequately capitalized	1. No brokered deposits, except with FDIC approval	
3. Undercapitalized	1. Suspend dividends and management fees 2. Require capital restoration plan 3. Restrict asset growth 4. Approval required for acquisitions, branching, and new activities 5. No brokered deposits	1. Order recapitalization 2. Restrict interaffiliate transactions 3. Restrict deposit interest rates 4. Restrict certain other activities 5. Any other action that would better carry out prompt corrective action
4. Significantly undercapitalized	1. Same as for Zone 3 2. Order recapitalization* 3. Restrict interaffiliate transactions* 4. Restrict deposit interest rates* 5. Pay of officers restricted	1. Any Zone 3 discretionary actions 2. Conservatorship or receivership if fails to submit or implement plan or recapitalize pursuant to order 3. Any other Zone 5 provision, if such action is necessary to carry out prompt corrective action
5. Critically undercapitalized	1. Same as for Zone 4 2. Receiver/conservator within 90 days* 3. Receiver if still in Zone 5 four quarters after becoming critically undercapitalized 4. Suspend payments on subordinated debt* 5. Restrict certain other activities	

*Not required if primary supervisor determines action would not serve purpose of prompt corrective action or if certain other conditions are met.

SOURCE: Federal Reserve Board of Governors, September 10, 1993.

Calculating Risk-Based Capital Ratios

A bank's capital is the numerator of the risk-based capital ratios. We begin by looking at the definition of Tier I and Tier II capital—the numerator of the new ratios—and then look at the definition of risk-adjusted assets—the denominator.

Capital.   A bank's capital is divided into Tier I and Tier II. Tier I capital is primary or core capital and must be a minimum of 4 percent of a bank's risk-adjusted assets, while Tier II, or supplementary capital, is the make-weight such that:

$$\text{Tier I Capital} + \text{Tier II Capital} \geq 8\% \text{ of Risk-Adjusted Assets}$$

Tier I Capital.   Look at the definitions of Tier I core capital and Tier II supplementary capital in Table 14–10.

Tier I capital is closely linked to a bank's book value of equity reflecting the concept of the core capital contribution of a bank's owners.[16] Basically, it includes the book value of common equity, plus an amount of perpetual (nonmaturing) preferred stock, plus minority equity interests held by the bank in subsidiaries minus goodwill. Goodwill is an accounting item that reflects the excess a bank pays over market value in purchasing or acquiring other banks or subsidiaries.

[16]However, loan loss reserves are assigned to Tier II capital on the basis that they often reflect losses that have already occurred, rather than losses or insolvency risks that may occur in the future.

Tier II Capital.   Tier II capital is a broad array of secondary capital resources. Tier II includes a bank's loan loss reserves up to a maximum of 1.25 percent of risk-adjusted assets plus various convertible and subordinated debt instruments with maximum caps.

Risk-Adjusted Assets.   Risk-adjusted assets is the denominator of the risk-based capital ratios. Two components comprise risk-adjusted assets:

Risk-adjusted assets = Risk-adjusted on-balance-sheet assets +
Risk-adjusted off-balance-sheet assets

Next, we look at each component separately.

Risk-Adjusted On-Balance-Sheet Assets.   Under the new capital plan, each bank assigns its assets to one of four categories of credit risk exposure: 0 percent, 20 percent, 50 percent, 100 percent. In Table 14–11, we list the key categories and assets in these categories. The main features are that cash assets; U.S. T-bills, notes and bonds of all maturities; and GNMA (Ginnie Mae) mortgage-backed securities—mortgage securitization packages backed by a government agency—are all zero risk based. In the 20 percent class are U.S. agency-backed securities, municipal issued general obligation bonds, FHLMC and FNMA mortgage-backed securities as well as interbank deposits.[17] In the 50 percent class are regular residential mortgage loans and other municipal (revenue) bonds. Finally, all other loans such as C&I, consumer, and credit card are in the 100 percent risk category. To figure the risk-adjusted assets of the bank, we would multiply the dollar amount of assets it has in each category by the appropriate risk weight.

Consider the balance sheet in Table 14–12 as an example. Then, the risk-adjusted value of the bank's on-balance-sheet assets would be:

$$\sum_{i=1}^{n} w_i a_i$$

where

w_i = Risk weight of the ith asset
a_i = Dollar (book) value of the ith asset on the balance sheet

Thus, in our example:

Risk-Adjusted On-Balance-Sheet Assets = 0(5) + 0(5) + 0(10) + .2(10) + .2(5)
+ .5(30) + 1(35) = 0 + 0 + 0 + 2 + 1 + 15 + 35 = \$53 million.

While the simple book value of on-balance-sheet assets is \$100 million, its risk-adjusted value is \$53 million.

Risk-Adjusted Off-Balance-Sheet Activities.   The risk-adjusted value of assets is only one component of the capital ratio denominator; the other is the credit risk-adjusted value of the bank's off-balance-sheet activities. The calculation of the risk-adjusted values of the off-balance-sheet activities involves some initial

---

[17]Bonds backed by the full taxing authority of a municipal government. FHLMC and Federal National Mortgage Association (FNMA) are quasi-government or government-backed mortgage securitization agencies. (See Chapter 21 for more details on these agencies.)

TABLE 14–10   Summary Definition of Qualifying Capital for Bank Holding Companies
(Using the Year-end 1992 Standards)

Components	*Minimum Requirements after Transition Period*
Core capital (Tier I)	Must equal or exceed 4 percent of weighted-risk assets.
Common stockholders' equity	No limit.
Qualifying cumulative and noncumulative perpetual preferred stock	Limited to 25 percent of the sum of common stock, minority interests, and qualifying perpetual preferred stock.
Minority interest in equity accounts of consolidated subsidiaries	Organizations should avoid using minority interests to introduce elements not otherwise qualifying for Tier I capital.
Less: Goodwill*	
Supplementary capital (Tier II)	Total of Tier II is limited to 100 percent of Tier I.†
Allowance for loan and lease losses	Limited to 1.25 percent of weighted-risk assets.
Perpetual preferred stock	No limit within Tier II.
Hybrid capital instruments, perpetual debt, and mandatory convertible securities	No limit within Tier II.
Subordinated debt and intermediate-term preferred stock (original weighted-average maturity of five years or more)	Subordinated debt and intermediate-term preferred stock are limited to 50 percent of Tier I; amortized for capital purposes as they approach maturity.‡
Revaluation reserves (equity and buildings)	Not included; organizations encouraged to disclose; may be evaluated on a case-by-case basis for international comparisons; and taken into account in making an overall assessment of capital.
Deductions (from sum of Tier I and Tier II)	
Investments in unconsolidated subsidiaries	As a general rule, one half of the aggregate investments would be deducted from Tier I capital and one half from Tier II capital.§
Reciprocal holdings of banking organizations' capital securities	
Other deductions (such as other subsidiaries or joint ventures) as determined by supervisory authority	On a case-by-case basis or as a matter of policy after formal rulemaking.
Total capital (Tier I + Tier II − Deductions)	Must equal or exceed 8 percent of weighted risk assets.

*Goodwill on the books of bank holding companies before March 12, 1988, would be grandfathered for the transition period.

†Amounts in excess of limitations are permitted but do not qualify as capital.

‡Amounts in excess of limitations are permitted but do not qualify as capital.

§A proportionately greater amount may be deducted from Tier I capital if the risks associated with the subsidiary so warrant.

SOURCE: Federal Reserve Board of Governors, Press Release, January 1989, Attachment II.

**TABLE 14–11   Summary of the Risk-Based Capital Standards for
On-Balance-Sheet Items**

Risk Categories

Category 1 (0% weight)
  Cash, Federal Reserve Bank balances. Securities of the U.S. Treasury, OECD governments, and
    some U.S. agencies.

Category 2 (20% weight)
  Cash items in the process of collection. U.S. and OECD interbank deposits and guaranteed claims.
    Some non-OECD bank and government deposits and securities. General obligation municipal bonds.
    Some mortgage-backed securities. Claims collateralized by the U.S. Treasury and some other
    government securities.

Category 3 (50% weight)
  Loans fully secured by first liens on one to four family residential properties. Other (revenue)
    municipal bonds.

Category 4 (100% weight)
  All other on-balance-sheet assets not listed above, including:
    loans to private entities and individuals, some claims on non-OECD governments and banks, real
    assets, and investments in subsidiaries.

SOURCE: Federal Reserve Board of Governors, Press Release, January 1989, Attachment III.

segregation of these activities. In particular, the calculation of the credit risk exposure or the risk-adjusted asset amount of contingent or guarantee contracts, such as letters of credit, differs from the calculation of the risk-adjusted asset amounts for foreign exchange and interest rate forward, option, and swap contracts. We consider the risk-adjusted asset value of off-balance-sheet guarantee type contracts and contingent contracts and then derivative or market contracts.

The Risk-Adjusted Asset Value of Off-Balance-Sheet Contingent Guarantee Contracts.   The beginning step in calculating the risk-adjusted asset values of these off-balance-sheet items is to convert them into credit equivalent amounts; that is, into amounts equivalent to an on-balance-sheet item. Consider the appropriate conversion factors in Table 14–13.[18]

From Table 14–13, note that standby letter of credit guarantees issued by banks to back commercial paper have a 100 percent conversion factor rating; this means they have the same credit risk as on-balance-sheet loans. Future performance-related SLCs and unused loan commitments of more than one year have a 50 percent conversion factor. Standard trade-related commercial letters of credit and banker's acceptances sold have a 20 percent conversion factor. Other loan commitments, those with less than one year to run, impose no credit risk on the bank and have a 0 percent credit conversion factor. To see how off-balance-sheet activities are incorporated into the risk-based ratio, we can extend the example of the bank in Table 14–13. Assume that in addition to having $53 million in risk-adjusted assets on its balance sheet, it also has the following off-balance-sheet contingencies or guarantees:

[18]Appropriate here means those used by the regulators and required to be used by banks rather than being equal to conversion factors that might be calculated from a contingent asset valuation (option) model. Indeed, regulators used no such valuation model in deriving the conversion factors in Table 14–13.

TABLE 14–12 A Bank's Balance Sheet
(in millions)

Weight		Assets	Liabilities	
	Cash	$5	Total Tier I plus	
0%	T-Bills	5	Tier II Capital	$10
	T notes and bonds	10		
20%	General obligation municipal bonds	10	Liabilities	90
	FNMA securities	5		
50%	Residential mortgages	30		
100%	Other Loans	35		
		100		100

1. $80 million two-year loan commitments to large U.S. corporations.
2. $10 million standby letter of credit backing an issue of commercial paper.
3. $50 million commercial letters of credit.

Credit Equivalent Amount
The credit risk exposure of an off-balance-sheet item calculated by multiplying the face value of an OBS instrument by a conversion factor.

To find out the risk-adjusted asset value for these off-balance-sheet items, we follow a two-step process: In the first step, we multiply the dollar amount outstanding of these items to derive the **Credit Equivalent Amounts** using the conversion factors (CF) listed in Table 14–13.

OBS Item	Face Value		Conversion Factor		Credit Equivalent Amount
Two-year loan commitment	$80	×	.5	=	$40
Standby letter of credit	10	×	1.0	=	10
Commercial letter of credit	50	×	.2	=	10

Thus, the credit equivalent amounts of loan commitments, standby letters of credit, and commercial letters of credit are respectively $40, $10, and $10 million. These conversion factors convert an off-balance-sheet item into an equivalent credit or on-balance-sheet item.

In the second step, we multiply these credit equivalent amounts by their appropriate risk weights. The appropriate risk weight in each case depends on the underlying counterparty to the off-balance-sheet activity such as a municipality, a government, or a corporation. For example, if the underlying party being guaranteed were a municipality issuing general obligation (GO) bonds, the bank would have issued an off-balance-sheet standby letter of credit backing the credit risk of a municipal GO issue, and the risk weight would be .2. However, in our example, the counterparty being guaranteed is a *private agent* in all three cases: a corporate loan

---

TABLE 14–13 Conversion Factors for Off-Balance-Sheet Contingent or Guarantee Contracts

Direct credit substitute standby letters of credit (100%)
Performance-related standby letters of credit (50%)
Unused portion of loan commitments with original maturity of more than one year (50%)
Commercial letters of credit (20%)
Bankers acceptances conveyed (20%)
Other loan commitments (0%)

SOURCE: Federal Reserve Board of Governors, Press Release, January 1989, Attachment IV.

commitment, a guarantee underlying commercial paper, and a commercial letter of credit. Thus, the appropriate risk weight in each case is one. Note that if the counterparty had been the central government, the risk weight would be zero. The appropriate risk weights for our example follow:

OBS Item	Credit Equivalent Amount		Risk Weight (w_i)		Risk-Adjusted Asset Amount
Two-year loan commitment	$40	×	1.0	=	$40
Standby letter of credit	10	×	1.0	=	10
Commercial letter of credit	10	×	1.0	=	10
					$60

The bank's risk-adjusted asset value of its OBS contingencies and guarantees is $60 million.

The Risk-Adjusted Asset Value of Off-Balance-Sheet Market Contracts or Derivative Instruments.   In addition to having OBS contingencies and guarantees, modern FIs heavily engage in buying and selling OBS futures, options, forwards, swaps, caps, and other derivative securities contracts for interest rate and foreign exchange management and hedging reasons as well as products to sell to their customers. Each of these positions potentially exposes banks to **counterparty credit risk,** that is, the risk the counterparty (or other side of a contract) will default when suffering large actual or potential losses on its position. Such defaults mean that a bank would have to go back to the market to replace such contracts at (potentially) less favorable terms.

Counterparty Credit Risk
The risk that the other side of a contract will default on payment obligations.

Under the risk-based capital ratio rules, we make a major distinction between exchange-traded derivative security contracts (e.g., Chicago Board of Trade's exchange traded options), and over-the-counter traded instruments (e.g., forwards, swaps, caps, and floors). The credit or default risk of exchange traded derivatives is approximately zero because when a counterparty defaults on its obligations the exchange itself adopts the counterparty's obligations in full. However, no such guarantees exist for bilaterally agreed, over-the-counter contracts originated and traded outside organized exchanges. Hence, most OBS futures and options positions have no capital requirements for a bank while most forwards, swaps, caps, and floors do.[19]

The calculation of the risk-adjusted asset values of OBS market contracts also requires a two-step approach: First, we calculate a conversion factor to create credit equivalent amounts. And second, we multiply the credit equivalent amounts by the appropriate risk weights.

Specifically, we convert the notional or face values of all nonexchange traded swap, forward, and other derivative contracts into credit equivalent amounts. The credit equivalent amount itself is divided into a *potential exposure* element and a *current exposure* element. That is:

$$\begin{array}{l}\text{Credit equivalent} = \text{Potential exposure} + \text{Current exposure} \\ \text{amount of OBS} \qquad\qquad (\$) \qquad\qquad\qquad (\$) \\ \text{derivative} \\ \text{security item}(\$)\end{array}$$

Potential Exposure
The risk of a counterparty to a derivative securities contract defaulting in the future.

The **potential exposure** component reflects the credit risk of the counterparty to the contract defaulting in the *future.* The probability of such an occurrence depends on future volatility of either interest rates for an interest rate contract or exchange rates for an exchange rate contract. The Bank of England and the Federal Reserve carried out an enormous number of simulations and found that FX rates were far more volatile than interest rates.[20] Thus, the potential exposure conversion factors in Table 14–14 are larger for foreign exchange contracts than for interest rate contracts. Also, note the larger potential exposure credit risk for longer-term contracts of both types.

Current Exposure
The cost of replacing a derivative securities contract at today's prices.

In addition to calculating the potential exposure of an OBS market instrument, a bank also has to calculate its **current exposure** with the instrument. This reflects the cost of replacing a contract should a counterparty default today. The bank calculates this replacement cost or current exposure by replacing the rate or price that was initially in the contract with the current rate or price for a similar contract and recalculates all the current and future cash flows that would be generated under current rate or price terms.[21] The bank would discount any future cash flows to give a current present-value measure of the replacement cost of the contract. Since each swap or forward is in some sense unique, this involves a considerable computer processing task for the FI's management information systems. Indeed, specialized service firms are likely to perform this task for smaller banks.[22]

Once the current and potential exposure amounts are summed to produce the credit equivalent amount for each contract, we multiply this dollar number by a risk weight to produce the final risk-adjusted asset amount for OBS market contracts. In general, the appropriate risk weight is .5 or 50 percent. That is:

[19]This may create some degree of preference among banks for using exchange-traded hedging instruments rather than over-the-counter instruments because using the former may save a bank costly capital resources.

[20]The Bank of England and the Federal Reserve employed a Monte-Carlo simulation approach in deciding on the size of the appropriate conversion factors. See C. W. Smith, C. W. Smithson, and D. S. Wilford, *Managing Financial Risk* (New York: Ballinger Publishing Company, 1990), pp. 255–56.

[21]For example, suppose a two-year forward foreign exchange contract was entered into in January 1993 at \$1.55/£. In January 1994, the bank has to evaluate the credit risk of the contract which now has one year remaining. To do this, it replaces the agreed forward rate \$1.55/£ with the forward rate on current one-year forward contracts, \$1.65/£. It then recalculates its net gain or loss on the contract, if it had to be replaced at this price. This is the contract's replacement cost.

[22]One large New York money center bank has to calculate, on average, the replacement cost of more than 6,000 different forward contracts alone.

TABLE 14–14 Credit Conversion Factors for Interest Rate and Foreign Exchange Contracts in Calculating Potential Exposure

Remaining Maturity	(1) Interest Rate Contracts	(2) Exchange Rate Contracts
One year or less	0	1.0%
Over one year	0.5%	5.0%

SOURCE: Federal Reserve Board of Governors, Press Release, January 1989, Attachment IV.

Risk-adjusted = Total credit equivalent amount × .5 (risk weight)
asset value of
OBS market
contracts

Continuing our example of calculating the risk-based capital ratio for a bank, suppose that the bank had taken one interest-rate hedging position in the fixed-floating interest rate swap market for 10 years with a notional dollar amount of $100 million and one two-year forward $/£ foreign exchange contract for $40 million. We calculate the credit equivalent amount for each item or contract as:

Type of Contract (Remaining Maturity)	Notional Principal	×	Potential Exposure Conversion Factor	=	Potential Exposure ($)	Replacement Cost	Current Exposure	=	Credit Equivalent Amount
10-year fixed-floating interest rate swap	$100	×	.005	=	$.5	3	3		$3.5
Two-year forward foreign exchange contract	$ 40	×	.05	=	2	−1	0		2

Let's look closely at these calculations. For the 10-year fixed-floating interest rate swap, the notional value (contract face value) of the swap is $100 million. Since this is a long-term, over one year interest rate market contract, its face value is multiplied by .005 to get a potential exposure or credit risk equivalent value of 0.5 million (see column 1 of Table 14–14). We add this potential exposure to the replacement cost (current exposure) of this contract to the bank. The replacement cost reflects the cost of having to enter into a new 10-year fixed-floating swap agreement at today's interest rates for the remaining life of the swap. Assuming that interest rates today are less favorable, on a present value basis the cost of replacing the existing contract for its remaining life would be $3 million. Thus, the total credit equivalent amount—current plus potential exposures—for the interest rate swap is $3.5 million.

Next, we can look at the foreign exchange two-year forward contract of $40 million face value. Since this is a long-term contract, the potential (future) credit risk is

$40 million $\times$ .05 or $2 million (see column 2 Table 14–14). However, its replacement cost is *minus* $1 million. That is, in this example our bank actually stands to gain if the counterparty were to default. Exactly why the counterparty would do this when it is in the money is unclear. However, regulators cannot permit a bank to gain from a default by a counterparty as this might produce all types of perverse risk-taking incentives. Consequently, if the replacement cost of a contract is negative, as in our example, current exposure has to be set equal to zero (as shown). Thus, the sum of potential exposure ($2) and current exposure ($0) produces a total credit equivalent amount of $2 million for this contract.

Since the bank just has these two OBS derivative contracts, summing the two credit equivalent amounts produces a total credit equivalent amount of $3.5 + $2 = $5.5 million for the bank's OBS market contracts. The next step is to multiply this credit equivalent amount with the appropriate risk weight. Specifically, to calculate the risk-adjusted asset value for the bank's OBS derivative or market contracts, we multiply the credit equivalent amount by the appropriate risk weight, which for virtually all over-the-counter derivative security products is .5 or 50 percent:

$$
\begin{array}{lll}
\text{Risk-adjusted} = & \$5.5 \text{ million} \times & 0.5 = \$2.75 \text{ million.} \\
\text{asset value of} & \text{(credit} & \text{(risk} \\
\text{OBS derivatives} & \text{equivalent} & \text{weight)} \\
& \text{amount)} &
\end{array}
$$

Calculating the Overall Risk-Based Capital Position of a Bank.   We can now calculate our bank's overall capacity adequacy in the light of the risk-based capital requirements. From our example, we have calculated:

1. Tier I plus Tier II capital = $10 million
2. Risk-adjusted assets on balance sheet = $53 million
3. Risk-adjusted assets off balance sheet =
   (*a*) Contingent/Guarantee items = $60 million
   (*b*) Market contracts/Derivative securities = $2.75 million

Thus, the total risk-based capital ratio is:

$$
\frac{\text{Total capital}}{\text{Risk-adjusted assets}} = \frac{(1)}{(2)+(3a)+(3b)} = \frac{10}{53+60+2.75} = \frac{10}{115.75}
$$
$$
= 8.64\%
$$

Since the minimum risk-based capital ratio required is 8 percent, this bank has adequate capital, exceeding the required minimum by 0.64 percent.

Interest Rate Risk and Risk-Based Capital.   Our bank's 8.64 percent is only adequate as long as it is not exposed to undue interest rate risk. The reason is that the risk-based capital ratio only takes into account the adequacy of a bank's capital to meet both its on- and off-balance sheet credit risks. Not explicitly accounted for is the insolvency risk emanating from interest rate risk (duration mismatches) and asset concentrations.

To meet this criticism, banks are required to hold additional capital if they are excessively exposed to interest rate risk. In Chapter 7, we discussed why the Federal Reserve views any net worth loss exposure as a percent of assets exceeding 1 percent as excessive and requires additional capital. Thus, if our bank had a net worth-assets exposure of 1.68 percent to interest rate shocks, it would be required to hold additional capital over and above the 8 percent risk-based capital ratio equal to:

$$(1.68\% - 1\%) \times \$100 \text{ million} = \$680,000$$

In our example, the bank with $10 million in capital and risk-adjusted assets of $115.75 million had an actual risk-based capital ratio of 8.64 percent. This meant that it had capital in excess of the 8 percent (minimum) level of $740,800. This $740,800 excess would be more than sufficient to meet the additional capital of $680,000 required by regulators for the bank's interest rate risk exposure.[23]

Criticisms of the Risk-Based Capital Ratio.   The risk-based capital requirement seeks to improve on the simple leverage ratio by: (1) more systematically accounting for credit risk differences among assets and (2) incorporating off-balance-sheet risk exposures. Unfortunately, it has a number of conceptual and applicability weaknesses.

1. *Risk weights.* It is unclear how closely the four risk weight categories reflect true credit risk. For example, residential mortgage loans have a 50 percent risk weight, while commercial loans have a 100 percent risk weight. Taken literally, these relative weights imply that commercial loans are exactly twice as risky as mortgage loans.[24]

2. *Balance sheet incentive problems.* The fact that different assets have different risk weights may induce bankers to engage in balance sheet asset allocation games. For example, given any amount of total capital, a bank can always increase its reported risk-based capital ratio by reducing its risk-adjusted assets, the denominator of the ratio. There are a number of interesting opportunities for an FI manager to do this under the new scheme. For example, residential mortgages have a 50 percent risk weight while GNMA mortgage-backed securities have 0 percent risk weight. Suppose a bank pools all its mortgages and then sells them to outside investors. If it then replaced the mortgages sold by buying GNMA securities backing similar pools of mortgages to those securitized, it could significantly reduce its risk-adjusted asset amount. Overall, the incentives and opportunities for balance sheet games may have increased, especially if bank managers believe certain asset and OBS risks are either over- or underpriced in terms of the risk-based capital weights.

3. *Portfolio aspects.* The new plan also ignores credit risk portfolio diversification opportunities. As we discuss in Chapter 8, when returns on assets have negative or low positive correlations, an FI may lower its portfolio risk through diversification. As constructed, the new capital adequacy plan is essentially a linear risk measure that ignores correlations or covariances among assets and asset groups such as residential mortgages and commercial loans.[25] That is, the banker weights each asset

---

[23]The risk-based capital ratios were fully implemented in January 1993. Some banks such as Citicorp had trouble meeting the 8 percent ratio and had to engage in asset sales (reducing risk-based assets) and capital raising exercises (increasing total capital) to meet the 8 percent target. However, all major banks managed to meet this requirement on the target date. After taking into account interest rate risk, the bank would have an excess capital cushion above the minimum regulatory required capital of $740,800 − $680,000 = $60,800.

[24]However, R. B. Avery and A. Berger show evidence that these risk weights do a good job in distinguishing between failing and nonfailing banks. See "Risk-Based Capital and Deposit Insurance Reform," *Journal of Banking and Finance* 15, 1991, pp. 847–74.

[25]In a portfolio context, it assumes that asset and OBS risks are independent of each other.

separately by the appropriate risk weight and then sums those numbers to get an over-all measure of credit risk. No account is taken of the covariances among asset risks (or risk weights).

4. *Bank specialness.* Giving private sector commercial loans the highest credit risk weighting may reduce the incentives for banks to make such loans relative to holding other assets. This may reduce the amount of bank loans to business as well as the degree of bank monitoring, and have associated negative externality effects on the economy. That is, one aspect of banks' special functions, bank lending, may be muted.[26]

5. *All commercial loans have equal weight.* Loans made to a AAA-rated company have a credit risk weight of one as do loans made to a CCC company. That is, within a risk-weight class such as commercial loans, no account is taken of credit risk quality differences. This may create perverse incentives for banks to pursue lower quality customers thereby increasing the risk of the bank.[27]

6. *Other risk.* While interest rate risk exposure has now been integrated into the risk-based capital requirements, the plan does not yet account for other risks such as foreign exchange rate risk, asset concentration risk, and operating risk. A more complete risk-based capital requirement would include these risks.[28]

Concept Questions

1. What are the major strengths of the risk-based capital ratios?
2. You are an FI manager with a total risk-based capital ratio of 6 percent. Discuss four strategies to meet the required 8 percent ratio in a short period of time without raising new capital.
3. Why isn't a capital ratio levied on exchange-traded derivative contracts?
4. What are three problems with the simple leverage ratio measure of capital adequacy?
5. What is the difference between Tier I and Tier II capital?
6. Identify one asset in each of the four risk-weight categories.

Capital Requirements for Other FIs

Property-Casualty Insurance

As we discuss in Chapter 2, in property-casualty insurance the insurer generally has two measures of risk exposure: First, the **pure loss ratio** measures the current and ex-

Pure Loss Ratio
The ratio between current and expected payouts to each dollar of premiums.

---

[26]This effect has been of great concern and controversy in recent years. Indeed, the high-risk weight given to commercial loans relative to securities has been blamed in part for inducing a credit crunch and a reorientation of bank portfolios away from commercial loans toward securities.

[27]One possible argument in support of the same risk weight for all commercial loans is that if the bank holds a well-diversified commercial loan portfolio, the unsystematic risk of each individual loan would be diversified away leaving only systematic credit risk. However, the betas or systematic risk sensitivity of loans may still differ across loans.

[28]Interestingly, the risk-based capital scheme proposed for life insurers has a more complete coverage of risks than the bank scheme. Also, the BIS has plans for introducing such measures by 1996. See BIS, "Prudential Supervision of Netting, Market Risks, and Interest Rate Risk," Basel, Switzerland, April 1993.

Combined Ratio
The loss ratio adjusted for expenses in settling claims now and in the future.

pected payouts on each dollar of premiums. Second, the **combined ratio** is essentially the loss ratio adjusted for expenses involved in settling claims now and in the future. There is a close link between the combined ratio and insurer profitability on underwriting.[29] Let:

$$P = \text{Premiums}$$

$$L = \text{Losses incurred}$$

$$E = \text{Expenses incurred}$$

$$\pi = \text{Profit on underwriting}$$

Then by definition: $P = L + E + \pi$

That is, each dollar of premiums can be allocated to meet losses on claims (L), to pay legal and other expenses (E), or to generate underwriting profits (π). Dividing by P or premiums and rearranging:

$$\frac{\pi}{P} = 1 - \left[\frac{L}{P} + \frac{E}{P} \right]$$

$$\frac{\pi}{P} = 1 - [\text{combined ratio}]$$

In the preceding equation, π/P is the profit the insurer earns on the premiums written and the combined ratio is the sum of payouts from premium income to meet losses and expenses. As can be directly inferred from the equation, the higher the combined ratio, the lower insurer profitability, since the combined ratio and insurer profitability are inversely related. In essence, if the combined ratio is 100 percent, a P-C insurer's profitability from underwriting a given P-C line is zero. However, this does not mean that the underwriting is totally unprofitable because the insurer also earns interest and returns from investing premium income between receiving premiums and paying out claims. Thus, a combined ratio of 100 percent implies that the insurer relies on investment income from the insurance line for overall profit. Indeed, even if the combined ratio rises above 100 percent, the P-C insurer can still be profitable as long as the investment portfolio is generating sufficiently high returns.[30]

Suppose that the combined ratio was 100 percent and the insurer's return on its assets was zero. The P-C insurer's overall profitability would be *zero*. Any unexpected increase in losses or expenses, such as the combined ratio rising above 100 percent due to a major storm or blizzard, would result in negative profits and threaten the insurer's solvency. State insurance regulators envisage this worst-case scenario in setting capital requirements for P-C insurers. In general, if the combined ratio unexpectedly rises above 100 percent and the insurer has zero returns on its assets, the insurer would have to draw on its capital and reserves—or its surplus—to meet claims or additional expenses. The larger this surplus, the longer it could continue in business even under this worst-case scenario. Consequently, many state regulators

---

[29]See S. E. Harrington, "Prices and Profits in the Liability Insurance Market," in *Liability: Perspectives and Policy,* ed. R. E. Litan and C. Winston (Washington, D.C.: The Brookings Institution, 1988), pp. 45–54.

[30]See Chapter 2 for more details of the combined ratio in P-C insurance.

TABLE 14–15 Profit and Performance for the Property-Liability Industry, 1972–88

Millions of dollars unless otherwise specified

Item	1972	1973	1974	1975	1976	1977	1978	1979	1980
Combined ratio (percent)	96.2	99.2	105.4	107.9	102.4	97.1	97.4	100.6	103.1
Ratio of net investment income/earned premiums	7.1	7.6	8.3	8.2	8.1	8.5	9.3	10.7	11.8
Before-tax operating income*	3,724	3,100	959	−322	2,405	6,928	8,586	7,978	7,729
After-tax operating income*	2,895	2,631	1,284	232	2,256	5,913	7,197	7,083	7,137
Realized capital gains	301	412	−154	139	286	329	57	300	533
Unrealized capital gains	2,836	−4,915	−6,999	4,035	3,803	−1,083	41	2,030	4,274
Net capital and surplus paid in†		−458	−1,084	−185	17	−78	−72	−736	−1,199	−1,495
Surplus at year-end*	23,812	21,389	16,270	19,712	24,631	29,300	35,379	42,395	52,174
Percent change in surplus	24.9	−10.2	−23.9	21.2	24.9	18.9	20.7	19.8	23.1
Percent change in net premiums written	10.1	8.1	6.2	11.0	21.8	19.8	12.8	10.3	6.0
Ratio of net premiums written/surplus	1.63	1.97	2.75	2.52	2.45	2.47	2.31	2.13	1.83
Ratio of liabilities/surplus	2.12	2.64	1.70	3.47	3.29	3.32	3.21	3.10	2.79
Ratio of loss reserves/surplus	1.12	1.42	2.13	2.00	1.91	1.94	1.94	1.91	1.77
Number of insolvencies	2	2	5	20	4	6	6	3	4

*Income and surplus calculated according to statutory accounting principles.

†Net capital and surplus paid in equals new capital and surplus paid in less dividends to stockholders.

SOURCE: Harrington, "Prices and Profits in the Liability Insurance Market" in Liability Perspectives and Policy, ed. R. E. Litan and C. Winston (Washington D. C.: The Brookings Institution, pp. 50–51 (1988) for years 1972–1985: A. M. Best, "Aggregates and Averages: Property-Casualty Insurance," Oldwick, N. J. (1989) for years 1986–1988, and NCIGF for insolvencies 1986–1988.

establish a maximum ratio on premiums or business that can be written relative to capital and surplus. For most states, this ratio is 3 to 1—or a maximum of $3 in premium written for every $1 in capital surplus held. The economic interpretation is as follows: Suppose that with zero investment income the combined ratio (losses plus expenses to premiums) rises by one third from 100 to 133 percent. Since for every $1 in premiums the insurer has kept a minimum of 33 cents in a surplus or capital fund, the insurer could actually meet and payout these claims from its capital reserves without becoming insolvent. In actuality, on average, P-C insurers hold surplus reserves far exceeding the $1 in capital to $3 in premuims requirement. This suggests that for a P-C insurer to become insolvent, it has to face extreme, unexpected upward jumps in its loss payouts and expenses (combined ratio) and/or unexpected drops in its asset returns.

In Table 14–15, we show the performance of the combined ratio, the net investment income-earned premium ratio (the investment return ratio), and the ratio of net premiums written to surplus (the capital ratio) along with other financial ratios of interest for all P-C insurers over the period 1972–88. As you can see, the combined ratio tends to follow a clear cycle (see also Chapter 2 for a discussion of the P-C insurance underwriting cycle). For example, in the early 1980s the combined ratio across all lines rose quite dramatically reaching a maximum of 118 percent in 1984. The years 1984–85 were very bad years for underwriting profitability; it was only because (1) investment returns were high in the 14–15 percent range and (2) the ratio of premiums written to surplus was well below 3—in fact, in the 1.8 to 1.9 range—that

TABLE 14–15 (*concluded*)

1981	1982	1983	1984	1985	1986	1987	1988
106.0	109.6	112.0	118.0	116.3	107.9	104.6	105.4
13.6	14.6	14.9	15.4	14.6	13.15	12.73	13.86
6,960	4,617	2,651	−3,609	−5,780	5,382	13,396	15,923
6,906	5,333	3,869	−1,942	−3,822	5,974	10,074	12,256
276	572	2,110	3,063	5,483	6,835	3,335	2,725
−2,666	2,908	1,358	−2,848	5,227	2,111	−3,076	2,703
−1,775	−1,248	−1,945	233	5,561	4,468	−167	−3,290
53,805	60,395	65,606	63,809	75,511	95,496	104,919	118,195
3.1	12.2	8.6	−2.7	18.3	24.1	9.9	12.7
3.9	4.7	4.8	8.4	22.0	21.7	7.9	4.5
1.85	1.72	1.67	1.86	1.92	1.9	1.8	1.7
2.95	2.84	2.80	3.15	3.12	2.9	3.0	3.0
1.90	1.85	1.87	2.11	2.05	1.93	2.07	2.05
6	9	4	20	20	17	11	16

no more than 20 P-C firms became insolvent. Thus, investment income is the first line of defense against a rising combined ratio (underwriting losses) and the premium-surplus (or capital) ratio, the second line of defense. After 1985, the combined ratio fell and P-C insurers faced easier underwriting conditions; however, this was partly offset by a fall in their investment income returns. Finally, even in this more favorable stage of the underwriting insurance cycle, on average, P-C insurers held premium-surplus ratios well below three; that is, held more capital than was required by regulation.

Securities Firms

Unlike the book value capital rules employed by bank and insurance company regulators, the capital requirements for broker-dealers set by the SEC's Rule 15C 3–1 in 1975 is close to a market value accounting rule. Essentially, broker-dealers have to calculate a market value for their net worth on a day-to-day basis and to ensure that their net worth-assets ratio exceeds 2 percent.

$$\frac{\text{Net-worth}}{\text{Assets}} \geq 2\%$$

The essential idea is that if a broker-dealer has to liquidate all assets at near market values, a capital cushion of 2 percent should be sufficient to satisfy all customer liabilities such as brokerage accounts held with the firm.

Specifically, to compute net capital the broker-dealer calculates book net worth and then makes a number of adjustments: (1) subtracting all assets such as fixed assets not readily convertible into cash and (2) subtracting securities that cannot be publicly offered or sold. Moreover, the dealer must make other deductions, or haircuts, reflecting potential market value fluctuations in assets. For example, the net capital rule requires haircuts on illiquid equities of up to 40 percent and on debt securities generally between 0 and 9 percent. Finally, other adjustments are required to reflect unrealized profits and losses, subordinated liabilities, contractual commitments, deferred taxes, options, commodities and commodity futures, and certain collateralized liabilities.

Thus, broker-dealers must make significant adjustments to the book value of net worth—the difference between the book values of assets and liabilities—to reach a market value net worth figure. This figure must exceed 2 percent of assets.

Life Insurance

The life insurance industry is moving toward adopting a risk-based capital scheme similar in nature to that adopted by banks and thrifts. While capital requirements are imposed at the state level, these are heavily influenced by recommendations from the National Association of Insurance Commissioners (NAIC). We describe the proposed NAIC model next.

The model begins by identifying four risks faced by the insurer:

C1 = Asset risk
C2 = Insurance risk
C3 = Interest rate risk
C4 = Business risk

C1: Asset Risk.   Asset risk reflects the riskiness of the asset portfolio of the life insurer. It is similar in spirit to the risk-adjusted asset calculations for banks and thrifts in that a credit risk weight is multiplied by the dollar or face value of the assets on the balance sheet. See Table 14–16.

Thus, the insurer with $100 million in common stocks would have a risk-based capital requirement of $30 million, while with $100 million in BBB corporate bonds only $1 million would be required.

Mortality Risk
The risk of death.

Morbidity Risk
The risk of ill health.

C2: Insurance Risk.   Insurance risk captures the risk of adverse changes in **mortality** and **morbidity risk.** As we discuss in Chapter 2, through mortality tables life insurers have an extremely accurate idea of the probabilities of an insured dying in any given year. However, epidemics such as AIDS can upset these predictions quite drastically. As a result, insurers adjust insurance in force for the current level of reserves, and multiply the resulting number by an insurance risk factor. Similar calculations are carried out for accident and health insurance which covers morbidity risk.

C3: Interest Rate Risk.   Interest rate risk in part reflects the liquidity of liabilities and their probability or ease of withdrawal as interest rates change. For example, guaranteed investment contracts (GICs) have similar characteristics to long-term, fixed-rate bank deposits and are often highly sensitive to interest rate movements. As we also discuss in Chapter 13, illiquidity problems have led to a number of insurer insolvencies in recent years. With respect to interest rate risk, insurers must divide liabilities into three risk classes: low risk (0.5 percent risk-based capital requirement), medium risk (1 percent capital requirement), and high risk (2 percent capital requirement).

**TABLE 14–16 Risk-Based Weights for Life
Insurer Assets**

Category	Proposed RBC Factor
I. Bonds	
U.S. Government	0%
Category 1: AAA-A	0.3
Category 2: BBB	1
Category 3: BB	4
Category 4: B	9
Category 5: CCC	20
Category 6: In or Near Default	30
II. Other	
Residential mortgages (Whole loan)	2%
Commercial mortgages	3
Preferred stock*	5
Common stock	30

*As of the original exposure draft. Subsequent proposals are 2.0 percent plus
the comparable bond factor.

C4: Business Risk.   As we discuss in Chapter 15, states have organized guarantee
funds that partially pay for insurer insolvencies by levying a charge on surviving
firms. Thus, the capital requirement for business risk is set to equal the maximum potential assessment by state guarantee funds (2 percent for life and annuity premiums
and 0.5 percent for health premiums for each surviving insurer). Also company-
specific fraud and litigation risk might require an additional capital charge.

   After calculating C1, C2, C3, and C4, the life insurance manager computes a
risk-based capital measure (RBC) based on the following equation:

$$RBC = \sqrt{(C1 + C3)^2 + C2^2} + C4$$

   As calculated, the RBC is the minimum required capital for the life insurer. The
insurer compares this risk-based capital measure to the actual capital and surplus
(total capital) held:

$$\frac{\text{Total surplus and capital}}{\text{Risk-based capital}}$$

If this ratio is greater than 1, the life insurance manager is meeting, or is above, the
minimum capital requirements. If the ratio falls below 1, the manager would be subject to regulatory scrutiny.[31]

---

[31]NAIC testing found that 87 percent of the industry had a total surplus and capital/RBC ratio above
one. This description of the life insurance risk-based capital ratio is based on L. S. Goodman, P. Fischer,
and C. Anderson, "The Impact of Risk-Based Capital Requirements on Asset Allocation for Life Insurance
Companies," *Insurance Executive Review,* Fall 1992, pp. 14–21; and P. J. Bouyoucos, M. H. Siegel, and
E. B. Raisel, "Risk-Based Capital for Insurers: A Strategic Opportunity to Enhance Franchise Value,"
Goldman Sachs, Industry Resource Group, September 1992.

Summary

This chapter has reviewed the role of an FI's capital in insulating it against credit, interest rate, and other risks. According to economic theory, capital or net worth should be measured on a market value basis, as the difference between the market value of assets and liabilities; in actuality, regulators use book value accounting rules. While a book value capital adequacy rule accounts for credit risk exposure in a rough fashion, it overlooks the effects of interest rate changes and interest rate exposure on net worth. We analyzed the specific capital rules adopted by banks and thrifts, insurance companies, and securities firms and discussed their problems and weaknesses. In particular, we looked at how bank, thrift, and life insurance regulators are now adjusting book value-based capital rules to account for both credit and interest rate risk as part of their imposition of risk-based capital adequacy ratios. As a result, actual capital requirements in banks, life insurance companies, and thrifts are moving closer to the market value-based net worth requirement of broker-dealers.[32]

Questions and Problems

1. *a.* Why do FIs hold capital? Which of these reasons are unique to depository institutions?
   b. Why do regulators stipulate minimum required capital levels?

2. *a.* How have the Basel capital regulations enhanced regulators' abilities to monitor bank capital positions?
   b. What is the difference between Tier 1 and Tier 2 capital?
   c. Identify at least one asset that falls into each of the four risk classifications.

3. *a.* Why is the market value of equity a better measure of a bank's ability to absorb losses and protect uninsured creditors than its book value of equity?
   b. In April of 1993, FASB adopted a rule that will require banks and other FIs to use the market value of assets on their financial statements. What are two of the shortcomings of this rule?

4. A book value solvent FI may actually be either solvent or insolvent from a financial perspective. Discuss.

5. What is the contribution to the asset base of the following items under the Basel requirements? Under the U.S. capital-assets ratio (simple leverage) rule?
   a. $10 million cash reserves.
   b. $50 million 91-day U.S. Treasury bills.
   c. $25 million cash items in the process of collection.
   d. $5 million U.K. government bonds.
   e. $5 million Australian short-term government bonds.
   f. $1 million general obligation municipal bonds.
   g. $40 million repurchase agreements (against U.S. Treasuries).
   h. $500 million one to four family home mortgages.
   i. $500 million commercial and industrial loans.
   j. $100,000 performance-related standby letters of credit to a blue chip corporation.
   k. $100,000 performance-related standby letters of credit to a municipality issuing general obligation bonds.
   l. $7 million commercial letter of credit to a foreign corporation.
   m. $3 million five-year loan commitment to an OECD government.
   n. $8 million bankers acceptance conveyed to a U.S. corporation.
   o. $17 million three-year loan commitment to a private agent.
   p. $17 million three-month loan commitment to a private agent.
   q. $30 million standby letter of credit to back a corporate issue of commercial paper.
   r. $4 million five-year interest rate swap with no current exposure (the counterparty is a private agent).
   s. $4 million five-year interest rate swap with no current exposure (the counterparty is a municipality).
   t. $6 million two-year currency swap with $500,000 current exposure (the counterparty is a private agent).

6. How does the primary capital assets ratio test impact the stringency of regulatory monitoring of bank capital positions?

7. *a.* Calculate the risk-adjusted asset base for a bank with (a) cash of $20 million, (b) general obligation municipal securities or $100 million, (c) single family home mortgages of $500 million, and (d) commercial loans of $300 million.
   b. If the bank has no off-balance sheet activity, what is the bank's minimum required level of Tier 1 capital? Tier 2 capital? Combined?
   c. If the bank has Tier 1 capital of $25 million and Tier 2 capital of $15 million, does the bank comply with the Basel international capital requirements?

---

[32]P-C insurance regulators are also reportedly considering adopting a risk-based capital scheme on the lines of that adopted by the life insurance industry.

8. *a.* Calculate the value of risk-adjusted assets for the following off-balance-sheet assets:

   6 month loan commitments: $500 million

   Commercial letters of credit: $50 million

   5 year loan commitments: $100 million

   Performance related standby letters of credit: $20 million

   Direct credit substitute standby letters of credit: $200 million

   NOTE: All counterparties are private agents except for the holders of the $200 million of direct credit substitute standby letters of credit. These werre issued to back an issue of general obligation municipal notes.

   b. If the bank has the same on-balance-sheet activity as the bank in question 1, what is the bank's minimum required level of Tier 1 capital? Tier 2 capital? Combined?

   c. If the bank has Tier 1 capital of $45 million and Tier 2 capital of $35 million, does the bank comply with the Basel international capital requirements?

9. Use the constant dividend growth model to fill in the missing figures in the following table:

Bank	Dividends ($ annual)	Earnings ($ annual)	Growth Rate (%)	Discount Rate (%)	P/E ($)
A	$1.50	$2.15	5%	7%	a
B	5.00	6.50	3	10	b
C	2.25	2.75	2	c	9.1
D	.50	d	15	20	10

10. Can the book value of capital ever be negative? Why or why not? What does this imply about the relevance of capital book values as an indicator of FI solvency?

11. Mark the following balance sheet to market:

    Book Values (in thousands)

Treasury portfolio	$1,123	Deposits	$2,500
Municipals	555	Money market borrowings	730
Loans	2,700	Notes	58
		Equity	1,090

    a. What is the ratio of book value of equity capital to total assets? Using this calculation, is the bank solvent?

    b. If the market value of the Treasury portfolio declined by 5 percent, what is the impact on the book value of equity?

    c. If in addition to the decline in the value of the bank's Treasury portfolio, the value of the bank's municipals declined by 10 percent, what would be the cumulative impact on the book value of equity?

    d. If additionally, the value of the loan portfolio declined by 35 percent, what would be the market value of capital?

    e. If additionally, the value of the bank's note liabilities declined by 7 percent, what would be the market value of capital?

    f. Use your answer to (*e*) to calculate the bank's capital to asset ratio. Is the bank solvent?

12. Explain some scenarios that would account for the decline in market values detailed in question 11 *b, c, d,* and *e.* (Be sure to consider at least two sources of risk exposure for each.)

13. What would account for the differences in the magnitude of the price declines for each of the market values in question 11 *b, c, d,* and *e*?

14. Consider the following bank's balance sheet. What is the bank's risk-adjusted asset base?

On-Balance-Sheet Items	Category	Face Value
Cash	1	$121,600
Short-term government securities (<92 days)	1	5,400
Long-term government securities (>92 days)	1	414,400
Federal Reserve balances	1	9,800
Repos secured by federal agencies	2	159,000
Claims on U.S. depository institutions	2	937,900
Short-term (<1 yr) claims on foreign banks	2	1,640,000
General obligation municipals	2	170,000
Claims on or guaranteed by federal agencies	2	26,500
Municipal revenue bonds	3	112,900
Loans	4	6,645,700
Claims on foreign banks (>1 yr.)	4	5,800

Off-Balance-Sheet Items:

Guaranteed by U.S. Government:	**(Risk Weight Category 1)**	
Loan commitments:		
< 1 year	0%	300
> 1 year	50	1,140
Standby letters of credit		
Performance related	50	200
Other	100	100
Backed by Domestic Depository Institution:	**(Risk Weight Category 2)**	
Loan commitments:		
< 1 year	0%	1,000
> 1 year	50	3,000
Standby letters of credit		
Performance related	50	200
Other	100	56,400
Commercial letters of credit	20	400
Backed by State or Local Government Revenues:	**(Risk Weight Category 3)**	
Loan commitments:		
> 1 year	50%	100
Standby letters of credit		
Nonperformance related	50	135,400
Extended to Corporate Customers:	**(Risk Weight Category 4)**	
Loan commitments:		
< 1 year	0%	2,980,000

Extended to Corporate Customers:	(Risk Weight Category 4)	
> 1 year	50	3,046,278
Standby letters of credit		
Performance related	50	101,543
Other	100	485,000
Commercial letters of credit	20	78,978
Note issuance facilities	50	20,154
Forward agreements	100	5,900
Category II Interest Rate Market Contracts:		
(Current exposure assumed to be zero.)		
< 1 year (Notional amount)	0%	2,000
> 1 year (Notional amount)	.5%	5,000

15. What is the total risk-based capital requirement of the bank in question 14? For Tier I capital? For Tier II capital? (Use the balance sheet in question 14.)

16. Using the primary capital-assets ratio requirement, what is the U.S. bank's minimum regulatory capital requirement? (Use the balance sheet in question 14.)

17. What is the bank's capital level if the par value of the bank's equity is $150,000; surplus value of equity is $200,000; qualifying perpetual preferred stock is $50,000? Does the bank meet Basel (Tier I) capital standards? Does the bank comply with the primary capital-assets ratio requirement? (Use the balance sheet in question 14.)

15

DEPOSIT INSURANCE AND OTHER LIABILITY GUARANTEES

Learning Objectives

In this chapter, you learn about deposit insurance and other liability guarantee programs. Deposit insurance has many attractive characteristics in that it deters bank runs and protects small and less-informed savers against losses to their wealth as a result of bank failures. However, deposit insurance also has a number of unattractive features that become important if the insurance contract does not price FI risk taking correctly. One such unattractive feature is moral hazard—the increased incentive for an insured FI to take more rather than less risk. You will learn how Congress is trying to maintain the attractive features of deposit insurance, such as its role in deterring liability runs, while eliminating or reducing its unattractive features by imposing greater discipline on bank depositors, bank owners, and bank regulators.

Introduction

In Chapter 13 we discussed the liquidity risks faced by FIs. Because of concerns about the asset quality or solvency of an FI, liability holders such as depositors and life insurance policyholders have incentives to engage in runs; that is, to withdraw all their funds from an FI. As we discussed in Chapter 13, the incentive to run is accentuated by the fact that banks and insurance companies follow a sequential servicing rule in meeting withdrawals. As a result, deposit and liability holders who are first in line to withdraw funds get preference over those last in line.

While a run on an unhealthy FI is not necessarily a bad thing—it can discipline the performance of managers and owners—there is a risk that runs on bad FIs can become contagious, in the sense of spreading to good or well-run FIs. In contagious run or panic conditions, liability holders do not bother to distinguish between good and bad FIs but rather seek to turn their liabilities into cash or safe securities as quickly as possible. This has a major contractionary effect on the supply of credit as well as the money supply.

Moreover, a contagious run on FIs can have other serious social welfare effects. In particular, a major run on banks can have an adverse effect on the level of savings and, therefore, inhibit the ability of individuals to transfer wealth through time to protect themselves against major risks such as future ill health or falling income in old age.

Because of such wealth, money supply, and credit supply effects, government regulators of financial service firms have introduced guarantee programs to deter runs

FIGURE 15–1

Number of failed banks by year (1934–1989)

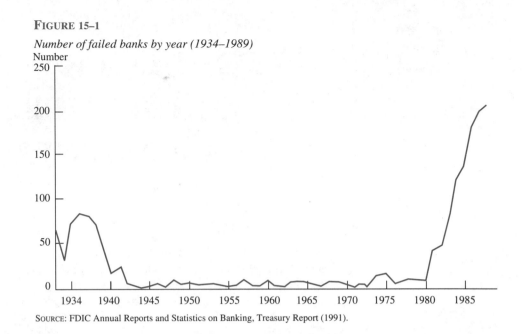

SOURCE: FDIC Annual Reports and Statistics on Banking, Treasury Report (1991).

by offering liability holders varying degrees of failure protection. Specifically, if a liability holder believes a claim is totally secure even if the FI is in trouble, there is no incentive to run. The liability holder's place in line no longer affects getting his or her funds back. Regulatory guarantee or insurance programs for liability holders deter runs and, thus, deter contagious runs and panics.

Federally backed insurance programs include the Federal Deposit Insurance Corporation or FDIC (created in 1933) for banks and thrifts, the Securities Investors Protection Corporation or SIPC (created in 1970) for securities firms, and the Pension Benefit Guaranty Corporation or PBGC (created in 1974) for private pension funds.[1] In addition, because of their state rather than federal regulation, state-organized guarantee funds back up most life and property-casualty insurance companies.

We analyze deposit insurance funds for banks and thrifts and then look at the special features of the guarantee funds for other FIs.

The History of Bank and Thrift Guarantee Funds

The FDIC

The FDIC was created in 1933 in the wake of the banking panics of 1930–33, when some 10,000 commercial banks failed. The original level of individual depositor insurance coverage at commercial banks was $2,500, which has since been increased to $100,000 in 1980. Between 1945 and 1980, commercial bank deposit insurance clearly worked; there were no runs or panics and the number of individual bank failures was very small. See Figure 15–1.

Beginning in 1980, however, bank failures accelerated with more than 1,039 failures in the decade ending in 1990. This number of failures was actually larger

---

[1]Until its insolvency in 1989, FSLIC (the Federal Savings and Loan Insurance Corporation) insured the deposits of most thrifts. Since 1989, both banks and thrifts are insured under the umbrella of the FDIC, as we discuss later.

than for the entire 1933–79 period. In 1991, the FDIC had to close an additional 124 banks, and through November 1992, it closed an additional 104. Moreover, the costs to the FDIC were often larger than for the mainly small bank failures in 1933–79. As the number and costs of these closures mounted in the 1980s, the FDIC fund became rapidly weakened. Any insurance fund becomes insolvent if the premiums collected and the reserves built up from investing premiums are insufficient to offset the cost of failure claims. The FDIC's resources were virtually depleted by early 1991 when it was given permission to borrow $30 billion from the Treasury. In response to this crisis, Congress passed the FDIC Improvement Act (FDICIA) in December 1991 to restructure the bank insurance fund and prevent its potential insolvency. Some observers argue that even with the increase in bank insurance premiums and the use of new failure resolution methods mandated under the FDIC Improvement Act, the bank insurance fund will not be solvent again until the year 2000 at the earliest. However, such a projection is uncertain and depends on how profitable the banking industry is over the next few years.[2]

FSLIC and Its Demise

FSLIC covered savings and loan associations (S&Ls); other thrifts, such as mutual savings banks, often chose to be insured under the FDIC rather than FSLIC.[3] Like the FDIC, this insurance fund was in relatively good shape until the end of the 1970s. Beginning in 1980, the fund's resources were rapidly depleted as more and more thrifts failed and had to be closed or merged. The causes of these failures were many, including fraud, risky lending, declining real estate values, and insider loans. A major reason was thrifts' exposure to interest rate risk due to their massive duration mismatches of assets and liabilities in 1979–82. In this period, interest rates rose to historically high levels resulting in a major fall in the market values of thrifts' long-term fixed-rate mortgage portfolios. Between 1980 and 1988, out of 3,998 FSLIC-insured institutions, 1,060 failed and required FSLIC assistance, while 798 engaged in voluntary mergers. As a result, by 1988 the FSLIC fund had a negative net worth—its present value of liabilities exceeded its assets—variously estimated at between $40 and $80 billion. Lacking the resources to close and resolve failing thrifts, the FSLIC had to follow a policy of forbearance toward the closure of failed and failing thrifts. This meant that many bad thrifts stayed open and their losses continued to accumulate.

In August 1989, Congress passed the Financial Institutions Reform Recovery and Enforcement Act (FIRREA) largely in response to the deepening crisis in the thrift industry and the growing insolvency of FSLIC. This act completely restructured the savings bank fund and transferred its management to the FDIC.[4] At the same time, the restructured savings bank insurance fund became the Savings Association Insurance Fund (SAIF). FDIC manages SAIF separately from the commercial bank fund, which is now called the Bank Insurance Fund (BIF). We present the organizational structure of FDIC and these funds in Figure 15–2.

Finally, the *Resolution Trust Corporation* (RTC), a new agency created by FIRREA, began resolving failed savings and loan assets through liquidations and restructuring of troubled savings banks by recapitalizations and mergers. The cost of

---

[2]See S. Labaton, "Business News," *New York Times*, September 16, 1992, p. D1.

[3]As we discussed in Chapter 1, credit union depositors enjoy a degree of coverage similar to bank, S&L, and savings bank depositors via coverage through the National Credit Union Insurance Fund.

[4]At that time, FSLIC ceased to exist.

FIGURE 15–2

FDIC, BIF, and SAIF

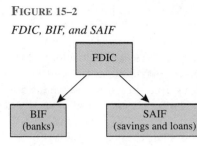

resolving the thrift industry crisis is currently estimated at somewhere between $180 and $200 billion in present value terms.

The Causes of the Depository Fund Insolvencies

There are two not necessarily independent views of why depository institution insurance funds became insolvent. In addition, some factors offer better explanations of FSLIC insolvency than FDIC insolvency, especially as the FSLIC insolvency was far worse than the current FDIC insolvency.

The Financial Environment

One view is that a number of external events or shocks adversely impacted U.S. banks and thrifts in the 1980s. The first of these was the dramatic rise in interest rates in the 1979–82 period. As we noted earlier, this rise in rates had a major negative effect on those thrifts funding long-term, fixed-rate mortgages with short-term deposits. The second event was the collapse in oil, real estate, and other commodity prices, that particularly harmed oil, gas, and agricultural loans in the southwestern United States. The third event was increased competition at home and abroad that eroded the value of bank and thrift charters during the 1980s (see Chapters 16 and 17).[5]

Moral Hazard

A second view is that these financial environment effects were catalysts for, rather than causes of, the crisis. At the heart of the crisis is deposit insurance itself, especially some of its contractual features. Although deposit insurance has deterred depositors and other liability holders from engaging in runs, in so doing it has also removed or reduced depositor discipline. Deposit insurance allows banks to borrow at rates close to the risk free rate and if they choose, to undertake high-risk asset investments. Bank managers knew that insured depositors had little incentive to restrict such behavior, either through fund withdrawals or by requiring risk premia on deposit rates since they were fully insured by the FDIC if the bank failed. Given this scenario, losses on oil, gas, and real estate loans in the 1980s are viewed as the outcome of bankers exploiting underpriced or mispriced risk under the deposit insurance contract. When the provision of insurance encourages rather than discourages risk

---

[5]As we discuss in Chapter 3, the value of a bank or thrift charter is the present value of expected profits from operating in the industry. As expected profits fall, so does the value of a bank or thrift charter.

Moral Hazard
The loss exposure faced by an insurer when the provision of insurance encourages the insured to take more risks.

Implicit Premiums
Deposit insurance premiums or costs imposed on a bank through activity constraints rather than direct monetary charges.

taking, this is called **moral hazard** because it increases the scope of the risk exposure faced by insurers.[6]

In the absence of depositor discipline, regulators could have priced risk taking by bankers, either through charging explicit deposit insurance premiums linked to bank risk or by charging **implicit premiums**, and better restricting and monitoring the risky activities of banks. This could potentially have substituted for depositor discipline; those banks that took more risk would have paid directly or indirectly for this risk-taking behavior. However, from 1933 until January 1, 1993 regulators levied deposit insurance on bank deposit size rather than on a risk basis. The 1980s were also a period of deregulation and capital adequacy forbearance rather than stringent activity regulation and tough capital requirements. Moreover, for the FSLIC, the number of bank examinations and examiners actually fell between 1981 and 1984.[7] Finally prompt corrective action for undercapitalized banks did not begin until the end of 1992 (see Chapter 14).

Concept Question

1. Why was interest rate risk less of a problem for banks than thrifts in the early 1980s?

Panic Prevention versus Moral Hazard

A great deal of attention has focused on the moral hazard reason for the collapse of the bank and thrift insurance funds. The less bank owners have to lose from taking risks, the greater are their incentives to take excessively risky asset positions. When asset investment risks or gambles pay off, bank owners make windfall gains in profits. Should they fail, however, the FDIC, as the insurer, bears most of the costs given that owners of banks—like owners of regular corporations—have limited liability. It's a heads I win, tails I don't lose (much) situation.

Actuarially Fairly Priced Insurance
Insurance pricing based on the perceived risk of the insured.

Note that even without deposit insurance the limited liability of bank owners or stockholders always creates incentives to take risk at the expense of fixed claimants such as depositors or debt holders.[8] The only difference between banks and firms is that mispriced deposit insurance, when risk taking is not **actuarially fairly priced in insurance** premiums, adds to the incentives of bank stockholders to take additional risk.

---

[6]The precise definition of moral hazard is that it is the loss exposure of an insurer (the FDIC) that results from the character or circumstances of the insured (here the bank).

[7]See L. J. White who points to a general weakness of thrift supervision and examination in the 1980s. The number of examinations fell from 3,210 in 1980 to 2,347 in 1984 and examinations per billion dollars of assets from 5.41 in 1980 to 2.4 in 1984. See *The S and L Debacle* (New York: Oxford University Press, 1991), p. 89.

[8]See K. John, T. John, and L. W. Senbet, "Risk Shifting Incentives of Depository Institutions: A New Perspective on Federal Deposit Insurance Reform," *Journal of Banking and Finance* 36, 1981, pp. 335–67. Thus, one possible policy to reduce excessive bank risk taking would be to eliminate limited liability for bank stockholders. A study by L. J. White found that bank failures in private banking systems with unlimited liability, such as that which existed in eighteenth-century Scotland, were rare. Indeed, in the United States double liability existed for bank stockholders prior to the introduction of deposit insurance; that is, on failure, the stockholders would lose their initial equity contribution and be assessed, by the receiver, an extra amount equal to the par value of their stock which would be used to pay creditors (over and above the liquidation value of the bank's assets). See "Scottish Banking and Legal Restrictions Theory: A Closer Look," *Journal of Money Credit and Banking* 22, 1990, pp. 526–36.

FIGURE 15–3

Bank run risk versus moral hazard risk trade-off

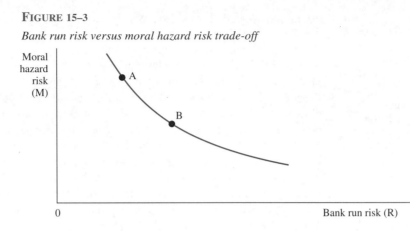

Nevertheless, even though mispriced deposit insurance potentially accentuates bank risk taking, we have also seen from Figure 15–1 that deposit insurance effectively deterred bank panics and runs of the 1930–33 kind in the postwar period. That is, deposit insurance ensured a good deal of stability to the credit and monetary system.

This suggests that ideally regulators should design the deposit insurance contract with the trade-off between moral hazard risk and bank panic or run risk in mind. For example, by providing 100 percent coverage of all depositors and reducing the probability of runs to zero, the insurer may be encouraging a significant degree of moral hazard risk-taking behavior among certain banks. On the other hand, a very limited degree of deposit insurance coverage might encourage runs and panics although moral hazard behavior itself would be less evident. We depict the potential trade-off between bank run risk and moral hazard risk in Figure 15–3.

In the 1980s, the insurance contract wound up at point *A* in Figure 15–3, where depositors had little incentive to engage in runs and bank owners and managers had strong incentives to engage in moral hazard risk-taking behavior.[9] By restructuring the deposit insurance contract, it may be possible to reduce moral hazard risk quite a bit without a very large increase in bank run risk. Such a point might be *B* in Figure 15–3. To some extent these were the objectives behind the passage of the FDIC Improvement Act (FDICIA) of 1991. Of course, Figure 15–3 is only illustrative. We don't know the actual shape of the moral hazard bank run risk trade-off as the deposit insurance contract changes; however, we expect the relationship to be inverse and pricing bank risk taking more explicitly should discourage moral hazard behavior.

Concept Questions

1. How would levying actuarially fairly priced deposit insurance premiums on banks change the trade-off in Figure 15–3?

---

[9]At this point, note that managers might not have the same risk-taking incentives as owners. This is especially true if managers are compensated through wage and salary contracts rather than through shares and share option programs. Where managers are on fixed wage contracts, their preferences as regards to risk lean toward being risk averse. That is, they are unlikely to exploit the same type of moral hazard incentives that stockowner-controlled banks would. This is because managers have little to gain if their banks do exceptionally well (their salaries are fixed) but will likely lose their jobs and human capital investments in a bank if they fail. A study by A. Saunders, E. Strock, and N. Travlos showed that stockowner-controlled banks tend to be more risky than manager-controlled banks. Thus, understanding the agency structure of the bank is important in identifying which banks are most likely to exploit risk-taking (moral hazard) incentives. See "Ownership Structure, Deregulation, and Bank Risk Taking," *Journal of Finance* 45, 1989, pp. 643–54.

2. Suppose the FDIC provided deposit insurance free of charge to banks and covered all depositors, roughly where would we be on the trade-off curve in Figure 15–3?

Controlling Bank Risk Taking

There are three ways in which a deposit insurance contract could be structured to reduce moral hazard behavior:

1. Increase stockholder discipline.
2. Increase depositor discipline.
3. Increase regulator discipline.

Specifically, redesigning the features of the insurance contract can either directly impact bank owners' and stockholders' risk-taking incentives or indirectly affect their risk-taking incentives by altering the behavior of depositors and regulators. In the wake of the insolvency of the FDIC, in 1991, the FDIC Improvement Act was passed with the objective of increasing discipline in all three areas.

Stockholder Discipline

Insurance Premiums.   One approach toward making stockholders' risk taking more expensive is to link FDIC insurance premiums to the risk profile of the bank. Below we look at ways in which this might be done including the risk-based premium scheme adopted by the FDIC in 1993.

Theory.   A major feature of the pre-1993 FDIC deposit insurance contract was the flat deposit insurance premium levied on banks and thrifts. Specifically, each year a bank paid a given sum or premium to the FDIC based on a fixed proportion of its domestic deposits.[10] Until 1989, the premium was 8.33 cents per $100 in domestic deposits.[11] As the FDIC fund became increasingly depleted, the level of the premium was raised several times but its risk-insensitive nature was left unaltered. By 1992, the premiums banks had to pay had risen to 23 cents per $100 of their domestic deposits, almost a tripling of their premiums since 1988.[12]

To see why a flat- or size-based premium schedule does not discipline a bank's risk taking, consider two banks of the same domestic deposit size as in Table 15–1. Banks A and B have domestic deposits of $100 million and would pay the same premium to the FDIC (.0023 × $100 million = $230,000 per annum). However, their risk-taking behavior is completely different. Bank A is excessively risky, investing all its assets in real estate loans. Bank B is almost risk free, investing all of its assets in government T-bills. We graph the insurance premium rates paid by the two banks compared to their asset risk in Figure 15–4.

In Figure 15–4, note that under the pre-1993 flat premium schedule, both banks A and B would have been charged the same deposit insurance premium based on bank size. Critics of flat premiums argue that the FDIC should act more like a private

---

[10]In actual practice, premiums are levied and paid semiannually.

[11]In the pre-1980 period, the FDIC was able to rebate some of these premiums as they felt they had adequate reserves at the time. See S. A. Buser, A. H. Chen, and E. J. Kane, "Federal Deposit Insurance, Regulatory Policy, and Optimal Bank Capital," *Journal of Finance* 36, 1981, pp. 51–60.

[12]This was also the 1992 rate for thrifts insured under SAIF.

TABLE 15–1 Flat Deposit Insurance Premiums and Risk Taking

Bank A				Bank B			
Assets		*Liabilities*		*Assets*		*Liabilities*	
Real estate loans	100	Domestic deposits	100	T-bills	100	Domestic deposits	100

property-casualty insurer. Under normal property-casualty insurance premium setting principles, insurers charge those with higher risks higher premiums. That is, low-risk parties (such as bank B) do not generally fully subsidize high-risk parties (such as bank A) as they did under the pre-1993 FDIC premium pricing scheme. If premiums increased as bank risk increased, banks would have reduced incentives to take risks. Therefore, the ultimate goal might be to price risk in an actuarially fair fashion, similar to a private property-casualty insurer, so that premiums reflect the expected private costs or losses to the insurer from the provision of deposit insurance.

Note that there are arguments against imposing an actuarially fair risk-based premium schedule. If the deposit insurer's mandate is not to act as if it were a private cost minimizing insurer such as a P-C insurance company, because of social welfare considerations, some type of subsidy to banks and thrifts can be justified. Remember that the FDIC is a quasi-government agency and broader banking market stability concerns and savers' welfare concerns might arguably override private cost minimizing concerns and require subsidies.[13] Other authors have argued that if an actuarially fair premium is imposed on a banking system that is fully competitive, banking itself cannot be profitable. That is, some subsidy is needed for banks to profitably exist.[14] However, while U.S. banking is competitive, it probably deviates somewhat from the perfectly competitive model.

Calculating the Actuarially Fair Premium.   Economists have suggested a number of approaches for calculating the fair premium that a cost-minimizing insurer should charge. One approach would be to set the premium equal to the expected severity times the frequency of losses due to bank failure plus some load or mark-up factor. This would exactly mimic the approach toward premium setting in the property-casualty industry. However, the most common approach has been to view the FDIC's provision of deposit insurance as virtually identical to the FDIC writing a put option on the assets of the bank that buys the deposit insurance.[15] We depict the conceptual idea in Figure 15–5.

In this framework, the FDIC charges a bank a premium $0P$ to insure a bank's deposits ($0D$). If the bank does well and the market value of the bank's assets is greater

[13]Most of the deposit insurance literature, however, assumes that the objective of the FDIC should be to minimize cost; see S. Acharya and J. F. Dreyfus, "Optimal Bank Reorganization Policies and the Pricing of Federal Deposit Insurance," *Journal of Finance* 44, 1988, pp. 1313–14. Also, the FDIC Improvement Act generally confirms cost minimization as an important objective defining FDIC's policies.

[14]See Y. S. Chan, S. I. Greenbaum, and A. V. Thakor, "Is Fairly Priced Deposit Insurance Possible?" *Journal of Finance* 47, 1992, pp. 227–46; and Buser, Chen, and Kane, "Federal Deposit Insurance."

[15]See, for example, R. C. Merton, "An Analytic Derivation of the Cost of Deposit Insurance and Loan Guarantees: An Application of Modern Option Pricing Theory," *Journal of Banking and Finance* 1, 1977, pp. 3–11; and E. Ronn and A. K. Verma, "Pricing Risk-Adjusted Deposit Insurance: An Option-Based Model," *Journal of Finance* 41, 1986, pp. 871–96.

FIGURE 15–4

Premium schedules relative to risk

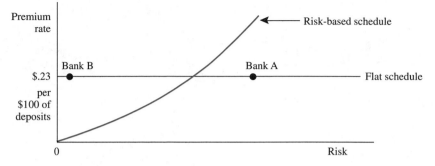

than $0D$—its net worth is positive—and it can continue in business. The FDIC would face no charge against its resources. If the bank is insolvent, possibly because of a bad or risky asset portfolio, such that the value of the bank's assets ($0A$) falls below $0D$ and its net worth is negative, the bank owners would "put the bank" back to the FDIC. If this happens, the FDIC will pay out, to the insured depositors, an amount $0D$ and and will liquidate the bank's assets ($0A$). As a result, the FDIC bears the cost of the insolvency (or negative net worth) equal to ($0D - 0A$) minus the insurance premiums paid by the bank ($0P$).

When valued in this fashion as a simple European put option, the FDIC's cost of providing deposit insurance increases with the level of asset risk (σ^2_A) and with the bank's leverage (D/A). That is, the actuarially fair premium ($0P$) is equivalent to the premium on a put option and as such should be positively related to both asset risk (σ^2_A) and leverage risk (D/A).[16]

Even though the option pricing model is a conceptually and theoretically elegant tool, it is difficult to apply in practice—especially as asset risk (σ^2_A) is not directly observable. Such risk can be proxied by using the variance of a bank's stock market return; however, less than 150 banks have their stocks traded on the three major exchanges (AMEX, NASDAQ, and NYSE) and there are some 12,500 banks. Even so, the option model framework is useful because it indicates that both leverageand asset quality (or risk) are important elements that should enter into any pricing model. Next, we look at the interim risk-based deposit premium scheme

---

[16]In Merton, "An Analytic Derivation," the value of a deposit insurance guarantee is shown to be the same as the Black-Scholes model for a European put option of maturity T (where T is the time period until the next premium assessment):

$$OP(T) = De^{-rT} \phi(X_2) - A\phi(X_1)$$

where:

$$X_1 = \{\log (D/A) - (r + \sigma^2_A/2) \, T\}/\sigma_A\sqrt{T}$$

$$X_2 = X_1 + \sigma_A\sqrt{T}$$

and ϕ is the standard normal distribution.

Other authors have relaxed many of Merton's assumptions including: (1) allowing for partial deposit coverage (Ronn and Verma, "Pricing Risk-Adjusted Deposit Insurance,"); (2) closure taking place when $D<A$ (i.e., forbearance) rather than $D = A$ (Ronn and Verma, and Acharya and Dreyfus, "Optimal Bank Reorganization,") (3) surveillance and monitoring involving costs (Merton "On the Cost of Deposit Insurance When There Are Surveillance Costs," *Journal of Business* 51, 1978, pp. 439–52); and (4) the option being American rather than European, that is, closure exercisable at any time during the insurance contract period rather than at the end (Merton, "On the Cost").

FIGURE 15–5

Deposit insurance as a put option

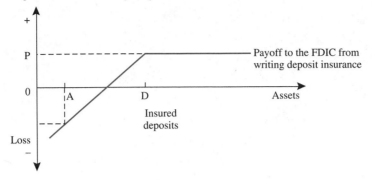

introduced by the FDIC in January 1993; it is directly linked to both bank leverage and asset quality.

Concept Questions

1. Bank A has a ratio of deposits to assets of 90 percent and a variance of asset returns of 10 percent. Bank B has a ratio of deposits to assets of 85 percent and a variance of asset returns of 5 percent. Which bank should pay the higher insurance premium?
2. If deposit insurance is similar to a put option, who exercises that option?
3. If you are managing a bank that is technically insolvent but has not yet been closed by the regulators, would you invest in Treasury bonds or real estate development loans? Explain your answer.

Implementing Risk-Based Premiums.   The FDIC Improvement Act requires the FDIC to establish risk-based premiums by January 1, 1994. The FDIC has to base these premiums on:[17]

1. Different categories and concentrations of assets.
2. Different categories and concentrations of liabilities—insured, uninsured, contingent, and noncontingent.
3. Other factors that affect the probability of loss.
4. The deposit insurer's revenue needs.

As an interim measure, the FDIC introduced a transitional risk-based deposit insurance program on January 1, 1993. Under this program that applies equally to all depository-insured institutions, a bank or thrift's risk would be ranked along a capital dimension and a supervisory dimension. That is, rankings are partly based on regulators' judgments regarding asset quality, loan underwriting standards, and other operating risks. Since each dimension has three categories, a bank or thrift could be placed in any one of nine cells. See these in Table 15–2.

---

[17]The FDIC is also allowed to reinsure up to 10 percent of an insured institution's risk and to use reinsurance prices to set the insured's premiums.

TABLE 15–2 Shifting the Deposit Insurance Burden

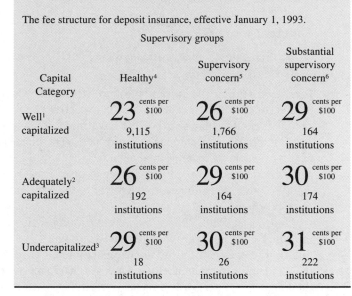

The fee structure for deposit insurance, effective January 1, 1993.

Capital Category	Supervisory groups		
	Healthy[4]	Supervisory concern[5]	Substantial supervisory concern[6]
Well[1] capitalized	23 cents per $100 — 9,115 institutions	26 cents per $100 — 1,766 institutions	29 cents per $100 — 164 institutions
Adequately[2] capitalized	26 cents per $100 — 192 institutions	29 cents per $100 — 164 institutions	30 cents per $100 — 174 institutions
Undercapitalized[3]	29 cents per $100 — 18 institutions	30 cents per $100 — 26 institutions	31 cents per $100 — 222 institutions

NOTE: Numbers in cells show premiums (large type) and the projected number of commercial banks in each cell.

[1]Total risk based ≥ 10 percent, Tier I risk based ≥ 6 percent, Tier I leverage ≥ 5 percent.

[2]Total risk based ≥ 8 percent, Tier I risk based ≥ 4 percent, Tier I leverage ≥ 4 percent.

[3]Does not meet the capital criteria for well or adequately capitalized depository institutions.

[4]Financially sound and only a few weaknesses.

[5]Weaknesses that if not corrected could result in significant risk to the fund.

[6]Substantial probability of loss to the fund unless effective corrective action is taken.

SOURCE: From *The New York Times,* September 16, 1992, p. D2. Copyright © 1992 by The New York Times Company. Reprinted by permission.

The best banks, those in cell 1 that are capitalized and healthy, pay an annual insurance premium of 23 cents per $100 of deposits while the worst banks pay 31 cents. The FDIC estimates that about 75 percent of the over 12,000 insured commercial banks and savings banks (with 51 percent of the bank deposit base) and 60 percent of the 2,300 insured thrifts (with approximately 43 percent of the thrift deposit base) are in the group paying the lowest premium. Only about 220 banks (2 percent of all insured commercial and savings banks) and 160 thrifts (7 percent of all insured thrifts) are in the group paying the highest insurance rate. According to FDIC estimates, banks will pay an average rate of about 25.4 cents per $100, compared to 25.9 cents per $100 for thrifts.[18]

The premiums introduced in 1993 are based in part on relatively objective measures of risk, such as risk-based capital, and subjective measures of risk reflecting the health of the institution. However, given only an 8-basis-point spread, or .08 percent, between the best and worst banks, there must be some doubts about the disciplining effects of risk-based premiums, at least as specified in the 1993 transitional scheme.

[18]See FDIC, Division of Research and Statistics, FIL-71-92, October 7, 1992.

Moreover, concerns have been raised regarding the heavy reliance on the subjective evaluation of regulators, given their performance during the thrift crisis.[19]

Concept Question

1. Make up a 3-point critique of the FDIC's risk-based premium scheme.

Increased Capital Requirements and Stricter Closure Rules. A second way to reduce stockholders' incentives to take excessive risks would be to (1) require higher capital ratios (so that stockholders have more at stake in taking risky investments) and (2) to impose stricter bank closure rules. The moral hazard risk-taking incentives of bank owners increase as their capital or net worth approaches zero and their leverage increases. For those thrifts allowed to operate in the 1980s with virtually no book equity capital and with negative net worth, the risk-taking incentives of their owners were enormous.

Indeed, in 1990, 395 thrifts were operating with zero capital and approximately the same number again with capital-assets ratios of between 0 and 3 percent. By failing to close such thrifts, regulators exhibited excessive **capital forbearance**. In the short term, forbearance may save the insurance fund some liquidation costs. In the long run, owners of bad banks or thrifts have continuing incentives to grow and take additional risks in the hope of a large payoff that could turn the institution around. This strategy potentially adds to the future liabilities of the insurance fund and to the costs of bank liquidation. We now know that huge additional costs were the actual outcome of the regulators' policy of capital forbearance in the thrift industry.

> **Capital Forbearance**
> Regulators allowing an FI to continue operating even when its capital funds are fully depleted.

As we discuss in Chapter 14, a system of risk-based capital requirements mandates that those banks and thrifts taking greater on- and off-balance-sheet credit and interest rate risks must hold more capital. Thus, risk-based capital is supporting risk-based deposit insurance premiums by increasing the cost of risk taking for bank stockholders.[20] In addition, the 1991 FDIC Improvement Act sought to significantly increase the degree of regulatory discipline over bank stockholders by introducing the prompt corrective action program. This imposes five capital zones for banks and thrifts with progressively harsher mandatory actions being taken by regulators as capital ratios fall. Under this carrot and stick approach, a bank or thrift is placed into receivership when its capital falls below some positive book value level such as 2 percent of assets for banks.

To the extent that the book value of capital somewhat approximates true net worth or the market value of capital, this enhances stockholder discipline by imposing additional costs on bank owners for risk taking. It also increases the degree of coinsurance, in regard to risks taken, between bank owners and regulators.

Concept Question

1. Do we need both risk-based capital requirements and risk-based premiums to discipline shareholders?

---

[19]See R. S. Carnell, "A Partial Antidote to Preserve Incentives: The FDIC Improvement Act of 1991" (Paper presented at the Conference on Rebuilding Public Confidence through Financial Reform, Ohio State University, Columbus, Ohio, June 15, 1992).

[20]On the assumption that new equity is more costly to raise than deposits for banks.

TABLE 15–3   Deposit Ownership Categories

Individual ownership, such as a simple checking account.

Joint ownership, such as the savings account of a husband and wife.

Revocable trusts, in which the beneficiary is a qualified relative of the settlor, and the settlor has the ability to alter or eliminate the trust.

Irrevocable trusts, where the beneficial interest is not subject to being altered or eliminated.

Interests in employee benefit plans where the interests are vested and thus not subject to being altered or eliminated.

Public units, that is, accounts of federal, state, and municipal governments.

Corporations and partnerships.

Unincorporated businesses and associations.

Individual retirement accounts (IRAs).

Keogh accounts.

Executor or administrator accounts.

Accounts held by banks in an agency or fiduciary capacity.

SOURCE: U.S. Department of the Treasury, "Modernizing the Financial System: Recommendations for Safer More Competitive Banks," Washington, D.C.: February 1991.

Depositor Discipline

An alternative, more indirect route to disciplining riskier banks is to create conditions for a greater degree of depositor discipline. Depositors could either require higher interest rates and risk premiums on deposits or ration the amount of deposits they are willing to hold in riskier banks.

Critics argue that under the current insurance contract neither insured depositors nor uninsured depositors have sufficient incentives to discipline riskier banks. To understand these arguments, we consider the risk exposure of both insured and uninsured depositors under the current deposit insurance contract.

Insured Depositors.   When the deposit insurance contract was introduced in 1933, the level of coverage per depositor was $2,500. This coverage cap has gradually risen through the years reaching $100,000 in 1980. The $100,000 cap concerns a depositor's beneficial interest and ownership of deposited funds. In actuality, by structuring deposit funds in a bank or thrift in a particular fashion, a depositor can achieve many times the $100,000 coverage cap on deposits. To see this, consider the different categories of deposit fund ownership available to an individual in Table 15–3.

A married couple with one daughter, where both husband and wife had **Individual Retirement Accounts (IRA)** and **Keogh** private pension plans at the bank, could garner a total coverage cap of $800,000 as a family: his individual deposit account, her individual deposit account, their joint deposit account, their daughter's deposit account held in trust, his IRA account, his Keogh account, her IRA account, and her Keogh account. By expanding the range of ownership in this fashion, the coverage cap for a family can rapidly approach $1 million or more.

Note that this coverage ceiling is *per bank*; wealthy and institutional investors can employ **deposit brokers** to spread their funds over many banks up to the per-

IRA and Keogh Accounts
Private pension plans held by individuals with banks or other FIs.

Deposit Brokers
Break up large deposits into smaller units at different banks to ensure full coverage by deposit insurance.

mitted cap. In this way, all of their deposits become explicitly insured. For example, a wealthy individual with $1 million in deposits could hire a deposit broker such as Merrill Lynch to split the $1 million into 10 parcels of $100,000 and deposit those funds at 10 different banks. During the 1980s, the greatest purchasers of brokered deposits were the most risky banks that had no, or limited, access to the borrowed funds market. These risky banks attracted brokered deposits by offering higher interest rates than relatively healthy banks. In fact, a high proportion of brokered deposits held by a bank became an early warning signal of its future failure risk. Neither the depositors nor fund brokers were concerned about the risk of these funds because every parcel of $100,000 was fully insured, including interest accrued up until time of failure.[21]

In 1984, the FDIC and FSLIC introduced a joint resolution intending to deny insurance coverage to funds invested by deposit brokers. After extensive congressional hearings, this resolution was ultimately rejected; however, in 1989 Congress passed the Financial Institutions Reform, Recovery and Enforcement Act (FIRREA). It specified that insured financial institutions failing to meet capital standards would be prohibited from accepting brokered deposits as well as from soliciting deposits by offering interest rates significantly higher than prevailing rates. The FDIC Improvement Act (FDICIA) of 1991 formalized these restrictions by allowing access to brokered deposits only to those banks and thrifts in Zone 1 capital range. Under the prompt corrective action plan, this means banks with total risk-based capital ratios exceeding 10 percent. Banks outside this range are generally precluded unless they receive specific approval from the FDIC. These restrictions became effective in June 1992.[22]

Finally, the FDIC Improvement Act left the insured depositor coverage cap unchanged at $100,000. While lowering the coverage cap would increase the incentives of depositors to monitor and run from more risky banks, it would also increase the bank failures and the probability of panics. Thus, the gains to the FDIC from covering a smaller dollar amount of deposits per head would have to be weighed against the possibility of more failures with their attendant liquidation costs. This suggests that setting the optimal level of the insurance cap per depositor per bank is a far from easy problem.[23]

Uninsured Depositors.   The primary intention of deposit insurance is to deter bank runs and panics. A secondary and related objective has been to protect the smaller, less informed saver against the reduction in wealth that would occur if that person were last in line when a bank fails. Under the current contract, the small, less informed depositor is defined by the $100,000 ceiling. Theoretically, at least, larger, informed depositors with more than $100,000 on deposit are at risk should a bank fail. As a result, these large uninsured depositors should be sensitive to bank risk and seek to discipline more risky banks by demanding either higher interest rates on their

---

[21]Technically, principal on deposits plus accrued interest up to $100,000 is covered.

[22]There were certain other provisions limiting coverage to an individual, including coverage of certain pension fund accounts (other than IRA and Keogh) and investment accounts. So-called pass-through insurance, where a bank manages pension funds on behalf of a large number of savers, such as investing in bank investment contracts or BICs, is fully covered by FDIC insurance up to $100,000 per head only if the bank is eligible to issue brokered deposits and/or meets the highest capital standards.

[23]For a modeling of this problem, see J. F. Dreyfus, A. Saunders, and L. Allen, "Deposit Insurance and Regulatory Forbearance: Are Caps on Insured Deposits Optimal?" *Journal of Money Credit and Banking*, forthcoming.

Too Big to Fail Banks
Regulators view these banks as being too big to be closed and liquidated without imposing a systemic risk to the banking and financial system.

deposits or withdrawing their deposits completely. Until recently, the manner in which bank failures have been resolved meant that both large and small depositors were often fully protected against losses. This was especially so where large banks got into trouble and were **too big to fail.** That is, they were too big to be liquidated by regulators either because of the draining effects on the resources of the insurance fund or for fear of contagious or systemic runs spreading to other major banks. Thus, although uninsured depositors tended to lose in small bank failures, in large bank failures the failure resolution methods employed by regulators usually resulted in implicit 100 percent deposit insurance. As a result, for large banks in particular, neither small nor large depositors had sufficient incentives to impose market discipline on riskier banks.

To understand these arguments, we look at the major ways bank failures were resolved before the passage of the FDIC Improvement Act in 1991. We also look at the new procedures required under the FDICIA to create greater exposure for uninsured depositors and to reduce the FDIC's failure resolution costs.

Failure Resolution Procedures Pre-FDICIA.   Pre-FDICIA, the three failure resolution methods were the payoff method, the purchase and assumption method, and the open assistance method. Before the passage of the FDICIA in 1991, the FDIC had to use liquidation (**the payoff method**) unless an alternative method was judged by the FDIC to cost less. This method of choosing the closure policy is "a less than liquidation cost requirement" and contrasts with a true "least-cost resolution" policy where the lowest cost method of all closure methods available would be selected.[24] Not until the passage of the FDICIA was the least cost resolution required of the FDIC. In addition, prior to 1991, the less than liquidation cost requirement could be overridden and the bank kept open in a restructured form if its continued operation was deemed essential for the local community. The FDICIA also repealed this "essentiality" provision.

Pay Off Method of Closure
Liquidation of the bank and paying off the bank's depositors.

Next, we look in more detail at the three principal methods of failure resolution employed by the FDIC pre-1991. Then we discuss how the FDICIA has changed the FDIC's strategy and, most important, the potential effects of these changes on increasing depositor discipline.

The Payoff Method (Liquidation).   The payoff method has resolved most small bank failures, where a merger was unavailable or too costly or where the bank's loss to the community would impose few local social costs. Under a payoff closure, regulators liquidate the assets of the bank and pay off the insured depositors in full (insured deposit payoff). They could also transfer these deposits in full to another local bank (insured deposit transfer). In Table 15–5, compare the relative sizes of these two payoff methods over the 1980–89 period. On liquidation, uninsured depositors and the FDIC, which assumes the claims of the insured depositors, have pro rata claims to the remaining value of the failed bank's assets.

To understand who gains and who potentially loses under the payoff (liquidation) method, consider the simple example of a failed bank in Table 15–6. The failed bank's liquidation value of assets is only $80 million. It has $50 million in outstanding claims held by small insured depositors whose claims individually are $100,000 or less and $50 million in uninsured depositor claims that individually exceed $100,000. The net worth of the failed bank is negative $20 million.

---

[24]See R. S. Carnell, "A Partial Antidote to Preserve Incentives: The FDIC Improvement Act of 1991."

TABLE 15–5 Failure Resolutions by Transaction Type, 1980–89

	Purchase and Assumptions (P&As)			Payoff (liquidation)			
Year	Traditional	Whole Bank[1]	Small Loan	Insured Deposit Transfers	Insured Deposit Payoffs	Open-Bank Assistance	Total
1980	7	0	0	0	3	1	11
	$ 218,331[1]	0	0	0	$ 17,832	$ 7,953,000	$ 8,189,163
1981	8	0	0	0	2	3	13
	4,808,042	0	0	0	51,018	4,599,000	9,458,060
1982	35	0	0	0	7	8	50
	11,046,997	0	0	0	585,418	8,543,000	20,175,415
1983	36	0	0	0	9	3	48
	7,026,923	0	0	0	164,037	2,890,000	7,026,923
1984	62	0	0	12	4	2	80
	1,905,924	0	0	$ 499,517	356,051	34,147,919	36,936,411
1985	87	0	0	7	22	4	120
	2,235,182	0	0	325,841	284,315	5,895,930	8,741,268
1986	98	0	0	19	21	7	145
	6,375,900	0	0	759,400	575,100	718,800	8,429,200
1987	114	19	0	40	11	19	203
	3,833,870	$ 584,092	0	2,190,700	348,300	2,551,115	9,508,077
1988	54	110	0	30	6	21	221
	1,523,979	37,351,973	0	1,153,000	123,700	13,539,018	53,691,670
1989	30	87	$ 58	22	9	1	207
	960,982	23,099,693	3,013,685	1,630,243	548,024	5,699	6,052,934
Total	531	216	58	130	94	69	1,098
	$39,936,130	$61,035,758	$3,013,685	$6,558,701	$3,053,795	$80,843,481	$168,209,121

[1]The second row in each year contains total assets in thousands of dollars.

[2]The whole bank P&As include some large bank failure transactions in which the acquirer has a contractual relationship with the Federal Deposit Insurance Corporation (FDIC) to service problem assets. This involves an ongoing loss exposure for the FDIC. The term *whole bank* P&A normally refers to a transaction in which the FDIC has no ongoing exposure.

SOURCE: Federal Deposit Insurance Corporation, U.S. Department of the Treasury, "Modernizing the Financial System," 1991.

On closure, the insured depositors receive a $50 million payoff in full.[25] The FDIC liquidates the $80 million in assets and shares it on an equal, or pro rata, basis with the uninsured depositors. Since the FDIC owns 50 percent of deposit claims and the uninsured depositors the other 50 percent, each gets $40 million on the liquidation of the bank's assets.

The allocation of the $20 million net worth loss of the bank among the three parties or claimants follows:[26]

[25]Instead of a payoff in full, in an insured deposit transfer their deposits are transferred in full to another local bank.

[26]We do not show the value of the equity holders' claims. Since they have junior claims to these three parties (the FDIC, the insured depositors, and uninsured depositors) their claims are reduced to zero on failure. If, however, the bank liquidation did not produce $80 million but rather due to a dramatic improvement in the economy $102 million, then the equity holders might receive the residual amount above $100 million which is $2 million. Even this, in reality, might be absorbed by legal costs and other administrative costs related to failure.

TABLE 15–6   Failed Bank Balance Sheet
(in millions)

Assets		Liabilities	
Asset (Liquidation value)	$80	Insured deposits	$ 50
		Uninsured deposits	50
	$80		$100

Loss (in millions)	
Insured depositors	$ 0
FDIC	10
Uninsured depositors	10
	$20

The negative $20 million net worth loss of the bank is shared pro rata by the FDIC and the uninsured depositors.[27] From this example, it is clear that if the payoff method were always used to resolve bank failures, uninsured depositors would have very strong incentives to monitor bank risk taking. They would also discipline owners by requiring higher risk premiums on their deposits and/or withdrawing their deposits from riskier banks.

While regulators frequently used the payoff method, prior to 1991, this was mostly for small failing banks. They used the second and third closure methods described next most often for large failing banks. As will become clear, these imposed much less discipline on uninsured depositors.

Concept Question

1. How would the losses of the bank have been shared in the previous example if insured deposits were 30 and uninsured deposits were 70?

Purchase and Assumption (P&A)
Merger of a failed bank with a healthy bank.

Purchase and Assumption (P&A).   As you can see in Table 15–5, there are three types of purchase and assumption resolutions. That most commonly used prior to the FDIC Improvement Act was the traditional P&A method; beginning in 1987 regulators tried whole bank P&As and since 1989 some small loan P&As.

Under a traditional purchase and assumption, a stronger healthy bank purchases and assumes both the insured and uninsured deposits of the failed bank, as well as its remaining good assets, mostly securities. The difference between the total deposits of the failed bank and the market value of the failed bank's good assets is met by a cash infusion from the FDIC minus any takeover premium the acquiring bank is willing to pay. For large bank failures, whole bank P&As transferred all assets, good and bad, with a lower initial FDIC cash infusion but with an option for the acquiring bank to put back uncollectible bad assets (up to some limit) to the FDIC at a later date.

---

[27]In insured deposit transfers, when the insured deposits of the failed bank are transferred to another bank and its assets liquidated, the acquirer of the insured deposits sometimes pays a premium to the FDIC reflecting the value of picking up new deposit customers. Any such premium would lower the costs of liquidation to the FDIC.

TABLE 15–7   A Traditional P&A Transaction

Assets		Liabilities	
Good assets	$ 80	Insured depositors	$ 50
			→ Good bank (acquirer)
FDIC cash infusion	20	Uninsured depositors	50
	$100		$100

Finally, a small loan P&A transfers all deposits and only the small good loans of the failing bank, such as auto loans, to an acquiring bank. The large bad loans and other loans are kept by the FDIC.

To understand the mechanics of a traditional P&A and who bears the losses, we look at a P&A of the same bank discussed in the *payoff* (liquidation) example earlier. See Table 15–7.

The P&A transfers all depositors, insured and uninsured, to the acquiring bank. Thus, neither the insured nor uninsured depositors lose. The full $20 million loss is borne by the FDIC through its cash injection to clean up the failed bank's bad assets prior to the merger with the acquiring bank minus any premium it can obtain from the acquiring bank.[28] For example a bank in New York may pay a premium to acquire a failing bank in Florida, because Florida is a high growth market. Also, given the current interstate banking barriers, this is one of the few ways a New York bank can do deposit business in Florida. We discuss these barriers in detail in Chapter 16.

To summarize the losses of the three parties in a traditional P&A:

Loss (in millions)	
Insured depositors	0
Uninsured depositors	0
FDIC	$20 (minus any merger premium)
Total	$20

Clearly, with a traditional P&A, large uninsured depositors are de facto insured depositors.

Concept Question

1. List four factors that might influence an acquirer to make a large merger premium bid for a failing bank.

Open Assistance.   The third main method of closure regulators used was **open assistance** (see Table 15–5). When very large banking organizations fail, such as Continental Illinois in 1984 with $36 billion in assets and First City Bancorporation

Open Assistance
Provision of FDIC loans or capital funds to keep a large failing bank open as part of a restructuring plan.

---

[28]In recent years, regulators have held auctions to select the acquiring bank. However, the bank that bids the highest premium does not always win; the FDIC takes into account the quality of the bidder as well. For example, a low-quality bank that acquires a failed bank in an auction might become a bigger problem bank in the future.

of Texas in 1987 with $11 billion in assets, it is often difficult, if not impossible, to find a bank sound and big enough to engage in a P&A. Moreover, regulators feared that smaller correspondent banks would be hurt by a large bank's closure and that big depositors and investors might lose confidence in all large U.S. banks if they used payoff and liquidation. An example of open assistance was the commitment of $870 million by the FDIC to an investor group headed by Robert Abboud to take over control of First City Bancorporation of Texas in September 1987. However, failure to close and liquidate a bad bank sends a strong and undesirable signal to large uninsured depositors at other big banks that their deposits are safe and that regulators will not permit big banks to fail. That is, all large uninsured depositors with big banks are really implicitly 100 percent insured, thereby alleviating depositors from any monitoring/market discipline responsibilities.[29] Such an implicit guarantee to uninsured depositors at large banks is often called the too big to fail guarantee.[30]

Failure Resolution Policies Post-FDICIA.   In the wake of the FDIC's growing deficit, the FDICIA sought to pass more of the costs of insured bank failures on to uninsured depositors, thereby enhancing their incentives to monitor banks and to control risk through interest rates and/or in their deposit placement decisions.

The FDICIA requested that by January 1, 1995, at the latest, a least cost resolution (LCR) strategy should be put in place by the FDIC. In applying the LCR strategy, the FDIC evaluates failure resolution alternatives on a present value basis and documents their assumptions in deciding which method to use. These decisions can be audited by the General Accounting Office, the government's audit watchdog.

However, there was a very important and controversial exception to using least cost resolution in all cases. Specifically, a systemic risk exemption applies where a large bank failure could cause a threat to the whole financial system. Then methods that could involve the full protection of uninsured depositors as well as insured depositors could be used. This appears to allow the too big to fail guarantee to large bank uninsured depositors prevalent in the pre-1991 system to carry over after the passage of the FDICIA. However, the act has restricted when this systemic risk exemption can be used. Such an exemption is allowed only if a two thirds majority of the boards of the Federal Reserve and the FDIC recommend it to the secretary of the treasury, and if the secretary of the treasury, in consultation with the president of the United States, agrees. Further, any cost of such a bail out of a big bank would have to be shared among all other banks by charging them an additional premium based on their size as measured by their domestic and foreign deposits as well as their borrowed funds excluding subordinated debt. Because large banks have more foreign

---

[29]For example, in the final restructuring arrangement for Continental Illinois, all depositors were protected; the FDIC assumed a large amount of problem loans and infused $1 billion new capital into the bank with a part convertible into a direct ownership interest. By taking an equity stake in the failed bank, the FDIC stood to gain, with outside equity owners, from any improvement in the performance of the bank as well. Indeed, in a number of open assistance programs, the FDIC holds long-term options or warrants that allow it to share in the upside of improved bank performance (if any). Nevertheless, the incentive to impose market discipline has still been eliminated for large uninsured depositors.

[30]See O'Hara and Shaw and Mei and Saunders who seek to calculate the value of such a too big to fail guarantee. O'Hara and Shaw find significant value while Mei and Saunders find little value from such guarantees. See M. O'Hara and W. Shaw, "Deposit Insurance and Wealth Effects; The Value of Being Too Big to Fail," *Journal of Finance* 45, 1990, pp. 1587–1600; and J. P. Mei and A. Saunders, "Bank Risk and Too Big to Fail Guarantees: An Asset Pricing Perspective" (Working Paper, Salomon Brothers Center, New York University, 1993).

TABLE 15–8 A Modified Payoff Resolution

(a) Failed				(b) Modified Payoff			
Assets		*Liabilities*		*Assets*		*Liabilities*	
Good assets	$80	Insured deposits	$50	Good assets	$80	Insured deposits	$50
		Uninsured deposits	50			Uninsured deposits	30
	$80		$100		$80		$80

In panel (b), beside the Liabilities: "Merger → with good bank"

Modified Payoff
Uninsured depositors take a loss or haircut on failure equal to the difference between their deposit claims and the estimated value of the failed bank's assets minus insured deposits.

deposits and borrowed funds, they will have to make bigger contributions (per dollar of assets) than smaller banks to any future bail-out of a large bank.

Consequently, with the exception of systemic risk, the least cost resolution strategy requires the FDIC to employ the method that imposes most failure costs on the uninsured depositors. To this end, the FDIC has been using a modified payoff or haircut method to resolve a number of post-1991 failures. For example, it used a form of **modified payoff** in the February 1993 takeover of First City Bancorporation of Texas by the Chemical Banking Corporation.[31] Uninsured depositors in the Dallas and Houston branches of the failed banking organization bore some significant losses. We describe a simplified form of the modified payoff or haircut method next. This allows us to compare the cost of this new approach to previous methods such as the traditional P&A and payoff methods.

In Table 15–8 the failed bank in panel *a* has only $80 million in good assets to meet the $50 million in deposit claims of insured depositors and the $50 million in claims of the uninsured depositors.[32] Under a modified payoff in panel *b* the FDIC would transfer the $80 million in assets to an acquiring bank along with the full $50 million in small insured deposits but only $30 million of the $50 million in uninsured deposits.[33] Notice that the uninsured depositors get protection only against losses up to the difference between the estimated value of the failed bank's assets and its insured deposits. In effect, the uninsured depositors are subject to a haircut to their original deposit claims of $20 million (or as a percentage, 40 percent of the value of their deposit claims on the failed bank). After the modified payoff, the uninsured depositors own $30 million in deposits in the acquiring bank and $20 million in receivership claims on the bad assets of the failed bank. Only if the FDIC as receiver can recover some value from the $20 million in bad assets, would the loss to the uninsured be less than $20 million.

To summarize the losses of the three parties under the modified payoff:

Loss (in millions)		
Insured depositors	=	0
FDIC	=	0
Uninsured depositors	=	$20

---

[31]Chemical purchased the bank from the FDIC that had seized it in October 1992 from the investor group to which it had provided open assistance in September 1987.

[32]That is, it has $20 million negative net worth.

[33]Unlike in a P&A, it would not inject cash into the failed bank prior to a merger with the acquiring bank.

As you can see from this simple example, the uninsured depositors bear all the losses and now have a much stronger incentive than before to monitor and control the actions of bank owners through imposing market discipline via interest rates and the amount of funds deposited.

Concept Question

1. Make up a simple balance sheet example to show a case where the FDIC can lose even when it uses modified-payoff to resolve a failed bank.

Regulatory Discipline

To bolster increased stockholder and depositor discipline, the FDICIA imposed additional regulatory discipline. The act perceived two areas of regulatory weakness: (1) in the frequency and thoroughness of examinations and (2) the forbearance shown to weakly capitalized banks in the pre-1991 period.

Examinations.   First, the act required improved accounting standards for banks, including working toward the market valuation of balance sheet assets and liabilities. This would improve the ability of examiners to monitor banks' net worth positions off-site and is consistent with monitoring the true net worth of the bank (see Chapters 5 and 6). Second, beginning in December 1992, the act required an annual on-site examination of every bank. Third, private accountants have been given a greater role in monitoring a bank's performance with independent audits being mandated. This is similar to the United Kingdom, where the 1987 Bank Act recommended an enhanced role for private auditors as a backup for regulatory examiners.

Capital Forbearance.   The introduction of the five prompt corrective action capital zones (see Chapter 14), along with the mandatory actions required of regulators in each of those zones (including closure) is symptomatic of a movement toward a regulatory policy based on rules rather than discretion. Such rules clearly direct the behavior of regulators to act in a certain manner even if they are reluctant to do so out of self-interest or for other reasons. The weakness of such rules is that if a policy is bad, then bad policy becomes more effective.[34]

The Discount Window

Deposit Insurance versus the Discount Window

The previous sections have described how a well-designed deposit insurance system imposes stockholder, depositor, and manager discipline. This system can potentially stop bank runs and extreme liquidity problems arising in the banking system without

---

[34]Similar arguments have been made in the area of monetary policy where proponents (such as monetarist Milton Friedman) have argued for a rules policy based on a constant growth rate of the money supply. However, most central bankers prefer discretion in deciding on the timing and size of monetary policy actions such as their open market operations.

TABLE 15–9 **The Spread between the Discount Rate and the Fed Funds Rate**

	1989	1990	1991
Federal funds	9.21	8.10	5.69
Discount window	6.93	6.98	5.45

SOURCE: *Federal Reserve Bulletin*, January 1993, Table A25.

introducing significant amounts of moral hazard risk-taking behavior among insured institutions.

Whether the FDICIA has priced risk accurately enough, to stop all but the most egregious cases of moral hazard, only time will tell. It has certainly increased the incentives of bank owners, uninsured depositors, and regulators to monitor and control bank risk. As such, the changes made under the act are considerable improvements over the old pre-1991 deposit insurance contract.

However, deposit insurance isn't the only mechanism by which regulators mitigate bank liquidity risk. A second mechanism has been the central banks' provision of a lender of last resort facility through the discount window.

The Discount Window

Discount Window
Central bank lender of last resort facility.

Traditionally, central banks such as the Federal Reserve have provided a **discount window** facility to meet the short-term, nonpermanent, liquidity needs of banks.[35] For example, suppose a bank has an unexpected deposit drain close to the end of a reserve requirement period, and cannot meet its reserve target. It can seek to borrow from the central bank's discount window facility. Alternatively, short-term seasonal liquidity needs due to crop planting cycles can also be met through discount window loans. Normally, such loans are made by a bank discounting short-term high-quality paper such as Treasury bills and bankers acceptances with the central bank. The rate at which such paper is discounted is called the discount rate and is set by the central bank. In the United States, the central bank has traditionally set the discount rate below market rates, such as the overnight federal funds rates, as we show in Table 15–9.[36]

The Discount Window Does Not Substitute for Deposit Insurance

There are a number of reasons why bank access to the discount window is unlikely to deter bank runs and panics the way deposit insurance does. The first reason is that to borrow from the discount window, a bank needs high-quality liquid assets to pledge as collateral. By definition, highly illiquid banks are unlikely to have such assets available to discount. The second reason is that borrowing is not automatic, unlike deposit insurance coverage, once premiums are paid. Specifically, banks gain access to the window only on a "need to borrow" basis. If the central bank considers that a borrowing request emanates from a profit motive because the discount rate is set

---

[35]In times of extreme crisis, the discount window can meet the liquidity needs of securities firms as well.

[36]However, as the level of market rates drops, it is possible for fed fund rates to lie below the discount rate. This occurred in October 1992 when fed funds were 2.96 percent and the discount rate was 3 percent.

below money market interbank rates, the borrowing request would be refused. That is, discount window loans are made at the discretion of the central bank. Third, discount window loans are meant to provide temporary liquidity for inherently solvent banks and not permanent long-term support for otherwise insolvent banks.

This narrow role of the discount window was confirmed in the 1991 FDICIA that limited the discretion of the Federal Reserve to make extended loans to troubled banks. Specifically, discount window loans to troubled, undercapitalized banks are limited to no more than 60 days in any 120-day period, unless both the FDIC and the institution's primary regulator certify that the bank is viable. Additional extensions of up to 60 days are allowed subject to regulator certification. Finally, any discount window advances to undercapitalized banks that eventually fail would lead to the Federal Reserve having to compensate the FDIC for incremental losses caused by the delay in keeping the troubled bank open longer than necessary.[37] Consequently, the discount window is a partial but not a full substitute for deposit insurance as a liquidity stabilizing mechanism.

Other Guarantee Programs

As we discuss in Chapter 13, other FIs are also subject to liquidity crises and liability holders run into problems resulting in insolvencies. To deter such runs and protect small claim holders, guarantee programs have appeared in other sectors of the financial services industry. We describe these programs and their similarities to and differences from deposit insurance next.

P-C and Life Insurance Companies

Both life insurance companies and property-casualty insurance companies are regulated at the state level. Unlike banks and thrifts, no federal guarantee fund exists for either life or P-C insurers. Beginning in the 1960s, most states began to sponsor state guarantee funds for firms selling insurance in that state.[38] These state guarantee funds have a number of important differences from deposit insurance. First, while these programs are sponsored by state insurance regulators, they are actually run and administered by the private insurance companies themselves.

Second, unlike SAIF or BIF, where the FDIC established a permanent reserve fund through banks paying annual premiums in excess of payouts to resolve failures, no such permanent guarantee fund exists for the insurance industry with the sole exception of the P-C and life guarantee funds for the state of New York. This means that contributions are paid into the guarantee fund by surviving firms only after an insurance company has failed.

Third, the size of the required contributions surviving insurers make to protect policyholders in failed insurance companies differs widely across states. In those states that have guarantee funds, each surviving insurer is normally levied a pro rata amount, according to the size of its statewide premium income. This amount either

---

[37]In practice, the Fed would be penalized by a loss in the interest income on discount window loans made to banks that eventually fail.

[38]However, Louisiana, New Jersey, and Washington, D.C., have no fund for life insurance industry failures while Colorado has only recently established one. Moreover, New York has a permanent fund into which insurers pay premiums regardless of the failure rate.

helps pay off small policyholders after the assets of the failed insurer have been liqui-dated or acts as a cash injection to make the acquisition of a failed insurer attractive. The definition of small policyholders generally varies across states from $100,000 to $500,000.[39]

Finally, because there is no permanent fund and the annual pro rata contributions are often legally capped, there is usually a delay before small policyholders get the cash surrender values of their policies or other payment obligations are met from the guarantee funds. This contrasts with deposit insurance, where insured depositors nor-mally receive immediate coverage of their claims. For example, the failure of Executive Life Insurance in 1991 left approximately $117.3 million in outstanding claims in Hawaii. But the Hawaii life insurance guarantee fund can raise only $13.1 million a year due to legal caps on surviving firms' contributions. This means that it may take up to nine years for surviving firms to meet the claims of Executive Life policyholders in Hawaii. In the failure of Baldwin United in 1983, the insurers them-selves raised additional funds, over and above the guarantee fund, to satisfy policy-holders' claims.

Thus, the private nature of insurance industry guarantee funds, their lack of per-manent reserves, and low caps on contributions means that they probably provide less credible protection to claimants than the bank and thrift insurance funds—even given the latter's parlous state. As a result, the incentives for insurance policyholders to engage in a run, should they perceive that an insurer has asset quality problems or in-surance underwriting problems, is quite strong even in the presence of such guarantee funds.

The Securities Investor Protection Corporation

Since the passage of the Securities Investor Protection Act in 1970 and the creation of the Securities Investor Protection Corporation (SIPC), securities firm customers have been given specific, but limited, protection against insolvencies. Basically, cus-tomers receive pro rata shares of a liquidated securities firm's assets with SIPC satis-fying remaining claims up to a maximum of $500,000 per individual. Between 1970 and 1988, 206 insolvencies cost the SIPC fund a total of $187 million; this is minis-cule in comparison to the payouts of the FDIC or FSLIC. Indeed, compared to either the banking or insurance funds, the SIPC losses have been very small. For example, even in the wake of the October 1987 stock market crash, the fund stood at $360 mil-lion at the end of 1988, with SIPC charging an annual assessment fee to its members of only $100 per annum.

The Pension Benefit Guarantee Corporation

In 1974 the Employee Retirement Income Security Act, or ERISA, established the Pension Benefit Guarantee Corporation (PBGC). Prior to 1974, an employee's pension benefits with a private corporation had very limited backing from that firm's assets. The establishment of the PBGC insured pension benefits against the under-funding of plans by corporations. In particular, ERISA made corporations liable for pension liabilities up to 30 percent of their net worth. Thus, if a pension plan had to be terminated due to a corporate merger, for example, the PBGC paid the difference between the plan's liabilities and 30 percent of the sponsor's net worth

[39]Since insurance industry guarantee fund premiums are size-based, they are similar to the pre-1993 flat insurance premiums under deposit insurance.

subject to an annual payment cap which is currently $29,250 a year. In 1985, Congress increased the pension plan sponsors' liability by giving the PBGC a secondary claim on the assets of corporations. And, in 1987, under the Pension Protection Act, Congress restricted the ability of firms to terminate underfunded plans in a reorganization unless the firm could show that such a termination was necessary for the continued existence of the firm.

Unlike the FDIC, however, the PBGC has virtually no regulatory or monitoring power over the pension plans it insures. Thus, it cannot restrict the risk-taking behavior of the plan managers through portfolio restrictions or implicit insurance premiums.[40] Moreover, the explicit premiums charged to corporations for plan coverage at first exhibited the same type of moral hazard incentives as those levied under deposit insurance. Given the lack of regulatory power of the PBGC, the moral hazard risk-taking incentives for plan sponsors are probably as great, if not greater, than those under deposit insurance.[41] Not surprisingly, in the 1970s, the PBGC operated with an ever-increasing deficit, which was reflected in the rising level of its nonrisk-related premium schedule. Starting with a flat fee of $1 per employee for insurance, this fee was raised to $2.60 in 1978 and to $8.50 in 1986. Finally in 1988, the fee increased to $16 per employee plus an additional $6 for every $1,000 that the plan was underfunded per employee. The $6 surcharge for underfunded programs, covering an estimated 8 percent of employees, was one of the first cases where a public guarantee fund has instituted a form of risk-related insurance premiums. Despite this, PBGC's deficit continues to rise, standing at $2.7 billion at the end of 1992.

---

[40]To the extent that regulation restricts the asset and liability activities of a firm or FI, it is similar to imposing an implicit premium or tax on the activities of the firm.

[41]See "Underfunded Pension Plans Raise Benefits, GAO Says," *New York Times*, February 5, 1993, p. D1.

Summary

In recent years, bank and other financial industry guarantee programs have been weakened and in some cases rendered insolvent. This suggests that all financial service industry guarantee programs need to be revised—not just those for depository institutions—so that liquidity risk protection can be provided (and financial system stability enhanced) without encouraging moral hazard behavior. To do this, risk-related premiums, risk-based capital, and increased market and regulatory discipline of FI owners and managers should be encouraged and strict closure rules for insolvent FIs should be implemented and enforced.

Questions and Problems

1. If you are managing a bank that is technically insolvent but has not yet been closed by the regulators, would you invest in Treasury bonds or risky loans? Why?

2. How does the FDIC Improvement Act of 1991 succeed in implementing a risk-based deposit insurance premium? What are the shortcomings of the procedure?

3. Deposit insurance in the United States has, since its inception, been structured to create the incentive to engage in excessive risk taking. If this is true, why did the system operate successfully for almost 50 years?

4. Contrast the three guarantee funds: the FDIC (Federal Deposit Insurance Corporation), the SIPC (Securities Investor Protection Corporation), and the PBGC (Pension Benefit Guarantee Corporation).

5. If the SIPC is subject to the same problems of moral hazard as the FDIC and the PBGC, what accounts for its relatively strong financial condition?

6. How would a risk-based deposit insurance pricing scheme impact the risk and profitability of the FI?

7. What are the difficulties in designing a risk-based deposit insurance pricing scheme?

8. What are the determinants of option based, risk-adjusted

deposit insurance premiums? What changes in each of these determinants increase the value of deposit insurance premiums?

9. Use the FDICIA pricing schedule that took effect in January 1993 to calculate the deposit insurance premium for the following banks, assuming that supervisors classified all three as healthy.

Capital

Bank	Insured Deposits	Tier I	Tier II
A	$150 million	11%	19%
B	700	1	4
C	305	5.5	4.5

10. A bank with insured deposits of $55 million and uninsured deposits of $45 million has assets valued at only $75 million. What is the cost to insured depositors, uninsured depositors, and the FDIC if:

   a. The payoff method of failure resolution is used?

   b. A purchase and assumption is arranged with no purchase premium?

   c. A purchase and assumption is arranged with a $5 million purchase premium?

   d. A purchase and assumption is arranged with a $25 million purchase premium?

   e. A modified payoff method of failure resolution is used?

11. An insolvent bank has liabilities worth $100 million and assets valued at only $50 million; $70 million of the liabilities are insured deposits and $30 million are uninsured.

   a. What is the FDIC's loss if the payoff method of failure resolution is used? What is the loss to insured depositors? What is the loss to uninsured depositors?

   b. What is the FDIC's loss if the modified payoff method of failure resolution is used? What is the loss to insured depositors? What is the loss to uninsured depositors?

   c. What determines the cost to the FDIC of a purchase and assumption?

   d. Contrast the preceding two methods of failure resolution. Be sure to discuss their impact on the incentive structure for surviving solvent banks.

   e. Discuss the rationale supporting the provision of federal deposit insurance. What are some other elements of the safety net available to banks in the United States?

   f. How does the open bank assistance failure resolution method contribute to the federal safety net in the United States?

12. A bank has the following balance sheet in billions:

Assets		Liabilities	
Cash	$ 1	Demand deposits	$40
Loans	44	Net worth	5

Loans have one year until maturity and are priced at par, paying 7 percent annual rates. Demand deposits are noninterest-bearing.

   a. The bank experiences a run on its demand deposits. Deposit withdrawals are financed through asset sales. If the bank attempts to conduct a fire sale of its loan portfolio by selling it in one day, the loans will be priced at a 35 percent annual rate. If the bank takes two days to package the loan sale, the loan sale rate will fall to 10 percent annually. It will take three days for the bank to get the true market value of its loan portfolio. What is the value of the bank's loan portfolio on day 1? Day 2? Day 3? (Use annual interest rates.)

   b. How much do depositors receive if all attempt complete withdrawals of their balances on day 1? Day 2? Day 3? What will be the impact on the bank's net worth at each point in time? (Assume that regulators do not step in to close the bank.)

   c. How would your answer differ if the preceding balance sheet were for a mutual fund? (Assume that all mutual fund investments are completely financed by fund shareholders, there is no net worth.)

   d. Contrast the experience of bank depositors with the experience of mutual fund shareholders in the event of financial distress.

   e. If regulators use the payoff method to close the bank on day 1, what is the payment to depositors if 70 percent of all demand deposits are insured? What is the cost to the FDIC? What is the cost to uninsured depositors and shareholders?

   f. If regulators used the modified payoff method to close the bank on day 1, how would your answers to part e change?

   g. If the bank is closed at the start of the run, but the FDIC waits until day 2 to liquidate the bank's asset portfolio, what are the cash flows if the payoff method is used?

13. Use the Black-Scholes option pricing model as applied by Merton (1977) to price deposit insurance for the following bank: (see footnote 16)

Debt, D = $95 million

Assets, A = $100 million

Asset risk, $\sigma_A = 18\%$

The risk-free rate, r, is 5%

The time until the next audit, T, is 1 year.

CHAPTER

16

PRODUCT EXPANSION

Learning Objectives

In this chapter you learn about the potential advantages and disadvantages to an FI seeking to expand its range of financial service products. U.S. regulations have segmented the financial services industry by creating barriers to entry between commercial banking and investment banking, commercial banking and insurance, and commercial bank and real sector activities. You will find that, despite these barriers, many FIs are creatively exploiting gaps and loopholes in a process of homemade deregulation. Finally, we evaluate the public policy arguments for maintaining regulatory barriers among the major sectors of the financial services industry.

Introduction

The U.S. financial system has traditionally been structured on separatist or segmented product lines. Regulatory barriers and restrictions have often inhibited the ability of an FI operating in one area of the financial services industry to expand its product set into other areas. This might be compared with FIs operating in Germany, Switzerland, and the United Kingdom, where a more **universal FI** structure allows any single financial services organization to offer a far broader range of banking, insurance, securities, and other financial services products.[1]

Universal FI
An FI that can engage in a broad range of financial service activities.

In this chapter we first analyze the problems and risks that can arise and have arisen for U.S. FIs constrained to limited financial service sectors or franchises. Second, we analyze the existing set of laws and regulations restricting product expansions for banks, insurance companies, and securities firms. In addition, we look at barriers to product expansion between the financial sector and the real or commercial sector of the economy. Third, we evaluate the advantages and disadvantages of allowing U.S. FIs to adopt more universal franchises similar to those found in many European countries.

Risks of Product Segmentation

In recent years, many financial service firms have faced return and risk problems due to constraints on product diversification. Arguably, product expansion restrictions have affected commercial banks the most. For example, to the extent that regulations have limited the franchise of banks to traditional areas such as deposit-taking and commercial-lending, banks have been increasingly susceptible to nonbank

---

[1] For a thorough analysis of universal banking systems overseas, see A. Saunders and I. Walter, *Universal Banking in the U.S.?* (New York: Oxford University Press, 1993).

Money Market Mutual Funds (MMMF)
Mutual funds that offer high liquidity, check writing ability and a money market return to smaller individual investors.

competition on both the liability and asset sides of their balance sheets. Specifically, the growth of **money market mutual funds** (MMMF) that offer checking account-like deposit services with high liquidity, stability of value, and an attractive return have proved very strong competition for bank deposit and transaction account products.[2]

From virtually no assets in 1972, MMMFs had acquired more than $400 billion by February 1993; this compares to transaction accounts of approximately $720 billion in commercial banks.

On the asset side of the balance sheet, the commercial and industrial (C&I) loans of banks have faced increased competition from the dynamic growth of the commercial paper market as an alternative source of short-term finance for large- and middle-sized corporations. For example, in January 1988, C&I loans outstanding were $565 billion versus $380 billion of commercial paper; in October 1992, C&I loans were $600 billion versus $550 billion of commercial paper outstanding.

This has meant that the economic value of narrowly defined bank franchises have declined at the same time that credit risk concerns and interest risk concerns have increased (see Chapters 5 to 8). In particular, product line restrictions inhibit the ability of an FI to optimize the set of financial services it can offer, potentially forcing it to adopt a more risky set of activities than it would have adopted if it could fully diversify.[3]

Product restrictions also limit the ability of FI managers to flexibly adjust to shifts in the demand for financial products by consumers and to shifts in costs due to technology and related innovations. We analyze the advantages and disadvantages of increased product line diversification in more detail after we have looked more closely at the major laws and regulations segmenting the U.S. financial services industry.

Segmentation in the U.S. Financial Services Industry

Commercial and Investment Banking Activities

Since 1864, the United States has passed through several phases in regulating the links between the commercial and investment banking industries. Simply defined, commercial banking is the activity of deposit taking and lending, while investment banking is the activity of underwriting, issuing, and distributing securities. Early legislation, such as the 1864 National Bank Act, prohibited nationally chartered banks from engaging in corporate securities activities such as underwriting and distribution of corporate bonds and equities. However, as the United States industrialized and the demand for corporate finance grew, the largest banks such as National City Bank (today's Citibank) found ways around this restriction by establishing state-chartered affiliates in which to do the underwriting. By 1927,

---

[2]As we discuss in Chapter 2, MMMF collect small savers' funds and invest in a diversified portfolio of short-term money market instruments. This allows the small saver indirect access to the wholesale money market and to the relatively more attractive rates in those markets.

[3]While it is true that banks earned very high profits in 1991 and 1992, this was in large part due to rapidly falling interest rates for deposits and the stickiness of consumer lending rates that dramatically increased bank margins in the consumer lending areas. Thus, the increased profitability of banks in the early 1990s may be more cyclical than secular (or long term).

these bank affiliates were underwriting approximately 30 percent of the corporate securities being issued. In that year the comptroller of the currency, the regulator of national banks, relaxed the controls on national banks underwriting securities within the bank, thereby allowing them to pursue an even greater market share of securities underwritings.

After the 1929 stock market crash, the United States entered a major recession and some 10,000 banks failed between 1930 and 1933. A commission of inquiry established in 1931 began looking into the causes of the crash. The Pecora Commission pointed to banks' securities activities and the inherent abuses and conflicts of interest when commercial and investment banking activities were mixed as a major cause. Today, many question the Pecora Commission findings, believing that the slow growth in bank reserves and the money supply by the Federal Reserve lay at the heart of the post-crash recession.[4]

Nonetheless, the commission's findings resulted in new legislation, the 1933 Banking Act or the Glass-Stegall Act, which was named after the two congressmen who most strongly promoted the legislation.

The Glass-Steagall Act sought to impose a rigid separation between commercial banking—taking deposits and making commercial loans—and investment banking—underwriting, issuing, and distributing stocks, bonds, and other securities. Sections 16 and 21 of the Act limited the ability of banks and securities firms to engage directly in each other's activities. While Sections 20 and 32 limited the ability of banks and securities firms to engage indirectly in such activities through separately established affiliates. For important excerpts from these sections of the Act, see Table 16–1.

Nevertheless, the Act defined three major securities underwriting exemptions. First, banks were to continue to underwrite new issues of Treasury bills, notes, and bonds. Thus, the largest banks today such as Citibank and Morgan Guaranty actively compete with Salomon Brothers and Goldman Sachs in government bond auctions as primary dealers. Second, banks were allowed to continue underwriting municipal general obligation (GO) bonds.[5]

Private Placement
The placement of a whole issue of securities with a single (or a few) large investors by a bank acting as a placing agent.

Firm Commitment Underwriting
An underwriter buys securities from an issuer and reoffers them to the public at a slightly higher price.

Third, banks were allowed to continue engaging in private placements of all types of bonds and equities, corporate and otherwise. In a **private placement,** a bank seeks to find a large buyer or investor for a new securities issue. As such, the bank acts as an agent for a fee. By comparison, in a public offering of securities, a bank would normally act as a direct principal and have an underwriting stake in the issue. This principal position, such as in **firm commitment underwriting,** involves buying securities from the issuer at one price and seeking to resell them to the public at a slightly higher price. Failure to sell these securities can result in a major loss to the underwriter of publicly issued securities. Thus, the Act distinguished between the private placements of securities, which was allowed, and public placement, which was not.

---

[4]For a major critique of the facts underlying the Pecora Commission's findings and the Glass-Steagall Act, see G. J. Benston, *The Separation of Commercial and Investment Banking: The Glass-Steagall Act Revisited and Reconsidered* (New York: St. Martins Press, 1989). For a monetary explanation of the 1930–33 contraction, see M. Friedman and A. J. Schwartz, *A Monetary History of the United States, 1867–1960* (Princeton University Press: Princeton, N. J., 1963).

[5]A municipal general obligation bond is a bond issued by a state, city, or local government whose interest and principal payments are backed by the full faith and credit of that local government; that is, its full tax and revenue base.

TABLE 16–1   Excerpts from the Banking Act of 1933 Relating to Securities Activities

Section 16

The business of dealing in securities and stock by the (national) association shall be limited to purchasing and selling such securities and stock without recourse, solely upon the order, and for the account of, customers, and in no case for its own account, and the association shall not underwrite any issues of securities or stock: Provided (specifies securities qualified for the association's own investment account). . . . The limitations and restriction herein contained are to dealing in, underwriting and purchasing for its own account, investment securities shall not apply to (specifies securities exempted).

(Section 5 extends these restrictions to Federal Reserve member banks.)

Section 20

No member bank shall be affiliated in any manner . . . with any corporation, association, business trust, or other similar organization engaged principally in the issue, flotation, underwriting, public sale, or distribution at wholesale or retail or through syndicate participation of stocks, bonds, debentures, notes, or other securities.

Section 21

It shall be unlawful . . . for any person, firm, corporation, association, business trust, or other similar organization, engaged in the business of issuing, underwriting, selling, or distributing, at wholesale or retail, or through syndicate participation, stock, bonds, debentures, notes, or other securities, to engage at the same time to any extent whatever in the business of receiving deposits subject to check or to repayment upon presentation of a passbook, certificate of deposit, or other evidence of debt or upon request of the depositor.

Section 32

No officer, director, or employee of any corporation or unincorporated association, no partner or employee of any partnership, and no individual, primarily engaged in the issue, flotation, underwriting, public sale, or distribution, at wholesale or retail, or through syndicate participation, of stocks, bonds, or other similar securities shall serve the same time as an officer, director, or employee of any member bank except in limited classes of cases in which the Board of Governors of the Federal Reserve System may allow such service by general regulations when in the judgment of said Board it would not unduly influence the investment policies of such member bank of the advice it gives its customers regarding investments.

SOURCE: G. G. Kaufman and L. R. Mote, "Glass-Steagall: Repeal by Regulatory and Judicial Interpretation," *Banking Law Journal* (September/October 1990), pp. 388–421.

For most of the 1933–63 period, commercial banks and investment banks generally appeared to be willing to abide by the letter and spirit of the Glass-Steagall Act. However, since 1963 both have sought to erode Glass-Steagall and enter into each other's activity areas.

For commercial banks, such as the largest money center banks (Citibank and Bankers Trust), the usual procedure has been to challenge "gray" areas in the Act and to leave it to the courts to decide on the validity of the activity. Thus, between 1963 and 1987, banks challenged restrictions on municipal revenue bond underwriting, commercial paper underwriting, discount brokerage, managing and advising open and closed-end mutual funds, and underwriting mortgage-backed securities.[6]

---

[6]Municipal revenue bonds are more risky than municipal GO bonds, since their interest and principal is only guaranteed by the revenue from the project they finance. One example would be the revenue from road tolls if the bond funded the building of a new section of highway.

FIGURE 16–1

Bank holding company and its bank and Section 20 subsidiary

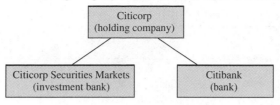

In some cases, the courts upheld activities such as a discount brokerage; in others an activity such as municipal bond underwriting was ruled contrary to Glass-Steagall.[7]

In the face of this onslaught and defacto erosion of the Act by legal interpretation, in April 1987 the Federal Reserve Board allowed commercial bank holding companies—such as Citicorp, the parent of Citibank—to establish separate **Section 20 affiliates.** In these Section 20 affiliates, they could conduct all their ineligible or gray area securities activities, such as commercial paper underwriting, mortgage-backed securities underwriting, and municipal revenue bond underwriting. Note the organizational structure of a bank holding company, its bank, and the Section 20 subsidiary or investment bank in Figure 16–1 for Citicorp.

These Section 20 subsidiaries did not violate Section 20 of the act, which restricts bank-securities firm affiliations, as long as the revenue generated from the subsidiaries' securities activities amounted to no more than 5 percent (currently 10 percent) of the total revenues they generated.[8]

Moreover, the Fed placed very stringent **firewalls,** or barriers, between the bank and its Section 20 securities affiliate to protect the bank from the risks of the affiliate's securities activities. These firewalls were both legal and economic in nature.[9]

Therefore, Citibank in our example could neither make loans to nor buy assets from its Section 20 securities affiliate, Citicorp Securities Markets (CSMI).

In 1989, the Federal Reserve expanded the set of permitted activities of selected Section 20 affiliates to include corporate bond underwriting and, in 1990, corporate equity underwriting as well. Thus, the wheel has almost come full circle; now commercial banking organizations hold widespread securities underwriting powers. In Table 16–2, we list bank holding companies allowed to establish Section 20

Section 20 Affiliate
A securities subsidiary of a bank holding company through which a banking organization can engage in investment banking activities.

Firewalls
Legal barriers separating the activities of a bank from those of its subsidiaries.

---

[7]To see the type of issues involved, discount brokerage was held to be legal since it was not viewed as being the same as full-service brokerage supplied by securities firms. In particular, a full-service brokerage combines both the agency function of securities purchase along with investment advice (e.g., hot tips). By contrast, discount brokers only carry out the agency function of buying and selling securities for clients; they do not give investment advice. For further discussion of these issues see M. Clark and A. Saunders, "Judicial Interpretation of Glass-Steagall: The Need for Legislative Action," *The Banking Law Journal* 97, 1980, pp. 721–40; and "Glass-Steagall Revised: The Impact on Banks, Capital Markets, and the Small Investor," *The Banking Law Journal* 97, 1980, pp. 811–40.

[8]This means that 90 percent of the revenues of the Section 20 subsidiary have to be generated from eligible securities activities such as government bond underwritings, which were permitted by the Glass-Steagall Act. Also note that the 10 percent revenue restriction has created incentives for banks to make the eligible business they put into these subsidiaries as big as possible on the basis that 10 percent of a very large number is itself a large number.

[9]For banks and the Section 20 securities affiliates, some 20 firewalls were established (see, General Accounting Office, "Bank Powers: Issues Relating to Banks Selling Insurance," GAO/GGO 90–113 (Washington D.C.: U.S. Government Printing Office, 1990). The idea of a firewall is to insulate or protect the bank (and thus the deposit insurance fund) from the risks of nonbank activities.

TABLE 16–2 **Bank Holding Companies with Section 20 Subsidiaries***

(As of December 31, 1992)

Banking Organization	Initial Order
Boston District:	
Fleet/Norstar Financial Corporation	10/88
New York District:	
The Bank of Nova Scotia†	4/90
Bankers Trust New York Corporation	4/87
Barclays Bank PLC‡	1/90
Canadian Imperial Bank of Commerce†	1/90
Chase Manhattan Corporation‡	5/87
Chemical Banking Corporation	5/87
Citicorp†	4/87
Deutsche Bank AG†	12/92
The Long-Term Credit Bank of Japan, Ltd.	5/90
Marine Midland Banks	7/87
J.P. Morgan & Co.†	4/87
The Royal Bank of Canada	1/90
The Toronto-Dominion Bank	5/90
Philadelphia District:	
Dauphin Deposit Corporation†	6/91
Cleveland District:	
Banc One Corporation	7/90
Huntington Bancshares, Inc.	11/88
PNC Financial Corporation	7/87
Richmond District:	
First Union Corporation	8/89
NationsBank Corporation	5/89
Atlanta District:	
Barnett Banks	1/89
South Trust Corporation	7/89
Synovus Financial Corporation	9/91
Chicago District:	
Amsterdam-Rotterdam Bank N.V.	6/90
The Bank of Montreal†	5/88
First Chicago Corporation	8/88
St. Louis District:	
Liberty National Bancorp	4/90
Minneapolis District:	
Norwest Corporation	12/90
San Francisco District:	
BankAmerica Corporation	3/92
Dai-Ichi Kangyo Bank, Ltd.	1/91
The Sanwa Bank, Ltd.	5/90

*Authorized to underwrite and deal in certain municipal revenue bonds, mortgage-related securities, commercial paper, and consumer-receivable related securities.

†Also has corporate debt and equity securities powers.

‡Also has corporate debt securities powers.

SOURCE: Federal Reserve Board, U.S. Department of the Treasury, "Modernizing the Financing System: Recommendations for Safer More Competitive Banks," Washington, D. C.: February 1991.

TABLE 16–3   **Selected Expanded Activities for State-Chartered Banks, May 1990**

Insurance Underwriting	Insurance Brokerage	Real Estate Equity Participation	Real Estate Development	Real Estate Brokerage	Securities Underwriting	Securities Brokerage/ No Underwriting
Delaware	Alabama	Arizona	Arizona	Georgia	Arizona	Arizona
Idaho	California	Arkansas	Arkansas	Iowa	California[4]	Connecticut
North Carolina	Delaware	California	California	Maine[16]	Delaware	Delaware
South Dakota	Idaho	Colorado	Colorado	Massachusetts	Florida	Florida
Utah[1]	Indiana[13]	Connecticut	Connecticut	New Jersey	Idaho	Georgia
	Iowa[14]	Florida	Florida	North Carolina	Indiana[5]	Idaho
	Nebraska	Georgia	Georgia	Oregon	Iowa	Indiana[17]
	New Jersey	Kentucky	Kentucky	Utah	Kansas[5]	Kansas
	North Carolina	Maine	Maine	Wisconsin	Maine	Iowa
	Oregon	Massachusetts	Massachusetts		Massachusetts	Maine
	South Carolina	Missouri	Michigan		Michigan	Michigan
	South Dakota	Nevada	Missouri		Missouri[7]	Minnesota
	Utah	New Hampshire	Nevada		Montana[8]	Nebraska
	Washington[15]	New Jersey	New Hampshire		Nebraska[9]	New Jersey
	Wisconsin	North Carolina	New Jersey		New Jersey	New York
	Wyoming	Ohio	North Carolina		North Carolina[10]	North Carolina
		Pennsylvania	Ohio		Pennsylvania[11]	Ohio
		Rhode Island	Oregon		Puerto Rico[12]	Pennsylvania[16]
		South Dakota	Rhode Island		Tennessee	Texas
		Tennessee[2]	South Dakota		Utah	Tennessee
		Utah	Utah		Washington	Utah
		Virginia	Virginia		West Virginia	Vermont
		Washington	Washington			West Virginia
		West Virginia	West Virginia			
		Wisconsin[3]	Wisconsin[3]			

NOTE: Expanded activities above those permitted national banks and bank holding companies under the Bank Holding Company Act. Extent of practice unknown.

[1]Grandfathered institutions.

[2]Banks not allowed to be active partners in real estate development.

[3]Wisconsin: Enacted expanded powers legislation 5/86. New legislation authorized the commissioner of banking to promulgate rules under which state banks may engage in activities that are authorized for other financial institutions doing business in the state.

[4]Underwrite mutual funds; law silent on other securities.

[5]Underwrite municipal revenue bonds and market mutual funds and mortgage-backed securities.

[6]Underwrite municipal bonds.

[7]Underwrite mutual funds and may underwrite securities to extent of the state legal loan limit.

[8]Limited to bonds.

[9]Underwrite U.S. government securities.

[10]U.S. government, federal farm loan act bonds and general obligation bonds of state and political subdivisions.

[11]Underwrite municipal and mortgage-related securities to extent permitted savings banks.

[12]May underwrite bonds of the U.S. and Puerto Rican governments, their political subdivisions and instrumentalities, and agencies.

[13]Cannot broker life insurance, all other types permitted.

[14]Property and casualty only.

[15]Banks located in small towns (5,000) may conduct insurance agency activities without geographic limitations.

[16]May own or operate brokerage firm established for the purpose of disposing of bank-owned property.

[17]May conduct discount brokerage.

SOURCE: Conference of State Bank Supervisors, U.S. Department of the Treasury, "Modernizing the Financial System. . ."

subsidiaries as of June 1990. Most of the largest U.S. commercial bank organizations are represented with J.P. Morgan's subsidiary (J.P. Morgan Securities) being the largest measured by its capital.

Indeed, as of September 1992, J.P. Morgan Securities was ranked seventh largest across all investment banks, for underwriting issues of domestic investment-grade

TABLE 16–4 Grandfathered Securities Affiliates of Foreign Banks Under Section 8 of the International Banking Act

Bank	Securities Affiliate	Percent
Julius Baer	Julius Baer Securities	100%
Campagnie Financiere de Paribas	A.G. Becker/Warburg	100
Bayerische Hypotheken Bank	ABD Securities	25
Berliner Handels and Frankfurter Bank.	BHF Securities	100
Bayerische Vereinsbank	Associated European Capital Corp.	95.1
Cho Heung Bank	Korean Associated Securities	9.1
Commerzbank	Europartners Securities	40
Credit Lyonnais	Europartners Securities	40
Credit Suisse	Swiss American Corp.	100
	Swiss American Securities, Inc. (First Boston)	80
Deutsche Bank	Atlantic Capital Corp.	100
Dresdner Bank	ABD Securities	75
	German American Securities (inactive)	100
Long-Term Credit Bank	Sanyo Securities (Tokyo)	5.44
Societe Generale (France).	Hudson Securities	100
Swiss Bancorp	Basle Securities Corp.	100
Union Bank of Switzerland	USB Securities, Inc.	100
Westdeutsche Landesbank	RWS Securities	100
Bank Hapoalim	Ampal (best efforts for parent)	100

NOTE: Securities affiliates were grandfathered under Section 8 of the International Banking Act of 1978.
SOURCE: Federal Reserve Board, U.S. Department of the Treasury, "Modernizing the Financial System . . ."

debt with Citicorp Securities Markets being ranked 13th. Also, in the first nine months of 1992, J.P. Morgan comanaged 14 initial public offerings of equity worth $1.16 billion and in June 1992 became the first Section 20 subsidiary to lead underwrite a U.S. public equity offering: an $157 million issue for Riverwood International, a paper products company.

The erosion of the product barriers between commercial and investment banking has also been helped by the fact that some 23 states allow state-chartered banks to engage in securities activities, beyond those permitted by Glass-Steagall for national banks (see Table 16–3). However, because state-chartered banks are smaller than nationally chartered banks, few state-chartered banks have actually taken advantage of such powers. Moreover, some 17 foreign banks can engage in securities activities because they were legally engaged in such activities prior to the passage of the International Banking Act of 1978. This act imposed the Glass-Steagall Act restrictions on the securities activities of all new foreign bank entrants to the United States. However, all foreign banks established prior to 1978 had their securities activities in the United States **grandfathered**.[10]

This has meant foreign banks have been allowed to pursue securities activities even though they have a competitive advantage over domestic banks. The grandfathered U.S. affiliates of foreign banks are in Table 16–4.

Grandfathered Affiliate
An existing affiliate that is allowed to continue operating even after the passage of restrictive laws regarding new entrants into an activity area.

_____

[10]Prior to 1978, foreign banks entering into the United States were largely regulated by state laws. Since these state laws often allowed more extensive securities activities than federal law, a number of major foreign banks engaged in securities activities through affiliates.

The erosion of the product barriers between the commercial and investment banking industries has not been all one way. Large investment banks such as Merrill Lynch have increasingly sought to offer banking products. For example, in the late 1970s, Merrill Lynch innovated the cash management account (CMA), which allowed investors to own a money market mutual fund with check writing privileges into which bond and stock sale proceeds could be swept on a daily basis. This allows the investor to earn interest on cash held in a brokerage account. In addition, many investment banks act as deposit brokers. As we discuss in Chapter 15, deposit brokers charge a fee to break large deposits into $100,000 deposit units and place them in banks across the country. Finally, investment banks have been major participants as traders and investors in the secondary market for LDC and other loans (see Chapters 12 and 22).

In sum, while the Glass-Steagall Act remains the defining piece of legislation concerning the mixing of commercial and investment banking, it is gradually being eroded through homemade deregulation by banks and securities firms.[11]

Nevertheless, although the product opportunities of banking organizations have increased, they are still constrained by limits. One is the 10 percent revenue rule applied to the ineligible activities of bank holding companies' Section 20 affiliates. Another is the extensive set of firewalls separating a bank's activities from its Section 20 affiliate's activities.

Concept Questions

1. Why do you think there is a 10 percent rather than a 50 percent maximum ceiling on the revenues earned from the ineligible underwriting activities of a Section 20 subsidiary?
2. What are the eligible or permissible underwriting activities of commercial banks under Glass-Steagall?
3. What was the rationale for the passage of the Glass-Steagall Act in 1933?
4. Looking at Table 16–3, what expanded activities have been authorized for state-chartered banks in the state where you live?

Banking and Insurance

Traditionally, there have been very strong barriers restricting the entry of banks into insurance. Insurance activities can be either of the property-casualty kind (homeowners insurance, auto insurance) or of the life/health kind (term life insurance). Moreover, we must make a distinction between a bank selling insurance as an agent by selling others' policies for a fee, and the bank acting as an insurance underwriter and bearing the direct risk of underwriting losses.

In general, the risks of insurance agency activities are quite low in loss potential when compared to insurance underwriting. Certain types of insurance tend to have natural synergistic links to bank lending products; for example, credit life insurance, mortgage insurance, and auto insurance.[12]

[11]While the 1991 Treasury Report to Congress recommended eliminating most of the restrictive provisions of the Glass-Steagall Act, the final piece of legislation—the FDIC Improvement Act of 1991—did not materially change the Glass-Steagall Act's provisions.

[12]See, Saunders and Walter, *Universal Banking,* for an elaboration of these arguments.

TABLE 16–5   Bank Holding Companies Insurance Activities

(A) Acting as agent, broker, or principal (i.e., underwriter) for credit-related life, accident, health, or unemployment insurance.

(B) For bank holding company finance subsidiaries, acting as agent or broker for credit-related property insurance in connection with loans not exceeding $10,000 ($25,000 in the case of a mobile home loan) made by finance company subsidiaries of bank holding companies.

(C) Acting as agent for any insurance activity in a place with a population not exceeding 5,000, or with insurance agency facilities that the bank holding company demonstrates to be inadequate.

(D) Any insurance agency activity engaged in by a bank holding company or its subsidiaries on May 1, 1982 (or approved as of May 1, 1982), including (i) insurance sales at new locations of the same bank holding company or subsidiaries in the state of the bank holding company's principal place of business or adjacent states, or any states in which insurance activities were conducted by the bank holding company or any of its subsidiaries on May 1, 1982, or (ii) insurance coverages functionally equivalent to those engaged in or approved by the Board as of May 1, 1982.

(E) Acting, on behalf of insurance underwriters, as supervisor of retail insurance agents who sell fidelity insurance and property and casualty insurance on bank holding company assets or group insurance for the employees of a bank holding company or its subsidiaries.

(F) Any insurance agency activity engaged in by a bank holding company (or subsidiary) having total assets of $50 million or less, except that life insurance and annuities sold under this provision must be authorized by (A), (B), or (C).

(G) Any insurance agency activity that is performed by a registered bank holding company, which was engaged in the insurance activity prior to January 1, 1971, pursuant to the approval of the Board.

NOTE: These are the seven statutory exemptions to the Bank Holding Company Act's prohibition on insurance activities under Title VI of the Garn-St Germain Depository Institutions Act of 1982, Public Law 97-320 (October 15, 1982).
SOURCE: S. D. Felgren, "Banks as Insurance Agencies: Local Constraints and Competitive Advances," Federal Reserve Bank of Boston, *New England Economic Review,* September–October 1985, pp. 34–39.

Nevertheless, banks are under very stringent restrictions when selling and underwriting almost every type of insurance. For example, national banks have been restricted to offering credit-related life, accident, health, or unemployment insurance. Moreover, they can act as insurance agents only in small towns of less than 5,000 people. Further, the Bank Holding Company Act of 1956 (and its 1970 Amendments) places severe restrictions on bank holding companies establishing separately capitalized insurance affiliates. The Garn-St Germain Depository Institutions Act of 1982 sets out these restrictions explicitly (see Table 16–5). Most states also have taken quite restrictive actions regarding the insurance activities of state-chartered banks (see columns 1 and 2 of Table 16–3). A few states—most notably Delaware—have passed liberal laws allowing state-chartered banks to underwrite and broker various types of property-casualty and life insurance. This has encouraged large bank holding companies such as Citicorp and Chase to enter Delaware and establish state-chartered banking subsidiaries with their own insurance affiliates. The Fed views such expansions as illegal and they are being actively challenged in the courts.

Unlike banks, insurance companies are regulated solely at the state level. This state level of regulation was reaffirmed by the McCarran–Ferguson Act of 1945.[13]

While few states explicitly restrict insurance companies from acquiring banks and, therefore, pursuing banking activities, banking laws have essentially restricted such expansions. In particular, the Bank Holding Company Act of 1956 has severely

[13]For an excellent discussion of the background to this Act, see K. J. Meier, *The Political Economy of Regulation: The Case of Insurance* (Albany: State University of New York Press, 1988).

Nonbank bank
A bank divested of its commercial loans and/or its demand deposits.

restricted the ability of insurance companies to own, or to be affiliated with, full-service banks. Nevertheless, beginning in the early 1980s, several insurance companies and commercial firms found indirect ways to engage in banking activities. This was through the organizational mechanism of establishing **nonbank bank** subsidiaries. The 1956 Bank Holding Company Act legally defined a bank as an organization that both accepts demand deposits and makes commercial and industrial loans. An insurance company could get around this restrictive provision by buying a full-service bank and then divesting its demand deposits or its commercial loans. This converted the bank into a nonbank bank. In 1987, Congress passed the *Competitive Equality Banking Act* (CEBA) in an attempt to block the nonbank bank loophole. This essentially prevented the creation of any new nonbank banks by redefining a bank as any institution that accepts and is accepted for deposit insurance coverage. This meant that any new nonbank bank established after 1987 would have to forgo deposit insurance coverage making it very difficult to raise deposits. Although nonbank banks established prior to 1987 were grandfathered by CEBA, their growth rates were capped.[14]

Note in Table 16–6 the nonbank banks operating at the end of 1990 and their large insurance company owners, such as Aetna, John Hancock, Prudential, Sun Life, and Travelers.

Concept Question

1. Is a bank that currently specializes in making just consumer loans and makes no commercial loans a nonbank bank?

Commercial Banking and Commerce

The 1864 National Bank Act severely limited the ability of nationally chartered banks, which were the nation's largest, to expand into commercial activities by taking direct equity stakes in firms. Today, the provisions of the National Bank Act limit participation by national banks in nonbank subsidiaries to those activities permitted by statute or regulation. Banks can only engage in commercial-sector activities "incidental to banking," and even then, only through service or subsidiary corporations with an aggregate limitation of 5 percent of bank assets. This is why corporate stocks or equities are conspicuously absent from bank balance sheets (see Chapter 1).

While the direct holdings of equity by national banks has been constrained as far back as 1864, restrictions on the commercial activities of bank holding companies are more recent phenomena. In particular, the 1970 Amendments to the 1956 Bank Holding Company Act required bank holding companies to divest themselves of nonbank related subsidiaries over a 10-year period following the amendment. When Congress passed the amendments, bank holding companies owned some 3,500 commercial-sector subsidiaries ranging from public utilities to transportation and manufacturing firms. Nevertheless, bank holding companies today can still hold up

---

[14]Specifically, nonbank banks established before March 5, 1987, were allowed to continue in business, but were limited to a maximum growth in assets of 7 percent during any 12-month period beginning one year after the act's enactment. It also permitted those nonbank banks allowed to remain in business to engage in only those activities in which they were engaged as of March 1987, and limited the cross-marketing of products and services by nonbank banks and affiliated companies.

TABLE 16–6   Nonbank Banks Reporting Pursuant to CEBA* and Still in Operation Listed Alphabetically by Holding Company

Holding Company	*Subsidiary*
Advest Group, Inc., Hartford, CT	Advest Bank, Hartford, CT
Aetna Life and Casualty Company, Hartford, CT	Liberty Bank & Trust, Gibbsboro, NJ
American Express Company, New York, New York	Boston Safe Deposit and Trust Co., Boston, MA
American Express Company, New York, NY	Advisory Bank & Trust Co., Minneapolis, MN
	American Express Centurion Bank, Newark, DE
Archer-Daniels-Midland Co., Decatur, IL	Hickory Point Bank and Trust, Decatur, IL
Bear Stearns Companies, Inc., New York, NY	Custodial Trust Company, Trenton, NJ
Bessemer Group, Inc., New York, NY	Bessemer Trust Co., N.A., New York, NY
	Bessemer Trust Co., Woodbridge, NJ
Capital Holding Co., Louisville, KY	First Deposit National Bank, Tilton, NH
Chrysler Corporation, Highland Park, MI	Automotive Financial Services, Inc., Highland Park, MI
Citadel Holding Corporation, Glendale, CA	Fidelity National Trust Co., Sherman Oaks, CA
CityFed Financial Corporation, Bedminster, NJ	City Trust Services, N.A., Elizabeth, NJ
Co-operative Bancorp, Acton, MA	Co-operative Bank of Concord, Concord, MA
	Quincy Co-operative Bank, Quincy, MA
Commercial Credit Co., Baltimore, MD	City Loan Bank, Lima, OH
	Commercial Credit Bank of Dallas Addison, TX
	Commercial Credit Bank, Baltimore, MD
	Commercial Credit Savings Bank, Pittsburgh, PA
	First National Bank of Wilmington, Newark, DE
Continental Corporation, New York, NY	International Central Bank & Trust Corp., Irvine, CA
Drexel Burnham Lambert Group, Inc., New York, NY	Commercial Trust Company, Hato Rey, PR
	Harbor Trust Co., Hoboken, NJ
Dreyfus Corp., New York, NY	Dreyfus Consumer Bank, East Orange, NJ
Eaton Vance Corporation, Boston, MA	Investors Bank & Trust Co., Boston, MA
Fidata Corporation, New York, NY	Fidata Trust Co., Massachusetts, New York, NY
	Fidata Trust Co., New York, New York, NY
First American Financial Co., Santa Ana, CA	First American Trust Company, Santa Ana, CA
First Boston, Inc., New York, NY	Universal Trust Co., Puerto Rico
First Franklin Corporation, Toccoa, GA	Liberty Bank & Trust, Toccoa, GA
FMR Corporation, Boston, MA	Fidelity Bank & Trust Co., Salem, NH
	Fidelity Management Trust Co., Boston, MA
Franklin Resources, Inc., San Mateo, CA	Pacific Union Bank & Trust Co., Menlo Park, CA
General Electric Company, Stamford, CT	Monogram Bank, Blue Ash, Ohio
Goldman, Sachs & Co., New York, NY	Broad Street Bank and Trust Co., Boston, MA†
Greyhound Financial Corp., Phoenix, AZ	Greyhound Commercial Bank, Washington, DC†
Gulf & Western, Inc., New York, NY	Associates National Bank, Concord, CA
Home Group, Inc., New York, NY	Premium Bank, Oceanside, CA
ITT Financial Corporation, St. Louis, MO	Lyndon Guaranty Bank of New York, Rochester, NY
	Lyndon Guaranty Bank of Ohio, Columbus, OH
J.C. Penney Company, Inc., New York, NY	J.C. Penney National Bank, Harrington, DE
John Hancock Subsidiaries, Inc., Boston, MA	First Signature Bank & Trust Co., Boston, MA
Leucadia National Corp., New York, NY	American Investment Bank, N.A., Salt Lake City, UT
Lomas & Nettleton Financial Corp., Dallas, TX	MBank USA (Lomas Bank USA), Wilmington, DE
Marsh & McLennan, Cos., Inc., New York, NY, and The Putnam Cos., Inc., Boston, MA	Putnam Fiduciary Trust Co., Boston, MA
McMahan's Valley Stores, Carlsbad, CA	Western Family Bank, N.A., Carlsbad, CA
Merrill Lynch & Co., Inc., New York, NY	Merrill Lynch Bank & Trust Co., Plainsboro, NJ
Montgomery Ward & Co., Inc., Chicago, IL	Clayton Bank & Trust Company, Clayton, DE
Prescott Holdings, Inc., Cleveland, OH	Prescott Merchants Bank, Washington, DC†
Prudential Insurance Co. of America, Newark, NJ	Prudential Bank & Trust Company, Atlanta, GA
Sargent Investors, Inc., Cranston, RI	Domestic Safe Deposit Co., Cranston, RI

TABLE 16–6 (*concluded*)

Holding Company	Subsidiary
Sears, Roebuck and Co., Chicago, IL	Greenwood Trust Company, New Castle, DE
	Hurley State Bank, Hurley, SD
Seperverde Holding Company, Flourtown, PA	Firstrust Savings Bank, Flourtown, PA
Society Corporation, Cleveland, OH	SBC Corporation, Washington, DC†
State Savings Bank, Columbus, OH	Century Bank, Cincinnati, OH
Sun Life Assurance Co. of Canada, Wellesley Hills, MA	New London Trust Co., New London, NH
Textron, Inc., Providence, RI	AVCO National Bank, Irvine, CA
Travelers Corp., Hartford, CT	Massachusetts Co., Inc., Boston, MA
TSO Financial Corporation, Horsham, PA	Colonial National Bank USA, Horsham, PA

*The Competitive Equality Banking Act of 1987.

†Indicates subsidiaries which were not open as of March 5, 1987. No determination has been made as to the status of these under CEBA.

SOURCE: House Committee on Banking, Housing, and Urban Affairs Task Force on the International Competitiveness of U.S. Financial Institutions, 1991.

to 4.9 percent of the voting shares in any commercial firm without regulatory approval.[15]

The 1956 Bank Holding Company Act has also effectively restricted acquisitions of banks by commercial firms (as was true for insurance companies). The major vehicle for commercial firm entry into commercial banking has been the nonbank bank or nonbank financial service firms that offer banking services. Note in Table 16–6 that some major nonfinancial corporations, such as Sears, Roebuck & Company and General Electric Company, owned nonbank banks at the end of 1990.

Nonbank Financial Service Firms and Commerce

By comparison with the barriers separating banking and either securities, insurance, or commercial sector activities, the barriers among nonbank financial service firms and commercial firms are generally much weaker. For example, in recent years insurance firms and commercial firms have faced few barriers to entering into either the investment banking industry or the finance company industry. Consider Table 16–7, the top 25 securities firms ranked by net worth as of January 1991. Looking at the top 10 firms, 5 had clear links with other financial service or commercial firms. Specifically, American Express owned Shearson, Lehman, Hutton (SLH); Phibro (a commodity trader) purchased Salomon Brothers before Salomon Brothers reversed the takeover; Prudential bought Bache Securities; Credit Suisse (a Swiss universal bank) was the dominant shareholder of First Boston; and Dean Witter was a subsidiary of Sears.[16]

In Table 16–8, we list the top 20 finance companies as of the end of 1990. As we discuss in Chapter 2, finance companies engage in asset-backed lending

---

[15]Under the Bank Holding Company Act, *control* is defined as when a holding company has an equity stake exceeding 25 percent in a subsidiary bank or affiliate.

[16]The 1993 sale of Shearson by American Express and of Dean-Witter by Sears, along with the proposed sale of Furman Selz—Xerox's brokerage and underwriting unit—may be indicative of a new trend by major commercial corporations to withdraw from nonbanking financial services. This suggests that the potential gains from being a diversified commercial and financial services holding company may be less than supposed. Indeed, both Sears and Xerox are selling their insurance and real estate brokerage subsidiaries as well.

TABLE 16–7   Top 25 Brokerage Firms, December 31, 1990
(Ranked by capital)

Firm	Capital (in mil. $)	Offices No.	Offices Rank	Employees No.	Employees Rank
1. Merrill Lynch	$9,567	510	2	39,000	1
2. Shearson Lehman	5,406	427	5	33,326	2
3. Goldman, Sachs	4,700	21	49	6,822	9
4. Salomon Brothers	4,420	17	51	4,520	14
5. Morgan Stanley	3,380	12	65	7,079	8
6. Paine Webber	1,553	267	7	12,746	5
7. First Boston	1,471	10	69	4,218	15
8. Dean Witter	1,405	499	3	16,609	4
9. Bear Stearns	1,388	13	62	5,558	10
10. Prudential-Bache	1,224	336	6	17,000	3
11. Smith Barney	1,012	98	11	7,200	7
12. Donaldson, Lufkin	919	16	54	3,250	16
13. Kidder, Peabody	620	55	22	5,067	12
14. Bank of Tokyo	602	. . .	. . .	1,059	33
15. Nomura Securities	520	3	. . .	620	49
16. J.P. Morgan	507	6	90	854	40
17. Citicorp Securities	474	3	. . .	343	82
18. A. G. Edwards	376	432	4	8,416	6
19. Wood Gundy Inc.	283	41	28	1,863	23
20. Kemper Securities	279	178	8	4,800	13
21. Charles Schwab	270	130	9	2,950	17
22. Daiwa Sec. America	270	3	. . .	400	72
23. UBS Securities	262	1	. . .	510	55
24. Oppenheimer & Co.	248	12	65	2,253	19
25. Dillon, Reed & Co.	242	5	. . .	584	52
Total, 25 firms	$41,398	3,095	610	187,047	567

SOURCE: *Standard & Poor's Industry Surveys,* December 5, 1991, pI. 39. Reprinted by permission.

(such as auto finance) and leasing usually financed by short-term debt issues such as commercial paper and long-term notes and bonds. As you can see, 7 of top 20 finance companies are captive subsidiaries of major commercial firms such as General Motors and General Electric. Although banks were prevented from purchasing non-failed savings and loans, until the passage of the 1989 Financial Institutions, Reform, Recovery, and Enforcement Act, commercial firms had been able to purchase single savings and loans under the Savings and Loan Holding Company Act of 1967. This act allowed companies such as Ford Motor Company, to acquire one savings and loan association under a holding company structure. In Table 16–9, we summarize the extensive entry of commercial and insurance firms into various financial service areas in recent years.

Activity Restrictions in the United States

We have just described the essentially separatist or segmented nature of the U.S. financial services industry. Although many of the barriers are gradually being eroded

TABLE 16–8   **The Twenty Largest Finance Companies**
Assets in Millions, End-1990

Rank		Assets	Parent Relationship/ Type of Parent	Concentration of Business
1	General Motors Acceptance Corp.	$105,103	Captive	Diversified
2	General Electric Capital Corp.	70,385	Nonfinancial firm	Diversified
3	Ford Motor Credit	58,969	Captive	Diversified
4	Chrysler Financial	24,702	Captive	Diversified
5	Household Financial	16,898	Independent	Consumer
6	Associates Corp. of North America	16,595	Nonfinancial firm	Diversified
7	Sears Roebuck Acceptance Corp.	15,373	Captive	Consumer
8	American Express Credit	14,222	Captive	Consumer
9	ITT Financial Corp.	11,665	Nonfinancial firm	Diversified
10	CIT Group	11,374	Bank holding company	Diversified
11	I.B.M. Credit	11,132	Captive	Diversified
12	Westinghouse Credit	10,336	Nonfinancial firm	Diversified
13	Security Pacific Financial Services System	9,928	Bank holding company	Diversified
14	Beneficial Corp.	9,270	Independent	Consumer
15	Transamerica Finance	8,501	Financial nonbank	Diversified
16	Heller Financial	7,512	Bank holding company	Diversified
17	Commercial Credit Corp.	7,138	Financial nonbank	Consumer
18	American General Finance	5,933	Financial nonbank	Consumer
19	Toyota Motor Credit	5,579	Captive	Consumer
20	Avco Financial	5,084	Nonfinancial firm	Consumer

SOURCE: From *American Banker,* November 8, 1990, p. 10. Reprinted by permission. E. M. Remolona and K. C. Wulfekuhler, Federal Reserve Bank of New York, *Quarterly Review,* Summer 1992, p. 26.

and are relatively light in some areas, restrictions fall particularly heavily on this nation's commercial banks. You can see this in Table 16–10, which compares the range of activities permitted to U.S. commercial banks with the range of product activities permitted to banks in other major industrialized countries. With the possible exception of Japan, U.S. banks are the most constrained of all the major industrialized countries in the range of nonbank product activities permitted.[17]

This has created considerable pressure on Congress to bring U.S. banks' activity powers in line with their global competitors and counterparts. Especially disturbing is the fact that at the end of 1992, no U.S. bank was in the world's top 20 (measured by assets). Citicorp was the highest at 23rd. While Congress did actively consider these issues in the debate leading up to the passage of the 1991 FDIC Improvement Act, it left the restrictions on nonbank activities defined under the Glass-Steagall Act, the Bank Holding Company Act and its amendments, and the Competitive Equality Bank Act largely intact. This was despite recommendations by the U.S. Treasury and others to relax the separations between banking and securities activities and banking and commerce.[18]

---

[17]Many of Japan's postwar regulations were modeled on those of the United States. Thus, Article 65 in Japan separates commercial banking from investment banking in a similar fashion to the Glass-Steagall Act. However, Japan has recently proposed a major deregulation that will considerably weaken the historic barriers between commercial and investment banking in that country.

[18]See the U.S. Treasury Report "Modernizing the Financial System . . ."(1991) for a description of these proposals. The prompt corrective action procedures implemented by the act did link the scope of permitted activities to the capitalization of the bank (see Chapter 14).

TABLE 16–9   Selected Diversified Financial Conglomerates

Firm (principal business)	Insurance	Real Estate	Securities	Depository Institution	Other Financial
Aetna Life & Casualty (Insurance)	X	X			X
American Can Company (Manufacturing)	X	X	X	X	X
American Express Co. (Diversified Financial)	X		X	X	X
American General Corp. (Diversified Financial)	X	X	X		X
Armco Inc. (Steel)	X			X	X
Avco Corp. (Defense Contracting)	X			X	X
BankAmerica Corp. (Banking)	X	X	X	X	X
Beneficial Corp. (Consumer Finance)	X			X	X
Borg-Warner Corp. (Manufacturing)	X		X		X
Chrysler Corp. (Manufacturing)	X	X			X
Citicorp (Banking)	X	X	X	X	X
Control Data Corp. (Computers)	X			X	X
Equitable Life Assurance Society of the U.S. (Insurance)	X	X	X		X
Ford Motor Company (Manufacturing)	X	X		X	X
General Electric (Manufacturing)	X	X	X		X
General Motors Corp. (Manufacturing)	X	X			X
Greyhound Corp. (Transportation)	X				X
Gulf & Western Industries Inc. (Commercial Conglomerate)	X	X		X	X
Household International Corp. (Consumer Finance)	X			X	X
ITT (Commercial Conglomerate)	X		X		X
Merrill Lynch Co. (Securities)	X	X	X	X	X
National Steel Corp. (Steel)		X		X	X
Parker Pen Company (Manufacturing)	X			X	X
J.C. Penny Company (Retail)	X	X		X	X
Prudential Insurance Company of America (Insurance)	X	X	X	X	X
RCA Corp. (Electronics)	X				X
Sears, Roebuck & Co. (Retail)	X	X	X	X	X
Transamerica Corp. (Insurance)	X	X			X
Westinghouse Electric Company (Manufacturing)		X	X		X

Other includes: credit cards, consumer lending, financing, leasing, factoring, investment advisory services, mutual fund management, data processing services, purchasing of installment contracts, trust services, venture capital services, merchant banking, pension fund management, traveler's checks, and money orders.

SOURCE: Subcommittee on Telecommunications, Consumer Protection, and Finance, *Restructuring Financial Markets: The Major Policy Issues,* July 1986, pp. 201–2.

In the next section, we look at the issues that have been raised and will continue to be raised whenever the question of expanded product powers for banks and other FIs arise.

Issues Involved in the Expansion of Product Powers

Whether the debate concerns bank expansion into securities activities, insurance, or commerce, similar issues arise. These include:

1. Safety and soundness issues.
2. Economy of scale and scope issues.
3. Conflict of interest issues.
4. Deposit insurance issues.

TABLE 16–10 Limits in Services of Commercial Banks

Bank Services	Belgium	Canada	France	West Germany	Italy	Japan	Luxem-bourg	Nether-lands	Switzer-land	United Kingdom	United States
Insurance:											
Brokerage	Y	N	Y	Y	N*	N	Y	Y	N	Y	N*
Underwriting	Y	N	N*	Y*	N*	N	Y	N	N	Y*	N
Equities:											
Brokerage	Y	Y*	Y	Y	Y	N	Y	Y	Y	Y	Y
Underwriting	Y	Y*	Y	Y	Y	N	Y	Y	Y	Y*	N
Investment	Y	Y	Y	Y	Y	Y	Y	Y	Y	Y*	N
Other underwriting:											
Government debt	Y	Y	Y	Y	Y	N	Y	Y	Y	Y*	Y
Private debt	Y	Y*	Y	Y	Y	N	Y	Y	Y	Y*	N
Mutual funds:											
Brokerage	Y	Y	Y	Y	Y	N	Y	Y	Y	Y	N
Management	Y	Y*	Y	Y	Y	N	Y	Y	Y	Y	N
Real estate:											
Brokerage	Y*	N	Y	Y	N	N	Y	Y	Y	Y	N*
Investment	Y	Y	Y	Y	Y	N	Y	Y	Y	Y	N
Other brokerage:											
Government debt	Y	Y	Y	Y	Y	Y	Y	Y	Y	Y	Y
Private debt	Y	Y	Y	Y	Y	Y	Y	Y	Y	Y	Y

NOTES: N = No, N* = No, with exceptions; Y = Yes; Y* = Yes, but not directly by the bank.
SOURCE: American Bankers Association, *International Banking Competitiveness,* March 1990, p. 82.

    5. Regulatory oversight issues.

    6. Competition issues.

In this section, we evaluate these issues in the context of banks entering into securities activities.

Consider the three alternative organizational structures for linking banking and securities activities in Figure 16–2. The bank holding company structure in panel *c* of the figure is the organizational form within which we will evaluate the six issues just identified. This is the form already adopted by U.S. regulators to accommodate bank organization expansions into nonbank activities such as the creation of Section 20 subsidiaries to engage in limited amounts of ineligible securities activities.

In Figure 16–2, panel *a* shows the fully integrated universal bank, where banking and securities activities are conducted in different departments. This is typical of the way in which large banks in Germany, such as Deutsche Bank, engage in securities activities. In panel *b* is the universal subsidiary model where a bank engages in securities activities through a separately owned securities affiliate. This is typical of the way in which commercial banks such as Barclay's in the United Kingdom conduct their securities activities. BZW is the bank's securities subsidiary. Note that the degree of bank-nonbank integration is much less with the holding company model than either the full or subsidiary universal banking model.[19]

For example, in the universal subsidiary model, the bank holds a direct ownership stake in the securities subsidiary. By comparison, in the holding company

---

    [19]For a comparative analysis of these three models, see Saunders and Walter, *Universal Banking.* The Japanese do not allow holding company structures for fear of recreating the *zaibatsu,* finance and commercial conglomerates that dominated the pre–Second World War Japanese economy.

FIGURE 16–2

Alternative organizational forms for nonbank product expansions
of banking organizations

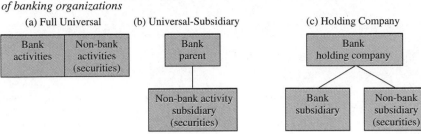

model, the bank and securities subsidiary are separate companies with their own equity capital; their link is that their equity is held by the same parent company, the bank holding company (such as Citicorp).[20]

Safety and Soundness Concerns

With respect to the securities activities of commercial banks, and the possible effects on their safety and soundness, two key questions arise: How risky is securities underwriting? And, if losses occur for a securities subsidiary, can this cause the affiliated bank to fail?

The Risk of Securities Underwriting. To understand the risk of securities underwriting, you must understand the mechanics of firm commitment securities offerings. While some corporate securities are offered on a **best efforts** basis in which the underwriter does not guarantee a price to the issuer and acts more like a placing or distribution agent, the dominant form of underwriting in the United States is a firm commitment offering.

In a firm commitment offering, the underwriter purchases securities directly from the issuing firm (say, at $99 per share) and then reoffers them to the public or the market at large at a slightly higher price, say, $99.50. The difference between the underwriter's buy price ($99) and the public offer price ($99.50) is the spread that compensates the underwriter for accepting the principal risk of placing the securities with outside investors as well as any administrative and distribution costs associated with the underwriting. In our simple example of a $0.50 spread, the maximum revenue the underwriter can gain from underwriting the issue is $0.50 × the number of shares issued. Thus, if 1 million shares were offered, the maximum gross revenue for the underwriting would be $0.50 × 1,000,000 = $500,000. Note that once the public offering has been made and the price specified in the prospectus, the underwriter cannot raise the price over the offering period. In this example the underwriter could not raise the price above $99.50, even after determining that the market valued the shares more highly.[21]

While the upside return from underwriting is normally capped, by comparison, the downside risk can be very large.

Best Efforts Underwriting
An underwriting where the investment banker acts as an agent rather than as a principal that bears risk.

---

[20]In general, the advantages of the full universal is greater resource flexibility and integration of commercial bank and investment bank product lines. Its perceived disadvantages include greater monopoly power and greater potential conflicts of interest.

[21]The offering period is usually a maximum of 10 business days.

The downside risk arises if the underwriter overprices the public offering, setting the public offer price higher than outside investors' valuations. As a result the underwriter would be unable to sell the shares during the public offering period, and would have to lower the price to get rid of the inventory of unsold shares, especially as this inventory is often financed through issuing commercial paper or RP agreements. In our example, if the underwriter has to lower the offering price to $99, the gross revenue from the underwriting would be zero, since this is the price paid to the issuing firm. Any price less than $99 generates a loss. For example, suppose that the issue could only be placed at $97, the underwriter's losses would be $2 $\times$ 1,000,000 shares = $2 million.

There are a number of possible reasons why an underwriter may take a big loss or big hit on an underwriting. The first is simply overestimating the market's demand for the shares. The second is that in the short period between setting the public offering price and seeking to sell the securities to the public there may be a major drop in security values in general.

The classic example of this second type of market risk was the sale of British Petroleum (BP) shares in October 1987 in the period surrounding the October 19, 1987, stock market crash. Underwriters set the bid price of the shares at £3.265 and the offer price at £3.30 on October 15, 1987, four days before the crash, and four large U.S. investment banks (such as Goldman Sachs) agreed to underwrite 22 percent of the issue or 505,800,000 shares. However, in the week following the October 19, 1987 crash BP's share price fell to a low of £2.65—so that the underwriters faced a loss of as much as £0.615 per share (£3.265 minus £2.65) or a loss of £311 million. Note that the maximum gross revenue the U.S. underwriters could have made, if all shares had been sold at the originally planned offer price of £3.30 was: [(£3.30 − £3.265) $\times$ 505.8 million] or £17,703,000. We show this profit and loss trade-off in Figure 16–3.

As you can see, firm commitment underwriting involves a potential payoff with a limited upside gain (£17,703,000) and a very large downside loss. As such, it is similar to the risks involved in *writing put* options on assets.[22]

Of course, the big hit described in the BP case is unusual for three reasons. First, most new issues are underpriced rather than overpriced. Second, in the United States the offer period is usually much shorter than in the BP example; and third, stock market crashes are fortunately rare. However, it is very much this big hit scenario that regulators are concerned about when it comes to the question of allowing banks to engage in securities underwriting through an affiliate.

Concept Question

1. All other things considered, which is likely to be more risky, underwriting corporate equities or underwriting corporate debt (bonds)? Explain your answer.

If Underwriting Losses Occur for the Securities Affiliate, Can this Cause a Bank to Fail? Proponents of allowing banking organizations to expand their securities activities argue that the answer to this question is no, as long as the bank subsidiary is

---

[22]The premium on the put could be thought of as being similar to the maximum revenue that could be earned on an underwriting.

FIGURE 16–3

Profit-loss function for BP share underwriting

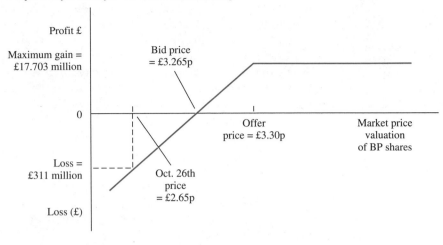

sufficiently insulated from the risk problems of the securities affiliate. As noted earlier, in a bank holding company structure, the bank is legally a separate corporation from the securities affiliate. As shown in Figure 16–4, its only link to its securities affiliate is indirect, through the holding company owning a controlling equity stake in both the bank and the securities affiliate. However, even this indirect link raises the concern that the effects of losses by the securities affiliate could threaten the safety of the bank unless additional firewalls or regulatory barriers are introduced to insulate the bank against such losses (see Figure 16–4).

There are at least three ways a bank could be harmed by losses of a securities affiliate in a holding company structure. First, a bank holding company might be tempted to drain capital and funds from the bank by requiring excessive dividends and fees from the bank (this is called upstreaming). The holding company could then downstream these funds to prevent the failing securities affiliate from insolvency. As a result, the bank would be weakened at the expense (or because) of the securities affiliate.

Currently, the Federal Reserve closely monitors bank dividend payments to holding company owners and must restrict dividend payments of the bank if it is undercapitalized under the prompt corrective action plan (see Chapter 14). Also Section 23B of the 1982 Federal Reserve Act limits the size of management and other fees banks can pay for services provided by the holding company to those normally established by the market for such services.

A second way in which a bank could be harmed is through interaffiliate loans. For example, the holding company may induce the bank to extend loans to the securities affiliate to keep it afloat, even though such loans are excessively risky. To prevent this, Section 23A of the Federal Reserve Act limits bank loans to any single nonbank affiliate to 10 percent of a bank's capital. If bank capital is approximately 5 percent of bank assets, this limits loans to an affiliate to .05 × .1 of bank assets, or 0.5 percent of bank assets. Currently, for Section 20 securities affiliates, firewalls prohibit banks from lending anything at all to the affiliate.[23]

---

[23]This also holds for the sale of assets by the affiliate to the bank.

FIGURE 16–4

The role of firewalls in protecting banks

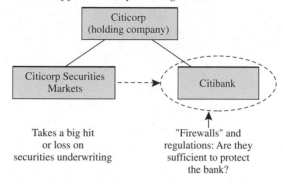

Takes a big hit
or loss on
securities underwriting

"Firewalls" and
regulations: Are they
sufficient to protect
the bank?

The third way in which a bank may be affected is through a contagious confidence problem. Specifically, if an affiliated securities firm gets into difficulty, it may result in a negative information signal to financial service consumers and investors regarding the quality of the management of the holding company and its bank affiliate. Such negative information can create incentives for large depositors and investors to withdraw their money from the bank in the manner described in Chapter 13. This bank run possibility seems more likely to occur if the bank and its securities affiliate were to share similar names and logos; for example, if Citibank and Citicorp Securities Markets had joint books, management, and office space and extensively cross-marketed each other's products. Currently, Section 20 securities affiliates of banks are required by firewall regulations to have separate books, separate offices, and separate managements. Also, there is an absolute prohibition on cross-marketing each other's products. However, in general they do retain names similar to their bank affiliates.

Obviously, a big hit taken by the securities affiliate can potentially threaten the safety and solvency of the affiliated bank, especially through the confidence effect. However, at least two countervailing risk-reducing effects may enhance the safety and soundness of a bank indirectly linked to a securities affiliate in a holding company framework. The first effect is a *product diversification benefit.* A well diversified financial services firm (bank holding company) potentially enjoys a far more stable earnings and profit stream over time than a product specialized bank. As demand and cost shifts reduce earnings in one activity area such as banking, offsetting demand and cost shifts may take place in other activity areas, such as securities or insurance, increasing bank holding company earnings. Advocates argue that a more stable and diversified earnings stream for the holding company enables it to act as a source of strength in keeping the affiliated bank well capitalized.

In the academic literature, a number of empirical studies have evaluated the gains from bank activity diversification by looking at the correlations of accounting earnings between segmented financial firms or industries and analyzing correlations between firms' stock market returns. Essentially, the lower these correlations, the greater are the potential gains from activity diversification and the lower the coefficient of variation (COV)—the standard deviation divided by the mean—of a banking organization's earnings flows. Other studies have sought to evaluate the potential effects of activity diversification on the risk of failure of banks (ROF) and to simulate the effects of bank-nonbank mergers (MS) on bank risk. We summarize the findings of a number of these COV, ROF, and MS studies in Table 16–11.

TABLE 16–11   Review of Selected Studies of the Risk of Nonbank Activities*

Study	Time Period	Methodology†	Nonbank Activities Reduce BHC Risk
Accounting **Industry data** Heggestad (1975)	1953–67	COV	Yes. Impermissible activities: insurance agents and brokers, and real estate agents, brokers, managers, holdings, and investment companies, and lessors of R.R., oil, and mining properties. Banking is among the riskiest activities based on the coefficient variation in profits. (Studied activities of one BHC prior to 1970 BHC Act amendments.)
Johnson and Meinster (1974)	1954–69 (annual data)	COV	Yes. Impermissible activities: insurance agents and brokers, portfolio holding and investment companies, and real estate agents, analysis brokers and managers. Studies 13 activities. Portfolio analysis based on earnings and cash flow conclude there are diversification benefits into nonbank activities but that the benefits are sensitive to the percentage of assets in each activity.
Wall and Eisenbeis (1984)	1970–80	COV	Yes. Impermissible activities: S&Ls, security brokers and dealers, life insurance, general merchandise stores, lessor of R.R. property. Permissible activities personal and business credit agency. Banking neither highest nor lowest risk based on coefficient of variation. Results are sensitive to time period.
Accounting **Firm data** Jessee and Seelig (1977)		COV	No. Risk reduction is not related to share of nonbank investment.
Meinster and Johnson (1979)	1973–77	ROF	Yes. BHCs effectively diversified but slightly increased probability of capital impairment with debt financing. (Sample of only 2 BHCs in 7 permissible activities of leasing, consumer finance, mortgage banking, bank management consulting, financial services, and foreign bank services.)
Litan (1985)	1978–83	COV	As likely to reduce volatility of BHC income as to increase it. (Sample of 31 large BHCs.)
Wall (1986)	1976–84	ROF	Nonbank activity either decreases BHC risk slightly or has no impact. The positive relationship between nonbank risk and BHC risk, BHC leverage, and bank risk is consistent with the possibility that management preferences influence the riskiness of the BHC's subsidiaries and determine the use of leverage to influence overall risk.
Boyd and Graham (1986)	1971–83, (1971–77 and 1978–83)	ROF	Entire period: no significant relationship between non-bank activity and any risk or return measures. Less stringent policy period (1971–77): no nonbank activity is positively related to risk. More stringent policy period (1978–83): weak negative relationship between nonbank activity and risk.
Boyd and Graham (1988)	1971–84 (annual data)	COV/ROF/MS	Study covers six impermissible activities. Yes for life insurance. The standard deviation and bankruptcy risk measures indicate risk is likely to increase for real estate development, securities firms, and property-casualty insurance activities, and increase slightly for other real estate and insurance agency and brokerage activities. BHC is lowest risk activity.
Brewer (1988)	1979–85	COV	Yes. One standard deviation increase in investment in nonbank subsidiaries leads to 6 basis point drop in BHC risk (approximately 7 percent).

TABLE 16–11 (*concluded*)

Study	Time Period	Methodology†	Nonbank Activities Reduce BHC Risk
Industry and firm data			
Stover (1982)	1959–68	Wealth maximization debt capacity	Yes. Impermissible activities: S&Ls, investment banking, land development, fire and casualty insurance. Measures equity returns and diversification benefits of 14 permissible and impermissible activities in wealth maximization model.
Boyd, Hanweck and Pithyachanyakul (1980)	1971–77	COV/ROF	Yes, but limited. Permissible activities: mortgage banking, factoring, consumer finance, credit card, loan servicing, investment: advisors, leasing (except auto), community welfare, data processing, credit life, accident and health insurance agents and underwriters and management consulting.
			No (any investment increases probability of bankruptcy). Permissible activities, commercial and sales finance, industrial banks, trust services, auto leasing. (Study only covered permissible activities.)
Market data			
Industry data			
Eisemann (1976)	1961–68 (monthly data)	Industry (portfolio) selection model (COV)	Yes. Banking is minimum risk activity. Lowest risk BHC includes permissible activity of sales finance and impermissible activities of insurance investment banking. Highest risk BHC includes permissible activity of data processing. Studies 20 activities.
Firm data			
Wall (1984)	Select dates	Bond returns	No significant effect.
Wall and Eisenbeis (1984)	Select dates (monthly data)	Bond returns	No. (Study only covered permissible activity of discount brokerage.)
Boyd and Graham (1988)	1971–84 (annual data)	COV/ROF/MS	Studies six impermissible activities. Yes for life insurance, insurance agency and brokerage, and property casualty insurance. Risk likely to increase for real estate development and securities firms and increase slightly for other real estate. Based on standard deviation, bankruptcy, and beta risk measures BHC is not lowest risk activity. Insurance agency and brokerage and property and casualty insurance are lowest risk activities.
Brewer (1988)	1979–85 (daily data)	COV	Yes. One standard deviation increase in investment in nonbank subsidiaries leads to an 8–11 percent basis point drop in BHC risk. Results are sensitive to the time period studied.
Brewer, Fortier, and Pavel (1988)	1980, 1982, and 1986, and 1979–1983	COV/MS	Yes. Impermissible activities of insurance agents and brokers, property and casualty and life insurance underwriting. Investment of 5 percent or less for any of the tested activities would not increase the variance of the BHC significantly, but investment of 25 percent or more for all but the above listed activities would increase the riskiness of the BHC significantly. Examination of the impact of total investment in nonbank activities regardless of the specific activities finds increases in nonbank activity tends to lower BHC risk significantly.

*Permissible activities refer to those nonbank activities currently permissible (May 1988) whether or not they were permissible at the time of the study. Impermissible activities also include activities not yet ruled upon by the Board at the time of the study.

†COV–analysis of coefficient of variation of rates of return of banking and nonbanking activities.

ROF–Risk of failure (bankruptcy analysis).

MS–simulated merger analysis.

SOURCE: From "Bank Risk from Nonbank Activities," by E. Brewer, D. Fortier, and C. Pavel, in *Economic Perspectives,* July–August 1988, pp. 14–26. Reprinted by permission of the Federal Reserve Bank of Chicago.

As you can see from Table 16–11, the majority of the studies find that bank holding company risk could be reduced by expansion into nonbank product lines. However, the optimal proportion of investment in individual nonbank product lines often falls in the 5 to 25 percent range. This suggests that excessive product expansions in some nonbank lines could actually increase the total risk exposure of a banking organization.

In addition to the potential risk-reducing gains of product diversification, by diversifying its earnings stream geographically, a bank holding company can generate additional risk reduction gains when there are regional imperfections in the costs of raising debt and equity (see Chapter 17).

Concept Question

1. What are three ways in which a securities affiliate's failure could harm a bank within a bank holding company structure?

Economies of Scale and Scope

A second issue concerning the expansion of banks into securities and other nonbank activities is the potential for additional economies of scale and scope. As we discuss in Chapter 10, there appears to be limited economy of scale opportunities for financial firms in the $100 million to $5 billion range. Moreover, most studies find cost-based economies of scope are negligible, although revenue-based economies may arise for the largest FIs. Arguably, the current very restrictive firewalls between banks and their Section 20 investment banking affiliates covering finance, management, and cross-marketing have severely limited economies of scope and related revenue and cost synergies. Such economies might only be generated in a more integrated universal banking structure of the German or British kind with fewer cross-marketing and finance firewalls between the bank and its nonbank product activities.[24]

Conflicts of Interest

A third issue, the potential for conflicts of interest, lies at the very heart of opposition to an expansion of banking powers into other financial service areas. Indeed, concerns regarding conflicts of interest provided the main foundation for the passage of the Glass-Steagall Act in 1933.[25]

The two principal questions that arise are: (1) what are the potential conflicts of interest arising from the expansion of banks' securities activities? and (2) what type of incentive structures change *potential* conflicts into *actual* conflicts?

Six Potential Conflicts of Interest.   We discuss the six most common potential conflicts of interest identified by regulators and academics below.[26]

---

[24]See T. F. Huertas, "Redesigning Regulation: The Future of Finance in the United States" (Jackson Hole, Wyoming, August 22, 1987, Mimeographed). Nevertheless, Saunders and Walter, *Universal Banking* could find no evidence of cost economies of scope for the world's 100 largest banks, many of which are universal banks.

[25]See Benston, *The Separation of Commercial and Investment Banking.*

[26]See A. Saunders, "Conflicts of Interest: An Economic View," in *Deregulating Wall Street,*

Salesperson's Stake.   Critics argue that when banks have the power to sell nonbank products, managers no longer dispense dispassionate advice to their customers as to which products to buy. Instead, they have a salesperson's stake in pushing the bank's own products, often to the disadvantage of the customer.

Stuffing Fiduciary Accounts.   Suppose a bank is acting as a securities underwriter and is unable to place these securities in a public offering. To avoid being exposed to potential losses (see Figure 16–3) the bank may stuff these unwanted securities in accounts managed by its own trust department and over which it has discretionary investment powers.

Bankruptcy Risk Transference.   Assume that a bank has a loan outstanding to a firm whose credit or bankruptcy risk has increased to the private knowledge of the banker. With this private knowledge, the banker may have an incentive to induce the firm to issue bonds underwritten by the bank's securities affiliate to an unsuspecting public. The proceeds of this bond issue could then be used to pay down the bank loan. As a result, the bank would have transferred the issuing firm's credit risk from itself to less-informed outside investors, while the securities affiliate also earned an underwriting fee.

Third-Party Loans.   To ensure that an underwriting goes well, a bank may make cheap loans to third-party investors on the implicit condition that this loan finance is used to purchase securities underwritten by its securities affiliate.

Tie-Ins.   A bank may use its lending powers to coerce or tie in a customer to the products sold by its securities affiliate. For example, it may threaten credit rationing unless the customer agrees to let the bank's securities affiliate do its securities underwritings.

Information Transfer.   In acting as a lender, the bank may become privy to certain inside information about its customers or its rivals that can be used in setting the prices or helping the distribution of securities offerings by its affiliate. This information could also flow from the securities affiliate to the bank.

Concept Question

1. Can you think of any more potential conflicts, in addition to the previous six, should commercial banks expand their investment banking activities?

Potential Conflicts of Interest and Their Actual Exploitation.   On their own, and unquestionably accepted, these conflicts appear to be extremely troublesome. Remember, however, there are specific and general checks and balances that mitigate against their exploitation. That is, many of these conflicts are likely to remain

ed. I. Walter (New York: John Wiley & Sons, 1985), pp. 207–30; E. J. Kelly, "Conflicts of Interest: A Legal View," in *Deregulating Wall Street*, pp. 231–54; and R. S. Kroszner and R. G. Rajan, "Is the Glass-Steagall Act Justified? A Study of U.S. Experience with Universal Banking before 1933" (Paper presented at the Western Finance Association, Vancouver, B.C., June 1993).

Chinese Wall
An internally imposed barrier within an organization that limits the flow of confidential client information among departments or areas.

potential rather than actual conflicts of interest. Specifically, many of these conflicts such as tie-ins and third-party loans, breach existing bank regulations and laws. Also, internal barriers or **Chinese walls** in most banks prohibit internal information transfers where they potentially conflict with the best interests of the customer. Further, sales of debt issues to a less-informed public to pay down bank loans may result in future lawsuits against the underwriter once investors discover their losses.[27]

More generally, conflicts of interest are only exploitable under three conditions: first, if markets for bank services are uncompetitive so that banks have monopoly power over their customers; for example, in making loans. Second, information flows between the customer and the bank are imperfect or asymmetric so that the bank possesses an information advantage over its customers. And third, the bank places a relatively low value on using its reputation as an asset. The discovery of having exploited a conflict can result in a considerable loss in future business and regulatory penalties. For instance, the recent case of Salomon Brothers squeezing the auction for U.S. Treasury notes and bonds (see Chapter 9). This suggests that potential conflicts are only likely to become actual conflicts under rather extreme conditions and/or incentives.[28]

Deposit Insurance

A possible argument against expanded powers is that the explicit and implicit protection given to banks by deposit insurance coverage gives banks a competitive advantage over other financial service firms (see Chapter 15). For example, because bank deposits up to $100,000 are covered by explicit deposit insurance, they are able to raise funds at subsidized, lower-cost rates than traditional securities firms. This may allow them to pass on these lower costs in cheaper loans to their affiliates. Currently, however, banks cannot make any loans at all to their Section 20 securities affiliates. Nevertheless, there still may be an indirect deposit insurance-related advantage to banking organizations undertaking securities activities when compared to traditional securities firms. This may result if bank regulators regard certain large banking organizations as being too big to fail (TBTF), thereby encouraging these institutions to take excessive risks such as placing aggressive underwriting bids for new issues. This effect would limit the underwriting shares of traditional investment banks, especially as TBTF guarantees do not appear to exist for them as shown in the failure of Drexel Burnham Lambert in February 1990. Consequently, TBTF guarantees tend to give banks some unfair competitive advantages.[29]

---

[27]In particular, the underwriter may be accused of lack of due diligence in not disclosing information in the new issue's prospectus.

[28]R. G. Rajan models these incentives in "A Theory of the Costs and Benefits of Universal Banking," C.R.S.P. Working Paper no. 346, University of Chicago, 1992.

[29]A recent study by L. Benveniste, M. Singh, and W. J. Wilhelm found very large stock return gains accruing to the biggest banks with Section 20 subsidiaries on the announcement of Drexel Burnham Lambert's bankruptcy. This may reflect investors' beliefs of increased profit opportunities for large bank-linked Section 20 subsidiaries in securities underwriting in future years. See "The Failure of Drexel Burnham Lambert: Evidence on the Implications for Commercial Banks" (Paper presented at the American Finance Association Conference, Anaheim, California, 1993).

Concept Question

1. Would risk-based deposit insurance introduced in 1993 alleviate concerns that deposit insurance provides an unfair subsidy to commercial banks relative to other financial service firms?

Regulatory Oversight

Currently, most bank holding companies with extensive nonbank subsidiaries face a diffuse and multilayered regulatory structure that would potentially hinder the monitoring and control of conflicts of interest abuses and excessive risk taking should banks be allowed to expand their securities activities. Specifically, for a bank holding company such as Citicorp, the Federal Reserve is the primary regulator. For its bank subsidiary such as Citibank, the comptroller of the currency, which is the charterer of national banks, shares regulatory oversight with the Federal Reserve and the FDIC. For its Section 20 securities subsidiary, the primary regulator is the SEC, although the Federal Reserve also has some oversight powers. It is far from clear that such a complex and overlapping regulatory structure is efficient from a public policy perspective.[30]

This is because it can lead to waste of monitoring and surveillance resources as well as unnecessary fights over bureaucratic turf. Furthermore, coordination problems can weaken monitoring and surveillance efficiency. Thus, a case can be made for subsuming all regulatory power in a single regulatory body should banks' securities powers be extended further.

Competition

The final issue concerns the effects of bank product expansions on competition in investment banking product lines. In securities underwriting, there are three primary reasons for believing that bank expansions would enhance competition. There is also one reason for believing that it would do the reverse; that is, increase both market concentration and the monopoly power of commercial banks over customers.

Pro-Competitive Effects. The three potential pro-competitive effects of banks' entry into securities activities are discussed below.

Increased Capital Market Access for Small Firms. Most large investment banks are headquartered in New York and the Northeast. As a result, small U.S. firms based in the Midwest and Southwest have often had a more difficult time accessing national capital markets than those of a similar size located in the Northeast. Consequently, the entry of regional and superregional banks into securities underwriting through securities affiliates could potentially expand the national capital market access of smaller firms.

---

[30]In the context of allowing banks to expand into insurance activities, the problem of aligning the differences between (largely) federal bank regulation and state-based insurance regulation would have to be faced.

Lower Commissions and Fees.   Greater competition for securities underwritings should work to reduce the underwriter's spread. That is, it should reduce the spread between the new issue bid price paid to the issuing firm and the offer price at which these shares are resold to the market. This potentially raises the new issue proceeds for the issuing firm by raising the underwriter's bid price. Such an effect was claimed when banks expanded their municipal bond underwritings, although this has been disputed.[31]

Reduce the Degree of Underpricing of New Issues.   The greatest risk to the underwriter is to price a new issue too high relative to the market's valuation of that security. That is, underwriters stand to lose when they overprice new issues. Given this, there is an incentive for underwriters to underprice new issues by setting the public offer price (OP) below the price established for the security in the secondary market once trading begins (P). The investment banker stands to gain through underpricing as it increases the probability of selling out the issue, without affecting the fixed underwriting spread. That is, a spread of $.50 at a bid-offer price of $93 and $93.50 produces the same gross-revenue (spread) of $.50 per share to the underwriter as a bid-offer price spread of $97 and $97.50. The major difference is that a lower offer price increases the demand for the shares by investors and the probability of selling the whole issue to the public very quickly. Both the underwriter and the outside investor may benefit from underpricing; the loser is the firm issuing the securities, which garners lower proceeds than if the offer price had been set at a higher price reflecting a more accurate market valuation. In the preceding example, the issuer receives only $93 per share rather than $97. Consequently, the underpricing of new issues is an additional cost of securities issuance borne by issuing firms. Most empirical research on the underpricing of U.S. new issues, or **initial public offerings** (IPOs), has found that they are underpriced in the range of 8 to 48 percent depending on the sample and time period chosen.[32] In contrast, **secondary issues** tend to be underpriced by less than 3 percent.[33]

If a major cause of IPO underpricing is a lack of competition among existing investment banks, then bank entry and competition should lower the degree of underpricing and increase the new issue proceeds for firms. Nevertheless, many economists argue that monopoly power is not the primary reason for the underpricing of new issues, but rather that underpricing reflects a risk premium that has to be paid to investors and investment bankers for information imperfections. That is, it is a risk premium for the information advantage possessed by issuers who better know the true quality of their firm's securities and its assets.[34]

IPO (Initial Public Offering)
A corporate equity or debt security offered to the public for the first time through an underwriter.

Secondary Issues
A new issue of equity or debt of firms whose securities are already traded in the market.

---

[31]For a review of this debate and the evidence, see W. L Silber, "Municipal Revenue Bond Costs and Bank Underwriting: A Survey of the Evidence," Monograph Series in Finance and Economics, Salomon Center for the Study of Financial Institutions, New York University, 1979.

[32]See the review of some 20 studies of underpricing by A. Saunders, "Why Are So Many Stock Issues Underpriced?" Federal Reserve Bank of Philadelphia, Business Review, March–April 1990, pp. 3–12.

[33]See C. F. Loderer, D. P. Sheehan, and G. B. Kadler, "The Pricing of Equity Offerings," *Journal of Financial Economics,* 1991, pp. 35–57.

[34]See R. Beatty and J. Ritter, "Investment Banking, Reputation, and the Underpricing of Initial Public Offerings," *Journal of Financial Economics* 15, 1986, pp. 213–32; and K. Rock, "Why New Issues Are Underpriced," *Journal of Financial Economics* 15, 1986, pp. 187–212. Also C. Muscerella and M. R. Vetsuypens, "A Simple Test of Baron's Model of IPO Underpricing," *Journal of Financial Economics* 24, 1989, pp. 125–36. They found out that when investment banks themselves (such as Morgan Stanley) went public, their stocks were also underpriced. This tends to support an information role in underpricing—although the average underpricing of investment banks was less than that found, on average, for other firms.

If this is so, bank entry may only reduce the degree of underpricing to the extent that it reduces the degree of information imperfection among issuers and investors. This might reasonably be expected given the specialized role of banks as delegated monitors (see Chapter 3).[35]

Anticompetitive Effects. While bank entry may be pro-competitive in the short-term, there still exists considerable concern about potential anticompetitive behavior in the long-term. The big money center banks, measured by either capital or assets, are many times larger than the biggest securities firms or insurance firms, for that matter. They may aggressively compete for business in the short run, trying to force traditional investment banks out of business. If successful, they would assume quasi-oligopoly positions, market concentration may rise, and in the long run, prices for investment banking services would rise rather than fall. Such a long-run outcome would outweigh any short term pro-competitive benefits.[36]

Summary

Looked at from a private financial service firm's perspective, product or activity expansion appears to offer a number of concrete private benefits. Most important are the potential gains from both regional and product diversification as well as from the potential generation of cost and revenue synergies. However, a set of important public policy or social welfare concerns relate to conflicts of interest, safety and soundness, competition and regulation. These latter concerns have restricted expansions of the financial product sets of traditional FIs such as commercial banks. Nevertheless, in recent years regulators and Congress have shown a greater appreciation of the potential benefits of financial service activity expansions although this has yet to be turned into major legislative changes for banks. Given that no U.S. bank is currently one of the world's top 20 banks, measured by assets, and that the 12 countries of the European Community have now adopted a *single capital market* in which full-service universal banking on German lines is viewed as the norm, larger and more powerful financial service conglomerates may pose an increasing competitive threat to financial firms headquartered in segmented financial systems such as the United States. If this occurs, it is likely to increase pressure on Congress and regulators to allow U.S. financial firms to expand their activities beyond the traditional boundaries defined by laws such as Glass-Steagall and the Bank Holding Company Act.

Questions and Problems

1. How does product segmentation reduce the risk of FIs? How does product segmentation increase the risk of FIs?

2. How does product segmentation reduce the profitability of FIs? How does product segmentation increase the profitability of FIs?

3. How does product segmentation reduce the profitability of nonfinancial firms? How does product segmentation increase the profitability of nonfinancial firms?

4. In the United States commercial banks specialize in customized products for difficult to evaluate transactions. Securities firms specialize in standardized products about which information is more easily obtainable. Discuss. Be sure to discuss the symbiosis between both types of FIs.

5. If you managed a U.S. bank and wanted to diversify your product line risk exposure, how would you do so under existing regulatory restrictions?

6. Why do you think that U.S. banks have been so aggressive in attempting to break down the barriers between traditional banking and other financial services activities?

7. The Garn-St Germain Act of 1982 explicitly stated that banking and insurance were not closely related. Discuss

---

[35]However, firewalls limit the efficiency with which the delegated monitor can transfer information to its affiliate.

[36]One possible reason for slow development of the German corporate bond market is that German universal banks wish to preserve their monopoly power over corporate debt. This may be best done by encouraging corporate loans rather than bond issues.

the distinction between insurance and traditional banking activities. Why do you think that this separation was maintained?

8. In many of the emerging capitalist economies of the Eastern European countries, commercial firms are allowed to open banks. State the pros and cons of this policy that allows the integration of banking and commerce.

9. The best efforts underwriting contract simply calls for payment of a commission (based on the ultimate sale price) while the firm commitment method entails a price guarantee where the underwriter writes a put option. Calculate the FI's underwriting fee under both the best efforts and firm commitment methods for the following initial public offerings:

a. The sale of 1 million shares of Ultrasonics, Inc. offered at $6.50 per share. The underwriter's bid price was $6. The best efforts commission rate was 50 basis points.

b. The sale of 1 million shares of Ultrasonics, Inc. offered at $5.50 per share. The underwriter's bid price was $6. The best efforts commission rate was 50 basis points.

10. What is the maximum possible underwriter's fee on both the best efforts and firm commitment underwriting contracts of an issue of 12 million shares at a bid price of $12.45 and an offer price of $12.60? What is the maximum possible loss? The best efforts underwriting commission is 75 basis points.

17

GEOGRAPHIC DIVERSIFICATION

Learning Objectives

In this chapter you will learn about the advantages and disadvantages of domestic and international expansions for FIs. The attractiveness of such expansions depends in part on whether they are de novo expansions, such as establishing new offices or branches, or expansions through mergers and acquisitions. It will be shown that the attractiveness of mergers and acquisitions depend on three sets of factors: regulation, cost and revenue synergies, and firm- and market-specific characteristics.

Introduction

Just as product expansion may enable an FI to reduce risk and increase returns, so may geographic expansion. Geographic expansions can have a number of dimensions. In particular, they can be either domestic within a state or region, or international by participating in an overseas market. Also, expansions can be effected through opening a new office or branch or by acquiring another FI. In this chapter we trace the potential benefits and costs to an FI from expanding domestically—especially through acquisition—and then go on to look at international or global expansions. In addition, we look at some empirical evidence on the gains from geographic expansions.

Domestic Expansions

De Novo Office
A newly established office.

In the United States, the ability of FIs to expand domestically is constrained by regulation. By comparison, no special regulations inhibit the ability of commercial firms such as General Motors, IBM, or Sears from establishing new or **de novo offices**, factories, or branches anywhere in the country. Nor are they prohibited from acquiring other firms—as long as they are not banks. While insurance companies face relatively few restrictions in expanding their business domestically, other FIs, especially banks, face a complex and changing network of rules and regulations. While such regulations may inhibit expansions, they also create potential opportunities to increase an FI's returns. In particular, regulations may create locally uncompetitive markets with monopoly economic rents that new entrants can potentially exploit. Thus, for the most innovative FIs, regulation can provide profit opportunities as well as costs. As a result, regulation is both an inhibitor and an incentive to engage in geographic expansions.[1]

---

[1] E. Kane has called this interaction between regulation and incentives the regulatory dialectic. See "Accelerating Inflation, Technological Innovation, and the Decreasing Effectiveness of Banking Regulation," *Journal of Finance* 36, 1981, pp. 335–67. Expansions that are geographic market extensions involving firms in the same product areas are part of a broader set of horizontal mergers.

In addition, the economic factors that impact commercial firm expansion and acquisition decisions are likely to impact the decisions of FIs as well. Two major groups of factors are cost and revenue synergies and firm/market specific attractions, such as the specialized skills of an acquired firm's employees or the markets of the firm to be acquired. Thus, the attractiveness of a geographic expansion, whether through acquisition, branching, or opening a new office, depends on a broad set of factors encompassing:

1. Regulation and the regulatory framework.
2. Cost and revenue synergies.
3. Firm or market specific factors.

We start by considering how the first factor, regulation, impacts an FI's geographic expansion decision. Specifically, we briefly discuss the restrictions applying to insurance companies and thrifts; then we look in more detail at regulations affecting commercial banks.

Regulatory Factors Impacting Geographic Expansion

Insurance Companies

As we discussed earlier, insurance companies are state-regulated firms. By establishing a subsidiary in one state, an insurance company normally has the opportunity to sell insurance anywhere in that state and often to market the product nationally by telemarketing and direct sales. To effectively deliver a financial service, however, it is often necessary to establish a physical presence in a local market. To do this, insurance companies establish subsidiaries and offices in other states. This is usually easy since the initial capital requirement for establishing a new subsidiary is set at relatively low levels by state regulators. Thus, most large insurance companies such as Aetna, All State, and Prudential have a physical presence in virtually every state in the union.

Thrifts

Historically, the ability of thrifts to branch or expand geographically—whether intrastate (within a state) or interstate (between states)—was under the power of the Federal Home Loan Bank Board. The newly established Office of Thrift Supervision assumed this power in 1989.[2] Generally, the policy was that a federally chartered thrift could not branch across state lines. Then, in the 1980s a considerable loosening of these restrictions occurred. Both the Garn-St Germain Act of 1982 and the Financial Institutions Reform Recovery and Enforcement Act (FIRREA) of 1989 allowed sound banks and thrifts to acquire failing thrifts across state lines and to run them either as separate subsidiaries or convert them into branches. For example, the Resolution Trust Corporation (RTC), established under FIRREA to resolve failing thrift institutions, has wide-ranging powers to enable out-of-state acquisitions of failing thrifts to lower the costs of failure resolution. Thus, the RTC has allowed banks to acquire thrifts and convert them into branches overriding state laws in Colorado, New

---

[2]As part of the FIRREA 1989 legislation.

Mexico, and Arkansas. The RTC has also allowed banks to acquire a thrift in another state and convert it into a branch. Bank of America did this in Utah. Thus, the crisis in the thrift industry is eroding the barriers to geographic expansion for this class of FIs.

Commercial Banks

Restrictions on Intrastate Banking.   At the beginning of the century, most U.S. banks were **unit banks** with a single office. Improving communications and customer needs resulted in a rush to branching in the first two decades of the twentieth century. Increasingly, this movement ran into opposition from the smallest unit banks and the largest money center banks. The smallest unit banks perceived a competitive threat to their retail business from the bigger branching banks; money center banks feared a loss of valuable correspondent business such as check clearing and other payment services. As a result, several states restricted the ability of banks to branch within the state. Indeed, some states prohibited intrastate branching per se, effectively constraining a bank to unit status. Over the years and in a very piecemeal fashion, states have liberalized their restrictions on within state branching. As we show in Table 17–1, in 1990 only two states absolutely prohibited branching, whereas nine other states had laws that allowed limited intrastate banking. This usually means setting up branches in counties bordering the county in which the bank's head office was established.

Unit Bank
A bank with a single office.

Concept Question

1. Looking at Table 17–1, is the state in which you reside restrictive toward intrastate banking?

Restrictions on Interstate Banking.   The defining piece of legislation affecting interstate branching was the McFadden Act passed in 1927 and amended in 1933. The McFadden Act and its amendments restricted nationally chartered banks' branching ability to the same extent allowed to state-chartered banks. Because states prohibit interstate banking for state-chartered banks in general, nationally chartered banks were similarly prohibited.[3]

Since 1927, given the prohibition on interstate branching, bank organizations expanding across state lines have relied on establishing subsidiaries rather than branches. Some of the biggest banking organizations have established **multibank holding companies** for this purpose. A multibank holding company (MBHC) is a parent company that acquires more than one bank as a direct subsidiary. While MBHCs had been around in the early part of the twentieth century, restrictions on interstate branching gave the bank acquisition movement an added impetus. By 1956, some 47 multibank holding companies were established, many in two or more states.[4]

In 1956, Congress recognized the potential loophole to interstate banking posed by the MBHC movement and passed the Douglas Amendment to the Bank Holding

Multibank Holding Company (MBHC)
A parent banking organization that owns a number of individual bank subsidiaries.

---

[3]It is arguable, contrary to conventional wisdom, that the McFadden Act actually enlarged the geographic expansion powers of nationally chartered banks since the prime regulator of nationally chartered banks had restricted national bank branching even within a state up until the Act's passage.

[4]In 1990, there were 157 interstate multibank holding companies, the growth reflecting the presence of regional banking pacts, see later.

TABLE 17–1 Summary of State Bank Expansion Laws

Statewide (40)	Limited (9)	Unit (2)
Alabama[2]	Arkansas[4]	Colorado
Alaska	Illinois	Wyoming
Arizona	Iowa	
California	Kentucky	
Connecticut	Louisiana[3]	
Delaware	Minnesota	
District of Columbia	Missouri[3]	
Florida[2,3]	New Mexico	
Georgia[2]	Tennessee[3]	
Hawaii[1]		
Idaho		
Indiana[2]		
Kansas[1,2]		
Maine		
Maryland		
Massachusetts		
Michigan		
Mississippi		
Montana[1,2]		
Nebraska[2]		
Nevada		
New Hampshire		
New Jersey		
New York		
North Carolina		
North Dakota[1,2]		
Ohio		
Oklahoma[2]		
Oregon		
Pennsylvania		
Rhode Island		
South Carolina		
South Dakota		
Texas		
Utah		
Vermont		
Virginia		
Washington		
West Virginia		
Wisconsin[3,5]		

[1]State has not enacted a law providing for entry from other states.
[2]Statewide branching by merger.
[3]Statewide branching permitted for national banks according to ruling of Comptroller of the Currency.
[4]Contiguous county branching Jan. 1, 1994, statewide Jan. 1, 1999.
[5]Statewide branching effective Aug. 1, 1989 for 1 year.
Revised: September 10, 1990.
SOURCE: Federal Reserve Board, U.S. Treasury, "Modernizing the Financial System . . ." (1991).

Company Act. This act permitted MBHCs to acquire bank subsidiaries only to the extent allowed by the laws of the state in which the proposed bank target resided. Because states prohibited out-of-state bank acquisitions, this essentially curtailed the growth of the MBHC movement until the emergence and expansion of regional banking pacts. Any MBHCs with out-of-state subsidiaries established prior to 1956 were **grandfathered;** that is, MBHCs were allowed to keep them. (One such example was First Interstate.)

The passage of the 1956 Douglas Amendment did not close all potential interstate banking loopholes. Since the amendment pertained to MBHC acquisitions, it still left open the potential for **one-bank holding company** (OBHC) geographic extensions. A OBHC is a parent bank holding company that has a single bank subsidiary and a number of other nonbank subsidiaries. By creating a OBHC and establishing across state lines various nonbank subsidiaries that sell financial services such as consumer finance, leasing, and data processing, a bank could almost replicate an out-of-state banking presence. However, doing interstate banking in this fashion was far more expensive than establishing either direct branches or full-service subsidiaries. Nevertheless, one bank holding expansions are excellent examples of Kane's regulatory dialectic.[5] That is, blocking one path to geographic expansion simply resulted in banks exploiting a loophole elsewhere if they believed it was net profitable to do so.

The OBHC movement grew tremendously from 117 banking organizations in 1956 to 1,318 in 1970, with all manner of financial and nonfinancial subsidiaries established both within the home state of the affiliated bank and across state lines. For example, some OBHCs even had ownership stakes in supermarket chains and railroads.

In 1970, Congress again acted, recognizing that bankers had creatively innovated yet another loophole to interstate banking restrictions. The 1970 Bank Holding Company Act Amendments effectively restricted the nonbank activities a OBHC could engage in to those "closely related to banking," as defined by the Federal Reserve under Section 4(c)(8) of the act. Further, acquisitions of nonbank subsidiaries after 1970 were subject to the approval of the Federal Reserve. Initially, the act permitted only six nonbank activities including consumer finance and credit cards. Moreover, subsidiaries engaged in activities not closely related to banking had to be divested by 1980.

Thus, the year 1970 and the passage of the Bank Holding Company Act Amendments are probably the low point of interstate banking in the United States. Since that time, four developments have resulted in major, but not complete, erosion of interstate banking restrictions. We describe these four developments next.

Grandfathered Subsidiary
A subsidiary established prior to the passage of a restrictive law and not subject to that law.

One-Bank Holding Company
A parent banking organization that owns one bank subsidiary and nonbank subsidiaries.

Concept Question

1. What is the difference between the interstate banking restrictions imposed under the 1956 Bank Holding Company Act and those passed under the 1970 Amendments to the Bank Holding Company Act?

Regional and National Banking Pacts.   Maine took the first step in eroding interstate banking restrictions in 1975 by passing a law that exploited a loophole in the

[5]Kane, "Accelerating Inflation."

Douglas Amendments of 1956. This loophole occurred because the law prohibited the acquisition of a bank across state lines unless directly permitted by the state in which the proposed target bank resided. To increase employment in, and growth of, its financial services industry, Maine passed a law allowing banks from any other state to enter and acquire local banks, even if the banks in Maine could not engage in such acquisitions in other states. This nationwide nonreciprocal bank acquisition law led to a rapid acquisition of Maine's banking assets by out-of-state bank holding companies. Indeed, by 1988 some 85 percent of bank assets in Maine were held by out-of-state banking organizations such as Citicorp.

Regional or Interstate Banking Pact
An agreement among states describing the conditions for entrance of out-of-state banks by acquisition.

In the early 1980s other states in New England sought to follow Maine's example by enacting their own **interstate banking pacts.** However, these laws were often more restrictive, in that they only allowed banks from a certain geographic region—in one case, New England—to enter their banking markets by acquisition. In particular, acquisition by out-of-state banks from New York and California were generally prohibited. This created some concern about the legality of these more restrictive regional pacts, until Connecticut's restrictive law was upheld by the U.S. Supreme Court in the face of a challenge to its legality by New York-based Citicorp in 1984.

Since then all but Hawaii have passed some form of interstate banking law or pact. There are three general types of interstate banking laws:

Nationwide (open entry). Nationwide laws allow an out-of-state bank to acquire an in-state target bank even if the acquirer's home state does not permit banks from the target's state similar acquisition powers.

Nationwide Reciprocal. An out-of-state acquirer can purchase a target bank as long as the acquirer's state allows other banks from the target's state to enter by acquisition as well. Big banking states such as New York and California currently have such laws. Thus, since January 1991, a New York bank can potentially acquire a California bank and vice versa.

Regional Reciprocal. These regional banking pacts allow banks from a regional group of states to acquire a target bank in a given state as long as there is reciprocity; that is, as long as home state banks can acquire targets in other regional pact states and vice versa. For example, Wisconsin's regional reciprocal law allows entry by acquisition for banks from Iowa, Illinois, Indiana, Kentucky, Michigan, Minnesota, Missouri, and Ohio as long as those states reciprocate by allowing acquisitions by Wisconsin banks in their markets.

In Table 17–2 we show the interstate banking laws as of July 1992.

Concept Questions

1. All other things being the same, which of the three types of pacts would an out-of-state bank find most attractive in considering entry? Explain your answer.
2. Why has Hawaii not passed any regional banking pact laws at all?

Purchase of Troubled Banks.   The acquisition of failing or troubled banks across state lines is a second way of eroding interstate banking barriers. Following the passage of the Garn-St Germain Act in 1982, the bankruptcy of the FSLIC, and the depletion of the FDIC's reserves, regulators have increasingly turned to out-of-state

TABLE 17–2   State Laws Allowing Interstate Banking as of July 1, 1992

Nationwide Entry		Regional or Contiguous State Entry with Reciprocity	Entry Not Allowed
Without Reciprocity	*With Reciprocity*		
Alaska	California	Alabama	Hawaii
Arizona	Connecticut	Arkansas[2]	Kansas[3]
Colorado	Delaware	District of Columbia	Montana[3]
Idaho	Illinois	Florida	North Dakota[3]
Maine	Indiana	Georgia	
Nevada	Kentucky	Iowa	
New Hampshire	Louisiana	Maryland	
New Mexico	Michigan	Massachusetts	
Oklahoma[1]	Nebraska	Minnesota	
Oregon	New Jersey	Mississippi	
Texas	New York	Missouri	
Utah	Ohio	North Carolina	
Wyoming	Pennsylvania	South Carolina	
	Rhode Island	Virginia	
	South Dakota	Wisconsin	
	Tennessee		
	Vermont		
	Washington		
	West Virginia		

[1]Bank holding companies from states not granting reciprocal entry to Oklahoma banking organizations must wait four years before making additional acquisitions.

[2]Entry into Arkansas is contingent on submission, approval, and compliance with an extensive plan guaranteeing certain levels of community service and investment.

[3]Passed laws after July 1992.

SOURCE: U.S. Treasury, "Modernizing the Financial System . . ." 1991 (updated).

acquisitions to resolve bank failures. Thus, for example, in 1987 Chemical Bank acquired Texas Commerce and gained a foothold in the Texas banking market.

Through its Texas Commerce unit, Chemical Bank acquired most of the banks of the failed First City Bancorporation of Texas in January 1993. In general, sound banks perceiving a profit opportunity willingly pay the FDIC a premium to acquire banks in markets where they cannot legally branch (see Chapter 15). In its acquisition of First City Bancorporation, Chemical paid $346.8 million for banks with a total of $4.4 billion in deposits and $6.6 billion in assets of varying quality. In addition, the 1982 Garn-St Germain Act allowed banks to acquire failing thrifts as well as banks; through this mechanism Citicorp has acquired thrifts in growing banking markets such as California and Florida. Finally, the passage of FIRREA in August 1989 extended the interstate acquisition powers of banks to encompass healthy thrifts as well.

Nonbank Banks.   A third way of eroding interstate banking barriers came from the establishment of nonbank banks (described in Chapter 16). Until 1987, a large U.S. bank could acquire a full-service out-of-state bank, divest it of its commercial loans, and legally operate it as a nonbank bank specializing in consumer finance.[6] However,

[6]For the purposes of the Bank Holding Company Act's restrictions on MBHC acquisitions, the definition of a bank was an institution that accepted demand deposits and made commercial and industrial loans. By stripping a bank of its commercial loans, it turned into a nonbank bank that was not subject to restrictions on interstate banking.

TABLE 17–3 **Organizational Structure of U.S. Banks**
(September 1992)

		Percent of Assets
Number of OBHCs	4,784	17.4%
Number of MBHCs	890 with 3,574 banks	70.8
Independent banks	3,538	11.3
Total banks	11,896	

Percent of assets calculated on total foreign and domestic assets.
SOURCE: Federal Reserve Board of Governors (private communication).

the Competitive Equality Banking Act (CEBA) effectively put an end to this loophole in 1987, although it grandfathered existing nonbank banks.

Expansion in OBHC Activities. A bank can virtually replicate a full interstate banking presence by establishing out-of-state nonbank subsidiaries. Norwest Corporation, a bank holding company from Minneapolis, has mortgage subsidiaries in 49 states and more than 770 consumer lending subsidiaries in 46 states. Moreover, in 1970, Section 4(c)(8) of the Bank Holding Company Act Amendments specified that permitted nonbank activities of bank holding companies had to be "closely related to banking" (as defined by the Federal Reserve). Even so, from a total of 6 activities in 1971, the permitted list has now expanded either by regulation or order of the Federal Reserve to close to 60.

Prospects for Future Deregulation. As just described, there has been a considerable erosion of interstate banking restrictions in the 1980s and early 1990s. Indeed, the U.S. Treasury strongly advised Congress to eliminate nationwide banking restrictions during the debate leading up to the passage of FDICIA in December 1991.[7] The principal arguments revolved around the costs or inefficiencies relating to regulatory avoidance. For example, nationwide banking expansion through multibank holding companies is potentially far more expensive than through branching. Separate corporations and boards of directors have to be established for each bank in a MBHC and it is hard to achieve the same level of economic and financial integration as with branches. In addition, because most of the major banking competitor countries such as Japan, Germany, France, and the United Kingdom have nationwide branching, it is consistent with creating a level playing field for U.S. banks internationally. Unfortunately, the final FDICIA legislation contained no material changes either to the McFadden Act or the Bank Holding Company Act. As a result, nationwide banking will gradually emerge in a piecemeal fashion through de facto deregulation and organizational innovations, along with further regional banking pact extensions.[8] Note the current structure of the U.S. banking industry in Table 17–3.

---

[7]U.S. Treasury, "Modernizing the Financial System . . ." (1991).

[8]This haphazard approach to creating a nationwide banking system has been called the Balkanization of banking.

Concept Question

1. On which does the restriction on nationwide branching have more of an effect, on a bank's ability to raise deposits or on its ability to make loans?

Cost and Revenue Synergies Impacting Geographic Expansion

One reason for an FI expanding or not expanding geographically by acquisition relates to the regulations defining its merger opportunities. Another reason relates to the exploitation of potential cost and revenue synergies from merging. Indeed, in recent years there has been a merger wave among banks, including some **megamergers** among large banks, driven by the desire to achieve greater cost and revenue synergies.

Megamerger
The merger of two large banks.

Cost Synergies

A frequent reason given for bank mergers is the potential cost synergies that may result from economies of scale, economies of scope, or managerial efficiency sources (often called **X efficiencies** because they are difficult to pin down in a quantitative fashion). For example, in April 1992, Bank of America acquired Security Pacific creating the second largest banking organization in the United States with assets of $190 billion. Specifically, for Bank America cost savings would potentially occur by ending duplication of branching activities and improving the managerial efficiency of some units of Security Pacific. As of early 1993, the corporate bank side of the two banks had been fully integrated and one third of all branches (500 in total) had been closed. The targeted savings in costs is $1.2 billion by 1995; an estimated $500 million had been achieved by the end of 1992.[9]

X Efficiency
Cost savings due to the greater managerial efficiency of the acquiring bank.

Another example of a cost-motivated megamerger was between Chemical Bank and Manufacturers Hanover in 1991. In the first two years of the merger, Chemical laid off 6,200 employees largely through branch closings. Nonetheless, Chemical's 350 branches makes it the largest branch bank in the New York City area and the nation's third largest bank. In addition, as one of the major credit card issuers, it has made significant cost gains from centralizing these operations.

Although Bank of America and Chemical Bank are interesting examples of megamergers, they are still essentially mergers in the same or closely related geographic banking markets. An important question is whether similar cost synergies are available for more geographically dispersed acquisitions, such as MBHCs exploiting regional banking pacts. For example, NCNB of North Carolina, a $7 billion bank in 1982, has used out-of-state acquisitions to expand into the renamed NationsBank which, with assets of $118 billion, is now the fourth largest U.S. bank. Its two major acquisitions were the 1988 purchase of the First Republic Bank of Texas and the 1991 purchase of C and S-Sovran, a bank holding company that combined branches and subsidiaries in states such as Virginia, the District of Columbia, and Georgia. The newly created NationsBank now has a strong presence in nine southern and southwestern states. On the cost side, savings targets are branching costs and the reorganization of back office systems; for example, the main NationsBank data center

---

[9]See *Euromoney,* "Do the Gains Outweigh the Losses," December 1992, p. 67.

was out sourced to Perot Systems in Texas. In 1992, NationsBank's profits of $350 million were reportedly above analysts' expectations.[10]

In a recent comprehensive study, A. Berger and D. Humphrey used data from 1981 to 1989 to analyze the cost savings from megamergers, which they defined as when the acquirer's and the target bank's assets exceeded $1 billion. They could find very little evidence of potential gains from economies of scale and scope. Indeed, what cost savings they could find were related to improved managerial efficiency (X efficiency).[11] The three major findings of their study were as follows: First, the managerial efficiency of the acquirer tends to be superior to that of the acquired bank. Second, the 57 megamergers analyzed produced small but significant X efficiency gains. Third (and perhaps surprisingly), the degree of cost savings in market overlap mergers (e.g., as in the Bank of America and Chemical cases) were apparently no greater than for geographic extension mergers (as in the NationsBank case). Overall, they could not find the sizable cost synergies of 30 percent or so that are often given as the motivational forces behind such mergers.[12]

Revenue Synergies

The revenue synergies argument has three dimensions: First, revenues may be enhanced by acquiring a bank in a growing market. Thus, acquisitions of banks in Florida and the Southwest by NationsBank are apparently a key part of its strategy to expand its retail banking network.

Second, the acquiring bank's revenue stream may become more stable if the asset and liability portfolio of the target institution exhibits different credit, interest rate, and liquidity risk characteristics from the acquirer. For example, real estate loan portfolios have shown very strong regional cycles in the 1980s. Specifically, U.S. real estate declined in value in the Southeast, followed by the Northeast, followed by California with a long and variable lag. Thus, a geographically diversified real estate portfolio may be far less risky than one in which both acquirer and target specialized in a single region.[13]

Third, there is an opportunity for revenue enhancement by expanding into markets that are less than fully competitive. That is, banks may be able to identify and expand geographically into those markets where *economic rents* potentially exist, but where such entry will not be viewed as being potentially anticompetitive by regulators. Indeed, to the extent that geographic expansions are viewed as enhancing the monopoly power of a bank by generating excessive rents, regulators may act to prevent a merger unless the merger produces potential efficiency gains that cannot be reasonably achieved by other means.[14] In recent years, the ultimate enforcement of antimonopoly laws and guidelines has fallen to the U.S. Department of Justice. In

---

[10]See *Euromoney,* "NationsBank: New Kid on the Block," December 1992, p. 63.

[11]X efficiencies are those cost savings not directly due to economies of scope or economies of scale. As such, they are usually attributed to superior management skills and other difficult-to-measure managerial factors. To date, the explicit measurement of what comprises these efficiencies, remains to be established in the empirical banking literature.

[12]A. Berger and D. B. Humphrey, "Megamergers in Banking and the Use of Cost Efficiency as an Antitrust Defense," *The Anti Trust Bulletin* 37, 1992, pp. 541–600.

[13]As a result, the potential revenue diversification gains for more geographically concentrated mergers such as Bank of America and Security Pacific are likely to be relatively low; for example, both are heavily exposed to California real estate loans.

[14]U.S. Department of Justice, "Horizontal Merger Guidelines," April 2, 1992.

TABLE 17–4 1982 Department of Justice Horizontal Merger Guidelines

Postmerger Market Concentration	*Level of Herfindahl-Hirschman Index*	*Postmerger Change in Herfindahl-Hirschman Index and Likelihood of a Challenged Merger*
Highly concentrated	Greater than 1,800	Greater than 100—likely to be challenged
		50 to 100—depends on other factors*
		Less than 50—unlikely to be challenged
Moderately concentrated	1,000 to 1,800	Greater than 100—likely to be challenged; other factors considered*
		Less than or equal to 100—unlikely to be challenged
Unconcentrated	Less than 1,000	Any increase—unlikely to be challenged

*In addition to the postmerger concentration of the market and the size of the resulting increase in concentration, the Department will consider the presence of the following factors in deciding whether to challenge a merger: ease of entry; the nature of the product and its terms of sale; market information about specific transactions; buyer market characteristics; conduct of firms in the market; and market performance. (For a detailed explanation of these factors see Sections III(B) and III(C) of the 1982 Department of Justice Merger Guidelines.)

Source: Department of Justice, Merger Guidelines, 1982.

particular, the Department of Justice has laid down guidelines regarding the acceptability or unacceptability of acquisitions based on the potential increase in concentration in the market in which an acquisition takes place, with the cost-efficiency exception just noted.[15]

These merger guidelines are based on a measure of market concentration called the Herfindahl-Hirschman Index (**HHI**). This index is created by taking the percentage market shares of each firm in a market, squaring them, and then adding these squared shares. Thus, in a market where a single firm had a 100 percent market share the HHI would be:

$$HHI = (100)^2 = 10,000$$

Alternatively, in a market in which there were an infinitely large number of firms of equal size, then:

$$HHI \simeq 0$$

Thus, the HHI must lie between 0 and 10,000.

Whether a merger will be challenged under the Department of Justice guidelines depends on the postmerger HHI level. As you can see in Table 17–4, the Department

The HHI
An index or measure of market concentration based on the squared market shares of market participants.

---

[15]The Federal Reserve also has the power to approve or disapprove mergers among state member banks and bank holding companies. The Comptroller of the Currency has similar powers over nationally chartered banks. The Federal Reserve's criteria is similar to the Department of Justice in that it takes into account the HHI (market concentration index). However, it also evaluates the risk effects of the merger. The Department of Justice has powers to review the decisions made by the bank regulatory agencies.

of Justice defines a *concentrated* market as having a postmerger HHI ratio of 1,800, a moderately concentrated market as having a ratio of 1,000 to 1,800, and an unconcentrated market as having a ratio of less than 1,000. In either a concentrated or moderately concentrated market, postmerger HHI increases of 100 or more may be challenged.[16] For example, consider a market that has three banks with the following shares:

Bank A = 50%

Bank B = 46%

Bank C = 4%

The premerger HHI for the market is

$$HHI = (50)^2 + (46)^2 + (4)^2 = 2,500 + 2,116 + 16 = 4,632$$

Thus, the market is highly concentrated according to the Department of Justice guidelines.

Suppose Bank A wants to acquire Bank C so that the postacquisition market would exhibit the following shares:[17]

$$A + C = 54\%$$

$$B = 46\%$$

The postmerger HHI would be:

$$HHI = (54)^2 + (46)^2 = 2,916 + 2,116 = 5,032$$

Thus, the increase or change in the HHI (ΔHHI) postmerger is

$$\Delta HHI = 5032 - 4632 = 400$$

Since the increase is 400, and is more than the 100 benchmark defined in the Department of Justice guidelines, the market is heavily concentrated and the merger could be challenged.[18]

Concept Questions

1. Suppose that five firms in a banking market each have a 20 percent equal market share. What is the HHI?

---

[16]In practice, it is only when the change exceeds 200 in banking that a challenge may occur. This is because banking is generally viewed as being more competitive than most industries.

[17]Here we consider the effect on the HHI of a within-market acquisition; similar calculations can be carried out for between market acquisitions.

[18]There are two problems of interpretation of the HHI in the context of banking and financial services. First, what is the relevant geographic scope of the market for financial services—national, regional, or city? Second, once that market is defined, do we view banks, thrifts, and insurance companies as separate or unique lines of business, or are they competing in the same financial market? That is, what defines the institutional scope of the market? In the case of financial services, it has been traditional to define markets on functional, or line of business criteria, so that commercial banking is a separate market from savings (thrift) banking and other financial services. Further, the relevant market area has usually been defined as highly localized, the standard metropolitan statistical areas (SMSAs) or rural areas (non-SMSAs). Unfortunately, such definitions become increasingly irrelevant in a world of greater geographic and product expansion. Indeed, logically, the use of HHIs should increasingly be based on regional market lines and include a broad financial service firm definition of the marketplace. Thus, in recent years the Federal Reserve has often included one half of thrift deposits in calculating bank market HHIs.

2. Suppose that two banks in question 1 merged, what is the postmerger HHI? Could it be challenged by the Justice Department?

Other Market- and Firm-Specific Factors Impacting Geographic Expansion Decisions

In addition to regulation and cost and revenue synergies, other factors may impact an acquisition decision. For example, an acquiring bank may be concerned about the solvency and asset quality of a potential target bank in another region. Thus,

TABLE 17–5 (*a*) **Variable Definitions and Expected Coefficient Signs**

	Variable	*Definition*	*Average*	*Expected Sign*
Bank variables	TREAS	Ratio of U.S. Treasury investments to total assets	.203	−
	LNTOAST	Ratio of net loans to total assets	.482	?
	PROV	Ratio of loan loss provision to net loans	.007	+
	CHARGOFF	Ratio of loan write-offs to net loans	.008	−
	ROEQ	Ratio of net income to equity capital	.091	+
	CAPDEV	(Ratio of loan loss allowance plus equity capital to assets) − .06	.030	−
Regulatory variables	UNIT	Equals 1 if acquired bank located in unit bank state and zero otherwise	.276	+
	MULTI	Equals 1 if state law permits multibank holding companies and zero otherwise	.002	?
	ELECT	Equals 1 if state law permits statewide electronic banking and zero otherwise	.397	−
Market structure variables	MS	Ratio of bank's total deposits to that of the market; its market share	.179	+
	HERF	The Herfindahl index of that target bank's market	.253	+
Other variables	PURCH	Equals 1 if the acquisition was a purchase of the acquired bank	.609	?
	COMB	Equals 1 if the acquisition involved a combination of cash and equity shares	.166	?

(*b*) **Bank Merger Premium Regression Equation Results***

$$
\begin{aligned}
\text{PREMIUM} = \quad & 1.927^{*\dagger} & - \quad & .771 \text{ TREAS}^{*\dagger} & - \quad & .574 \text{ LNTOAST}^{*\dagger} & + \quad & 10.438 \text{ PROV} \\
& (9.27) & & (-2.76) & & (-1.96) & & (1.41) \\
- \quad & 6.684 \text{ CHARGOFF} & - \quad & 1.786 \text{ CAPDEV}^{*\dagger} & + \quad & .510 \text{ ROEQ}^{*\dagger} & + \quad & .096 \text{ UNIT}^{*\dagger} \\
& (-1.08) & & (-1.76) & & (2.10) & & (1.66) \\
- \quad & .506 \text{ MULTI} & - \quad & .061 \text{ ELECT} & - \quad & .306 \text{ MS}^{*\dagger} & + \quad & .392 \text{ HERF}^{*\dagger} \\
& (-1.26) & & (-1.19) & & (-1.66) & & (1.70) \\
- \quad & .176 \text{ PURCH}^{*\dagger} & - \quad & .171 \text{ COMB}^{*\dagger} & & (-2.85) & & (-2.20)
\end{aligned}
$$

$R^2 = .121$ Number of Observations = 264   F-statistic = 2.68*†

*T-statistics in parentheses below estimated coefficients.

†Coefficient on variable or test statistic significant at the 10 percent level.

Source: From "Bank Merger Premiums: Analysis and Evidence," by Beatty, Smirlock, and Santomero, *The Salomon Center Monograph Series on Economic and Finance,* 1987. Reprinted by permission.

important factors influencing the acquisition decision may include the target bank's leverage and capital ratio, its loss reserves, and the amount of nonperforming loans in its portfolio.

A study by R. P. Beatty, A. M. Santomero and M. L. Smirlock analyzed the factors potentially impacting the attractiveness of bank mergers and identified some 13 factors or variables, many of them bank specific. In particular, they analyzed 149 bank acquisitions over the period 1984–85; they measured the attraction of the merger by the size of the **merger premium** the acquired bank was willing to pay for a target bank. Analytically, we measure this premium by the ratio of the purchase price of the target bank's equity to its book price or the market to book ratio (see Chapter 14).

The variables analyzed, their average values, and the expected direction of their effect on the merger premium appear in Table 17–5, panel *a*, with the regression results in panel *b*. As you can see, 6 of the 13 variables are bank-specific variables measuring the quality of the bank, and 3 variables are regulatory variables reflecting the degree of barriers to entry into the market of the target bank. Two variables are market structure variables reflecting the possibilities of revenue synergies and rents from entry, as measured by the market HHI and the deposit share of the target bank. Panel *b* indicates that the highest merger premiums are paid for well-managed banks in relatively uncompetitive environments.[19]

Merger Premium
The ratio of the purchase price of a target bank's equity to its book value.

Concept Question

1. Suppose you are a manager of a bank looking at another bank as a target in an acquisition. What three characteristics of the target bank would most attract you? What three characteristics would most discourage you?

The Success of Geographic Expansions

As you can see, a variety of regulatory and economic factors impact the attractiveness of geographic expansions to an FI manager. In this section, we evaluate some of the empirical evidence on the success of market extension mergers. There are at least two levels at which such an evaluation can be done: First, how did investors react when an interstate bank merger was announced? Second, once interstate bank mergers have taken place, do they produce, in aggregate, the expected gains in efficiency and profitability?[20]

Investor Reaction

Researchers have conducted a number of studies on both nonbank and bank mergers looking at the announcement effects of mergers on bidding and target firms' share values. They measure the announcement effect by the reaction of investors in the stock market to the news of a merger event. In particular, economists have been interested in whether a merger announcement generates positive **abnormal returns**— risk-adjusted stock returns above normal levels—for the bidding and/or target firms. Unlike for commercial firms, where the typical study finds that only target firms'

Abnormal Returns
Risk-adjusted stock returns above expected levels.

---

[19]R. P. Beatty, A. M. Santomero, and M. L. Smirlock, "Bank Merger Premiums . . ."

[20]We have already noted that the Berger and Humphrey "Megamergers in Banking" study casts doubts on the actual size of the cost savings from megamergers.

shareholders gain from merger announcements through significantly positive abnormal returns, studies in banking generally find that both the acquiring bank and the target bank gain.[21] For example, M. Millon-Cornett and S. De studied interstate merger proposals during 1982–86. They found that on the day of the merger announcement, bidding bank stockholders enjoyed positive abnormal returns of 0.65 percent while target bank shareholders enjoyed 6.08 percent abnormal returns. They also found that bidding bank returns were higher for those banks seeking to acquire targets in states with more restrictive banking pact laws that prohibited nationwide entry and where the target bank was not a failed bank. Studies by A. Desai and R. Stover and C. James and P. Weir also report significant abnormal returns for bidding bank stockholders even for intrastate mergers.[22]

Postmerger Performance

Even though the expectation, on announcement, might be favorable for enhanced profitability and performance as a result of an interstate geographic expansion, are such mergers actually proving successful in the postmerger period? M. Millon-Cornett and H. Tehranian have looked at the postacquisition performance of large bank mergers between 1982 and 1987. Using operating cash flow (defined as earnings before depreciation, goodwill, interest on long-term debt and taxes) divided by assets as a performance measure, they found that merged banks tended to outperform the banking industry. They found that superior performance resulted from improvements in these banks' ability to (1) attract loans and deposits, (2) increase employee productivity, and (3) enhance asset growth. K. Spong and J. D. Shoenhair studied the postmerger performance of banks that merged interstate in 1985, 1986, and 1987; they found that acquired banks either maintained or increased earnings and demonstrated some success in controlling and reducing overhead and personnel costs. The acquired banks also tended to become more active lenders.[23]

Thus, both the announcement effect studies and the postmerger performance studies generally support the existence of gains from domestic geographic expansions by U.S. commercial banks.

Concept Question

1. If the abnormal returns on target banks are usually positive, does this mean that managers of acquiring banks tend to overpay the shareholders of the target bank?

---

[21]See, for example, N. Travlos, "Corporate Takeover Bids, Methods of Payment, and Bidding Firm Stock Returns," *Journal of Finance* 42, 1987, pp. 943–63.

[22]M. Millon-Cornett and S. De, "Common Stock Returns in Corporate Takeover Bids: Evidence of Interstate Bank Mergers," *Journal of Banking and Finance* 15, 1991, pp. 273–95; A. Desai and R. Stover, "Bank Holding Company Acquisitions, Stockholders Returns, and Regulatory Uncertainty," *Journal of Financial Research* 8, 1985, pp. 145–56; and C. James and P. Weir, "Returns to Acquirers and Competition in the Acquisition Market: The Case of Banking," *Journal of Political Economy* 95, 1983, pp. 355–70. However, in a study of 118 bank mergers between 1970 and 1984 G. Hawawini and I. Swary found that bidding banks stock returns decreased on average by 1.5 percent, see G. Hawawini and I. Swary, *Mergers and Acquisitions in the U.S. Banking Industry,* North-Holland: Amsterdam, 1990, p. 211.

[23]M. Millon-Cornett and H. Tehranian, " Changes in Corporate Performance Associated with Bank Acquisitions," *Journal of Financial Economics* 31, 1992, pp. 211–34; and K. Spong and J.D. Shoenhair, "Performance of Banks Acquired on an Interstate Basis," Federal Reserve Bank of Kansas City, *Financial Industry Perspectives,* December 1992, pp. 15–23.

Global or International Expansions

Many FIs can potentially diversify domestically but only the very largest can aspire to diversify beyond national frontiers. There are at least three ways an FI can establish a global or international presence: (1) selling financial services from its domestic offices to foreign customers, such as a loan originated in the New York office of Chase made to a Brazilian manufacturer; (2) selling financial services through a branch, agency, or representative office established in the foreign customer's country, such as making a loan to the Brazilian customer through Chase's branch in Brazil; and (3) selling financial services to a foreign customer through subsidiary companies in the foreign customer's country, such as Chase buying a Brazilian bank and using that wholly owned bank to make loans to the Brazilian customer. Note that these three methods of global activity expansion are not mutually exclusive; an FI could use all three, simultaneously, to expand the scale and scope of its operations.

U.S. banks, insurance companies, and securities firms have all expanded abroad in recent years, often through branches and subsidiaries; this has been reciprocated by the entrance and growth of foreign FIs in U.S. financial service markets. Next, we concentrate on the global growth of banking; we begin with U.S. bank expansions abroad and the factors motivating these expansions and then move on to foreign bank expansions into the United States.

U.S. Banks Abroad

While some U.S. banks such as Citibank and J. P. Morgan have had offices abroad since the beginning of the century, the major phase of growth began in the early 1960s following the passage of a law restricting domestic U.S. banks' ability to lend to U.S. corporations that wanted to make investments overseas. The major law restricting this activity, the Overseas Direct Investment Control Act of 1964, was eventually repealed; however, it created incentives for U.S. banks to establish offices offshore to service the overseas funding and other business needs of their U.S. clients. This offshore funding and lending in dollars created the beginnings of a market we now call the Eurodollar market. The term Eurodollar transaction usually denotes a banking transaction booked externally to the boundaries of the United States, often through an overseas branch or subsidiary.[24]

Factors Encouraging U.S. Bank Expansions Abroad. Regulation of offshore lending was the original impetus for the early growth of the Eurodollar market and the associated establishment of U.S. branches and subsidiaries abroad. Other regulatory and economic factors have encouraged the growth of U.S. offshore banking; these factors have included:

The Dollar as an International Medium of Exchange. The growth of international trade after the Second World War and the use of the dollar as an international medium of exchange encouraged foreign corporations and investors to demand dollars. A convenient way to do this was using U.S. banks' offshore offices

---

[24]That is, the definition of a Euro transaction is more general than a transaction booked in Europe. In fact, any deposit in dollars taken externally to the United States normally qualifies that transaction as a Euro transaction.

to intermediate such fund flows between the United States and foreign demand. Today, trade-related transactions underlie much of the activity in the Eurodollar market.

Political Risk Concerns.   Political risk concerns among countries from the old Eastern or Communist bloc and Latin America have led to enormous flows of dollars offshore, often to U.S. branches and subsidiaries in the Cayman Islands and the Bahamas, where there are very stringent bank secrecy rules.

Domestic Activity Restrictions.   As we discuss in Chapter 16, U.S. banks have faced considerable activity restrictions at home regarding their securities, insurance, and commercial activities. However, with certain exceptions, Federal Reserve Regulation K has allowed U.S. banking offices abroad to engage in the permitted banking activities of the foreign country, even if such activities were not permitted in the United States. For example, U.S. banks setting up subsidiaries overseas can engage in leasing real property, act as general insurance agents, and underwrite and deal in foreign corporate securities (up to a maximum commitment of $2 million).

Technology and Communications Improvements.   The improvements in telecommunications and other communications technologies such as CHIPS (the international payment system) as well as the development of proprietary communication networks by large FIs, have allowed U.S. parent banks to extend and maintain real-time control over their overseas operations at a decreasing cost. The decreasing operating costs of such expansions have made it feasible to locate offices in an even wider array of international locations.

In Table 17–6, we show the recent growth in foreign assets of U.S. branches abroad in total and for the two primary locations of U.S. bank offshore business, the United Kingdom and the Bahamas and Cayman Islands. As you can see, there has been very little growth since 1989 when total foreign branch assets reached $545 billion. We discuss the reasons for this and the factors deterring bank expansions abroad next.

Factors Deterring U.S. Expansions Abroad.   In Table 17–6, the static 1989–92 asset position of overseas branches suggests that U.S. banks are questioning the return-risk benefits of international expansion and that some may have started to contract the scale and scope of their overseas operations. Potential factors deterring international expansions include:

TABLE 17–6   Foreign Branches of U.S. Banks
(in billions)

	1989	1990	1991	1992 (Sept)
1. Total payable in any currency	$545.4	$557.0	$548.9	$544.7
2. Total payable in U.S. dollars	382.5	379.5	363.9	346.7
3. Total payable in any currency (United Kingdom)	162.0	184.8	175.6	161.1
4. Total payable in any currency (Bahamas and Cayman Islands)	176.0	162.3	168.3	145.4

SOURCE: *Federal Reserve Bulletin,* January 1993, Table 3.14.

Capital Constraints.   The phasing in of the 1993 risk-based capital requirements over the 1988–92 period meant that a number of large global U.S. banks, such as Citicorp, had to scale back their activities to be in a position to meet the 8 percent target (see Chapter 14).

LDC Lending.   The loan reschedulings of Brazil, Mexico, and other countries during the 1980s resulted in an increased reluctance of U.S. banks to extend new loans to LDCs—other than those directly linked to the refinancing and restructuring of old loans (see Chapter 12).

Competition.   In the 1980s, the United States faced extensive and increasing competition from Japanese and other foreign banks for Euro business. Aiding the Japanese banks was their access to a large domestic savings base at a relatively low funding cost, given the relatively slow pace of deregulation in the Japanese domestic financial markets. In addition, the largest Japanese city banks followed a conscious strategy of maximizing foreign asset growth by accepting very small margins on their overseas business. Thus, in the 1980–90 period, BIS figures show that the average gross profit margin (return on assets minus cost of funds) for Japanese banks was approximately half that of U.S. banks.[25] Given the risk exposure, this made it increasingly difficult for U.S. banks to compete profitably in the offshore lending markets making further expansions less attractive.[26]

Foreign Banks in the United States

Just as U.S. banks can profitably expand into overseas markets, foreign banks have historically viewed the United States as an attractive market for entry.

Organizational Form.   The five primary forms of entry by foreign banks into the U.S. market are:

Subsidiary.   A foreign bank subsidiary has its own capital and charter; it operates the same as any U.S. domestic bank with access to both retail and wholesale markets.

Branch.   A branch bank is a direct expansion of the parent bank into an overseas or U.S. banking market. As such, it is reliant on its parent bank, such as Sumitomo Bank in Japan, for capital support; normally it has access to both wholesale and retail deposit and funding markets.

Agency.   An agency is a restricted form of entry; this organizational form restricts access of funds to those borrowed on the wholesale and money markets. A special case of an agency is a New York Agreement Company that has both agency functions and limited investment banking functions as well.

---

[25]BIS Annual Reports.

[26]However, in recent years as their capital requirements became more binding and problems with their domestic loan portfolios mounted (especially real estate loans) Japanese banks have shown signs of retrenchment. For example, The Banker (2/28/93) reported that measured by overseas presence, or percentage of banking business (assets) overseas, only nine Japanese banks appeared in the list of the top 50 global banks in 1992 compared to 12 in 1991. For example Sakurabank's overseas assets fell by 9.5 percent between 1991 and 1992. However, note that all the major U.S. banks—except J. P. Morgan and Citibank—also retrenched their overseas (foreign asset) presence in 1992 compared to 1991.

Edge Act Corporation.   An Edge Act Corporation is a specialized organizational form open to U.S. domestic banks since 1919 and to foreign banks since 1978. These banks specialize in international trade-related banking transactions or investments.

Representative Office.   Even though a representative office neither books loans nor deposits in the United States, it acts as a loan production office, generating loan business for its parent bank at home. This is the most limited organizational form for a foreign bank entering the United States.[27]

Trends and Growth.   There has been a rapid and persistent expansion of foreign banks into the United States. From approximately 4 percent of total bank assets in 1973, their share increased to 21 percent at the end of 1990, with total assets amounting to $785 billion. Of this total, some $154.5 billion were assets of foreign bank subsidiaries and $626.4 billion of agencies and branches. Thus, the primary form of entry has been the agency or branch. In Figure 17–1, we indicate the growth of foreign bank agencies and branches in the United States and their assets over the 1980–92 period. These foreign agencies and branches came from 57 countries and operated 565 offices, of which Japanese banks had an approximate 60 percent share.[28] Most of these branches and agencies are state-licensed but are subject to increasing federal regulation, which we discuss next.

Regulation of Foreign Banks in the United States.   Prior to 1978, foreign branches and agencies entering the United States were licensed mostly at the state level. As such, their entry, regulation, and oversight was almost totally confined to the state level. Beginning in 1978 with the passage of the *International Banking Act* (IBA) and the more recent passage of the Foreign Bank Supervision Enhancement Act (FBSEA), Title II of the FDICIA, of December 1991, federal regulators are exerting increasing control over foreign banks operating in the United States.

The International Banking Act of 1978.
   Pre-IBA. Before its passage in 1978, foreign agencies and branches entering the United States with state licenses had some competitive advantages and disadvantages relative to most domestic banks. On the one hand, as state-licensed organizations, they were not subject to the Federal Reserve's reserve requirement, Federal Reserve audits/exams, interstate branching restrictions (the McFadden Act), or restrictions on corporate securities underwriting activities (the Glass-Steagall Act). However, they had no access to the Federal Reserve's discount window (i.e., lender of last resort); no direct access to Fedwire and, thus, the fed funds market; and no access to FDIC deposit insurance.

   Their inability to gain access to deposit insurance effectively precluded them from the U.S. retail banking markets and its deposit base. As a result, prior to 1978 foreign banks in the United States largely concentrated on wholesale banking.

---

[27]Also note the existence of International Banking Facilities (IBF) in the United States since 1981. These are specialized vehicles that are allowed to take deposits from and make loans to foreign (non-U.S.) customers only. As such, they are essentially offshore banking units that operate onshore. Most are located in New York, Illinois, and California and are generally free of U.S. bank regulation and taxes. In September 1992, IBF assets were $292 billion; $232 billion were in New York, $33.7 billion in California, and $17.6 billion in Illinois.

[28]Japanese banks also had a 41 percent share of foreign bank subsidiary assets in 1990.

FIGURE 17–1

Growth in the number and assets of foreign banks and their branches and agencies in the United States, December 1980–June 1992

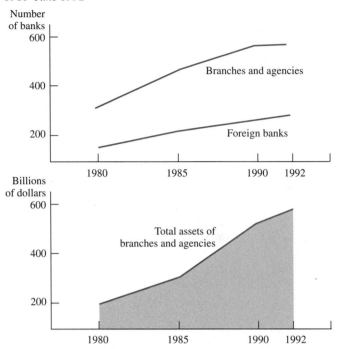

Data are plotted from year-end to year-end. The number of foreign countries with branch and agency operations in the United States was 34 in 1980, 49 in 1985, 54 in 1990, and 57 as of June 1992.

Source: *Federal Reserve Bulletin,* January 1993, p. 2

National Treatment
Regulating foreign banks in the same fashion as domestic banks or creating a level playing field.

Post-IBA. The unequal treatment of domestic and foreign banks as regards to federal regulation, and lobbying by domestic banks regarding the unfairness of this situation, provided the impetus for Congress to pass the International Banking Act in 1978. The fundamental regulatory philosophy underlying the IBA was one of **national treatment.** This philosophy attempted to lay down a level playing field for both domestic and foreign banks in U.S. banking markets. As a result of this act, foreign banks were required to hold Federal Reserve specified reserve requirements if their worldwide assets exceeded $1 billion, made subject to Federal Reserve examinations, and made subject to both the McFadden and Glass-Steagall Acts. With respect to the latter, an important grandfather provision was inserted into the act which allowed foreign banks established in the United States prior to 1978 to keep their illegal interstate branches and securities-activity operations. That is, interstate and security activity restrictions were only applied to new foreign banks entering the United States after 1978.[29]

If anything, the passage of the IBA accelerated the expansion of foreign bank activities in the United States. A major reason for this was that for the first time the

---

[29]For example, in 1978 some 60 foreign banks had branches in at least three states. As noted earlier, the McFadden Act prevents domestic banks from interstate branching.

IBA gave foreign banks access to the Federal Reserve's discount window (lender of last resort facility), Fedwire, and FDIC insurance.

In particular, access to FDIC insurance allowed access to retail banking. For example, in 1979 alone foreign banks acquired four large U.S. banks (Crocker, National Bank of North America, Union Planters, and Marine Midland). In addition, in the early 1980s the Bank of Tokyo, Mitsubishi Bank, and Sanwa Bank invested $1.3 billion in California bank acquisitions so that by 1988, Japanese banks had acquired a 25.2 percent share of California's banking market assets.

The Foreign Bank Supervision Enhancement Act (FBSEA) of 1991.   Along with the growth of foreign bank assets in the United States came concerns about foreign banks' rapidly increasing share of U.S. banking markets as well as about the weakness of regulatory oversight of many of these institutions. This latter concern was compounded by three events that focused attention on the weaknesses of foreign bank regulation. The first event was the collapse of the Bank of Credit and Commerce International (BCCI) which had a highly complex international organizational structure based in the Middle East and Luxembourg and had ownership stakes in two large U.S. banks. BCCI was not subject to any consolidated supervision by a home country regulator; this quickly became apparent after its collapse when massive fraud, insider lending abuses, as well as money-laundering operations were discovered. The second event was the issuance of more than $1 billion in unauthorized letters of credit to Saddam Hussein's Iraq by the Atlanta agency of the Italian bank, Banca Nazionale del Lavoro. The third event was the unauthorized taking of deposit funds by the U.S. representative office of the Greek National Mortgage Bank of New York.

These events and related concerns led to the passage of the Foreign Bank Supervision Enhancement Act (FBSEA) of 1991. The objective of this act was to extend federal regulatory authority over foreign banking organizations in the United States, especially where these organizations have entered using state licenses. The act has five main features that have significantly enhanced the powers of federal bank regulators over foreign banks in the United States.[30]

1. *Entry.* Under FBSEA, the Fed's approval is now needed to establish a subsidiary, branch, agency, or representative office in the United States. The approval applies to both a new entry or an entry by acquisition. To get Fed approval, a number of standards have to be met, two of which are mandatory. First, the foreign bank must be subject to comprehensive supervision on a consolidated basis by a home country regulator. Second, that regulator must furnish all the information needed by the Federal Reserve to evaluate the application. Both standards are aimed at avoiding the lack of disclosure and lack of centralized supervision associated with BCCI's failure.

2. *Closure.* The act also gives the Federal Reserve power to close a foreign bank if its home country supervision is inadequate, if it has violated U.S. laws, or if it is engaged in unsound and unsafe banking practices.

3. *Examination.* The Federal Reserve has the power to examine each office of a foreign bank, including its representative offices. Further, each branch or agency has to be examined at least once a year.

---

[30]See S. Bellanger, "Stormy Weather: The FBSEA's Impact on Foreign Banks," *Bankers Magazine,* November–December 1992, pp. 25–31; M. Gruson, "Are Foreign Banks Still Welcome in the United States?" *Bankers Magazine,* September–October 1992, pp. 16–21.

4. *Deposit Taking.* Only foreign subsidiaries with access to FDIC insurance can take retail deposits under $100,000. This effectively rolls back the provision of the IBA that gave foreign branches and agencies access to FDIC insurance.

5. *Activity Powers.* Beginning on December 19, 1992, state-licensed branches and agencies of foreign banks could not engage in any activity not permitted to a federal branch.

Overall then, the FBSEA considerably increases the Federal Reserve's authority over foreign banks and adds to the regulatory burden or costs of entry into the United States for foreign banks. This may make the post-FBSEA U.S. banking market much less attractive for foreign banks than it had been over the 1970–91 period. In addition, it may lead to more restrictive regulatory moves by Japan and the European Community against U.S. banks entering their markets.

Concept Question

1. Why would a foreign bank prefer to establish a branch in the United States rather than a subsidiary?

Advantages and Disadvantages of International Expansion

So far, we have laid out the historical and recent trends affecting the expansion of FIs both into and outside the United States. Now we look at the economic and regulatory advantages and disadvantages of international expansions to the individual FI seeking to generate additional returns or to better diversify its risk.

Advantages

These are the six major advantages of international expansion:[31]

Risk Diversification. As with domestic geographic expansions, an FI's international activities potentially enhance its opportunity to diversify the risk of its earning flows. Often, domestic earnings flows from financial services are strongly linked to the state of that economy. Therefore, the less integrated the economies of the world are, the greater the potential for earnings diversification through international expansions.[32]

Economies of Scale. To the extent that economies of scale exist, by expanding its activities beyond domestic boundaries an FI can potentially lower its average operating costs.

---

[31]See, for example, L. Goldberg and A. Saunders, "The Causes of U.S. Bank Expansion Overseas: The Case of Great Britain,"*Journal of Money Credit and Banking* 12, 1980, pp. 630–44; Goldberg and Saunders,"The Growth of Organizational Forms of Foreign Banks in the U.S.,"*Journal of Money Credit and Banking* 13, 1981, pp. 365–74; Goldberg and Saunders, "The Determinants of Foreign Banking Activity in the United States," *Journal of Banking and Finance* 5, 1981, pp. 17–32, and C. W. Hultman and L. R. McGee, "Factors Affecting the Foreign Banking Presence in the United States," *Journal of Banking and Finance* 13, 1989, pp. 383–96.

[32]This, of course, assumes that stockholders are sufficiently undiversified to value FIs diversifying on their behalf.

Innovations.   An FI can generate extra returns from new product innovations if it can sell such services internationally rather than just domestically. For example, consider complex financial innovations, such as securitization, caps, floors, and options, that FIs have innovated in the United States and sold to new foreign markets with few domestic competitors.

Funds Source.   International expansion allows an FI to search for the cheapest and most available sources of funds. This is extremely important given the very thin profit margins in domestic and international wholesale banking. Also it reduces the risk of fund shortages (credit rationing) in any one market.

Customer Relationships.   International expansions also allow an FI to maintain contact with and service the needs of domestic multinational corporations. Indeed, one of the fundamental factors determining the growth of FIs abroad has been the parallel growth of foreign direct investment and foreign trade by globally oriented multinational corporations from the FI's home country.

Regulatory Avoidance.   To the extent that domestic regulations such as activity restrictions and reserve requirements impose constraints or taxes on the operations of an FI, seeking out low regulatory tax countries can allow an FI to lower its net regulatory burden and to increase its potential net profitability.

Disadvantages

These are the three major disadvantages of international expansion:

Information/Monitoring Costs.   While global expansions allow an FI the potential opportunity to better diversify its geographic risk, the absolute level of exposure in certain areas such as lending can be high, especially if the FI fails to diversify in an optimal fashion. For example, the FI may fail to choose a loan portfolio combination on the efficient lending frontier (see Chapter 8). Foreign activities may also be more risky for the simple reason that monitoring and information collection costs are often higher in overseas markets. For example, Japanese and German accounting standards differ significantly from the generally accepted accounting principles (GAAP) used by U.S. firms. In addition, language, legal, and cultural problems can impose further transaction costs on international activities. Finally, because the regulatory environment is controlled locally and regulation imposes a different array of net costs in each market, a truly global FI would face the problem of having to master the various rules and regulations in each market.

Nationalization/Expropriation.   To the extent that an FI expands by establishing a local presence through investing in fixed assets, such as branches or subsidiaries, an FI faces the political risk that a change in government may lead to the nationalization of those fixed assets.[33] Further, if overseas FI depositors take losses following a nationalization, they may seek legal recourse from the FI in U.S. courts rather than from the nationalizing government. For example, it has taken many years to resolve

---

[33]Such nationalizations have occurred with some frequency in African countries.

the outstanding claims of depositors in Citicorp's branches in Vietnam following the Communist takeover and expropriation of those branches.[34]

Fixed Costs.   The fixed costs of establishing overseas organizations may be extremely high. A U.S. FI seeking an organizational presence in the Tokyo banking market faces real estate prices some five to six times higher than in New York. Such relative costs can be even higher if an FI chooses to enter by buying a Japanese bank rather than establishing a new toehold operation. The reason is the considerable cost of acquiring Japanese equities measured by price-earnings ratios despite the falls in the Nikkei Index in 1991 and 1992. These relative cost considerations become even more important if there is uncertainty about the expected volume of business to be generated and, thus, revenue flows from foreign entry. The failure of U.S. acquisitions to realize expected profits following the 1986 "big bang" deregulation in the United Kingdom is a good example of unrealized revenue expectations vis à vis the high fixed costs of entry and the costs of maintaining a competitive position.[35]

Concept Question

1. Looking at the benefits and costs listed above, why have so few U.S. banks established branches in Russia?

Summary

In this chapter, we have examined the potential return-risk advantages and disadvantages from both domestic and international geographic expansions. While regulatory considerations and costs are fundamental to such decisions, several other economic factors play an important role in the net return or benefit-cost calculus for any given FI. For example, considerations such as earnings diversification and economies of scale and scope, add to the potential benefits from geographic expansions. However, there are also costs or risks of geographic expansion such as monitoring costs, expropriation of assets and the costs of market entry. Managers need to carefully weigh each of these factors before making a geographic expansion decision, whether domestic or international.

Questions and Problems

1. In Chapter 7, we examined the issue of FI efficiency of operation. Many empirical studies found little or no evidence of economies of scale and scope for U.S. banks and thrifts. This conclusion may be a result of the regulatory structure in the U.S. that has historically discouraged geographic diversification. Discuss.

2. The Justice Department measures market concentration using the Herfindahl index of market share. What problems does this measure have for (a) multiproduct FIs; (b) FIs with global operations?

3. How does the existence of an active takeover market impact the Justice Department's measure of concentration?

4. How do limitations on geographic diversification increase FI profitability? How do limitations on geographic diversification decrease FI profitability?

5. What was the impetus for bank regulations to limit intra- and interstate diversification? How have bank regulators attempted to limit geographic diversification? How have banks attempted to circumvent such regulations?

---

[34]See G. Dufey and I. Giddy, "Eurocurrency Deposit Risk," *Journal of Banking and Finance* 8, 1984, pp. 567–89.

[35]Also, in aggregate, foreign banks in Japan (including U.S. banks) have less than a 1 percent share of Japanese bank assets.

6. What are some of the synergies between the following prohibited financial activities and traditional banking?

   a. Real estate syndication.
   b. Contract data entry services.
   c. Acting as a specialist in French franc options on the Philadelphia Stock Exchange.
   d. Acceptance of deposit accounts linked to credit card accounts.

7. What are some of the risks associated with performing the following prohibited financial activities and traditional banking?

   a. Real estate syndication.
   b. Contract data entry services.
   c. Acting as specialist in French franc options on the Philadelphia Stock Exchange.
   d. Acceptance of deposit accounts linked to credit card accounts.

8. Should the McFadden Act be repealed? Why or why not?

9. Both the International Banking Act of 1978 and the FDIC Improvement Act of 1991 extend U.S. banking laws to international banks operating in the United States. How does this effect their ability to integrate U.S. operations into their global banking network? How does this effect the regulators ability to oversee foreign banking activity in the United States?

10. The Justice Department has been asked to review a merger request for a market in which there are the following four FIs.

FI	Assets
1	$ 12 million
2	25 million
3	102 million
4	3 million

    a. What is the Herfindahl Index for the existing market?
    b. If FI 1 acquires FI 4, what will be the impact on the market's level of concentration?
    c. If FI 3 acquires FI 4, what will be the impact on the market's level of concentration?
    d. What is likely to be the Justice Department's response regarding the two merger applications?

11. Why do you think that U.S. banks have been so aggressive in attempting to break down the barriers to geographic expansion?

12. If you managed a U.S. bank and wanted to diversify geographically, how would you do so under existing regulatory restrictions?

18

FUTURES AND FORWARDS

Learning Objectives

In this chapter you will start to learn how FIs can use the derivative markets to hedge their interest rate, foreign exchange, and credit risk exposures. An FI manager can use forward and futures contracts to alter the FI's risk-return trade-off. In particular, futures and forwards might be routinely used to hedge every asset and liability position or selectively to hedge so that the FI retains some risk exposure and a potentially higher return. In addition, you will learn how these contracts can hedge an FI's duration gap.

Introduction

In this chapter we start by defining the features of forward and futures contracts and compare these with spot contracts and markets. We then analyze how these contracts can hedge three major risks faced by FIs: interest rate risk, foreign exchange risk, and credit risk.

Forward and Futures Contracts

To understand the essential nature and characteristics of forward and futures contracts, we can compare them with spot contracts. We show appropriate time lines for each of the three contracts in Figure 18–1.

Spot Contract

A spot contract is an agreement between a buyer and seller at time 0, when the seller of the asset agrees to deliver the asset immediately and the buyer of the asset agrees to pay for that asset immediately.[1] Thus, the unique feature of a spot market is the immediate and simultaneous exchange of cash for securities, or what is often called delivery versus payment. A spot bond quote of $97 for a 20-year maturity bond would be the price the buyer would have to pay the seller, per $100 of face value, for immediate delivery of the 20-year bond.

---

[1] Technically, physical settlement and delivery may take place one or two days after the contractual spot agreement in bond markets. In equity markets, delivery and cash settlement normally occur five business days after the spot contract agreement.

FIGURE 18–1

Contract time lines

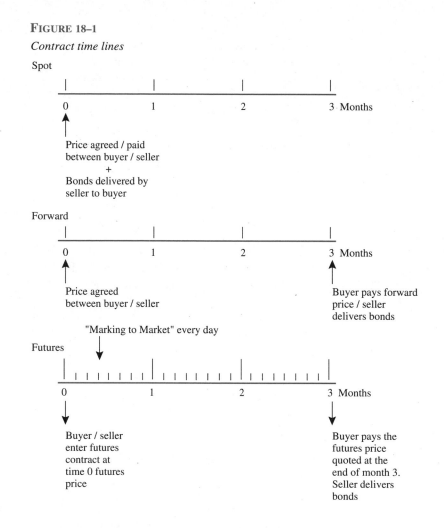

Forward Contract

A forward contract is an agreement between a buyer and seller, at time 0, when there is a contractual agreement that an asset will be exchanged for cash at some later date. For example, in a three-month forward contract to deliver 20-year bonds, the buyer and seller would agree on a price and quantity today (time 0) but the delivery (or exchange) of the 20-year bond for cash would not occur until three months hence. If the forward price agreed to at time 0 was $97 per $100 of face value, in three months' time the seller would deliver $100 of 20-year bonds and receive $97 from the buyer. This is the price the buyer would have to pay no matter what happens to the spot price of 20-year bonds during the three months between when the contract was entered into and when the bonds are delivered for payment.

Futures Contract

A futures contract is normally arranged through an organized exchange. It is an agreement between a buyer and seller at time 0 that an asset will be exchanged for cash at some later date. As such, a futures contract is very similar to a forward contract. The difference is that whereas the price of a forward contract is fixed over the

Marking-to-Market
The process by which the prices on outstanding futures contracts are adjusted each day to reflect current futures market conditions.

life of the contract ($97 per $100 of face value for three months), futures contracts are **marked-to-market** daily. This means the contract's price is adjusted each day as the futures price for the contract changes. Therefore, daily cash flows pass between the buyer and seller in response to this marking-to-market process. This can be compared to a forward contract where the whole cash payment from buyer to seller occurs at the end of the contract period.[2]

Concept Question

1. What are the major differences between a spot and a futures contract?

Forward Contracts and Hedging Interest Rate Risk

Naive Hedge
When a cash asset is hedged on a direct (dollar for dollar basis) with a forward or futures contract.

To see the usefulness of forward contracts in hedging the interest rate risk of an FI, we can consider a simple example of a **naive hedge.** Suppose an FI portfolio manager held 20-year $1 million face value bonds on the balance sheet. Currently, at time 0, these bonds are valued by the market at $97 per $100 of face value or $970,000 in total. At time 0, the manager receives a forecast that interest rates are expected to rise by 2 percent from their current level of 8 percent to 10 percent over the next three months. Knowing that rising interest rates mean that bond prices will fall, the manager stands to make a capital loss on the bond portfolio. Having read Chapters 5 and 6, the manager is an expert in duration and has calculated the weighted-average life of the 20-year maturity bonds to be exactly 9 years. Thus, the manager can predict a capital loss or change in bond values (ΔP) from the duration equation of Chapter 6.[3]

$$\frac{\Delta P}{P} = -D \cdot \frac{\Delta R}{1 + R}$$

where

ΔP = Capital loss on bonds = ?

P = Initial value of bond position = $970,000

D = Duration of the bonds = 9 years

ΔR = Change in forecast yield = .02

$1 + R$ = 1 plus the current yield on 20-year bonds = 1.08

$$\frac{\Delta P}{\$970,000} = -9 \cdot \left[\frac{.02}{1.08} \right]$$

$$\Delta P = -9 \times \$970,000 \times \left[\frac{.02}{1.08} \right] = -\$161,666.67$$

As a result, the FI portfolio manager would expect to make a capital loss on the bond portfolio of $161,666.67 (as a percentage loss ($\Delta P/P$) = 16.67%) or as a fall in

---

[2]Aside from the marking-to-market process, the two major differences between forwards and futures are (1) forwards are tailor-made contracts while futures are standardized contracts; (2) forward contracts are bilateral contracts subject to counterparty default risk, while the default risk on futures is significantly reduced by the futures exchange guaranteeing to indemnify counterparties against credit or default risk.

[3]For simplicity, we ignore issues relating to convexity here.

Cross-Hedging as Intermarket Trading

John Merrick
Lehman Brothers

A cross-hedge is a spread position matching a cash security against a futures contract in a nonidentical, but related market. Suppose that a fixed income trader with a sizable position in illiquid off-the-run two-year Treasury notes turns bearish on the market. The trader needs to sell something, but what? Selling the illiquid cash Treasury position quickly would entail unacceptably high price concessions. Selling the on-the-run two-year Treasury short would hedge the position, but the off-the-runs the trader owns would probably underperform the newly shorted on-the-run issue in a market sell-off. Hence, the hedge could be expected to lose money if the trader's scenario is correct.

Alternatively, the trader could sell a strip of Eurodollar futures against the Treasuries. The resulting long cash Treasuries/short Eurodollar futures position would be classified as a cross-hedge, since it matches a cash position (Treasury notes) against futures contracts on a different underlying instrument (three-month Eurodollar deposits). Cross-hedges are usually less efficient than own-market hedges because price changes in the two individual markets are less than perfectly correlated. Nevertheless, the trader may prefer the Eurodollar cross-hedge if Euros appear to be priced expensively to Treasuries, especially since Euros tend to underperform Treasuries in bear markets. Searching for the right hedge turns out to be just another trading decision. Cross-hedging becomes just a form of intermarket trading.

Yield spreads between the Treasury and Eurodollar deposit markets fluctuate both because of credit and supply considerations. The TED spread—three-month T-bill futures to three-month Eurodollar futures—has been the traditional way to trade movements in the yield spread.

However, there is no reason to confine Treasury versus Eurodollar trading to the three-month area. In fact, cash Treasury Note/Eurodollar yield spread trading—the Term TED—is possible out to five-year maturities. The basic idea is to value the Treasury note using a spread derived from Eurodollar futures strips to each individual Treasury cash flow (coupons and principal) date.

To trade the Term TED, buy or sell individual cash Treasury notes against specially constructed strips of Eurodollar futures.[1] When the Term TED spread is expected to widen, buy the Treasury note and sell the offsetting Eurodollar strip. When the Term TED spread is expected to tighten, sell the Treasury note and buy the offsetting Eurodollar strip.

Keys to the Trade

- *Price the Treasury note through a Zero Trader's Eyes:* Select a target Treasury note (e.g., an off-the-run two-year) and—like a Zero Trader—view it as a set of coupon and maturity value cash flow sizes and dates.

- *Define the Spread:* The *Term TED Spread* is the basis point adjustment necessary to each implied Eurodollar futures rate such that the sum of the present values of each of the note's cash flows—discounted at the spread-adjusted Eurodollar strip rate—equals the note's current market value.

- *Structure the Hedge:* Hedge the Treasury note with a specific strip of Eurodollar futures contracts implied by the sum of duration-weighted hedges of the note's individual cash flows.

- *To Buy the Spread:* Buy the Treasury note and sell the appropriate Eurodollar contract strip.

- *To Sell the Spread:* Sell the Treasury note and buy the appropriate Eurodollar contract strip.

---

[1]See "Using Eurodollar Strips to Hedge and Trade Treasury Notes," G. Courtadon and D. Nadler. Lehman Brothers, January 1988; and "Trading the Term TED Spread," John Merrick and Nomi Prins, Lehman Brothers, October 1991.

BIOGRAPHICAL SUMMARY
John Merrick is a Vice President with Lehman Brothers Multimarket Trading. Prior to joining Lehman in 1988, he was Associate Professor of Finance at the New York University Graduate School of Business Administration. He received his Ph.D. in Economics from Brown University.

price from $97 per $100 face value to $80.833 per $100 face value. To offset this loss—in fact, to reduce the risk of capital loss to zero—the manager may hedge this position by taking an off-balance-sheet hedge, such as selling $1 million face value of 20-year bonds for forward delivery in three months' time.[4] Suppose that at time 0, the portfolio manager can find a buyer willing to pay $97 for every $100 of 20-year bonds delivered in three months' time.

Now consider what happens to the FI portfolio manager if the gloomy forecast of a 2 percent rise in interest rates proves to be true. The portfolio manager's bond position has fallen in value by 16.67 percent, equal to a capital loss of $161,667. After the rise in interest rates, the manager can buy $1 million face value of 20-year bonds in the spot market at $80.833 per $100 of face value, a total cost of $808,333, and deliver these bonds to the forward contract buyer. Remember that the forward contract buyer agreed to pay $97 per $100 of face value for the $1 million of face value bonds delivered, or $970,000. As a result, the portfolio manager makes a profit on the forward transaction of:

$$\begin{array}{ccc} \$970,000 & - & \$808,333 & = & \$161,667 \\ \text{(price paid by} & & \text{(cost of purchasing} \\ \text{forward buyer to} & & \text{bonds in the spot market} \\ \text{forward seller)} & & \text{at } t = \text{month 3 for delivery} \\ & & \text{to the forward buyer)} \end{array}$$

As you can see, the on-balance-sheet loss of $161,667 is exactly offset by the off-balance-sheet gain of $161,667 from selling the forward contract. Thus, the FI's net interest rate exposure is zero or in the parlance of finance it has **immunized** its interest rate risk.

Immunized
Fully hedged or protected against adverse movements in interest rates (or other asset prices).

Hedging Interest Rate Risk with Futures Contracts

Even though some hedging of interest rate risk does take place using forward contracts—such as forward rate agreements commonly used by insurance companies and banks prior to mortgage loan originations—most FIs hedge interest rate risk either at the micro-level (called microhedging) or at the macro-level (called macrohedging) using futures contracts. See Figure 18–3, found later in the chapter, for a list of interest rate futures contracts currently available. Before looking at futures contracts, we explain the difference between microhedging and macrohedging and between routine hedging and selective hedging.

Microhedging

Microhedging
Using a futures (forward) contract to hedge a specific asset of liability.

An FI is **microhedging** when it employs a futures or a forward contract to hedge a particular asset or liability risk. For example, earlier we considered a simple example of microhedging asset side portfolio risk, where an FI manager wanted to insulate the value of the institution's bond portfolio fully against a rise in interest rates. An example of microhedging on the liability side of the balance sheet might be when an FI is attempting to lock in a cost of funds to protect the FI against a possible rise in

---

[4]Since a forward contract involves delivery of bonds in a future time period, it does not appear on the balance sheet, which records only current and past transactions. Thus, forwards are one example of off-balance-sheet items.

short-term interest rates, by taking a short (sell) position in futures contracts on CDs or T-bills. In microhedging, the FI manager often tries to pick a futures or forward contract whose underlying deliverable asset is closely matched to the asset (or liability) position being hedged. In the earlier example, we had an unrealistic example of exact matching of the asset in the portfolio with the deliverable security underlying the forward contract (20-year bonds). Such exact matching cannot be achieved often and this produces a residual unhedgable risk termed **basis risk**. We discuss basis risk in detail later; it arises mainly because the prices of the assets or liabilities that an FI wishes to hedge are imperfectly correlated over time with the prices on the futures or forward contract used to hedge risk.

Basis Risk
A residual risk that arises because the movement in a spot (cash) asset's price is not perfectly correlated with the movement in the price of the asset delivered under a futures or forward contract.

Macrohedging
Hedging the entire duration gap of an FI.

Macrohedging

Macrohedging occurs when an FI manager wishes to use futures or other derivative securities to hedge the entire balance sheet duration gap. This contrasts to microhedging, where an FI manager identifies specific assets and liabilities and seeks out individual futures and other derivative contracts to hedge those individual risks. Note that macrohedging and microhedging can lead to quite different hedging strategies and results. In particular, a macrohedge takes a whole portfolio view and allows for individual asset and liability interest sensitivities or durations to net out each other. This can result in a very different aggregate futures position than when an FI manager disregards this netting or portfolio effect and hedges only individual asset and liability positions on a one-to-one basis.[5]

Routine Hedging versus Selective Hedging

Routine Hedging
Seeking to hedge all interest rate risk exposure.

Routine hedging is when an FI reduces its interest rate or other risk exposure to its lowest possible level by selling sufficient futures to offset the interest rate risk exposure of its whole balance sheet or cash positions in each asset and liability. For example, this might be achieved by macrohedging the duration gap as described next. However, since reducing risk also reduces return, not all FI managers seek to do this. In Figure 18–2, we show the trade-off between return and risk and the minimum risk fully hedged portfolio.[6]

Hedging Selectively
Only partially hedging the gap or individual assets and liabilities.

Rather than a fully hedged position, many FIs choose to bear some interest rate risk as well as credit and FX risks because of their comparative advantage as FIs (see Chapter 3). One possibility is that an FI may choose to **hedge selectively** its portfolio. For example, an FI manager may generate expectations regarding future interest rates before deciding on a futures position. As a result, the manager may selectively hedge only a proportion of its balance sheet position. Alternatively, the FI manager may decide to remain unhedged or even to overhedge by selling more futures than required by the cash position, although regulators may view the latter as speculative. Thus, the fully hedged position—and the minimum risk portfolio—becomes one of several choices depending, in part, on managerial interest rate expectations, managerial objectives, and the nature of the return-risk trade-off from hedging. Finally, an FI

---

[5]P. H. Munter, D. K. Clancy, and C. T. Moores found that macrohedges provided better hedge performance than microhedges in a number of different interest rate environments. See "Accounting for Financial Futures: A Question of Risk Reduction," *Advances in Accounting* 3, 1986, pp. 51–70.

[6]The minimum risk portfolio is not shown as zero here because of basis risk that prevents perfect hedging. In the absence of basis risk, a zero risk position becomes possible.

FIGURE 18–2

The effects of hedging on risk and return

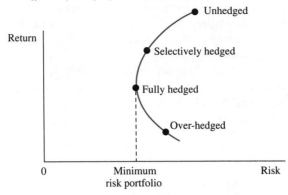

may selectively hedge in an attempt to arbitrage profits between a spot asset's price movements and movements in a futures price (see box).

Macrohedging with Futures

How many futures contracts an FI should buy or sell depends on the size and direction of its interest rate risk exposure and the return-risk trade-off from fully or selectively hedging that risk. In Chapter 6, we showed that an FI's net worth exposure to interest rate shocks was directly related to its leverage adjusted duration gap as well as its asset size. Again, this is

$$\Delta E = -\left[D_A - kD_L\right] \cdot A \cdot \frac{\Delta R}{1 + R}$$

where

$$\Delta E = \text{Change in an FI's net worth}$$

$$D_A = \text{Duration of its asset portfolio}$$

$$D_L = \text{Duration of its liability portfolio}$$

$$k = \text{Ratio of an FI's liabilities to assets } (L/A)$$

$$A = \text{Size of an FI's asset portfolio}$$

$$\frac{\Delta R}{1 + R} = \text{Shock to interest rates}$$

To see how futures might fully hedge a positive or negative portfolio duration gap, consider the following example for an FI where:

$$D_A = 5 \text{ years}$$

$$D_L = 3 \text{ years}$$

Suppose the FI manager receives information from an economic forecasting unit that rates are expected to rise from 10 to 11 percent, that is,

$$\Delta R = 1\% = .01$$

$$1 + R = 1.10$$

and the FI's initial balance sheet is:

Assets (in millions)	Liabilities (in millions)
A = $100	L = $ 90
	E = 10
$100	$100

The FI manager wants to calculate the potential loss to the FI's net worth (E), if the forecast of rising rates proves to be true. As we showed in Chapter 6,

$$\Delta E = -\left(D_A - kD_L\right) \cdot A \cdot \frac{\Delta R}{1+R}$$

so that

$$\Delta E = -\left(5 - (.9)(3)\right) \times \$100 \times \frac{.01}{1.1} = -\$2.09 \text{ million}$$

The bank could expect to lose −$2.09 million in net worth should the interest rate forecast turn out to be correct. Since the FI started with a net worth of $10 million, the loss of $2.09 million is almost 21 percent of its initial net worth position. Clearly, as this example illustrates, the impact of the rise in interest rates could be quite threatening to the FI and its insolvency risk exposure.

The Risk-Minimizing Futures Position.   The FI manager's objective to hedge fully the balance sheet exposure would be fulfilled by constructing a futures position such that if interest rates do rise by 1 percent to 11 percent, as in the prior example, the FI would make a gain on the futures position to just offset the loss of balance sheet net worth of $2.09 million.

When interest rates rise, the price of futures contracts falls, since this price reflects the value of the underlying bond that is deliverable against the contract. How much a bond price falls when interest rates rise depends on its duration. Thus, we would expect the price of the 20-year T bond futures contract to be more sensitive to interest rate changes than the price of the 3-month T-bill futures contract since the former futures price reflects the price of the 20-year T bond deliverable on contract maturity. Thus, the sensitivity of the price of a futures contract depends on the duration of the deliverable bond underlying the contract, or,

$$\frac{\Delta F}{F} = -D_F \frac{\Delta R}{1+R}$$

where

$$\Delta F = \text{Change in dollar value of futures contracts}$$

$$F = \text{Dollar value of the initial futures contracts}$$

$$D_F = \text{Duration of the bond to be delivered against the futures}$$
$$\text{contracts such as a 20-year 8 percent coupon T bond.}$$

$$\Delta R = \text{Expected shock to interest rates}$$

$$1 + R = 1 \text{ plus the current level of interest rates}$$

This can be rewritten as:

$$\Delta F = -D_F \cdot F \cdot \frac{\Delta R}{1+R}$$

The left side of this expression (ΔF) shows the dollar gain or loss on a futures position when interest rates change. To see this dollar gain or loss more clearly, we can decompose the initial dollar value position in futures contracts, F, into its two component parts:

$$F = N_F \times P_F$$

The dollar value of the outstanding futures position depends on the number of contracts bought or sold (N_F) and the price of each contract (P_F).

Futures contracts are homogenous in size. Thus, futures exchanges sell T bond futures in minimum units of $100,000 of face value; that is, one T bond futures ($N_F = 1$) = $100,000. Whereas they sell T-bill futures in larger minimum units: one T-bill futures (N_F) = $1,000,000.

The price of each contract quoted in the newspaper is the price per $100 of face value for delivering the underlying bond. Looking at Figure 18–3, a price quote of 112 15/32 on April 19, 1993, for the T bond futures contract maturing in June 1993 means that the buyer would be required to pay $112,468.75 if this were the price on contract maturity for one T bond contract and the 20-year, 8 percent T bonds were delivered by the seller in June.[7]

In actuality, the seller of the futures contract has a number of alternatives other than an 8 percent coupon 20-year bond that can be delivered against the T bond futures contract. If only one bond could be delivered, a shortage or squeeze might develop making it very hard for the short-side or seller to deliver. In fact, the seller has quite flexible delivery options; apart from delivering the 20-year, 8 percent coupon bond, the seller can deliver bonds that range in maturity from 15 years upwards. Often up to 25 different bonds may qualify for delivery. When a bond other than the 20-year benchmark bond is delivered, the buyer pays a different invoice price for the futures contract based on a **conversion factor** that calculates the price of the deliverable bond if it were to yield 8 percent divided by face value. Suppose $100,000 worth of 18-year, 10 percent semiannual coupon Treasury bonds were valued at a yield of 8 percent. This would produce a fair present value of the bond at approximately $119,000. The conversion factor for the bond would be 1.19 (or $119,000/$100,000). This means the buyer would have to pay the seller the conversion factor of 1.19 times the published price of $112 15/32. That is, the futures price would be 1.19 × $112,468.75 = $133,837.81.[8]

Conversion Factor
A factor used to figure the invoice price on a futures contract when a bond other than the benchmark bond is delivered to the buyer.

---

[7]In practice, the futures price changes day to day and gains or losses would accumulate to the seller/buyer over the period between when the contract is entered into and when it matures. See our later discussion of this unique marking-to-market feature.

Note that the FI could sell contracts in T bonds maturing at later dates. However, while contracts exist out to December 1994 (or just under two years into the future), they tend to be infrequently traded and therefore relatively illiquid. For example, in Table 18–3 the nearby (June 1993) contract has open interest (contracts outstanding) of 374,140 compared to only 116 contracts for December 1994. This also means that if the FI's hedging horizon exceeds two years, it will have to rollover its futures position into a new contract as it matures. This involves transaction costs and an element of price uncertainty (or basis risk) on the rollover date. An alternative would be to enter into a long-term tailor-made forward contract *or* to enter into a swap contract (see Chapter 20).

[8]In practice, the seller exploits the delivery option by choosing the cheapest bond to deliver; that is,

FIGURE 18–3

Futures contracts on interest rates (April 19, 1993)

INTEREST RATE

TREASURY BONDS (CBT)—$100,000; pts. 32nds of 100%

	Open	High	Low	Settle	Chg	Yield Settle	Chg	Open Interest
June	112-05	112-17	111-29	112-15	+ 9	6.846	− .024	347,140
Sept	110-29	111-08	110-21	111-07	+ 10	6.953	− .027	22,529
Dec	109-22	109-31	109-12	109-31	+ 9	7.062	− .025	4,719
Mr94	....	....	....	108-25	+ 9	7.167	− .025	4,071
June	107-10	107-20	107-05	107-19	+ 9	7.274	− .025	507
Sept	....	....	....	106-16	+ 9	7.373	− .026	90
Dec	105-06	105-17	105-05	105-16	+ 9	7.466	− .026	116

Est vol 235,000; vol Fri 326,793; op int 379,191, +11,576.

TREASURY BONDS (MCE)—$50,000; pts. 32nds of 100%

	Open	High	Low	Settle	Chg	Yield Settle	Chg	Open Interest
June	112-08	112-17	111-29	112-16	+ 9	6.843	− .024	11,337

Est vol 2,800; vol Fri 3,776; open int 11,414, +174.

TREASURY NOTES (CBT)—$100,000; pts. 32nds of 100%

	Open	High	Low	Settle	Chg	Yield Settle	Chg	Open Interest
June	112-19	112-27	112-14	112-25	+ 5	6.261	− .020	195,245
Sept	111-07	111-15	111-08	111-15	+ 5	6.428	− .020	6,126
Dec	110-05	110-08	110-00	110-08	+ 5	6.585	− .020	249

Est vol 31,031; vol Fri 42,460; open int 201,624, +450.

5 YR TREAS NOTES (CBT)—$100,000; pts. 32nds of 100%

	Open	High	Low	Settle	Chg	Yield Settle	Chg	Open Interest
June	111-17	11-215	11-145	111-21	+ 2.5	5.315	− .017	150,457
Sept	....	....	....	110-18	+ 2.5	5.552	− .017	1,414

Est vol 15,000; vol Fri 17,734; open int 159,877, +2,543.

2 YR TREAS NOTES (CBT)—$200,000, pts. 32nds of 100%

	Open	High	Low	Settle	Chg	Yield Settle	Chg	Open Interest
June	107-02	07-037	07-015	07-037	+ 1	4.250	− .016	16,396

Est vol 500; vol Fri 1,073; open int 16,396, +30.

30-DAY FEDERAL FUNDS (CBT)-$5 million; pts. of 100%

	Open	High	Low	Settle	Chg	Settle	Chg	Open Interest
Apr	96.99	96.99	96.98	96.98	....	3.02	....	2,213
May	97.00	97.00	97.00	97.00	....	3.00	....	2,679
June	97.00	97.00	97.00	97.00	− .01	3.00	+ .01	2,264
July	96.99	96.99	96.99	96.99	....	3.01	....	1,556
Aug	96.97	96.97	96.97	96.97	− .01	3.03	+ .01	1,030
Sept	96.93	96.93	96.93	96.93	....	3.07	....	979
Oct	....	....	....	96.91	....	3.09	....	417
Nov	....	....	....	96.86	....	3.14	....	348

Est vol 555; vol Fri 1,476; open int 11,491, +304.

TREASURY BILLS (CME)—$1 mil.; pts. of 100%

	Open	High	Low	Settle	Chg	Discount Settle	Chg	Open Interest
June	97.09	97.11	97.09	97.10	+ .01	2.90	− .01	27,570
Sept	96.99	97.01	96.98	97.01	+ .01	2.99	− .01	9,194
Dec	96.73	96.77	96.73	96.77	....	3.23	....	2,809
Mr94	96.63	96.66	96.63	96.66	....	3.34	....	754

Est vol 1,224; vol Fri 2,508; open int 40,327, +496.

Source: *The Wall Street Journal,* April 20, 1993, p. C14. Reprinted by permission of *The Wall Street Journal.*
© 1993 Dow Jones & Company, Inc. All Rights Reserved Worldwide.

bonds whose conversion factor is most favorable (being based on an 8 percent yield) relative to the true price of the bond to be delivered (which reflects the actual level of yields). See S. Figlewski, *Hedging with Financial Futures for Institutional Investors: From Theory to Practice* (Cambridge, Mass.: Ballinger, 1986).

We can now solve the problem of how many futures contracts to sell to fully macrohedge an FI's on-balance-sheet interest rate risk exposure. We have shown that:

1. *Loss on Balance Sheet.* The loss of the net worth for an FI when rates rise is equal to

$$\Delta E = -\left(D_A - kD_L\right) A \frac{\Delta R}{1+R}$$

2. *Gain off Balance Sheet on Futures.* The gain off balance sheet from selling futures is equal to[9]

$$\Delta F = -D_F\left(N_F \times P_F\right) \frac{\Delta R}{1+R}$$

Fully hedging can be defined as selling a sufficient number of futures contracts (N_F) so that the loss of net worth on the balance sheet (ΔE) when rates rise is just offset by the gain from off-balance-sheet selling of futures when rates rise or:

$$\Delta F = \Delta E$$

Substituting in the appropriate expressions for each

$$-D_F\left(N_F \times P_F\right) \frac{\Delta R}{1+R} = -\left(D_A - kD_L\right) A \frac{\Delta R}{1+R}$$

canceling $\Delta R/1 + R$ on both sides,[10]

$$D_F \left(N_F \times P_F\right) = \left(D_A - kD_L\right) A$$

Solving for N_F (the number of futures to sell)

$$N_F = \frac{\left(D_A - kD_L\right) A}{D_F \cdot P_F}$$

From the equation for N_F, we can now solve for the correct number of futures positions to sell (N_F) in the context of our earlier example where the bank was exposed to a balance sheet loss of net worth (ΔE) amounting to $2.09 million when interest rates rose. In that example:

$$D_A = 5 \text{ years}$$

$$D_L = 3 \text{ years}$$

$$k = .9$$

$$A = \$100 \text{ million}$$

Thus, the N_F equation reads:

$$N_F = \frac{\left(5 - (.9)(3)\right) \$100 \text{ million}}{D_F \cdot P_F}$$

---

[9] When futures prices fall, the buyer of the contract compensates the seller, here the FI. Thus, the FI gains when the price of futures falls.

[10] This amounts to assuming that the interest changes of the cash asset position match those of the futures position; that is, there is no basis risk. This assumption is relaxed later.

Suppose the current futures price quote is $97 per $100 of face value for the benchmark 20-year, 8 percent coupon bond underlying the nearby futures contract; the minimum contract size is $100,000; and the duration of the deliverable bond is 9.5 years:

$$D_F = 9.5 \text{ years}$$

$$P_F = \$97,000$$

Inserting these numbers into the expression for N_F, we can now solve for the number of futures to sell:[11]

$$N_F = \frac{\left(5 - (.9) \cdot (3)\right) \times \$100 \text{ million}}{9.5 \times \$97,000}$$

$$= \frac{\$230,000,000}{\$921,500}$$

$$= 249.59 \text{ contracts to be sold}$$

Since the FI cannot sell a part of a contract, the number of contracts should be rounded down to the nearest whole number, or 249 contracts.[12] Next, we double-check that selling 249 T bond futures contracts will indeed hedge the FI against a sudden increase in interest rates from 10 to 11 percent, or a 1 percent interest rate shock.

On Balance Sheet. You have already seen that when rates rise by 1 percent, the FI takes a net worth loss (ΔE) of $2.09 million on the balance sheet:

$$\Delta E = -\left(D_A - kD_L\right) A \frac{\Delta R}{1 + R}$$

$$-\$2.09 \text{ million} = -\left(5 - (.9)(3)\right) \times 100 \text{ million} \times \left(\frac{.01}{1.1}\right)$$

Off Balance Sheet. The value of the off-balance-sheet futures position (ΔF) falls by approximately $2.09 million when the FI sells 249 futures contracts in the T bond futures market. Such a fall in value of the futures contracts means a positive cash flow to the futures seller as the buyer compensates the seller for a lower futures price through the marking-to-market process. This requires a cash flow from the buyer's margin account to the seller's margin account as the price of a futures contract falls.[13] The change in the value of the futures position is

---

[11]For further discussions of this formula, see Figlewski, *Hedging with Financial Futures*, and E. Brewer, "Bank Gap Management and the Use of Financial Futures," Federal Reserve Bank of Chicago, *Economic Perspectives*, March–April 1985. Also note that if the FI intends to deliver any bond other than the 20-year benchmark bond, the P_F has to be multiplied by the appropriate conversion factor (c). If $c = 1.19$, then $P_F = 97 \times 1.19 = \$115.43$ per $100 of face value and the invoice price per contract would be $115,430.

[12]The reason for rounding down rather than rounding up is technical. The target number of contracts to sell is that which minimizes interest rate risk exposure. By slightly underhedging rather than overhedging, the FI can generate the same risk exposure level but the underhedging policy produces a slightly higher return (see Figure 18–1).

[13]An example of marking-to-market might clarify how the seller gains when the price of the futures contract falls. Suppose on day 1 the seller entered into a 90-day contract to deliver 20-year T bonds at $P = 97$. The next day, because of a rise in interest rates the futures contract, which now has 89 days to maturity, is trading at $96 when the market closes. Marking-to-market requires the prices on all contracts entered

$$\Delta F = -D_F \left(N_F \times P_F\right) \frac{\Delta R}{1+R}$$

$$= -9.5 \left(249 \times \$97,000\right) \left(\frac{.01}{1.1}\right)$$

$$= -\$2.086 \text{ million}$$

Thus, as the seller of the futures, the FI makes a gain of \$2.086 million. As a result, the net gain/loss on and off the balance sheet is

$$\Delta E - \Delta F = -\$2.09 + \$2.086 = -\$0.004 \text{ million}$$

This small remaining net loss of \$.004 million to equity or net worth reflects the fact that the FI couldn't achieve the perfect hedge—even in the absence of basis risk—as it needed to round down the number of futures to the nearest whole contract from 249.59 to 249 contracts.

Suppose instead of using the 20-year T bond futures to hedge, it had used the three-month T-bill futures.[14] We can use the same formula to solve for N_F in the case of T-bill futures:

$$N_F = \frac{\left(D_A - kD_L\right) A}{D_F \cdot P_F}$$

$$= \frac{\left(5 - (.9)(3)\right) \$100 \text{ million}}{D_F \cdot P_F}$$

Assuming $P_F = \$97$ per \$100 of face value or \$970,000 per contract (the minimum contract size is \$1,000,000) and D_F .25 (the duration of a three-month T-bill that is the discount instrument deliverable under the contract).[15] Then:

$$N_F = \frac{\left(5 - (.9)(3)\right) \$100 \text{ million}}{.25 \times \$970,000} = \frac{\$230,000,000}{\$242,500}$$

$$N_F = 948.45 \text{ contracts to be sold}$$

Rounding down to the nearest whole contract $N_F = 948$.

As this example illustrates, we can hedge an FI's on-balance-sheet interest rate risk when its $D_A > kD_L$ by selling either T bond or T-bill futures. In general, fewer T bond than T-bill contracts need to be sold. In our case, 948 T-bill versus 249 T bond contracts. This suggests that on a simple transaction cost basis the FI might normally prefer to use T bond futures. However, other considerations can be important especially if the FI holds the futures contracts until the delivery date. The FI needs to be

---

into on the previous day(s) to be marked-to-market at each night's closing (settlement) price. As a result, the price of the contract is lowered to \$96 per \$100 of face value, but in return for this lowering of the price from \$97 to \$96, the buyer has to compensate the seller to the tune of \$1 per \$100 of face value. Thus, given a \$100,000 contract, there is a cash flow payment of \$1,000 on that day from the buyer to the seller. Note that if the price had risen to \$98, the seller would have had to compensate the buyer \$1,000. The marking-to-market process goes on until the futures contract matures. If over the period futures prices have mostly fallen, then the seller accumulates positive cash flows on the futures position. It is this accumulation of cash flows that can be set off against losses in net worth on the balance sheet.

[14]As Figure 18–3 shows, three-month T-bill futures are an alternative interest rate futures contract to the long-term bond futures contract.

[15]We assume the same futures price (\$97) here for purposes of comparison. Of course, the actual prices of the two futures contracts are very different (see Figure 18–3).

concerned about the availability of the deliverable set of securities and any possible supply shortages or squeezes. Such liquidity concerns may favor T-bills.[16]

Concept Questions

1. Why does the FI have to sell more T-bill futures given that the size of each T-bill futures contract is 10 times the size of each T bond futures contract?
2. Suppose the FI had the reverse duration gap from the case just considered. That is, the duration of its assets were shorter ($D_A = 3$) than the duration of its liabilities ($D_L = 5$). (This might be the case of a bank that borrows with long-term notes or time deposits to finance floating-rate loans.) What should its futures position be?
3. Suppose:

$$D_A = 4.5$$

$$k = .9$$

$$D_L = 5$$

So that:

$$(D_L - kD_L) = (4.5 - (.9)(5)) = 0$$

How many futures should an FI buy or sell to minimize interest rate risk?

The Problem of Basis Risk

Because spot bonds and futures on bonds are traded in different markets, the shift in yields $\Delta R/1 + R$ affecting the values of the on-balance-sheet cash portfolio may differ from the shift ($\Delta R_F/1 + R_F$) in yields affecting the value of the underlying bond in the futures contract; that is, spot and futures prices or values are not perfectly correlated. This lack of perfect correlation has been called *basis risk*. In the previous section, we assumed a naive world of no basis risk in which $\Delta R/1 + R = \Delta R_F/1 + R_F$. Let's suppose this were not the case. How can the formula to solve for the risk minimizing N_F be fixed to account for greater or less rate volatility and, hence, price volatility in the futures market relative to the spot or cash market? Returning to our on-balance-sheet exposure we have:

$$\Delta E = -(D_A - kD_L) \times A \times \Delta R/1 + R$$

and for the off-balance-sheet futures position:

$$\Delta F = -D_F(N_F \times P_F) \times \Delta R_F/1 + R_F$$

setting $$\Delta E = \Delta F$$

and solving for N_F, we have

---

[16]However, when rates change the loss of net worth on the balance sheet and the gain on selling the futures are instantaneous, therefore delivery need not be a concern. Indeed, because of the daily marking-to-market process, an FI manager can close out a futures position by taking an exactly offsetting position. That is, a manager who had originally sold 100 futures contracts could close out a position on any day by buying 100 contracts. Because of the unique marking-to-market feature, the marked-to-market price of the contracts sold equals the price of any new contracts bought on that day.

$$N_F = \frac{\left(D_A - kD_L\right) \cdot A \cdot \Delta R/1 + R}{D_F \cdot P_F \cdot \Delta R_F /1 + R_F}$$

Dividing the top and bottom of the RHS by $\Delta R/1 + R$ and letting the ratio $(\Delta R_F/1 + R_F)/(\Delta R/1 + R)) = b$, we have:

$$N_F = \frac{\left(D_A - kD_L\right) A}{D_F \cdot P_F \cdot b}$$

The only difference between this and the previous formula is an adjustment for basis risk (b), which measures the degree to which the futures price yields move more or less than spot bond price yields. In our example, let $b = 1.1$. This means that for every 1 percent change in discounted spot rates ($\Delta R/1 + R$), the implied rate on the deliverable bond in the futures market moves by 1.1 percent. That is, futures prices are more sensitive to interest-rate shocks than spot market prices. Solving for N_F, we have:

$$N_F = \frac{\left(5 - (.9)(3)\right) \$100 \text{ million}}{9.5 \times \$97,000 \times 1.1}$$

$$= 226.9 \text{ contracts}$$

or 226 contracts rounding down. This compares to 249 when we assumed equal rate shocks in both the cash and futures markets ($\Delta R/1 + R = \Delta R_F/1 + R_F$). The reason that we need fewer contracts is that futures rates and prices are more volatile, so that selling fewer futures would be sufficient to provide the same change in ΔF (the value of the futures position) than before when we implicitly assumed $b = 1$.

Note that if futures rates or prices had been less volatile than spot rates or prices, we would have had to sell more than 249 contracts to get the same dollar gain in the futures position as was lost in net worth on the balance sheet so that $\Delta E = \Delta F$.

Concept Question

1. Suppose the basis risk measure $b = .8$. How many futures should have been sold using the 20-year bond and 3-month T-bill contracts in the previous example?

Next, we look at the important issue of measuring the basis risk adjustment in the preceding formula. One method is to look at the ratio between $\Delta R/1 + R$ and $\Delta R_F/1 + R_F$ today. Since this is only one observation, we might better analyze their relationship by investigating their relative behavior in the recent past. We can do this by running an ordinary least squares linear regression of implied futures rate changes on spot rate changes with the slope coefficient of this regression giving an estimate of the degree of comovement of the two rates over time. We discuss this regression procedure in greater detail next in connection with calculating basis risk when hedging with FX futures.[17]

---

[17]Another problem with the simple duration gap approach to determining N_F is that it is assumed that yield curves are flat. This could be relaxed by using duration measures that allow for nonflat yield curves (see Chapter 6).

Hedging Foreign Exchange Risk

Just as forwards and futures can hedge an FI against losses due to interest rate changes, so can these contracts hedge against foreign exchange risk.

Forwards

In Chapter 11 we analyze how an FI could use forward contracts to reduce the risks due to currency fluctuations when it mismatched the currencies of its asset and liability portfolios. In that chapter, we consider the simple case of an FI that raised all its liabilities in dollars but invested half of its assets in British pound sterling-denominated loans and the other half in dollar-denominated loans. Its balance sheet looked as follows:

Assets	Liabilities
U.S. loans ($) $100 million	U.S. CDs $200 million
U.K. loans (£) $100 million	

All assets and liabilities were of a one-year maturity and duration. Because the bank was net long in pound sterling assets, it faced the risk that over the period of the loan the pound would depreciate against the dollar so that the proceeds of the pound loan (along with the dollar loan) would be insufficient to meet the required payments on the maturing dollar CDs. Then, the bank would have to meet such losses out of its net worth; that is, its insolvency risk would increase.

In Chapter 11, we show that by selling both the pound loan principal and interest forward one year, at the known forward exchange rate at the beginning of the year, the FI could hedge itself against losses on its pound loan position due to changes in the dollar/pound exchange rate over the succeeding year. Note the hedging strategy for hedging (£100 million) of British pound sterling loans with forwards in Figure 18–4.

Futures

Instead of using FX forward contracts to hedge foreign exchange risk, the FI could use FX futures contracts. The major contracts available are in Figure 18–5. As indicated by the trading data on April 19, 1993, measured by open interest or the number of contracts outstanding at the end of the day, the deutsche mark, Japanese yen, Swiss franc, and British pound were the most popular currencies for futures positions.

Consider a U.S.-based FI wishing to hedge a one-year British pound loan of £100 million principal plus £15 million interest (or £115 million) against the risk of the pound falling in value against the dollar over the succeeding year.

As you can see, as of April 19, 1993, there were two British pound futures contracts: the June 1993 contract and the September 1993 contract. Thus, the futures market did not allow the FI to institute a long-term one-year hedge that day. The longest maturity contract available matured in just over five months, in September 1993. However, measured by open interest, this contract is quite illiquid compared to the nearby June 1993 contract. Thus, the FI could use futures only by rolling over the hedge into a new futures contract on maturity. Considerations such as the transactions

Figure 18–4

Hedging a long position in pound assets through sale of pounds forward

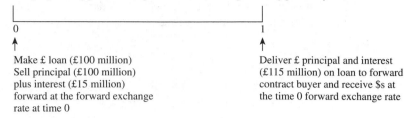

Make £ loan (£100 million)
Sell principal (£100 million)
plus interest (£15 million)
forward at the forward exchange
rate at time 0

Deliver £ principal and interest
(£115 million) on loan to forward
contract buyer and receive $s at
the time 0 forward exchange rate

costs from having to roll over the hedge and uncertainty regarding the prices of new futures contracts, may make hedging through forwards or swaps relatively more attractive to those FIs that want to lock in a longer-term hedge (see Chapter 20).

However, let's suppose the FI still wants to hedge fully via the futures markets. How many futures should it sell? The answer to this question is that it should sell the amount that produces a sufficient profit on the pound futures contract just to offset any exchange-rate losses on the pound loan portfolio should the pound fall in value relative to the dollar. There are two cases to consider:

1. The futures dollar/pound price is expected to change in exactly the same fashion as the spot dollar/pound price over the course of the year. That is, futures and spot price changes are perfectly correlated; there is no basis risk.

2. Futures and spot prices, while expected to change in the same direction, are not perfectly correlated (there is basis risk).

Perfect Correlation between Spot and Futures Prices.   On April 19, 1993, *The Wall Street Journal* reported:

S_t = Spot exchange rate ($/£):$1.54 per £1

f_t = Futures price ($/£) for the nearby contract (June 1993): $1.52 per £1

Suppose the FI made a £100 million loan at 15 percent interest and wished to hedge fully the risk that the dollar value of the proceeds would be eroded by a declining British pound sterling over the year. Also, suppose that the FI manager receives a forecast that in one year's time (on April 19, 1994) the spot and futures will be:

$$S_{t+1} = \$1.49 \text{ per } £1$$

$$f_{t+1} = \$1.47 \text{ per } £1$$

So that, ΔS_t = 5 cents

Δf_t = 5 cents

For a manager who believes this forecast of a depreciating pound against the dollar, the correct full-hedge strategy would be to cover the £115 million expected earnings on the British loan by selling or shorting £115 million of British pound futures contracts on April 19, 1993. Here, we are assuming that the FI manager continuously rolls over the futures position into new futures contracts and will get out of futures on April 19, 1994.

As you can see from Figure 18–5, the size of each British pound futures contract is £62,500. Therefore the number (N_F) of futures to be sold is

FIGURE 18–5

Foreign currency futures contracts (April 19, 1993)

CURRENCY

	Open	High	Low	Settle	Change	Lifetime High	Low	Open Interest
JAPAN YEN (CME)–12.5 million yen; $ per yen (.00)								
June	.8940	.9030	.8940	.8997	+ .0079	.9030	.7745	74,839
Sept	.9000	.9026	.8972	.8997	+ .0079	.9026	.7945	3,491
Dec	.9000	.9030	.9000	.9002	+ .0079	.9030	.7970	670
Est vol 25,042; vol Fri 22,114; open int 79,003, +1,336.								
DEUTSCHEMARK (CME)–125,000 marks; $ per mark								
June	.6149	.6218	.6143	.6211	+ .0076	.6920	.5883	107,302
Sept	.6103	.6155	.6102	.6149	+ .0076	.6720	.5860	6,968
Dec	....	....	....	.6103	+ .0076	.6650	.5830	245
Est vol 40,115; vol Fri 47,597; open int 114,524, −2,869.								
CANADIAN DOLLAR (CME)–100,000 dlrs.; $ per Can $								
June	.7917	.7949	.7917	.7947	+ .0032	.8360	.7532	18,934
Sept	.7902	.7908	.7897	.7903	+ .0033	.8335	.7515	1,664
Dec	.7860	.7860	.7855	.7854	+ .0034	.8310	.7470	870
Mr94	.7810	.7810	.7810	.7809	+ .0035	.7860	.7550	782
Est vol 3,082; vol Fri 1,311; open int 22,198, −278.								
BRITISH POUND (CME)–62,500 pds.; $ per pound								
June	1.5200	1.5358	1.5120	1.5354	+ .0176	1.9100	1.4020	37,322
Sept	1.5176	1.5250	1.5150	1.5250	+ .0174	1.5580	1.3980	1,290
Est vol 12,046; vol Fri 12,307; open int 38,678, −2,186.								
SWISS FRANC (CME)–125,000 francs; $ per franc								
June	.6740	.6800	.6733	.6793	+ .0074	.8070	.6405	39,769
Sept	.6737	.6775	.6735	.6769	+ .0074	.7100	.6380	1,241
Dec	.6750	.6750	.6750	.6754	+ .0073	.6865	.6400	223
Est vol 21,195; vol Fri 21,253; open int 41,233, −2,847.								
AUSTRALIAN DOLLAR (CME)–100,000 dlrs.; $ per A.$								
June	.7147	.7176	.7147	.7170	+ .0014	.7210	.6590	3,063
Est vol 216; vol Fri 283; open int 3,080, +66.								
U.S. DOLLAR INDEX (FINEX)–1,000 times USDX								
June	92.08	92.08	90.98	91.03	− 1.17	97.20	82.55	6,811
Sept	93.00	92.56	92.26	92.13	− 1.17	97.10	91.75	1,186
Est vol 3,000; vol Fri 2,494; open int 8,002, −144.								
The index: High 91.28; Low 90.30; Close 90.33 −.98								

SOURCE: *The Wall Street Journal,* April 20, 1993, p. C14. Reprinted by permission of *The Wall Street Journal.* © 1993 Dow Jones & Company, Inc. All Rights Reserved Worldwide.

$$N_F = \frac{£115,000,000}{£62,500} = \frac{\text{Size of long position}}{\text{Size of a pound futures contract}}$$

$$= 1,840 \text{ contracts to be sold}$$

Next, look at whether losses on the long asset position (the British loan) would just offset gains on the futures should the FI sell 1,840 British pound futures contracts and should spot and futures prices change in the direction and amount expected.

Loss on British Pound Loan. The loss on the British pound loan in dollars would be:

$$[£ \text{ Principal} + \text{Interest}] \times \Delta S_t$$

$$[£115 \text{ million}] \times [\$1.54/£ - \$1.49/£] = \$5.75 \text{ million}$$

That is, the dollar value of the British pound loan proceeds would be $5.75 million less should the pound depreciate from $1.54/£ to $1.49/£, in the spot market over the year.

Gain on Futures Contracts.

$$[N_F \times £62{,}500] \times \Delta f_t$$

$$[1{,}840 \times £62{,}500] \times (\$1.52/£ - \$1.47/£) = \$5.75 \text{ million}$$

By selling 1,840 futures contracts of £62,500 each, the seller makes $5.75 million as the futures price falls from $1.52/£ at the contract initiation on April 19, 1993, to $1.47/£ at the futures position termination on April 19, 1994. This cash flow of $5.75 million results from the marking-to-market of the futures contract. As the futures price falls due to the daily marking-to-market, the pound futures contract buyer has the contract repriced to a lower level in dollars to be paid per pound but has to compensate the seller out of his or her margin account for the difference between the original contract price and the new lower marked-to-market contract price. Thus, over the one year the buyer compensates the seller by a net of 5 cents per £1 of futures purchased. That is, $1.52/£1 minus $1.47/£1 as the futures price falls, or a total of 5 cents × the number of contracts (1,840) × the pound size of each contract (62,500). Note that on April 19, 1994, when the principal and interest on the pound loan is paid by the borrower, the FI seller of the pound futures terminates its position in 1,840 short contracts by taking an opposing position of 1,840 long in the same contract. This effectively ends any net cash flow implications from futures positions beyond this date.

Finally, in this example we have ignored the interest income effects of marking-to-market. In reality, the $5.75 million from the futures position would be received by the FI seller over the course of the year. As a result, this cash flow can be reinvested at the current short-term dollar interest rate and generate a cash flow more than $5.75 million. Given this, an FI hedger can sell slightly fewer contracts in anticipation of this interest income. The number of futures that could be sold, below the 1,840 suggested, would depend on the level and pattern of short-term rates over the hedging horizon as well as the precise expected pattern of cash flows from marking-to-market. In general, the higher the level of short-term interest, the more an FI manager could **tail the hedge** in this fashion.[18]

Tail the Hedge
Reducing the number of futures contracts that are needed to hedge a cash position because of the interest income that is generated from re-investing the marking-to-market cash-lows generated by the futures contract.

Imperfect Correlation between Spot and Futures Prices (Basis Risk). Suppose, instead, the FI manager did not believe that the spot exchange rate and futures price on the dollar/pound contract would fall exactly in tandem. Instead, let the forecast for one year's time be:

$$S_{t+1} = \$1.49/£1$$

$$f_{t+1} = \$1.49/£1$$

So that, in expectation, over the succeeding year:

$$\Delta S_t = 5 \text{ cents}$$

$$\Delta f_t = 3 \text{ cents}$$

---

[18]See Figlewski, *Hedging with Financial Futures*, for further discussion. One way to do this is to discount the calculated hedge ratio (the optimal number of futures to sell per $1 of cash position) by a short-term interest rate such as the federal funds rate.

This means that the dollar/pound futures price is expected to depreciate less than the spot dollar/pound. This basis risk arises because spot and futures contracts are traded in different markets with different demand and supply functions. Given this, even though futures and spot prices are normally highly correlated, this correlation is often less than one.

Because futures prices and spot prices do not always move exactly together, this can create a problem for an FI manager seeking to hedge the long position of £115 million with pound futures. Suppose that the FI manager ignored the fact that the spot pound is expected to depreciate faster against the dollar than the futures price for pounds and continued to believe that selling 1,840 contracts would be the best hedge. That manager could be in for a big (and nasty) surprise in one year's time. To see this, consider the loss on the cash asset position and gain on the futures position under a new scenario where the dollar/pound spot rate falls by 2 cents more than dollar/pound futures over the year.

Loss on British Pound Loan. The expected fall in the spot value of the pound by 5 cents over the year results in a loss of:

$$[£115 \text{ million}] \times [\$1.54 - \$1.49] = \$5.75 \text{ million}$$

Gain on Futures Position. The expected gain on the futures position is

$$[1,840 \times £62,500] \times [\$1.52 - \$1.49] = \$3.45 \text{ million}$$

Thus, the net loss to the FI is

Net loss = Loss on British pound loan − Gain on British pound futures

Net loss = $5.75 − $3.45

Net loss = $2.3 million

Such a loss would have to be charged against the FI's profits and implicitly its net worth or equity.[19] As a result, the FI manager needs to take into account the lower sensitivity of futures prices relative to spot exchange rate changes by selling more than 1,840 futures contracts to hedge fully the British pound loan risk.

To see how many more contracts are required, we need to know how much more sensitive spot exchange rates are relative to futures prices. Let h be the ratio of ΔS_t to Δf_t

$$h = \frac{\Delta S_t}{\Delta f_t}$$

Then, in our example:

$$h = \frac{\$.05}{\$.03} = 1.66$$

That is, spot rates are 66 percent more sensitive than futures prices, or—put slightly differently—for every 1 percent change in futures prices, spot rates change by 1.66 percent.[20]

---

[19]In actuality, as long as the futures position is a hedge, such losses can be deferred and written off over the life of the hedge (see *FASB Statement No. 52*, on Foreign Currency Translation of Gains and Losses). We discuss accounting issues further in the section on accounting rules and futures contracts.

[20]Of course, this can always be expressed the other way around in that a 1 percent change in spot prices lead, on average, to only a 0.6 percent change in futures prices.

Hedge Ratio
The dollar value of futures contracts that should be sold per $ of cash position exposure.

An FI manager could use this ratio, h, as a **hedge ratio** to solve the question of how many futures should be sold to hedge the long position in the British pound when the spot and futures prices are imperfectly correlated. Specifically, the value of h means that for every £1 in the long asset position, £1.66 futures contracts should be sold. To see this, let's look at the FI's losses on its long asset position in pound loans relative to the gains on its selling pound futures.

Loss on British Pound Loans. As before, its losses are

$$[£115 \text{ million}] \times [\$1.54/£ - \$1.49/£] = \$5.75 \text{ million}$$

Gains on British Pound Futures Position. Taking into account the degree to which spot exchange rates are more sensitive than futures prices—the hedge ratio (h)—means that we can solve for the number of futures (N_F) to sell as:

$$N_f = \frac{\text{Long asset position} \times h}{\text{Size of one futures contract}}$$

$$N_f = \frac{£115 \text{ million} \times 1.66}{£62,500} = 3,054.4 \text{ contracts}$$

or rounding down to the nearest whole contract, 3,054 contracts. Selling 3,054 British pound futures results in expected profits of:

$$[3,054 \times £62,500] \times [\$1.52/£ - \$1.49/£] = \$5.73 \text{ million}$$

The difference of $0.02 million is due to rounding.

Estimating the Hedge Ratio

In the previous example, we showed that the number of FX futures that should be sold to hedge fully foreign exchange rate risk exposure depends crucially on expectations regarding the correlation between the change in the dollar/pound spot rate (ΔS_t) and the change in its futures price (Δf_t). When:

$$h = \frac{\Delta S_t}{\Delta f_t} = \frac{\$.05}{\$.05} = 1$$

there is no basis risk. Both the spot and futures are expected to change together by the same absolute amount and the FX risk of the cash position should be hedged dollar for dollar by selling FX futures. When basis risk is present, the spot and futures are expected to move imperfectly together:

$$h = \frac{\Delta S_t}{\Delta f_t} = \frac{\$.05}{\$.03} = 1.66$$

The FI must sell a greater number of futures than when basis risk is absent.

Unfortunately, without perfect foresight we cannot know exactly how exchange rates and futures prices will change over some future time period. If we did, we would have no need to hedge in the first place! Thus, a common method to calculate h is to look at the behavior of ΔS_t relative to Δf_t over the *recent past* and to use this past behavior as a prediction of the appropriate value of h in the future. One

FIGURE 18–6

Monthly changes in ΔS_t *and* Δf_t *in 199X*

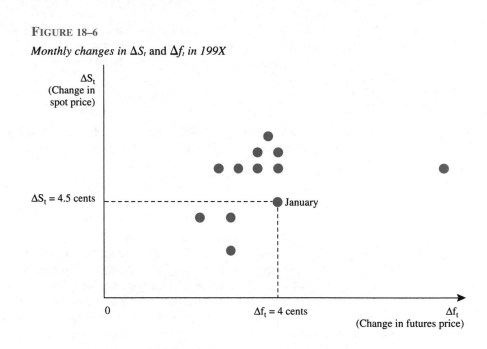

way to estimate this past relationship is to run an ordinary least squares regression of recent changes in spot prices on recent changes in futures prices.[21]

Consider Figure 18–6, where we plot hypothetical monthly changes in the spot pound/dollar exchange rate (ΔS_t) against monthly changes in the futures pound/dollar price (Δf_t) for the year 199X. Thus we have 12 observations from January through December.

For information purposes, the first observation (January) is labeled in Figure 18–6. In January, the dollar/pound spot rate rose by 4.5 cents and the dollar/pound futures price rose by 4 cents. Thus, the pound appreciated in value over the month of January but the spot exchange rate rose by more than the futures price. In some other months, as implied by the scatter of points in Figure 18–6, the futures price rose by more than the spot rate.

Concept Question

1. Circle an observation in Figure 18–6 that shows futures price changes exceeding spot price changes.

An ordinary least squares (OLS) regression fits a line of best fit to these monthly observations such that the sum of the squared deviations between the observed values of ΔS_t and its predicted values (as given by the line of best fit) are minimized. This line of best fit reflects an intercept term α and a slope coefficient β. That is:

$$\Delta S_t = \alpha + \beta \, \Delta f_t + U_t$$

---

[21]When we calculate *h* (the hedge ratio) we could use the ratio of the most recent spot and futures changes. However, this would amount to basing our hedge ratio estimate on *one* observation of the change in S_t and f_t. This is why the regression model, which uses many past observations, is usually preferred by market participants, although regulators appear to prefer the former (see the section on accounting guidelines, regulations, and macrohedging versus microhedging).

where the U_t are the regression's residuals (the differences between actual values of ΔS_t and its predicted values based on the line of best fit).

Definitionally β, or the slope coefficient, of the regression equation is equal to:

$$\beta = \frac{\text{Cov}\left(\Delta S_t, \Delta f_t\right)}{\text{Var}\left(\Delta f_t\right)}$$

That is, the covariance between the change in spot rates and change in futures prices divided by the variance of the change in futures prices. Suppose ΔS_t and Δf_t moved perfectly together over time, then

$$\text{Cov}\left(\Delta S_t, \Delta f_t\right) = \text{Var}\left(\Delta f_t\right)$$

$$\text{and } \beta = 1$$

If spot rate changes are greater than futures price changes, then $\text{Cov}\left(\Delta S_t, \Delta f_t\right) > \text{Var}\left(\Delta f_t\right)$ and $\beta > 1$. Conversely, if spot rate changes are less sensitive than futures price changes over time then $\text{Cov}\left(\Delta S_t, \Delta f_t\right) < \text{Var}\left(\Delta f_t\right)$ and $\beta < 1$.

Moreover, the value of β, or the estimated slope of the regression line, has theoretical meaning as the hedge ratio (h) that minimizes the risk of a portfolio of spot assets and futures contracts.[22] Put more simply, we can use the estimate of β from the regression model as the appropriate measure of h (the hedge-ratio) to be used by the FI manager. For example, suppose we used the 12 observations on ΔS_t and Δf_t in 199X to estimate an OLS regression equation (the equation of the line of best fit in Figure 18–6). And, this regression equation takes the form:

$$\Delta S_t = .015 + 1.2 \, \Delta f_t$$

$$\text{Thus, } \alpha = .015$$

$$\beta = 1.2$$

Using $\beta = 1.2$ as the appropriate risk minimizing hedge ratio (h) for the portfolio manager, we can solve our earlier problem of determining the number of futures contracts to sell to protect the FI from FX losses on its £115 million loan:

$$N_F = \frac{\text{Long position in £ assets} \times \beta \text{ (the estimated value of the hedge ratio } h \text{ using past data)}}{\text{Size of one £ futures contract}}$$

$$N_F = \frac{£115 \text{ million} \times 1.2}{£62,500} = 2,208 \text{ contracts}$$

Thus, using the past relationship between ΔS_t and Δf_t as the best predictor of their future relationship over the succeeding year dictates that the FI manager should sell 2,208 contracts.

The degree of confidence the FI manager may have in using such a method to determine the appropriate hedge ratio depends on how well the regression line fits the scatter of observations. The standard measure of the goodness fit of a regression line is the R^2 of the equation, where the R^2 is the square of the correlation coefficient between ΔS_t and Δf_t,

---

[22]For proof of this, see L. H. Ederington, "The Hedging Performance of the New Futures Markets," *Journal of Finance* 34, 1979, pp. 157–70.

$$R^2 = \rho^2 = \left[\frac{\left(\mathrm{Cov}\left(\Delta S_t, \Delta f_t \right) \right)}{\sigma_{\Delta s_t} \cdot \sigma_{\Delta f_t}} \right]^2$$

The term in brackets [   ] is the statistical definition of a correlation coefficient. If changes in the spot rate (ΔS_t) and changes in the futures price (Δf_t) are perfectly correlated, then

$$R^2 = \rho^2 = (1)^2 = 1$$

and all observations between ΔS_t and Δf_t lie on a straight line. By comparison, an $R^2 = 0$ indicates that there is no statistical association at all between ΔS_t and Δf_t.

Hedging Effectiveness
The (squared) correlation between past changes in spot asset prices and futures prices.

Since we are using futures contracts to hedge the risk of loss on spot asset positions, the R^2 of the regression measures the degree of **hedging effectiveness** of the futures contract. A low R^2 would mean that we might have little confidence that the slope coefficient β from the regression is actually the true hedge ratio. As the R^2 approaches one, our degree of confidence increases in the use of futures contracts, with a given hedge ratio (h) estimate, to hedge our cash asset-risk position.

Concept Questions

1. Suppose the $R^2 = 0$ in a regression of ΔS_t. Would you still use futures contracts to hedge? Explain your answer.
2. In running a regression of ΔS_t on Δf_t, the regression equation is $\Delta S_t = .51 + .95 \, \Delta f_t$ and $R^2 = .72$. What is the hedge ratio? What is the measure of hedging effectiveness?

Hedging Credit Risk

In Chapter 8, we demonstrated that by diversifying their loan portfolios across different borrowers, sectors, and regions, FIs could diversify away much of the borrower-specific or unsystematic risk of the loan portfolio. Of course, the ability of an FI manager to diversify sufficiently depends in part on the size of the loan portfolio under management. Thus, the potential ability to diversify away borrower-specific risk increases with the size of the FI.

As a result, for big well-diversified FIs, their credit risk exposure may be largely nondiversifiable systematic risk. In particular, the returns on the loan portfolio may come to be uniquely reliant on general macrofactors relating to the state of the economy. Such macrofactors could include the growth of national income, inflation, and unemployment. In Figure 18–7, we show the relationship between the expected payoffs on a large FI's portfolio of loans and the possible states of the economy from bad to good.

Looking at Figure 18–7, in the very bad economic state, such as a major recession, many loans go into default and the value of the loan portfolio has to be marked down through writeoffs and loan restructurings. In the bad state, some loans go into default but the major problem may be in receiving interest payments from borrowers on a timely basis. Finally, in the good economic state—such as a major economic expansion—virtually all borrowers pay off both principal and interest. Note that the relationship between payoffs from the loan portfolio and the state of the economy is nonlinear. That is, in the very good economic states, the best the FI can do is for all

FIGURE 18–7

The relationship between the payoff on an FI loan portfolio and the state of the economy

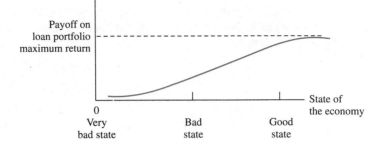

borrowers to pay their promised interest and principal. Thus, the upside payoff on the loan portfolio is limited. By comparison, as we move away from good economic states to bad economic states, writeoffs on principal and interest increase and payoffs from the loan portfolio approach zero in the limit.[23]

Futures Contracts and Credit Risk Hedging

An FI manager sufficiently concerned about the likelihood of bad economic states occurring in the near term and the systematic losses this may impose on the loan portfolio could consider the possibility of hedging. In this chapter, we consider the use of stock index futures by an FI to hedge the systematic credit risk of its portfolio.

The reason that stock index futures may be useful is that stock prices should reflect the underlying current and expected present values of the earnings and dividends of the firms in the economy. In good economic states, firms' earnings prospects improve; normally, a rise in stock market prices and stock market index values reflects this. Similarly, in bad economic states, stock market prices and values generally (but not always) fall.

In Figure 18–8, we list the major stock index futures. The major domestic index futures contract is the Standard & Poor's 500 Stock Average (S&P 500). As you can see, the cost of one index futures contract is $500 times the S&P 500 index value. Thus, on April 19, 1993, the settlement price of the nearby June 1993 contract for the S&P 500 was 446.95. If an FI manager purchased one contract, the price would have been 446.95 × $500 = $223,475.

Suppose the economy moves into a recession and the stock market index and futures prices on the index start to fall. The seller of the futures contract would start to receive a positive cash flow from the futures buyer through the marking-to-market process. In particular, assume the S&P 500 futures price falls from a settlement price of 446.95 on index futures on April 19, 1993, to 400 on April 19, 1994.[24] As the S&P 500 futures contract is marked-to-market, the buyer has to compensate the seller. The cash flow the buyer would send to the seller over the year is

---

[23]This section is based in part on analysis in D. F. Babbel, "Insuring Banks against Systematic Credit Risk," *Journal of Futures Markets* 9, 1989, pp. 487–506.

[24]Again, we assume that existing futures contracts positions are rolled over into new contract positions on maturity. In the context of Figure 18–8, the S&P 500 futures contract would need to be rolled over on June 1993 if the FI manager had chosen to hedge using the most liquid nearby contract. Alternatively, the manager could have chosen to hedge with the longer December 1993 contract. This contract is less liquid; however, the hedger in our example would need to roll over the futures position a fewer number of times.

FIGURE 18–8

Stock index futures (April 19, 1993)

INDEX

S&P 500 INDEX (CME) $500 times index

	Open	High	Low	Settle	Chg	High	Low	Open Interest
June	448.90	449.75	446.10	446.95	− 2.60	458.10	391.00	167,597
Sept	449.50	450.15	446.90	447.55	− 2.60	458.55	391.00	3,937
Dec	447.85	450.80	447.50	448.25	− 2.45	459.30	429.70	940

Est vol 40,525; vol Fri 41,290; open int 172,482, −778.
Indx prelim High 449.14; Low 445.85; Close 447.46 −1.48

S&P MIDCAP 400 (CME) $500 times Index

June	161.30	161.70	160.30	160.75	− .65	167.50	138.60	9,044

Est vol 428; vol Fri 205; open int 9,055, −42.
The index: High 161.43; Low 160.67; Close 161.10 −.20

NIKKEI 225 Stock Average (CME) −$5 times Index

June	20110.	20140.	20045.	20070.	− 285.0	20860.	14550.	16,936

Est vol 852; vol Fri 1,149; open int 17,018, +416.
The index: High 20254.09; Low 19890.47; Close 20112.34 −185.52

NYSE COMPOSITE INDEX (NYFE) 500 times index
not avaiable
Est vol n.a.; vol Fri 2,553; open int 3,394, −189.
The index: High n.a.; Low n.a.; Close n.a.

MAJOR MKT INDEX (CBT) $500 times index

May	356.15	356.75	354.35	355.25	− .65	364.30	346.75	1,678
June	355.90	355.90	354.40	355.10	− .60	363.75	339.75	127

Est vo¹ 1,000; vol Fri 1,997; open int 4,105, +15.
The index: High 357.18; Low 354.40; Close 356.31 −.27

SOURCE: *The Wall Street Journal,* April 20, 1993, p. C14. Reprinted by permission of *The Wall Street Journal.*
© 1993 Dow Jones & Company, Inc. All Rights Reserved Worldwide.

$$(446.95 - 400) \times \$500 = \$23,475$$

As a result, for every index contract sold, the FI manager can expect to make a profit on index futures as the index falls in value.[25] Consequently, the cash flow profits the FI manager gets from selling futures when bad economic states arise can offset losses from the loan portfolio due to increased systematic credit risk. See this hedging outcome in Figure 18–9.

However, when using index futures to hedge systematic credit risk, an FI manager may face a large number of practical and conceptual problems. Selling futures may produce sufficient cash flows to offset credit losses in bad economic states, as shown in Figure 18–10. However, in good economic states the seller of futures contracts loses as the index rises and the marking-to-market cash flows favor the contract buyer. Unfortunately, such losses are not likely to be compensated fully by gains on the loan portfolio since the return on this portfolio has a limited upside return potential; that is, the full repayment of loan interest and principal. See this asymmetric effect in Figure 18–10.

---

[25]Note that index futures are cash settlement contracts. This means that should the contract mature, the seller never seeks to deliver all the stocks in the S&P 500 (this would be extremely difficult and costly), but rather makes a cash settlement with the buyer based on the final day's marking-to-market of the contract.

FIGURE 18–9

Hedging systematic credit risk with index futures sales

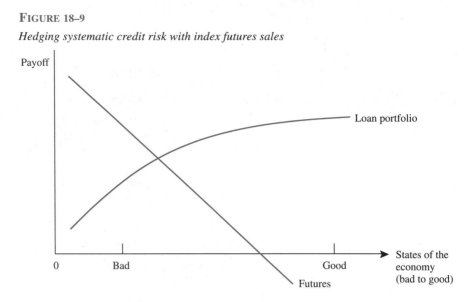

As you can see in this figure, selling index futures may allow the FI manager to generate a more predictable payoff return on the credit portfolio in bad economic states. In good states, the sale of index futures results in losses that may more than offset gains in returns on the loan portfolio. Thus, in general, a manager would prefer a derivative securities product that limits the risk of losses in good economic states while still producing profits in bad states. Products that have such an asymmetric payoff and can potentially do this are *put options* on the stock market index (see Chapter 19). Buying put options limits the risk of loss on the derivative product, when good economic states arise, to a fixed premium while allowing for potential upside returns in bad states similar to those enjoyed from selling index futures.

Another problem is one of basis risk. Managers must determine how close and stable the correlation is between stock index futures prices and the general macroeconomic conditions affecting the systematic credit risk exposure to losses of the FI's loan portfolio. Clearly, the stronger this correlation, the smaller the basis risk and the better the hedging effectiveness of index futures to protect the FI manager against systematic credit risk. In actuality, we would expect basis risk to pose a severe problem to an FI manager seeking to calculate a hedge ratio.

Concept Question

1. What was the quarterly correlation between changes in the S&P 500 and changes in GNP over the 1989–92 period?

Accounting Guidelines, Regulations, and Macrohedging versus Microhedging

A number of accounting rules and regulations determine whether an FI uses macrohedging or microhedging as well as affect the FI's choice of hedging instrument.

FIGURE 18–10

Net payoff on credit risk hedging with index futures

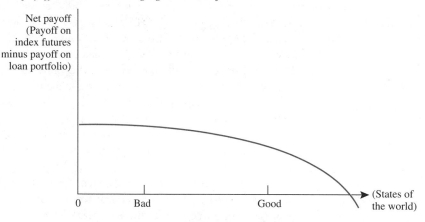

Accounting Rules and Futures Contracts

The Financial Accounting Standards Board (FASB) has made a number of rulings regarding the accounting and tax treatment of futures transactions.[26] In hedge accounting, a futures position is a hedge transaction if it can be linked to a particular asset or liability. An example would be using the T bond futures contract to hedge a bank's holdings of long-term bonds as investments. If this hedging condition is met, then when the bank's on-balance-sheet position is carried at book value it can defer gains or losses on its futures contract until the position is closed out. Any gains or losses are then amortized over the remaining life of the asset or liability; that is, they are reflected in bank income slowly. Requiring that hedges be linked to an identifiable asset or liability mitigates against pursuing macrohedging or aggregate duration gap hedging. Since this type of hedge cannot be directly associated with any particular underlying asset or liability it is often viewed as speculative; this requires immediate recognition of losses and gains in the profit and loss statement. Unfortunately, while FASB accounting rules require a close correlation between the instrument being hedged and the futures contract, FASB doesn't actually define quantitatively what it means by a close correlation nor the precise statistical technique that could establish that such a close correlation exists.[27]

This has resulted in some disputes among FI managers and regulators. Perhaps the most publicized was the closure of Franklin Savings Bank in February 1990.[28] Franklin Savings Bank operated in a nontraditional fashion for thrifts. It relied heavily on brokered deposits for growth of assets, growing from $0.5 billion in 1982 to more than $9 billion by the end of 1989. More importantly, it invested heavily in junk bonds and mortgage-backed securities and took very active positions in futures, swaps, and options. At the end of 1989, it had a notional value of $1.7 billion in long-term futures (short positions) with $119 million in futures contract losses it wished to defer.

---

[26]FASB, *Statement Number 80* (1984) "Accounting for Futures Contracts" is probably the most important.

[27]See Brewer, "Bank Gap Management."

[28]The following discussion is based on S. Holifield, M. Madaris, and W. H. Sackley, "Correlation and Hedge Accounting Standards: The Case of Franklin Savings" (Working Paper, Ohio State University, Columbus, Ohio, 1993, Mimeographed).

The dispute revolved around whether these losses could be deferred. In particular, the Office of Thrift Supervision (OTS) challenged the deferral of such losses and required their immediate recognition, which would have rendered Franklin Savings insolvent. The basis for the OTS challenge was the statistical technique used to calculate its hedge ratio. Franklin used the absolute value method, which is essentially the regression model approach (or β), to calculate the hedge ratio. The OTS preferred the net offset method, which is essentially the same as taking the ratio of the change in the spot price to the change in the futures price ($\Delta S_t/\Delta f_t$) over the hedge period.[29] The OTS apparently required the futures price to covary within a range of 70 to 130 percent of the movement in the spot asset's price.

As it turned out, Franklin's hedge program satisfied this criterion using the absolute value method and failed the criterion using the regulator-preferred net offset method. Eventually, the courts supported the OTS stance that Franklin's method of hedge ratio calculation was not consistent with the GAAP principles laid down by the FASB. As a result, Franklin's request for loss deferral was denied and it was placed under the conservatorship of the RTC in 1990.

Futures and Forward Policies of Regulators

The main bank regulators, the Federal Reserve, the FDIC, and the Comptroller of the Currency, have issued uniform guidelines for trading in futures and forwards.[30] These guidelines require a bank (1) to establish internal guidelines regarding its hedging activity, (2) to establish trading limits, and (3) to disclose large contract positions that materially affect bank risk to shareholders and outside investors. Overall, the policy of regulators is to encourage the use of futures for hedging and to discourage their use for speculation, although on a practical basis it is often difficult to distinguish between the two.

Finally, as noted in Chapter 14, futures contracts are not subject to risk-based capital requirements with respect to credit risk; by contrast, OTC forward contracts are potentially subject to capital requirements. Other things being equal, the risk-based capital requirements favor the use of futures over forwards.

Summary

In this chapter, we have analyzed the risk-management role of futures and forwards. We have seen that while they are close substitutes, they are not perfect substitutes. A number of characteristics such as maturity, flexibility, marking-to-market, and capital requirements differentiate these products and make one or the other more attractive to any given FI manager. These products might be used to partially or fully hedge at least three types of risk commonly faced by an FI: interest rate risk, foreign exchange risk, and credit risk.

[29]See S. Abbott, "Franklin Case Points Out Thrift Accounting Difficulties," *Futures*, July 1990, pp. 58–60; and Holifield, Madaris, and Sackley, "Correlation and Hedge Accounting."

[30]See B. C. Gendreau, "The Regulation of Bank Trading in Futures and Forward Markets," in *Below the Bottom Line: The Use of Contingencies and Commitments by Commercial Banks* (Washington, D.C.: Federal Reserve Board of Governors, 1982).

Questions and Problems

1. Suppose you purchase a Treasury bond futures contract at 95.
   a. What obligation, if any, is required as a result of this position?
   b. What type of a hedge does this future position represent?
   c. Assume that the Treasury bond futures price falls to 94. Mark your position to market.
   d. Assume that the Treasury bond futures price rises to 97. Mark your position to market.

2. a. What is the duration of a $1 million face value 91 day Treasury bill futures contract?
   b. What is the duration of a 20-year, 8% coupon (paid semiannually) Treasury bond (deliverable against the Treasury bond futures contract) selling at par?
   c. What is the impact on the Treasury bond price if interest rates increase 50 basis points?
   d. If you purchased a Treasury bond futures contract at 95 and interest rates rose 50 basis points, what would be the change in the value of your futures position?
   e. What is the meaning of the following Treasury bond futures price quote: 101-13?

3. Why is it generally more efficient for FIs to employ a macrohedge than a series of microhedges?

4. Consider the following balance sheet:

Assets ($000)		Liabilities ($000)	
Duration = 10 years	$950	Duration = 2 years	$860
		Equity	$ 90

   a. What is the FI's duration gap?
   b. What is the FI's interest rate risk exposure?
   c. How can the FI use futures and forward contracts to put on a macrohedge?
   d. What is the impact on the FI's equity value if all interest rates increase by 1%? (That is, $\frac{\Delta R}{1+R} = .01$.)
   e. Suppose that the FI put on the macrohedge in part c using Treasury bond futures that are currently priced at 96. What is the impact on the FI's futures position if all interest rates increase by 1%? (That is, $\frac{\Delta R}{1+R} = .01$. Assume that the deliverable Treasury bond has a duration of 9 years.)
   f. If the FI wanted to put on a perfect macrohedge, how many Treasury bond futures contracts would be needed?

5. a. How does consideration of basis risk change your answers to question 4?
   b. Compute the number of futures contracts required to construct a perfect macrohedge (as in question 4) if
   $$\frac{\Delta R_F/(1+R_F)}{\Delta R/(1+R)} \equiv b = .90.$$
   c. Explain what is meant by a b = .90.
   d. Explain your answer to part b.

6. Suppose that an FI has assets denominated in British pound sterling of $125 million and sterling liabilities of $100 million.
   a. What is the FI's net exposure?
   b. What is the FI's currency risk exposure?
   c. How can the FI use futures or forward contracts to hedge its FX rate risk?
   d. What are the number of futures contracts to be utilized to fully hedge the FI's currency risk exposure?
   e. If the British pound falls from $1.60/£ to $1.50/£, what would be the impact on the FI's cash position?
   f. If the British pound futures price falls from $1.55/£ to $1.45/£, what would be the impact on the FI's futures position?
   g. Using the information in parts e and f, what can you conclude about basis risk?

7. a. If the British pound futures price fell from $1.55/£ to $1.43/£ in question 6, part f, what would be the impact on the FI's futures position?
   b. Does your answer to part a differ from your answer to question 6, part f? Why or why not?
   c. How would you fully hedge the FX rate risk exposure in question 6 using the futures price change of part a?

8. An FI sells a June $1 million 91-day Eurodollar futures contract at an IMM Index price of 90.99 on April 30th and then repurchases it on May 20th at a price of 90.70. What is the cumulative cash flow from this transaction?

Use the following information to answer questions 9–18.

Rate Sensitivity Report ($ millions)

Maturity	Overnight	1–30 days	31–91 days	92–181 days	>182 days
Assets					
FF & RP	20				
Loans	0	10	15	80	65
Liabilities					
FF & RP	50				
Euros	5	25	40	0	60
Deposits					20

Balance Sheet ($ millions)

Assets	Amount $ m	Duration years	Liabilities	Amount $ m	Duration years
Cash	30	0	Core deposits	20	y
FF & RP	20	.01	FF & RP	50	.01
Loans (variable)	105	.97	Euro CDs	130	.97
Loans (fixed)	65	x	Net worth	20	
	220			220	

NOTES TO THE BALANCE SHEET:
Currently the FF and repo (FF & RP) rate is 8.5 percent. Variable rate loans are priced at 4 percent over LIBOR where LIBOR is currently at 11 percent. Fixed rate loans are all 5 year maturities with 12 percent interest, paid annually. Core deposits are all fixed rate for two years, at 8 percent paid annually. Euro CDs are all variable rate.

9. Assuming a 91-day planning period, what is the bank's repricing risk exposure?

10. If you wanted to hedge $25 million of the bank's funding gap using 91-day Treasury bill futures, what would your position be if the futures price was quoted at 94.5? Calculate the number of future contracts in the hedge as well as their dollar price using the discount formula:

$$P = FV\left(1 - \frac{dt}{360}\right)$$ where P = dollar price, FV = face value, d = discount yield, and t = days until maturity.

11. If you *do not* put on the above hedge position and all interest rates increased by 25 basis points ($\Delta R = .0025$), what would be the impact on the bank's underlying cash position? What would be the futures hedge profit or loss?

12. Calculate the bank's duration gap. (Hint: You must compute x and y.)

13. Using the bank's duration gap, what will be the impact on the market value of equity if all interest rates increase by 50 basis points? (i.e., $\frac{\Delta R}{1+R} = .0050$)

14. In conceptual terms, how can you use Treasury bill futures to hedge the impact of interest rate changes on the market value of the bank's equity?

15. Specifically, how would you put on the hedge in question 14? Be sure to specify the number of Treasury bill futures contracts (quoted at an IMM Index price of 94.5) required to hedge perfectly the bank's interest-rate risk exposure. (Assume no basis risk.) Recall that the IMM Index price = 100 minus the discount yield.

16. How would the hedge position change if there was basis risk, such that when 91-day T-bill futures prices decline 50 basis points, the cash prices decline 75 basis points?

17. Evaluate the futures cash flows for the hedge in question 15 if all interest rates increase 50 basis points. (Assume no basis risk.).

18. Do you think that most real world FIs would completely hedge their interest rate risk exposure as in questions 15 and 16? Why or why not?

19

OPTIONS, CAPS, FLOORS AND COLLARS

Learning Objectives

In this chapter you learn how FIs are using option-type contracts to hedge their interest rate, FX, and credit risks. In addition, you learn how some FIs are developing specialized option contracts, such as caps, floors, and collars, to sell as financial products to customers to generate increased revenues. The special payoff features of put and call options offer FIs a degree of hedging flexibility that may be unavailable when FIs use only futures or forward contracts.

Introduction

Just as there is a wide variety of forward and futures contracts available for an FI to use in hedging, there is an even wider array of option products including exchange traded options; over-the-counter options; options embedded in securities; and caps, collars, and floors.

In this chapter, we mostly concentrate on the use of fixed-income or interest rate options to hedge interest rate risk; we discuss the role of options in hedging foreign exchange and credit risks as well. We start by reviewing the four basic options strategies; buying a call, writing a call, buying a put, and writing a put.[1]

Basic Features of Options

In describing the features of the four basic option strategies FIs might employ, we discuss their return payoffs in terms of interest rate movements. Specifically, we consider bond options whose payoff values are inversely linked to interest rate movements in a manner similar to bond prices and interest rates in general (see Chapter 5).

Buying a Call Option on a Bond

Call option
Gives a purchaser the right, but not the obligation, to buy the underlying security from the writer of the option at a prespecified exercise price.

See the first strategy, buying a call option on a bond, in Figure 19–1. A **call option** gives the purchaser the right (but not the obligation) to buy the underlying security—

---

[1]There are two basic option contracts, puts and calls. However, an FI could potentially be a buyer or seller (writer) of each.

FIGURE 19–1

Payoff function for the buyer of a call option on a bond

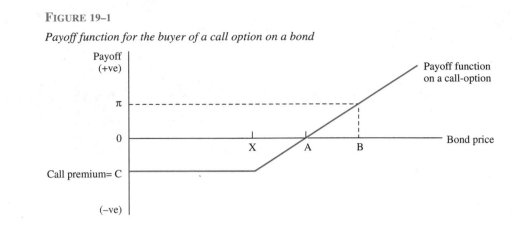

a bond—at a prespecified exercise or strike price (*X*). In return, the buyer of the call option must pay the writer or seller an upfront fee known as a call premium (*C*). This premium is an immediate negative cash flow for the buyer of the call who potentially stands to make a profit should the underlying bond's price rise above the exercise price by an amount exceeding the premium.

As we show in Figure 19–1, if the price of the bond underlying the option rises to price *0B*, the buyer makes a profit of *0π*, which is the difference between the bond price (*0B*) and the exercise price of the option (*0X*) minus the call premium (*C* = *XA*). If it rises to *0A*, the buyer of the call has broken even in that the profit from exercising the call (*0A–0X*) just equals the premium payment for the call (*C*).

Notice two important things about bond call options in Figure 19–1:

1. As interest rates fall, bond prices rise and the potential for a positive (+ve) payoff for the buyer of the call option on a bond increases.

2. As interest rates rise, bond prices fall and the potential for a negative (−ve) payoff (loss) for the buyer of the call option increases. However, the losses of the buyer are truncated by the amount of the upfront premium payment (*C*) made to purchase the call option.

Thus, unlike interest rate futures, whose prices and payoffs move symmetrically with changes in the level of rates, the payoffs on bond call options move asymmetrically with interest rates (see Chapter 18).

Writing a Call Option on a Bond

The second strategy is writing a call option on a bond. In writing a call option on a bond, the writer or seller receives an upfront fee or premium and must stand ready to sell the underlying bond to the purchaser of the option at the exercise price X. Note the payoff from writing a call option on a bond in Figure 19–2.

There are two important things to notice about this payoff function:

1. When interest rates *rise* and bond prices *fall,* there is an increased potential for the writer of the call to receive a positive payoff or profit. However, this profit has a maximum equal to the call premium (*C*) charged up front to the buyer of the option.

2. When interest rates fall and bond prices rise, the writer has an increased potential to take a loss. Since bond prices are theoretically unbounded in the

FIGURE 19–2

Payoff from writing a call option on a bond

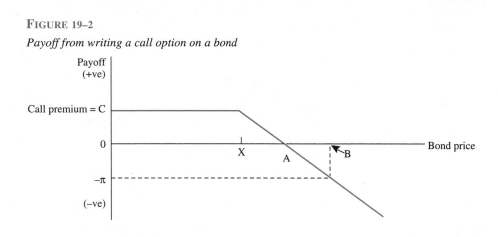

upward direction, although they must return to par at maturity, these losses could be very large.

In Figure 19–2, a fall in interest rates and a rise in bond prices to *0B*, results in the writer of the option losing 0π.

Buying a Put Option on a Bond

Put Option

Gives a purchaser the right, but not the obligation, to sell the underlying security to the writer of the option at a prespecified exercise price.

The third strategy is buying a put option on a bond. The buyer of a **put option** on a bond has the right (but not the obligation) to sell the underlying bond to the writer of the option at the agreed exercise price (*X*). In return for this option, the buyer of the put option pays a premium to the writer (*P*). We show the potential payoffs to the buyer of the put option in Figure 19–3. Note that:

1. When interest rates rise and bond prices fall, the buyer of the put has an increased probability of making a profit from exercising the option. Thus, if bond prices fall to 0D, the buyer of the put option can purchase bonds in the bond market at that price and put them (sell them) back to the writer of the put at the higher exercise price *X*. As a result, the buyer makes a profit, after deducting the cost of the put premium, of πp in Figure 19–3.

2. When interest rates fall and bond prices rise, the probability of the buyer of a put losing increases. However, the maximum loss is limited to the size of the upfront put premium (*P*).

Writing a Put Option on a Bond

The fourth strategy is writing a put option on a bond. In writing a put option on a bond, the writer or seller receives a fee or premium (*P*) in return for standing ready to buy bonds at the exercise price (*X*) should the buyer of the put choose to exercise the option to sell. See the payoff function for writing a put option on a bond in Figure 19–4. Note that:

1. If interest rates rise and bond prices fall, the writer of the put is exposed to potentially large losses (e.g., $-\pi p$ if bond prices fall to *0D* in Figure 19–4).

2. If interest rates fall and bond prices rise, the writer has an enhanced probability of making a profit. However, the writer's maximum profit is constrained to equal the put premium (*P*).

FIGURE 19–3

Buying a put option on a bond

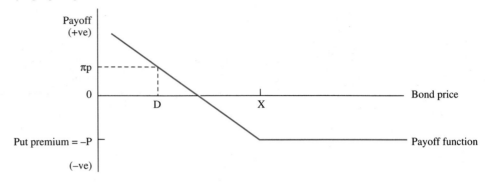

FIGURE 19–4

Writing a put option on a bond

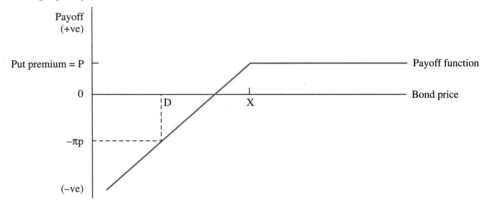

Writing versus Buying Options

For many smaller FIs, the relevant strategy set is constrained to buying rather than writing options. There are two reasons for this, one economic and the other regulatory. However, as we note later, large FIs such as money center banks often both write and buy options including caps, floors, and collars that are complex forms of interest rate options.

Economic Reasons for Not Writing Options

In writing an option, the upside profit potential is truncated, whereas the payoffs on the downside losses are not. While such risks may be offset by writing a large number of options, at different exercise prices and/or hedging an underlying portfolio of bonds, the downside risk exposure of the writer may still be significant. To see this,

FIGURE 19–5

Writing a call option to hedge the interest rate risk on a bond

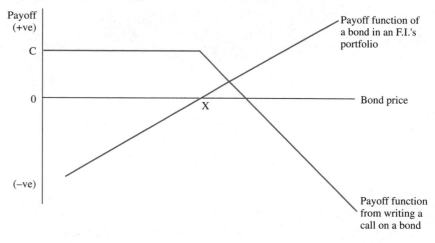

FIGURE 19–6

Buying a put option to hedge the interest rate risk on a bond

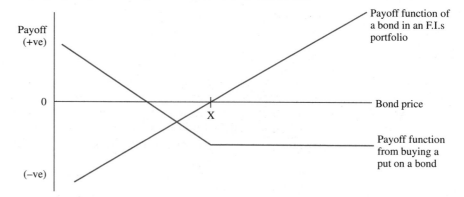

look at Figure 19–5, where an FI is long in a bond in its portfolio and seeks to hedge the interest rate risk on that bond by writing a bond call option.

As you can see, writing the call may hedge the FI when rates fall and bond prices rise; that is, the increase in the value of the bond is offset by losses on the written call. When the reverse occurs and interest rates rise, the FI's profits from writing the call may be insufficient to offset the loss on its bonds. This is because the upside profit (per call written) is truncated and is equal to the premium income (C).

By contrast, hedging the FI's risk by buying a put option on a bond offers the manager a much more attractive alternative. You can see this from Figure 19–6, the gross payoff of the bond and the payoff from buying a put option on a bond, and in Figure 19–7, the net payoff or the difference between the bond and option payoff.

Note that:

1. Buying a put option truncates the downside losses on the bond following interest rate rises to some maximum amount and scales down the upside

FIGURE 19–7

Net payoff of buying a bond put and investing in a bond

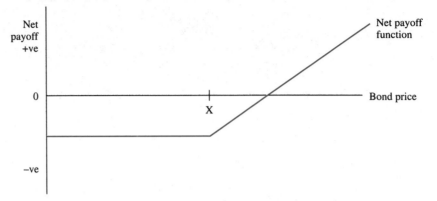

profits by the cost of bond price risk insurance—the put premium—leaving some positive upside profit potential.

2. The combination of being long in the bond and buying a put option on a bond mimics the payoff function of buying a call option (compare Figures 19–1 and 19–7).

Regulatory Reasons

There are also regulatory reasons why FIs buy options rather than write options. Regulators view writing options, especially naked options that do not identifiably hedge an underlying asset or liability position, as risky because of the potentially unlimited loss potential. Indeed, in the past, bank regulators have prohibited banks from writing puts or calls in certain areas of risk management.

Concept Question

1. Suggest two simple option-hedging strategies for an FI whose duration is $D_A - kD_L < 0$.

The Mechanics of Hedging a Bond or Bond Portfolio

You have seen how buying a put option on a bond can potentially hedge the interest rate risk exposure of an FI that holds bonds as part of its asset investment portfolio. In this section, we use a simple example to demonstrate how buying a put option works mechanically as a hedging device, and how the FI manager can calculate the fair value of the premium to pay for buying a put option on a bond.

In calculating the fair value of an option, two alternative models can be used: the binomial model and the Black-Scholes model. The Black-Scholes model produces a closed-form solution to the valuation of call or put options. Although it works well for stocks, the Black-Scholes model has two major problems when employed to value bond options: First, it assumes that short-term interest rates are constant, which

FIGURE 19–8

The variance of a bond's price

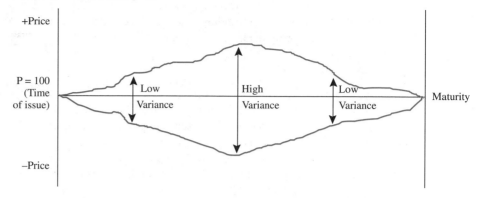

they generally are not. And second, it assumes a constant variance of returns on the underlying asset.[2] The problem with applying the Black-Scholes formula to bonds is the way bond prices behave between issuance and maturity.[3] You can see this in Figure 19–8, where a bond is issued at par; that is, at 100 at time of issue. If interest rates fall, its price may rise above 100; and if interest rates rise, its price may fall

---

[2]The Black-Scholes formulas for a put and a call are

$$P = X\,e^{-rT}\,N\left[-D+\sigma\sqrt{T}\right]-SN\left[-D\right]$$

$$C = SN\left[D\right]-X\,e^{-rT}N\left[D-\sigma\sqrt{T}\right]$$

where

S = Price of the underlying asset

X = Exercise price

T = Time to option expiration

r = Instantaneous riskless interest rate

$$D = \frac{\ln(S/X)+\left(r+\sigma^2/2\right)T}{\sigma\sqrt{T}}$$

$\ln\left[\,\cdot\,\right]$ = Natural logarithm

σ = Volatility of the underlying asset

$N\left[\,\cdot\,\right]$ = Cumulative normal distribution function; that is, the probability of observing a value less than the value in brackets when drawing randomly from a standardized normal distribution

[3]There are models that modify Black-Scholes to allow for nonconstant variance. These include Merton, who allows variance to be time dependent; Ball and Tourous, who allow bond prices to change as a stochastic process with a variance that first increases and then decreases (the Brownian bridge process); and the Schaefer-Schwartz model that assumes that the standard deviation of returns is proportional to a bonds duration. See R. C. Merton, "On the Pricing of Corporate Debt: The Risk Structure of Interest Rates," *Journal of Finance* 29, 1974, pp. 449–70; C. Ball and W. N. Tourous, "Bond Price Dynamics and Options," *Journal of Financial and Quantitative Analysis* 18, 1983, pp. 517–31; and S. Schaefer and E. S. Schwartz, "Time Dependent Variance and The Pricing of Bond Options," *Journal of Finance* 42, 1987, pp. 1113–28.

below 100. However, as the bond approaches maturity, all price paths must lead to 100, the face value of the bond or principal paid by the issuer on maturity. Because of this **pull-to-maturity,** the variance of bond prices are nonconstant over time rising at first and then falling as the bond approaches maturity. We evaluate the mechanics of hedging using bond put options in a simple binomial framework next.

Pull-to-Maturity
The tendency of the variance of a bond's price or return to decrease as maturity approaches.

Hedging with Bond Options Using the Binomial Model

Let's suppose that an FI manager has purchased a zero-coupon bond with exactly two years to maturity. A zero-coupon bond, if held to maturity, pays its face value of $100 on maturity in two years. Assume that the FI manager pays $80.45 per $100 of face value for this zero-coupon bond. This means that if held to maturity, the FI's annual yield to maturity (R_2) from this investment would be:

$$P_2 = \frac{100}{\left(1+R_2\right)^2}$$

$$80.45 = \frac{100}{\left(1+R_2\right)^2}$$

$$\left(1+R_2\right)^2 = \frac{100}{80.45}$$

$$1+R_2 = \sqrt{\frac{100}{80.45}}$$

$$R_2 = \sqrt{\frac{100}{80.45}} - 1 = .115 = 11.5\%$$

Now, fearing unexpected deposit withdrawals, the FI manager may be forced to liquidate and sell this two-year bond before maturity. As we discuss in Chapter 13, Treasury securities are important liquidity sources for an FI. We assume here that the manager may have to sell the bond at the end of the first year. Because of uncertainty about future interest rates, the FI manager faces the risk that if interest rates rise over the next year, the bond would have to be sold at a low price if liquidated early at end of the first year.

Suppose, that the current yield on one-year discount bonds (R_1) is $R_1 = 10$ percent. Also, assume a forecast that next year's one-year interest rate (r_1) will rise to either 13.82 percent or 12.18 percent.

If one-year interest rates rise from $R_1 = 10$ percent this year to $r_1 = 13.82$ percent next year, the FI manager would only be able to sell the zero-coupon bond with one year remaining to maturity for a price of:

$$P_1 = \frac{100}{\left(1+r_1\right)} = \frac{100}{(1.1382)} = \$87.86$$

If, on the other hand, one-year interest rates rose to 12.18 percent, the manager could expect to sell the bond with one year remaining to maturity for:

$$P_1 = \frac{100}{\left(1+r_1\right)} = \frac{100}{(1.1218)} = \$89.14$$

In these equations, r_1 stands for the two possible one-year rates that might arise one year into the future.[4] That is:

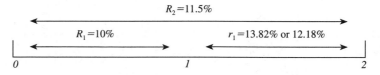

Assume the manager believes that one-year rates (r_1) one year from today will be 13.82 percent or 12.18 percent with an equal probability. This means that the expected one-year rate one year from today would be:

$$[E(r_1)] = .5\,(.1382) + .5\,(.1218) = .13 = 13\%$$

Thus, the expected price, if the bond has to be sold at the end of the first year is,[5]

$$E(P_1) = \frac{100}{(1.13)} = \$88.5$$

Assume that the FI manager wants to ensure that the bond sale produces at least $88.5 per $100, or else the FI has to find alternative and very costly sources of liquidity. For example, banks having to borrow from the central bank's discount window incur the direct and indirect penalty costs involved.

One way for the bank to ensure that it receives at least $88.5 on selling the bond at the end of year is to buy a put option on the bond at time 0 with an exercise price of $88.5 at time 1. If the bond is trading below $88.5 at the end the year, say, at $87.86, the FI can exercise its option and put the bond back to the writer of the option who would have to pay the FI $88.5. If, however, the bond is trading above the $88.5 level, say, at $89.14, the FI does not have to exercise its option and instead can sell the bond in the open market for $89.14.

What premium should the FI manager pay for buying this put option or bond insurance at time 1? To calculate this, look at Figure 19–9, which shows the possible paths of the zero-coupon bond's price from purchase to maturity over the two-year period.[6] The FI manager purchased the bond at $80.45 with two years to maturity. Given expectations of rising rates, there is a 50 percent probability that the bond with one year left to maturity would trade at $87.86 and a 50 percent probability that it would trade at $89.14. Note that between $t = 1$ or one year left to maturity, and maturity $(t = 2)$, there must be a pull to par on the bond; that is, all paths must lead to a price of $100 on maturity.

Figure 19–9 shows the binomial tree or lattice. We show the value of the option in Figure 19–10.

---

[4]Note that if one-year bond rates next year equaled the one-year bond rate this year, $R_1 = r_1 = 10$ percent, then the bond could be sold for $P_1 = \$90.91$.

[5]Note that the interest rates assumed in this example are consistent with arbitrage-free pricing under current term structure conditions. (See T. S.Y. Ho and S. B. Lee, "Term Structure Movements and Pricing Interest Rate Contingent Claims," *Journal of Finance* 61, 1986, pp. 1001–1029.) That is, the expectations theory of interest rates implies that the following relationship must hold:

$$(1+R_2)^2 = (1+R_1) \cdot (1+E(r_1))$$

As you can easily see when the interest rates from our example are inserted, $R_1 = 10\%$, $R_2 = 11.5\%$, $E(r_1) = 13\%$, this equation holds.

[6]This example is based on R. Litterman and T. Iben, "Corporate Bond Valuation and the Term Structure of Credit Spreads," *Journal of Portfolio Management,* 1989, pp. 52–64.

FIGURE 19–9

Binomial model of bond prices: Two-year zero-coupon bond

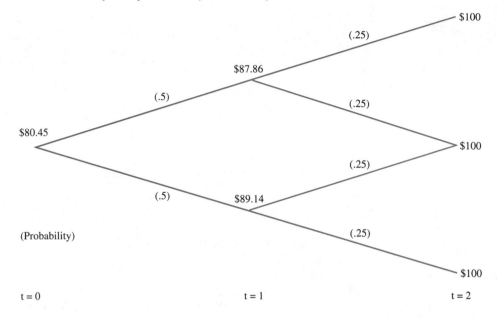

t = 0	t = 1	t = 2

The option in Figure 19–10 can only be exercised at the end of year 1 ($t = 1$). If the zero-coupon bond with one year left to maturity trades at $87.86, the option is worth $88.5 − $87.86 in time 1 dollars, or $0.64. If the bond were trading at $89.14, the option would have no value since the bond could be sold at a higher value than the exercise price of $88.5 on the open market. This suggests that in time 1 dollars the option is worth:

$$.5\,(0.64) + .5\,(0) = \$0.32$$

However, the FI is evaluating the option and paying the put premium at time $t = 0$; that is, one year before the date when the option might be exercised. Thus, the fair value of the put premium (P) the FI manager should be willing to pay is the discounted present value of the expected payoff from buying the option. Since one-year interest rates (R_1) are currently 10 percent, this implies:

$$P = \frac{\$0.32}{1 + R_1} = \frac{\$0.32}{(1.1)} = \$0.29$$

or approximately 29 cents per $100 bond option purchased.

Further, as you can easily see, the option becomes increasingly valuable as the variability of interest rates increases. Conceptually, the branches of the binomial tree diagram become more widely dispersed as variability increases. For example, suppose one-year interest rates on the upper branch were expected to be 14.82 percent instead of 13.82 percent. Then, the price on a one-year, zero-coupon bond associated with a one-year yield of 14.82 percent is $87.09 and the value of the put option with the same exercise price of $88.5 is

$$P = \frac{.5\,(1.41) + .5\,(0)}{1.1}$$

$$= 64 \text{ cents.}$$

FIGURE 19–10

The value of a put option on the two-year zero-coupon bond

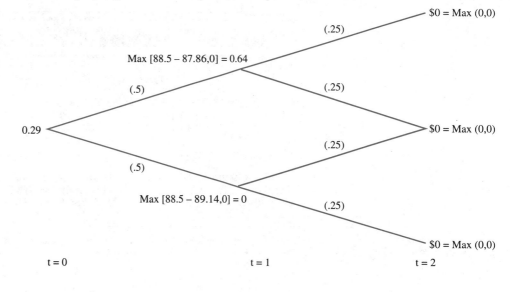

Thus, the familiar result from option pricing theory holds

$$\frac{\delta P}{\delta \sigma} > 0$$

That is, the value of the put option increases with the increases in underlying variance of asset returns.

Concept Question

1. Calculate the value of the option in the previous example if the exercise price (*X*) = $88.

Actual Bond Options

We have presented a simple example of how FIs might use bond options to hedge exposure to liability withdrawal and forced liquidation of assets in a world of interest rate variability. In actuality, FIs have a wide variety of over-the-counter (OTC) and exchange traded options available. In Figure 19–11, we show exchange traded interest rate options on the Chicago Options Exchange (CBOE).

As you can see from this figure, there is one interest rate put option on long interest rates. The April 1993 put option on long-term rates with an exercise (or strike) price of 60 was trading at a premium of 7/16ths. However, both the volume of put option trading and open interest are very small. This is not because interest rate or bond options aren't used, although the **open interest** is relatively small, but rather because the preferred method of hedging is an option on an interest rate futures contract. See these **futures options** on bonds in Figure 19–12. Bond or interest rate futures options are generally preferred to options on the underlying bond because they

Open Interest
The outstanding stock of put or call contracts.

Futures Option
An options contract that when exercised results in the delivery of a futures contract as the underlying asset.

FIGURE 19–11

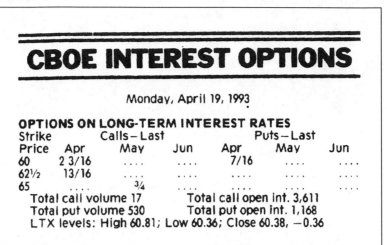

CBOE INTEREST OPTIONS

Monday, April 19, 1993

OPTIONS ON LONG-TERM INTEREST RATES

Strike	Calls–Last			Puts–Last		
Price	Apr	May	Jun	Apr	May	Jun
60	2 3/16	....	....	7/16	....	....
62½	13/16	....	....	....	....	....
65	....	¾	....	....	....	....

Total call volume 17   Total call open int. 3,611
Total put volume 530   Total put open int. 1,168
LTX levels: High 60.81; Low 60.36; Close 60.38, −0.36

combine the favorable liquidity, credit risk, homogeneity, and marking-to-market features of futures with the same asymmetric payoff functions as regular puts and calls (see Chapter 18).

Specifically, when the FI hedges by buying put options on futures, if interest rates rise and bond prices fall, the exercise of the put results in the FI delivering a futures contract to the writer at an exercise price higher than the cost of the bond future currently trading on the futures exchange. The futures price itself reflects the price of the underlying deliverable bond such as a 20-year, 8 percent coupon T bond; see Figure 19–12. As a result, a profit on futures options may be made to offset the loss on the market value of bonds held directly in the FI's portfolio. If interest rates fall while bond and futures prices rise, the buyer of the futures option will not exercise the put and the losses on the futures put option are limited to the put premium. Thus, if the FI had bought one May 1993 T bond futures put option at a strike price of $108, the most it could have lost is 1/64th (0.01 as shown in Figure 19–12) times $100,000 or $1,562.50. Offsetting these losses, however, would be an increase in the market value of the FI's underlying bond portfolio. Unlike futures positions in Chapter 18, a net upside profit potential remains when interest rates fall and FIs use put options on futures to hedge interest rate risk.

Using Options to Hedge the Interest Rate Risk of the Balance Sheet

Our previous simple example shows how a bond option could hedge the interest rate risk on an underlying bond position in the asset portfolio. Next, we determine if an option position can hedge the interest rate risk of the balance sheet; that is, macro-hedging rather than microhedging. As with futures, the use of hedge accounting by regulators and hedging selectivity—the need and desire to bear some interest risk for return on equity reasons—favors microhedging over macrohedging.

FIGURE 19–12

FUTURES OPTIONS PRICES

INTEREST RATE

T-BONDS (CBT)
$100,000; points and 64ths of 100%

Strike	Calls—Settle			Puts—Settle		
Price	May	Jun	Sep	May	Jun	Sep
108	4-30	4-37	4-16	0-01	0-07	1-04
110	2-31	2-54	2-62	0-01	0-23	1-49
112	0-46	1-30	1-61	0-14	0-62	2-46
114	0-04	0-38	1-12	1-38	2-08	3-61
116	0-01	0-12	0-45	....	3-46	....
118	....	0-02	0-26	5-33	7-06	

Est. vol. 60,000;
Fri vol. 68,119 calls; 54,566 puts
Op. int. Fri 329,642 calls; 314,362 puts

T-NOTES (CBT)
$100,000; points and 64ths of 100%

Strike	Calls—Settle			Puts—Settle		
Price	May	Jun	Sep	May	Jun	Sep
110	2-50	2-57	2-39	0-01	0-08	1-12
111	1-52	2-04	2-01	0-02	0-18	1-38
112	0-56	1-22	1-33	0-06	0-36	2-05
113	0-16	0-50	1-07	0-30	1-00	2-42
114	0-02	0-26	0-51	....	1-40	3-21
115	0-01	0-11	0-34	....	2-25	....

Est. vol. 20,000;
Fri vol. 11,823 calls; 9,775 puts
Op. int. Fri 98,206 calls; 126,523 puts

MUNICIPAL BOND INDEX (CBT)
$100,000; pts. & 64ths of 100%

Strike	Calls—Settle			Puts—Settle		
Price	Jun	Sep	Dec	Jun	Sep	Dec
98	3-11	....	....	0-13	....	....
99	2-22	....	....	0-25	....	....
100	1-39	....	....	0-42	....	....
101	0-63	....	....	1-02	....	....
102	0-31	....	....	....	....	....
103	0-10	....	....	....	....	....

Est. vol. 50;
Fri vol. 5 calls; 0 puts
Op. int. Fri 3,288 calls; 5,261 puts

5 YR TREAS NOTES (CBT)
$100,000; points and 64ths of 100%

Strike	Calls—Settle			Puts—Settle		
Price	May	Jun	Sep	May	Jun	Sep
11000	1-42	1-47	1-29	0-01	0-07	....
11050	1-10	1-20	1-11	0-01	0-11	1-07
11100	0-44	0-59	0-60	0-03	0-18	1-24
11150	0-18	0-40	0-47	0-08	0-31	....
11200	0-05	0-25	0-36	....	0-47	....
11250	....	0-14				

Est. vol. 1,800;
Fri vol. 784 calls; 2,361 puts
Op. int. Fri 42,407 calls; 67,854 puts

EURODOLLAR (CME)
$ million; pts. of 100%

Strike	Calls—Settle			Puts—Settle		
Price	Jun	Sep	Dec	Jun	Sep	Dec
9625	0.52	0.45	0.26	.0004	0.03	0.21
9650	0.28	0.25	0.14	0.01	0.08	0.34
9675	0.06	0.09	0.06	0.04	0.17	0.50
9700	0.01	0.02	0.03	0.24	0.35	0.72
9725	.0004	.0004	0.02	0.48	0.58	0.96
9750	.0004	.0004	0.01	0.73	....	....

Est. vol. 28,094;
Fri vol. 35,088 calls; 24,509 puts
Op. int. Fri 528,092 calls; 538,843 puts

LIBOR — 1 Mo. (CME)
$3 million; pts. of 100%

Strike	Calls—Settle			Puts—Settle		
Price	Apr	May	Jun	Apr	May	Jun
9625	0.56	0.58	0.57	.0004	.0004	.0004
9650	0.31	0.33	0.33	.0004	.0004	0.01
9675	0.06	0.08	0.09	.0004	0.01	0.02
9700	.0004	0.00	0.01	0.19	0.17	0.19
9725	....	....	.0004	....	....	....
9750	....	....	....	....	....	....

Est. vol. 0;
Fri vol. 295 calls; 500 puts
Op. int. Fri 4,896 calls; 1,978 puts

TREASURY BILLS (CME)
$1 million; pts. of 100%

Strike	Calls—Settle			Puts—Settle		
Price	Jun	Sep	Dec	Jun	Sep	Dec
9650	0.60	0.53	0.39	.0004	0.03	0.12
9675	0.35	0.31	0.21	.0004	0.05	0.19
9700	0.11	0.13	....	0.01	0.12	....
9725	0.01	0.04	....	0.16	0.28	....

Est. vol. 60;
Fri vol. 20 calls; 1 puts
Op. int. Fri 508 calls; 1,143 puts

EURODOLLAR (LIFFE)
$1 million; pts. of 100%

Strike	Calls—Settle			Puts—Settle		
Price	Jun	Sep	Dec	Jun	Sep	Dec
9625	0.52	0.46	0.27	0.00	0.05	0.23
9650	0.27	0.26	0.15	0.00	0.10	0.36
9675	0.06	0.09	0.08	0.04	0.18	0.54
9700	0.01	0.03	0.04	0.24	0.37	0.75
9725	0.00	0.01	0.02	0.48	0.60	0.98
9750	0.00	0.00	0.01	0.73	0.84	1.22

Est. vol. Mon, 0 calls; 0 puts
Op. int. Fri, 2,375 calls; 2,910 puts

LONG GILT (LIFFE)
£50,000; 64ths of 100%

Strike	Calls—Settle			Puts—Settle		
Price	Jun	Sep	....	Jun	Sep	....
103	2-55	2-59	....	0-09	1-03	....
104	2-01	2-18	....	0-19	1-26	....
105	1-19	1-48	....	0-37	1-56	....
106	0-49	1-19	....	1-03	2-27	....
107	0-26	0-61	....	1-44	3-05	....
108	0-12	0-43	....	2-30	3-51	....

Est. vol. Mon, 8,892 calls; 3,794 puts
Op. int. Fri, 38,560 calls; 57,979 puts

SOURCE: *The Wall Street Journal,* April 20, 1993, p. C14. Reprinted by permission of *The Wall Street Journal.*
© 1993 Dow Jones & Company, Inc. All Rights Reserved Worldwide.

FIGURE 19–13

*Buying put options on the bank's stocks to hedge the interest rate gap risk
exposure of the bank*

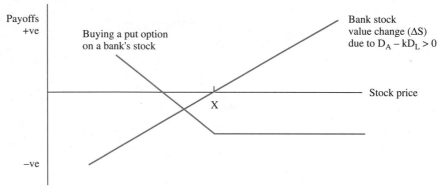

In Chapter 6 we showed that an FI's net worth exposure to an interest rate shock could be represented as:

$$\Delta E = -\left(D_A - kD_L \right) \cdot A \cdot \frac{\Delta R}{1 + R}$$

where

$$\Delta E = \text{Change in the FI's net worth}$$

$$\left(D_A - kD_L \right) = \text{FI's duration gap}$$

$$A = \text{Size of the FI's assets}$$

$$\frac{\Delta R}{1 + R} = \text{Size of the interest rate shock}$$

$$k = \text{FI's leverage ratio} \left(L/A \right)$$

The interest sensitivity of the FI's equity is similar to a bond with a duration of $[D_A - kD_L]$. For example, if $D_A = 2$, $k = .9$, and $D_L = 1.5$, then the behavior of a bank's equity or net worth to interest rate changes should mimic the behavior of a bond of 0.65 years duration. Thus, hedging macro or balance-sheet interest rate risk with bond put options would be a direct expansion of the micro risk management problem; namely, modeling a particular path of interest rates and putting on the appropriate hedge position with put options.

An alternative route—particularly for those FIs whose primary source of risk is interest rate risk—might be to try to hedge the FI's gap or net worth risk via buying options on the FI's underlying stocks. In an efficient capital market, fluctuations in the bank's net worth due to interest rate changes should also be reflected in the value of the bank's common stock, $\Delta E \rightarrow \Delta S$.[7]

---

[7]See, for example, M. J. Flannery and C. M. James, "The Effect of Interest Rate Changes on the Common Stock Returns on Financial Institutions," *Journal of Finance* 39, 1984, pp. 1141–53; and J. Aharony, A. Saunders, and I. Swary, "The Effects of a Shift in Monetary Policy Regime on the Profitability and Risk of Commercial Banks," *Journal of Monetary Economy* 17, 1986, pp. 493–506. See Figure 19–13.

Exchange traded options

Monday, April 19, 1993

Volume, close, net change and open interest of the 1,400 most active equity and 100 most active long-term contracts. Volume figures are unofficial. Open interest is total outstanding for all exchanges and reflects previous trading day. **CB**-Chicago Board Options Exchange. **AM**-American Stock Exchange. **PB**-Philadelphia Stock Exchange. **PC**-Pacific Stock Exchange. **NY**-New York Stock Exchange. a-Underlying stock on primary market. c-Call. p-Put.

MOST ACTIVE CONTRACTS

Option/Strike				Vol	Exch	Last	Net Chg	a-Close	Open Int
Cisco	May	35		85	CB	9	− 5/8	43	105
Cisco	Jul	35		64	CB	9 3/8	− 1	43	258
Cisco	Jul	37 1/2	p	100	CB	1 7/8	+ 3/16	43	1,616
Cisco	May	40		152	CB	4 1/4	− 1	43	435
Cisco	May	40	p	80	PC	1 3/8	+ 1/8	43	2,635
Cisco	May	40	p	672	CB	1 3/16	+ 1/16	43	2,635
Cisco	Jul	42 1/2		70	CB	4 1/2	− 1/2	43	565
Cisco	Jul	42 1/2		298	PC	4 1/8	− 2 1/8	43	565
Cisco	May	45		935	CB	1 13/16	− 7/16	43	9,759
Cisco	May	45	p	271	CB	3 3/4	+ 15/16	43	197
Cisco	Jun	45		115	CB	2 7/16	+ 2 7/16	43	...
Cisco	Jul	45		236	CB	3 3/8	− 5/8	43	806
Cisco	May	50		296	CB	1/2	− 1/4	43	773
Cisco	Jul	50		196	CB	1 9/16	− 9/16	43	4,121
Citicp	May	30		1,723	CB	15/16	− 5/16	29 1/4	7,070
Citicp	May	30	p	621	CB	1 13/16	+ 5/8	29 1/4	1,102
Citicp	Jul	30		136	CB	1 3/4	− 5/16	29 1/4	13,219
Citicp	Jul	30	p	492	CB	2 3/8	+ 5/8	29 1/4	6,025
Citicp	Oct	30		113	CB	2 1/2	− 3/8	29 1/4	6,214
Citicp	Oct	30	p	920	CB	2 7/8	+ 1/8	29 1/4	2,759
Citicp	May	35		789	CB	3/16	...	29 1/4	1,712
Citicp	Jul	35		127	CB	1/2	− 1/16	29 1/4	1,133
Citicp	Oct	35		792	CB	7/8	− 1/4	29 1/4	2,323
ClerCd	May	7 1/2		75	AM	1 5/8	+ 1 1/4	9 1/8	418

SOURCE: *The Wall Street Journal,* April 20, 1993, p. C13. Reprinted by permission of *The Wall Street Journal.* © 1993 Dow Jones & Company, Inc. All Rights Reserved Worldwide.

If interest rates rise, the net worth of the bank and the value of its shares fall below their current levels. That is, equity holders take capital losses on their position in this bank's stock. By buying put options on the bank's stock, equity holders can hedge the risk of adverse increases in rates while enjoying some of the upside net worth gains resulting from falls in the level of interest rates. Of course, this strategy of taking a put position in the bank's own stock options also hedges stock return risk due to adverse changes in other factors that impact stock returns as well, including credit and FX risks. Thus, one would expect a considerable basis risk between the movements of net worth due to gap (interest rate risk exposure) and to movements in the FI's underlying stock price, which may be influenced by factors other than interest rate changes. Consequently, such a hedging strategy may only be a possible substitute for bond options when the bank is particularly prone to interest rate risk. A number of banks have options on their stock; in Figure 19–14, we show the traded options on Citicorp's stock.

FIGURE 19–15

Hedging FX risk by buying a put option on sterling

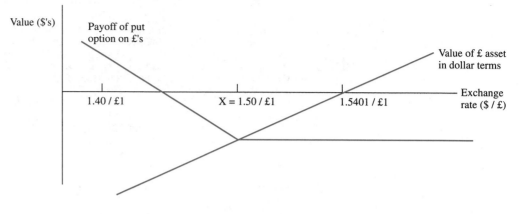

Using Options to Hedge Foreign Exchange Risk

Just as an FI can hedge a long position in bonds against interest rate risk through bond options or futures options on bonds, a similar opportunity is available to micro-hedge long or short positions in a foreign currency asset against foreign exchange risk.

To see this, suppose that an FI bought or is long in, a sterling asset in April 1993. This sterling asset is a one-month T-bill paying £100 million in May 1993. Since the FI's liabilities are in dollars, it may wish to hedge the FX risk that the pound sterling will depreciate over the forthcoming month. Suppose that if the pound were to fall from the current exchange rate of $1.5401/£1 to a rate less than $1.50/£1, the bank would make a loss on its British T-bill investment when measured in dollar terms. For example, if the pound depreciated from $1.5401/£1 to $1.40/£1—well below an assumed breakeven $1.50/£1—the £100 million asset would be worth only $140 million on maturity instead of the expected $154.01 million when purchased. If the foreign exchange rate depreciation is sufficiently severe, the bank might be unable to meet its dollar liability commitments used to fund the T-bill purchase. To offset this exposure, the bank may buy one month put options on sterling at an exercise price of $1.50/£1. Thus, if the exchange rate does fall to $1.40/£1 at the end of the month, the FI manger can put the £100 million proceeds from the T-bill on maturity to the writer of the option. Then, the bank receives $150 million, instead of the $140 million if the pounds were sold at the open market spot exchange rate at the end of the month. If the pound actually appreciates in value, or does not depreciate below $1.50/£1, the option expires unexercised and the proceeds of the £100 million asset would be realized by the FI manager by a sale of pounds for dollars in the spot foreign exchange market one month into the future. See Figure 19–15.

Note the cost of this one-month hedge and the number of put options required in Figure 19–16, which shows the cost of buying a one-month European option on the British pound on the Philadelphia Options Exchange. As you can see, the premium cost of a May 1993 put option (as of April 19, 1993) was 0.85 cents per pound or ($.0085 per £). Since each contract has a size of £31,250, the dollar premium cost per put contract would be $265.63. If the bank wished to microhedge its whole £100 million position in the sterling assets, it would need to buy:

Currency put options (April 19, 1993)

OPTIONS
PHILADELPHIA EXCHANGE

Option & Underlying	Strike Price	Calls—Last			Puts—Last		
		May	Jun	Sep	May	Jun	Sep
50,000 Australian Dollars-European Style.							
CAD	71	r	r	1.47	r	r	r
50,000 Australian Dollars-cents per unit.							
ADollr.....	68	r	r	r	r	0.10	0.52
71.91	72	0.41	r	r	r	r	r
31,250 British Pound-German Mark cross.							
BPd-GMk	250	1.02	2.40	r	r	r	r
246.49 ..	256	r	0.94	r	r	r	r
31,250 British Pounds-European Style.							
BPound .	155	r	r	r	r	4.10	r
154.01 ..	145	r	r	r	r	0.70	r
31,250 British Pounds-cents per unit.							
BPound .	145	r	r	r	r	0.63	r
154.01 ..	150	r	4.50	r	0.85	2.27	r
154.01 ..	152½	r	r	r	2.03	r	r
154.01 ..	155	1.23	2.08	r	r	r	r

$$\frac{£100,000,000}{£31,250} = 3,200 \text{ contracts (puts)}$$

Thus, the total premium cost of this put position would be $850,000. This is the cost of buying foreign currency risk insurance in the options market against a major fall in the value of the pound.

As with bonds, instead of taking a direct position in an option on the underlying pound asset, the bank could have bought put options on foreign currency futures contracts. A put position in one foreign currency futures contract with expiration in May 1993 and exercise price of $1.50/£ would have cost the bank a premium of $.0068 per pound on April 19, 1993. Since each pound sterling futures option contract is £62,500 in size, the cost would have been $425 per contract. If we ignore the question of basis risk, that is, the imperfect correlation between the dollar/pound exchange rate on the spot and futures on options markets, the optimal number of futures options purchased would be:

$$\frac{£100,000,000}{£62,500} = 1,600 \text{ contracts}$$

with a total premium cost of $680,000.[8] Note the futures option contracts for foreign currencies in Figure 19–17.

---

[8]There are a number of reasons why the cost of the two option positions should differ including differences in basis risk, market liquidity, contract maturity, and the American-style nature of the futures option, which may be exercised before the expiration date versus the European-style nature of the cash option, which may be exercised only on the expiration date.

FIGURE 19–17

Futures options on currencies (April 19, 1993)

CURRENCY

JAPANESE YEN (CME)
12,500,000 yen; cents per 100 yen

Strike Price	Calls—Settle May	Jun	Jly	Puts—Settle May	Jun	Jly
8900	1.46	1.87	....	0.49	0.90	....
8950	1.15	1.58	....	0.68	1.11	....
9000	0.89	1.33	....	0.92	1.36	....
9050	0.68	1.11	1.14	....	....	....
9100	0.52	0.92	....	....	....	....
9150	0.38	....	....	....	....	....

Est. vol. 10,223;
Fri vol. 4,183 calls; 2,917 puts
Op. int. Fri 30,830 calls; 28,354 puts

DEUTSCHEMARK (CME)
125,000 marks; cents per mark

Strike Price	Calls—Settle May	Jun	Jly	Puts—Settle May	Jun	Jly
6100	1.42	1.78	1.71	0.31	0.67	....
6150	1.09	1.48	....	0.48	0.87	1.47
6200	0.80	1.21	1.24	0.69	1.10	1.74
6250	0.56	0.98	1.03	0.95	1.37	....
6300	0.39	0.79	0.87	1.28	1.67	....
6350	0.26	0.62	....	....	2.00	....

Est. vol. 24,931;
Fri vol. 11,656 calls; 15,276 puts
Op. int. Fri 164,102 calls; 125,274 puts

CANADIAN DOLLAR (CME)
100,000 Can.$, cents per Can.$

Strike Price	Calls—Settle May	Jun	Jly	Puts—Settle May	Jun	Jly
7850	1.06	1.23	....	0.09	0.27	....
7900	0.68	0.89	....	0.21	0.42	....
7950	0.37	0.60	....	0.40	0.63	....
8000	0.17	0.39	....	0.70	0.92	....
8050	0.07	0.24	....	....	1.26	....
8100	0.02	0.14	....	....	1.66	....

Est. vol. 209;
Fri vol. 45 calls; 65 puts
Op. int. Fri 3,483 calls; 4,339 puts

BRITISH POUND (CME)
62,500 pounds; cents per pound

Strike Price	Calls—Settle May	Jun	Jly	Puts—Settle May	Jun	Jly
1475	6.30	6.90	....	0.28	0.90	....
1500	4.22	5.10	....	0.68	1.58	2.76
1525	2.52	3.60	3.96	1.48	2.56	....
1550	1.34	2.42	....	2.80	3.88	....
1575	0.64	1.56	2.04	4.60	5.50	....
1600	0.28	0.96	1.42	....	7.38	....

Est. vol. 1,067;
Fri vol. 1,585 calls; 636 puts
Op. int. Fri 15,603 calls; 10,192 puts

SWISS FRANC (CME)
125,000 francs; cents per franc

Strike Price	Calls—Settle May	Jun	Jly	Puts—Settle May	Jun	Jly
6700	1.39	1.86	....	0.46	0.93	....
6750	1.08	1.58	....	0.65	1.15	....
6800	0.82	1.32	....	0.89	1.39	....
6850	0.60	1.09	....	1.17	1.66	....
6900	0.43	0.90	....	1.50	1.97	....
6950	0.30	0.73	....	....	....	....

Est. vol. 2,056;
Fri vol. 1,727 calls; 1,116 puts
Op. int. Fri 10,581 calls; 13,755 puts

U.S. DOLLAR INDEX (FINEX)
1,000 times index

Strike Price	Calls—Settle May	Jun	Jly	Puts—Settle May	Jun	Jly
89	....	....	....	0.23	0.60	....
90	....	....	....	0.48	0.94	....
91	0.92	1.42	....	0.89	1.39	....
92	0.51	0.98	....	1.48	1.94	....
93	0.25	0.65	....	2.22	2.61	....
94	0.11	0.41	....	3.07	3.36	....

Est. vol. 793;
Fri vol. 125 calls; 127 puts
Op. int. Fri 965 calls; 1,498 puts

SOURCE: *The Wall Street Journal,* April 20, 1993. p. C14.
Reprinted by permission of *The Wall Street Journal.*
© 1993 Dow Jones & Company, Inc. All Rights Reserved Worldwide.

Using Options to Hedge Credit Risk

Options also have a potential use in hedging the credit risk of an FI. Although FIs are always likely to be willing to bear some credit risk, as part of the intermediation process (i.e., exploiting their comparative advantage to bear such risk), options may allow them to modify that level of exposure selectively. As we discuss in Chapter 18, the payoff function for a well-diversified loan portfolio has a high degree of systematic risk. In good economic states, the loan portfolio has a payoff close to the aggregate amount of promised interest plus principal on the loan portfolio; that is, loan losses would be small. However, in bad economic states, the loan portfolio is likely to suffer significantly increased credit risk and losses.

In Chapter 18, we stated that an FI could seek an appropriate systematic credit risk hedge by selling index futures, since the market factor underlying movements in the stock index may be correlated with expansionary/recessionary states of the economy. However, even if there is a close correlation between movements in the stock market index and underlying economic states (or low basis risk) while hedging the downside credit risk of the loan portfolio, selling index futures produces potentially negative outcomes in very good economic states. As a result, index options, because of the asymmetric nature of their payoffs, may offer a better credit risk hedging choice than index futures.

In Figure 19–18, we assume the FI manager is buying index put options to hedge the credit risk of a well-diversified loan portfolio. The put option mitigates credit losses on the loan portfolio and can even produce a net profit in bad economic states. In good economic states, the favorable payoff of the loan portfolio is partially offset by the cost of the put premium on the option. However, if constructed correctly, the hedged put option strategy can produce a positive return in the good economic states as well.[9] We show the main put index options potentially available for hedging systematic credit risk in Figure 19–19.

Caps, Floors, and Collars

Cap
A cap is a call option on interest rates often with multiple exercise dates.

Buying a **cap** means buying a call option or a succession of call options on interest rates. Specifically, if interest rates rise above the cap rate, the seller of the cap, which is usually a bank, compensates the buyer, for example, another FI, in return for an up-front premium. As a result, buying an interest rate cap is like buying insurance against an (excessive) increase in interest rates. The exercise dates in a cap agreement can be one or many.

Floor
A floor is a put option on interest rates often with multiple exercise dates.

Buying a **floor** means buying a put option on interest rates. If interest rates fall below the floor rate, the seller of the floor compensate the buyers in return for an up-front premium. As with caps, there can be one or many exercise dates.

Collar
A position taken simultaneously in a cap and a floor.

A **collar** occurs when an FI takes a simultaneous position in a cap and a floor, such as buying a cap and selling a floor. Thus, these three over-the-counter instruments are special cases of options; FI managers use them like bond options and bond futures options to hedge the interest rate risk of FIs' portfolios.[10]

---

[9]For more details on the best strategy, see D. F. Babbel, "Insuring Banks against Systematic Credit Risk," *Journal of Futures Markets*, 9, 1989, pp. 487–506.

[10]Bank for International Settlement (BIS) figures put the aggregate face value amount used internationally at $577 billion in 1991.

FIGURE 19–18

Buying put index options to hedge credit risk

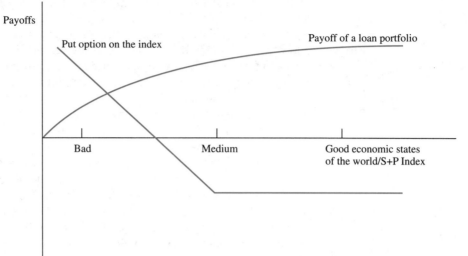

In general, FIs purchase interest rate caps if they are exposed to losses when interest rates rise. Usually this happens if they are funding assets with floating rate liabilities such as notes indexed to LIBOR (or some other cost of funds) and they have fixed rate assets, or they are net long in bonds, or in a macrohedging context, their duration gap is $D_A - kD_L > 0$. By contrast, FIs purchase floors when they have fixed costs of debt and have variable rates (returns) on assets, are net short in bonds, or else $D_A - kD_L < 0$. Finally, FIs purchase collars when they are concerned about excessive volatility of interest rates and to finance cap or floor positions.

Caps

For simplicity let us assume that a bank buys a 9 percent cap at time 0 from another bank with a notional face value of $100 million. In return for paying an upfront premium, the seller of the cap stands ready to compensate the buying bank whenever the interest rate index defined under the agreement is above the 9 percent cap rate on the dates specified under the cap agreement. This effectively converts the cost of the bank's floating-rate liabilities into fixed-rate liabilities. In this example, we assume that the purchasing bank buys a cap at time 0 with cap exercise dates at the end of the first year and end of the second year. That is, the cap has a three year maturity from initiation until the final exercise dates with exercise dates at the end of year 1 and year 2.[11]

Thus, the buyer of the cap would demand two cash payments from the seller of the cap if rates lie above 9 percent at the end of the first year and at the end of the

---

[11]There is no point exercising the option at the end of year 0 (i.e., having three exercise dates) since interest rates for year 0 are set at the beginning of that year and are contractually set throughout. As a result, the bank does not bear interest rate uncertainty until the end of year 0 (i.e., interest uncertainty exists only in years 1 and 2).

FIGURE 19–19

Standard & Poor's 500 index options (April 19, 1993)

S & P 500 INDEX-AM(SPX)

Strike		Vol.	Close	Net Chg.	Open Int.
Jun	30 c	1,350	116	− 2 5/8	550
Jun	30 p	1,350	1/16	...	1,220
Jun	350 p	810	1/8	...	10,514
Jun	375 p	13	1/4	...	8,660
Jun	380 p	77	5/16	+ 1/16	2,185
May	400 c	5	47 3/4	− 1 1/4	32
Jun	400 p	300	3/4	...	19,888
May	410 c	1	39 1/4	− 1/4	28
May	410 p	13	3/8	...	678
Jun	410 p	10	1 3/16	+ 1/16	6,630
May	415 p	605	1/2	...	505
Jun	415 p	2,225	1 9/16	+ 1/8	3,631
May	420 p	3,303	3/4	+ 1/8	9,722
Jun	420 p	787	2 1/8	+ 1/8	11,493
May	425 p	1,330	1	+ 1/8	3,331
Jun	425 p	14,475	2 11/16	+ 3/8	16,453
Jul	425 p	510	4 1/4	+ 4 1/4	...
May	430 c	101	19	− 1 1/4	3,251
May	430 p	4,741	1 1/2	+ 3/16	13,583
Jun	430 c	5	20 3/4	− 1 3/8	2,782
Jun	430 p	911	3 5/8	+ 1/2	7,559
May	435 c	33	14 3/8	− 1/2	1,572
May	435 p	3,401	2 1/4	+ 1/2	7,464
Jun	435 p	6	4 1/8	+ 1/4	10,884
Jul	435 p	75	5 3/4	+ 5 3/4	...
May	440 c	559	10 1/2	− 7/8	6,966
May	440 p	767	3 1/8	+ 1/4	7,057
Jun	440 c	2	12 5/8	− 1 5/8	5,865
Jun	440 p	748	5 1/2	+ 1/2	5,097
Jul	440 p	380	7 3/8	+ 7 3/8	...
May	445 c	453	6 7/8	− 5/8	13,517
May	445 p	1,376	4 7/8	+ 7/8	9,429
Jun	445 c	30	9 3/4	− 1	8,123
Jun	445 p	206	7 1/8	+ 5/8	6,538
Jul	445 p	10	9 1/2	+ 9 1/2	...
May	450 c	2,317	4 1/8	− 1	14,547
May	450 p	3,260	7 1/4	+ 1 3/8	14,458
Jun	450 c	578	6 3/4	− 1 1/8	29,909
Jun	450 p	604	9 1/4	+ 3/4	21,523
Jul	450 p	50	12	+ 12	...
May	455 c	1,106	2	− 7/8	7,096
May	455 p	87	9 7/8	+ 7/8	1,069
Jun	455 c	100	4 5/8	− 7/8	3,266
Jun	455 p	3	12 1/2	+ 1 1/2	821
Jul	455 c	900	6 1/2	+ 6 1/2	...
May	460 c	1,528	1	− 7/16	8,993
May	460 p	40	13 7/8	+ 1 3/8	1,492
Jun	460 c	358	2 7/8	− 5/8	14,793
Jun	460 p	18	15 3/4	+ 1 1/2	171
May	465 c	1,427	7/16	− 3/16	10,176
Jun	465 c	476	1 3/4	− 5/16	1,798
May	470 c	90	1/8	− 1/8	13,204
May	470 p	225	23 3/8	− 1/2	5
Jun	470 c	972	13/16	− 5/16	10,316
May	475 c	210	1/16	− 1/16	6,006
Jun	475 c	20	1/2	− 5/16	5,074
Jul	475 c	1,150	1 1/8	+ 1 1/8	...
Jun	480 c	20	5/16	+ 3/16	4,783

Call vol....... 17,637 Open Int.......387,403
Put vol....... 49,699 Open Int.......490,088

S & P 500 INDEX-PM(NSX)

Strike		Vol.	Close	Net Chg.	Open Int.
Jun	250 c	100	196 1/4	+ 6 1/4	6,403
Jun	250 p	100	1/16	...	12,163
Jun	425 c	5	24 1/2	− 2 1/2	9,338
Jun	425 p	11	2 11/16	+ 5/16	7,739
Jun	500 c	100	1/8	+ 1/16	800
Jun	500 p	100	52 1/2	− 6	800

Call vol.......... 209 Open Int........63,237
Put vol.......... 233 Open Int.......128,746

SOURCE: *The Wall Street Journal,* April 20, 1993, p. C15.
Reprinted by permission of *The Wall Street Journal.*
© 1993 Dow Jones & Company, Inc. All Rights Reserved Worldwide.

FIGURE 19–20

Hypothetical path of interest rates

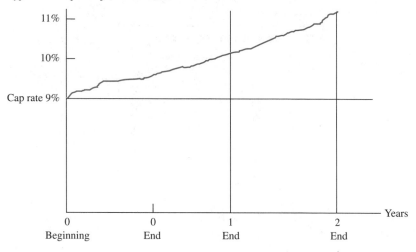

second year on the cap exercise dates. In practice, cap exercise dates usually closely correspond to payment dates on liabilities; for example, coupon dates on floating-rate notes. Consider one possible scenario in Figure 19–20.

In Figure 19–20, the seller of the cap has to pay the buyer of the cap the amount shown in Table 19–1. In this scenario, the cap buying bank would receive $3 million (undiscounted) over the life of the cap to offset any rise in the cost of liability funding or market value losses on its bond/asset portfolio. However, the interest rates in Figure 19–20 are only one possible scenario. Consider the possible path to interest rates in Figure 19–21.

In this interest rate scenario, rates fall below 9 percent at the end of the first year to 8 percent and at the end of the second year to 7 percent on the cap exercise dates. Thus, the cap seller makes no payments. This example makes it clear that buying a cap is similar to buying a call option on interest rates in that when the option expires out of the money because the interest rate is below the cap level, the cap seller makes no payments to the buyer. Conceptually, buying this cap is like buying a complex call option on an interest rate or a put option on a bond price with a single exercise price or interest rate and two exercise dates, the end of year 1 and the end of year 2.

The problem for the FI manager is to calculate the fair value of this 9 percent cap in the face of interest rate uncertainty. In particular, the FI manager does not know whether interest rates will be 10 percent at the end of year 1 or 8 percent. Similarly, the manager does not know whether interest rates will be 11 percent or 7 percent at the end of year 2. Nevertheless, to buy interest rate risk insurance in the form of a cap, the manager has to pay an upfront fee or premium to the seller of the cap. Next, we solve for the fair value of the cap premium in the framework of the binomial model introduced earlier to calculate the premium on a bond option.[12]

Consider Figure 19–22, the binomial tree for the cap contract entered into at the

---

[12]For more details and examples, see R. C. Stapleton and M. Subrahmanyam, "Interest Rate Caps and Floors," in *Financial Options: From Theory to Practice,* ed. S. Figlewski (Homewood, Ill.: Business One–Irwin, 1990), pp. 220–80.

FIGURE 19–21

Hypothetical path of interest rates

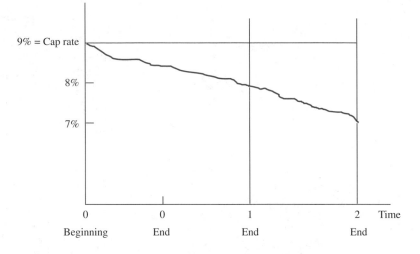

TABLE 19–1 Payments Under the Cap

End of Year	Cap Rate	Actual Interest Rate	Interest Differential	Payment by Seller to Buyer
1	9%	10%	1%	$1 million
2	9%	11%	2%	$2 million
			Total	$3 million

beginning of year 0 and where the cap is exercised at the end of the first and end of the second year.[13] The current (time 0) value of the cap or the fair cap premium would be the sum of the present value of the cap option exercised at the end of year 1 plus the present value of the cap option exercised at the end of year 2:

$$\text{Fair premium} = P = \text{PV of year-1 option} + \text{PV of year-2 option}$$

PV of Year Two Option.   At the end of year 2, there are three possible interest rate scenarios: 11 percent, 9 percent, and 7 percent. With a cap exercise price of 9 percent, and the 9 percent or 7 percent scenarios realized, the cap would have no value to the buyer. In other words, it would expire out of the money. The only interest rate scenario where the cap has exercise value to the buyer at the end of the second year, is if rates rise to 11 percent. With rates at 11 percent, the interest differential would be 11 percent − 9 percent, or 2 percent. But since there is only a 25 percent probability that interest rates will rise to 11 percent at the end of the second year, the expected value of this interest differential is

$$.25 \times 2\% = 0.5\%$$

With a $100 million cap, therefore, the expected cash payment at the end of year

---

[13]Interest rates are normally set at the *beginning* of each period and paid at the *end* of each period.

FIGURE 19–22

Interest rate cap at 9 percent cap rate

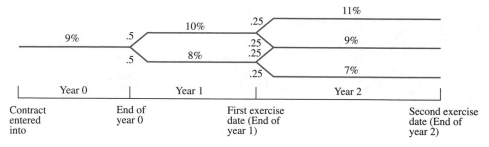

2 would be $0.5 million. However, to calculate the fair value of the cap premium in current dollars, the expected cash flow at end of year 2 has to be discounted back to the present (time 0).

$$PV_2 = \frac{0.5}{(1.09)(1.1)(1.11)} = .3757$$

where 9 percent, 10 percent, and 11 percent are the appropriate one-year discount rates for payments in years 0, 1, and 2. Thus, the fair present value of the option at the end of year 2 is .3757 or $375,700, given the $100 million face value of the cap.

PV of Year One Option.   We can also derive the present value of the option exercised at the end of the first year. At the end of year 1, there are two interest rate scenarios: Interest rates could rise to 10 percent or fall to 8 percent. If rates fall to 8 percent, the 9 percent cap has no value to the buyer. However, if rates rise to 10 percent, this results in a positive interest differential of 1 percent at the end of year 1. However, the expected interest differential is only .5 of 1 percent since this is the probability that rates will rise from 9 percent to 10 percent between the beginning of year 0 and end of year 1:

$$.5 \times 1\% = 0.5\%$$

In dollar terms, with a $100 million cap, the expected value of the cap at the end of year 1 is $0.5 million. To evaluate the time 0 or present value of a cap exercised at the end of time period 1, this expected cash flow has to be discounted back to the beginning of time 0 using the appropriate one-year discount rates. That is,

$$PV_1 = \frac{0.5}{(1.09)(1.1)} = .417$$

or $417,000, given the $100 million face value of the cap. As a result, the fair value of the premium the bank should be willing to pay for this cap is

$$\text{Cap premium} = PV_1 + PV_2$$

$$= \$417,000 + \$375,700$$

$$= \$792,700$$

That is, under the interest rate scenarios implied by this simple binomial model, the bank should pay no more than $792,700 or 0.792 percent of notional face value in buying the cap from the seller.

FIGURE 19–23

A 4 percent floor

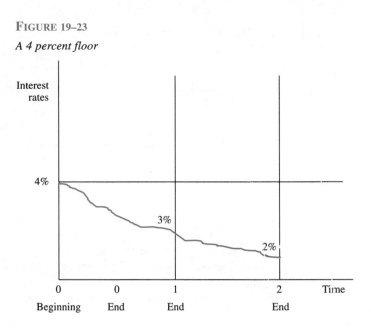

Concept Questions

1. Suppose in the previous example that in year 2 the highest and lowest rates were 12 percent and 6 percent instead of 11 percent and 7 percent. Calculate the fair premium on the cap.
2. What is the value of the cap if the highest interest rate over the next two years is expected to be 8.5 percent?

Floors

A floor is the direct opposite of a cap; it is a put option or a collection of put options on interest rates. Here, the FI manager who buys a floor is concerned about falling interest rates. Perhaps the FI is funding liabilities at fixed rates and has floating rate assets, or maybe it is short in some bond position and will lose if it has to cover the position with higher-priced bonds after interest rates fall. In a macrohedging sense, the FI could face a duration gap where the duration of assets is less than the adjusted duration of liabilities ($D_A - kD_L < 0$). For an example of the payoff from buying a floor, see Figure 19–23.

In this simple example, the floor is set at 4 percent and the buyer pays an upfront premium to the seller of the floor. While caps can be viewed as buying a complex call option on interest rates, a floor can be viewed as buying a complex put option on interest rates. In our example, the floor has two exercise dates, the end of year 1 and the end of year 2.

If the interest scenario in Figure 19–23 was the actual interest rate path followed, then the payments from the seller to the buyer would be as shown in Table 19–2. However, since the buyer of the cap is uncertain about the true path of interest rates—rates could rise and not fall—such profits are only probabilistic. That is, the buyer would have to use a model similar to the binomial model for caps to calculate the fair upfront premium to be paid for the floor at time 0.

TABLE 19–2 Hypothetical Floor Payments

End of Year	Cap Rate	Actual Interest Rate	Interest Differential	Payment by Seller to Buyer
1	4%	3%	1%	$1 million
2	4%	2%	2%	$2 million
			Total	$3 million

Concept Question

1. Assume two exercise dates at end of year 1 and end of year 2. Suppose the bank buys a floor of 4 percent at time 0. The binomial tree suggests that rates at the end of year 1 could be 3 percent ($p = .5$) or 5 percent ($p = .5$) and at the end of year 2, rates could be 2 percent ($p = .25$), 4 percent ($p = .5$) or 6 percent ($p = .25$). Calculate the fair value of the floor premium.

Collars

Financial institutions whose managers are very risk averse and overly concerned about the exposure of their portfolios to increased interest rate volatility may seek to protect themselves against such increases. One method of hedging such risk is through buying a cap and a floor together. This is usually called a collar. In Figure 19–24, we illustrate the essential risk-protection features of a collar when an FI buys a 9 percent cap and a 4 percent floor.

The shaded areas in Figure 19–24 show the interest rate payment regions (> 9 percent or < 4 percent) where the cap or floor is in the money and the buyer potentially receives either a cap or floor payment from the seller. If interest rates fall in the range of 4 through 9 percent, the buyer of the collar receives no compensation from the seller. In addition, the buyer has to pay two upfront premiums, one for the cap and one for the floor to the cap and floor sellers. As is clear, buying a collar is similar to simultaneously buying a complex put and call bond option, or straddle.

An alternative and more common use of a collar is to finance the cost of purchasing a cap. In our earlier example of the $100 million cap, the fair cap premium was $792,000 or 0.792 percent of the notional face value of the cap. That is, the cost (C) of the cap was:

$$C = NV_c \times pc$$

$$= \$100 \text{ million} \times .00792$$

$$= \$792,000$$

To purchase the cap, the bank has to pay this premium to the cap seller in upfront dollars.

Many large banks more exposed to rising interest rates than falling interest rates—perhaps because they are heavily reliant on interest sensitive sources of liabilities—seek to finance a cap by selling a floor at the same time.[14] In so doing, they

---

[14]In this context, the sale of the floor is like the sale of any revenue-generating product.

FIGURE 19–24

Payoffs from a collar

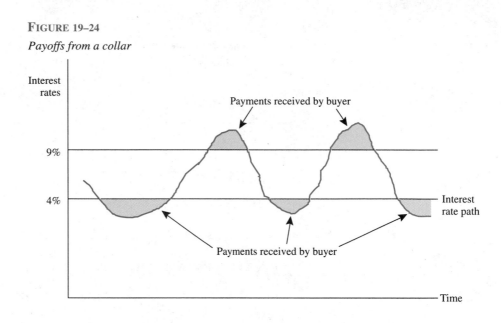

generate upfront revenues; this floor premium can finance the cost of the cap purchase or the cap premium. Nevertheless, they give up potential profits should rates fall rather than rise. Indeed, when rates fall, the floor is more likely to be triggered and the bank would have to compensate the buyer of the floor.

After a bank buys a cap and sells a floor, its net cost of the cap is:[15]

$$C = (NV_c \times pc) - (NV_f \times pf)$$

$$C = \text{Cost of cap} - \text{Revenue on floor}$$

where

$$NV_f = \text{Notional principal of the floor}$$

$$pf = \text{Premium rate on the floor}$$

Suppose that while buying the cap, the bank sold a two-year $100 million notional face value floor at a premium of .75 percent. The net upfront cost of purchasing the cap is reduced to:

$$C = (\$100 \text{ million} \times .00792) - (\$100 \text{ million} \times .0075) = \$42,000$$

Note that if the bank is willing to raise the floor exercise interest rate and thereby expose itself to increasing risk if rates fall, it can generate higher premiums on the floor it sells. Like any option, as the exercise price or rate moves from being out of the money when current rates are above the floor to being in the money when current rates are below the floor, the floor buyer would be willing to pay a higher premium to the writer (the bank). Given this, the buyer of the cap could set the floor rate with notional face values of $100 million each so that the floor premiums earned by the FI just equal the cap premium paid:

---

[15]See K. C. Brown and D. J. Smith, "Recent Innovations in Interest Rate Risk Management and the Reintermediation of Commercial Banking," *Financial Management* 17, 1988, pp. 45–58.

FIGURE 19–25

In-the-money floor and out-of-the-money cap

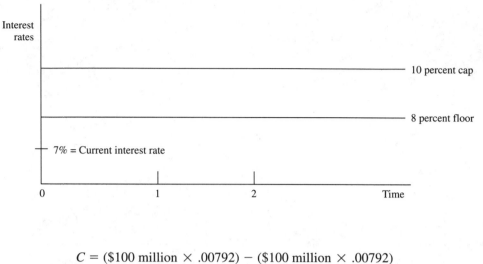

$$C = (\$100 \text{ million} \times .00792) - (\$100 \text{ million} \times .00792)$$
$$\text{cap cost} \qquad\qquad\qquad \text{floor revenue}$$

$$C = 0$$

When $pc = pf$, the cap buyer-floor seller can reduce the cap's net cost of purchase to zero. Indeed, if the cap buyer bought a very out-of-the-money cap and sold a very in-the-money floor, as shown in Figure 19–25, the net cost of the cap purchase could actually be negative. In recent years, FIs have offered a number of cap-floor innovations as financial products to customers.

In Figure 19–25, the current interest rate is 7 percent while the cap rate is 10 percent. Thus, rates would have to rise at least 3 percent for the cap buyer to receive a payment at the end of year 1. By contrast, the 8 percent floor is already 1 percent above the current 7 percent rate. If rates stay the way they are until the end of year 1, the bank seller of the floor is already exposed to a 1 percent notional face value loss in writing the floor.

If the out-of-the-money cap can be bought at a premium of .792 percent but the in-the-money floor is sold at a premium of .95 percent, then the (net) cost of the cap purchase is:

$$C = (NV_c \times pc) - (NV_f \times pf)$$

$$= \$792,000 - \$950,000$$

$$= -\$158,000$$

Raising the floor exercise rate and, thus, the floor premium can also be combined with mismatching the notional principal amounts of the cap and the floor to produce a zero-net cost financing for the cap. That is, there is no reason why both the floor and cap agreements have to be written against the same notional face values ($NV_c = NV_f = \$100$ million).

Suppose the out-of-the-money cap can be bought at a premium of .792 percent and the in-the-money floor sold at a .95 percent premium. An FI manager might want to know what notional principal on the floor or contract size is necessary to finance a $100 million cap purchase at zero net upfront cost. That is:

$$C = (NV_c \times pc) - (NV_f \times pf) = 0$$

$$(\$100 \text{ million} \times .00792) - (NV_f \times .0095) = 0$$

Solving for NV_f

$$NV_f = \frac{(\$100 \text{ million} \times .00792)}{.0095} = \frac{(NV_c \times pc)}{pf}$$

$$= \$83.37 \text{ million}$$

Clearly, the higher premium rate on the floor requires a lower notional face value floor amount to generate sufficient premium income upfront to finance the cap's purchase. In general, to fund fully the cap purchase ($C = 0$), the relationship between premium rates and notional value should be:

$$\frac{NV_f}{NV_c} = \frac{pc}{pf}$$

Concept Question

1. A bank buys a $100 million cap at a premium of .75 percent and sells a floor at .85 percent premium. What size of floor should be sold so that the net cost of the cap purchase is zero?

Caps, Floors, Collars, and Credit Risk

One important feature of buying caps, collars, and floors for hedging purposes is the implied credit risk exposure involved that is absent for exchange traded futures and options. Since these are multiple exercise over-the-counter contracts, the buyer of these instruments faces a degree of counterparty credit risk. To see this, consider the cap example just discussed. Suppose the writer of the cap defaulted on the $1 million due at the end of the first year if interest rates rose to 10 percent. The buyer would not only fail to collect on this in the money option but would also lose a potential payment at the end of year 2. In general, a default in year 1 would mean that the cap buyer would have to find a replacement contract for year 2 (and any succeeding years thereafter) at the cap rate terms or premiums prevailing at the end of year 1, rather than at the beginning of year 0. These cap rates may be far less favorable than under the original cap contract (reflecting the higher interest rate levels of time 1). In addition, the buyer could incur further transaction and contracting costs in replacing the original contract. Because of the often long-term nature of cap agreements, occasionally extending up to 10 years, only FIs that are the most creditworthy are likely to be able to write and run a large cap/floor book without the backing of external guarantees such as standby letters of credit. As we discuss in the next chapter, swaps have similar credit risk exposures due to their long-run contractual nature and their OTC origination.

Summary

In this chapter, we evaluated a wide range of option-type contracts that are available to FI managers to hedge the risk exposures of individual assets, portfolios of assets and the balance sheet gap itself. We illustrated how these options—some of which are exchange traded and some of which are sold OTC—can hedge the interest rate, credit, and FX risks of FIs. In particular, we described how the unique nature of the asymmetric payoff function of option-type contracts often makes them more attractive to FIs over other hedging instruments such as forwards and futures.

Questions and Problems

1. *a.* What two option positions can you undertake to generate positive cash flows in the event that interest rates decline?

   b. How might an FI use the options positions in *(a)* as a hedge? Describe two plausible hedge transactions.

   c. Is the FI indifferent between the two options positions in part *a* to accomplish the hedging goals of part *b*? Why or why not?

2. Suppose that a pension fund manager anticipates the purchase of a 20 year 8% coupon Treasury bond at the end of two years' time. Interest rates are assumed to change only once a year at the end of the year. At that time it is equally probable that interest rates will increase 1% or decrease 1%. The Treasury bond, when purchased in two years, will pay interest semiannually. Currently, the Treasury bond is selling at par.

   a. What is the pension fund managers' interest rate risk exposure?

   b. How can the pension fund manager use options to hedge that interest rate risk exposure?

   c. What are the possible Treasury bond prices at the end of the year? At the end of two years?

   d. If options on $100,000 20 year 8% coupon Treasury bonds (both puts and calls) have a strike price of 101, what will be the possible (intrinsic) values of your options position at the end of one year? At the end of two years?

   e. What is the option premium? (Use an 8% discount factor.)

3. Suppose that an American insurance company issued $10 million of one year zero coupon GICs (Guaranteed Investment Contracts) denominated in deutsche marks at a rate of 5%. The insurance company holds no DM-denominated assets and has neither bought nor sold DM in the foreign exchange market.

   a. What is the insurance company's net exposure in DM?

   b. What is the insurance company's risk exposure to foreign exchange rate fluctuations?

   c. How can the insurance company use futures to hedge the risk exposure in part *b*? How can it use options to hedge?

   d. If the strike price is DM 1.50 per U.S. dollar and the spot price is DM 1.55 per U.S. dollar, what is the intrinsic value (upon expiration) of a call option on DM? What is the intrinsic value (upon expiration) of a DM put option? (Note: DM futures options traded on the Chicago Mercantile Exchange are set at 125,000 DM per contract.)

   e. If the June delivery call option premium is 32 cents per DM and the June delivery put option is 10.7 cents per DM, what is the dollar premium cost per contract? (Assume that today's date is April 15th!)

   f. Why is the call option premium lower than the put option premium?

4. Contrast the use of financial futures options with the use of options on cash instruments in constructing interest rate hedges.

5. A U.S. bank extends a loan commitment for 6.25 million yen to be taken down, with certainty, in 90 days. Today's spot exchange rate is 143.40 yen/$ (quoted as 69.73 or $.006973/yen).

   What is the bank's foreign exchange risk exposure?

6. How can the bank's exchange risk exposure be hedged using futures and options?

7. Using the following information, set up the dollar cash flows paid by the bank in 90 days to honor its loan commitment if the bank takes: *(a)* an unhedged cash position, *(b)* a forward hedged position (use a 90 day forward rate of 70.02), *(c)* two possible options hedged positions. (Calculate the dollar cash flows for all possible exchange rates assuming that the spot exchange rate in 90 days can vary from 135 yen/$ to 155 yen/$ in 5 yen increments.)

   6,250,000 yen – 100ths of a cent

Strike Price		Call	Put
69.73	70	1.40	.15
69.73	73	.40	.97

8. Contrast the forward and options hedges. Compare their relative costs as well as the quality of the hedge.

9. Use the following information to price a collar by

purchasing an in the money cap and writing an out of the money floor. Assume a binomial options pricing model where there is equal probability of interest rates increasing 2 percent or decreasing 2 percent.

Spot rates are 7 percent. The cap rate is 7 percent. The floor rate is 4 percent. The notional value is $1 million. All interest payments are annual payments as a percent of notional value. All payments are made at the end of the year 1 and the end of year 2.

10. Use the following information to price a collar by purchasing an out of the money cap and writing an in the money floor.

Spot rates are 4 percent. The cap rate is 7 percent. The floor rate is 4 percent. The notional value is $1 million. All interest payments are annual payments as a percent of notional value. All payments are made at the end of the year 1 and the end of year 2.

11. Contrast the total cash flows associated with the collar position in question 9 against the collar in question 10. Do the goals of banks that use a collar in question 9 differ from those that put on the collar in question 10? If so, how?

Use the following information to answer questions 12–15.

Rate Sensitivity Report ($ millions)

Maturity	Overnight	1–30 days	31–91 days	92–181 days	>182 days
Assets:					
FF & RP	20				
Loans	0	10	15	80	65
Liabilities:					
FF & RP	50				
Euros	5	25	40	0	60
Deposits					20

Balance Sheet ($ millions)

Assets	Amount $ m	Duration years	Liabilities	Amount $ m	Duration years
Cash	30	0	Core deposits	20	y
FF & RP	20	.01	FF & RP	50	.01
Loans (variable)	105	.97	Euro CDs	130	.97
Loans (fixed)	65	x	Net worth	20	
	220			220	

NOTES TO THE BALANCE SHEET:
Currently the FF and repo (FF & RP) rate is 8.5 percent. Variable rate loans are priced at 4 percent over LIBOR where LIBOR is currently at 11 percent. Fixed rate loans are all 5 year maturities with 12 percent interest, paid annually. Core deposits are all fixed rate for two years, at 8 percent paid annually. Euro CDs are all variable rates.

12. Use the following quote from the financial pages to put on an options hedge for the bank's duration gap position. What is the options hedge position if the bank wants to hedge perfectly its interest rate risk exposure? What is the up front premium cost of the options hedge? (Assume no basis risk. Hint: You must use the solution to questions 6 and 11 at the end of Chapter 15.)

91 day Treasury Bill Futures

Strike Price	Calls-Last	Puts-Last
95.00	52 bp	11bp

13. What is the profit (loss) at expiration per contract on the options hedge in question 12 if all interest rates increase by 50 basis points?

14. Compare the options hedge profit (in question 13) with the futures hedge profit (question 13 in Chapter 15).

15. What alternative options hedges could be used to protect the bank against interest rate risk?

20

SWAPS

Learning Objectives

In this chapter you will learn about swaps and how these OTC instruments can hedge interest rate and FX risks over the long term. Also, many FIs rely on fees from dealing in swaps as both agents and principals. Swaps have special credit risk exposures relative to loans and other OTC instruments such as forward contracts. We explain the way in which each party to a swap manages its credit risk exposure.

Introduction

The market for swaps has grown enormously in recent years. The Bank for International Settlement (BIS) estimates the notional face value of outstanding swaps of all kinds at close to $4 trillion, far greater than the markets for futures, options and caps, floors and collars (see Table 20–1). Commercial banks and investment banks are major participants in the market as counterparties (taking one side of a swap arrangement) or as dealers trading swaps as products. In particular, a dealer can act as an intermediary or third party by putting a swap together and/or creating an OTC secondary market for swaps. This massive growth of the swap market, especially in the 1980s, raised regulatory concerns regarding the credit risk exposures of banks engaging in this market. It was one of the motivations behind the introduction of the 1992 BIS-sponsored risk-based capital adequacy reforms described in Chapter 14.

The four generic types of swaps in order of their quantitative importance, are interest rate swaps, currency swaps, commodity swaps, and equity swaps.[1] While the instrument underlying the swap may change, the basic principle of a swap agreement is the same in that there is a restructuring of asset or liability cash flows in a preferred direction by the transacting parties. Next, we consider the role of the two major generic types of swap—interest rate and currency—in hedging FI risk. We then go on to examine the credit risk characteristics of these instruments and their possible use in hedging and arbitraging credit risk.

Interest Rate Swaps

Interest Rate Swap Basics

By far, the largest segment of the global swap market (more than $3 trillion) is comprised of interest rate swaps. Conceptually, an interest rate swap is a succession of

---

[1]There are also *swaptions*. An option to enter into a swap agreement at some preagreed contract terms (e.g., a fixed rate of 10 percent) at some time in the future in return for the payment of an upfront premium.

TABLE 20–1 Markets for Selected Derivative Instruments
(Notional Principal Amounts Outstanding)

(in billions of U.S. $ equivalent)	1986	1987	1988	1989	1990	1991
Exchange traded*	$ 583	$ 725	$1,300	$1,762	$2,284	$3,518
Interest rate futures	370	488	895	1,201	1,454	2,159
Interest rate options†	146	122	279	387	600	1,072
Currency futures	10	14	12	16	16	18
Currency options†	39	60	48	50	56	59
Stock market index futures	15	18	28	42	70	77
Options on stock						
market indexes†	3	23	38	66	88	132
Over the counter‡	500e	867	1,330	2,402	3,451	4,449
Interest rate swaps§	400e	683	1,010	1,503	2,312	3,065
Currency and cross-currency						
interest rate swaps§	100e	184	320	449	578	807
Other instruments§‖	—	—	—	450	561	577
Memorandum item						
Total international claims of	$4,031	$5,187	$5,540	$6,498	$7,578	$7,497
BIS-reporting banks						

e: estimate

*Excludes options on individual shares and commodity-contract derivatives.

†Calls plus puts.

‡Only data collected by International Swap Dealers Association (ISDA).

§Contracts between ISDA members.

‖ Caps, collars, floors, and swaptions.

SOURCE: Bank for International Settlement, "Recent Developments in International Interbank Relations," October, 1992.

forward contracts on interest rates arranged by two parties.[2] As such, it allows an FI to put in place a long-term hedge sometimes for as long as 15 years. This reduces the need to rollover contracts if reliance had been placed on futures or forward contracts to achieve such long-term hedges.

In a swap, the **swap buyer** agrees to make a number of fixed interest rate payments on periodic settlement dates to the **swap seller.** The seller of the swap, in turn, agrees to make floating rate payments to the buyer of the swap on the same periodic settlement dates. The fixed-rate side—by convention the swap buyer—generally has a comparative advantage in making fixed-rate payments while the floating-rate side—by convention the swap seller—generally has a comparative advantage in making variable or floating-rate payments. In undertaking this transaction, the FI that is the fixed-rate payer is seeking to transform the variable rate nature of its liabilities into fixed-rate liabilities to better match the fixed returns earned on its assets. Meanwhile the FI that is the variable rate payer seeks to turn its fixed-rate liabilities into variable rate liabilities to better match the variable returns on its assets.

To explain the role of a swap transaction in hedging FI interest rate risk, we use a simple example. Consider two FIs, the first is a money center bank that has raised $100 million of its funds by issuing four-year medium-term notes with 10 percent annual fixed coupons rather than relying on short-term deposits to raise funds. See

Swap Buyer
By convention, makes the fixed-rate payments in an interest rate swap transaction.

Swap Seller
By convention, makes the floating-rate payments in an interest rate swap.

---

[2]See, C. W. Smith, C. W. Smithson and D. S. Wilford, *Managing Financial Risk* (Cambridge, Mass.: Ballinger Publishing, 1990). For example, a four-year swap with annual swap dates involves four net cash flows between the parties to a swap. This is essentially similar to arranging four forward contracts: a one-year, two-year, three-year, and four-year contract.

TABLE 20–2   Money Center Bank Balance Sheet

Assets		Liabilities	
C&I loans (rate indexed to LIBOR) =	$100 Million	Medium-term notes (coupons fixed) =	$100 Million

TABLE 20–3   The Savings Bank Balance Sheet

Assets		Liabilities	
Fixed-rate mortgages =	$100 Million	Short-term CDs (one year) =	$100 Million

Table 20–2. On the asset side of its portfolio, the bank makes commercial and industrial (C&I) loans whose rates are indexed to annual changes in the London Interbank Offered Rate (LIBOR). As we discuss in Chapter 8, banks currently index most large commercial and industrial loans to either LIBOR or the federal funds rate in the money market.

As a result of having floating-rate loans and fixed-rate liabilities in its asset-liability structure, the money center bank has a negative duration gap—the duration of its assets is shorter than that of its liabilities.

$$D_A - kD_L < 0$$

One way for the bank to hedge this exposure would be to shorten the duration or interest rate sensitivity of its liabilities by transforming them into short-term floating-rate liabilities that better match the duration characteristics of its asset portfolio. To do this, it can sell an interest rate swap, that is, enter into a swap agreement to make the floating-rate payment side of a swap agreement.

The second party to the swap is a thrift institution (savings bank) that is heavily invested in $100 million worth of fixed-rate residential mortgages of long duration. To finance this residential mortgage portfolio, the savings bank has had to rely on short-term certificates of deposit with an average duration of one year (see Table 20–3). On maturity, these CDs have to be rolled over at the current market rate.

Consequently, the savings bank's asset-liability balance sheet structure is the reverse of the money center bank's, that is:

$$D_A - kD_L > 0$$

The savings bank could hedge its interest rate risk exposure by transforming the short-term floating rate nature of its liabilities into fixed-rate liabilities, which better match the long-term maturity/duration structure of its assets. One way to do this is to buy a swap, that is, take the fixed payment side of a swap agreement.

The opposing balance sheet and interest rate risk exposures of the money center bank and the savings bank provide the necessary conditions for an interest rate swap agreement between the two parties. This swap agreement can be arranged directly between the parties. However, it is likely that an FI—another bank or an investment bank—would act either as a broker or an agent receiving a fee to bring the two

FIGURE 20–1

Fixed floating rate swap

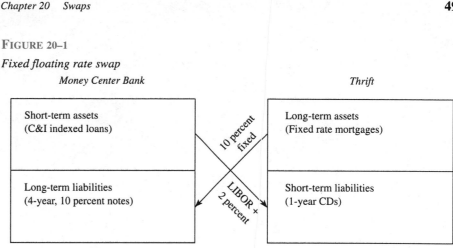

parties together or to intermediate fully by accepting the credit risk exposure and guaranteeing the cash flows underlying the swap contract. By acting as a principal as well as an agent, the FI can add a credit risk premium to the fee. However, the credit risk exposure of a swap to an FI is somewhat less than that on a loan (see later). Conceptually, when a third-party FI fully intermediates the swap, that FI is really entering into two separate swap agreements with the bank and with the savings bank.

Plain Vanilla
Standard agreement without any special features.

For simplicity, we consider a **plain vanilla** fixed-floating rate swap where a third-party intermediary acts as a simple broker or agent by bringing together two banks with opposing interest rate risk exposures to enter into a swap agreement or contract. In this example, the notional value of the swap is $100 million—equal to the assumed size of the money center bank's medium-term note issue—and the maturity of four years is equal to the maturity of the bank's note liabilities. The annual coupon cost of these note liabilities is 10 percent, and the bank's problem is that the variable return on its assets may be insufficient to cover the cost of meeting these coupon payments if market interest rates, and therefore asset returns, *fall*. By comparison, the fixed returns on the thrifts mortgage asset portfolio may be insufficient to cover the interest cost of its CDs should market rates *rise*. As a result, the swap agreement might dictate that the thrift should send fixed payments of 10 percent per annum of the notional $100 million value of the swap to the bank to allow the bank to fully cover the coupon interest payments on its note issue. In return, the bank sends annual payments indexed to one-year LIBOR to help the thrift cover the cost of refinancing its one-year renewable CDs. Suppose that one-year LIBOR is currently 8 percent and the bank agrees to send annual payments at the end of each year equal to one-year LIBOR plus 2 percent to the thrift.[3] We depict this fixed floating rate swap transaction in Figure 20–1.

In analyzing this swap, one has to distinguish between how it should be priced at time 0 (now); that is, how the exchange rate of fixed (10 percent) for floating (LIBOR + 2 percent) is set when the swap agreement is initiated, and the actual realized cash flows on the swap. As we discuss in the next section, *fair pricing* on initiation of the swap depends on the market's expectations of future short-term rates while realized cash flows on the swap depend on the actual market rates (here LIBOR) that materialize over the life of the swap contract.

---

[3]These rates implicitly assume that this is the cheapest way each party can hedge its interest rate exposure. For example, LIBOR + 2 percent is the cheapest way in which the money center bank can transform its fixed-rate liabilities into floating rate.

FIGURE 20–2

Actual path of one-year LIBOR over the four years of the swap agreement

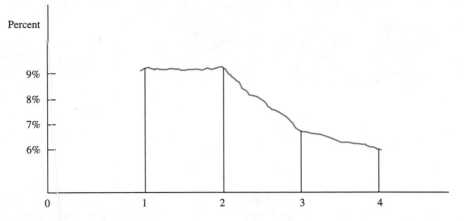

Concept Question

1. Which of the two FIs in the previous example has its liability costs fully hedged and which is only partially hedged? Explain your answer.

Realized Cash Flows on an Interest Rate Swap

We assume that the realized or actual path of interest rates (LIBOR) over the four-year life of the contract would look similar to Figure 20–2. Given this actual path of LIBOR, we can see that at the end of each year's settlement date for the four-year swap the rates would be:

End of Year	LIBOR
1	9%
2	9%
3	7%
4	6%

Money Center Bank Payments to the Savings Bank.   The money center bank's variable payments to the thrift were indexed to these rates by the formula,

$$(\text{LIBOR} + 2\%) \times \$100 \text{ million}$$

Savings Bank Payments to the Money Center Bank.   By contrast, the fixed annual payments the thrift made to the bank were the same each year: 10% × $100 million. We summarize the actual or realized cash flows among the two parties over the four years in Table 20–4. As you can see in the table, the savings bank's net gains from the swap in years 1 and 2 are $1 million per year. The enhanced cash flow offsets the increased cost of refinancing its CDs in a higher interest rate environment; that is, it is hedged against rising rates. By contrast, the bank makes net gains on the swap in years 3 and 4 when rates fall; thus, the bank is hedged against falling rates. The positive cash flow from the swap offsets the decline in the variable returns on

TABLE 20–4   Realized Cash Flows on the Swap Agreement
(in millions)

End of Year	One Year LIBOR	One Year LIBOR + 2 percent	Cash Payment by MCB	Cash Payment by Savings Bank	Net Payment Made by MCB
1	9%	11%	$11	$10	+1
2	9	11	11	10	+1
3	7	9	9	10	−1
4	6	8	8	10	−2
Total			39	40	−1

the money center bank's asset portfolio. Overall, the money center bank made a net dollar gain of $1 million in nominal dollars; its true realized gain would be the present value of this amount.

In effect, the bank has transformed its four-year fixed-rate liability notes into a variable rate liability (a floating-rate swap payment to the savings bank). Meanwhile, the thrift has transformed its variable rate liability of one-year CDs into a fixed-rate liability (a 10 percent fixed-rate swap payment to the bank).

In this example, note that, absent default/credit risk, only the money center bank is really fully hedged. This is because the annual 10 percent payments it receives from the savings bank at the end of each year allows it to meet the promised 10 percent coupon rate payments to its note holders regardless of the return it gets on its variable rate assets. By contrast, the savings bank receives variable rate payments based on LIBOR plus 2 percent. However, it is quite possible that the CD rate the savings bank has to pay on its deposit liabilities doesn't exactly track the LIBOR-indexed payments sent by the bank. That is, the savings bank is subject to basis risk exposure on the swap contract. There are two possible sources of this basis risk: First, CD rates do not exactly match the movements of LIBOR rates over time since the former are determined in the domestic money market and the latter in the overseas Eurodollar market. Second, the credit/default risk premium on the savings bank's CDs may increase over time; thus, the +2 percent add-on to LIBOR may be insufficient to hedge the savings bank's cost of funds. The savings bank might be better hedged if it required the bank to send it floating payments based on U.S. domestic CD rates rather than LIBOR. To do this, the bank would probably require additional compensation since it would then be bearing basis risk. Its asset returns would be sensitive to LIBOR movements while its swap payments were indexed to U.S. CD rates.

Off-Market Swaps
Swaps that have nonstandard terms that require one party to compensate another.

Swaps can always be molded or tailored to the needs of the transacting parties as long as one party is willing to compensate the other party for accepting nonstandard terms or **off-market swap** arrangements—usually in the form of an upfront fee or payments. Relaxing a standardized swap can include special interest rate terms and indexes as well as allowing for varying notional values underlying the swap. For example, in the case we just considered, the notional value of the swap was fixed at $100 million for each of the four annual swap dates. However, swap notional values can be allowed either to decrease or increase over a swap contract's life. This flexibility is useful where one of the parties has heavy investments in mortgages (in our example, the savings bank) and the mortgages are fully amortized. Fully amortized means that the annual and monthly cash flows on the mortgage portfolio reflect repayments of both principal and interest such that the periodic payment is kept constant (see Chapter 21). Fixed-rate mortgages normally have larger payments of interest than principal in the early years, with the interest component falling as mortgages approach maturity. One possibility would be for the savings bank to enter into a mortgage swap to hedge the amortizing nature of the mortgage portfolio or alternatively to allow the notional value of the swap to decline at a rate similar to the decline in the principal component of the mortgage portfolio.[4]

Pricing an Interest Rate Swap

We now discuss fair pricing of the swap at the time the parties enter into the swap agreement. As with much of financial theory, there are important no arbitrage conditions that should hold in setting rates in a fixed-floating rate swap agreement. The most important no arbitrage condition is that the expected present value of the cash flow payments made by the fixed-rate payer, the buyer, should equal the expected present value of the cash flow payments made by the seller:

Expected fixed payment PV = Expected floating payment PV

If this no arbitrage condition doesn't hold, one party usually has to compensate the other with an upfront payment equal to the difference between the two expected present values of the cash flows.

The fixed-rate payment of the swap is usually priced off the newly issued or **on-the-run** yield curve of U.S. Treasury notes and bonds. Thus, if four-year Treasuries are currently yielding 10 percent, then a quote of 10.25 percent (bid) and 10.35 percent (offer) would mean that the commercial or investment bank acting as a swaps dealer is willing to buy or become the fixed-rate payer in a swap agreement at a contractual swap rate of 10.25 percent. It is also willing to take the other side of the swap (become the fixed-rate receiver) if the swap fixed rate is set higher at 10.35 percent. The 10-basis-point spread is the dealer's spread, or the return for intermediating the swap. As discussed earlier, in intermediating the FI has to cover the credit risk assumed in the swap transaction plus cover its costs of search and intermediation as well. In the next subsection, we develop an example of how a swap might be priced.

On-the-run Issues
New issues of Treasury securities.

Pricing a Swap: An Example*

We develop an example of swap pricing under simplified assumptions by applying the no arbitrage condition and pricing swaps off the Treasury yield curve. This provides an understanding of why expected cash flows from the swap agreement can differ from actual or realized cash flows. It also explains why, when yield curves slope upward, the fixed-rate payer (swap buyer) faces an inherent credit risk in any swap contract.

Assume that in a four-year swap agreement the fixed-rate payer makes fixed-rate payments at the end of each year. Also assume that while these payments are made at

---

[4]For further details of nonstandard swaps, see P. A. Abken, "Beyond Plain Vanilla: A Taxonomy of Swaps," Federal Reserve Bank of Atlanta, *Economic Review,* March–April 1991, pp. 21–29.

FIGURE 20–3

T-bond par yield curve

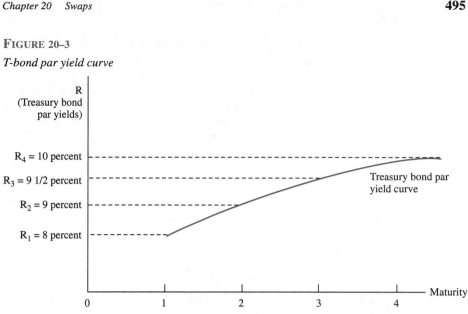

the end of each year, interest rates are determined at the beginning of each year.[5] That is:

Since this is a four-year swap agreement, the fixed-rate payer knows in advance the annual interest rate to pay each year:

$$\overline{R}_1 = \overline{R}_2 = \overline{R}_3 = \overline{R}_4 = \text{fixed}$$

Treasury Par Yield Curve
The yield curve that reflects newly issued bonds whose coupons and yields are the same (i. e., the bonds are priced at par or 100).

Let R be priced off of the current **Treasury** bond **par yield curve** for four-year on-the-run Treasury note issues. See the assumed current par yield curve in Figure 20–3.

Suppose newly issued four-year Treasury bonds are currently yielding 10 percent and that the fixed-rate payments on the swap are set at 10 percent for each of the four years:

$$\overline{R}_i = 10\% \qquad i, = 1, \ldots 4.$$

Here we ignore the usual markup in the swap market over Treasuries for simplicity.

For the no arbitrage condition to hold, the present value of these fixed payments made must equal the expected stream of variable one-year payments received from the floating-rate payer. If we assume that the expectations theory of interest rates holds, we can extract the expected one-year rates (payments) from the Treasury yield curve (see Chapter 8). We wish to determine:

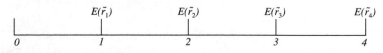

---

[5]This is not always the case.

where $E(\tilde{r}_i)$ are the expected one-year (forward) interest payments to be made at the end of years 1, 2, 3, and 4 respectively.

Extracting these expected one-year forward rates is a little awkward. We begin by extracting the spot or zero-coupon discount bond yield curve from the coupon par yield curve on Treasury bonds; then we derive expected one-year forward rates from this zero-coupon yield curve. The reason we need to extract the zero-coupon discount yield curve is that this yield curve reflects the time value of money for single payments (bonds) at 1 year, 2 years, 3 years, and 4 years' time. Unfortunately, the yield to maturity on a coupon bond is a complex weighted-average of the time value of money discount yields on zero-coupon bonds. Specifically, a yield to maturity on a coupon bond is the internal rate of return on that bond, or the single interest rate (yield) that equates the promised cash flows on the bond to its price. Such a yield is not the same as the time value of money. For example, assuming annual coupon payments, the 10 percent yield to maturity on the four-year T bond is a complex average of the yields to maturity on a one-year, two-year, three-year, and four-year zero-coupon discount bond.

To see this, consider the cash flows on the four-year coupon par value Treasury bond:

$$100 = P_4 = \frac{10}{\left(1 + R_4\right)} + \frac{10}{\left(1 + R_4\right)^2} + \frac{10}{\left(1 + R_4\right)^3} + \frac{110}{\left(1 + R_4\right)^4}$$

and the yield to maturity on this par bond, $R_4 = 10$ percent. Thus:

$$P_4 = \frac{10}{(1.1)} + \frac{10}{(1.1)^2} + \frac{10}{(1.1)^3} + \frac{110}{(1.1)^4} = 100$$

Treasury Strip
A zero-coupon or deep-discount bond.

Conceptually, this coupon bond could be broken down and sold as four separate zero-coupon bonds with one year, two years, three years, and four years to maturity. This is similar to how the U.S. Treasury currently creates zero-coupon bonds through its **Treasury Strips** program.[6] That is,

$$P_4 = \underbrace{\frac{10}{\left(1 + R_4\right)} + \frac{10}{\left(1 + R_4\right)^2} + \frac{10}{\left(1 + R_4\right)^3} + \frac{110}{\left(1 + R_4\right)^4}}_{\text{Coupon bond value}}$$

$$= \underbrace{\frac{10}{\left(1 + d_1\right)} + \frac{10}{\left(1 + d_2\right)^2} + \frac{10}{\left(1 + d_3\right)^3} + \frac{110}{\left(1 + d_4\right)^4}}_{\text{Sum of four separate zero-coupon bond values}}$$

The first relationship is the value of the coupon bond, while the second is the value of four stripped coupon and principal discount bonds of 10, 10, 10, and 110 each sold separately to different investors. The time value of money for single payments in each of the four years, or required discount yields, are d_1, d_2, d_3, d_4. Further, this equation confirms that the yield to maturity on the four-year coupon bond, when sold as a whole bond (R_4), is a complex average of the discount rates on four different

---

[6]Apart from semiannual rather than annual coupon stripping, the other major difference in practice is that final coupon payment of 10 is separated and sold independently from the 100 face value—even though both are paid at the same time and have the same time value of money.

zero-coupon bonds: d_1, d_2, d_3, d_4, where the d_i's are discount yields on single payment bonds of i years to maturity, $i = 1, 2, 3$, and 4:

$$P_1^D = \frac{10}{(1 + d_1)}$$

$$P_2^D = \frac{10}{(1 + d_2)^2}$$

$$P_3^D = \frac{10}{(1 + d_3)^3}$$

$$P_4^D = \frac{110}{(1 + d_4)^4}$$

$$\text{and } P_4 = \sum_{i=1}^{4} P_i^D$$

where the P_i^D represent the market values of the four different stripped or zero-coupon bonds. The no arbitrage condition requires that the values of the four zero-coupon bonds sum to the price of the four-year Treasury coupon bond (P_4) when sold as a whole.

To derive the expected forward one year rates implied by the yield curve, we need to calculate the discount yields themselves, d_1, d_2, d_3, and d_4.

Solving the Discount Yield Curve.* To calculate the discount yields, we use a process of forward iteration. From Figure 20–3, which shows the T bond yield curve, we note that one-year par value coupon Treasury bonds are currently yielding 8 percent:

$$P_1 = \frac{108}{(1 + R_1)} = \frac{108}{1.08} = 100$$

$$R_1 = 8\%$$

Because the one-year coupon bond has exactly one year left to maturity, and thus only one final payment of interest (8) and principal (100), its valuation is exactly the same as a one-year zero-coupon bond with one payment (of 108) at the end of the year. Thus, by definition under no arbitrage:

$$R_1 = d_1 = 8\%$$

Once we have solved for d_1, we can go on to solve for d_2 by forward iteration.

Specifically, from the par coupon yield curve we can see that two-year coupon-bearing bonds are yielding 9 percent:

$$P_2 = \frac{9}{(1 + R_2)} + \frac{109}{(1 + R_2)^2} = \frac{9}{(1.09)} + \frac{109}{(1.09)^2} = 100$$

$$R_2 = 9\%$$

The no arbitrage condition between coupon bonds and zero coupon bonds implies that:

$$P_2 = \frac{9}{(1.09)} + \frac{109}{(1.09)^2} = \frac{9}{(1+d_1)} + \frac{109}{(1+d_2)^2} = 100$$

Since we have solved for $d_1 = 8$ percent we can directly solve for d_2:

$$100 = \frac{9}{(1.08)} + \frac{109}{(1+d_2)^2}$$

$$d_2 = 9.045\%$$

Similarly, we know from the current par T bond yield curve that three-year coupon-bearing bonds are yielding $9\frac{1}{2}$ percent. Also, no arbitrage requires:

$$P_3 = \frac{9\frac{1}{2}}{(1+R_3)} + \frac{9\frac{1}{2}}{(1+R_3)^2} + \frac{109\frac{1}{2}}{(1+R_3)^3} = \frac{9\frac{1}{2}}{(1+d_1)} \frac{9\frac{1}{2}}{(1+d_2)^2} + \frac{109\frac{1}{2}}{(1+d_3)^3} = 100$$

$$R_3 = 9\frac{1}{2}\%$$

To solve for d_3, the yield on a three-year zero-coupon bond, we have

$$100 = \frac{9\frac{1}{2}}{(1.08)} + \frac{9\frac{1}{2}}{(1.09045)^2} + \frac{109\frac{1}{2}}{(1+d_3)^3}$$

Thus, since d_1 and d_2 have already been determined, $d_3 = 9.58$ percent.

Finally, to solve for the discount rate on a four-year zero-coupon bond (d_4), we know:

$$P_4 = 100 = \frac{10}{(1+R_4)} + \frac{10}{(1+R_4)^2} + \frac{10}{(1+R_4)^3} + \frac{110}{(1+R_4)^4}$$

$$= \frac{10}{(1+d_1)} + \frac{10}{(1+d_2)^2} + \frac{10}{(1+d_3)^3} + \frac{110}{(1+d_4)^4}$$

$$R_4 = 10\%$$

To solve for d_4, we have:

$$100 = \frac{10}{(1.08)} + \frac{10}{(1.09045)^2} + \frac{10}{(1.0958)^3} + \frac{110}{(1+d_4)^4}$$

As a result, since d_1, d_2, and d_3 were solved, $d_4 = 10.147$ percent.

In Figure 20–4, we plot the derived zero-coupon discount bond yield curve alongside the coupon par yield curve. As you can see, the derived zero-coupon yield curve slopes upward faster than the coupon bond yield curve. This result is a mathematical relationship and comes from the no arbitrage derivation of the zero-coupon curve from the T bond par yield curve. There is an intuitive explanation for this result as well. Remember that $R_4 = 10$ percent, the yield to maturity or internal rate of return on a four-year coupon bond, can be conceptually viewed as a complex weighted average of the discount rates on four successive one-year zero-coupon bonds (d_1, d_2, d_3, and d_4).

Since R_4 at 10 percent is higher than $d_1 = 8$ percent, $d_2 = 9.045$ percent, and $d_3 = 9.58$ percent, then d_4 (10.147 percent) must be above R_4 (10 percent) if R_4 is to be a weighted-average of the individual zero-coupon discount rates. This same reasoning applies to why $R_3 < d_3$ and $R_2 < d_2$.

Note, however, that if the coupon yield curve were flat, then $R_i = d_i$ for every maturity. If the coupon yield curve were downward sloping, the discount or zero-

FIGURE 20–4

Discount yield curve versus par yield curve

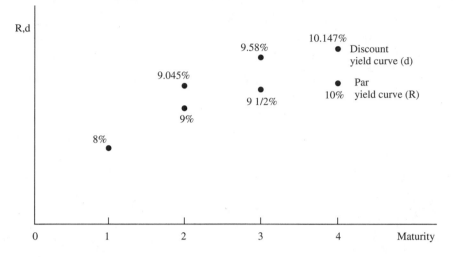

coupon yield curve would lie below the coupon yield curve (for the converse reason used to explain why it must be above when the coupon yield curve is rising). We can now go ahead and solve for the expected one-year floating rates implied by the zero-coupon yield curve.

We are assuming floating interest rate payments are made at the end of each year based on the one-year interest rates that are set at the beginning of each year. We can use the zero-coupon bond yield curve to derive the expected one-year forward rates that reflect the expected floating swap payments at the end of each year.

Concept Question

1. Suppose the par T bond yield curve slopes downward and $R_1 = 12$ percent, $R_2 = 11$ percent, $R_3 = 10$ percent, $R_4 = 9$ percent; derive d_1, d_2, d_3, and d_4.

Solving for the Implied Forward Rates/Floating Payments on a Swap Agreement*

End of Year 1 Payment.   The expected end of year 1 payment $E(r_1)$ must be equal to the current one-year rate set for one-year discount bonds at time 0 since floating rates paid at the end of a period are assumed to depend on rates set or expected at the beginning of that period. That is, the expected first year floating payment equals the current one-year discount rate.

$$E(\tilde{r}_1) = d_1 = 8 \text{ percent}$$

End of Year 2 Payment.   To determine the end of year 2 payment, we need to solve the expected one-year interest rate or forward rate in year 2. This is the rate that reflects expected payments at the end of year 2. We know that no arbitrage requires:[7]

$$\left(1+d_2\right)^2 = \left(1+d_1\right)\left(1+E(\tilde{r}_2)\right)$$

---

[7]Under the pure expectations theory of interest rates.

That is, the yield from holding a two-year zero-coupon bond to maturity must equal the expected yield from holding the current one-year zero-coupon bond to maturity times the expected yield from investing in a new one-year zero-coupon bond in year 2. Rearranging this equation, we have

$$\left(1+E(\tilde{r}_2)\right)=\frac{(1+d_2)^2}{(1+d_1)}$$

Since we have already solved for $d_2 = 9.045$ percent and $d_1 = 8$ percent, we can solve for $E(\tilde{r}_2)$:

$$1+E(\tilde{r}_2)=\frac{(1.09045)^2}{(1.08)}$$

$$E(\tilde{r}_2)=10.1\%$$

End of Year 3 Payment.   In a similar fashion,

$$\left(1+E(\tilde{r}_3)\right)=\frac{(1+d_3)^3}{(1+d_2)^2}$$

Substituting in the d_2 and d_3 values from the zero-coupon bond yield curve we have:

$$1+E(\tilde{r}_3)=\frac{(1.0958)^3}{(1.09045)^2}$$

$$E(\tilde{r}_3)=10.658\%$$

End of Year 4 Payment.   Using the same procedure,

$$1+E(\tilde{r}_4)=\frac{(1+d_4)^4}{(1+d_3)^3}=\frac{(1.10147)^4}{(1.0958)^3}$$

$$E(\tilde{r}_4)=11.866\%$$

These four expected one-year payments by the floating-rate payer are plotted against the fixed-rate payments by the buyer of the swap in Figure 20–5. Although expecting to pay a net payment $(\bar{R} - E(\tilde{r}_1))$ of 2 percent to the floating-rate seller in the first year, the fixed-rate payer expects to receive net payments of 0.1 percent, 0.568 percent and 1.866 percent from the floating rate seller in years 2, 3, and 4. This has important credit risk implications. It implies that when the yield curve is upward sloping, the fixed-rate payer can expect not only to pay more than the floating-rate payer in the early years of a swap agreement but also to receive higher cash flows from the seller or floating-rate payer in the later years of the swap agreement. Thus, the fixed-rate payer faces the risk that should expected rates actually be realized, the floating-rate payer may have an incentive to default toward the end of the swap agreement as a net payer. In this case, the swap buyer might have to replace the swap at less favorable market conditions in the future.[8]

---

[8]This example is based on the discussion in C. W. Smith, C. W. Smithson, and L. M. Wakeman, "The Market for Interest Rate Swaps," *Financial Management* 17, 1988, pp. 34–44.

FIGURE 20–5

Fixed and expected floating swap payments

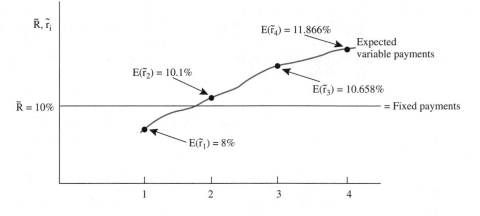

Finally, note that in this section we have been comparing expected cash flows in the swap agreement under no arbitrage conditions. Should the term structure shift after the swap has been entered into, then realized one-year rates (and payments) would not equal expected rates for the floating-rate payer. In our example, if the term structure shifts then:

$$r_2 \neq E(\tilde{r}_2)$$

$$r_3 \neq E(\tilde{r}_3)$$

$$r_4 \neq E(\tilde{r}_4)$$

where r_2, r_3, and r_4, are realized or actual one-year rates on new one-year discount bonds issued in years 2, 3, and 4 respectively. Of course, the floating-rate payer has to make payments on actual or realized rates rather than expected rates as we discussed in the first section of this chapter.

Concept Question

1. The current T bond par yield curve shows $R_1 = 8$ percent, $R_2 = 9$ percent, $R_3 = 10$ percent. Suppose you enter a $100 million three-year swap as the floating-rate paying party. What do you expect to receive over the three years? What do you expect to pay?

Currency Swaps

Just as swaps are long-term contracts that can hedge interest rate risk exposure, they can also be used to hedge currency risk exposures of FIs (see Table 20–1). In the following section, we consider a simple plain vanilla example of how currency swaps can immunize FIs against exchange-rate risk when they mismatch the currencies of their assets and liabilities.

Fixed-Fixed Currency Swaps

Consider a U.S. bank with fixed-rate assets all denominated in dollars. However, it is financing part of its asset portfolio with a £50 million issue of four-year medium-term British pound sterling notes that have a fixed annual coupon of 10 percent. By comparison, there is a U.K. bank that has all its assets denominated in sterling; however, it is partly funding those assets with a $100 million issue of four-year medium-term dollar notes with a fixed annual coupon of 10 percent.

These two banks are exposed to opposing currency risks. The U.S. bank is exposed to the risk that the dollar will depreciate against the pound over the next four years making it more costly to cover the annual coupon interest payments and the principal repayment on its pound-denominated notes. On the other hand, the U.K. bank is exposed to the dollar appreciating against the pound, making it more difficult to cover the dollar coupon and principal payments on its four-year $100 million note issue out of the sterling cash flows on its assets.

One solution to these exposures is for the U.K. and U.S. banks to enter into a currency swap under which the U.K. bank undertakes to send annual payments in pounds to cover the coupon and principal repayments of the U.S. bank's sterling note issue, while the U.S. bank would send annual dollar payments to the U.K. bank to cover the interest and principal payments on its dollar note issue.[9] In so doing, the U.K. bank has transformed fixed-rate dollar liabilities into fixed-rate sterling liabilities that better match the sterling fixed-rate cash flows from its asset portfolio. Similarly, the U.S. bank has transformed fixed-rate sterling liabilities into fixed-rate dollar liabilities that better match the fixed-rate dollar cash flows from its asset portfolio. In undertaking this exchange of cash flows, the two parties normally agree on a fixed-exchange rate for the cash flows at the beginning of the period.[10] In this example, the fixed-exchange rate would be $2/£1. We summarize the currency swap in Figure 20–6 and the realized cash flows in Table 20–5.

In this example, both liabilities bear a fixed 10 percent interest rate. This is not a necessary requirement for the fixed fixed currency swap agreement. For example, suppose that U.S. note coupons were 5 percent per annum while U.K. note coupons were 10 percent. The swap dollar payments of the U.S. bank in Table 20–5 would remain unchanged but the U.K. bank's sterling payments would be reduced by £2.5 million (or $5 million) in each of the four years. This difference could be met either by some upfront payment by the U.K. bank to the U.S. bank reflecting the difference in the present value of the two fixed cashflows, or by annual payments that result in zero net present value differences among the fixed-fixed currency swap participants' payments. Also note that should the exchange rate change from the rate agreed in the swap ($2/£1) either one or the other side would be losing in the sense that a new swap might be entered into at a more favorable exchange rate to one party. Specifically, if the dollar were to appreciate against the pound over the life of the swap, the agreement would become more costly for the U.S. bank. If, however, the dollar depreciated, the U.K. bank would find the agreement increasingly costly over the swap's life.

---

[9] In a currency swap, it is usual to include both principal and interest payments as part of the swap agreement. For interest rate swaps, it is usual to include just interest rate payments. The reason for this is that both principal and interest are exposed to FX risk.

[10] As with interest rate swaps, this exchange rate reflects the contracting parties' expectations as to future exchange rate movements.

FIGURE 20–6

Fixed-fixed pound/dollar currency swap

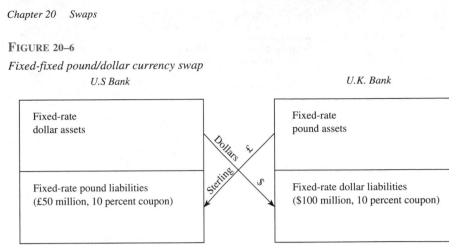

By combining an interest rate swap of the fixed-floating type described earlier with a currency swap, we can also produce a fixed-floating currency swap that is a hybrid of the two plain vanilla swaps we have considered so far.

Concept Question

1. If the net cash flows in the fixed-fixed currency swap in Table 20–5 are zero, why does either bank enter into the swap agreement?

Fixed-Floating Currency Swap

Consider a U.S. bank that holds mostly floating-rate short-term U.S. dollar-denominated assets. It has partly financed this asset portfolio with a £50 million, four-year note issue with fixed 10 percent annual coupons denominated in sterling. By comparison, a U.K. bank with mostly long-term fixed rate assets denominated in sterling has partly financed this portfolio with $100 million short-term dollar-denominated Euro CDs whose rates reflect changes in one-year LIBOR plus a 2 percent premium. As a result, the U.S. bank is faced with both an interest rate risk and a foreign exchange risk. Specifically, if dollar short-term rates fall and the dollar depreciates against the pound, it may face a problem in covering its promised fixed-coupon and principal payments on the pound-denominated note. Consequently, it may wish to transform its fixed-rate, pound-denominated liabilities into variable-rate, dollar-denominated liabilities. The U.K. bank also faces interest rate and foreign exchange rate risk exposure. If U.S. interest rates rise and the dollar appreciates against the pound, the U.K. bank would find it more difficult to cover its promised coupon and principal payments on its dollar-denominated CDs out of the cash flows from its fixed-rate pound asset portfolio. Consequently, it may wish to transform its floating-rate short-term, dollar-denominated liabilities into fixed-rate pound liabilities.

Each bank can achieve its objective of liability transformation by engaging in a fixed-floating currency swap. Each year, the two banks swap payments at some prearranged dollar/pound exchange rate, assumed to be $2/£1. The U.K. bank sends fixed payments in pounds to cover the cost of the U.S. bank's pound note issue, while the U.S. bank sends floating payments in dollars to cover the U.K. bank's floating-rate dollar CD costs.

TABLE 20–5   Cash Flows under the Fixed-Fixed Currency Swap Agreement

	Cash Flow Payments		Payments by U. K. Bank in $s (at $2/£1 Exchange Rate)	Net Cash Flow ($s)
End of Year	U.S. Bank ($s)	U.K. Bank (£s)		
1	$ 10	£ 5	$ 10	0
2	10	5	10	0
3	10	5	10	0
4	110	55	110	0

TABLE 20–6   Fixed-Floating Currency Swap
(in millions)

Year	LIBOR	LIBOR + 2 percent	Floating Rate Payment by U.S. Bank ($s)	Fixed Rate Payment by U. K. Bank		Net Payment by U.S. Bank ($s)
				(£s)	($ at $2/£1)	
1	9%	11%	$ 11	£ 5	$ 10	+$1
2	7	9	9	5	10	−1
3	8	10	10	5	10	0
4	10	12	112	55	110	+2
Total net payment						+$2

Given the realized LIBOR rates in column 2, we show the relevant payments among the contracting parties in Table 20–6. As you can see from Table 20–6, the realized cash flows from the swap result in a net nominal payment of $2 million by the U.S. bank to the U.K. bank, over the life of the swap.

Concept Question

1. Suppose in Table 20–6 that the U.S. bank had agreed to make floating payments of LIBOR + 1 percent instead of LIBOR + 2 percent. What would its net payment have been to the U.K. bank over the four-year swap agreement?

Credit Risk and Swaps

While hedging interest rate risk and FX rate risk have been important reasons for the growth of swaps, FIs have originated a significant number of swaps to arbitrage differences in the pricing of credit risk in the markets for short-term floating-rate and long-term fixed-rate debt. This type of swap—where an FI might be on either side—is generally called a **quality swap.**

Quality Swap
A fixed floating rate swap between two parties of different credit ratings.

Quality Swap

To understand how a quality swap works, let's look at an example. Consider a money center U.S. bank with predominantly interest sensitive, floating-rate, dollar-denominated assets. Because of its good profit and capital adequacy performance, the rating agencies give it an AAA credit rating (the highest possible). Consider a life insurance company with predominantly fixed-rate, long-term dollar assets such as government bonds and mortgages in its portfolio. Because of general concerns about the performance of the insurer and its property portfolio, its debt rating is currently BBB (the bottom of the investment grade rating).

Because the bank has a short duration of assets and the life insurer has a long duration of assets, direct hedging would dictate that the bank borrow short-term in the floating-rate market and the insurance company borrow long-term in the fixed-rate market. The motivation behind the quality swap is that these parties can achieve the same hedging outcome at a cheaper price by borrowing in the wrong market and then entering into a swap. The bank would borrow long-term fixed and the insurer short-term floating; and then they would enter into a swap agreement whereby the insurer sends fixed payments to cover the bank's fixed cost of debt and the bank sends floating-rate payments to cover the insurer's floating cost of debt. The net result of this swap transaction is that the bank has transformed a fixed debt liability into a floating liability that matches the duration structure of its assets. Similarly, the insurer has transformed the floating-rate liability into a fixed-rate liability that better matches the relatively long-term duration of its assets.

The question arises as to how and why borrowing in the wrong market and then swapping payments lowers the costs of funding for both parties over the costs of direct hedging. To understand the rationale for a quality swap, consider the representative cost of funds facing the AAA bank and the BBB insurer in the floating-rate and fixed-rate markets for debt (see Table 20–7).

From Table 20–7 you can see that the high credit quality AAA bank's rate advantage in borrowing in the short-term floating-rate market is only $\frac{1}{2}$ percent compared to its 2 percent advantage in the long-term debt market. While the bank has a borrowing cost advantage over the insurer in both markets, it has the greater *comparative* advantage in the long-term debt market. To exploit this comparative advantage and to generate gains from trade, the bank can borrow in the debt market where its *comparative advantage* is greatest (fixed long-term) and the insurer can borrow in the debt market where its *comparative disadvantage* is least (floating short-term); then, the two can engage in a swap. The net quality spread—the difference between the quality or credit risk spreads in the fixed and floating markets—can then be shared among the bank and the insurer. That is, the **net quality spread** reflects the potential aggregate gains from trade resulting from a quality swap. In the example in Table 20–7, the net quality spared is:

$$\text{Net quality spread} = \text{Spread in fixed-rate market} - $$
$$\text{Spread in floating-rate market} = 2\% - \tfrac{1}{2}\% = 1\tfrac{1}{2}\%$$

That is, the combined debt costs of the participants can theoretically be reduced by $1\frac{1}{2}$ percent. To see how these gains arise and are shared, let's follow each part of the swap transaction in detail.

The Bank. The bank borrows long-term fixed-rate at 10 percent. It then wishes to convert this fixed-rate liability into a floating-rate liability by selling a swap (i.e., being the floating-payment party). It contracts to send floating payments to the insurer equal to LIBOR plus 1 percent, which exactly matches the insurer's cost of debt when borrowing short-term. In return, it receives from the insurer fixed payments equal to 11 percent per annum. These fixed payments exactly match the bank's

Net Quality Spread
The net interest rate spread between rates paid by high-quality borrowers relative to low-quality borrowers in the long-term (fixed) and short-term (floating) rate markets.

TABLE 20–7   Quality Spreads in the Fixed- and Floating-Rate Markets

	Floating-Rate Market	*Fixed-Rate Market*
Insurer (BBB)	LIBOR + 1 percent	12 percent
Bank (AAA)	LIBOR + $\frac{1}{2}$ percent	10 percent
Quality spread	$\frac{1}{2}\%$	2%

Net quality spread = $2\% - \frac{1}{2}\% = 1\frac{1}{2}\%$

10 percent cost of debt plus an additional 1 percent markup payment. As a result, the bank's net cost of funds (shown by a negative sign) is:

1. Direct fixed-rate borrowing cost = −10 percent
2. Fixed-rate payment received from insurer = +11 percent
3. Floating payment to insurer = − (LIBOR + 1 percent)
4. Net payments = −10 percent + 11 percent − (LIBOR + 1 percent) = −LIBOR

As you can see, the post swap cost of funds to the bank is LIBOR. If it had engaged in direct hedging by borrowing in the short-term floating market directly, its cost of funds would have been higher at LIBOR + $\frac{1}{2}$ percent. That is, the quality swap has saved the bank $\frac{1}{2}$ percent in financing costs.

The Insurer.   The insurer borrows short-term floating-rate at LIBOR + 1 percent. It then participates in the quality swap with the bank as the buyer, the fixed-rate payer, to convert its floating-rate liabilities into fixed-rate liabilities. The insurer agrees to send fixed-rate payments to the bank equal to 11 percent and to receive floating-rate payments from the bank equal to LIBOR + 1 percent. As a result, the insurer has transformed its floating-rate debt liabilities into fixed-rate liabilities. The insurer's net cost of funds is

1. Direct floating-rate borrowing cost = −(LIBOR + 1 percent)
2. Floating-rate payment received from the bank = (LIBOR + 1 percent)
3. Fixed rate payment made to bank = −11 percent
4. Net payment = −(LIBOR + 1 percent) + (LIBOR + 1 percent) − 11 percent = −11 percent

As you can see the after-swap cost of funds to the insurer is 11 percent. This compares to the cost of direct hedging in the fixed-rate market by the insurer of 12 percent. That is, the quality swap has saved the insurer 1 percent in debt costs.

The $1\frac{1}{2}$ percent net quality spread is shared between the bank and the insurer, with $\frac{1}{2}$ percent going to the bank and 1 percent to the insurer:

$$
\underset{\text{(Net quality spread)}}{1\frac{1}{2}\%} \quad = \quad \underset{\text{(Debt cost savings bank)}}{\frac{1}{2}\%} \quad + \quad \underset{\substack{\text{(Debt cost} \\ \text{savings insurer)}}}{1\%}
$$

Note that the $1\frac{1}{2}$ percent could be shared between the two parties very differently. In fact, the degree to which the $1\frac{1}{2}$ percent is shared reflects the relative bargaining power of the two parties. The only limitation is that each needs to make some positive gains from entering into the quality swap. As a result, each party's share must be positive for a win-win situation to arise.

Nevertheless, many observers are skeptical about whether the net quality spread reflects a true arbitrage opportunity. Indeed, if this were the case, the market forces of demand and supply would probably eliminate these spread differentials over time. Only gross inefficiencies or barriers to the entry of good credit-rated parties into credit markets and quality swap deals would prevent such an equalizing of fixed-floating spreads.[11] Few believe that credit markets are so inefficient that quality spreads of $1\frac{1}{2}$ percent or more could persist for any length of time, nor that credit risk in each market is so grossly mispriced. One view is that the supposed gains from a quality swap are really illusory and come from ignoring the value of important option features on loans.[12] That is, borrowing fixed directly or borrowing floating and converting these liabilities into fixed via the swap are not the same from an options perspective. This is because a direct fixed-rate borrower (the insurer in our case) always has the option to pay back a fixed-rate loan early; that is, to prepay or put the fixed-rate loan back to the lender should fixed market rates fall. However, the synthetic fixed-rate borrowing created via the quality swap does not provide such an opportunity. This synthetic loan cannot be prepayed. Thus, the 1 percent savings to the insurer may reflect, in part, the sale or give-up of a valuable prepayment (or refinancing) option that exists when fixed-rate borrowing occurs directly.

Concept Questions

1. For AAA borrowers, short-term rates are 10 percent and long-term rates are $10\frac{1}{2}$ percent. For BBB borrowers short-term rates are 11 percent and long-term rates are 13 percent. What is the net quality spread?
2. In a swap, how is the net quality spread shared between the AAA and BBB firms?

Other Credit Risk Concerns

The growth of the OTC swap market was one of the major motivating factors underlying the imposition of the BIS risk-based capital requirements in January 1993 (see Chapter 14). The fear was that in any such long-term OTC contract, the out-of-the-money counterparty would have incentives to default on a swap contract to deter future and current losses. Consequently, the BIS requirements imposed a required capital ratio for banks against their holdings of both interest rate and currency swaps. Many analysts have argued that these new capital requirements will work against the growth of the swap market in the future since they can be viewed as a cost or tax on market participants.

---

[11]This assumes that there are enough good credit parties available. If not, then the good credit parties with AAA ratings have implicit monopoly power. In recent years, only one U.S. banking organization, J. P. Morgan, has consistently been rated AAA.

[12]See Smith, Smithson, and Wakeman, "The Market for Interest Rate Swaps," and Chapter 8.

Not only do regulators have a heightened awareness of credit risk but so do market participants. Both Merrill Lynch and Salomon Brothers are heavy participants as intermediaries in the swap market; for example, they act as counterparty guarantors to both the fixed and floating sides in swaps. To do this successfully and to maintain market share, a high if not the highest credit rating is increasingly required. For example, both Merrill Lynch (in November 1991) and Salomon Brothers (in February 1993) were rated only single As. To achieve AAA ratings, they established separately capitalized subsidiaries in which to conduct their swap business. Merrill Lynch had to invest $350 million and Salomon, $175 million in these swap subsidiaries.

This raises some questions: What exactly is the default risk on swaps? Is it high or low? Is it the same or different from the credit risk on loans? In fact, there are three major differences between the credit risk on swaps and the credit risk on loans. As a result, the credit risk on a swap is generally much less than on a loan. We discuss these differences next.

Netting and Swaps.   One factor that mitigates the credit risk on swaps is the netting of swap payments. On each swap payment date, a fixed payment is made by one party and a floating payment by another. However, in general, each party calculates the net difference between the two payments, and a single payment for the net difference is made by one party to the other. This netting of payments implies that the default exposure of the in-the-money party is limited to the net payment rather than either the total fixed or floating payment. Further, when two parties have large numbers of contracts outstanding against each other, they tend to net across contracts. This process is called netting by novation and further reduces the potential risk of loss if some contracts are in the money and others out of the money to the same counterparty. However, note that netting by novation hasn't been fully tested in all international courts of law. For example, in 1990 a number of U.K. municipal authorities engaged in swaps with U.S. and U.K. banks and investment banks. These municipal authorities, after taking major losses on some swap contracts, defaulted on further payments. The U.K. High Court supported the municipal authorities' right to default by stating that their entering into such swaps had been outside their powers of authority in the first place. This still has not stopped these municipal authorities from seeking to collect on in-the-money swaps.[13]

Payment Flows Are Interest and not Principal.   While currency swaps involve swaps of interest and principal, interest rate swaps involve swaps of interest payments only measured against some notional principal value. This suggests that the default risk on such swaps is less than on a regular loan, where both interest and principal are exposed to credit risk.

Standby Letters of Credit.   In cases where swaps are made between parties of different credit standing, such that one party perceives a significant risk of default by the other party, then the poor-quality credit risk party may be required to buy a standby letter of credit (or another form of performance guarantee) from a third-party

---

[13]Nevertheless, in April 1993 the BIS circulated a draft proposal supporting the bilateral netting of swap contracts in calculating risk-based capital requirements. It is estimated that this will reduce banks capital requirements against swaps by up to 40 percent.

high quality (AAA) FI, such that if default occurs, the standby letter of credit would provide the swap payments in lieu of the defaulting party. Further, increasingly, low-quality counterparties are required to post collateral in lieu of default. This collateral is an incentive mechanism working to deter swap defaults.[14]

---

[14]One solution being considered by market participants (such as the International Association of Swap Dealers) is to use collateral to mark-to-market a swap contract in a similar way in which futures are marked-to-market to prevent credit risk building up over time. Remember, a swap contract is like a succession of forwards. Note that in 1992 a swap futures contract began trading in Chicago; such swap futures are marked-to-market.

Summary

This chapter has evaluated the role of swaps as risk management vehicles for FIs. We analyzed the major types of swaps: interest rate and currency swaps as well as quality swaps that are linked to a supposed credit risk arbitrage. Swaps have special features of long maturity, flexibility, and liquidity that make them attractive alternatives relative to shorter-term hedging vehicles such as futures, forwards, options, and caps discussed in Chapters 18 and 19. However, even though the credit risk of a swap is less than on a loan because of their OTC nature and long maturities, their credit risk is still generally greater than on other OTC derivative instruments such as floors and caps. Also, the credit risk on swaps compares unfavorably with that of exchange traded futures and options whose credit risk is approximately zero.

Questions and Problems

1. Compare swap cash flows to cash flows using: (1) forward contracts and (2) options. Be sure to discuss:

   a. Frequency of marking to market.
   b. Credit risk exposure.
   c. Transaction costs.

2. Forward, futures, and options contracts had been used by FIs to hedge risk for many years before swaps were invented. If FIs already had these hedging instruments, why did they need swaps?

3. Use the following three-year swap information to construct a swap hedge. One year maturity notes are currently priced at par and pay a coupon rate of 5 percent annually. Two year maturity notes are currently priced at par and pay a coupon rate of 5.5 percent annually. Three year maturity notes are currently priced at par and pay a coupon rate of 5.75 percent annually. The terms of a three-year swap of $100 million notional value are: 5.45 percent annual fixed payments in exchange for floating rate payments tied to the annual discount yield.

   a. If an insurance company buys this swap, what can you conclude about the interest rate risk exposure of the company's underlying cash position? (Hint: Buying a swap entails an agreement to make fixed-rate liability payments in lieu of floating rate-interest payments.)

   b. What are the end of year cash flows expected over the three-year life of the swap? (Hint: Be sure to convert par value coupon yields to discount yields and then solve for the implied forward rate.)

   c. What are end of year actual cash flows that occur over the three year life of the swap if rates are ultimately revealed to be $d_2 = 4.95$ percent and $d_3 = 6.1$ percent?

4. Two multinational corporations enter their respective debt markets to issue $100 million of 2 year notes. Firm A can borrow at a fixed annual rate of 11 percent or a floating rate of LIBOR + 50 basis points, repriced at the end of the year. Firm B can borrow at a fixed annual rate of 10 percent or a floating rate of LIBOR, repriced at the end of the year.

   a. If Firm A is a positive duration gap insurance company and Firm B is a money market mutual fund, in what market(s) should both firms borrow so as to reduce their interest rate risk exposures?

   b. In which debt market does Firm A have a comparative advantage over Firm B?

   c. Although Firm A is riskier that Firm B, and therefore must pay a higher rate in both the fixed and floating rate markets, there are possible gains to trade. Set up a swap to exploit Firm A's comparative advantage over Firm B. What are the total gains from the swap trade? (Assume a swap intermediary fee of 10 basis points.)

   d. The gains from the swap trade can be apportioned between Firm A and B through negotiation. What terms of trade would give all the gains to Firm A? What terms of trade would give all the gains to Firm B?

e. Assume swap pricing that allocates all the gains from the swap to Firm A. If A buys the swap from B and pays the swap intermediary's fee, what are the end of year net cash flows if LIBOR = 8.25 percent?

f. If A buys the swap in part (e) from B and pays the swap intermediary's fee, what are the end of year net cash flows if LIBOR = 11 percent? (Be sure to net swap payments against cash market payments for both firms.)

g. If all barriers to entry and pricing inefficiencies between Firm A's debt markets and Firm B's debt markets are eliminated, how would that affect the swap transaction?

5. The swap market has grown into a more than $4 trillion global market serviced by swap intermediaries with international scope. What is your view of future growth in this market?

6. We have considered three categories of hedge instruments—futures and forwards, options, and swaps. Contrast these hedge instuments with reference to: (1) marking to market of cash flows; (2) credit risk exposure; and (3) hedge transactions cost.

7. A German bank issues a $100 million three-year Eurodollar CD at a fixed annual rate of 7 percent. The proceeds of the CD are loaned out to a German company for three years at a fixed rate of 9 percent. The spot exchange rate is DM 1.50/US$.

a. Is this a profitable transaction ex ante? What are the cash flows if exchange rates are unchanged over the next three years? What is the risk exposure of the bank's underlying cash position? How can the German bank reduce that risk exposure?

b. If the US dollar is expected to appreciate against the Deutschemark (DM) at a rate of 10 percent a year, what will be the cash flows on this transaction?

c. If the German bank swaps US$ payments for DM payments at the spot exchange rate, what are the cash flows on the swap? What are the cash flows on the entire hedged position? (Assume that the US$ appreciates against the DM at a rate of 10 percent annually.)

d. What are the cash flows on the swap and the hedged position if actual spot exchange rates are as follows:

End of year 1: DM 1.55/US$
End of year 2: DM 1.47/US$
End of year 3: DM 1.48/US$

8. a. Consider the German bank's cash position in problem 7. What would be the bank's risk exposure if the fixed rate German loan was financed with a *floating*

rate US$ 100 million three year Euro CD? What type(s) of hedge is appropriate if the German bank wants to reduce its risk exposure?

b. The annual Eurodollar CD rate is set at LIBOR where LIBOR at the end of years 1, 2, and 3 is expected to be 7, 8, and 9 percent respectively. What are the cash flows on the bank's unhedged cash position? (Assume no change in exchange rates.)

c. What are the cash flows on the bank's unhedged cash position if exchange rates are as follows:

End of year 1: DM 1.55/US$
End of year 2: DM 1.47/US$
End of year 3: DM 1.48/US$

d. What are both the swap and total hedged position cash flows if the bank swaps its floating rate US$ CD payments in exchange for 7.75 percent fixed rate, DM payments at current spot exchange rates (DM 1.50/US$)?

e. Use the following spot rates for par value coupon bonds to forecast expected future spot rates. (Hint: Forecast expected future spot rates using implied forward rates.)

1 year 7%
2 year 8.5%
3 year 9.2%

f. Use the rate forecasts in part e to calculate the cash flows on a 8.75 percent fixed to floating rate swap of US dollars to German Deutschemark at DM 1.50.

9. Consider the following swap of *assets*. Use the following balance sheet information to construct a swap hedge against interest rate risk exposure.

Balance Sheet ($millions)

Rate sensitive assets	50	Rate sensitive liabilities	75
Fixed rate assets	150	Fixed rate liabilities	100
		Net worth	25

NOTES: Rate sensitive assets are repriced quarterly at the 91 day Treasury bill rate plus 150 basis points. Fixed-rate assets have 5 years until maturity and are paying 9 percent annually. Rate sensitive liabilities are repriced quarterly at the 91 day Treasury bill rate plus 100 basis points. fixed rate liabilities have 2 years until maturity and are paying 7 percent annually. Currently, the 91 day Treasury bill rate is 6.25 percent.

a. What is the bank's current net interest income? If Treasury bill rates increase 150 basis points, what will be the change in the bank's net interest income?

b. What is the bank's repricing or funding gap? Use the repricing model to calculate the change in the bank's net interest income if interest rates increase 150 basis points.

c. What is the bank's interest rate risk exposure? How can swaps be used as an interest rate hedge?

Use the following information to construct a swap of asset cash flows. The bank is a price taker in both the fixed rate (at 9 percent) and rate sensitive asset (at a 91 day Treasury bill rate + 1.5 percent) markets. A securities dealer is a price taker in another fixed rate market (paying 8.5 percent) and another floating rate asset market (paying the 91 day T-bill rate + 1.25 percent). (All interest is paid annually.)

d. If the securities dealer is running a long book, what is its interest rate risk exposure? How can the bank and the securities dealer use a swap to hedge their respective interest rate risk exposures? What are the total potential gains to the swap trade?

e. Consider the following two year swap of asset cash flows. An annual fixed rate asset cash inflow of 8.6 percent in exchange for a floating rate asset cash inflow of T-bill + 125 basis points. The total swap intermediary fee is 5 basis points. How are the swap gains apportioned between the bank and the securities dealer if they each hedge their interest rate risk exposures using this swap?

f. What are the swap net cash flows if T-bill rates at the end of the first year are 7.75 percent and at the end of the second year are 5.5 percent? (Assume a notional value of $107.14 million.)

g. What are the sources of the swap gains to trade? What are the implications for the efficiency of cash markets?

Use the following information to answer questions 10–12.

Rate Sensitivity Report ($millions)

Maturity	Overnight	1–30 days	31–91 days	92–181 days	>182 days
Assets:					
FF & RP	20				
Loans	0	10	15	80	65
Liabilities:					
FF & RP	50				
Euros	5	25	40	0	60
Deposits					20

Balance Sheet ($millions)

Assets	Amount $m	Duration years	Liabilities	Amount $m	Duration years
Cash	30	0	Core deposits	20	y
FF & RP	20	.01	FF & RP	50	.01
Loans (variable)	105	.97	Euro CDs	130	.97
			Net worth	20	
Loans (fixed)	65	x			
	220			220	

NOTES TO THE BALANCE SHEET: Currently the FF and repo (FF & RP) rate is 8.5 percent. Variable rate loans are priced at 4 percent over LIBOR where LIBOR is currently at 11 percent. Fixed rate loans are all 5 year maturities with 12 percent interest, paid annually. Core deposits are all fixed rate for two years, at 8 percent paid annually. Euro CDs are all variable rate.

10. Use the following interest rate swap price information to determine which swap hedge is appropriate given the bank's duration gap position. Currently, LIBOR is 7.5 percent. (Use your answer to question 5 in Chapter 15 to determine the bank's interest rate risk exposure.)

Cash Market Prices: Fixed rate loan assets pay 12 percent and variable rate loan assets pay LIBOR plus 4 percent.

A swap intermediary offers the following two alternatives:

Swap I: Trade the interest income on the bank's fixed rate assets for variable rate assets paying LIBOR plus 4.25 percent.

Swap II: Trade the bank's variable rate interest income for fixed rate assets paying 12.35 percent.

11. If the Swap I counterparty's fixed rate cash assets offer 12.10 percent and the Swap II counterparty's floating rate cash assets offer LIBOR plus 4.05 percent, what are the total gains to each of the swap trades? What is the maximum potential swap intermediary fee?

12. What is the end of year profit (loss) per $100 million notional value on the swap hedge if all interest rates increase by 50 basis points? What is the bank's net cash inflow if the swap intermediary's fee is 5 basis points?

13. FIs can hedge interest rate risk exposure using forward, futures, options, and swap contract. Contrast these four derivative financial instruments making reference to:
a. credit risk exposure.
b. transactions costs.
c. frequency of marking to market.

14. Consider the following currency swap of coupon interest on the following assets:

5% (annual coupon) fixed rate US$1 million bond

5% (annual coupon) fixed rate bond denominated in Deutschemark (DM)

Spot exchange rates: DM 1.5 per US$1

a. What is the face value of the DM bond if the investments are equivalent at spot rates?
b. What are the end of year cash flows assuming no change in spot exchange rates? What are the net cash flows on the swap?
c. What are the cash flows if spot exchange rates fall to DM 0.5 per US$1? What are the net cash flows on the swap?
d. What are the cash flows if spot exchange rates rise to DM 2.25 per US$1? What are the net cash flows on the swap?

e. Describe the underlying cash position that would prompt the FI to hedge by swapping dollars in exchange for Deutschemark.

15. Consider the following fixed to floating rate currency swap of assets:

5% (annual coupon) fixed rate US$1 million bond.

(Annual coupon) floating rate bond denominated in Deutschemark (DM) set at LIBOR. Currently LIBOR is 4.00%. Face value is DM 1.5 million.

Spot exchange rates: DM 1.5 per US$1

a. What are the end of year cash flows assuming no change in spot exchange rates? What are the net cash flows on the swap at spot exchange rates?

b. If the one year forward rate is DM 1.538 per US$, what are the end of year net cash flows on the swap? (Assume LIBOR unchanged.)

c. If LIBOR increases to 6 percent, what are the end of year net cash flows on the swap? (Evaluate at the forward rate.)

21

SECURITIZATION

Learning Objectives

In this chapter you learn about asset securitization and why banks and other FIs are increasingly using this "technology" to transform their balance sheets. Asset securitization involves the FI packaging and selling assets backed by securities rather than holding assets on its balance sheet until maturity. Asset securitization is attractive to many FIs because it reduces the duration of asset portfolios, increases the liquidity of assets, provides a new means of finance, reduces the costs of regulation, and acts as a new source of fee income.

Introduction

Along with futures, forwards, options, and swaps, asset securitization—the packaging and selling of loans and other assets backed by securities—is a mechanism that FIs have used to hedge their interest rate exposure gaps better. In addition, the process of securitization has allowed FI asset portfolios to become more liquid, provided an important source of fee income (with FIs acting as servicing agents for the assets sold), and helped to reduce the effects of regulatory taxes such as capital requirements, reserve requirements, and deposit insurance premia.

In this chapter, we investigate the role of securitization in improving the return risk trade-off for FIs. We describe the three major forms, or vehicles, of asset securitization and analyze their unique characteristics. The major forms of asset securitization are the pass-through security, the collateralized mortgage obligation (CMO), and the asset-backed security. Chapter 22 deals with a more primitive form of asset securitization—loan sales—whereby loans are sold or traded to other investors and no new securities are created.

Forms of Securitization

The Pass-Through Security

While many different types of loans and assets on FIs' balance sheets are currently being securitized, the original use of securitization came as a result of government-sponsored programs to enhance the liquidity of the residential mortgage market. These programs indirectly subsidize the growth of home ownership in the United States.

Given this, we begin by analyzing the securitization of residential mortgage loans. Three government agencies or government-sponsored enterprises are directly involved in creation of mortgage-backed pass-through securities. Informally they are known as Ginnie Mae, Fannie Mae, and Freddie Mac.

GNMA.   The Government National Mortgage Association, or "Ginnie Mae," began in 1968 when it split off from FNMA. GNMA is a directly owned government agency with two major functions. The first is sponsoring mortgage-backed securities programs by FIs such as banks, thrifts, and mortgage bankers. The second is acting as a guarantor to investors in mortgage-backed securities regarding the timely pass-through of principal and interest payments on their sponsored bonds. In other words, GNMA provides **timing insurance,** which we describe more fully later. In acting as a sponsor and payment-timing guarantor, GNMA supports only those pools of mortgages that comprise mortgage loans whose default or credit risk is insured by one of three government agencies: the Federal Housing Administration (FHA), the Veterans Administration (VA), and the Farmers Home Administration (FMHA). The mortgage loans insured by these agencies are targeted at groups that might otherwise be disadvantaged in the housing market such as low-income families, young families, and veterans. As such, the maximum mortgage under the FHA/VA/FMHA-GNMA securitization program is capped. In recent years, the cap has been around $153,000.

Timing Insurance
A service provided by a sponsor of pass-through securities (such as GNMA) guaranteeing the bondholder interest and principal payments at the calendar date promised.

FNMA.   Originally created in 1938, the Federal National Mortgage Association, or "Fannie Mae," is the oldest of the three mortgage-backed security sponsoring agencies. While it is now a private corporation owned by shareholders with stocks traded on major exchanges, in the mind of many investors it still has implicit government backing that makes it equivalent to a government-sponsored agency.[1] Indeed, supporting this view is the fact that FNMA has a secured line of credit available from the U.S. Treasury should it need funds in an emergency. FNMA is a more active agency than GNMA in creating pass-through securities. While GNMA merely sponsors such programs, FNMA actually helps create pass-throughs by buying and holding mortgages on its balance sheet; it also issues bonds directly to finance those purchases.

Specifically, FNMA creates mortgage-backed securities (MBS) by purchasing packages of mortgage loans from banks and thrifts; it finances such purchases by selling MBS to outside investors such as life insurers or pensions funds. In addition, it engages in swap transactions whereby FNMA swaps MBS with an FI for original mortgages. Since FNMA securities carry FNMA guarantees as to the full and timely payment of interest and principal, the FI receiving the MBS can then resell them on the capital market or can hold them in its portfolio. Unlike GNMA, the FNMA securitizes conventional mortgage loans as well as FHA/VA insured loans, as long as the conventional loans have acceptable loan to value or collateral ratios normally not exceeding 80 percent. Conventional loans with high loan to value ratios usually require additional private sector credit insurance before they are accepted into FNMA securitization pools.

FHLMC.   The Federal Home Loan Mortgage Corporation, or "Freddie Mac," performs a similar function to FNMA except that its major securitization role has historically involved savings banks. Like FNMA, it is a stockholder-owned corporation

---

[1]See R. W. Spahr and M. A. Sunderman, "The Effect of Prepayment Modeling in Pricing Mortgage-Backed Securities," *Journal of Housing Research* 3, 1992, pp. 381–400.

with a line of credit from the Treasury. Further, like FNMA, it buys mortgage loan pools from FIs and swaps MBS for loans. The FHLMC also sponsors conventional loan pools as well as FHA/VA mortgage pools and guarantees timely payment of interest and ultimate payment of principal on the securities it issues.

The Incentives and Mechanics of Pass-Through Security Creation.   In beginning to analyze the securitization process, we trace through the mechanics of a mortgage pool securitization. Thus, we gain insights about the return risk benefits of this process to the mortgage originating FI as well as the attractiveness of these securities to investors. Given that more than $2 trillion of mortgage-backed securities are outstanding—the majority sponsored by the GNMA—we analyze an example of the creation of a GNMA pass-through security next.[2]

Suppose a bank has just originated 1,000 new residential mortgages in its local area. The average size of each mortgage is $100,000; thus, the total size of the new mortgage pool is

$$1,000 \times \$100,000 = \$100 \text{ million}$$

Because each mortgage is less than $153,000, each receives credit risk insurance protection from the FHA. This insurance costs a small fee to the originating bank. In addition, each of these new mortgages has an initial stated maturity of 30 years and a mortgage rate—often called the mortgage coupon—of 12 percent per annum. Suppose that the bank originating these loans relies mostly on liabilities such as demand deposits as well as its own capital or equity to finance its assets. Under current capital adequacy requirements, each $1 of new residential mortgage loans has to be backed by some capital. Since the risk-adjusted value of residential mortgages is 50 percent of face-value and the risk-based capital requirement is 8 percent, the bank capital needed to back the $100 million mortgage portfolio would be

$$\text{Capital requirement} = \$100 \text{ million} \times .5 \times .08 = \$4 \text{ million}$$

Even though the difference between $100 million and $4 million is $96 million, the bank must issue more than $96 million in liabilities (here demand deposits) due to a 10 percent noninterest-bearing reserve requirement imposed on these liabilities by the Federal Reserve.[3] Note that since there is currently a 0 percent reserve requirement on CDs and time deposits, the FI would need no extra funds to pay reserve requirements if it used CDs to fund the mortgage portfolio. The reserve requirement on demand deposits is an additional tax, over and above the capital requirement on funding the bank's residential mortgage portfolio.[4]

Given these considerations, the bank's initial post-mortgage balance sheet may look like that in Table 21–1. This balance sheet reflects the $4 million capital requirement that has to be held against mortgage asset and the 10 percent reserve requirements on demand deposits (106.6 $\times$ .1 = 10.66). This leaves $96 out of the $106.66 million in demand deposits raised to fund the mortgage portfolio of $100 million.

---

[2]At the end of the second quarter 1992, outstanding GNMA mortgage pools were $1.34 trillion; FNMA, $.413 trillion; and FHLMC, $.383 trillion.

[3]The first $46.8 million is subject to only a 3 percent reserve requirement, with a 10 percent reserve ratio levied on the rest. We ignore this distinction in this simple example.

[4]Implicitly viewing the capital requirement as a tax assumes that regulators set the minimum level above the level that would be privately optimal.

TABLE 21–1 Bank Balance Sheet
(in millions)

	Assets		Liabilities	
Cash reserves	$ 10.66	Demand deposits	$106.66
Long-term mortgages	100.00	Capital	4.00
	$110.66		$110.66

In addition to the capital and reserve requirement taxes, the bank also has to pay an annual insurance premium to the FDIC based on the size of its deposits. Taking the 1993 deposit insurance premium of 23 basis points for the highest-quality banks, the fee would be:

$$\$106.66 \text{ million} \times .0023 = \$245{,}318$$

Although the bank is earning a 12 percent mortgage coupon on its mortgage portfolio, it is facing three levels of regulatory taxes:

1. Capital requirements.
2. Reserve requirements.
3. FDIC insurance premiums.

Thus, one incentive to securitize is to reduce the regulatory tax burden on the FI to increase its "after-tax" return. In addition to facing regulatory taxes on its residential mortgage portfolio earnings, the bank in Table 21–1 has two risk exposure problems:

Gap Exposure or $D_A > kD_L$. The FI funds the 30-year mortgage portfolio out of short-term deposits; thus, it has a duration mismatch.[5] This would be true even if the mortgage assets has been funded with short-term CDs, time deposits, or other purchased funds.

Illiquidity Exposure. The bank is holding a very illiquid asset portfolio of long-term mortgages and no excess reserves; it is exposed to the potential liquidity shortages discussed in Chapter 13, including the risk of having to conduct mortgage asset fire sales to meet large unexpected demand deposit withdrawals.

One possible solution to this duration mismatch and illiquidity risk problem is to lengthen the bank's on-balance-sheet liabilities through issuing longer-term deposits or other liability claims, such as medium-term notes. Another solution is to engage in interest rate swaps to transform the bank's liabilities into those of a long-term, fixed-rate nature (see Chapter 20). These techniques do not resolve the problem of regulatory taxes and the burden they impose on the FI's returns.

By contrast, creating GNMA pass-through securities can largely resolve the duration and illiquidity risk problems on the one hand and reduce the burden of regulatory taxes on the other. This requires the bank to securitize the $100 million in residential mortgages by issuing GNMA pass-through securities. In our example, the bank can do this since the 1,000 underlying mortgages each have FHA/VA mortgage insurance, the same stated mortgage maturity of 30 years and coupons of 12 percent.

---

[5]As we discuss in Chapters 6 and 7, core demand deposits usually have a duration of less than three years. Depending on prepayment assumptions, mortgages normally have durations of at least 4.5 years.

Therefore, they are eligible for securitization under the GNMA program if the bank is an approved lender (which we assume it is).

The bank begins the securitization process by packaging the $100 million in mortgage loans and removing them from the balance sheet by placing them with a third-party trustee off the balance sheet. This third-party trustee may be another bank of high creditworthiness or a legal trustee. Next, the bank determines that (1) the GNMA will guarantee, for a fee, the timing of interest and principal payments on the bonds issued to back the mortgage pool, and (2) the bank itself will continue to service the pool of mortgages for a fee, even after they are placed in trust. Then, an issue of GNMA pass-through securities is made backed by the underlying $100 million pool of mortgages. These GNMA securities or pass-through bonds are sold to outside investors in the capital market.

Now, we consider the attractiveness of these bonds to investors; some may be other FIs such as banks, thrifts, and insurance companies. In particular, investors in these bonds are protected against two levels or types of default risk:

Default risk by the mortgagees. Suppose that because of falling house prices—such as happened in Houston, Texas, in the early 1980s—a homeowner walked away from a mortgage, leaving behind a low-valued house to be foreclosed at a price below the outstanding mortgage. This might expose the mortgage bondholders to losses unless there are external guarantors. Through FHA/VA housing insurance, government agencies bear the risk of default, thereby protecting bondholders against such losses.

Default risk by bank/trustee. Suppose the bank that originated the mortgages went bankrupt or the trustee absconded with the mortgage interest and principal due to bondholders. Because it guaranteed the prompt timing of interest and principal payments on GNMA securities, GNMA would bear the cost of making the promised payments in full and on time to GNMA bondholders.

Given this default protection, the GNMA bondholders (or investors') returns from holding these bonds would be the monthly repayments of interest and principal on the 1,000 mortgages in the pool, after the deduction of a mortgage servicing fee by the mortgage-originating bank and a monthly timing insurance fee to be paid to GNMA. The total sum of these fees is around 50 basis points, or $\frac{1}{2}$ percent, with approximately 6 basis points going as a fee to GNMA for timing insurance and the remaining 44 basis points going to the mortgage originator as a servicing fee. As a result, the stated coupons on the GNMA bonds would be set at approximately $\frac{1}{2}$ percent below the coupon rate on the underlying mortgages. In our example:

Mortgage coupon rate	=	12.00%
minus		
Servicing fee	=	0.44
minus		
GNMA insurance fee	=	0.06
GNMA pass-through bond coupon	=	11.50%

Suppose that GNMA issues $100 million face value bonds at par to back the pool of mortgage loans. The minimum size of a single bond is $25,000; each bondholder gets a pro rata monthly share of all the interest and principal received by the bank, minus servicing costs and insurance fees passed through to investors in the bonds. Thus, if a life insurance company bought 25 percent of the GNMA bond issue

FIGURE 21–1

Summary of GNMA pass through

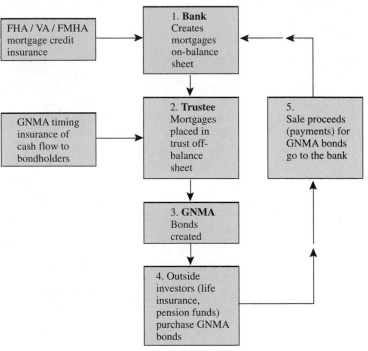

or (1,000 bonds × $25,000 each = $25 million) it would get a 25 percent share of the 360 promised monthly payments from the mortgages comprising the mortgage pool.

Every month, each mortgagee makes a payment to the bank. The bank aggregates these payments and passes the funds through to GNMA bond investors via the trustee net of servicing fee and insurance fee deductions. To make things easy, most fixed-rate mortgages are **fully amortized** over the mortgage's life. This means that as long as the mortgagee does not seek to prepay the mortgage early within the 30-year period, due to either moving or refinancing should mortgage rates fall, bondholders can expect to get a constant stream of payments each month analogous to the stream of income on other fixed-coupon, fixed-income bonds.

The problem is that mortgagees do not act in such a mechanistic fashion. For a variety of reasons, they move from houses and refinance their mortgages (especially when current mortgages rates are below their mortgage coupon rate). This propensity to **prepay** means that *realized* coupons/cash flows on pass-through securities can often deviate substantially from the stated or expected coupon flows in a no prepayment world. This unique prepayment risk provides the attraction of pass-throughs to some investors, but leads other more risk averse investors to avoid these instruments. Before we analyze in greater detail the unique nature of prepayment risk, we summarize the steps followed in the creation of a pass-through in Figure 21–1. Then, we analyze how this securitization has helped solve the duration, illiquidity, and regulatory tax problems of the FI manager.

In the previous discussion, we traced the GNMA from the origination of mortgages on the balance sheet (Box 1) through to the sale of GNMA bonds to out-

Fully Amortized
An equal periodic repayment on a loan that reflects part interest and part principal over the life of the loan.

Prepay
A borrower pays back a loan before maturity to the FI that originated the loan.

TABLE 21–2   The Bank's Balance Sheet Postsecuritization
(in millions)

Assets		Liabilities	
Cash reserves	$ 10.66	Demand deposits	$106.66
Cash proceeds from mortgage securitization	100.00	Capital	4.00
	$110.66		$110.66

side investors (Box 4 in Figure 21–1). To close the securitization process, the cash proceeds of the sale of GNMA bonds (Box 5) net of any underwriting fees go to the originating bank. As a result, the bank has substituted long-term mortgages for cash by using the GNMA securitization mechanism. Abstracting from the various fees and underwriting costs in the securitization process, the balance sheet of the bank might look as in Table 21–2 immediately after the securitization has taken place.

There has been a dramatic change in the balance sheet exposure of the bank. First, $100 million illiquid mortgage loans have been replaced by $100 million cash. Second, the duration mismatch has been reduced since both D_A and D_L are now low. Third, the bank has an enhanced ability to deal with and reduce its regulatory taxes. Specifically, capital requirements can be reduced since the risk-adjusted asset value of cash is zero compared to a risk-adjusted asset value of 50 percent for residential mortgages. Reserve requirement and deposit insurance premiums are also reduced if the bank uses part of the cash proceeds from the GNMA sale to pay off or retire demand deposits and downsize its balance sheet.

Of course, keeping an all or highly liquid asset portfolio and/or downsizing is a way of reducing regulatory taxes, but these strategies are hardly likely to enhance an FI's profits. The real logic of securitization is that the cash proceeds from the mortgage/GNMA sale can be reused to create or originate new mortgages, which in turn can be securitized. In so doing, the bank is acting more like an asset (mortgage) broker than a traditional asset transformer, as we discuss in Chapter 3. The advantage of being an asset broker is that bank profits from mortgage pool servicing fees plus up-front points and fees from mortgage origination. At the same time, the bank no longer has to bear the illiquidity and duration mismatch risks and regulatory taxes that arise when it acts as an asset transformer and holds mortgages to maturity on its balance sheet. Put more simply, the bank's profitability becomes more fee dependent than interest rate spread dependent.

The limits of this securitization process clearly depend on the supply of mortgages (and other assets) that can be securitized and the demand by investors for pass-through securities. As was noted earlier, the unique feature of pass-through securities from the demand side perspective of investors is prepayment risk. To understand the unique nature of this risk and why it might deter or limit investments by other FIs and investors, we next analyze the characteristics of pass-through securities more formally.

Concept Questions

1. Should an FI with $D_A < kD_L$ seek to securitize its assets? If so, why?
2. Is acting as a fee reliant asset broker a risk free strategy for an FI? If not, why not?
3. The credit risk on pools of jumbo (high face value) mortgages is insured by private insurers. List three reasons why the cost of private credit-risk insurance on these pools is likely to exceed that on GNMA pools.

Prepayment Risk on Pass-Through Securities.   To understand the effects of prepayments on pass-through security returns, you have to understand the nature of the cash flows received by investors from the underlying portfolio of mortgages. In the United States, most conventional mortgages are fully amortized. This means that the mortgagee pays back to the mortgage lender (mortgagor) a constant amount each month that contains some principal and some interest. While the total monthly promised payment remains unchanged, the interest component declines throughout the life of the mortgage contract and the principal component increases.

The problem for the bank is to figure a constant monthly payment that exactly pays off the mortgage loan at maturity. This constant payment is formally equivalent to a monthly annuity paid by the mortgagee. Consider our example of 1,000 mortgages comprising a $100 million mortgage pool that is to be paid off monthly over 360 months at an annual mortgage coupon rate of 12 percent:

Size of pool = 100,000,000
Maturity = 30 years ($n = 30$)
Number of monthly payments = 12 ($m = 12$)
r = Annual mortgage coupon rate = 12 percent
R = Constant monthly payment to pay off the mortgage over its life

Thus, we wish to solve for R from the following equation:

$$100,000,000 = \left[R\left(1+\frac{r}{m}\right)^{-1} + R\left(1+\frac{r}{m}\right)^{-2} + \ldots\ldots\ldots + R\left(1+\frac{r}{m}\right)^{-360} \right]$$

$$= R\left[\left(1+\frac{r}{m}\right)^{-1} + \left(1+\frac{r}{m}\right)^{-2} + \ldots\ldots\ldots + \left(1+\frac{r}{m}\right)^{-360} \right]$$

The term in square brackets is a geometric expansion that in the limit equals:

$$100,000,000 = \left[\frac{1 - \dfrac{1}{\left(1+\dfrac{r}{m}\right)^{m \cdot n}}}{\dfrac{r}{m}} \right] \times R$$

The term in square brackets is the present value of annuity factor, *PVAF*, or $100,000,000 = R \, [PVAF]$. Rearranging to solve for R, the required equal monthly payment on the mortgages, we have:

$$R = \frac{100,000,000}{PVAF}$$

TABLE 21–3 Fully Amortized Mortgages

Month	Outstanding Balance Payment	Fixed Monthly (R)	Interest Component	Principal Component	Principal Remaining
1	$100,000,000	$1,028,610	$1,000,000	$28,610	$99,971,390
2	99,971,390	1,028,610	999,714	28,896	99,942,494
.	.	.	.	.	.
.	.	.	.	.	.
.	.	.	.	.	.
360	.	.	.	.	.

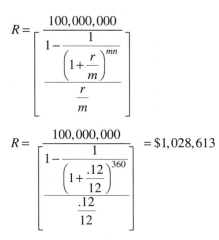

$$R = \dfrac{100,000,000}{\left[\dfrac{1 - \dfrac{1}{\left(1 + \dfrac{r}{m}\right)^{mn}}}{\dfrac{r}{m}}\right]}$$

$$R = \dfrac{100,000,000}{\left[\dfrac{1 - \dfrac{1}{\left(1 + \dfrac{.12}{12}\right)^{360}}}{\dfrac{.12}{12}}\right]} = \$1,028,613$$

As a result, $R = \$1,028,613$. Or, given 1,000 individual mortgages, $1,028.61 per mortgage rounding to the nearest cent. Thus, payments by the 1,000 mortgagees of an average monthly mortgage payment of $1,028.61 each pays off the mortgages outstanding over 30 years, assuming no prepayments.

The aggregate monthly payments of $1,028,610 comprise different amounts of principal and interest each month.[6] In Table 21–3, we break down the aggregate monthly amortized mortgage payments of $R = \$1,028,610$ into their interest and principal components. In month 1, the interest component is 12 percent divided by 12 (or 1 percent) times the outstanding balance on the mortgage pool ($100 million). This comes to $1,000,000, meaning that the remainder of the aggregate monthly payment, or $28,610, can be used to pay off outstanding principal on the pool. At the end of month 1, the outstanding principal balance on the mortgages has been reduced by $28,610 to $99,971,390. In month 2 and thereafter, the interest component declines and the principal component increases, but the two still sum to $1,028,610. Thus, in month 2 the interest component has declined to $999,714 (or 1 percent of the outstanding principal at the beginning of month 2) and the principal component of the payment has increased to $28,896. We show graphically the changing nature of these payments in Figure 21–2.

---

[6]Because of the rounding of each monthly payment to the nearest cent, we assume that aggregate monthly cash flows are 1,000 × $1,028.61 cents = $1,028,610.

Figure 21–2

Interest and principal components of the fully amortized mortgage

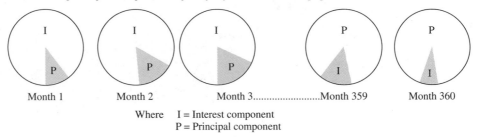

Where   I = Interest component
              P = Principal component

While 12 percent is the coupon or interest rate the housebuyers pay on the mortgages, the rate passed through to GNMA investors is 11½ percent reflecting an average 6 basis point insurance fee paid to GNMA and a 44 basis point servicing fee to the originating bank. The servicing fees are normally paid monthly, rather than as lump-sum single payments upfront, to create the appropriate collection/servicing incentives over the life of the mortgage for the originating bank. For example, the bank's incentive to act as an efficient collection/servicing agent over 360 months would probably decline if it received a single large upfront fee in month 1 and nothing thereafter.

The effect of the ½ percent fee is to reduce the cash flows passed through to the bondholders. As can be checked, using a *PVAF* that reflects an 11.5 percent annual rate rather than a 12 percent annual rate, GNMA bondholders would collectively receive $990,291 per month over the 30 years instead of $1,028,610 under conditions of no prepayments.

As we have shown so far, the cash flows on the pass-through directly reflect the interest and principal cash flows on the underlying mortgages minus service and insurance fees. However, over time mortgage rates change. Let *Y* be the current annual mortgage coupon rate, which could be higher or lower than 12 percent, and *y* be the yield on newly issued par value GNMA pass-through bonds. With no prepayments, the market value of the 12 percent mortgage coupon pool (11½ percent actual coupons) could be calculated as:

$$V = \frac{\$990,291}{\left(1+\dfrac{y}{12}\right)^1} + \frac{\$990,291}{\left(1+\dfrac{y}{12}\right)^2} + \cdots + \frac{\$990,291}{\left(1+\dfrac{y}{12}\right)^{360}}$$

If *y* is less than 11½ percent, the market value of the pool would be greater than its original value and if *y* is greater than 11½ percent, the pool would decrease in value. However, valuation is more complex than this since we have ignored the prepayment behavior of the 1,000 mortgagees. In effect, prepayment risk has two principal sources:

Refinancing. As the coupon rates on new mortgages fall, there is an increased incentive for individuals in the pool to pay off old high-cost mortgages and to refinance at lower rates. However, refinancing involves transaction costs and recontracting costs. Many banks and thrifts charge prepayment penalty fees on the outstanding mortgage balance prepaid. In addition, there are often origination costs or points for new mortgages to consider along with the cost of appraisals and credit checks. As a

FIGURE 21–3

The prepayment relationship

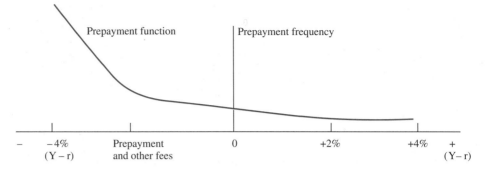

result, mortgage rates may have to fall by some amount below the current coupon rate before there is a significant increase in prepayments in the pool.[7]

Housing Turnover. The other factor that affects prepayments is the propensity of the mortgagees in the pool to move before their mortgages reach maturity. The decision to move or turn over a house may be due to a complex set of factors, such as the level of house prices, the size of the underlying mortgage, the general health of the economy, and even the season (e.g., spring is a good time to move). In addition, if the existing mortgage is an **assumable mortgage,** the buyer of the house takes over the outstanding mortgage's payments. Thus, the sale of a house in a pool does not necessarily imply that the mortgage has to be prepaid. By contrast, nonassumability means a one-to-one correspondence between sale of a house and mortgage prepayment. Most GNMA pools allow mortgages to be assumable; the reverse holds true for pass-throughs sponsored by FNMA and FHLMC.

In Figure 21–3, we plot the prepayment relationship frequency of a pool of mortgages to the spread between the current mortgage coupon rate (*Y*) and the mortgage coupon rate (*r*) in the existing pool (12 percent in our example). As you can see, when the current mortgage rate (*Y*) is above the rate in the pool (*Y* > *r*), mortgage prepayments are small, reflecting monthly forced turnover as people have to relocate due to jobs, divorces, marriages, and other considerations. Even when the current mortgage rate falls below *r*, those remaining in the mortgage pool do not rush to prepay because upfront refinancing, contracting, and penalty costs are likely to outweigh any present value savings from lower mortgage rates. However, as current mortgage rates continue to fall, the propensity for mortgage holders to prepay increases significantly. Conceptually, mortgage holders have a very valuable call option on the mortgage when this option is in the money.[8] That is, when current mortgage rates fall sufficiently low so that the present value savings of refinancing outweigh the exercise price (the cost of prepayment penalties and other fees and costs), the mortgage would be called.

Assumable Mortgage
The mortgage contract is transferred from the seller to the buyer of a house.

---

[7]Follian and Tzany found that only when the mortgage rate fell below the coupon rate by 60 basis points was there an incentive to refinance a mortgage with an average of 10 years left to maturity. As might be expected, this required differential declines as the holding period increases.

[8]The option is a call option on the value of the mortgage since falling rates increase the value of calling the old mortgage and refinancing a new mortgage at lower rates for the owner of the call option who is the mortgagee. See M. J. Brennan and E. S. Schwartz, "Savings Bonds, Retractable Bonds, and Callable Bonds," *Journal of Financial Economics* 5, 1977, pp. 67–88. This option can also be viewed as a put option on interest rates.

FIGURE 21–4

The effects of prepayments on pass-through bondholders' cash flows

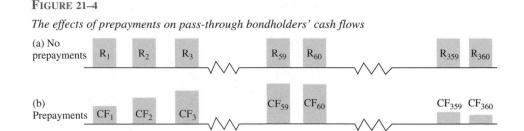

Since the bank has sold the mortgage cash flows to GNMA investors and must by law pass-through all payments received (minus servicing and guarantee fees), investors' cash flows directly reflect the rate of prepayment. As a result, instead of receiving an equal monthly cash flow, R, as under a no prepayment scenario, the actual cash flows (CF) received on these securities by investors fluctuate monthly with the rate of prepayments. (See Figure 21–4.)

In a no prepayment world, each month's cash flows are the same $R_1 = R_2 = \ldots = R_{360}$. However, in a world with prepayments, each month's realized cash flows from the mortgage pool can differ. In Figure 21–4, we show a rising level of cash flows from month 3 onwards peaking in month 60 reflecting the effects of early prepayments by some of the 1,000 mortgagees in the pool. This leaves less outstanding principal and interest to be paid in later years. For example, should 300 mortgagees fully prepay by month 60, only 700 mortgagees would remain in the pool at this date. The effect of prepayments is to lower dramatically the principal and interest cash flows received in the later months of the pool's life. For instance, in Figure 21–4, the cash flow received by GNMA bondholders in month 360 is very small relative to month 60 and even months 1 and 2. This reflects the decline in the pool's outstanding principal.

The lowering of current mortgage interest rates and faster prepayments has some good news and bad news effects on the current market valuation of the 12 percent mortgage pool, that is, the $11\frac{1}{2}$ percent GNMA bond.

Good News Effects.   First, lower market yields reduce the discount rate on any mortgage cash flow and increase the present value of any given stream of cash flows. This would also happen for any fixed-income security.

Second, lower yields lead to faster prepayment of the mortgage pool's principal. As a result, instead of having principal payments skewed toward the end of the pool's life, the principal is received (paid) back much faster.

Bad News Effects.   First, with early prepayment come fewer interest payments in absolute terms. Thus, instead of receiving scheduled interest payments over 360 months, some of these payments are irrevocably lost as principal outstanding is paid early, that is, mortgage holders are not going to pay interest on mortgage loans they no longer have outstanding.

Second, faster cash flows due to prepayments induced by interest rate falls can only be reinvested at lower interest rates when they are received. That is, instead of reinvesting monthly cash flows at 12 percent, investors may only reinvest at lower rates such as 8 percent.

Next we consider three cases:

FIGURE 21–5

GNMA bond price-yield curve

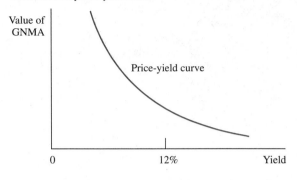

Good News Effects Outweigh Bad News Effects.   In the first case, the value of GNMA bonds rises as mortgage yields fall. This produces the usual inverse relationship between bond prices and yields common to most fixed-income securities (see Figure 21–5).

Bad News Effects Outweigh Good News Effects.   In the second case, the value of GNMA bonds actually falls when mortgage yields fall. That is, the loss in absolute interest payments and reduced reinvestment income due to prepayments outweigh any favorable effects of earlier principal payments and the present value discount effect. We show this in Figure 21–6.

The slope of the GNMA's price-yield curve exhibits a positive slope (or negative duration), which is the reverse of the normal inverse shape as in Figure 21–5. Remember from Chapter 6 that duration measures the interest sensitivity of a bond at a given yield. Then in this special case:

$$\frac{\Delta P}{P} = -(-D)\frac{\Delta R}{1+R} = +D\frac{\Delta R}{1+R}$$

Thus, a small positive shock to yields ($\Delta R/(1+R)$) leads to an increase in the value of the bond ($\Delta P/P$) by an amount proportional to the GNMA's duration.

The Good News Effects and the Bad News Effects Dominate over Different Ranges of Yields.   In the third case, these effects sometimes produce a whipsaw relationship between prices and yields on GNMA bonds (see Figure 21–7). As yields fall below 12 percent, the bad effects of prepayments increasingly dominate the good effects and as prepayments increase, the value of the GNMA bond falls. However, as rates rise above 12 percent, prepayment rates fall to reflect those mainly due to forced mortgage turnover. With lower prepayments, the normal discount effect of rate changes on bond values increasingly dominates. This produces the usual inverse relationship between bond values and yields at rates above 12 percent.

Concept Questions

   1. Are pass-through securities more likely to exhibit negative duration in high or low interest rate environments?

Figure 21–6

GNMA bond price-yield curve

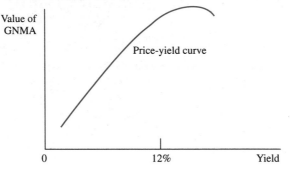

Figure 21–7

The price-yield curve whipsaw effect

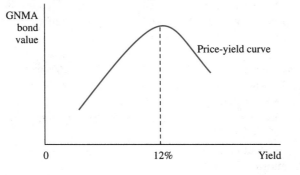

2. How would a reduction in mortgage and service fees and insurance fees affect the price of a GNMA security?

3. Taking the example in Table 21–3, calculate the principal and interest payments on a mortgage in months 10, 180, and 360.

Prepayment Models.   Clearly managers running FI investment portfolios need to factor in assumptions about the prepayment behavior of mortgages before they can assess the fair value and risk of their GNMA and FNMA/FHLMC bond portfolios. Next, we consider three alternative ways to model prepayment effects using the Public Securities Association (PSA) prepayment model, other empirical models, and option valuation models.

To begin, we look carefully at the results of one prepayment model. Look at the reported prices and yields on pass-through securities in Table 21–4. The first column in the table shows the sponsor of the issue (GNMA/FNMA/FHLMC), the stated maturity of the issue (30 years or 15 years), the mortgage coupons on the mortgages in each pool (e.g., 8 percent), and information about the maximum delay between the receipt of interest by the servicer/sponsor and the actual payment of interest to bondholders. The Gold next to FHLMC indicates a maximum stated delay of 55 days; this is the same as FNMA and 10 days more than GNMA. The remaining term in column two, reflects the remaining stated maturity of the underlying mortgages in the pool assuming no prepayments, an extreme and unlikely scenario. The third column

---

PROFESSIONAL PERSPECTIVES

The Mortgage Prepayment Option

Prafulla G. Nabar, Ph.D.
Lehman Brothers

The pricing of the prepayment option distinguishes the process of valuation for mortgage-backed securities (MBSs) from that for other fixed income securities such as treasuries. The prepayment option allows the mortgagee to prepay the mortgage, either partly or fully, at any time during its life. The investor in the MBS thus holds a short position in the prepayment option and a long position in the fixed income security whose cash flows consist of the monthly payments on the underlying mortgages.

At Lehman Brothers, the valuation of the prepayment option begins with the estimation of prepayment probabilities, using our prepayment model, for each of the future months through the life of the MBS. In our prepayment model, prepayments are considered to be caused by either housing turnover or mortgage refinancing. Housing turnover, which results from the sale of the house or default on the mortgage, is modeled as a function of a seasoning curve, seasonality and activity in the housing market. The seasoning curve is based on the premise that up to a certain mortgage age, the newer a mortgage the lesser the propensity to prepay it.

Seasonality accounts for the fact that people tend to change houses more during certain months of the year. Housing market activity captures the effect of the economic conditions and the supply of new housing. Refinancing takes into account the mortgagee's incentive to refinance the mortgage. This incentive depends on the mortgage rate prevailing in the market at each point in time. In addition, it depends on the slope of the yield curve since mortgage holders have an incentive to refinance into mortgages of lesser maturities at lower rates that depend on the slope of the yield curve. Refinancing also accounts for the burnout of a pool of mortgages as measured by the reluctance shown by the mortgagees in that pool to refinance their mortgages in the past. The prepayment probabilities are then used to compute the expected cash flows from the MBS to be used in the valuation of the security.

BIOGRAPHICAL SUMMARY
Prafulla G. Nabar is a Senior Analyst with Lehman Brothers. Before joining Lehman Brothers, he taught at New York University and Southern Methodist University.

Weighted-Average Life (WAL)
The product of the time when principal payments are received and the amount of principal received divided by total principal outstanding.

shows the weighted-average life of the bond reflecting an assumed prepayment schedule. This weighted-average life is not the same as duration, which measures the weighted-average time to maturity based on the relative present values of cash flows as weights. Rather, it is a significant simplification of the duration measure seeking to concentrate on the expected timing of payments of principal. Technically, **weighted-average life (WAL)** is measured by:

$$WAL = \frac{\Sigma \, \text{Time} \times \text{Expected principal received}}{\text{Total principal outstanding}}$$

For example, consider a loan with two years to maturity and $100 million in principal. Investors expect $40 million of the principal to be repaid at the end of year 1 and the remaining $60 million at maturity.

Time	Expected Principal Payments	Time × Principal
1	$ 40	$ 40
2	60	120
	$100	$160

$$WAL = \frac{160}{100} = 1.6 \text{ years}$$

TABLE 21–4 Pass-Through Securities
(April 19, 1993)

MORTGAGE-BACKED SECURITIES

Representative issues, quoted by Salomon Brothers Inc.

	REMAINING TERM (Years)	WTD-AVG LIFE (Years)	PRICE (MAY) (Pts.-32ds)	PRICE CHANGE (32ds)	CASH FLOW YIELD*	YIELD CHANGE (Basis pts.)
30-YEAR						
GNMA 8.0%	29.6	9.0	105-12	+ 8	7.11%	− 4
FHLMC Gold 8.0%	29.2	4.4	104-30	+ 5	6.55	− 2
FNMA 8.0%	29.3	4.4	104-23	+ 5	6.56	− 2
GNMA 9.0%	29.3	3.6	107-22	+ 4	6.33	− 3
FHLMC Gold 9.0%	28.2	2.3	106-16	+ 5	5.70	− 3
FNMA 9.0%	28.3	2.2	106-19	+ 5	5.47	− 4
GNMA 10.0%	29.0	2.7	110-14	unch	5.44	+ 1
FHLMC Gold 10.0%	27.2	1.4	108-25	+ 5	3.34	− 6
FNMA 10.0%	27.6	1.5	109-01	+ 5	3.06	− 6
15-YEAR						
GNMA 8.0%	14.5	5.8	105-27	+ 6	6.70%	− 4
FHLMC Gold 8.0%	14.2	4.3	105-07	+ 6	6.49	− 4
FNMA 8.0%	14.7	4.0	105-01	+ 6	6.38	− 3

*Based on projections from Salomon's prepayment model, assuming interest rates remain unchanged from current levels

SOURCE: *The Wall Street Journal,* April 20, 1993, p. c21. Reprinted by permission of *The Wall Street Journal.* © 1993 Dow Jones & Company, Inc., All Rights Reserved Worldwide.

FIGURE 21–8

PSA prepayment model

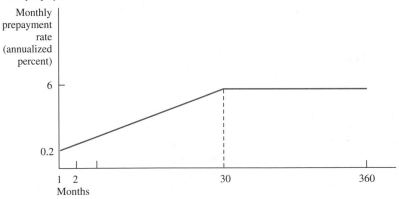

As you can see from Table 21–4, the *WAL*s of these pools are all nine years or less. The fourth column shows the prices of these pass-through securities quoted in 1/32nds—similar to treasuries—and the fifth column shows changes in price measured in 1/32nds. The sixth column shows the yield on these securities based on Salomon Brothers' prepayment model. That is, *The Wall Street Journal* reports the

The Economics of Securitization

Jerry Waldron
Citicorp Futures Corporation of Chicago

When a home loan is made, the financial institution is faced with a hold or sell decision. If the probability of default is lower than average, then the institution chooses to hold the loan and earn a return attributable to its high credit underwriting standards. If the loan has an average probability of default and meets certain conditions, such as loan size and a LTV (loan to value) ratio, then the loan can be sold to either FHLMC or FNMA. If the loan does not conform to FHLMC or FNMA standards, the loan can still be securitized with a little extra effort.

Both FHLMC and FNMA are government agencies designed to promote housing. These agencies, relying on diversification to reduce their credit exposure, combine mortgages into geographically diverse pools that they securitize and sell to investors. In purchasing an agency backed-MBS, investors receive a guarantee that they will receive full payment of principal and interest. As a result, the investor assumes no credit risk, but does assume the risk that the mortgages will prepay.

How much prepayment risk investors assume depends on how the security is structured. The simplest structure is a straight pass-through in which investors receive scheduled principal and interest payments and any additional principal repayment during the month. The prepayment risk associated with pass-throughs creates an interest rate risk profile that is undesirable to some investors. These investors can acquire other types

of MBS products. A CMO is a structured mortgage product designed to take advantage of the shape of the yield curve by assigning cash flows to discrete tranches. Each tranche varies in the amount of prepayment risk it absorbs, thereby allowing investors greater flexibility in choosing an interest rate risk profile.

The ability to separate credit risk and interest rate risk and to reengineer interest rate risk profiles has lead to the growth in the multibillion dollar MBS market. This process is not confined to mortgages; other active asset-backed markets include credit card receivables, auto loans, and home equity loans.

BIOGRAPHICAL SUMMARY

JERRY WALDRON is a financial economist experienced at applying quantitative investment management techniques to fixed income portfolios and derivative securities. He recently joined Citicorp Futures Corporation in Chicago where he is Vice President of Research and Sales. His Ph.D. in Economics is from Duke University (1983). He also holds an M.B.A. in Finance (1980) from Wright State University and a B.S. in Economics (1975) from Villanova University. His previous work experience includes his position as Vice President of Financial Risk Management for the Federal Home Loan Bank of San Francisco (1989-1993) where he was responsible for designing and executing MBS trading strategies in the context of managing a $5 billion MBS portfolio, overseeing interest rate risk management practices, managing unsecured credit exposure of $25 billion derivative security portfolio, and developing new financial products. While in the San Francisco area, he taught M.B.A. level courses in Investments and also in Financial Markets & Institutions at Golden Gate University. Other academic experience includes courses taught at New York University and Memphis State University in operations research, strategic management, and option pricing theory & trading.

yield on the bond given the contractual income and principal cash flows and expected prepayment cash flows over its life based on one investment bank's prepayment projections. That is, taking the quoted price (P) and the cash flow projections (CF_i) in each month, so that yield (y) solves for:

$$P = \frac{CF_1}{\left(1+\dfrac{y}{12}\right)^1} + \frac{CF_2}{\left(1+\dfrac{y}{12}\right)^2} + \text{........} + \frac{CF_{360}}{\left(1+\dfrac{y}{12}\right)^{360}}$$

Note that the prepayment projection depends on the assumption that the current mortgage rate remains unchanged. If it changes, prepayment rates and yields change

FIGURE 21–9

Deviations from 100 percent PSA

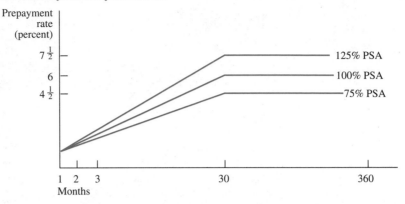

(often dramatically). The final column (column 7) shows the one-day change in yields in basis points.

Next we consider three approaches developed by analysts interested in modeling prepayment behavior.

Because of its technical nature, the option valuation model sub-section is starred (*).

PSA Model.   The prepayment model developed by the Public Securities Association (PSA) is an empirically based model that reflects an average rate of prepayment based on the past experience of pools of FHA-insured mortgages.

Essentially, the PSA model assumes that the prepayment rate starts at 0.2 percent (per annum) in the first month, increasing by 0.2 percent per month for the first 30 months, until the annualized prepayment rate reaches 6 percent. This model assumes the prepayment rate then levels off at a 6 percent annualized rate for the remaining life of the pool.[9] See Figure 21–8. Issuers or investors who assume that their mortgage pool prepayments exactly match this pattern are said to assume 100 percent PSA behavior. Realistically, the actual prepayment rate on any specific mortgage pool backing a specific pass-through security may differ from PSA's assumed pattern for general and economic reasons including:

1. The level of the pool's coupon relative to the current mortgage coupon rate (the weighted-average coupon).
2. The age of the mortgage pool.
3. Whether the payments are fully amortized or not.
4. Assumability of mortgages in the pool.
5. Size of the pool.
6. Conventional or nonconventional mortgages (FHA/VA).
7. Geographic location.
8. Age and job status of mortgagees in the pool.

One approach would be to approximately control for these factors by assuming some fixed deviation of any specific pool from PSA's assumed average or benchmark

---

[9]Or, after month 30, prepayments are made at approximately ¹/₂ percent per *month*.

FIGURE 21–10

Estimated prepayment function for a given pool

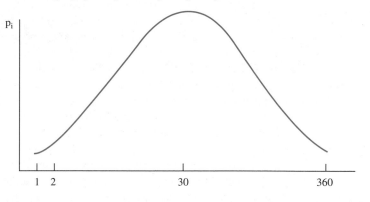

pattern. For example, one pool may be assumed to be 75 percent PSA and another 125 percent PSA. The former has a slower prepayment rate than historically experienced; the latter, a faster rate. Note these in Figure 21–9 relative to 100 percent PSA.

Other Empirical Models.   FIs that are trading, dealing, and issuing pass-throughs have developed their own proprietary empirical models of prepayment behavior to get a pricing edge on other issuers/investors. Clearly, the FI that can develop the best, most accurate, prepayment model stands to make large profits either in originating and issuing such bonds or in trading such instruments in the secondary market. As a wide variety of empirical models have been developed, we briefly look at the types of methodology followed.

Specifically, most empirical models are proprietary versions of the PSA model in which FIs make their own estimates of the pattern of monthly prepayments. From this modeling exercise, an FI can estimate either the fair price or fair yield on the pass-through. Of course, those FIs that make the most profits from buying and selling pass-throughs over time are the ones that have most accurately predicted actual prepayment behavior.

In constructing an empirical valuation model FIs begin by estimating a prepayment function from observing the experience of mortgage holders prepaying during any particular period on mortgage pools similar to the one to be valued. This is conditional, of course, on the mortgages not having been prepaid prior to that period. These conditional prepayment rates in month i (p_i) for similar pools would be modeled as functions of the important economic variables driving prepayment, for example, $p_i = f$ (mortgage rate spread, age, collateral, geographic factors, **burn-out factor**). This modeling should take into account the idiosyncratic factors affecting this specific pool, such as its age and burnout factor, as well as market factors affecting prepayments in general such as the mortgage rate spread.[10]

Burn-Out Factor
The aggregate percent of the mortgage pool that has been prepaid prior to the month under consideration.

_____

[10]A burnout factor is a summary measure of a pool's prepayments in total prior to month *i*. As such, it is meant to capture heterogeneity of prepayment behavior within any given pool rather than between pools. See E. S. Schwartz and W. N. Tourous, "Prepayment and the Valuation of Mortgage-Backed Securities," *Journal of Finance* 44, 1989, pp. 375–92.

Once the frequency distribution of the p_is is estimated, as shown in Figure 21–10, the bank can calculate the expected cash flows on the mortgage pool under consideration and estimate its fair yield given the current market price of the pool.[11]

The next subsection is starred (*) and is left as reading for those interested in the finer points of theoretically modeling prepayment behavior.

***Option Models.* *** The third class of models uses option pricing theory to figure the fair yield on pass-throughs and, in particular, the fair yield spread of pass-throughs over treasuries. These so-called option-adjusted spread models focus on the prepayment risk of pass-throughs as the essential determinant of the required yield spread of pass-through bonds over treasuries. As such, they are open to the criticism that they fail to properly include nonrefinancing incentives to prepay and the variety of transaction costs and recontracting cost involved in refinancing. Recent research has tried to integrate the option model approach with the empirical model approach.[12]

Stripped to its basics, the option model views the fair price on a pass-through such as a GNMA as being decomposable into two parts:[13]

$$P_{GNMA} = P_{TBOND} - P_{PREPAYMENT\ OPTION}$$

That is, the value of a GNMA bond to an investor (P_{GNMA}) is equal to the value of a standard noncallable Treasury bond of the same duration (P_{TBOND}) minus the value of the mortgage holder's prepayment call option ($P_{PREPAYMENT\ OPTION}$). Specifically, the ability of the mortgage holder to prepay is equivalent to the bond investor writing a call option on the bond and the mortgagee owning or buying the option. If interest rates fall, the option becomes more valuable as it moves into the money and more mortgages are prepaid early by having the bond called or the prepayment option exercised. This relationship can also be thought of in the yield dimension:

$$Y_{GNMA} = Y_{TBOND} + Y_{OPTION}$$

The investors' required yield on a GNMA should equal the yield on a similar duration T bond plus an additional yield for writing the valuable call option. That is, the fair yield or **option-adjusted spread** between GNMAs and T bonds should reflect the value of this option.

To gain further insight into the option model approach and its strengths and weaknesses, we can develop an example along the lines of S. D. Smith showing how to calculate the value of the option adjusted spread on GNMAs.[14] To do this, we make a number of simplifying assumptions indicative of the restrictive nature of many of these models. Our assumptions:

[11]A commonly used empirical model is the proportional hazards model. This model produces a prepayment function similar to that in Figure 21–10 where, other things being equal, conditional prepayment rates are typically low in the early years of a mortgage, increase as the age of the mortgage increases and then diminish with further seasoning (see Schwartz and Tourous).

[12]See, J. P. Kau et al., "A Generalized Valuation Model for Fixed-Rate Residential Mortgages," *Journal of Money Credit and Banking* 24, 1992; W. Archer and D. C. Ling, "Pricing Mortgage-Backed Securities: Should Contingent-Claim Models Be Abandoned for Empirical Models of Prepayments?" (Paper presented at the AFA Conference, Anaheim, California, January 1993.)

[13]For an excellent review of these option models see R. W. Spahr and M. A. Sunderman, "The Effect of Prepayment Modeling."

[14]S. D. Smith, "Analyzing Risk and Return for Mortgage-Backed Securities," Federal Reserve Bank of Atlanta, *Economic Review,* January–February 1991, pp. 2–11.

1. The only reasons for prepayment are due to refinancing mortgages at lower rates; there is no prepayment for turnover reasons.
2. The current discount (zero coupon) yield curve for T bonds is flat (this could be relaxed).
3. The mortgage coupon rate is 10 percent on an outstanding pool of mortgages with an outstanding principal balance of $1,000,000.
4. The mortgages have a three-year maturity and pay principal and interest only once at the end of each year. Of course, real-world models would have 15- or 30-year maturities and pay interest and principal monthly. These assumptions are made for simplification purposes only.
5. Mortgage loans are fully amortized and there is no servicing fee: again, this could be relaxed.

Thus, the annual fully amortized payment under no prepayment conditions is

$$R = \frac{1,000,000}{\left[\dfrac{1 - \dfrac{1}{(1+.10)^3}}{.1}\right]} = \frac{1,000,000}{2.48685} = \$402,114$$

In a world without prepayments, no default risk, and current mortgage rates (y) of 9 percent, we would have the GNMA bond selling at a premium over par:

$$P_{GNMA} = \frac{R}{(1+y)} + \frac{R}{(1+y)^2} + \frac{R}{(1+y)^3}$$

$$P_{GNMA} = \frac{\$402,114}{(1.09)} + \frac{\$402,114}{(1.09)^2} + \frac{\$402,114}{(1.09)^3}$$

$$P_{GNMA} = 1,017,869$$

6. Because of prepayment penalties and other refinancing costs, mortgagees do not begin to prepay until mortgage rates, in any year, fall 3 percent or more below the mortgage coupon rate for the pool (10% in this example).
7. Interest rate movements over time change a maximum of 1 percent up or down each year. The time path of interest rates follow a binomial process.
8. With prepayments present, cash flows in any year can either be the promised payment $R = \$402,114$, the promised payment ($R$) plus repayment of any outstanding principal, or zero if all mortgages have been prepaid or paid off in the previous year.

In Figure 21–11, we show the assumed time path of interest rates over the three years with associated probabilities (p).

End of Year 1.   Since rates can only change up or down by 1 percent per annum, the farthest they can be expected to fall in the first year is to 8 percent. At this level, no mortgage holder would prepay since any mortgage rate savings would be offset by the penalty costs of prepayment; that is, by the assumption it is only worth prepaying when the mortgage rate falls at least 3 percent below its coupon rate.

As a result, the GNMA pass-through investor could expect to receive, $R = \$402,114$ with certainty. Thus, $CF_1 = \$402,114$.

FIGURE 21–11

Mortgage rate changes: Assumed time path

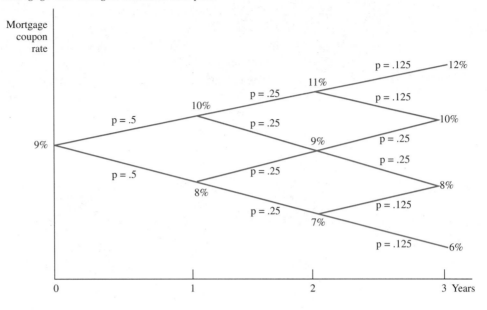

End of Year 2. In year 2, there are three possible mortgage interest rate scenarios. However, the only one that triggers prepayment is when mortgage rates fall to 7 percent (3 percent below the 10 percent mortgage coupon rate of the pool). According to Figure 21–11, this occurs with only a 25 percent probability. If prepayment does not occur with 75 percent probability, the investor receives $R = \$402,114$. If prepayment occurs with 25 percent probability, the investors receive:

$$R + \text{principal balance remaining at end of year 2.}$$

We can calculate the principal balance remaining at end of year 2 as follows: At the end of the first year, we divide the amortized payment, $R = \$402,114$, into a payment of interest and payment of principal. With a 10 percent mortgage coupon rate, the payment of interest component would be $.10 \times \$1,000,000 = \$100,000$; and the repayment of principal component $= \$402,114 - \$100,000 = \$302,114$. Thus, at the beginning of the second year, there would be $\$1,000,000 - \$302,114 = \$697,886$ principal outstanding. At the end of the second year, the promised amortized payment of $R = \$402,114$ can be broken down to an interest component 10 percent $\times \$697,886 = \$69,788.6$ and a principal component amount of $\$402,114 - \$69,788.6 = \$332,325.4$, leaving a principal balance at the end of year 2 of $\$1,000,000 - \$302,114 - \$332,325.4 = \$365,560.6$.

Consequently, if yields fall to 7 percent, the cash flow received by the investor in year 2 would be:

$$R + \text{principal balance outstanding at end of year 2} =$$
$$\$402,114 + \$365,560.6 = \$767,674.6$$

Thus, expected cash flows at the end of year 2 would be

$$CF_2 = .25(\$767,674.6) + .75(\$402,114)$$

$$= \$191,918.64 + \$301,585.5$$

$$= \$493,504.15$$

End of Year 3. Since there is a 25 percent probability that mortgages would be prepaid in year 2, there must be a 25 percent probability that the investor would receive no cash flows at the end of year 3 since mortgage holders owe nothing in this year if all mortgages have already been paid off early in year 2. However, there is also a 75 percent probability that mortgages would not be prepaid at the end of year 2. So, at the end of year 3 (maturity), the investor has a 75 percent probability of receiving the promised amortized payment $R = \$402,114$. The expected cash flow in year 3:

$$CF_3 = .25(0) + .75(\$402,114) = \$301,585.5$$

Derivation of the Option-Adjusted Spread. As just discussed, we conceptually divide the required yield on a GNMA, or other pass-throughs, with prepayment risk, into the required yield on T bonds plus a required spread for the prepayment call option given to the mortgage holders:

$$P = \frac{E(CF_1)}{(1+d_1+O_s)} + \frac{E(CF_2)}{(1+d_2+O_s)^2} + \frac{E(CF_3)}{(1+d_3+O_s)^3}$$

where

P = Price of GNMA

d_1 = Discount rate on one-year, zero-coupon Treasury bonds

d_2 = Discount rate on two-year, zero-coupon Treasury bonds

d_3 = Discount rate on three-year, zero-coupon Treasury bonds

O_s = Option adjusted spread on GNMA

Assume that the T bond yield curve is flat so that

$$d_1 = d_2 = d_3 = 8\%$$

We can now solve for O_s:

$$1,017,869 = \frac{\$402,114}{(1+.08+O_s)} + \frac{\$493,504}{(1+.08+O_s)^2} + \frac{\$301,585.5}{(1+.08+O_s)^3}$$

Solving for O_s, we find:

$$O_s = 0.96\% \text{ (to two decimal places)}$$

$$Y_{GNMA} = Y_{TBOND} + O_s$$

$$= 8\% + 0.96\%$$

$$= 8.96\%$$

You can see that when prepayment risk is present, the expected cash flow yield at 8.96 percent is 4 basis points less than the required 9 percent yield on the GNMA when no prepayment occurs. The slightly lower yield is because the positive effects of early prepayment (such as earlier payment of principal) dominate the negative effects (such as loss of interest payments). Note, however, that this

FIGURE 21–12

The creation of a CMO

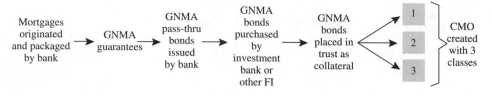

result might well be reversed if we were to alter our assumptions by allowing a wider dispersion of possible interest rate changes and having heavier penalties for prepayment.

Nevertheless, the option-adjusted spread approach is useful for FI managers in that they can place lower bounds on the yields they are willing to accept on GNMA and other pass-through securities before they place them in their portfolios. Realistically, some account has to be taken of nonrefinancing prepayment behavior and patterns, otherwise significant mispricing may occur.

Concept Questions

1. In the context of the option model approach, list three ways in which transaction and other contracting costs are likely to interfere with the accuracy of its predictions regarding the fair price or interest spread on a pass-through security.

2. Suppose interest rates are more volatile, how will this impact the option-adjusted spread?

The Collateralized Mortgage Obligation (CMO)

While pass-throughs are still the primary mechanism for securitization, the CMO is a second and growing vehicle for securitizing bank assets. Innovated in 1983 by the FHLMC and First Boston, the CMO is a device for making mortgage-backed securities more attractive to investors. The CMO does this by repackaging the cash flows from mortgages and pass-through securities in a different fashion to attract different types of investors. While a pass-through security gives each investor a pro rata share of any promised and prepaid cash flows on a mortgage pool, the CMO is a multiclass pass-through with a number of different bondholder classes or tranches. Unlike a pass-through each bondholder class has a different guaranteed coupon just like a regular T bond, but more importantly, the allocation of early cash flows due to mortgage prepayments are such that at any one time all prepayments go to retiring the principal outstanding of only one class of bondholders leaving the other classes prepayment protected for a period of time.

CMO
Collateralized mortgage obligation is a mortgage-backed bond issued in multiple classes or tranches.

Creation of CMOs.   **CMOs** can be created either by packaging and securitizing whole mortgage loans, or more usually by placing existing pass-throughs in a trust off the balance sheet. The trust or third-party bank holds the GNMA pass-through as collateral and issues new CMO securities, the trust issues these CMOs in 3 to 17 different classes. We show a three-class or tranche CMO in Figure 21–12.

As you can see, issuing CMOs is often equivalent to double securitization. Mortgages are packaged, and a GNMA pass-through is issued. An investment bank

FIGURE 21–13

The creation of a CMO

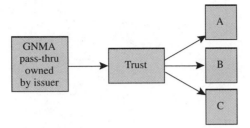

such as Goldman Sachs or another CMO issuer, such as FHLMC, a commercial bank, or a savings bank, may buy this whole issue or a large part of the issue. Goldman Sachs would then place these GNMA securities as collateral with a trust and issue three new classes of bonds backed by the GNMA securities as collateral.[15] As a result, the investors in each CMO class have a sole claim to the GNMA collateral should the issuer fail. The investment bank or other issuer creates the CMO to make a profit, by repackaging the cash flows from the single-class GNMA pass-through into cash flows more attractive to different groups of investors. The sum of the prices at which the three CMO bond classes can be sold normally exceed that of the original pass-through:

$$\sum_{i=1}^{3} P_{i,CMO} > P_{GNMA}$$

To understand the gains from repackaging, you must understand how CMOs restructure prepayment risk to make it more attractive to different classes of investors. We explain this in the following simple example.

The Value Additivity of CMOs.   Suppose an investment bank buys a $150 million issue of GNMAs and places them in trust as collateral. It then issues a CMO with these three classes also depicted in Figure 21–13:

> Class A: annual fixed coupon 7 percent, class size $50 million
>
> Class B: annual fixed coupon 8 percent, class size $50 million
>
> Class C: annual fixed coupon 9 percent, class size $50 million

Under a CMO, each class has a guaranteed or fixed coupon.[16] By restructuring the GNMA as a CMO, the bank can offer investors who buy bond class C a high degree or mortgage prepayment protection compared to a pass-through. Those who buy class B receive an average degree of prepayment protection; and those who take class A, virtually no prepayment protection.

Each month, mortgagees in the GNMA pool pay principal and interest on their mortgages; each payment includes the promised amortized amount (R) plus any additional payments as some of the mortgage holders prepay principal either to refinance their mortgages or because they have sold their houses and are relocating. These cash flows are passed-through to the owner of the GNMA bonds, in our example Goldman Sachs. The CMO issuer uses the cash flows to pay promised coupon interest to the

---

[15]These trusts are sometimes called REMICs or real estate mortgage investment conduits.

[16]In some cases, coupons are paid monthly, in others quarterly, and in still others, semiannually.

FIGURE 21–14

Allocation of cash flows to owners of CMO tranches

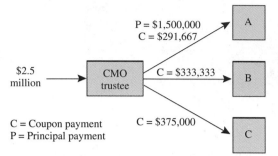

three classes of CMO bondholders. Suppose that in month 1 the promised amortized cash flows (*R*) on the mortgages underlying the GNMA pass-through collateral are $1 million, but there is an additional $1.5 million cash flow as a result of early mortgage prepayments. Thus, the cash flows in the first month available to pay promised coupons to the three classes of bondholders would be:

$$R + \text{prepayments} = \$1 \text{ million} + \$1.5 \text{ million} = \$2.5 \text{ million}$$

This cash flow is available to the trustee who uses it in the following fashion:

1. *Coupon Payments.* Each month (or more commonly, each quarter or half-year) the trustee pays out the guaranteed coupons to the three classes of bondholders at annualized coupon rates of 7 percent, 8 percent, and 9 percent respectively. Given the stated principal of $50 million for each class, the class A (7 percent coupon) bondholders receive approximately $291,667 in coupon payments in month 1; the class B (8 percent coupon) receive approximately $333,333 in month 1; and the class C (9 percent coupon) receive approximately $375,000 in month 1. Thus, the total promised coupon payments to the three classes amount to $1,000,000 (equal to *R*, the no prepayment cash flows in the GNMA pool).

2. *Principal Payments.* The trustee has $2.5 million available to pay out as a result of promised mortgage payments plus early prepayments, but the total payment of coupon interest amounts to $1 million. For legal and tax reasons, the remaining $1.5 million has to be payed out to the CMO bondholders. The unique feature of the CMO is that the trustee would pay this remaining $1.5 million only to class A bondholders to retire these bondholders' principal. At the end of month 1, only $50 million − $1.5 = $48.5 million class A bonds would remain outstanding, compared to $50 million class B and $50 million class C. See these payment flows shown graphically in Figure 21–14.

Let's suppose that in month 2 the same thing happens. The cash flows from the mortgage/GNMA pool exceed the promised coupon payments to the three classes of bondholders. Again, the trustee uses any excess cash flows to pay off or retire the principal of class A bondholders. If the excess cash flows again amount to $1.5 million, at the end of month 2 there would be only $48.5 − $1.5 = $47 million of class A bonds outstanding.

FIGURE 21–15

*Allocation of cash flows to remaining tranches
of CMO bonds*

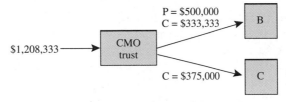

Given any positive flow of prepayments, it is clear that within a few years the class A bonds would be fully retired. In practice, this often occurs between 1.5 and 3 years after issue. After the trustee retires class A, only classes B and C remain.

As before, out of any cash flows received from the mortgage/GNMA pool, the trustee pays the bondholders their guaranteed coupons, $C_B = \$333,333$ and $C_C = \$375,000$ for a total of \$708,333. Suppose that total cash flows received by the trustee are \$1,208,333 in the first month after the total retirement of class A bonds, reflecting amortized mortgage payments by the remaining mortgagees in the pool plus any new prepayments. The excess cash flows of \$1,208,333 − \$708,333 = \$500,000 would then go to retire the principal outstanding of CMO bond class B. At the end of that month, there would be only \$49.5 million class B bonds outstanding. See this shown graphically in Figure 21–15.

As the months pass, the trustee would use any excess cash flows over and above the promised coupons to class B and C bondholders to retire bond class B's principal. Eventually, all of the \$50 million principal on class B bonds would be retired; in practice, 5 to 7 years after CMO issue. After class B bonds are retired, all remaining cash flows would be dedicated to paying the promised coupon of class C bondholders and retiring the \$50 million principal on class C bonds. In practice, class C bonds can have an average life as long as 20 years.

Class A, B, and C Bond Buyers.
Class A.   These bonds have the shortest average life with a minimum of prepayment protection. They are, therefore, of great interest to investors seeking short-duration mortgage-backed assets to reduce the duration length of their mortgage-related asset portfolios. In recent years, savings banks and commercial banks have been large buyers of CMO class A securities.

Class B.   These bonds have some prepayment protection and expected durations of 5 to 7 years depending on the level of interest rates. Mostly pension funds and life insurance companies purchase these bonds, although some banks and thrifts buy this bond class as well.

Class C.   Because of their long expected duration, they are highly attractive to insurance companies and pension funds seeking long-term duration assets to match their long-term duration liabilities. Indeed, because of their failure to offer prepayment protection, regular GNMA pass-throughs may not be of much attraction to these institutions. Class C CMOs, with their high but imperfect degree of prepayment protection, may be of greater interest to the FI managers of these institutions.

In summary, by splitting bondholders into different classes and by restructuring cash flows into forms more valued by different investor clienteles, the CMO issuer stands to make a profit.

Other CMO Classes.   CMOs can always have more than the three classes described in the previous example. Indeed, issues of up to 17 different classes have been made. Clearly, the 17th class bondholders would have an enormous degree of prepayment protection since the first 16 classes would have had their bonds retired before the principal outstanding on this bond class would be affected by early prepayments. In addition, trustees have created other special types of classes as products to attract investor interest; we discuss these next.

Z Class
Is an accrual class of a CMO that only makes a payment to bondholders when preceding CMO classes have been retired.

Class Z.   Frequently, CMO issues contain a **Z class** as the last regular class. The Z implicitly stands for zero but these are not really zero-coupon bonds. This class has a stated coupon such as 10 percent and accrues interest for the bondholder on a monthly basis at this rate. The trustee does not pay this interest, however, until all other classes of bonds are fully retired. When the other classes have been retired, the Z class bondholder receives the promised coupon and principal payments plus accrued interest payments. Thus, the Z class has characteristics of both a zero-coupon bond (no coupon payments for a long period) and a regular bond.

Class R.   In placing the GNMA collateral with the trustee, the CMO issuer normally uses very conservative prepayment assumptions. If prepayments are slower than expected, there is often excess collateral left over in the pool when all regular classes have been retired. Further, trustees often reinvest funds or cash flows received from the underlying instrument (GNMA) in the period prior to paying interest on the CMOs. In general, the size of any excess collateral and interest on interest gets bigger when rates are high and the timing of coupon intervals is semiannual rather than monthly. This residual **R class** or "garbage class" is a high-risk investment class that gives the investor the rights to the over-collateralization and reinvestment income on the cash flows in the CMO trust. Because the value of the returns in this bond class increases when interest rates increase, while normal bond values fall with interest rate increases, class R often has a negative duration. Thus, it is potentially attractive to banks and thrifts seeking to hedge their regular bond and fixed-income portfolios.[17]

R Class
The residual class of a CMO giving the owner the right to any remaining collateral in the trust after all other bond classes have been retired plus any reinvestment income earned by the trust.

Consider the example of a CMO with classes A, B, C, Z, and R in Table 21–5. From Table 21–5, you can see that the underlying pass-through bond held as collateral is a FNMA 9.99 percent coupon bond with an original maturity of 30 years, an issue size of $500 million, and a prepayment rate assumed to be twice the size assumed by the PSA model (200 percent PSA). The five CMO bond classes are issued in different amounts, with the largest class being B. Note that the principal amounts of the five classes sum to $500 million.

Concept Questions

1. Would thrifts or insurance companies prefer Z class strips? Explain your answer.

---

[17]As discussed earlier, negative duration implies that bond prices increase with interest rates; that is, the price-yield curve is positively sloped.

TABLE 21–5   CMO with Five Bond Classes

Fannie Mae REMIC Trust 1987-I

Dollars in millions

Collateral Type	Coupon	Amount	Original Term	Average Remaining Term	Assumed Prepayment Rate
FNMA	9.99%	$500	360 Mos.	349 Mos.	200% PSA

Bonds Class	A	B	C	Z	R
Amount	$150.9	$238.6	$85.5	$24.0	$1.0
Bond type	Fixed	Fixed	Fixed	Accrual	Residual
Coupon (percent)	7.95	9.35	9.60	9.99	503.88
Price	99.8099	99.3083	N/A	89.4978	1445.1121
Yield (bond equivalent)	7.85	9.55	N/A	10.86	10.30
Weighted-average life (yrs.)	1.6	5.9	11.2	18.4	3.6
Benchmark Treasury (yr.)	2	5	N/A	20	N/A
Spread over Treasury (basis points)	15	125	N/A	180	N/A

NOTE: All data on the above table is as of the pricing date (FNMA has retained Class C).
Pricing Date 8/18/87
Accrual Date 9/01/87
First Payment 10/25/87
Payment Frequency/Delay: Monthly pay, 25-day delay
SOURCE: GAO/GGD-88-111 (1988).

2. Are Z class CMO strips exactly the same as T bond strips? If not, why not?

3. In our example, the coupon on the class C bonds was assumed to be higher than on the class B bonds, and the coupon on class B bonds was assumed to be higher than on class A bonds. Under what term structure conditions might this not be the case?

The Mortgage-Backed Bond (MBB)

Mortgage-(Asset) Backed Bonds
Bonds collateralized by a pool of assets.

Mortgage- or **asset-backed bonds** are the third asset securitization vehicle. These bonds differ from pass-throughs and CMOs in two key dimensions: First, while pass-throughs and CMOs help banks and thrifts remove mortgages from their balance sheets as forms of off-balance-sheet securitization, mortgage-backed bonds (MBBs) normally remain on the balance sheet. Second, while pass-throughs and CMOs have a direct link between the cash flows on the underlying mortgages and the cash flows on the bond vehicles, with MBBs the relationship is one of collateralization, there is no direct link between the cash flow on the mortgages backing the bond and the interest and principal payments on the bond.

Essentially, an FI issues a MBB so that if the FI fails, the MBB bondholders have a first claim to a segment of the FI's mortgage assets. Practically speaking, the FI segregates a group of mortgage assets on its balance sheet and pledges this group as collateral backing the bond issue. A trustee normally monitors the segregation of assets and makes sure that the market value of the collateral exceeds the principal owed to bondholders. That is, FIs back most MBB issues by excess collateral. This excess

TABLE 21–6   Balance Sheet of Potential MBB Issuer
(in millions)

Assets		Liabilities	
Long-term mortgages	$20	Insured deposits	$10
		Uninsured deposits	10
	$20		$20

collateral backing of the bond, plus the priority rights of the bondholders, generally ensures that these bonds can be sold with a high credit rating such as AAA. In contrast, the FI when evaluated as a whole could be rated as BBB or even lower. A high credit rating results in lower coupon interest than if default risk is significant (see Chapter 8). To explain the potential benefits to an FI from issuing MBBs, and the sources of any gains, we examine the following simple example.

Consider a bank with $20 million in long-term mortgages as assets. It is financing these mortgages with $10 million in short-term uninsured deposits (wholesale deposits over $100,000) and $10 million in insured deposits (under $100,000 retail deposits). Here we ignore the issues of capital and reserve requirements. Look at this balance sheet structure in Table 21–6.

This balance sheet poses problems for the FI manager: First, the bank has a positive duration gap ($D_A > kD_L$). Second, because of this interest rate risk and the potential default risk on the bank's mortgage assets, uninsured depositors are likely to require a positive and potentially significant risk premium paid on their deposits. By contrast, the insured depositors may require approximately the risk-free rate on their deposits as they are fully insured by the FDIC (see Chapter 15).

To reduce its duration gap exposure and to lower its funding costs, the bank might segregate $12 million of the mortgages on the asset side of its balance sheet and pledge them as collateral backing a $10 million long-term MBB issue. Because of this over-collateralization, the mortgage-backed bond issued by the bank may cost less to issue, in terms of required yield, than uninsured deposits; that is, it may well be rated AAA while uninsured deposits might be rated BBB. The FI can therefore use the proceeds of the $10 million bond issue to retire the $10 million of uninsured deposits.

Consider the bank's balance sheet after the issue of the MBBs in Table 21–7. It might seem that the bank has miraculously engineered a restructuring of its balance sheet that has resulted in a better matching of D_A to D_L and a lowering of funding costs. The bond issue has lengthened the average duration of liabilities by replacing short-term deposits and lowered funding costs as bond coupon rates are below uninsured deposit rates. However, this outcome is only because the $10 million insured depositors do not worry about risk exposure since they are 100 percent insured by the FDIC. The result of the MBB issue and the segregation of $12 million of assets as collateral backing the $10 million bond issue is that the $10 million insured deposits are now only backed by $8 million in free or unpledged assets. If smaller depositors weren't insured by the FDIC they would surely demand very high risk premiums to hold these risky deposits. The implication of this is that the bank only gains because the FDIC is willing to bear enhanced credit risk through its insurance guarantees to depositors.[18] As a result, the bank is really gaining at the

---

[18]And, does not make the risk based deposit insurance premium sufficiently large to reflect this risk.

TABLE 21–7   Bank's Balance Sheet after MBB Issue
(in millions)

Assets		Liabilities	
Collateral = (market value of segregated mortgages)	$12	MBB issue	$10
		Insured deposits	10
Other mortgages	8		
	$20		$20

expense of the FDIC. Consequently, it is not surprising that the FDIC is concerned about the growing use of this form of securitization by risky banks and thrifts.

Other than regulatory discouragement and the risk of regulatory intervention, there are other private return reasons why a bank might prefer the pass through/CMO forms of securitization to that of issuing MBBs. The first is that MBBs tie-up mortgages on the bank's balance sheet for a long time. This increases the illiquidity of the asset portfolio. Second, the amount of mortgages tied up is enhanced by the need to over-collateralize to ensure a high-quality credit risk rating for the bond issue; in our example, the over-collateralization was $2 million. Third, by keeping the mortgages on the balance sheet, the bank continues to be liable for capital adequacy and reserve requirement taxes. Because of these problems, MBBs are the least used of the three basic vehicles of securitization.

Concept Question

1. Would a AAA FI ever issue mortgage-backed bonds? Explain your answer.

Innovations in Securitization

We now turn our attention to the growing innovations in FI's asset securitization. We discuss two major innovations and their use in return risk management by FIs, mortgage pass-through strips and the extension of the securitization concept to other assets.

Mortgage Pass-Through Strips

The mortgage pass-through strip is a special type of CMO with only two classes. The fully amortized nature of mortgages means that any given monthly payment, R, contains an interest component and a principal component. Beginning in 1987, investment banks and other FI issuers stripped out the interest component from the principal component and sold each payment stream separately to different bond class investors. They sold an interest only (IO) class and a principal only (PO) class; these two bond classes have very special cash flow characteristics, especially regarding the interest rate sensitivity of these bonds.

We show this stripping of the cash flows in Figure 21–16. We next consider the effects of interest rate changes on the value of each of these stripped instruments.

FIGURE 21–16

IO/PO strips

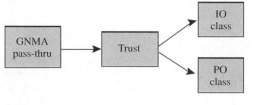

IO Strip

A bond sold to investors whose cash flows reflect the monthly interest payments received from a pool of mortgages.

IO Strips.   The owner of an **IO strip** has a claim to the present value of interest payments by the mortgagees in the GNMA pool; that is, to the IO segments of each month's cash flow received from the underlying mortgage pool:

$$P_{IO} = \frac{IO_1}{\left(1+\dfrac{y}{12}\right)} + \frac{IO_2}{\left(1+\dfrac{y}{12}\right)^2} + \frac{IO_3}{\left(1+\dfrac{y}{12}\right)^3} + \ldots\ldots + \frac{IO_{360}}{\left(1+\dfrac{y}{12}\right)^{360}}$$

When interest rates change, they affect the cash flows received on mortgage. We concentrate on two effects: the discount effect and the prepayment effect on the price or value of IOs denoted by P_{IO}.

Discount Effect.   As interest rates (y) fall, the present value of any cash flows received on the strip—the IO payments—rises, increasing the value (P_{IO}) of the bond.

Prepayment Effect.   As interest rates fall, mortgagees prepay their mortgages. In absolute terms, the number of IO payments the investor receives is likely to shrink. For example, the investor might receive only 100 monthly IO payments instead of the expected 360 in a no prepayment world. The shrinkage in the size and value of IO payments reduces the value (P_{IO}) of the bond.

Specifically, one can expect that as interest rates continue to fall below the mortgage coupon rate of the bonds in the pool, the prepayment effect gradually dominates the discount effect, so that over some range the price or value of the IO bond falls as interest rates fall. Note the price-yield curve in Figure 21–17 for an IO strip on a pass-through bond with 10 percent mortgage coupon rates.

Negative Duration

When the price of a bond increases or decreases as yields increase or decrease.

The price-yield curve slopes upward in the interest rate range below 10 percent. This means as current interest rates rise or fall, IO values or prices rise or fall. As a result, the IO is another rare example of a **negative duration** asset that is very valuable as a portfolio hedging device for an FI manager when included with regular bonds whose price-yield curves show the normal inverse relationship. That is, while as interest rates rise the value of the regular bond portfolio falls, the value of an IO portfolio may rise. Note in Figure 21–17, that at rates above the pool's mortgage coupon of 10 percent, the price-yield curve changes shape and tends to perform like any regular bond. In recent years, thrifts have been major purchasers of IOs to hedge the interest rate risk on the mortgages and other bonds held as assets in their portfolios. We depict the hedging power of IOs in Figure 21–18.

PO Strip

A bond sold to investors whose cash flows reflect the monthly principal payments received from a pool of mortgages.

PO Strips.   We consider next the **PO strip** whose value (P_{PO}) is defined by:

$$P_{PO} = \frac{PO_1}{\left(1+\dfrac{y}{12}\right)} + \frac{PO_2}{\left(1+\dfrac{y}{12}\right)^2} + \frac{PO_3}{\left(1+\dfrac{y}{12}\right)^3} + \ldots\ldots + \frac{PO_{360}}{\left(1+\dfrac{y}{12}\right)^{360}}$$

FIGURE 21–17

Price yield curve of a 10 percent strip

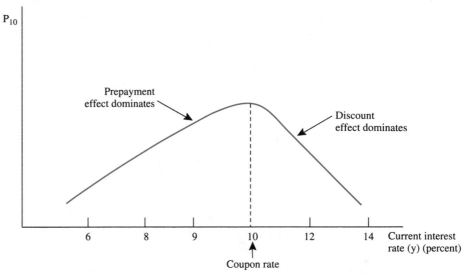

where the PO_i represents the mortgage principal components of each monthly payment by the mortgage holders. This includes both the monthly amortized payment component of R that is principal, plus any early prepayments of principal by the mortgagees. Again, we consider the effects on a POs value (P_{PO}) of a change in interest rates.

Discount Effect. As yields (y) fall, the present value of any principal payments must increase and the value of the PO strip rises.

Prepayment Effect. As yields fall, the mortgage holders pay off principal early. Consequently, the PO bondholder receives the fixed principal balance outstanding on the pool of mortgages earlier than stated. Thus, this prepayment effect must also work to increase the value of the PO strip.

As interest rates fall, both the discount and prepayment effects point to a rise in the value of the PO strip. The price-yield curve reflects an inverse relationship but with a steeper slope than for normal bonds; that is, PO strip bond values are very interest rate sensitive especially for yields below the stated mortgage coupon rate. We show this in Figure 21–19 for a 10 percent PO strip. (Note that a regular coupon bond is affected only by the discount effect.) As you can see, when yields fall below 10 percent, the market value or price of the PO strip can increase very fast. At rates above 10 percent, it tends to behave like a regular bond (as the incentive to prepay disappears).

Concept Question

1. Would an FI with $D_A < kD_L$ be interested in buying an IO strip for hedging purposes?

The IO-PO strip is a classic example of financial engineering. From a given GNMA pass-through bond, two new bonds have been created: the first with an upward sloping price-yield curve over some range and the second with a steeply downward

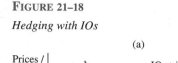

FIGURE 21-18

Hedging with IOs

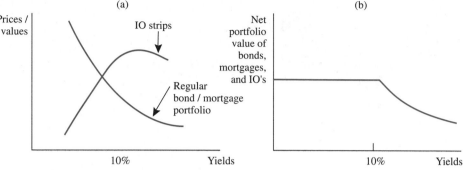

sloping price-yield curve over some range. Each class is attractive to different investors and investor segments. The IO is attractive to thrifts and banks as on-balance-sheet hedging vehicles. The PO is attractive to those financial institutions that wish to increase the interest rate sensitivity of their portfolios and to investors or traders who wish to take a naked or speculative position regarding the future course of interest rates. This high and complex interest sensitivity has resulted in major traders such as J. P. Morgan and Merrill Lynch suffering considerable losses on their investments in these instruments when interest rates moved unexpectedly against them.

Securitization of Other Assets

While the major use of the three securitization vehicles—pass throughs, CMOs, and mortgage-backed bonds—has been in packaging fixed-rate mortgage assets, these techniques can and have been used for other assets including:

> Automobile loans.
> Credit card receivables (Certificates of Amortizing Revolving Debts).
> Small business loans guaranteed by the Small Business Administration.
> Commercial and industrial loans.
> Junk bonds.
> Adjustable rate mortgages.

Junk bonds and certificates of amortizing revolving debts are two examples of securitizing other assets.

Junk Bonds. In the 1980s, a small number of California-chartered savings banks had built up large holdings of long duration junk bonds in their asset portfolios. Most of these bonds were funded by short-term liabilities. Imperial Corporation of America, a San Diego-based thrift holding company packaged together $180 million of its junk bond holdings, segregated them on the balance sheet as collateral, and issued a $100 million junk bond asset-backed bond. Because the junk bonds provided excess collateral of 80 percent over the face value of the newly issued bonds, and even though the junk bonds themselves were individually rated from B to BBB, bond rating agencies gave the $100 million Imperial bonds a high investment grade rating. According to estimates, even if interest rates rose dramatically and 40 percent of the

FIGURE 21–19

Price yield curve of a PO strip

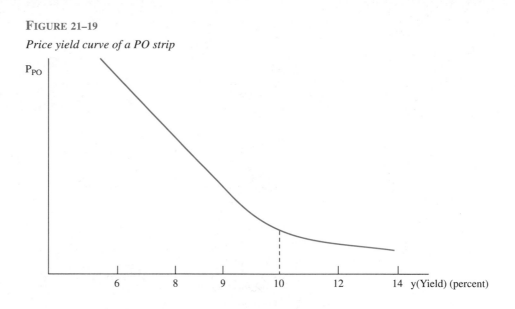

underlying junk bond issues defaulted, the bond investors' principal was still fully protected. This example is one of adapting the MBB securitization technology to junk bond assets.

Certificates of Amortizing Revolving Debts (CARDs).   Chase Manhattan Bank is a major sponsor of credit cards. The bank segregates a set of credit card account receivables and sells them to an off-balance-sheet trust. Chase retains the role of servicing the credit card pool, including collection, administration, and bookkeeping of the underlying credit card accounts. As an example, it sold $280 million of receivables to a trust. The trust, in turn, issued asset-backed securities (**CARDs**) in which investors had a pro rata claim on the cash flows from the credit-card receivables. As the trust received payments on the credit card receivables each month, they were paid through to the bondholders. In practice, bonds of a lesser principal amount than the $280 million credit card pool may be issued. In this example, $250 million in bonds were issued, with the difference—$30 million—being a claim retained by Chase. The reason for this is that credit card holders can either increase or repay their credit card balances at any time. The risk of variations in principal outstanding and, thus, collateral for the bonds is borne solely by the bank (i.e., the $30 million component), while the investors' collateral claim remains at $250 million until maturity unless a truly exceptional rate of debt repayment occurs. Indeed, Chase's segment is structured to bear even the most extreme cases of early repayment of credit card debts.

We show this credit card example in Figure 21–20. It is clear from Figure 21–20 that this securitization of credit card assets is similar in technology to the pass-through mortgage bond.

CARDs
Asset-backed securities backed by credit card receivables.

Can All Assets Be Securitized?

The extension of securitization technology to other assets raises questions about the limits of securitization and whether all assets and loans can be securitized.

FIGURE 21–20

The structure of a credit card securitization

TABLE 21–8   Benefits versus Costs of Securitization

Benefits	Costs
1. New funding source (Bonds versus deposits)	1. Costs of public/private credit risk insurance and guarantees
2. Increased liquidity of bank loans	2. Costs of over-collateralization
3. Enhanced ability to manage the duration gap $(D_A - kD_L)$	3. Valuation and packaging costs (the cost of asset heterogeneity)
4. If off balance sheet, the issuer saves on: reserve requirements, deposit insurance premiums, and capital adequacy requirements	

Conceptually the answer is yes they can, as long as it is profitable to do so or the benefits to the FI from securitization outweigh the costs of securitization.[19] In Table 21–8, we summarize the benefits versus the costs of securitization.

From Table 21–8, given any set of benefits, the more costly and difficult it is to find asset packages of sufficient size and homogeneity, the more difficult and expensive it is to securitize. For example, commercial and industrial (C&I) loans have maturities running from a few months up to eight years; further, they have varying interest rate terms (fixed, LIBOR-floating, federal funds rate floating) and fees. In addition, they contain differing covenants and are made to firms in a wide variety of industries. Given this, it is difficult for C&I loan pools to be valued by investors, insurers, and bond rating agencies.[20] The harder it is to value such asset pools, the greater the costs of securitization due either to over-collateralization or credit risk insurance. Thus, the potential boundary to securitization may well be defined by the relative degree of heterogeneity of an asset type or group. It is not surprising that 30-year fixed-rate residential mortgages were the first assets to be securitized since they are the most homogeneous of all assets in bank balance sheets. Moreover, the existence of secondary markets for houses provides price information that allows for reasonably accurate market valuations of the underlying asset to be made in the event of mortgage defaults.

Concept Question

1. Outline the benefits and costs to an FI from securitizing auto loans.

---

[19]See C. Pavel, "Securitization," Federal Reserve Bank of Chicago, *Economic Perspectives,* 1985, pp. 16–31.

[20]Despite this there has been some securitization of C&I loans. These are called CLOs. A CLO (collateralized loan obligation) is modeled on the CMO. A bank collects a diversified pool of loans and places them in a trust, and usually three tranches of securities are issued against the pool. Normally, there is a senior tranche, a subordinated tranche, and a tranche that has similar features to the residual tranche of CMOs. Approximately $1.5 billion have been issued so far in 11 deals since Continental Bank instigated the first deal in December 1988. Most have been concerned with securitizing highly leveraged loans made to finance mergers and acquisitions (see Chapter 22).

The Future of Securitization

Neil D. Baron
Fitch Investors Service, Inc.

The volume of securitized transactions should remain high for financial institutions subject to regulatory capital requirements as long as these capital requirements remain at current or higher percentages of their assets. Moreover, the ability of other financial institutions as well as industrial companies to achieve low-cost funding by the issuance of highly rated securities should provide high volumes of securitization in the future.

The cost of securitization could rise, however, on adoption of the Federal Financial Institutions Examination Council's pending proposal. It would require third-party providers of credit enhancement (e.g., through the issuance of letters of credit or purchase of subordinated interests in asset pools) to maintain capital against the entire asset pool instead of against the amount of the credit enhancement, as is presently required. If substantial, the increased cost of credit enhancements could affect the volume of many securitizers inasmuch as securitization of all but a few asset types requires credit enhancement of some sort.

Recent changes by the National Association of Insurance Commissioners in capital requirements for commercial mortgages held by insurance companies are likely to result in increased securitization of commercial mortgages into rated securities, which generally require lower capital levels than the mortgages themselves.

The present administration is considering facilitating the securitization of small- and medium-sized business loans to induce banks to increase the origination of these loans. The belief is that broader and lower-cost funding sources for these businesses will stimulate the economy.

In addition, securitization of health-care receivables is being considered by the administration as a method to lower the cost of financing to health-care providers. This in turn could reduce the cost of health care to consumers, much as the secondary mortgage market has reduced the cost of mortgages and, consequently, housing.

Securitization is in its infancy in Europe, Canada, and Australia and almost nonexistent in Japan. It is likely to experience growth in all these places.

In summary, securitization has served a number of purposes: It has provided companies with the ability to directly access the capital market for broader funding sources. It, by definition, allows the structuring of securities to achieve ratings higher than the ratings of the unsecured debt of the originators, thereby providing for lower cost of funding. Securitization is also an asset-liability management tool and reduces interest rate risk to originators. In addition, securitization reduces capital requirements by removing assets from RAP and GAAP on balance sheets. Finally, it creates safe and predictable securities for investors. As long as these needs exist to a material extent, securitization will survive and grow.

BIOGRAPHICAL SUMMARY

Neil D. Baron is Vice Chairman and General Counsel of Fitch Investors Service, Inc.

Prior to joining Fitch, Mr. Baron was a partner in the law firm of Booth & Baron in New York City. His practice has included advice regarding legal issues associated with corporate, municipal, and international finance. His primary focus has been on structured financings, including letters of credit, structured municipal debt, and the securitization of domestic, United Kingdom, and Australian single family and commercial mortgages; industrial company trade receivables; equipment and real estate leases; franchise fees; consumer receivables such as car loans, boat loans and credit card accounts; and bank portfolio loans. He has advised commercial banks, investment banks, financial guarantors, Standard & Poor's Corporation, the White House, the Federal Home Loan Bank Board, the U.S. Agency for International Development, the governments of Chile and Israel, and others with respect to these areas. He has testified before U.S. Senate committees with regard to the effect of proposed legislation on the capital markets. He has lectured for the Securities Institute, the Banking Law Institute, the Institute for International Finance, the Practising Law Institute, the *New York Law Journal*, the Business Research Institute, the Municipal Bond Attorneys Workshop, the International and American Bar Associations, and the Securities and Exchange Commission. He has also lectured at Yale, Cardozo, and Columbia Law Schools. He has published various articles in his areas of expertise.

A graduate of the Case Western Reserve University School of Law, Mr. Baron was admitted to the Bar in New York in 1969. He is a member of the American, Inter-American, New York State, and New York City Bar Associations.

Summary

A final word might be said about the implications of securitization for FIs' strategic behavior. In Chapter 3, we distinguished between FIs that are asset transformers and those that are asset brokers. By becoming increasingly reliant on securitization, banks and thrifts are moving away from being asset transformers that originate and hold assets to maturity; they are becoming asset brokers more reliant on servicing and other fees. This makes banks and thrifts look more similar to securities firms. Thus, over time, we expect the traditional financial technology differences between commercial banking and investment banking to diminish as more and more loans and assets are securitized.

Questions and Problems

1. Outline the costs and benefits of securitizing auto loans.

2. Your thrift institution has just originated 200 residential mortgages averaging $200,000 each.

   a. Use the Basel risk-adjusted capital requirements to calculate the minimum required capital on the mortgage portfolio.

   b. If the thrift finances the mortgages by issuing demand deposits, how much are required? (Assume a reserve ratio of 10 percent.)

   c. What are the thrift's reserve requirements? What are total assets?

   d. What is the thrift's deposit insurance premium if it is the lowest quality institution? (Hint: Use the FDICIA of 1991 procedure discussed in Chapter 15.)

3. Consider a GNMA mortgage pool with principal of $20 million. The maturity is 30 years with a monthly mortgage payment of 10% per annum. (Assume no prepayments.)

   a. What is the monthly mortgage payment (100 percent amortizing) on the pool of mortgages?

   b. If the GNMA insurance fee is 6 basis points and the servicing fee is 44 basis points, what is the yield on the GNMA pass-thru?

   c. What is the monthly payment on the GNMA in part b?

   d. Calculate the first monthly servicing fee paid to the originating banks.

   e. Calculate the first monthly insurance fee paid to GNMA.

4. Calculate the value of (a) the mortgage pool and (b) the GNMA pass-thru in question 3 if interest rates increased 100 basis points. (Assume no prepayments.)

5. A bank originates a pool of 500 thirty year mortgages, each averaging $150,000, with an annual mortgage coupon rate of 8 percent. If the GNMA insurance fee is 6 basis points and the bank's servicing fee is 19 basis points:

   a. What is the present value of the mortgage pool?

   b. What is the monthly mortgage payment?

   c. For the first two payments, what portion is interest and what is principal repayment?

   d. What are the expected monthly cash flows to GNMA bondholders?

   e. What is the present value of the GNMA pass-thru bonds? (Assume that the risk adjusted market annual rate of return is 8 percent compounded monthly.)

   f. Would actual cash flows to GNMA bond holders deviate from expected cash flows as in part d? Why or why not?

   g. What are the bank's and GNMA's expected monthly cash flows?

   h. If all of the mortgages in the pool are completely prepaid at the end of the second month, what is the pool's weighted average life? (Hint: Use your answer to part c.)

   i. What is the price of the GNMA pass-thru if its weighted average life is equal to your solution for part h? (Assume no change in market interest rates.)

   j. What is the price of the GNMA pass-thru with a weighted average life equal to your solution for part h if market yields decline by 50 basis points?

6. If 150 $200,000 mortgages are expected to be prepaid in 3 years and the remaining 150 $200,000 mortgages in a $60 million 15 year mortgage pool are to be prepaid in 4 years, what is the weighted average life of the mortgage pool? Mortgages are fully amortized with mortgage coupon rates set at 10 percent to be paid *annually*.

7. Use the options prepayment model to calculate the yield on a $12 million five year fully amortized mortgage pass-thru where the mortgage coupon rate is 7 percent paid annually. Market yields are 8 percent paid annually. Assume that there is no servicing or GNMA guarantee fee.

   a. What is the annual payment on the GNMA pass-thru?

   b. What is the present value of the GNMA pass-thru?

   c. Interest rates movements over time are assumed to change a maximum of 1 percent per year. Both an increase of 1 percent and a decrease of 1 percent in interest rates are equally probable. If interest rates fall 3 percent below current mortgage rates, all mortgages in the pool are completely prepaid. What are the GNMA's expected annual cash flows?

d. The Treasury bond yield curve is flat at a discount yield of 6 percent. What is the option adjusted spread on the GNMA?

8. What would be the impact on GNMA pricing if the pass-thru was not fully amortized? What is the present value of a $10 million pool of 15 year mortgages with an 8.50 percent monthly mortgage coupon p.a. if market rates are 5 percent? The GNMA guarantee fee is assumed to be 6 basis points and the bank servicing fee 44 basis points.

   a. Assume that the GNMA is fully amortized.

Challenge Question:

   b. Assume that the GNMA is only half amortized. (There is a lump sum payment at the maturity of the GNMA that equals 50 percent of the mortgage pool's face value.)

9. What factors affect prepayment probability?

10. Consider $200 million of thirty year mortgages with a coupon of 10 percent p.a. paid quarterly.

    a. What is the quarterly mortgage payment?

    b. What are the interest repayments over the first year of life of the mortgages? What are the principal repayments?

    Construct a 30 year CMO using this mortgage pool as collateral. There are three tranches (where A offers the least protection against prepayment and C offers the most). A $50 million Tranche A makes quarterly payments of 9 percent p.a.; a $100 million Tranche B makes quarterly payments of 10 percent; and a $50 million Tranche C makes quarterly payments of 11 percent.

    c. Assume non-amortization of principal and no prepayments. What are the total promised coupon payments to the three classes? What are the principal payments to each of the three classes for the first year?

d. If, over the first year, the trustee receives quarterly prepayments of $10 million on the mortgage pool, how are the funds distributed?

e. How are the cash flows distributed if payments in the first half of the second year prepayments are $20 million quarterly?

f. How can the CMO-issuer earn a positive spread on the CMO?

11. Use the mortgage pool in question 7 to construct both an IO and a PO strip. Calculate their present values assuming a market interest rate of 6 percent paid annually.

12. How does securitization impact the FI's role as a delegated monitor?

13. How does the FI use securitization to manage its risk exposure? (Be sure to consider interest rate, currency, liquidity, and credit risks.)

14. *a.* What is the yield to maturity on a 15 year mortgage with a rate of 6.75 percent (paid monthly) and a 1 percent (up front, lump sum) origination fee? What are the monthly cash flows? (Assume 100 percent amortization and no prepayments.)

    b. What is the yield to maturity on the 15 year mortgage in part *a* if instead of an up front origination fee there was a monthly servicing fee of 50 basis points? What are the monthly cash flows? Allocate those monthly cash flows between the FI servicing the mortgage and the ultimate holder of the mortgage.

    c. What is the yield to maturity if the mortgage is prepaid in four months? (A lump sum is paid at the end of the fourth month to repay the entire principal balance). Assume the up front origination fee and no monthly servicing fee (i.e., the mortgage in part *a*). (Hint: Calculate monthly interest payments using the monthly coupon rate assuming zero amortization.)

    d. What is the yield to maturity on the mortgage in part *c* if there is neither an up front origination fee nor a monthly servicing fee?

LOAN SALES

Learning Objectives

In this chapter you learn about loan sales and how they differ from other types of securitization in that no new securities are created. Loan sales comprise a number of different submarkets including the sale of loans made to finance mergers and acquisitions and leveraged buyouts. You will also learn that while a large number of regulatory and economic factors create incentives for banks to sell loans, the recent trend of the market has been one of decline rather than growth.

Introduction

Correspondent Banking
A relationship entered into between a small bank and a big bank in which the big bank provides a number of deposit, lending, and other services.

Highly Leveraged Transaction (HLT) Loan
A loan made to finance a merger and acquisition, a leveraged buyout results in a high leverage ratio for the borrower.

Banks and other FIs have sold loans among themselves for over 100 years. In fact, a large part of **correspondent banking** involves small banks making loans that are too big for them to hold on their balance sheets—either for lending concentration, risk, or capital adequacy reasons—and selling parts of these loans to large banks in bigger cities with whom they have a long-term deposit-lending correspondent relationship. In turn, the bigger city banks often sell parts of their loans called participations to smaller banks. Even though this market has existed for many years, it grew slowly until the early 1980s when it entered a period of spectacular growth, largely due to expansion in **highly leveraged transaction (HLT) loans** to finance leveraged buyouts (LBOs) and mergers and acquisitions (M&As). Specifically, the volume of loans sold by U.S. banks grew from less than $20 billion in 1980 to $285 billion in 1989. In recent years, the volume of loan sales has fallen almost equally as dramatically along with the decline in LBOs and M&As. For example, in June 1991, the volume of loan sales was $125 billion, less than half the peak 1989 figure.

In this chapter we describe the structure of the market for bank loan sales and then examine reasons why banks and other FIs seek to buy and sell loans. Finally, we discuss the reasons underlying the market's recent decline and ask whether this is likely to be a temporary or permanent phenomenon.

The Bank Loan Sale Market

Definition of a Loan Sale

A bank loan sale is when a bank originates a loan and sells it either with or without recourse to an outside buyer. If the loan is sold without recourse, once the loan is sold, not only is it removed from the bank's balance sheet but also the bank has no

Recourse
The ability of a loan buyer to sell it back to the originator should the loan go bad.

explicit liability if the loan eventually goes bad. Thus, the buyer bears all the credit risk. If, however, the loan is sold with **recourse,** under certain conditions, the buyer can put the loan back to the selling bank; therefore, the bank retains a contingent credit risk liability. In practice, most loans are sold without recourse because a loan sale is only technically removed from the balance sheet when the buyer has no future credit risk claim on the bank. Importantly, loan sales involve no creation of new types of securities such as pass-throughs, CMOs, and MBBs described in Chapter 21; as such they are a primitive form of securitization in that loan selling creates a secondary market for loans.

Concept Question

1. Which loans should have the highest yields: (*a*) loans sold with recourse or (*b*) loans sold without recourse?

Types of Loan Sale

The U.S. loan sales market has three segments; two involve the sale and trading in domestic loans, while the third involves LDC loan sales and trading. Since we fully described the LDC loan sales market in Chapter 12, we concentrate on the domestic loan sales market here.

Traditional Short-term.   In the traditional short-term segment of the market, banks sell loans with short maturities, often one to three months. This market has characteristics similar to commercial paper issued by corporations in that loan sales have similar maturities and issue size. Loan sales, however, usually have yields that are 1 to 10 basis points above those of commercial paper of similar rating. In particular, the loan sale market in which a bank originates and sells a short-term loan of a corporation is a close substitute to the issuance of commercial paper—either directly or through dealers—for the 1,000 or so largest U.S. corporations. The key characteristics of the short-term loan sale market are

- Secured by assets of the borrowing firm.
- Loans to investment grade borrowers or better.
- Short-term (90 days or less).
- Yield closely tied to the commercial paper rate.
- Sold in units of $1 million and up.

Until 1984 and the emergence of the HLT and LDC loan markets, these were the predominant loan sales.

HLT Loan Sales.   With the growth in mergers and acquisitions and LBOs, especially during the period 1985–89, a new segment in the loan sales market appeared. What constitutes an HLT loan has often caused dispute. However, in October 1989, the three U.S. federal bank regulators adopted a definition of an HLT as one that involves (1) a buyout, acquisition, or recapitalization, and (2) either doubles the company's liabilities and results in a leverage ratio higher than 50 percent, or results in a leverage ratio higher than 75 percent, or is designated as an HLT by a syndication agent.

HLT loans have the following general characteristics:

- Are secured by assets of the borrowing firm (usually senior secured).
- Are long term (often 6 to 8 years maturity).
- Float with LIBOR, the prime rate, or a CD rate (normally 200–275 basis points above).
- Have strong covenant protection.

Nevertheless, HLTs tend to be quite heterogeneous with respect to the size of the issue, the interest payment date, interest indexing, and prepayment features.

After origination, some HLT borrowers such as Revco, Circle K, and Allied Department Stores suffered periods of **financial distress.** As a result, a distinction is often made between the market for distressed and nondistressed HLTs. Market convention views a distressed HLT as a loan that sells for less than 90 percent of face value.

Financial Distress
A period when a borrower is unable to meet a payment obligation to lenders and other creditors.

In Table 22–1, we show a Bear, Stearns quote sheet from their HLT loan trading desk. Approximately six banks make a market in this debt, either as brokers or (less commonly) as broker-dealers. Most of these are investment banks that view trading in this debt as similar to trading in junk bonds. Moreover, these same investment banks were often involved in the original HLT transactions. There is also one large foreign bank acting as a market marker—ING bank, formerly NMB Post Bank Group of the Netherlands—that has moved into HLT trading as part of its overall business strategy.

As you can see from Table 22–1, bid-offer spreads are very wide by normal securities market standards, often exceeding 300 basis pints. For example, for Maxwell Communications' distressed loan with the highest outstanding dollar volume ($3 billion), the bid was 33 percent of face value and the offer 36 percent of face value.

Concept Question

1. Which have higher yields, junk bonds or HLT loans? Explain your answer.

Size of the Loan Sales Market

The best source of information about aggregate trends in the market for U.S. loan sales by U.S. banks is from the Quarterly Reports of Condition (Call Reports) filed by banks with the Federal Reserve. Since 1983:Q2 banks have had to report their loan sales on Schedule L of the Call Report. Since 1987:Q2 banks have reported loan purchases as well. We show the ratio of loan sales to total assets (LS/TA) for each quarter between 1983:Q2 and 1991:Q2 in column 1 of Table 22–2.

The market's development can be divided into three phases:
(1) The period up to 1986:Q4, when most of the growth is attributable to traditional loan sales. (2) The period 1987:Q1 to 1989:Q3, characterized by dramatic growth with loan sales as a percent of assets increasing nearly $2\frac{1}{2}$ times. And (3) a period after 1989:Q4 of almost as dramatic a decline in volume with loan sales falling to 3.72 percent of bank assets as of 1991:Q2. The second and third phases are clearly attributable to the dramatic growth in HLT loan sales by the largest U.S. banks in the 1987–89 period followed by a dramatic fall off as the market for new HLT loans dried up.

These data do not distinguish between the different types of loan sales or between primary loan sales and loan resales or secondary market trading in loans. For

TABLE 22-1 **High Yield Report's Bellwether Group**
Indicative Price Ranges on Traded Bank Debt (Prices as of noon, Thursday, Aug. 20, 1992)

Issuer	Type of Loan	Original Maturity	Interest Rate on Original Facility	Amount Outstanding in Millions*	Indicative Bid-Offer Price Range†	Change from Last Week's Price Range
Ames Department Stores	Term	1991	Libor + 1.375 or	$317	43–45	Unch.
	Revolver		Prime + 2.375	85	31–35	—
Brent Walker Group	Term + Accrued Int.	1997	Libor + 2	£1.2 bill		Unch.
Circle K	Term	—	Prime + 1.5 or CD + 2	280	45–48	
Drexel	CBI-As X-Cash	1995	NA	2.5	182–185	200–210
Federated	A Notes (Pvt)	2000	—	473	99–99.5	97–99
	B Notes (Pub)	2000	—	555	100.25–100.5	100–100.12
	C Notes (Pvt)	2000	—	Called	—	—
	D Notes (Pub)	1997	—	Called	—	—
	Converts (Pvt)	2004	—	307	69–70	69.5–70.5
	Common (Pub)	—	—	23	14.25	14.50
	Common (Rstd)	—	—	57	13.25–14	13.25–13.87
Gillett Holdings	Term	—	Libor + 2.75 or	130	89–92	86–88
	Revolver	—	Prime + 1.5			
Hillsborough Holdings	Term	1991	Libor + 2.25 or	81	89–90	Unch.
	Revolver		Prime + 1.5	242		
L. J. Hooker	Aussie-4A	NA	NA	—	16–18	Unch.
	U.S.-4B	NA	NA	—	16–18	Unch.
Integrated Resources Inc.		1995	Prime	239	37–40	Unch.
Interco Inc.	As	1991–93	—	1,665	99–100	97–99
	Bs		—		90.5–91	NC
Insilco Corp.	Term	1990–96	Prime + 1.5	248	96–98	96–99

R. H. Macy & Co.	Swiss	1994	10.41	550	73–74	Unch.
	Term	1994	Libor + 2.25 or	270	69–70	Unch.
	Revolver	—	Prime + 1.25	600	69–70	Unch.
Maxwell Communications	Mult. Tranche Financing	NA	Various	3,000	33–36	34–36
Memorex-Telex	B. Tranche	1995	Various	150	33–36	34–36
Olympia & York Resources	Term	NA	Various	—	35–40	38–42
Petrolane Inc.	Term	1996	Libor + 2.125 + or Prime + 1.125	297	80–82	Unch.
Revco D. S. Inc.	New, Secured Bank Notes	1997	11%	306	100.62–100.75	Unch.
West Point Acquisition	Revolver	1989	Libor + 2.5 or Prime + 1.5	796	92–98	92–94
WPP Group	—	—	—	—	60–65	Unch.

*All amounts are estimated. In case of revolver, amount of original commitment or, if in bankruptcy, pre-petition funded amount.

†Will depend on a number of factors, including size of transaction and terms of documentation.

SOURCE: From *High Yield Report*, August 24, 1992. Reprinted by permission of Bear, Stearns & Co. Inc.

TABLE 22–2 Loan Sales and Loan Purchases
(Industry Proportions Measured in Percent)

Time Period	LS/TA	LP/TA
1983:Q2	1.22%	
1983:Q3	1.36	
1983:Q4	1.56	
1984:Q1	1.42	
1984:Q2	1.41	
1984:Q3	1.58	
1984:Q4	2.01	
1985:Q1	2.08	N/A
1985:Q2	2.35	
1985:Q3	2.97	
1985:Q4	2.80	
1986:Q1	2.36	
1986:Q2	2.89	
1986:Q3	3.23	
1986:Q4	3.71	
1987:Q1	5.56	
1987:Q2	6.56	0.53%
1987:Q3	6.29	0.72
1987:Q4	6.43	0.55
1988:Q1	7.66	0.58
1988:Q2	7.99	0.56
1988:Q3	8.38	0.57
1988:Q4	9.00	0.62
1989:Q1	8.56	0.53
1989:Q2	8.47	0.58
1989:Q3	8.89	0.56
1989:Q4	7.66	0.59
1990:Q1	6.35	0.49
1990:Q2	5.55	0.48
1990:Q3	5.03	0.47
1990:Q4	4.86	0.51
1991:Q1	3.95	0.39
1991:Q2	3.72	0.50

LS = Loan sales
LP = Loan purchases
TA = Total bank assets
N/A = Not available
SOURCE: Bank Call Reports, Federal Reserve

example, the Loan Pricing Corporation reports that between 1985 and 1990 there were 2,316 HLT deals, with total volume of $416 billion. The volume of secondary market trading in these loans was estimated at no more than $10 billion for 1992.[1] This compares to junk bonds with an outstanding market size of approximately $200 billion and an annual amount traded of approximately $100 billion. We discuss next the reasons for the low volume of secondary market trading in loans.

---

[1]See "In Distress but Booming," *The Independent,* February 19, 1993.

Types of Loan Sales Contract

There are two basic types of loan sale contracts or mechanisms by which loans can be transferred between seller and buyer, participations and assignments. Currently, assignments comprise the bulk of loan sales trading.

Participations.   The unique features of **participations in loans** are

- The holder (buyer) is not a party to the underlying credit agreement so that the initial contract between loan seller and borrower remains in place after the sale.
- The loan buyer can exercise only partial control over changes in the loan contract's terms. The holder can only vote on material changes to the loan contract, such as the interest rate or collateral backing.

The economic implication of these features is that the buyer of the loan participation has a double-risk exposure, a risk exposure to the borrower as well as a risk exposure to the selling bank. Specifically, if the selling bank fails, the loan participation bought by a outside party may be characterized as an unsecured obligation of the bank, rather than as a true sale, if there are grounds for believing that some explicit or implicit recourse existed between the loan seller and buyer. Alternatively, the borrowers' claims against a failed selling bank may be set off against its loans, reducing the amount of loans outstanding and adversely impacting the buyer of a participation in those loans. As a result of these exposures, the buyer bears a double monitoring cost as well.

Assignments.   Because of the monitoring costs and risks involved in participations, loans are sold on an assignment basis in more than 90 percent of the cases on the U.S. domestic market. The key features of an **assignment** are

- All rights are transferred on sale, meaning the loan buyer now holds a direct claim on the borrower.
- Transfer of U.S. domestic loans is normally associated with a Uniform Commercial Code filing (as proof that a change of ownership has been perfected).

While ownership rights are generally much clearer in a loan sale by assignment, frequently contractual terms limit the seller's scope regarding to whom the loan can be sold. In particular, the loan contract may require either the bank agent or the borrower to agree to the sale and/or the sale may be restricted to a certain class of institutions such as those that meet certain net worth/net asset size conditions. (A bank agent is a bank that distributes interest and principal payments to lenders in loan syndications with multiple lenders.)

Currently, the trend appears to be toward loan contracts being originated with very limited assignment restrictions. This is true in both the U.S. domestic and LDC loan sales markets. The most tradeable loans are those that can be assigned without buyer restrictions. Even so, one has to distinguish between floating-rate and fixed-rate assignment loans. In floating rate loans, most loan sales by assignment occur on the loan repricing date, which may be two or four times a year, due to complexities for the agent bank in calculating and transferring accrued interest—especially given the heterogeneous nature of floating-rate loan indexes such as fed funds plus, T bond plus, or LIBOR plus. In addition, the nonstandardization of **accrued interest** payments in fixed-rate loan assignments (trade date, assignment date, coupon payment date) adds complexity and friction to this market. Moreover, while the bank agent may have a full record of the initial owners of the loans, it does not always have an up-to-date record of loan ownership changes and related transfers following trades. This means that great difficulties often occur for the borrower, bank agent, and the loan buyer in ensuring that the current holder of the loan receives the interest and principal payments due.

Finally, the buyer of the loan often needs to verify the original loan contract and to establish the full implications of the purchase regarding the buyer's rights to collateral if the borrower defaults.

Because of these contractual problems, trading frictions, and costs, some loan sales take as long as three months to complete; reportedly, up to 50 percent eventually fail to be completed at all. In many cases, the incentive to renege on a contract arises because market prices move away from those originally agreed so the counterparty finds reasons to delay the completion of a loan sale and/or eventually refuses to complete the transaction.[2]

The Buyers and Sellers

Vulture Fund
A specialized fund that invests in distressed loans.

The Buyers.   Out of the wide array of potential buyers, some are concerned with only a certain segment of the market for regulatory and strategic reasons. In particular, an increasingly specialized group of buyers of distressed HLT loans contains investment banks and **vulture funds.**

Investment banks are predominately involved because (1) they utilize similar investment skills as in junk bond trading; and (2) they were often closely associated with the HLT distressed borrower in underwriting the original junk bond/HLT deals. As such, large investment banks such as Salomon; Merrill Lynch; and Goldman Sachs are relatively more informed agents in this market, either as market makers or in taking short-term positions on movements in the discount from par.

Vulture funds are specialized funds established to invest in distressed loans. This investment can be active, especially for those seeking to use the loans purchased for bargaining in a restructuring deal; this generates a restructuring outcome and thus returns that strongly favor the loan purchaser. Alternatively, such loans may be held as a passive investment, as just one high-yield security in a well-diversified portfolio of distressed securities. Many vulture funds are, in fact, managed by investment banks. Most secondary market trading in U.S. loan sales occurs in this segment of the market.

For the nondistressed HLT market and the traditional U.S. domestic loan sales market, the five major buyers are other domestic banks, foreign banks, insurance companies and pension funds, closed-end bank loan mutual funds, and nonfinancial corporations.

Other Domestic Banks.   The interdomestic loans sales market is at the core of the traditional market and revolves around correspondent banking and *regional banking/branching restrictions* (such as the McFadden Act of 1927 and the Bank Holding Company Act of 1956 and its 1970 Amendments). Restrictions on nationwide banking have often led to banks originating regionally undiversified and often borrower undiversified loan portfolios.

---

[2]See "In Distress but Booming," *The Independent,* February 19, 1993.

TABLE 22–3 **Assets of Retail Bank Loan Funds**

Funds	Assets $M	Percent Invested in C&I Loans	Date of Initial Offering	Current Rate of Return
Allstate Prime Income Trust	$ 191	N/A	Nov-89	8.00%
Eaton Vance Prime Rate Fund	1,740	85%	Jul-89	9.60
Merrill Lynch Prime Fund	1,700	N/A	Oct-89	8.50
Pilgrim Prime Rate Trust	1,100	85–95	May-88	9.96
Van Kampen Prime Rate Trust	465	96.5	Oct-89	10.00
Total assets of bank loan funds	5,196			

SOURCE: From *Loan Pricing Report,* April 1990, p. 13. Reprinted by permission.

Small banks often sell loan participations to their large correspondents to improve regional/borrower diversification and to avoid regulatory imposed single borrower loan concentration ceilings. (A loan to a single borrower should not exceed 15 percent of a bank's capital.) This arrangement can also work in the other direction, with larger banks selling participations to smaller banks. The traditional interbank market, however, has been shrinking. In Table 22–1, column 2 shows the decline in the loan purchase/total asset ratio for domestic banks between 1987 and 1991. This is due to at least three factors: First, the traditional correspondent banking relationship is breaking down in a more competitive market. Second, concerns about counterparty risk and moral hazard have increased (e.g., Penn Square, a small bank, made bad loan sales to its larger correspondent bank Continental Illinois in the early 1980s). And third, the barriers to nationwide banking are being eroded, especially through the expansion of regional banking pacts and loan production offices (see Chapter 17).

Foreign Banks.   Foreign banks remain the dominant buyer of domestic U.S. loans. Due to the costs of branching and the post-1978 restrictions on interstate branching by foreign banks under the International Banking Act, the loan sales market allows foreign banks to achieve a well-diversified domestic U.S. loan portfolio without developing a nationwide banking network. However, renewed interest in asset **downsizing,** especially among Japanese banks, may mean that this source of demand will likely contract in the near future (see Chapter 17).

Downsizing
Shrinking the asset-size of an FI.

Insurance Companies and Pensions Funds.   Subject to meeting liquidity and quality or investment grade regulatory restrictions, insurance companies and pension funds are important buyers of long-term maturity loans.

Closed-End Bank Loan Mutual Funds.   Established in 1988, these leveraged mutual funds, such as Merrill Lynch Prime Fund, invest in domestic U.S. bank loans. Recent figures—see Table 22–3—put their asset size at approximately $5 billion and their number at five. While they could purchase loans on the secondary market, such as loan resales, the largest funds have moved into primary loan syndications because of the attractive fee income available. Indeed, some money center banks, such as Citibank and Chemical Bank, have actively encouraged closed-end fund participation in primary loan syndications.

PROFESSIONAL PERSPECTIVES

The Secondary Market for Distressed and High Yield Bank Loans

Geoffrey A. Gold
ING Bank

The secondary market for highly leveraged transaction (HLT) bank loans has expanded exponentially during the past three years from roughly $1 billion in turnover and a handful of participants involved in 1989 to more than $11 billion of turnover (Goldsheets 1/25/93) and more than 50 participants in the distressed sector alone. The impetus for the development of this market was the 1989–90 crash of the junk bond market and the two-year period of large-scale bankruptcies and restructurings that followed. Companies such as Federated Department Stores, Revco Corporation, Interco Inc. and Lomas Financial Corporation are among the well-known examples of overleveraged, junk bond-financed LBOs that relied on the bankruptcy process to fix their irrational capital structures. Moreover, many commercial banks had large portfolios of loans to these companies at a time when capital requirements under the BIS guidelines were becoming increasingly important and U.S. regulators were pressuring banks to reduce levels of nonperforming loans. In addition, banks with large portfolios of nonperforming loans were being penalized with weak stock prices in the equity markets. To reduce nonperforming loan levels, banks either willingly or unwillingly reduced this exposure. In other words, banks either had balance sheets strong enough to allow them to comfortably absorb losses on the nonperforming loans they sold or, alternatively, their financial stability was so fragile that they had to sell to improve their balance sheets.

In a recent study for the Foothill Group, Ed Altman (Max Heine Professor of Finance, Stern School of Business, New York University) estimated that $130–200 billion of distressed bank loans and other private paper was in existence in mid-1992. While on the one side, banks wanted to sell loans, on the other side, traditional bankruptcy investors and certain savvy junk bond investors saw a tremendous opportunity to earn very high rates of return by investing in the senior secured portion of the capital structure of a company. Thus, all the ingredients necessary for the development of a secondary market were present.

Bank Loan Buyers

Generally, bank loan buyers can be divided into two major groups, active strategic buyers and passive financial buyers. Strategic buyers are involved because they want to own companies or divisions. Between 1985 and 1989, this was accomplished by making a bid for the equity of a company. It could now be accomplished by buying up debt that was expected to be converted into equity during a company's bankruptcy process. Carl Ichan, Leon Black, and more recently Ronald Perelman are the best-known examples of strategic investors.

Financial buyers did not necessarily desire to own companies, but recognized an opportunity to earn excess rates of return by purchasing senior debt, and sometimes providing input directly in the restructuring process. The old debt would be exchanged for new debt and perhaps equity in a rationally capitalized company. The early players in this category included Trust Company of the West, Fidelity, Foothill Group, and Mutual Shares. Also, aggressive hedge fund money managers shooting for 20 percent plus rates of return gravitated toward this market as the M&A game dried up in the late 1980s. ING estimates that more than $3 billion of capital is currently available for investment in bank loans.

continued

Nonfinancial Corporations.   There are some corporations that buy loans, but this activity is limited to the very largest U.S. and European companies, and amounts to no more than 5 percent of total U.S. domestic loan sales.[3]

---

[3]Nonfinancial corporations are bigger buyers in the LDC loan sales market as part of debt-equity swaps (see Chapter 12).

Transferability

Selling banks transfer loans to buyers through assignment agreements or participations. The process of negotiating these legal documents generally takes between two and three weeks. Since the early days in 1990, the transfer process has become much more standardized, leading to cleaner and faster closings. The cleanest method of transfer is by an assignment in which all rights and obligations of the original lender are passed through directly to the new buyer, who then has a direct relationship with the borrower and the agent bank. If this cannot be accomplished for any reason, transfer takes place through a participation agreement in which the original lender maintains borrower and agent bank relationships but passes all economic interests on to the buyer.

Market Structure

The bank loan product fits into three broad categories: par or near par loans, late stage or recently restructured loans, and distressed/bankrupt situations. Par/near par loans generally trade between 95 and 100 percent of face value and are generated by bank financing of healthy but leveraged companies. As junk bond financing became revitalized in 1992 after a 2 1/2 year hiatus, so too did bank financing. Demand for leveraged loans was led by regional U.S. banks and foreign banks that had been starved for new product over the past couple of years. The Goldsheets estimates that volume exceeded $40 billion in this sector in 1992 and examples of borrowers included Burlington Industries, Grand Union, Lexmark Intl., and Hospital Corp. of America.

The next level of risk in this continuum involves loans to companies that have recently been restructured and/or recently emerged from bankruptcy with a healthy capital structure. The loans usually trade between 85 and 93 percent of face value, pay current interest, and are not in imminent danger of default. Buyers of these loans often anticipate improvement in the health of the underlying company and a potential for refinancing in the near future. Naturally, the riskiest and potentially most financially rewarding situations fit into the bankruptcy/distressed category. Loans in this category can trade as low as 20 percent of face (not a common occurrence), but are normally priced between 50 and 70 percent. In this sector, 1991 and 1992 were exceptional years as the average rate of return exceeded 30 percent for many players. Prices increased rapidly as more money entered the market based on the results of early situations like Federated and Revco in which loan prices doubled between bankruptcy filing and emergence from Chapter 11.

The Future

While the future for the par/near par market seems bright due to an improving economy and robust demand for public refinancings, the prospects for the traditional corporate distressed market are uncertain. The easy money has been made as the big junk bond-financed LBOs and leveraged recapitalizations of the 1980s have been restructured and refinanced. Market participants are being forced to look at small- and middle-market companies requiring much more active participation and longer investment periods. Also, investors have begun to look overseas for new opportunities. This latter approach brings the added risks of currency fluctuations, unfamiliar and different legal systems, and more limited public financial disclosure. As the number of new opportunities diminishes and the risk reward relationship deteriorates (too much money chasing too little product), the smart money will gravitate to new and unexploited emerging markets such as distressed real estate.

BIOGRAPHICAL SUMMARY

Geoffrey Gold received his Master of Business Administration from the Stern School of Business at New York University. He holds a Bachelor of Arts degree from Colgate University.

Geoffrey Gold joined ING Bank in 1986. Since June 1991 he has been a trader/portfolio manager in the Domestic Asset Management Group. He specializes in distressed/bankruptcy situations and bank debt. As a member of the Capital Markets Group from 1987 to June 1991, he traded Latin American debt, focusing on special situations, Central America, and the Caribbean.

The Sellers.   The sellers of domestic loans and HLT loans are major money center banks, foreign banks, investment banks, and the Resolution Trust Corporation.

Major Money Center Banks.   Loan selling has been dominated by the largest money center banks. In recent years, market concentration on the loan selling side

---

TABLE 22–4   Distribution of Loan Sales by U.S. Banks

	Top 10 Banks	*Next 40*	*Others*
1986:Q4	60%	18%	22%
1990:Q3	86%	10%	4%

SOURCE: Asset Sales Report, June 1991

---

has been accentuated by the growth of HLTs and the important role major money center banks have played in originating loans in HLT deals.

Table 22–4 shows the distribution of loan sales in 1986:Q4 (at the genesis of the HLT market) and 1990:Q3 after the HLT surge. The top 10 money center banks' share of loan sales rose from 60 to 86 percent with just two banks, Bankers Trust and Security Pacific, accounting for more than 50 percent of sales at the market's peak. However, post-1990 developments suggest that future trends are likely to be toward decreased rather than increased concentration in sales. Specifically, as the market for new HLT deals has collapsed, the largest banks have reduced the size of their domestic loan sales departments. Consequently, we might expect the distribution of loan sales across banks to look more like 1986, than 1990, in the future.

Foreign Banks.   To the extent that foreign banks are sellers rather than buyers of loans, these come out of branch networks such as Japanese-owned banks in California (6 of the 10 largest retail banks in California are Japanese-owned) or through their market making activities. One of the six major market makers in the U.S. loan sales market (especially the HLT market) is ING Bank.

Investment Banks.   Similar to the role of ING bank, investment banks such as Salomon and Bear, Stearns act as loan sellers either as part of their market making function or as active traders. Again, these loan sales are generally confined to large HLT transactions.

The Resolution Trust Corporation (RTC).   Since being established in 1989, the RTC has had to resolve more than 650 problem savings banks, either through merger, closure, or conservatorship. By March 1992, the RTC had disposed of nearly $240 billion in assets with a further $123 billion in assets to liquidate. Of these, the RTC estimates 75 percent comprise highly illiquid assets that are virtually impossible to sell at a positive price.[4] Recent projections suggest that another 250 savings banks may have to be resolved even in the current, relatively favorable, interest rate environment. With respect to the U.S. commercial and industrial loan sale market, the RTC dispositions, mostly through *auctions,* have had a relatively moderate supply-side effect largely because the bulk of RTCs assets have been securities and mortgages. For example, of the $123 billion in assets remaining to be sold in mid-1992, only 4 percent were *performing* loans (some of which may have been consumer loans). The 23 percent *delinquent* loans were mostly of a loss nature with market values significantly below the 40 to 70 percent of par value normally found in the distressed HLT market. While the RTC seeks to improve the salability of delinquent

---

[4]For example, a real estate development loan for a motel built on a chemical dump.

loans by mixing them in packages with performing loans prior to auction, the limited amount of performing loans on the RTC's books significantly inhibits this strategy. Further, the activities of the RTC are being constrained by congressional reluctance to provide the funds RTC estimates it needs to resolve the remaining problem banks.

Why Banks and Other FIs Sell Loans

We have described the growth cycle and characteristics of the loan sales market in the previous section. However, to better understand the market you need to be able to answer the question, Why do banks sell loans? There are a large number of interrelated economic and regulatory reasons to explain loan sales; some are similar to those discussed for securitization in Chapter 21. We discuss six major reasons next.

Loan Diversification.   Regulators limit the amount a bank can loan to a single borrower to a proportion of a bank's capital. In recent years, this loan concentration-capital ratio has been 15 percent. As a result, if a borrower requires a loan larger than permitted by this credit concentration restriction, its demand can only be satisfied by the bank selling the **overline** amount to outside investors. Further, even if the 15 percent limit has not been reached, a bank can still achieve a greater diversification by selling the loans of firms in which it has the highest concentration (see Chapter 8).

Overline
The amount of a loan in excess of a borrower's loan concentration limit.

Reserve Requirements.   Regulatory requirements, such as noninterest-bearing reserve requirements that a bank has to hold at the central bank, are a form of tax that adds to the cost of funding the loan portfolio. Taxes such as reserve requirements create an incentive for banks to remove loans from the balance sheet by selling them without recourse to outside parties.[5]

Broker versus Asset Transformer Technology.   Banks have a comparative advantage in originating and monitoring loans; yet, if such loans are held to maturity on its books, the bank faces both interest rate and credit risks. Both of these risks can be removed or limited if, instead of acting as an asset transformer, the bank originates and monitors loans but sells the loans along with the associated credit and interest rate risk to a third-party investor. In originating and selling loans in this fashion, the bank acts as a loan broker. Moreover, the bank can often immediately report any fee income earned in this manner as current income, whereas interest earned on direct lending can only be accrued (as income) over time. As a result, loan sales can boost a bank's reported income under current accounting rules.

Capital Costs.   Like reserve requirements, the capital adequacy requirements imposed on banks are a burden as long as required capital exceeds the amount the bank believes to be privately beneficial. For tax reasons, debt is a cheaper source of funds

---

[5]Under current reserve requirement regulations (Regulation D, amended May 1986), bank loan sales with recourse are regarded as a liability and hence are subject to reserve requirements. The reservability of loan sales extends to when a bank issues a credit guarantee as well as a recourse provision. Loans sold without recourse (or credit guarantees by the selling bank) are free of reserve requirements. With the elimination of reserve requirements on nontransaction accounts and the lowering of reserve requirements on transaction accounts in 1991, the reserve tax effect is likely to become a less important feature driving bank loan sales (as well as the recourse/nonrecourse mix) in the future.

than equity capital. Thus, banks struggling to meet a required capital (K) − assets (A) ratio can boost this ratio by reducing assets (A) rather than boosting capital (K) (see Chapter 14). One way to downsize or reduce A and boost the K/A ratio is through loan sales.

Liquidity Risk.   In addition to credit risk and interest rate risk, holding loans on the balance sheet can increase the overall illiquidity of the bank's assets. This illiquidity is a problem because bank liabilities tend to be highly liquid. Asset illiquidity can expose the bank to harmful liquidity squeezes whenever depositors unexpectedly withdraw their deposits. To mitigate a liquidity problem, a bank's management can sell some of its loans to outside investors. Thus, the bank loan market has created a secondary market in loans that has significantly reduced the illiquidity of bank loans held as assets on the balance sheet.

Glass-Steagall and Securities Law Interpretations.   Loan sales are also a substitute for securities underwriting. Because the 1933 Glass-Steagall Act prohibited banks from underwriting corporate equity and bonds, this has raised questions about the underwriting of loans for sale in the secondary market.[6]

Case law has been almost unanimous in deciding that a loan or loan participation sold by one bank to another financial institution is not a security for the purposes of Federal Securities Acts (or state securities laws). For example, in *Reves* v. *Ernst & Young,* a family resemblance test was laid down by the Supreme Court. Essentially, the family resemblance test presumes that all debt notes are securities unless they bear a strong family resemblance to certain types of loans including commercial loans. The *Reves* decision requires focusing not on what is distributed but to whom and how it is distributed. In particular, a loan sale offering to sophisticated institutional investors is unlikely to be viewed as a security. Indeed, in a June 1992, Court of Appeals decision regarding a Security Pacific Loan Participation, the family resemblance test was upheld. Specifically, Security Pacific was held not liable to reimburse institutions that purchased short-term interest in loans made by Security Pacific to the now bankrupt Integrated Resources Inc., under a loan participation sales program. The court held that sophisticated investors were bound by a disclaimer in the master participation agreement, exonerating Security Pacific from any duty to pass on the unfavorable information which it possessed about the financial condition of Integrated to the loan participation buyer.

The Declining Loan Sales Market

The loan sales market is currently in decline despite the apparent attractiveness of loan sales to many FIs. Here are some reasons why.

Moral Hazard.   Clearly, banks have an incentive to sell their worst loans and keep their best. This incentive is especially strong if loans are sold without recourse. The bank, as a loan monitor, usually possesses superior information about the quality of the loans sold. Due to their inferior information, investors may be averse to buying loans in a recessionary period such as 1990–92, when the average quality of loans declined.

---

[6]Underwriting is the origination, sale, and distribution of a security or loan.

Loss of Bank Monitoring.   When a buyer purchases a loan without recourse from a bank, the buyer often relies on the bank to continue monitoring the borrower. However, other than reputational considerations, the bank has little incentive to expend resources in monitoring the borrower when it no longer has a loan at risk.[7] Academics such as G. Gorton and G. Pennacchi have argued that the reason why banks continue monitoring is because they extend an implicit guarantee to buyers to repurchase their loans should they go into default.[8] If this is true, some monitoring can be expected to continue by the bank after a sale, but the onus is still on the buyer to expend resources to monitor the borrower. This adds to the costs of loan purchase.

Reductions in M&A/LBO Activity.   The end of the 1980s saw a dramatic shrinkage in LBO and merger and acquisition activity. Along with this came the bankruptcy of Drexel Burnham Lambert in February 1990 and the general shrinkage of the new issue junk bond market. In many LBOs and M&As, bank senior debt played a crucial financing role often alongside very junior junk bond issues. As megamerger deals faded, so did the need for money center banks such as Bankers Trust and Security Pacific to originate and sell off senior HLT loan participations in such deals to other banks.

Regulatory Pressure.   At the end of 1989, bank regulators showed increasing concern about the growth of banks' participation in M&A/LBO deals. They viewed HLT lending as potentially risky despite the apparent seniority of bank loans in any financing package. A major concern was that the restructuring firm's assets were often overvalued and/or that the cash flows generated by these firms were unlikely to be sufficient to meet promised debt payments on the senior loans. The result has been separate regulatory reporting by banks of their HLT loans and more stringent scrutiny of these loans by bank examiners and other regulators since 1989.

Access to the Commercial Paper Market.   With the advent of Section 20 subsidiaries in 1987, large banks have enjoyed much greater powers to underwrite commercial paper directly without legal challenges by the securities industry that underwriting by banks was contrary to the Glass-Steagall Act. This has meant that the need to underwrite or sell short-term bank loans as an imperfect substitute for commercial paper underwriting is now much less important. In addition, more and more smaller middle market firms are gaining direct access to the commercial paper market. As a result, they have less need to rely on bank loans to finance their short-term expenditures.

Credit Crunch.   Many argue that the 1990–1992 recession made bankers less willing to lend. Even so, the evidence of a credit crunch—a shift to the left in the supply of credit at each interest rate—has not been established beyond dispute.[9] The conventional wisdom is that the supply of commercial loans has been more constrained in

[7]One contractual solution to this problem has been the loan sale strip. A bank sells the first stream of payments on a loan to an outside buyer and retains the later payments on its books. As a result, the bank retains a strong incentive to monitor the borrower even over the period when promised loan payments have been sold since the bank wants to ensure that the borrower will be around to make the promised payments to it in later periods.

[8]G. Gorton and G. Pennacchi, "Are Loan Sales Really Off Balance Sheet?" in *Off-Balance-Sheet Activities,* ed. J. Ronen, A. Saunders, and A. C. Sondhi (New York: Quorum Books, 1989), pp. 19–40.

[9]See, A. Berger and G. Udell, "Does Risk-Based Capital Allocate Bank Credit?" *Journal of Money Credit and Banking,* 1994, Forthcoming.

the early 1990s compared to the 1980s. If the volume of primary loans declines, it is not surprising that the volume of loan sales should also decline. Others have argued, however, that the decline in loan volumes may in large part reflect the lower demand for loans by borrowers rather than a contraction of supply by lenders.

Legal Concerns.   A number of legal concerns are hampering the loan sale market's growth, especially for distressed HLT loans. In particular, while banks are normally secured creditors, this status may be attacked by other creditors if the firm enters bankruptcy. For example, **fraudulent conveyance** proceedings have been brought against the secured lenders to Revco, Circle K, Allied Stores, and RJR Nabisco. Such legal suits are one of the factors that have slowed the growth of the distressed loan market. Indeed, in many of the most recent HLT sales, buyers have demanded a put option feature that allows the loan buyer to put the loan back to the seller at the purchase price if a transaction is proved to be fraudulent under the *Uniform Fraudulent Conveyance Act.* Further, a second type of distressed-firm risk may result if, in the process of a loan workout, the bank lender acts more like an equity owner than as an outside debtor. For example, the bank may get involved in the day-to-day running of the firm and make strategic investment and asset sales decisions. This could open up claims that the bank's loans should be treated like equity rather than secured debt. That is, the bank's loans may be subordinated in the claims priority-ranking.

Fraudulent Conveyance
When a transaction such as a sale of securities or transference of assets to a particular party is ruled as illegal.

A Temporary Decline in the Loan Sales Market?

At the moment, it is unclear whether the downward trend in domestic loan sales in the first few years of the 1990s reflects a temporary decline in loan sale volume or a long-term secular decline. Note that at least three factors on the horizon point to an enhanced volume of loan sales in the future.

BIS Capital Requirements.   The BIS 8 percent risk-based capital rules regarding a 100 percent risk weighting of commercial loans means that bankers will continue to have strong incentives to sell commercial loans to other FIs and investors, to downsize their balance sheets, and boost bank capital ratios.

Market Value Accounting.   The Securities and Exchange Commission and the Federal Accounting Standards Board have both advocated the replacement of book value accounting with market value accounting (see Chapter 5). In addition, the duration-based capital requirements for interest rate risk to be introduced by the Federal Reserve in 1993 and proposed internationally by the Bank for International Settlements (BIS) have moved banks toward a market value accounting framework. The effect of marking-to-market is to make bank loans look more like securities and, thus, make them easier to sell and/or trade.

Asset Brokerage and Loan Trading.   The greater emphasis of large money center banks, such as Bankers Trust and J. P. Morgan, as well as investment banks on trading and trading income suggests that significant attention will still be paid to those segments of the loan sales market where price volatility is high and thus potential trading profits can be made. Most HLT loans have floating rates so that their underlying values are in large part insulated from swings in the level of interest rates (unlike fixed-income securities such as Treasury bonds). The low credit quality of many of these loans and their long maturities create an enhanced potential for credit risk volatility. As a result, a short-term three-month secured loan to a AAA-rated company is unlikely to show as significant future credit risk volatility compared to eight-year HLT loans to a distressed company. This suggests that trading in distressed HLT loans will always be attractive for banks that use their specialized credit monitoring skills as asset traders rather than asset transformers, in participating in the market.

Summary

Loan sales provide a primitive alternative to the full securitization of loans through bond packages. The new loan sales market appeared to be born in the early 1980s and allowed banks to sell off short-term and long-term loans of both high and low credit quality. Yet, despite its rapid growth, the loan sales market appears to have fallen into a recent decline. At the moment, it is not possible to say whether the dramatic decline in loan sale volume is temporary or permanent.

Chapter Questions

1. Contrast loan sales with loan securitization (the creation of a pass-thru security based on a pool of underlying loans).
   a. List their similarities and differences.
   b. List each one's advantages and disadvantages.
2. What are the determinants of loan sale prices?
3. Why are yields higher on loan sales than they are for similar maturity and issue size commercial paper issues?
4. Contrast loan participations with loan assignments with respect to:
   a. transactions cost.
   b. monitoring incentives.
   c. risk exposure.
5. Why have FIs been very active in loan securitization issuance of pass-thru securities while they have reduced their volume of loan sales? Under what circumstances would you expect loan sales to dominate loan securitization?
6. Who are the buyers of U.S. loans and why do they participate in this activity?

7. Who are the sellers of U.S. loans and why do they participate in this activity?
8. Why has the volume of loan sales declined in recent years? How did the development of the market in pass-thru securities affect this trend?
9. *a.* Do you expect the volume of loan sales to increase in the future? Why or why not?
   b. Do you expect the issuance of pass-thru securities to increase in the future? Why or why not?
   c. How are your answers to questions *a* and *b* related to one another?
10. Use bond valuation methods to price the following (non-amortizing) loans for sale:
    a. A \$2 million 2 year C & I loan paying 10 percent interest p.a. (on a quarterly basis) and yielding 9 percent p.a.
    b. A \$2 million 2 year C & I loan paying 10 percent interest p.a. (on a quarterly basis) and yielding 10.5 percent p.a.
    c. A \$500,000 15 year jumbo mortgage paying 7 percent interest p.a. (monthly) and yielding 6.55 percent p.a.

23

LIABILITY AND LIQUIDITY MANAGEMENT

Learning Objectives

In this chapter you learn about asset and liability management and how these techniques can be employed to control liquidity risk in FIs. You also learn about regulator-imposed reserve requirements and how they constrain management's choice of liquid assets and the size of the liquid asset portfolio. We explain how liability and liquidity management are complementary to one another. You will also have a better understanding of the wide range of instruments available to the modern FI manager to control liquidity risk exposure.

Introduction

Depository institutions as well as life insurance companies are especially exposed to liquidity risk (see Chapter 13). The essential feature of this risk is that an FI's assets are relatively illiquid in the face of sudden withdrawals (or nonrenewals) of liability claims. The classic case is a bank run where depositors demand cash as they withdraw their claims from a bank and the bank is unable to meet these demands because of the relatively illiquid nature of its assets. For example, it could have a large portfolio of non-marketable small business loans.

To reduce the risk of a liquidity crisis, FIs can insulate their balance sheets from liquidity risk by efficiently managing their liquid asset positions or managing the liability structure of their portfolios. We address both management issues. In reality, an FI manager can optimize over both liquid asset and liability structures to insulate the FI against liquidity risk.

Liquid Asset Management

A liquid asset can be turned into cash quickly and at a low transactions cost with little or no loss in principal value. Specifically, a liquid asset is traded in a thick market where even large transactions in that asset do not move the market price or will move it very little. Good examples of liquid assets are newly issued Treasury bills, Treasury notes, and Treasury bonds. The ultimate liquid asset is, of course, cash. While it is obvious that an FI's liquidity risk can be reduced by holding large amounts of assets such as cash, T-bills, and T bonds, FIs usually face a return or interest earnings penalty from doing this. Because of their low liquidity and default risks, such assets often bear low returns reflecting their essentially risk free nature. By contrast, illiquid assets often have to promise additional returns or risk premiums to compensate an FI for the relative lack of marketability and often greater default risk of the instrument.

On the other hand, holding relatively small amounts of liquid assets exposes an FI to enhanced illiquidity and run risk problems. Excessive illiquidity risk can result in insolvency and can even lead to contagious effects that negatively impact other FIs (see Chapter 13). Consequently, regulators have often imposed minimum liquid asset reserve requirements on FIs. In general, these liquid asset requirements differ in nature and scope across FIs, and even across countries. They depend on the illiquidity risk exposure perceived for the type of FI and other regulatory objectives that relate to minimum liquid asset requirements.

Specifically, regulators often set minimum liquid asset requirements for at least two other reasons beyond simply ensuring that FIs can meet expected and unexpected liability withdrawals. The two other reasons are monetary policy reasons and taxation reasons.

Monetary Policy Reasons

Many countries set minimum liquid asset reserve requirements with the objective of strengthening monetary policy. Specifically, setting a minimum ratio of liquid reserve assets to deposits limits the ability of banks and bank-related institutions to expand lending and enhances the central bank's ability to control the money supply. In this context, requirements that depository institutions hold minimum ratios of liquid assets to deposits allow the central bank to gain greater control over the money supply and its growth as part of its overall macrocontrol objectives.

Taxation Reasons

Another reason for minimum requirements on FI liquid asset holdings is to force FIs to invest in government financial claims rather than private-sector financial claims. That is, minimum required liquid asset reserve requirements are an indirect way in which governments can raise additional "taxes" from FIs. Requiring banks to hold cash in the vault or cash reserves at the central bank (when there is no interest rate compensation paid) involves a resource transfer from banks to the central bank. In fact, the profitability of many central banks is contingent on the size of the **reserve requirement tax** they can levy on banks under their jurisdiction.

Reserve Requirement Tax
The cost of holding reserves when the central bank pays no interest on them and inflation is present to erode the purchasing power value of those balances.

Concept Question

1. Can we view reserve requirements as a tax when the consumer price index (CPI) is falling?

The Composition of the Liquid Asset Portfolio

The composition of an FI's liquid asset portfolio, especially among cash and government securities, is partly determined by earnings considerations and partly by the type of minimum liquid asset reserve requirements imposed by the central bank. In many countries, such as the United Kingdom, reserve ratios have historically been imposed to encompass both cash and liquid government securities such as T-bills. Thus, a 20 percent **liquid-assets ratio** would require a bank to hold cash plus government securities in a ratio of $1 to $5 of deposits. Also, many states in the

Liquid-Assets Ratio
A minimum ratio of liquid assets-total assets set by the central bank.

United States impose liquid asset ratios on life insurance companies and savings banks that require minimum cash and government securities holdings in their balance sheets. By contrast, the minimum liquid-asset requirements on banks in the United States have been cash-based and have excluded government securities. Currently, banks in the United States are required to hold a 10 percent minimum cash reserve ratio against demand deposits above $46.2 million and 3 percent against the rest.[1] As a result, government securities are less useful, in that they are not given official reserve status and at the same time yield lower promised returns than loans. Nevertheless, many banks view government securities holdings as performing a useful **buffer reserve** function. In times of liquidity crisis when significant drains on cash reserves occur, these securities can be turned into cash quickly, and with very little loss of principal value, because of the deep nature of the markets in which these assets are traded.

Buffer Reserves
Nonreserve assets that can be quickly turned into cash.

Concept Question

1. In general, would it be better to hold 3-month T-bills or 10-year T notes as buffer assets? Explain your answer.

Return-Risk Trade-Off for Liquid Assets

In optimizing its holdings of liquid assets, an FI has to trade the benefit of cash immediacy for lower returns. In addition, the FI manager's choice is one of constrained optimization in the sense that liquid-asset reserve-requirements imposed by regulators set a minimum bound on the level to which liquid reserve assets can fall in the balance sheet. Thus, an FI facing little risk of liquidity withdrawals and holding only a small amount of liquid assets for prudential reasons would find that it is forced to hold more than is privately optimal due to minimum reserve restrictions imposed by regulators.

In the next section, we examine the risk return trade-off in running a liquid asset position, and the constraints imposed on this position by regulation, by looking at a detailed example of FI liquidity management. This example is for U.S. banks under the current minimum reserve requirements imposed by the Federal Reserve. However, many of the issues and trade-offs are readily generalizable to any FI facing liability withdrawal risk under conditions where minimum liquid asset reserve ratios are imposed by regulators.

The Liquid-Asset Reserve Management Problem for U.S. Banks

The issues involved in the optimal management of a liquid asset portfolio are illustrated by the problems faced by the money desk manager in charge of a U.S. bank's reserve position. In the context of U.S. bank regulation, we concentrate on a bank's management of its cash reserves, defined as vault cash and cash deposits held by the bank at the Federal Reserve.[2] Since January 1991, banks in the United States have

---

[1]As of February 1993, these were the requirements. This minimum figure is adjusted by the Federal Reserve each year to reflect the growth of deposits. Specifically, the figure is adjusted by 80 percent of the change in transaction accounts held by all depository institutions. The reserve ratio was reduced from 12 to 10 percent for transaction accounts over $46.8 million in April 1992.

[2]However, banks that are not members of the Federal Reserve System—mostly very small banks—may maintain reserve balances with a Federal Reserve Bank indirectly (on a pass-through basis) with certain approved institutions, such as correspondent banks.

had to hold a 3 percent cash reserve against the first $46.2 million of transaction accounts (such as demand deposits) and 10 percent against the rest.[3] Historically, banks in the United States also had to hold a reserve ratio against time deposits; however, this was reduced from 3 to 0 percent at the beginning of 1991.

While knowing the target reserve ratio—here assumed to be 10 percent of demand deposits—the bank reserve manager requires two additional pieces of information to manage the position. First, over what period's deposits do they compute the bank's reserve requirement? And second, over what period or periods do we have to maintain the target reserve requirement just computed?

The U.S. system is complicated by the fact that the period for which the bank manager computes the required reserve target differs from the period during which the reserve target is maintained or achieved. We describe the computation and maintenance periods for bank reserves next.

Reserve Computation Period
Period over which required reserves are calculated.

Computation Period.   A U.S. bank reserve manager has to think of the world as being divided into two-week periods for the purposes of bank reserve management. The **reserve computation period** always begins on a Tuesday and ends on a Monday 14 days later. Consider ABC bank's reserve manager who wants to assess the bank's minimum cash reserve requirement target. Let's suppose that the manager knows the bank's demand deposit position at the close of the banking day on each of the 14 days over the period Tuesday, July 21, to Monday, August 3. Of course, in reality, the manager only knows these deposit positions with certainty at the very end of the two-week period. Consider the realized demand deposit positions of ABC bank in Table 23–1.

The first thing to note from Table 23–1 is that the minimum daily average reserves a bank must maintain in the reserve maintenance period is computed as a percent of the daily average demand deposits held by the bank over the two-week computation period:

Minimum daily average reserves in = Reserve × Daily average demand deposits
the reserve maintenance period   ratio   in the reserve computation period

$$\$130.57 \text{ million} = 10\% \times \$1,305.7 \text{ million}$$

That is, the ABC bank must maintain a daily average minimum of $130.57 million in reserves (vault cash plus deposits held by the bank at the Federal Reserve) over the reserve maintenance period. Note that this daily average target is calculated by taking a 14-day average of demand deposits even though the bank is closed for 4 of the 14 days (two Saturdays and two Sundays). Effectively, Friday's deposit figures count three times compared to other days in the business week. This means that the bank manager who can engage in a strategy whereby deposits are lower on Fridays, on average, can lower the bank's reserve requirements. This may be important if required liquid asset reserve holdings are above the level that is optimal from the bank's perspective to handle liquidity drains due to expected and unexpected deposit withdrawals.

---

[3]The Garn-St Germain Depository Institutions Act of 1982 (Public Law 97–320) requires that $2 million of reservable liabilities (transaction accounts, nonpersonal time deposits, and Eurocurrency liabilities) of each depository institution be subject to a zero percent reserve requirement. The Federal Reserve adjusts the amount of reservable liabilities subject to this zero percent reserve requirement each year for the succeeding calendar year by 80 percent of the percentage increase in the total reservable liabilities of all depository institutions, measured on an annual basis as of June 30. In February 1993, this figure was $3.8 million.

TABLE 23–1 Demand Deposits of ABC Bank

Date	Million Dollars
Tuesday, July 21	$ 1,420
Wednesday, July 22	1,410
Thursday, July 23	1,360
Friday, July 24	1,200
Saturday, July 25	1,200
Sunday, July 26	1,200
Monday, July 27	1,250
Tuesday, July 28	1,240
Wednesday, July 29	1,290
Thursday, July 30	1,320
Friday, July 31	1,350
Saturday, August 1	1,350
Sunday, August 2	1,350
Monday, August 3	1,340
Total	$18,280
Daily average demand deposits	$ 1,305.7

One strategy employed in the past is for a bank to send deposits offshore on a Friday when a reduction in deposits effectively counts for 3/14ths of the two-week period and to bring them back on the following Monday when an increase counts for just 1/14th of the two-week period. This action effectively reduces the average demand deposits in the balance sheet of the bank over the 14-day period by 2/14ths times the amount sent offshore and thus the reserves it needs to hold. Analysts have labeled this the **weekend game.**[4]

Weekend Game
Lowering deposit balances on Fridays since that day's figures count three times for reserve accounting purposes.

Note that the $130.57 million figure is a minimum reserve target. The bank manager may hold excess cash reserves above this minimum level if the privately optimal or prudential level for the bank exceeds the regulatory specified minimum level because this bank is especially exposed to deposit withdrawal risk. In addition, the bank manager may hold some buffer reserves in the form of government securities that can be turned into cash quickly if deposit withdrawals are unusually high or to preempt the early stages of a bank run.

Reserve Maintenance Period
Period over which actual reserves have to meet or exceed the required reserve target.

Contemporaneous Reserve Accounting System
When the reserve computation and reserve maintenance periods overlap.

Maintenance Period. We have computed a daily average minimum cash reserve requirement for ABC bank but have yet to exactly delineate the two-week period over which the bank manager has to maintain this $130.57 million daily average reserve target. Suppose that the **reserve maintenance period** was set as the same two-week period over which reserve requirements were computed (July 21 to August 3). Obviously, this **contemporaneous reserve accounting system** would impose an extreme level of stress on the bank reserve manager, who would not know the exact reserve target until the two-week period was over on August 3. Implicitly, on any day

---

[4]In fact, the weekend game is a special case of bank window dressing, which is to undertake transactions in a manner that reduces reported deposits below their true or actual figures. For a discussion of window dressing in banking and the incentives for bankers to window dress, see L. Allen and A. Saunders, "Bank Window Dressing: Theory and Evidence," *Journal of Banking and Finance* 16, 1992, pp. 585–624.

FIGURE 23–1

Almost contemporaneous reserve requirements

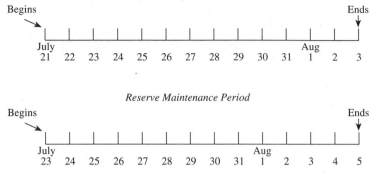

before then, the manager would face reserve target uncertainty. For example, on Monday, July 27, the manager knows the deposit levels for 7 of the 14 days but is unclear as to what deposits are going to be for the last 7 days. The manager can estimate deposits based on projections of deposit flows from deposit behavior observed over the first seven days but these will always be subject to error. Since required reserves are the product of the reserve ratio and average daily deposits over a 14-day period, and the latter are not fully observed with certainty until the end of the period. Thus, the manager must face some uncertainty about the true level of the reserve target. Of course, as the days pass and the end of the 14 days approaches, the degree of uncertainty as to the true reserve target diminishes; there is a gradual resolution of uncertainty about the true reserve target for the bank as the period evolves.[5]

Because a bank manager would not know the true minimum reserve target until the two weeks are up on August 3, regulators have set the two-week reserve maintenance period to make the achievement of reserve targets slightly easier than if the two-week reserve maintenance period ran exactly synchronous to the two-week reserve calculation period (i.e., full contemporaneous reserve accounting). In actuality, regulators give bank managers a two-day leeway, or grace period; the 14-day maintenance period for meeting the reserve target begins 2 days after and ends two days after the two-week reserve computation period.

In our example, the reserve computation period runs from Tuesday, July 21, to Monday, August 3, but the reserve maintenance period runs from Thursday, July 23, to Wednesday, August 5. As a result, for the last two days of the reserve maintenance period, August 4 and 5, the bank manager knows the minimum reserve target (here $130.57 million per day) with absolute certainty. However, for the first 12 days of the reserve maintenance period the manager would still be uncertain as to the final daily average target. We show this almost contemporaneous reserve accounting system in Figure 23–1.

Basically, the reserve manager has two days, August 4 and August 5, to correct any major undershooting or overshooting of the required reserve target over the preceding 12 days when there was target uncertainty.

---

[5]For a further discussion of this resolution of uncertainty see P. A. Spindt and J. R. Hoffmeister, "The Micromechanics of the Federal Funds Market: Implications for Day of the Week Effects in Funds Rate Variability," *Journal of Financial and Quantitative Analysis* 23, 1988, pp. 401–16.

TABLE 23–2   ABC Bank's Actual Daily Reserve Positions over the July 23–August 5 Reserve Maintenance Period

Date	Million Dollars	
Thursday, July 23	$129	
Friday, July 24	130	
Saturday, July 25	130	
Sunday, July 26	130	
Monday, July 27	128	
Tuesday, July 28	127	
Wednesday, July 29	132	
Thursday, July 30	131	
Friday, July 31	129	
Saturday, August 1	129	
Sunday, August 2	129	
→ Monday, August 3	130	[Last day of the reserve computation period]
Tuesday, August 4	?	
Wednesday, August 5	?	[Last day of the reserve maintenance period]

Table 23–2 looks at ABC bank's reserve position as of the close of the day on August 3, when the final reserve target can be calculated with certainty and there are two days left in the reserve maintenance period to make adjustments to reserves held to meet the required target.

On the close of the Monday, August 3, banking day, the average daily cash reserve position of the ABC bank (over the first 12 days of the reserve maintenance period) was $1,554 million/12 = $129.5 million. However, based on deposits held over the full reserve computation period, the manager must hold an average reserve level of $130.57 million per day over the full 14-day reserve maintenance period. Thus, as of that Monday evening, the manager can easily calculate that over the preceding 12 days the minimum reserve target was short by $130.57 million − $129.5 million = $1.07 million per day, or cumulatively 12 × $1.07 million = $12.84 million.

This presents the manager with a clear target for the two remaining days of the reserve maintenance period—Tuesday, August 4, and Wednesday, August 5. The manager must hold an average of $130.57 on each of those days plus make up the cumulative shortfall of $12.84 million over the previous 12 days. The bank manager must hold a total average of:

$$\frac{\$130.57 + \$130.57 + \$12.84}{2} = \$136.99 \text{ million}$$

over the last two days of the reserve maintenance period. While the manager could hold different amounts of reserves on each of these two days, such as $131.99 million on Tuesday, and $141.99 million on Wednesday, they must average to at least $136.99, so that over the full 14-day period the manager can meet the regulatory imposed minimum reserve ratio target.[6]

---

[6]While the $130.57 million daily average is the sum of the vault cash and deposits held by the ABC bank at the central bank, the vault cash component is, in fact, given at the time the reserve maintenance period begins. The vault cash component is calculated over a two-week period that ends two weeks prior

Undershooting/Overshooting of the Reserve Target.

Undershooting.   What happens if at the end of the reserve maintenance period on August 5, the bank holds less than the regulatory required daily minimum reserve ratio, that is, less than $130.57 daily average million in our example? The Federal Reserve allows the bank to make up to a 2 percent daily average error without penalty. Thus, if the bank is 2 percent in the red on its reserve target to the tune of $2\% \times \$130.57$ million = $2.61 million, it has to make this up in the next two-week reserve maintenance period that runs from August 6, to August 19. If the reserve short-fall exceeds 2 percent, the bank is liable to explicit and implicit penalty charges from the Federal Reserve. The explicit charges include the imposition of a penalty interest rate charge equal to the central bank's discount rate plus a markup, while the implicit charges can include more frequent monitoring, examinations, and surveillance if bank regulators view the undershooting of reserve requirements as reflecting an unsafe and unsound practice by the bank's manager. Such a view is likely to be taken only if the bank consistently undershoots its reserve targets.

In undershooting the target, the bank manager has to weigh the explicit and implicit costs of undershooting against any potential benefits. Specifically, it may be beneficial to undershoot if the privately optimal or prudential reserve position of the bank is less than the regulatory set minimum and/or there are very high opportunity costs of meeting the reserve requirement targets. There may be high opportunity costs of meeting reserve targets if interest rates and loan demands are high so that the cost of forgone loans on future profits may be significant.

For a bank below the reserve target, there are two principal ways to build up reserves to meet the target as the reserve maintenance period comes to an end: (1) by liquidating assets through selling off some buffer assets such as Treasury bills, or (2) by borrowing in the interbank market for reserves, especially in the federal funds and repurchase agreement markets, which we describe later. The bank manager is likely to choose the least costly method of meeting any reserve deficiency such as borrowing fed funds if this rate is less than the cost of selling off liquid assets. The manager may be reluctant to fund the whole gap in this manner, however, if the costs of adjusting to an undershooting are high and the privately optimal amount of reserves are less than the regulatory required minimum amount.

In the past, such cost considerations have led some bank managers to use the Federal Reserve's discount window to borrow the required funds to meet reserve shortfalls. The reason for this is that the cost of borrowing from the discount window is the discount rate, an administered rate set by the Federal Reserve. Since this rate is not market determined and is adjusted only weekly, it usually lies below fed funds and government security rates and offers a very attractive borrowing cost to a bank with deficient reserves as the reserve maintenance period comes to an end. However, discount window loans are really only meant to be used by banks on a need rather than a profit basis. That is, by banks that are solvent but face sudden liquidity crises due to deposit withdrawals caused by seasonality in deposit flows, or some other similar lender of last resort need. Specifically, discount window borrowings

---

to the beginning of the reserve computation period. For example, suppose that vault cash had been $10 million on average held at the bank during the period ending two weeks before the reserve computation period started. This means that the true or real target for the bank manager is to maintain reserves on deposit at the Federal Reserve equal to a daily average of $130.57 million − $10 million = $120.57 million over the 14-day reserve maintenance period. That is, effectively, the minimum reserve target is really a minimum target for deposits held on reserve at the Federal Reserve (the central bank).

are not meant to be a cheap source of funds to meet reserve requirements or because the interbank federal funds rate is more costly than the Federal Reserve's discount rate.[7] Despite this, it is evident that discount window borrowings do increase when market rates rise well above the discount rate and tend to fall when the market rate–discount rate spread narrows. Thus, some bank managers appear to be gaming the Federal Reserve by claiming that their borrowings are due to sudden liquidity needs when, in fact, they reflect borrowings to arbitrage the spread between the discount and market rates and to profit from the lender of last resort discount window facility.

Finally, note that any such gaming behavior is extremely dangerous, not only on moral grounds but also on economic grounds; if a bank is caught, it could theoretically lose its bank charter. At best, bank managers seeking to exploit the availability of cheap discount window finance are likely to borrow on a highly randomized basis that is difficult for central bank regulators to detect.

Overshooting.   The cost of overshooting, or holding cash reserves in excess of the minimum required level, depends on whether the bank perceives its prudent level of reserves to meet expected and unexpected deposit withdrawals to be above or below the regulatory imposed minimum reserve requirement.

If its required minimum reserves are above what managers perceive as optimal, the first 2 percent of excess reserves can be carried forward and the Federal Reserve allows them to count toward meeting the reserve requirement in the next two-week maintenance period. After that, any excess reserves held above the required minimum plus 2 percent are a drag on bank earnings, since every dollar that is held as excess reserves either in cash or central bank deposits earns no interest and could have been lent out at the bank lending rate. For example, if the bank's lending rate to its best customers is 12 percent, the bank and its shareholders have suffered an opportunity cost loss of 12 percent for every dollar of excess cash reserves held by the bank.

By contrast, if the bank manager perceives that its required minimum level of reserves is below what it privately needs for expected and unexpected deposit withdrawal exposure, the FI would overshoot the required minimum reserve target. This policy would maintain the liquidity position of the bank at a prudently adequate level. In choosing to overshoot the target, the manager must consider the least cost instrument in which to hold such reserves.

Thus, while some excess reserves might be held in highly liquid noninterest-bearing cash form, at least part of any excess reserve position might be held in buffer assets such as short-term securities or Treasury bills that earn interest but are not quite as liquid as cash. The proportions held between cash and Treasury bills depend in large part on yield spreads.

For example, suppose the loan rate is 12 percent, the T-bill rate is 7 percent, and the interest earned on excess cash holdings is 0 percent. The opportunity cost of a forgone return to the bank from holding excess reserves in cash form or T-bill form is:

$$\text{Opportunity cost cash} = 12\% - 0\% = 12\%$$
$$\text{Opportunity cost T-bills} = 12\% - 7\% = 5\%$$

---

[7]For more on the use of fed funds versus the discount window as a borrowing source, see T. Ho and A. Saunders, "A Micro Model of the Federal Funds Market," *Journal of Finance* 40, 1985, pp. 977–88; and M. Smirlock and J. Yawitz, "Asset Returns, Discount Rate Changes, and Market Efficiency," *Journal of Finance* 40, 1985, pp. 1141–58.

TABLE 23–3   **Reserves and Excess Reserves of U.S. Banks**
(in millions)

	1989 (Dec)	1990 (Dec)	1991 (Dec)	1992 (Nov)
Total reserves	$62,810	$59,120	$55,532	$54,664
Required reserves	61,887	57,456	54,553	53,620
Excess reserves	923	1,664	979	1,043

Thus, T-bills have a significantly lower opportunity cost than cash, and the manager has to weigh the 7 percent net opportunity cost saving of holding excess reserves in T-bill form against the ease with which such instruments can be sold and turned into cash to meet liability withdrawals or liquidity crunches. In Table 23–3, we show excess cash reserves of U.S. banks between 1989 and 1992. As you can see, because of their opportunity cost, excess reserves are invariably kept at very low levels at around 2 percent of required reserves.

Liquidity Management as a Knife Edge Management Problem.   The management of an FI's liquidity position is something of a knife edge situation because holding too many liquid assets penalizes a bank's earnings and, thus, its stockholders. An FI manager who holds excessive amounts of liquid assets is unlikely to survive for long. Similarly, a manager who excessively undershoots the reserve target faces enhanced risks of liquidity crises and regulatory intervention. Again, such a manager's tenure at the FI may be relatively short-lived.

Avoiding the costs of excess overshooting or undershooting is made even more difficult for U.S. banks because the exact minimum required reserve target is not known until two days before the end of reserve maintenance period. This makes the optimal management of the reserve position of a bank similar to a complex dynamic control problem with a moving target. While there have been a number of quite sophisticated attempts to come to grips with this management control problem, there is still room for more work and analysis to be done.[8]

Concept Question

1. Prior to 1984, U.S. banks operated under a lagged reserve accounting system in which the reserve computation period ended one week before the reserve maintenance period. Did the reserve manager face any uncertainty at all in managing a bank's reserve position? Explain your answer.

Liability Management

Liquidity and liability management are closely related; one aspect of liquidity risk control is to build up a prudential level of liquid assets. Another aspect is to manage

---

[8]For a sample of studies that have applied management science and mathematical techniques to the optimization of an FI's reserve position, see W. Poole, "Commercial Bank Reserve Management in a Stochastic Model: Implications for Monetary Policy," *Journal of Finance* 23, 1968, pp. 769–91; and Spindt and Hoffmeister, "The Micro Mechanics."

FIGURE 23–2

Funding risk versus cost

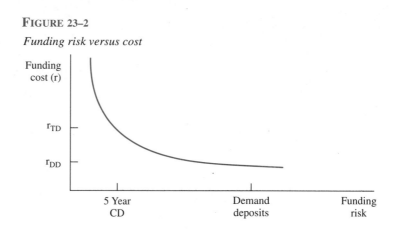

the FI's liability structure so that it reduces the need for large amounts of liquid assets to meet liability withdrawals. However, excessive use of purchased funds can result in a liquidity crisis if investors lose confidence in the bank and refuse to rollover such funds (as Continental Illinois found out in 1984).

Funding Risk and Cost

Unfortunately, constructing a low-cost, low-withdrawal-risk liability portfolio is more difficult than it sounds. This is because those liabilities, or sources of FI funds, that are the most subject to withdrawal risk, are often the least costly. That is, an FI has to trade off the benefits of attracting liabilities at a low funding cost, with a high chance of withdrawal, against liabilities with a high funding cost and low liquidity. For example, demand deposits are relatively low funding cost vehicles for banks but can be withdrawn instantaneously.[9] By contrast, a five-year, fixed-term certificate of deposit may have a relatively high funding cost but can only be withdrawn before the five-year maturity is up after the payment of a substantial interest rate penalty.

Thus, in structuring the liability, or funding, side of the balance sheet, the FI manager faces a trade-off along the lines suggested in Figure 23–2.

Although we have discussed commercial banks funding risk, thrifts and other FIs face a similar trade-off.[10] For example, investment banks can finance through overnight funds (RPs and broker deposits) or longer-term sources such as notes and bonds, while finance companies have a choice between commercial paper and longer-term notes and bonds.

In the next section, we look at the spectrum of liabilities available to a bank manager in seeking to actively impact liquidity risk exposure through the choice of liability structure.

---

[9]Depositors do not always exercise this option; therefore, some demand deposits behave like longer-term core deposits.

[10]The trade-off faced by thrifts is essentially the same as that faced by banks with the exception of thrifts' access to borrowings from Federal Home Loan banks, while banks tend to have more direct access to the federal funds and repurchase agreement markets.

Choice of Liability Structure

In this section, we take a more detailed look at the withdrawal risk and funding cost characteristics of the major liabilities available to a modern bank manager.

Demand Deposits

Withdrawal Risk.   Demand deposits have a high degree of withdrawal risk. Withdrawals can be instantaneous and largely expected by the bank manager, such as preweekend cash withdrawals, or unexpected in economic crisis situations (so-called bank runs).

Costs.   In the United States, demand deposits have paid zero explicit interest since the 1930s by law. This does not mean that they are a costless source of funds for banks or that banks have no price or interest mechanisms available to partially control the withdrawal risk associated with these contracts.

Despite the zero explicit interest paid on demand deposit accounts, competition among banks and FIs has resulted in the payment of implicit interest, or payments of interest in kind, on these accounts. Specifically, in providing demand deposits that are checkable accounts, a bank has to provide a whole set of associated services from provision of checkbooks, to clearing of checks, to sending out statements with cleared checks. Because such services absorb real resources of labor and capital, they are costly for banks to provide. One way in which banks can recapture these costs is through charging fees, such as 10 cents a check cleared. To the extent that these fees do not cover the bank's cost of providing such services, the depositor receives a subsidy or an implicit interest payment. For example, if it costs the bank 15 cents to clear a check, the customer receives a 5 cent subsidy. We can calculate such implicit yields for each service or an average implicit interest rate for each demand deposit account. For example, an average implicit interest rate for a bank's demand deposits might be calculated as:

$$\begin{array}{c} \text{Average implicit} \\ \text{interest rate} \\ \text{(IIR)} \end{array} = \dfrac{\begin{array}{c}\text{Bank's average management} \\ \text{costs per account per annum}\end{array} - \begin{array}{c}\text{Fees earned per} \\ \text{account per annum}\end{array}}{\text{Average annual size of account}}$$

Suppose that:

$$\begin{array}{rl} \text{Bank's average management} = & \$150 \\ \text{costs per account per annum} & \\ \text{Fees earned per account per annum} = & 100 \\ \text{Average annual size of account} = & 1{,}200 \end{array}$$

Then:

$$IIR = \frac{\$150 - \$100}{\$1{,}200} = 4.166\%$$

The payment of implicit interest means that the bank manager is not absolutely powerless to mitigate deposit withdrawals, especially if rates on competing instruments are rising. In particular, the FI could lower check clearing fees which would in turn raises implicit interest payments to deposits. Recognize that such payments are payments in kind or subsidies and are not paid in actual dollars and cents as is interest earned on competing instruments. Nevertheless, implicit payments of interest are tax free while explicit interest payments are taxable. Finally, demand deposits have an additional cost in the form of noninterest-bearing reserve requirements the bank has to hold at the Federal Reserve.

Interest-Bearing Checking Accounts

Withdrawal Risk.   Since 1980, banks in the United States have been able to offer checkable deposits that pay interest and are withdrawable on demand; they are called Negotiable Order of Withdrawal accounts or **NOW accounts.**[11] The major distinction between these instruments and traditional demand deposits is that the depositor has to maintain a minimum account balance to earn interest. If the minimum balance falls below some level, such as $500, these accounts formally convert to a status equivalent to demand deposits and earn no interest. The payment of explicit interest and the existence of the minimum balance requirement makes them potentially less prone to withdrawal risk than demand deposits. Nevertheless, they are still highly liquid instruments from the depositor's perspective.

NOW Account
Negotiable order of withdrawal account that is like a demand deposit account but has a minimum balance requirement.

Costs.   Like demand deposits, the bank can affect the potential withdrawability of these accounts by payment of implicit interest or fee subsidies such as not charging the full cost of check clearance. However, the manager has two other ways to impact the yield paid to the depositor. The first is varying the minimum balance requirement. By lowering the minimum balance requirement, say from $500 to $250, a larger portion of a NOW account becomes subject to interest payments and thus the explicit return and attractiveness of these accounts increases.[12] The second is to vary the explicit interest rate payment itself, such as increasing it from 5 to $5\frac{1}{4}$ percent. Thus, the bank manager has three pricing mechanisms to increase or decrease the attractiveness and therefore impact the withdrawal rate of NOW accounts: implicit interest payments, minimum balance requirements, and explicit interest payments.[13]

For example, consider a depositor who holds on average $250 per month for the first three months of the year, $500 per month for the next three months, and $1,000 per month for the final six months of the year in a NOW account. The NOW account pays 5 percent per annum interest if the minimum balance is $500 or more. The depositor writes an average of 50 checks per month and pays a service fee of 10 cents for each check, but it costs the bank 15 cents to process each check. The account holder's gross interest return, consisting of implicit plus explicit interest, is:

$$\text{Gross interest return} = \text{Explicit interest} + \text{Implicit interest}$$

$$= \$500 \ (.05)(.25) + \$1000 \ (.05)(.5) + (\$.15 - \$.10) \ (50) \ (12)$$

$$= \$6.25 + \$25 + \$30 = \$61.25$$

---

[11]There are also Super-Now accounts that have very similar features to NOW accounts but require a larger minimum balance.

[12]Subject to any regulatory requirement on the minimum balance.

[13]As transactions accounts, these deposits are also subject to reserve requirements at the same rate as on demand deposits as well as deposit insurance premiums. Given a 5 percent NOW account rate, a 10 percent reserve ratio, and a 23 basis point insurance premium, and ignoring implicit interest, the effective cost of the marginal dollar of NOW accounts to the issuing bank is

$$\text{Effective cost} = [r_{NOW}/1-R] + \text{premium} = [.05/.90] + .0023 = .0579 \text{ or } 5.79\%.$$

Suppose that the minimum balance was lowered from \$500 to \$250 and check service fees were lowered from 10 cents to 5 cents per check, then:

$$\text{Gross interest return} = \$250(.05)(.25) + \$500(.05)(25) + \$1000$$
$$(.05)(.5) + (\$.15 - \$.05)(50)(12)$$

$$= \$3.125 + \$6.25 + \$25 + \$60$$

$$= \$94.37$$

Passbook Savings

Withdrawal Risk. Passbook savings are generally less liquid than demand deposits and NOW accounts for two reasons: the first is that they are noncheckable and usually involve physical presence at the bank for withdrawal. Second, the bank has the legal power to delay payment or withdrawal requests for as long as one month. While this is rarely done and withdrawal requests are normally met with immediate cash payment, the legal right to delay provides an important withdrawal risk control to bank managers.

Costs. Since these accounts are noncheckable, any implicit interest rate payments are likely to be small; thus, the principal costs to the bank are the explicit interest payments on these accounts. In recent years, banks have normally paid slightly higher explicit rates on passbook savings than on NOW accounts.

Money Market Deposit Accounts (MMDAs)

MMDAs
Money market deposit accounts are retail savings accounts with some limited checking account features.

Withdrawal Risk. Introduced in 1982 under the Garn-St Germain Act, MMDAs are an additional liability instrument banks can use to control their overall withdrawal risk; in particular, the risk of funds disintermediating from banks and flowing to money market mutual funds (MMMFs). To make banks competitive with the money market mutual funds offered by groups such as Vanguard and Fidelity, **MMDAs** have to be liquid, but not as liquid as demand deposits and NOW accounts. In the United States, MMDAs are checkable but subject to restrictions on the number of checks written on each account per month, the number of preauthorized automatic transfers per month, and the minimum denomination of the amount of each check. For example, a customer with a MMDA may make a maximum of six preauthorized transfers of which no more than three can be checks of at least \$500 each. In addition, MMDAs impose minimum balance requirements on depositors.

Costs. The major cost of MMDAs and the pricing mechanism to control withdrawal risk is the explicit interest rate paid to depositors. Since MMDAs are in direct competition with MMMFs, the bank manager can affect their net withdrawal rate by varying the rate paid on such accounts. In particular, while the rate paid by MMMFs on their shares directly reflects the rates earned on the underlying money market assets in which the portfolio manager invests, such as commercial paper, bankers acceptances, repurchase agreements, and T-bills, the rates paid on MMDAs by bank managers are not directly based on any underlying portfolio of money market assets. In general, bank managers have considerable discretion to alter the rates paid on MMDAs, and thus, the spread on MMMF-MMDA accounts. This can directly impact the rate of withdrawals and withdrawal risk on such accounts. Allowing MMDA rates to have a large negative spread with MMMFs increases the net withdrawal rate on such accounts.

Retail Time Deposits and CDs

Withdrawal Risk.   By contractual design, time deposits and retail certificates of deposit reduce the withdrawal risk of bank issuers. Retail CDs are fixed-maturity instruments with face values under $100,000. In a world of no early withdrawal requests, the bank knows the exact scheduling of interest and principal payments to depositors holding such deposit claims, since these payments are contractually specified. As such, the bank manager can directly control fund inflows and outflows by varying the maturities of the time deposits and CDs it offers to the public. In general, banks offer time deposits and CDs with maturities varying from two weeks to eight years.

In cases where depositors wish to withdraw before the maturity of their time deposit or CD contract, banks are empowered by regulation to impose penalties on the withdrawing depositor equal to a certain number of months' interest depending on the maturity of the deposit. However, while this does impose a friction or transactions cost on withdrawals, it is unlikely to stop withdrawals when the depositor has exceptional liquidity needs. Also, withdrawals may increase if the bank is perceived to be insolvent, despite the presence of interest penalties and the existence of deposit insurance coverage up to $100,000. Nevertheless, under normal banking conditions, these instruments have relatively low withdrawal risk compared to transaction accounts such as demand deposits and NOW accounts and can be used as an important liability management tool to control withdrawal/liquidity risk.

Costs.   Similar to passbook savings, the major costs of these accounts are explicit interest payments. Short-term CDs are often competitive with T-bills and their rates are set with the T-bill rate in mind. Note that depositors who buy CDs are subject to state and local taxes on their interest payments, whereas T-bill investors do not pay state and local taxes on T-bill interest income.[14] Finally, time deposits and CDs do not, at present, require the bank to hold noninterest-bearing reserves at the central bank.

Wholesale CDs

Withdrawal Risk.   Wholesale CDs were innovated by banks in the early 1960s as a contractual mechanism for giving the depositor liquidity without imposing withdrawal risk on the bank. The unique feature of these liability instruments is not so much their large minimum denomination size of $100,000 or more, but that

---

[14]Thus, the marginal investor would be indifferent between Treasury bills and insured bank CDs when:

$$r_{TB} = r_{CD}(1 - T_L)$$

where r_{TB} is the rate on T-bills, r_{CD} is the CD rate and T_L is the local income tax rate. T. Cook estimates the average local tax rate at 8 percent. Thus, if the T-bill rate is 3 percent, insured CDs would have to pay:

$$r_{CD} = r_{TB}/(1 - T_L) = 3.00\%/(1 - .08) = 3.26\%.$$

See T. Cook, "Treasury Bills," in *Instruments of the Money Market,* Federal Reserve Bank of Richmond, 1986, pp. 81–93.

Negotiable Instrument
An instrument whose ownership can be transferred in the secondary market.

they are **negotiable instruments.** That is, they can be resold by title assignment in a secondary market to other investors. This means, for example, that if IBM had bought a $1 million three-month CD from Citibank, and for unexpected liquidity reasons needs funds after only one month has passed, it can sell this deposit to another outside investor in the secondary market. This does not impose any obligation on Citibank in terms of an early funds withdrawal request. Thus, a depositor can sell a relatively liquid instrument without causing adverse withdrawal risk exposure for the bank. Essentially, the only withdrawal risk is that these wholesale CDs are not rolled over and reinvested by the holder of the deposit claim on maturity.[15]

Costs.   The rates banks pay on these instruments are competitive with other wholesale money market rates, especially those on commercial paper and T-bills. This competitive rate aspect is enhanced by the highly sophisticated nature of investors in such CDs, such as money market mutual fund managers, and the fact that these deposits are not explicitly covered by explicit deposit insurance guarantees, which are capped at $100,000. To the extent that these CD's are offered by large banks perceived as being too big to fail, the required credit risk premium on CDs is less than that required for similar quality instruments issued by the private sector (e.g., commercial paper). In addition, required interest yields on CDs reflect investors' perceptions of the depth of the secondary market for CDs. In recent years, the liquidity of the secondary market in CDs appears to have diminished as dealers have withdrawn and the credit risk problems of the largest banks increased. This has increased the relative cost of issuing such instruments by banks.[16]

Federal Funds

Withdrawal Risk.   The liabilities just described are all deposit liabilities, reflecting deposit contracts issued by banks in return for cash. However, banks not only fund their assets through issuing deposits but can also borrow in various markets for purchased funds. Since the funds generated from these purchases are borrowed funds and are not deposits, they are subject to neither reserve requirements (like demand deposits and NOW accounts) nor deposit insurance premium payments to the FDIC (like all the domestic deposits described earlier).[17] The largest market available

---

[15]Wholesale CDs are also offered offshore, in which case they are called Eurodollar CDs. Eurodollar CDs may sell at slightly different rates from domestic CDs because differences in demand and supply for CDs between the domestic and Euromarket and differences in credit risk perceptions of depositors buying a CD from an overseas branch (e.g., Citibank in London) rather than a domestic branch (Citibank in New York). To the extent that it is believed that banks are too big to fail, a guarantee that only extends to domestic branches, then a higher risk premium may be required of overseas CDs. Indeed, FDICIA has severely restricted the ability of the FDIC to rescue overseas depositors of a failed U.S. bank.

[16]In addition, for all the liability instruments considered so far (with the exception of Euro CDs) the bank has to pay a FDIC insurance premium of between 23 and 31 basis points depending on its perceived riskiness (see Chapter 13). For example, consider an AAA bank issuing CDs at 3.26 percent, at which rate a depositor might just be indifferent to holding T-bills at 3.00 percent, given a local tax rate of 8 percent. However, the cost to the bank of the CD issue is not 3.26 percent but rather:

$$\text{Effective CD cost} = 3.26\% + \text{insurance premium} = 3.26\% + 0.23\% = 3.49\%.$$

Thus, deposit insurance premiums add to the cost of deposits as a source of funds.

[17]Foreign deposits are not subject to deposit insurance premiums. However, in the exceptional event of a very large bank failure where all deposits are protected, under the 1991 FDICIA, the FDIC is required to levy a charge on surviving large banks proportional to their total asset size. To the extent that assets are funded by foreign liabilities, this is an implied premium on foreign deposits.

for banks for purchased funds is the federal funds market. While banks with excess reserves can invest some of this excess in liquid assets such as T-bills and short-term securities, an alternative is to lend excess reserves for short intervals to other banks seeking increased short-term funding. The interbank market for excess cash reserves is called the federal funds market. In the United States, federal funds are short-term uncollateralized loans made by one bank to another; more than 90 percent of such transactions have maturities of one day. The bank that purchases funds shows them as a liability on its balance sheet while the bank that sells them shows them as an asset.

For the liability funding bank, there is no risk that the fed funds borrowed can be withdrawn within the day, although there is settlement risk at the end each day (see Chapter 10). However, there is some risk that they will not be rolled over by the lending bank the next day if this is desired by the borrowing bank. In reality, this has occurred only in periods of extreme crisis such as the failure of Continental Illinois in 1984. Nevertheless, since fed funds are uncollateralized loans, fed funds selling banks normally impose maximum bilateral limits or credit caps on a funds-borrowing bank. This may constrain the ability of a bank to expand its federal funds borrowing position very rapidly if this was part of its overall liability management strategy.

Costs.   The cost for the purchasing bank is the federal funds rate. The federal funds rate can vary considerably both within the day and across days. In particular, the federal funds rate shows a lot of variability around the last days of each two-week reserve maintenance period; that is, around the second Tuesday and Wednesday of each successive period.[18] For example, the fed funds rate can rise as high as 30 percent and fall close to zero on some Wednesdays. This is because federal funds are a major liability tool used by banks in offsetting deposit withdrawals that deplete a bank's cash reserve position. Suppose that ABC bank had experienced a large unexpected withdrawal of demand deposits on the afternoon of the second Wednesday of the reserve maintenance period. As deposits are withdrawn, the bank's cash/liquid asset reserve position is depleted in meeting these deposit withdrawals. To offset the possible undershooting of its required minimum and prudential reserve target, the bank can purchase immediately available funds on the interbank federal funds market. Since it has few other alternative market sources on the second Wednesday afternoon and it fears the regulatory penalties from reserve target undershooting, the bank is often willing to pay a high rate to borrow such funds. The rate it pays depends on how many banks are short in reserves on that Wednesday, compared to those banks wanting to generate a one-day return by selling excess reserves on the federal funds market that day. Similarly, if a bank has excess reserves on the last afternoon of the reserve maintenance period, it would prefer to lend them out for one day—even at rates as low as 0.5 percent—since this is better than earning 0 percent on excess cash reserves held at the Federal Reserve.[19]

---

[18]For evidence of this, see A. Saunders and T. Urich, "The Effects of Shifts in Monetary Policy and Reserve Accounting Regimes on Bank Reserve Management Behavior in the Federal Funds Market," *Journal of Banking and Finance* 12, 1988, pp. 523–35.

[19]The minimum required rate would have to exceed the fees the Federal Reserve charges for effecting wire transfers over Fedwire.

Repurchase Agreements (RPs)

Withdrawal Risk.   RPs are collateralized federal funds transactions. In a federal funds transaction, the bank with excess reserves sells fed funds for one day to the purchasing bank. The next day, the purchasing bank returns the fed funds plus one day's interest reflecting the fed funds rate. Since there is a credit risk exposure to the selling bank in that the purchasing bank may be unable to repay the fed funds the next day, it may seek collateral backing for the one-day loan of fed funds. In an RP transaction, the funds-selling bank receives government securities as collateral from the funds-purchasing bank. That is, the funds-purchasing bank temporarily exchanges securities for cash.[20] The next day, this transaction is reversed with the funds-purchasing bank sending back the fed funds borrowed plus interest (the RP rate): it receives in return or repurchases its securities used as collateral in the transaction.

As with the fed funds market, the RP market is a highly liquid and flexible source of funds for banks needing to increase their liabilities and to offset deposit withdrawals. Moreover, like federal funds, these transactions can be rolled over each day. The major liability management flexibility difference between fed funds and RPs is that a fed funds transaction can be entered into at any time in the banking day as long as the Fedwire is open (see Chapter 10).[21] In general, it is difficult to effect an RP borrowing late in the day since the fed funds sending bank has to be satisfied with the type and quality of the securities collateral proposed by the funds-borrowing bank. While this collateral is normally T-bills, T notes, T bonds, and mortgage-backed securities, the maturities and other features such as callability or coupons may be unattractive to the funds seller. Negotiations over the collateral package can delay RP transactions and make them more difficult to arrange than simple uncollateralized fed funds loans.

Costs.   Because of their collateralized nature, RP rates normally lie below federal funds rates. Also, RP rates generally show less interday fluctuation than fed funds over the reserve maintenance period, especially over the last two days of the reserve maintenance period. This is in part due to the lesser intraday flexibility of RPs relative to fed fund transactions.

Other Borrowings

While fed funds and RPs have been the major sources of borrowed funds, banks have utilized a host of other borrowing sources to supplement their liability management flexibility. We describe these briefly in the following sections.

Bankers Acceptances.   Banks often convert off-balance-sheet letters of credit into on-balance-sheet bankers acceptances (BA) by discounting the letter of credit when it is presented by the holder for acceptance. Further, these BAs may then be resold to money market investors. Thus, BA sales to the secondary market are an additional funding source.

---

[20]Since Treasury securities are of a book-entry form, the title to ownership is transferred along a securities Fedwire, in a similar manner to cash transfers.

[21]Normally, Fedwire closes at 6:30 P.M. EST.

Commercial Paper.   Although a bank itself cannot issue commercial paper, its parent holding company can; that is, Citicorp can issue commercial paper but Citibank cannot. This provides banks owned by holding companies—most of the largest banks in the United States—with an additional funding source. Specifically, when the bank itself finds funding tight, it can utilize the funds downstreamed from its holding company's issue of commercial paper. Indeed, Citicorp is one of the largest issuers of commercial paper in the United States. Note that funds downsteamed to a bank are subject to reserve requirements, detracting from the attractiveness of this mechanism as a regular funding source.

Medium-Term Notes.   A number of banks in search of more stable sources of funds with low withdrawal risk have begun to issue medium-term notes, often in the five- to seven-year range. These notes are additionally attractive because they are subject to neither reserve requirements nor deposit insurance premiums.

Discount Window Loans.   As discussed earlier, banks facing temporary liquidity crunches can borrow from the central bank's discount window at the discount rate.

Concept Questions

1. Since transaction accounts are subject to both reserve requirements and deposit insurance premiums, whereas fed funds are not, why shouldn't a bank fund all its assets through fed funds? Explain your answer.
2. What are the major differences between fed funds and repurchase agreements?

Liquidity and Liability Structures for U.S. Banks

In this section, we summarize the preceding discussion by looking at some balance sheet data for U.S. banks. In Table 23–4, we show the liquid asset/nonliquid asset composition of insured U.S. banks in 1992 versus 1960. We use 1960 as a benchmark year since the next year (1961) is widely viewed as the date when banks first began to actively manage their liabilities, with Citibank's innovation of wholesale CDs.

As you can see, the ratio of traditional liquid to illiquid assets has declined since 1960 with cash plus securities in 1992 comprising 28 percent of the asset balance sheet of insured banks versus 52 percent in 1960. However, it is arguable that such a comparison misrepresents and overstates the fall in bank asset liquidity, since bank loans themselves have become significantly more liquid over this 30-year period. As we discuss in Chapters 21 and 22, bank loans are increasingly being securitized and/or sold in the secondary market. This has fundamentally altered the illiquidity of bank loan portfolios and has made them more similar to securities than hitherto. The more liquid the loan portfolio, the less the need for large amounts of traditional liquid assets, such as cash and securities, to act as buffer reserves against unexpected liability withdrawals.

In Table 23–5, we look at a breakdown of the liability composition of banks over the 1960 to 1992 period. The most striking feature of Table 23–5 has been the shift by banks away from funds sources with relative high withdrawal risk such as transaction accounts (demand deposits and NOW accounts) and passbook savings accounts,

TABLE 23–4   **Liquid Assets versus Nonliquid Assets for Insured Commercial Banks, 1960 and 1992**

	Percentage	
Assets	*1960*	*1992 (Sept.)*
Cash	20%	6%
Government and agency securities	24	17
Other securities*	8	5
Loans†	46	63
Other assets	2	9
	100%	100%

*Other securities = state and local, mortgage-backed plus others.
†Loans = C&I, mortgage, consumer, and others.
SOURCE: *Federal Reserve Bulletin,* various issues.

TABLE 23–5   **Liability Structure of Insured Commercial Banks, 1960 and 1992**

	Percentage	
Liabilities	*1960*	*1992 (Sept.)*
Transaction accounts	61%	20%
Passbook savings	22	20
Retail CDs and time deposits	7	18
Wholesale CDs	0	11
Borrowings and other liabilities	2	23
Bank capital	8	8
	100%	100%

SOURCE: *Federal Reserve Bulletin,* various issues.

to accounts or instruments over which a bank has greater potential control over the supply such as liability managed accounts. Specifically, the sum of transaction and passbook savings accounts fell from 83 percent in 1960 to 40 percent in 1992. By contrast, wholesale CDs plus borrowed funds (fed funds, RPs plus other borrowed funds) have expanded from 2 percent in 1960 to 34 percent in 1992. However, having a liability management strategy that reduces liability withdrawal risk doesn't come without a cost. As implied in Figure 23–2, there is often a trade-off between withdrawal risk and funding cost. As banks have sought to reduce their withdrawal risk by relying more on borrowed and wholesale funds, this added to their interest expense.

Finally, too heavy a reliance on borrowed funds can be a risky strategy in itself. Even though withdrawal risk may be reduced if lenders in the market for borrowed funds have confidence in the borrowing bank, perceptions that the bank is risky can lead to nonrenewals of fed fund and RP loans and the non rollover of wholesale CDs and other purchased funds as they mature. The best example of a bank that failed partly due to excessive reliance on large CDs and purchased funds was Continental

Illinois in 1984 with more than 80 percent of its funds borrowed from wholesale lenders. Consequently, excessive reliance on borrowed funds may be as bad an overall liability management strategy as excessive reliance on transaction accounts and passbook savings. Thus, a well-diversified portfolio of liabilities may be the best strategy to balance withdrawal risk and funding cost considerations.

Summary

Liquidity and liability management issues are intimately linked for the modern FI. Many factors, both cost and regulatory, impact an FI manager's choice of the amount of liquid assets to hold. An FI's choice of liquidity is something of a knife edge situation, trading off the costs and benefits of undershooting or overshooting regulatory specified (and prudentially specified) reserve asset targets. Reserve asset management is analogous to a constrained dynamic control problem with a moving target.

A bank can manage its liabilities in a fashion that affects the overall withdrawal risk of its funding portfolio and, therefore, the need for liquid assets to meet such withdrawals. However, reducing withdrawal risk often comes at a cost. This is because liability sources that are easier to control from a withdrawal risk perspective are often more costly for the bank to utilize.

Questions and Problems

1. *a.* From the viewpoint of the FI, what are the costs and benefits of holding liquid assets?
   b. From the viewpoint of the bank regulator, what are the costs and benefits of holding liquid assets?
   c. Contrast your answers to parts *a* and *b*.
   d. How does the regulator induce bank behavior in line with regulatory policy goals?

2. Contrast the different methods utilized by Central Banks to induce FIs to meet "socially desirable" levels of liquidity.

3. Prior to February of 1984, reserve requirements in the U.S. were computed on a lagged reserve accounting system. Under lagged reserve accounting the reserve computation period preceded the reserve maintenance period by two weeks.
   a. Contrast the contemporaneous reserve accounting (CRA) system with the lagged reserve accounting (LRA) system.
   b. Under which accounting system, CRA or LRA, were bank reserves higher? Why?
   c. Under which accounting system, CRA or LRA, was bank uncertainty higher? Why
   d. Why do you think that the Fed moved from LRA to CRA?

4. *a.* What is the "weekend game"?
   b. Contrast the bank's ability and incentive to play the weekend game under LRA as opposed to CRA.

5. Under CRA, when is the uncertainty about the reserve requirement resolved? Discuss the feasibility of making large reserve adjustments during this period of complete information.

6. Contrast the following liabilities with respect to funding risk and funding cost:
   a. Demand deposits.
   b. Certificates of deposit.
   c. Federal funds.
   d. Eurodollar deposits.

7. Use the following end of day balance sheet posting balances to calculate the bank's reserve requirement.

Date	Demand Deposits ($billions)	Cash Reserves ($billions)
Mon., Dec. 8	10	2
Tues., Dec. 9	11	1.9
Wed., Dec. 10	9.9	1.5
Thurs., Dec. 11	10.2	1.3
Fri., Dec. 12	8.8	1.5
Mon., Dec. 15	8.75	1.1
Tues., Dec. 16	8.5	1.2
Wed., Dec. 17	7.9	1
Thurs., Dec. 18	7.5	.8
Fri., Dec. 19	7.3	.9
Mon., Dec. 22	6.2	.3
Tues., Dec. 23	5.9	.4
Wed., Dec. 24	5.5	.1

a. For the above time period, what is the reserve computation period? What is the reserve maintenance period?

b. What are the bank's daily average demand deposit balances over the reserve computation period?

c. What are the bank's daily average reserves over the reserve maintenance period?

d. Has the bank met its reserve requirement? (Ignore the 3 percent reserve requirement on the first $46.8 million of demand deposits.)

e. If a glitch in FedWire transfers caused reserve balances on Friday, December 12th to fall to zero, what would be the impact on the bank's reserve position?

f. How can the bank compensate if the effect of FedWire problem (part e) is discovered on Tuesday morning, December 23rd?

g. Discuss the feasibility of the actions outline in part f.

8. Under LRA the seven day reserve computation period began on a Thursday and ended on the following Wednesday. The corresponding seven day reserve maintenance began on a Thursday 14 days after the start of the reserve computation period. Using the bank's posting balances in question 7:

a. State the dates of the first reserve computation and maintenance periods.

b. Calculate the average daily deposit balance over the reserve computation period.

c. Calculate the average daily reserve requirement over the reserve maintenance period. (Use a 10 percent reserve ratio.)

d. Is the bank in compliance with reserve requirements under LRA? Why or why not?

e. Compare your answers to your answers to question 7.

9. Calculate the average implicit interest rate on the following noninterest bearing accounts.

a. A $1 million account with average management costs of $150,000 and fees earned of $35,000.

b. A $150,000 account with average management costs of $25,000 and fees earned of $5,000.

c. A $1,000 account with average management costs of $1,000 and fees earned of $750.

d. Which account is least costly for the bank?

10. Calculate (in dollars and percent) the gross interest return (cost from the bank's viewpoint) of the following NOW accounts:

a. A $1 million deposit with a $5,000 minimum balance and no service charges paying 5.5 percent interest. The cost to the bank of processing each check is 15 cents. An average of 500 checks are processed each year.

b. A $10,000 deposit with a $5,000 minimum balance and a 5 cent per check service charge paying 5.5 percent interest. The cost to the bank of processing each check is 15 cents. An average of 250 checks are processed each year.

c. A $1,000 deposit with a $500 minimum balance and a 25 cent per check service charge paying 5.5 percent interest. The cost to the bank of processing each check is 15 cents. An average of 25 checks are processed each year.

d. Which account is least costly for the bank?

APPENDIXES

TABLE A–1 **Future value of \$1 at the end of *t* periods** $= (1 + r)^t$

	Interest rate								
Period	1%	2%	3%	4%	5%	6%	7%	8%	9%
1	1.0100	1.0200	1.0300	1.0400	1.0500	1.0600	1.0700	1.0800	1.0900
2	1.0201	1.0404	1.0609	1.0816	1.1025	1.1236	1.1449	1.1664	1.1881
3	1.0303	1.0612	1.0927	1.1249	1.1576	1.1910	1.2250	1.2597	1.2950
4	1.0406	1.0824	1.1255	1.1699	1.2155	1.2625	1.3108	1.3605	1.4116
5	1.0510	1.1041	1.1593	1.2167	1.2763	1.3382	1.4026	1.4693	1.5386
6	1.0615	1.1262	1.1941	1.2653	1.3401	1.4185	1.5007	1.5869	1.6771
7	1.0721	1.1487	1.2299	1.3159	1.4071	1.5036	1.6058	1.7138	1.8280
8	1.0829	1.1717	1.2668	1.3686	1.4775	1.5938	1.7182	1.8509	1.9926
9	1.0937	1.1951	1.3048	1.4233	1.5513	1.6895	1.8385	1.9990	2.1719
10	1.1046	1.2190	1.3439	1.4802	1.6289	1.7908	1.9672	2.1589	2.3674
11	1.1157	1.2434	1.3842	1.5395	1.7103	1.8983	2.1049	2.3316	2.5804
12	1.1268	1.2682	1.4258	1.6010	1.7959	2.0122	2.2522	2.5182	2.8127
13	1.1381	1.2936	1.4685	1.6651	1.8856	2.1329	2.4098	2.7196	3.0658
14	1.1495	1.3195	1.5126	1.7317	1.9799	2.2609	2.5785	2.9372	3.3417
15	1.1610	1.3459	1.5580	1.8009	2.0789	2.3966	2.7590	3.1722	3.6425
16	1.1726	1.3728	1.6047	1.8730	2.1829	2.5404	2.9522	3.4259	3.9703
17	1.1843	1.4002	1.6528	1.9479	2.2920	2.6928	3.1588	3.7000	4.3276
18	1.1961	1.4282	1.7024	2.0258	2.4066	2.8543	3.3799	3.9960	4.7171
19	1.2081	1.4568	1.7535	2.1068	2.5270	3.0256	3.6165	4.3157	5.1417
20	1.2202	1.4859	1.8061	2.1911	2.6533	3.2071	3.8697	4.6610	5.6044
21	1.2324	1.5157	1.8603	2.2788	2.7860	3.3996	4.1406	5.0338	6.1088
22	1.2447	1.5460	1.9161	2.3699	2.9253	3.6035	4.4304	5.4365	6.6586
23	1.2572	1.5769	1.9736	2.4647	3.0715	3.8197	4.7405	5.8715	7.2579
24	1.2697	1.6084	2.0328	2.5633	3.2251	4.0489	5.0724	6.3412	7.9111
25	1.2824	1.6406	2.0938	2.6658	3.3864	4.2919	5.4274	6.8485	8.6231
30	1.3478	1.8114	2.4273	3.2434	4.3219	5.7435	7.6123	10.063	13.268
40	1.4889	2.2080	3.2620	4.8010	7.0400	10.286	14.974	21.725	31.409
50	1.6446	2.6916	4.3839	7.1067	11.467	18.420	29.457	46.902	74.358
60	1.8167	3.2810	5.8916	10.520	18.679	32.988	57.946	101.26	176.03

TABLE A–1 (*concluded*)   (*concluded*)

					Interest rate					
10%	12%	14%	15%	16%	18%	20%	24%	28%	32%	36%
1.1000	1.1200	1.1400	1.1500	1.1600	1.1800	1.2000	1.2400	1.2800	1.3200	1.3600
1.2100	1.2544	1.2996	1.3225	1.3456	1.3924	1.4400	1.5376	1.6384	1.7424	1.8496
1.3310	1.4049	1.4815	1.5209	1.5609	1.6430	1.7280	1.9066	2.0972	2.3000	2.5155
1.4641	1.5735	1.6890	1.7490	1.8106	1.9388	2.0736	2.3642	2.6844	3.0360	3.4210
1.6105	1.7623	1.9254	2.0114	2.1003	2.2878	2.4883	2.9316	3.4360	4.0075	4.6526
1.7716	1.9738	2.1950	2.3131	2.4364	2.6996	2.9860	3.6352	4.3980	5.2899	6.3275
1.9487	2.2107	2.5023	2.6600	2.8262	3.1855	3.5832	4.5077	5.6295	6.9826	8.6054
2.1436	2.4760	2.8526	3.0590	3.2784	3.7589	4.2998	5.5895	7.2058	9.2170	11.703
2.3579	2.7731	3.2519	3.5179	3.8030	4.4355	5.1598	6.9310	9.2234	12.166	15.917
2.5937	3.1058	3.7072	4.0456	4.4114	5.2338	6.1917	8.5944	11.806	16.060	21.647
2.8531	3.4785	4.2262	4.6524	5.1173	6.1759	7.4301	10.657	15.112	21.199	29.439
3.1384	3.8960	4.8179	5.3503	5.9360	7.2876	8.9161	13.215	19.343	27.983	40.037
3.4523	4.3635	5.4924	6.1528	6.8858	8.5994	10.699	16.386	24.759	36.937	54.451
3.7975	4.8871	6.2613	7.0757	7.9875	10.147	12.839	20.319	31.691	48.757	74.053
4.1772	5.4736	7.1379	8.1371	9.2655	11.974	15.407	25.196	40.565	64.359	100.71
4.5950	6.1304	8.1372	9.3576	10.748	14.129	18.488	31.243	51.923	84.954	136.97
5.0545	6.8660	9.2765	10.761	12.468	16.672	22.186	38.741	66.461	112.14	186.28
5.5599	7.6900	10.575	12.375	14.463	19.673	26.623	48.039	85.071	148.02	253.34
6.1159	8.6128	12.056	14.232	16.777	23.214	31.948	59.568	108.89	195.39	344.54
6.7275	9.6463	13.743	16.367	19.461	27.393	38.338	73.864	139.38	257.92	468.57
7.4002	10.804	15.668	18.822	22.574	32.324	46.005	91.592	178.41	340.45	637.26
8.1403	12.100	17.861	21.645	26.186	38.142	55.206	113.57	228.36	449.39	866.67
8.9543	13.552	20.362	24.891	30.376	45.008	66.247	140.83	292.30	593.20	1178.7
9.8497	15.179	23.212	28.625	35.236	53.109	79.497	174.63	374.14	783.02	1603.0
10.835	17.000	26.462	32.919	40.874	62.669	95.396	216.54	478.90	1033.6	2180.1
17.449	29.960	50.950	66.212	85.850	143.37	237.38	634.82	1645.5	4142.1	10143.
45.259	93.051	188.88	267.86	378.72	750.38	1469.8	5455.9	19427.	66521.	*
117.39	289.00	700.23	1083.7	1670.7	3927.4	9100.4	46890.	*	*	*
304.48	897.60	2595.9	4384.0	7370.2	20555.	56348.	*	*	*	*

*The factor is greater than 99,999.

TABLE A–2 **Present value of \$1 to be received after *t* periods** $= 1/(1 + r)^t$

					Interest rate				
Period	1%	2%	3%	4%	5%	6%	7%	8%	9%
1	0.9901	0.9804	0.9709	0.9615	0.9524	0.9434	0.9346	0.9259	0.9174
2	0.9803	0.9612	0.9426	0.9246	0.9070	0.8900	0.8734	0.8573	0.8417
3	0.9706	0.9423	0.9151	0.8890	0.8638	0.8396	0.8163	0.7938	0.7722
4	0.9610	0.9238	0.8885	0.8548	0.8227	0.7921	0.7629	0.7350	0.7084
5	0.9515	0.9057	0.8626	0.8219	0.7835	0.7473	0.7130	0.6806	0.6499
6	0.9420	0.8880	0.8375	0.7903	0.7462	0.7050	0.6663	0.6302	0.5963
7	0.9327	0.8706	0.8131	0.7599	0.7107	0.6651	0.6227	0.5835	0.5470
8	0.9235	0.8535	0.7894	0.7307	0.6768	0.6274	0.5820	0.5403	0.5019
9	0.9143	0.8368	0.7664	0.7026	0.6446	0.5919	0.5439	0.5002	0.4604
10	0.9053	0.8203	0.7441	0.6756	0.6139	0.5584	0.5083	0.4632	0.4224
11	0.8963	0.8043	0.7224	0.6496	0.5847	0.5268	0.4751	0.4289	0.3875
12	0.8874	0.7885	0.7014	0.6246	0.5568	0.4970	0.4440	0.3971	0.3555
13	0.8787	0.7730	0.6810	0.6006	0.5303	0.4688	0.4150	0.3677	0.3262
14	0.8700	0.7579	0.6611	0.5775	0.5051	0.4423	0.3878	0.3405	0.2992
15	0.8613	0.7430	0.6419	0.5553	0.4810	0.4173	0.3624	0.3152	0.2745
16	0.8528	0.7284	0.6232	0.5339	0.4581	0.3936	0.3387	0.2919	0.2519
17	0.8444	0.7142	0.6050	0.5134	0.4363	0.3714	0.3166	0.2703	0.2311
18	0.8360	0.7002	0.5874	0.4936	0.4155	0.3503	0.2959	0.2502	0.2120
19	0.8277	0.6864	0.5703	0.4746	0.3957	0.3305	0.2765	0.2317	0.1945
20	0.8195	0.6730	0.5537	0.4564	0.3769	0.3118	0.2584	0.2145	0.1784
21	0.8114	0.6598	0.5375	0.4388	0.3589	0.2942	0.2415	0.1987	0.1637
22	0.8034	0.6468	0.5219	0.4220	0.3418	0.2775	0.2257	0.1839	0.1502
23	0.7954	0.6342	0.5067	0.4057	0.3256	0.2618	0.2109	0.1703	0.1378
24	0.7876	0.6217	0.4919	0.3901	0.3101	0.2470	0.1971	0.1577	0.1264
25	0.7798	0.6095	0.4776	0.3751	0.2953	0.2330	0.1842	0.1460	0.1160
30	0.7419	0.5521	0.4120	0.3083	0.2314	0.1741	0.1314	0.0994	0.0754
40	0.6717	0.4529	0.3066	0.2083	0.1420	0.0972	0.0668	0.0460	0.0318
50	0.6080	0.3715	0.2281	0.1407	0.0872	0.0543	0.0339	0.0213	0.0134

TABLE A–2 *(concluded)*

					Interest rate					
10%	12%	14%	15%	16%	18%	20%	24%	28%	32%	36%
0.9091	0.8929	0.8772	0.8696	0.8621	0.8475	0.8333	0.8065	0.7813	0.7576	0.7353
0.8264	0.7972	0.7695	0.7561	0.7432	0.7182	0.6944	0.6504	0.6104	0.5739	0.5407
0.7513	0.7118	0.6750	0.6575	0.6407	0.6086	0.5787	0.5245	0.4768	0.4348	0.3975
0.6830	0.6355	0.5921	0.5718	0.5523	0.5158	0.4823	0.4230	0.3725	0.3294	0.2923
0.6209	0.5674	0.5194	0.4972	0.4761	0.4371	0.4019	0.3411	0.2910	0.2495	0.2149
0.5645	0.5066	0.4556	0.4323	0.4104	0.3704	0.3349	0.2751	0.2274	0.1890	0.1580
0.5132	0.4523	0.3996	0.3759	0.3538	0.3139	0.2791	0.2218	0.1776	0.1432	0.1162
0.4665	0.4039	0.3506	0.3269	0.3050	0.2660	0.2326	0.1789	0.1388	0.1085	0.0854
0.4241	0.3606	0.3075	0.2843	0.2630	0.2255	0.1938	0.1443	0.1084	0.0822	0.0628
0.3855	0.3220	0.2697	0.2472	0.2267	0.1911	0.1615	0.1164	0.0847	0.0623	0.0462
0.3505	0.2875	0.2366	0.2149	0.1954	0.1619	0.1346	0.0938	0.0662	0.0472	0.0340
0.3186	0.2567	0.2076	0.1869	0.1685	0.1372	0.1122	0.0757	0.0517	0.0357	0.0250
0.2897	0.2292	0.1821	0.1625	0.1452	0.1163	0.0935	0.0610	0.0404	0.0271	0.0184
0.2633	0.2046	0.1597	0.1413	0.1252	0.0985	0.0779	0.0492	0.0316	0.0205	0.0135
0.2394	0.1827	0.1401	0.1229	0.1079	0.0835	0.0649	0.0397	0.0247	0.0155	0.0099
0.2176	0.1631	0.1229	0.1069	0.0930	0.0708	0.0541	0.0320	0.0193	0.0118	0.0073
0.1978	0.1456	0.1078	0.0929	0.0802	0.0600	0.0451	0.0258	0.0150	0.0089	0.0054
0.1799	0.1300	0.0946	0.0808	0.0691	0.0508	0.0376	0.0208	0.0118	0.0068	0.0039
0.1635	0.1161	0.0829	0.0703	0.0596	0.0431	0.0313	0.0168	0.0092	0.0051	0.0029
0.1486	0.1037	0.0728	0.0611	0.0514	0.0365	0.0261	0.0135	0.0072	0.0039	0.0021
0.1351	0.0926	0.0638	0.0531	0.0443	0.0309	0.0217	0.0109	0.0056	0.0029	0.0016
0.1228	0.0826	0.0560	0.0462	0.0382	0.0262	0.0181	0.0088	0.0044	0.0022	0.0012
0.1117	0.0738	0.0491	0.0402	0.0329	0.0222	0.0151	0.0071	0.0034	0.0017	0.0008
0.1015	0.0659	0.0431	0.0349	0.0284	0.0188	0.0126	0.0057	0.0027	0.0013	0.0006
0.0923	0.0588	0.0378	0.0304	0.0245	0.0160	0.0105	0.0046	0.0021	0.0010	0.0005
0.0573	0.0334	0.0196	0.0151	0.0116	0.0070	0.0042	0.0016	0.0006	0.0002	0.0001
0.0221	0.0107	0.0053	0.0037	0.0026	0.0013	0.0007	0.0002	0.0001	*	*
0.0085	0.0035	0.0014	0.0009	0.0006	0.0003	0.0001	*	*	*	*

*The factor is zero to four decimal places.

TABLE A–3 Present value of an annuity of $1 per period for t periods $= [1 - 1/(1 + r)^t]/r$

Number of periods	Interest rate								
	1%	2%	3%	4%	5%	6%	7%	8%	9%
1	0.9901	0.9804	0.9709	0.9615	0.9524	0.9434	0.9346	0.9259	0.9174
2	1.9704	1.9416	1.9135	1.8861	1.8594	1.8334	1.8080	1.7833	1.7591
3	2.9410	2.8839	2.8286	2.7751	2.7232	2.6730	2.6243	2.5771	2.5313
4	3.9020	3.8077	3.7171	3.6299	3.5460	3.4651	3.3872	3.3121	3.2397
5	4.8534	4.7135	4.5797	4.4518	4.3295	4.2124	4.1002	3.9927	3.8897
6	5.7955	5.6014	5.4172	5.2421	5.0757	4.9173	4.7665	4.6229	4.4859
7	6.7282	6.4720	6.2303	6.0021	5.7864	5.5824	5.3893	5.2064	5.0330
8	7.6517	7.3255	7.0197	6.7327	6.4632	6.2098	5.9713	5.7466	5.5348
9	8.5660	8.1622	7.7861	7.4353	7.1078	6.8017	6.5152	6.2469	5.9952
10	9.4713	8.9826	8.5302	8.1109	7.7217	7.3601	7.0236	6.7101	6.4177
11	10.3676	9.7868	9.2526	8.7605	8.3064	7.8869	7.4987	7.1390	6.8052
12	11.2551	10.5753	9.9540	9.3851	8.8633	8.3838	7.9427	7.5361	7.1607
13	12.1337	11.3484	10.6350	9.9856	9.3936	8.8527	8.3577	7.9038	7.4869
14	13.0037	12.1062	11.2961	10.5631	9.8986	9.2950	8.7455	8.2442	7.7862
15	13.8651	12.8493	11.9379	11.1184	10.3797	9.7122	9.1079	8.5595	8.0607
16	14.7179	13.5777	12.5611	11.6523	10.8378	10.1059	9.4466	8.8514	8.3126
17	15.5623	14.2919	13.1661	12.1657	11.2741	10.4773	9.7632	9.1216	8.5436
18	16.3983	14.9920	13.7535	12.6593	11.6896	10.8276	10.0591	9.3719	8.7556
19	17.2260	15.6785	14.3238	13.1339	12.0853	11.1581	10.3356	9.6036	8.9501
20	18.0456	16.3514	14.8775	13.5903	12.4622	11.4699	10.5940	9.8181	9.1285
21	18.8570	17.0112	15.4150	14.0292	12.8212	11.7641	10.8355	10.0168	9.2922
22	19.6604	17.6580	15.9369	14.4511	13.1630	12.0416	11.0612	10.2007	9.4424
23	20.4558	18.2922	16.4436	14.8568	13.4886	12.3034	11.2722	10.3741	9.5802
24	21.2434	18.9139	16.9355	15.2470	13.7986	12.5504	11.4593	10.5288	9.7066
25	22.0232	19.5235	17.4131	15.6221	14.0939	12.7834	11.6536	10.6748	9.8226
30	25.8077	22.3965	19.6004	17.2920	15.3725	13.7648	12.4090	11.2578	10.2737
40	32.8347	27.3555	23.1148	19.7928	17.1591	15.0463	13.3317	11.9246	10.7574
50	39.1961	31.4236	25.7298	21.4822	18.2559	15.7619	13.8007	12.2335	10.9617

TABLE A–3 *(concluded)*

					Interest rate				
10%	12%	14%	15%	16%	18%	20%	24%	28%	32%
0.9091	0.8929	0.8772	0.8696	0.8621	0.8475	0.8333	0.8065	0.7813	0.7576
1.7355	1.6901	1.6467	1.6257	1.6052	1.5656	1.5278	1.4568	1.3916	1.3315
2.4869	2.4018	2.3216	2.2832	2.2459	2.1743	2.1065	1.9813	1.8684	1.7663
3.1699	3.0373	2.9137	2.8550	2.7982	2.6901	2.5887	2.4043	2.2410	2.0957
3.7908	3.6048	3.4331	3.3522	3.2743	3.1272	2.9906	2.7454	2.5320	2.3452
4.3553	4.1114	3.8887	3.7845	3.6847	3.4976	3.3255	3.0205	2.7594	2.5342
4.8684	4.5638	4.2883	4.1604	4.0386	3.8115	3.6046	3.2423	2.9370	2.6775
5.3349	4.9676	4.6389	4.4873	4.3436	4.0776	3.8372	3.4212	3.0758	2.7860
5.7590	5.3282	4.9464	4.7716	4.6065	4.3030	4.0310	3.5655	3.1842	2.8681
6.1446	5.6502	5.2161	5.0188	4.8332	4.4941	4.1925	3.6819	3.2689	2.9304
6.4951	5.9377	5.4527	5.2337	5.0286	4.6560	4.3271	3.7757	3.3351	2.9776
6.8137	6.1944	5.6603	5.4206	5.1971	4.7932	4.4392	−3.8514	3.3868	3.0133
7.1034	6.4235	5.8424	5.5831	5.3423	4.9095	4.5327	3.9124	3.4272	3.0404
7.3667	6.6282	6.0021	5.7245	5.4675	5.0081	4.6106	3.9616	3.4587	3.0609
7.6061	6.8109	6.1422	5.8474	5.5755	5.0916	4.6755	4.0013	3.4834	3.0764
7.8237	6.9740	6.2651	5.9542	5.6685	5.1624	4.7296	4.0333	3.5026	3.0882
8.0216	7.1196	6.3729	6.0472	5.7487	5.2223	4.7746	4.0591	3.5177	3.0971
8.2014	7.2497	6.4674	6.1280	5.8178	5.2732	4.8122	4.0799	3.5294	3.1039
8.3649	7.3658	6.5504	6.1982	5.8775	5.3162	4.8435	4.0967	3.5386	3.1090
8.5136	7.4694	6.6231	6.2593	5.9288	5.3527	4.8696	4.1103	3.5458	3.1129
8.6487	7.5620	6.6870	6.3125	5.9731	5.3837	4.8913	4.1212	3.5514	3.1158
8.7715	7.6446	6.7429	6.3587	6.0113	5.4099	4.9094	4.1300	3.5558	3.1180
8.8832	7.7184	6.7921	6.3988	6.0442	5.4321	4.9245	4.1371	3.5592	3.1197
8.9847	7.7843	6.8351	6.4338	6.0726	5.4509	4.9371	4.1428	3.5619	3.1210
9.0770	7.8431	6.8729	6.4641	6.0971	5.4669	4.9476	4.1474	3.5640	3.1220
9.4269	8.0552	7.0027	6.5660	6.1772	5.5168	4.9789	4.1601	3.5693	3.1242
9.7791	8.2438	7.1050	6.6418	6.2335	5.5482	4.9966	4.1659	3.5712	3.1250
9.9148	8.3045	7.1327	6.6605	6.2463	5.5541	4.9995	4.1666	3.5714	3.1250

TABLE A–4   **Future value of an annuity of $1 per period for t periods = $[(1 + r)^t - 1]/r$**

Number of periods	Interest rate								
	1%	2%	3%	4%	5%	6%	7%	8%	9%
1	1.0000	1.0000	1.0000	1.0000	1.0000	1.0000	1.0000	1.0000	1.0000
2	2.0100	2.0200	2.0300	2.0400	2.0500	2.0600	2.0700	2.0800	2.0900
3	3.0301	3.0604	3.0909	3.1216	3.1525	3.1836	3.2149	3.2464	3.2781
4	4.0604	4.1216	4.1836	4.2465	4.3101	4.3746	4.4399	4.5061	4.5731
5	5.1010	5.2040	5.3091	5.4163	5.5256	5.6371	5.7507	5.8666	5.9847
6	6.1520	6.3081	6.4684	6.6330	6.8019	6.9753	7.1533	7.3359	7.5233
7	7.2135	7.4343	7.6625	7.8983	8.1420	8.3938	8.6540	8.9228	9.2004
8	8.2857	8.5830	8.8932	9.2142	9.5491	9.8975	10.260	10.637	11.028
9	9.3685	9.7546	10.159	10.583	11.027	11.491	11.978	12.488	13.021
10	10.462	10.950	11.464	12.006	12.578	13.181	13.816	14.487	15.193
11	11.567	12.169	12.808	13.486	14.207	14.972	15.784	16.645	17.560
12	12.683	13.412	14.192	15.026	15.917	16.870	17.888	18.977	20.141
13	13.809	14.680	15.618	16.627	17.713	18.882	20.141	21.495	22.953
14	14.947	15.974	17.086	18.292	19.599	21.015	22.550	24.215	26.019
15	16.097	17.293	18.599	20.024	21.579	23.276	25.129	27.152	29.361
16	17.258	18.639	20.157	21.825	23.657	25.673	27.888	30.324	33.003
17	18.430	20.012	21.762	23.698	25.840	28.213	30.840	33.750	36.974
18	19.615	21.412	23.414	25.645	28.132	30.906	33.999	37.450	41.301
19	20.811	22.841	25.117	27.671	30.539	33.760	37.379	41.446	46.018
20	22.019	24.297	26.870	29.778	33.066	36.786	40.995	45.762	51.160
21	23.239	25.783	28.676	31.969	35.719	39.993	44.865	50.423	56.765
22	24.472	27.299	30.537	34.248	38.505	43.392	49.006	55.457	62.873
23	25.716	28.845	32.453	36.618	41.430	46.996	53.436	60.893	69.532
24	26.973	30.422	34.426	39.083	44.502	50.816	58.177	66.765	76.790
25	28.243	32.030	36.459	41.646	47.727	54.865	63.249	73.106	84.701
30	34.785	40.568	47.575	56.085	66.439	79.058	94.461	113.28	136.31
40	48.886	60.402	75.401	95.026	120.80	154.76	199.64	259.06	337.88
50	64.463	84.579	112.80	152.67	209.35	290.34	406.53	573.77	815.08
60	81.670	114.05	163.05	237.99	353.58	533.13	813.52	1253.2	1944.8

TABLE A–4 *(concluded)*

					Interest rate					
10%	12%	14%	15%	16%	18%	20%	24%	28%	32%	36%
1.0000	1.0000	1.0000	1.0000	1.0000	1.0000	1.0000	1.0000	1.0000	1.0000	1.0000
2.1000	2.1200	2.1400	2.1500	2.1600	2.1800	2.2000	2.2400	2.2800	2.3200	2.3600
3.3100	3.3744	3.4396	3.4725	3.5056	3.5724	3.6400	3.7776	3.9184	4.0624	4.2096
4.6410	4.7793	4.9211	4.9934	5.0665	5.2154	5.3680	5.6842	6.0156	6.3624	6.7251
6.1051	6.3528	6.6101	6.7424	6.8771	7.1542	7.4416	8.0484	8.6999	9.3983	10.146
7.7156	8.1152	8.5355	8.7537	8.9775	9.4420	9.9299	10.980	12.136	13.406	14.799
9.4872	10.089	10.730	11.067	11.414	12.142	12.916	14.615	16.534	18.696	21.126
11.436	12.300	13.233	13.727	14.240	15.327	16.499	19.123	22.163	25.678	29.732
13.579	14.776	16.085	16.786	17.519	19.086	20.799	24.712	29.369	34.895	41.435
15.937	17.549	19.337	20.304	21.321	23.521	25.959	31.643	38.593	47.062	57.352
18.531	20.655	23.045	24.349	25.733	28.755	32.150	40.238	50.398	63.122	78.998
21.384	24.133	27.271	29.002	30.850	34.931	39.581	50.895	65.510	84.320	108.44
24.523	28.029	32.089	34.352	36.786	42.219	48.497	64.110	84.853	112.30	148.47
27.975	32.393	37.581	40.505	43.672	50.818	59.196	80.496	109.61	149.24	202.93
31.772	37.280	43.842	47.580	51.660	60.965	72.035	100.82	141.30	198.00	276.98
35.950	42.753	50.980	55.717	60.925	72.939	87.442	126.01	181.87	262.36	377.69
40.545	48.884	59.118	65.075	71.673	87.068	105.93	157.25	233.79	347.31	514.66
45.599	55.750	68.394	75.836	84.141	103.74	128.12	195.99	300.25	459.45	700.94
51.159	63.440	78.969	88.212	98.603	123.41	154.74	244.03	385.32	607.47	954.28
57.275	72.052	91.025	102.44	115.38	146.63	186.69	303.60	494.21	802.86	1298.8
64.002	81.699	104.77	118.81	134.84	174.02	225.03	377.46	633.59	1060.8	1767.4
71.403	92.503	120.44	137.63	157.41	206.34	271.03	469.06	812.00	1401.2	2404.7
79.543	104.60	138.30	159.28	183.60	244.49	326.24	582.63	1040.4	1850.6	3271.3
88.497	118.16	158.66	184.17	213.98	289.49	392.48	723.46	1332.7	2443.8	4450.0
98.347	133.33	181.87	212.79	249.21	342.60	471.98	898.09	1706.8	3226.8	6053.0
164.49	241.33	356.79	434.75	530.31	790.95	1181.9	2640.9	5873.2	12941.	28172.3
442.59	767.09	1342.0	1779.1	2360.8	4163.2	7343.9	22729.	69377.	*	*
1163.9	2400.0	4994.5	7217.7	10436.	21813.	45497.	*	*	*	*
3034.8	7471.6	18535.	29220.	46058.	*	*	*	*	*	*

*The factor is greater than 99,999.

REFERENCES

Abbott S. "Franklin Case Points Out Thrift Account Difficulties." *Futures,* July 1990, pp. 58–60.

Abken, P. A. "Beyond Plain Vanilla: A Taxonomy of Swaps." Federal Reserve Bank of Atlanta, *Economic Review,* March–April 1991, pp. 21–29.

Acharya, S., and I. Diwan. "Debt Conversion Schemes of Debtor Countries as a Signal of Creditworthiness: Theory and Evidence." Working Paper, Stern School of Business, New York University, June 1987.

Acharya, S., and J. F. Dreyfus. "Optimal Bank Reorganization Policies and the Pricing of Federal Deposit Insurance." *Journal of Finance* 44, December 1988, pp. 1313–14.

Aharony, J.; A. Saunders; and I. Swary. "The Effects of a Shift in Monetary Policy Regime on the Profitability and Risk of Commercial Banks." *Journal of Monetary Economy* 17, 1986, pp. 493–506.

Allen, L., and A. Saunders. "Bank Window Dressing: Theory and Evidence." *Journal of Banking and Finance* 16, 1992, pp. 585–624.

——— "Forbearance and Valuation of Deposit Insurance as a Callable Put." *Journal of Banking and Finance* 17, 1993, (forthcoming).

Altman, E. I. "Managing the Commercial Lending Process." In *Handbook of Banking Strategy,* ed. R. C. Aspinwall and R. A. Eisenbeis. New York: John Wiley, 1985, pp. 473–510.

——— "Measuring Corporate Bond Mortality and Performance." *Journal of Finance* 44, 1989, pp. 909–22.

——— "How 1989 Changed the Hierarchy of Fixed Income Security Performance." In *Recent Developments in Finance,* ed. A. Saunders. Homewood Ill.: Business One Irwin, 1990, pp. 19–30.

——— "Default Risk, Mortality Rates, and the Performance of Corporate Bonds." *The Research Foundation of The Institute of Chartered Financial Analysts,* 1989.

——— "Valuation, Loss Reserves, and Pricing of Commercial Loans." Working Paper, Salomon Center, New York University, 1992.

Amemiya, T. "Qualitative Response Models: A Survey." *Journal of Economic Literature* 19, 1991, pp. 483–536.

Archer, W., and D. C. Ling. "Pricing Mortgage-Backed Securities: Should Contingent-Claim Models Be Abandoned for Empirical Models of Prepayments?" Paper presented at the AFA Conference, Anaheim, California, January 1993.

Avery, R. B., and A. Berger. "Loan Commitments and Bank Risk Exposure." *Journal of Banking and Finance* 15, 1991, pp. 173–92.

——— "Risk-Based Capital and Deposit Insurance Reform." *Journal of Banking and Finance* 15, 1991, pp. 847–74.

Babbel, D. F. "Insuring Banks Against Systematic Credit Risk." *Journal of Futures Markets* 9, 1989, pp. 487–506.

Ball, C., and W. N. Tourous. "Bond Price Dynamics and Options." *Journal of Financial and Quantitative Analysis* 18, 1983, pp. 517–31.

Beatty, R., and J. Ritter. "Investment Banking, Reputation, and the Underpricing of Initial Public Offerings." *Journal of Financial Economics* 15, 1986, pp. 213–32.

Bellanger, S. "Stormy Weather: The FBSEA'S Impact on Foreign Banks." *Bankers Magazine,* November–December 1992, pp. 25–31.

Benston, G. J.; G. A. Hanweck; and D. B. Humphrey. "Scale Economies in Banking." *Journal of Money Credit and Banking* 14, 1982, pp. 436–55.

——— *The Separation of Commercial and Investment Banking: The Glass-Steagall Act Revisited and Reconsidered,* New York: St. Martin's Press, 1989.

Benston, G. J., and G. G. Kaufman. "Risk and Solvency Regulation of Depository Institutions: Past Policies and Current Options." Monograph Series in Finance and Economics, 1988–1, Salomon Center, New York University, 1988.

Benveniste, L.; M. Singh; and W. J. Wilhelm. "The Failure of Drexel Burnham Lambert: Evidence on the Implications for Commercial Banks." Paper presented at the AFA Conference, Anaheim, California, 1993.

Berger, A., and D. Humphrey. "The Dominance of Inefficiencies over Scale and Product Mix in Banking." *Journal of Monetary Economics* 28, 1991.

Berger, A., and D. B. Humphrey. "Megamergers in Banking and the Use of Cost Efficiency as an AntiTrust Defense." *The AntiTrust Bulletin* 37, 1992, pp. 541–600.

Berger, A., and G. Udell. "Does Risk-Based Capital Allocate Bank Credit?" *Journal of Money Credit and Banking,* 1994 (forthcoming).

Berger, A., and G. Udell. "Lines of Credit, Collateral, and Relationship Lending in Small Firm Finance." Working paper, Stein Business School, New York University, March 1993.

Berger, A.; D. Hancock; and D. B. Humphrey. "Bank Efficiency Derived from the Profit Function." *Journal of Banking and Finance,* 1993 (forthcoming).

Berlin, M. "Loan Commitments: Insurance Contracts in a Risky World." Federal Reserve Bank of Philadelphia, *Business Review,* May–June 1986, pp. 3–12.

Berlin, M., and L. Mester. "Debt Covenants and Renegotiation." *Journal of Financial Intermediation* 2, 1992, pp. 95–133.

Bierwag, G. O.; G. G. Kaufman; and A. Toevs. "Duration: Its Development and Use in Bond Portfolio Management." *Financial Analysts Journal* 39, 1983, pp. 15–35.

Black, F., and M. Scholes. "The Pricing of Options and Corporate Liabilities." *Journal of Political Economy* 81, 1973, pp. 637–59.

Boehmer, E., and W. L. Megginson. "Determinants of Secondary Market Prices for Developing Country Syndicated Loans." *Journal of Finance* 45, 1990, pp. 1517–40.

Boot, A. W. A., and A. V. Thakor. "Off-Balance-Sheet Liabilities, Deposit Insurance, and Capital Regulations." *Journal of Banking and Finance* 15, 1991, pp. 825–46.

Bouyoucos, P. J.; M. H. Siegel; and E. B. Raisel. "Risk-Based Capital for Insurers: A Strategic Opportunity to Enhance Franchise Value." Goldman, Sachs, Industry Resource Group, September 1992.

Boyd, J. H., and E. C. Prescott. "Financial Intermediary Coalitions." *Journal of Economic Theory* 38, 1986, pp. 211–32.

Brennan, M. J., and E. S. Schwartz. "Savings Bonds, Retractable Bonds, and Callable Bonds." *Journal of Financial Economics* 5, 1977, pp. 67–88.

Brewer, E. "Bank Gap Management and the Use of Financial Futures." Federal Reserve Bank of Chicago, *Economic Perspectives,* March–April 1985.

Brewer, E.; D. Fortier; and C. Pavel. "Bank Risk from Nonbank Activities." Federal Reserve Bank of Chicago, *Economic Perspectives,* July–August 1988, pp. 14–26.

Brown, K. C., and D. J. Smith. "Recent Innovations in Interest Rate Risk Management and the Reintermediation of Commercial Banking." *Financial Management* 17, 1988, pp. 45–58.

Bulow, J., and K. Rogoff. "A Constant Recontracting Model of Sovereign Debt." *Journal of Political Economy* 97, 1989, pp. 155–78.

Buser, S. A.; A. H. Chen; and E. J. Kane. "Federal Deposit Insurance, Regulatory Policy, and Optimal Bank Capital." *Journal of Finance* 36, 1981, pp. 51–60.

Canina, L., and S. Figlewski. "The Informational Content of Implied Volatility." *Review of Financial Studies* (forthcoming), 1994.

Carnell, R. S. "A Partial Antidote to Perverse Incentives: The FDIC Improvement Act of 1991." Paper presented at a Conference on Rebuilding Public Confidence through Financial Reform, Ohio State University, Columbus, Ohio, June 25, 1992.

Chan, Y. S.; S. I. Greenbaum; and A. V. Thakor. "Is Fairly Priced Deposit Insurance Possible?" *Journal of Finance* 47, 1992, pp. 227–46.

Clark, J. A. "Economies of Scale and Scope at Depository Financial Institutions: A Review of the Literature." Federal Reserve Bank of Kansas City, *Economic Review,* September–October 1988, pp. 16–33.

Clark, M., and A. Saunders. "Judicial Interpretation of Glass-Steagall: The Need for Legislative Action." *The Banking Law Journal* 97, 1980, pp. 721–40.

———— "Glass-Steagall Revised: The Impact On Banks, Capital Markets, and the Small Investor." *The Banking Law Journal* 97, 1980, pp. 811–40.

Coats, P. K., and L. F. Fant. "Recognizing Financial Distress Patterns: Using a Neural Network Tool." Working Paper, Department of Finance, Florida State University, September 1992.

Cook, T. Q. "Treasury Bills." *Instruments of the Money Market.* Richmond, Va.: Federal Reserve Bank of Richmond, 1986, pp. 81–93.

Desai, A., and R. Stover. "Bank Holding Company Acquisitions, Stockholder Returns, and Regulatory Uncertainty." *Journal of Financial Research* 8, 1985, pp. 145–56.

Diamond, D. W. "Financial Intermediaries and Delegated Monitoring." *Review of Economic Studies* 51, 1984, pp. 393–414.

Diamond, D. W., and P. H. Dybvig. "Bank Runs, Deposit Insurance and Liquidity." *Journal of Political Economy* 91, 1983, pp. 401–19.

Dreyfus, J. F.; A. Saunders; and L. Allen. "Deposit Insurance and Regulatory Forbearance: Are Caps on Insured Deposits Optimal?" *Journal of Money Credit and Banking* (forthcoming) 1994.

Dufey, G., and I. Giddy. "Eurocurrency Deposit Risk." *Journal of Banking and Finance* 8, 1984, pp. 567–58.

Ederington, L. H. "The Hedging Performance of the New Futures Markets." *Journal of Finance* 34, 1979, pp. 157–70.

Eichengreen, B., and R. Portes. "The Anatomy of Financial Crises." In *Threats to International Financial Stability,* ed. R. Portes and A. K. Swoboda. Cambridge: Cambridge University Press, 1987, pp. 10–51.

Fama, E. "What's Different about Banks?" *Journal of Monetary Economics* 15, 1985, pp. 29–39.

Federal Reserve Bank of Richmond. *Instruments of the Money Market,* 6th ed. Richmond, Va.: Federal Reserve Bank of Richmond, 1986.

Federal Reserve Board of Governors, "Revisions to Risk-Based Capital Standards to Account for Concentration of Credit Risk and Risks on Nontraditional Activities." *Memoranda*, Washington, D.C., March 26, 1993.

Federal Reserve Board of Governors, "Risk-Based Capital and Interest Rate Risk." Press Release, Washington, D.C., July 30, 1992.

Felgren, S. D. "Banks as Insurance Agencies: Legal Constraints and Competitive Advances." Federal Reserve Bank of Boston, *New England Economic Review,* September–October 1985, pp. 34–49.

Fields, J. "Expense Preference Behavior in Mutual Life Insurers." *Journal of Financial Services Research* 1, 1988, pp. 113–30.

Fields, J., and N. B. Murphy. "An Analysis of Efficiency in the Delivery of Financial Services: The Case of Life Insurance Agencies." *Journal of Financial Services Research* 2, 1989, pp. 343–56.

Figlewski, S. *Hedging with Financial Futures for Institutional Investors: From Theory to Practice.* Cambridge Mass.: Ballinger, 1986.

Flannery, M. J., and C. M. James. "The Effect of Interest Rate Changes on the Common Stock Returns of Financial Institutions." *Journal of Finance* 39, 1984, pp. 1141–53.

Gendrau, B. C. "The Regulation of Bank Trading in Futures and Forward Markets." *Below the Bottom Line: The Use of Contingencies and Commitments by Commercial Banks.* Washington, D.C.: Federal Reserve Board of Governors, 1982.

General Accounting Office. "Bank Powers: Issues Relating to Banks Selling Insurance." GAO/GGO 90–113, Washington, D.C.: U.S. Government Printing Office, September 1990.

Giddy, I.; A. Saunders; and I. Walter. "Securities Clearance and Settlement." Stern School of Business, New York University, 1993, Mimeographed.

Gilligan, T.; M. L. Smirlock; and W. Marshall. "Scale and Scope Economies in the Multiproduct Banking Firm." *Journal of Monetary Economics* 13, May 1984, pp. 393–405.

Gilligan, T., and M. L. Smirlock. "An Empirical Study of Joint Production and Scale Economies in Commercial Banking." *Journal of Banking and Finance* 8, 1984, pp. 67–78.

Gilson, S. C.; K. John; and L. Lang. "An Empirical Study of Private Reorganization of Firms in Default." *Journal of Financial Economics,* 1990, pp. 315–53.

Goldberg, L., and A. Saunders. "The Causes of U.S. Bank Expansion Overseas: The Case of Great Britain." *Journal of Money Credit and Banking* 12, 1980, pp. 630–44.

——— "The Growth of Organizational Forms of Foreign Banks in the U.S." *Journal of Money Credit and Banking* 13, 1981, pp. 365–74.

——— "The Determinants of Foreign Banking Activity in the United States." *Journal of Banking and Finance* 5, 1981, pp. 17–32.

Goldberg, L.; G Hanweck; M. Kennan; and A. Young. "Economies of Scale and Scope in the Securities Industry." *Journal of Banking and Finance* 15, 1991, pp. 91–108.

Goldberg, M. "Commercial Letters of Credit and Bankers Acceptances." In *Below the Bottom Line: The Use of Contingencies and Commitments by Commercial Banks.* Washington, D.C.: Federal Reserve Board of Governors, 1982.

Golinger, T. L., and J. B. Morgan. "Calculation of an Efficient Frontier for a Commercial Loan Portfolio." *Journal of Portfolio Management,* Winter 1993, pp. 39–46.

Goodman, L. S.; P. Fisher; and C. Anderson. "The Impact of Risk-Based Capital Requirements on Asset Allocation for Life Insurance Companies." Merrill Lynch, *Insurance Executive Review,* Fall 1992, pp. 14–21.

Gorton, G., and G. Pennacchi. "Are Loan Sales Really Off Balance Sheet?" *Off-Balance-Sheet Activities,* ed. J. Ronen, A. Saunders, and A. C. Sondhi, New York: Quorum Books, 1989, pp. 19–40.

Grammatikos, T.; A. Saunders; and I. Swary. "Returns and Risks of U.S. Bank Foreign Currency Activities." *Journal of Finance* 41, 1986, pp. 670–81.

Grammatikos, T., and A. Saunders. "Additions to Bank Loan Loss Reserves: Good News or Bad News?" *Journal of Monetary Economics* 25, 1990, pp. 289–304.

Grosse, T. "The Debt/Equity Swap in Latin America—In Whose Interest?" *Journal of International Financial Management and Accounting* 4, Spring 1992, pp. 13–39.

Grossman, S. J., and O. D. Hart. "Corporate Financial Structure and Managerial Incentives." *The Economics of Information and Uncertainty,* ed. J. McCall. Chicago: Chicago University Press, 1982.

Gruson, M. "Are Foreign Banks Still Welcome in the United States?" *Bankers Magazine,* September–October 1992, pp. 16–21.

Haraf, W. S. "The Collapse of Drexel Burnham Lambert: Lessons for Bank Regulators." *Regulation,* Winter 1991, pp. 22–25.

Harrington, S. E. "Prices and Profits in the Liability Insurance Market." In *Liability: Perspectives and Policy,* ed. R. E. Litan and C. Winston. Washington, D.C.: The Brookings Institution, 1988, pp. 45–54.

Hawawini, G. "Controlling the Interest Rate Risk of Bonds: An Introduction to Duration Analysis and Immunization Strategies." *Finanzmarket and Portfolio Management* 1, 1986–1987, pp. 8–18.

Herring, R. J. "Innovations to Enhance Liquidity: The Implications for Systemic Risk." Wharton School, University of Pennsylvania, October 1992, Mimeographed.

Ho, T., and A. Saunders. "A Catastrophe Model of Bank Failure." *Journal of Finance* 35, 1980, pp. 1189–1207.

——— "The Determinants of Bank Interest Rate Margins: Theory and Evidence." *Journal of Financial and Quantitative Analysis* 16, 1981, pp. 581–600.

——— "Fixed-Rate Loan Commitments, Takedown Risk, and the Dynamics of Hedging with Futures." *Journal of Financial and Quantitative Analysis* 18, 1983, pp. 499–516.

——— "A Micro Model of the Federal Funds Market." *Journal of Finance* 40, 1985, pp. 977–88.

Holifield, S.; M. Madis; and W. H. Sackley. "Correlation and Hedge Accounting Standards: The Case of Franklin Savings." Working Paper, Ohio State University, Columbus, Ohio, 1993, Mimeographed.

Huertas, T. F. "Redesigning Regulation: The Future of Finance in the United States." Federal Reserve—Central Bankers Symposium, Jackson Hole, Wyoming, August 22, 1987, Mimeographed.

Hultman, C. W., and R. I. McGee. "Factors Affecting the Foreign Bank Presence in the U.S." *Journal of Banking and Finance* 13, 1989, pp. 383–96.

Humphrey, D. B. "Payments Finality and Risk of Settlement Failure." In *Technology and the Regulation of Financial Markets: Securities, Futures, and Banking,* ed. A. Saunders and L. J. White. Lexington, Mass.: Lexington Books, 1986, pp. 97–120.

Hunter, W. C.; S. Timme; and W. K. Yang. "An Examination of Cost Subadditivity and Multiproduct Production in Large U.S. Commercial Banks." *Journal of Money Credit and Banking* 22, 1990, pp. 504–25.

Jacklin, C. S. "Demand Deposits, Trading Restrictions, and Risk Sharing." *Contractual Arrangements for Intertemporal Trade,* ed. E. Prescott and N. Wallace. Duluth: University of Minnesota, 1987.

James, C. "Some Evidence on the Uniqueness of Bank Loans." *Journal of Financial Economics* 19, 1987, pp. 217–35.

——— "Losses Realized in Bank Failures." *Journal of Finance* 66, 1991, pp. 123–42.

James, C., and P. Weir. "Borrowing Relationships, Intermediation, and the Costs of Issuing Public Securities." *Journal of Financial Economics* 28, 1990, pp. 149–71.

——— "Returns to Acquirers and Competition in the Acquisition Market: The Case of Banking." *Journal of*

Political Economy 95, 1983, pp. 355–70.

John, K.; T. John; and L. W. Senbet. "Risk Shifting Incentives of Depository Institutions: A New Perspective on Federal Deposit Insurance Reform." *Journal of Banking and Finance* 15, 1991, pp. 895–915.

Kane, E. "Accelerating Inflation, Technological Innovation and the Decreasing Effectiveness of Banking Regulation." *Journal of Finance* 36, 1981, pp. 335–67.

Kaufman, G. G. "Measuring and Managing Interest Rate Risk: A Primer." Federal Reserve Bank of Chicago, *Economic Perspectives,* 1984, pp. 16–29.

——— "Bank Contagion: Theory and Evidence." Working Paper, Loyola University, Center for Financial and Policy Studies, Chicago, Illinois, 93–1, 1993.

Kau, J. P.; D. C. Keenan; W. J. Muller III; and J. F. Epperson. "A Generalized Valuation Model for Fixed-Rate Residential Mortgages." *Journal of Money Credit and Banking* 24, 1992.

Kelly, E. J. "Conflicts of Interest: A Legal View." *Deregulating Wall Street,* ed. I. Walter. New York: John Wiley & Sons, 1985, pp. 231–54.

Kolari, J., and A. Zardkoohi. *Banks' Costs, Structure, and Performance.* Lexington Mass.: D.C. Heath, 1987.

Koppenhaver, G. O. "Standby Letters of Credit." Federal Reserve Bank of Chicago, *Economic Perspectives,* 1987, pp. 28–38.

Kroszner, R. S., and R. G. Rajan. "Is the Glass-Steagall Act Justified? A Study of U.S. Experience with Universal Banking before 1933." Paper presented at the Western Finance Association, Vancouver, B.C., June 1993.

Lawrence, C. "Banking Costs, Generalized Functional Forms, and Estimation of Economies of Scale and Scope." *Journal of Money, Credit and Banking* 21, 1989, pp. 368–79.

Lawrence, C, and R. Shay. "Technology and Financial Intermediation in the Multiproduct Banking Firm: an Econometric Study of U.S. Banks." *Technological Innovation Regulation and the Monetary Economy.* Cambridge, Mass.: Ballinger, 1986.

LeCompte, R. L. B., and S. D. Smith. "Changes in the Cost of Intermediation: The Case of Savings and Loans." *Journal of Finance* 45, pp. 1337–46.

Litterman R., and T. Iben. "Corporate Bond Valuation and the Term Structure of Credit Spreads." *Journal of Portfolio Management* 1989, pp. 52–64.

Loderer, C. F.; D. P. Sheehan; and G. B. Kadler. "The Pricing of Equity Offerings." *Journal of Financial Economics,* 1991, pp. 35–57.

Madalla, A. S. *Limited-Dependent and Qualitative Variables in Econometrics.* Cambridge: Cambridge University Press, 1983.

Madura, J., and E. Zarruk. "Impact of the Debt Reduction Plan on the Value of LDC Debt." *International Review of*

Economics and Finance 1, 1992, pp. 177–87.

Mei, J. P., and A. Saunders. "Bank Risk and Too Big to Fail Guarantees: An Asset Pricing Perspective." Working Paper, Salomon Center, New York University, 1993.

Meier, K. J. *The Political Economy of Regulation: The Case of Insurance.* Albany: State University of New York Press, 1988.

Melnik A., and S. Plaut. "Loan Commitment Contracts, Terms of Lending and Credit Allocation." *Journal of Finance* 41, 1986, pp. 425–36.

Merton, R. C. "On the Pricing of Corporate Debt: The Risk Structure of Interest Rates." *Journal of Finance* 29, 1974, pp. 449–70.

——— "An Analytic Derivation of the Cost of Deposit Insurance and Loan Guarantees: An Application of Modern Option Pricing Theory." *Journal of Banking and Finance* 1, 1977, pp. 3–11.

——— "On the Cost of Deposit Insurance When There Are Surveillance Costs." *Journal of Business* 51, 1978, pp. 439–52.

Mester, L. "Efficient Production of Financial Services: Scale and Scope Economies." Federal Reserve Bank of Philadelphia, *Economic Review,* January–February 1987, pp. 15–25.

Mester, L. J. "Traditional and Nontraditional Banking: An Information Theoretic Approach." *Journal of Banking and Finance* 16, 1992, pp. 534–66.

Millon-Cornett, M., and S. De. "Common Stock Returns in Corporate Takeover Bids: Evidence of Interstate Bank Mergers." *Journal of Banking and Finance* 15, 1991, pp. 273–95.

Millon-Cornett, M., and H. Tehranian. "Changes in Corporate Performance Associated with Bank Acquisitions." *Journal of Financial Economics* 31, 1992, pp. 211–34.

Morgan, J. B. "Managing A Loan Portfolio Like an Equity Fund." *Bankers Magazine,* January–February 1989, pp. 228–35.

Munter, P. H.; D. K. Clancy; and C. T. Moores. "Accounting for Financial Futures: A Question of Risk Reduction." *Advances in Accounting* 3, 1986, pp. 51–70.

Muscerella, C., and M. R. Vetsuypens. "A Simple Test of Baron's Model of IPO Underpricing." *Journal of Financial Economics* 24, 1989, pp. 125–36.

Nabar, P.; S. Park; and A. Saunders. "Prime Rate Changes: Is There an Advantage in Being First?" *Journal of Business* 66, 1993, pp. 69–92.

Noulas, A.; S. C. Ray; and S. M. Miller. "Returns to Scale and Input Substitution for Large U.S. Banks." *Journal of Money Credit and Banking* 22, 1990, pp. 94–108.

Office of Technology Assessment. *U. S. Banks and International Telecommunications Background Paper,* OTA-BP-TCT-100. Washington, D.C.: U.S. Government Printing Office, September 1992.

O'Hara, M., and W. Shaw. "Deposit Insurance and Wealth Effects: The Value of Being Too Big to Fail," *Journal of Finance* 45, 1990, pp. 1587–1600.

Pavel, C. "Securitization." Federal Reserve Bank of Chicago, *Economic Perspectives,* 1985, pp. 16–31.

Pennacchi, G. G. "Loan Sales and the Cost of Bank Capital." *Journal of Finance* 43, 1988, pp. 375–96.

Poole, W. "Commercial Bank Reserve Management in a Stochastic Model: Implications for Monetary Policy." *Journal of Finance* 23, 1968, pp. 769–91.

Pyle, D. "Pricing Deposit Insurance: The Effects of Mismeasurement." Working Paper, University of California, Berkeley, 1983.

Reilly, F. K. *Investment Analysis and Portfolio Management,* 3rd ed. Chicago: Dryden Press, 1989.

Rock, K. "Why New Issues Are Underpriced." *Journal of Financial Economics* 15, 1986, pp. 187–212.

Ronn, E., and A. K. Verma. "Pricing Risk-Adjusted Deposit Insurance: An Option-Based Model." *Journal of Finance* 41, 1986, pp. 871–96.

Ross, S., and R. Westerfield. *Corporate Finance.* St. Louis: Times Mirror–Mosby College Publishing, 1988.

Saunders, A. "Bank Safety and Soundness and the Risks of Corporate Securities Activities." In *Deregulating Wall Street,* ed. I. Walter. New York: John Wiley & Sons, 1985, pp. 171–206.

——— "Conflicts of Interest: An Economic View." In *Deregulating Wall Street,* ed. I. Walter. New York: John Wiley & Sons, 1985, pp. 207–30.

——— "Why Are So Many New Stock Issues Underpriced?" In Federal Reserve Bank of Philadelphia, *Business Review,* March–April 1990, pp. 3–12.

Saunders, A., and T. Urich. "The Effects of Shifts in Monetary Policy and Reserve Accounting Regimes on Bank Reserve Management Behavior in the Federal Funds Market." *Journal of Banking and Finance* 12, 1988, pp. 523–35.

Saunders, A.; E. Strock; and N. G. Travlos. "Ownership Structure, Deregulation, and Bank Risk Taking." *Journal of Finance* 45, 1989, pp. 643–54.

Saunders, A., and I. Walter. *Universal Banking in the U.S.?* New York: Oxford University Press, 1993.

Saunders, A., and B. Wilson. "Informed and Uninformed Depositor Runs and Panics: Evidence from the 1929–33 Period." Working Paper, Salomon Center, New York University, March 1993.

Schaefer, S., and E. S. Schwartz. "Time Dependent Variance and the Pricing of Bond Options." *Journal of Finance* 42, 1987, pp. 1113–28.

Schwartz, G. S., and W. N. Tourous. "Prepayment and the Valuation of Mortgage-Backed Securities." *Journal of Finance* 44, 1989, pp. 375–92.

Shaffer, S., and E. David. "Economies of Superscale in Commercial Banking." *Applied Economics* 23, 1991, pp. 283–93.

Silber, W. L. "Municipal Revenue Bond Costs and Bank Underwriting: A Survey of the Evidence." Monograph Series in Finance and Economics. New York: Salomon Center for the Study of Financial Institutions, 1979.

Sinkey, J. F. *Commercial Bank Financial Management in the Financial Services Industry,* 4th ed. New York: Macmillian Publishing, 1992.

Smirlock, M., and J. Yawitz. "Asset Returns, Discount Rate Changes, and Market Efficiency." *Journal of Finance* 40, 1985, pp. 1141–58.

Smith, C. W.; C. W. Smithson; and L. M. Wakeman. "The Market for Interest Rate Swaps." *Financial Management* 17, 1988, pp. 34–44.

Smith, C. W., and R. M. Stultz. "The Determinants of Firms' Hedging Policies." *Journal of Financial and Quantitative Analysis* 20, 1985, pp. 391–406.

Smith, C. W.; C. W. Smithson; and D. S. Wilford. *Managing Financial Risk.* Cambridge, Mass.: Ballinger Publishing, 1990.

Smith, S. D. "Analyzing Risk and Return for Mortgage-Backed Securities." Federal Reserve Bank of Atlanta, *Economic Review,* January–February 1991, pp. 2–11.

Spahr, R. W., and M. A. Sunderman. "The Effect of Prepayment Modeling in Pricing Mortgage-Backed Securities." *Journal of Housing Research* 3, 1992, pp. 381–400.

Spong, K., and J. D. Shoenhair. "Performance of Banks Acquired on an Interstate Basis." Federal Reserve Bank of Kansas City, *Financial Industry Perspectives,* December 1992, pp. 15–23.

Spindt, P. A., and J. R. Hoffmeister. "The Micromechanics of the Federal Funds Market: Implications for Day of the Week Effects in Funds Rate Variability." *Journal of Financial and Quantitative Analysis* 23, 1988, pp. 401–16.

Stapleton, R. C., and M. Subrahamanyam. "Interest Rate Caps and Floors." In *Financial Options: From Theory to Practice,* ed. S. Figlewski. Homewood, Ill.: Business One-Irwin, 1991, pp. 220–80.

Stiglitz, J., and A. Weiss. "Credit Rationing in Markets with Imperfect Information." *American Economic Review* 71, 1981, pp. 393–410.

Stigum, M. *The Money Market,* 3rd ed. Homewood, Ill.: Dow-Jones Irwin, 1990.

Swary, I. "Stock Market Reaction to Regulatory Action in the Continental Illinois Crisis." *Journal of Business* 59, 1986, pp. 451–73.

Thakor, A. V., and G. Udell. "An Economic Rationale for the Pricing Structure of Bank Loan Commitments." *Journal of Banking and Finance* 11, 1987, pp. 271–90.

Thakor, A. V. "Toward a Theory of Bank Loan Commitments." *Journal of Banking and Finance* 6, 1982, pp. 55–84.

Travlos, N. "Corporate Takeover Bids, Methods of Payment, and Bidding Firm Stock Returns." *Journal of Finance* 42, 1987, pp. 943–63.

Turvey, C. G. "Credit Scoring for Agricultural Loans: A Review with Applications." *Agricultural Finance Review* 51, 1991, pp. 43–54.

Wall, L., and D. R. Peterson. "The Effect of Continental Illinois Failure on the Financial Performance of Other Banks." *Journal of Monetary Economics* 1990, pp. 77–99.

Walter, I. *Secret Money: The World of International Financial Secrecy.* London: George Allen and Unwin, 1985.

Walter, I., and A. Saunders. *Global Competitiveness of New York City as a Financial Center.* Occasional Papers in Business and Finance. New York: Stern Business School, 1992.

White, L. H. "Scottish Banking and the Legal Restrictions Theory: A Closer Look." *Journal of Money Credit and Banking* 22, 1990, pp. 526–36.

White, L. J. *The S and L Debacle.* New York: Oxford University Press, 1991.

Yawitz, J. B. "Risk Premia on Municipal Bonds." *Journal of Financial and Quantitative Analysis* 13, 1978, pp. 475–85.

Yoshioka, K., and T. Nakajima. "Economies of Scale in Japan's Banking Industry." Bank of Japan, Monetary and Economic Studies, September 1987.

INDEX